THE STORY OF THE
DAVIS CUP

THE STORY
OF THE
DAVIS CUP

Alan Trengove

In association with the
International Tennis Federation

Stanley Paul
London   Melbourne   Sydney   Auckland   Johannesburg

Stanley Paul & Co. Ltd

An imprint of Century Hutchinson Ltd

Brookmount House, 62–65 Chandos Place, London WC2N 4NW

Century Hutchinson Publishing Group (Australia) Pty Ltd
16–22 Church Street, Hawthorn, Melbourne, Victoria 3122

Century Hutchinson Group (NZ) Ltd
32–34 View Road, PO Box 40–086, Glenfield, Auckland 10

Century Hutchinson Group (SA) Pty Ltd
PO Box 337, Bergvlei 2012, South Africa

First published 1985
© Alan Trengove 1985

The title 'Davis Cup' connotes the international tennis competition held under the auspices of the International Tennis Federation and its member national associations and is a registered trademark of the International Tennis Federation.

Set in Linotron Bembo by Input Typesetting Ltd, London

Printed and bound in Great Britain by Anchor Brendon Ltd,
Tiptree, Essex

ISBN 0 09 159860 5

CONTENTS

Acknowledgements

I wish to thank Philippe Chatrier, the president, and Shirley Wood-head, the general secretary, of the International Tennis Federation for their cooperation in making the records of the Davis Cup Nations and the ITF available for research. My thanks also go to Alan Little, librarian of the All England Club, for allowing me to make use of the Wimbledon library, and to Ed Fabricius for permission to use the USTA library I was also able to study a number of Davis Cup programmes at the offices of the Lawn Tennis Association of Australia.

Joe McCauley provided me with invaluable assistance by referring me to a number of articles and helping to fill gaps in the record of results.

The newspapers I consulted comprised, in the main, the *Boston Globe*, the *New York Times*, the *Times of London*, the *Melbourne Argus*, the *Melbourne Age* and the *Sydney Morning Herald*. The most useful periodicals were *American Lawn Tennis* (1907–51) *British Lawn Tennis and Squash* (1936–60), *Tennis Magazine* of USA, *World Tennis* and *Tennis Magazine* of Australia. An article by Dr Kevin Fewster titled 'Advantage Australia: Davis Cup Tennis 1950–59', published in the *Meanjin Magazine* in 1984, was especially helpful. In addition, the *USTA Yearbook* and its British equivalent, *World of Tennis*, provided easy-to-read statistics and summaries.

For permission to reproduce copyright photographs, the author and publishers would like to thank Russ Adams, Le-Roye Productions, Photo Source, *Melbourne Herald*, H. J. Entink and Pressens Bild AB.

The principal books to which I referred were as follows:

Austin, H. W., *Lawn Tennis Bits & Pieces*. Low, Marston & Co., London, 1930.

Brookes, Dame Mabel, *Crowded Galleries*. Heinemann, London, 1956.

Clerici, Gianni, *The Ultimate Tennis Book*. Follett, Chicago, 1975.

Collins, Bud, and Hollander, Zander (ed.), *Bud Collins' Modern Encyclopedia of Tennis*. Doubleday, New York, 1980.

Coombes, D. C., *A History of the Davis Cup*. Hennel Locke, London, 1949.

Danzig, Allison, and Schwed, Peter (ed.), *The Fireside Book of Tennis*. Simon & Schuster, New York, 1972.

Deford, Frank, *Big Bill Tilden*. Gollancz, London, 1977.

Evans, Richard, *Nastase*. Aidan Ellis, London, 1978.

Evans, Richard, *McEnroe: A Rage for Perfection*. Sidgwick & Jackson, London 1982.

Fraser, Neale, *Power Tennis*. Stanley Paul, London, 1962.

Hillyard, G. W., *Forty Years of First-Class Tennis*. Williams and Norgate, London, 1924.

Hoad, Lew, with Jack Pollard, *My Game*. Hodder & Stoughton, London, 1958.

Hopman, Harry, *Aces & Places*. Cassell, London, 1957.

Kidston, R. M., *Lawn Tennis in Australia*, Edwards, Dunlop & Co., Sydney, 1912.

Kramer, Jack, with Frank Deford, *The Game: My 40 Years in Tennis*. Putnam, New York, 1979.

Lacoste, J. R., *Lacoste on Tennis*. London, 1931.

Laney, A. L., *Covering the Court*. New York, 1915.

Merrihew, S. W., *The Quest of the Davis Cup*. American Lawn Tennis, Inc., New York, 1928.

Metzler, Paul, *Tennis Styles and Stylists*, Angus & Robertson, Sydney, 1969.

Myers, A. W., *Lawn Tennis at Home and Abroad*, London, 1903.

Myers, A. W., *Captain Anthony Wilding*, London, 1916.

Myers, A. W., *Story of the Davis Cup*, London, 1913.

Myers, A. W., *Twenty Years of Lawn Tennis*, London, 1916.

Pails, Dinny, *Set Points*. Currawong, Sydney, 1952.

Perry, F. J., *My Story*. Hutchinson, London, 1933.

Potter, E. C., *Kings of the Court*. New York, 1936.

Robertson, Max (ed.), *The LTAA Book of the Game*. Max Parrish, London, 1951.

ACKNOWLEDGEMENTS

Robertson, Max (ed.), *The Encyclopedia of Tennis*. Allen & Unwin, London, 1974.

Smythe, Sir John, VC, *Jean Borotra: The Bounding Basque*. Stanley Paul, London, 1974.

Talbert, Bill with Gordon Greer, *Bill Talbert's Weekend Tennis*. Doubleday, New York, 1970.

Tilden, William, *Match Play & The Spin of the Ball*, Methuen, London, 1928.

Tilden, William, *Aces, Places & Faults*, London, 1938.

Tilden, William, *My Story*. Hellman & Williams, New York, 1948.

Tingay, Lance, *The Guinness Book of Tennis Facts & Feats*. Guinness, London, 1983.

USLTA staff, *USLTA Official Encyclopedia of Tennis*, Harper & Row, New York, 1972.

Whitington, R. S., *An Illustrated History of Australian Tennis*. Macmillan, Melbourne, 1975.

Wilding, A. F., *On the Court and Off*. Methuen, London, 1911.

FOREWORD

by Philippe Chatrier
President, International Tennis Federation

The Davis Cup, the greatest international team event in tennis, is one of the brightest jewels in the International Tennis Federation's domain. Like the four Grand Slam tournaments in Paris, Wimbledon, the US Open and in Australia, it is a fundamental symbol of stability in a game which for ever seems to be experiencing change.

It was therefore with considerable interest that I heard that Alan Trengove, a most respected Australian journalist, whose fascination with, and love of, tennis is so apparent, was producing what is basically a history of the Davis Cup.

Since its inception at Boston in 1900 the Davis Cup has been a byword for importance and excellence in tennis. The revival of its status in the last few years, after it had passed through what has to be admitted was a period of decline, has been one of the most outstanding success stories in the game.

For all the marvellous tennis we see in the major tournaments and the awesome individual talents of some of our leading men and women champions, I doubt if there is anything that can generate such widespread emotion and atmosphere as international team events which catch patriotic attention. In this the Davis Cup has no peer.

Despite the limited number of nations that have celebrated victory in the Davis Cup and the emphatic supremacy of the United States and Australia over the years, the structure of the competition is such that its magical appeal can touch every nation, and I am happy to say that the number of countries wishing to take part continues to grow.

Trengove, after endless hours of diligent research, many of them spent in the Wimbledon library and our own International Tennis Federation offices in London last summer, reflects both the changing moods surrounding the Davis Cup and the exploits of some of the greatest Davis Cup players, from the Dohertys to John McEnroe, whose alliegiance to the United States team has been a prime example for others to follow.

Davis Cup memories and stories are part of tennis legend. In France, we still recall with great fondness those six unbelievable years when the Musketeers reigned supreme between 1927 and 1932. In Britain, they threw a dinner to honour the British team who started their four-year run of success fifty years earlier in 1933.

In those days, of course, travel between countries was by no means so easy, quick and commonplace as it is today. Journeys between North America and Europe, for instance, would then have been counted in days rather than hours, and from Europe to Australia in weeks.

For that reason, Davis Cup ties were quite frequently arranged to coincide with the major championships such as Wimbledon, when all the players would be together in one place. Indeed, the record books are full of matches staged between two countries using a third as the neutral but most convenient venue.

This still sometimes happens. The New Zealand team, for instance, instead of going all the way back home to play Sweden in the week after Wimbledon in 1983, agreed to stage their tie at Eastbourne, one of England's most famous and picturesque tennis centres.

Trengove touches on this aspect of the Davis Cup and many more, including those personalities, famous and sometimes possibly infamous, who have added colour, class, controversy and, above all, credibility to the world of tennis.

The ITF is very pleased to be associated with this book which I am sure will be as fascinating as it is informative, establishing its presence in any tennis library.

INTRODUCTION

On the eve of the Davis Cup semifinal between America and
Australia in Portland, Oregon, in 1981 the American captain, Arthur
Ashe, was asked to speak at a dinner to which several former Davis
Cup players had been invited. It was a nostalgic occasion marked
by the camaraderie and tremendous goodwill that were manifest
among the guests. All had been influenced in some way by the
Davis Cup, and indeed in a few cases the cup had provided them
with their most vivid and powerful memories. Ashe's particular
theme was the tradition of friendly rivalry that had evolved between
the United States and Australia since the two nations first played
each other in the Davis Cup seventy-six years before. He spoke of
how important that rivalry had been in his own life and of the
friendships he had made Down Under. Then suddenly he could say
no more, for he was choked with emotion. Harry Hopman, the
quick-witted septuagenarian who had captained all the great
Australian teams of the fifties and sixties, was quickly on his feet
with some lighthearted reminiscences of Ashe designed to give
Arthur time to recover. But when Ashe, normally a cool and
unflappable man, resumed speaking he was still so deeply affected
by his feelings that he could not express more than another few
words before breaking down again. Such is the sentimental hold
that the Davis Cup has over many of those who have played in the
competition.

In doing the research for this book I came across an article which
Ashe had written for *World Tennis* on the Davis Cup and world
politics. I would have thought the high point of his career would
have been winning Wimbledon at the fairly late age of thirty-two,

the first black man ever to do so, but, no, Ashe revealed that for him the highlight was helping to capture the Davis Cup for his country in 1968, an achievement that ended in tears when he lost the final 'dead' rubber to Bill Bowrey of Australia. The lowest point, said Ashe, was also provided by the Davis Cup when, a year earlier, he had lost both his singles against two obscure Ecuadorians whom in a tournament he would have been expected to beat soundly.

Ashe's eloquent words, written in 1977, are worth repeating.

In this era of planned obsolescence the Davis Cup endures as few other . . . institutions have done before it. The Davis Cup is not a place or a player, a cup or a contest, a name or a notion. It is an *idea*, and it will always be just that. Furthermore, it is not an accident that the word *ideal* is derived from the word *idea*. Dwight Davis must have been an idealist when in 1900 he went to the trouble of donating the huge silver bowl, a symbol of friendly tennis rivalry.

Players who have played Davis Cup frequently, have gone to war against one another later, only to return after the wars are over to play again. Some have seen their countries conquer and be conquered, and the names of countries changed. The Davis Cup rules have changed, political systems have changed, even the cup itself has changed, but the idea and its ideals are immutable. The court is always 78 feet by 36 feet, and the highest standards of sportsmanship are demanded within those lines. Few countries can measure up to these ideals. Perhaps that is why only the idea lives on. . . .

Dwight Filley Davis of St Louis, Missouri, was a Harvard student when in 1900 he offered a large silver punchbowl for international competition. Neither Davis nor anybody else then realized the extent to which the competition would grow. Originally, only America and the British Isles contested the trophy, but by the First World War France, Belgium, Austria, Australasia, Germany and Canada had also entered teams. By 1984 a record number of sixty-two nations were playing in the competition, and no fewer than seventy-two had been involved at one time or another. Up to 1927 the only three nations to win the cup were America, Great Britain and Australasia (which split into separate Australian and New Zealand teams in 1923), all predominantly grass-court strongholds. In 1927 the so-called Four Musketeers of France, Réné Lacoste, Henri

Cochet, Jean Borotra and Jacques Brugnon, ended the Anglo-Saxon domination by winning the cup in Philadelphia in one of the great epics of French sports history. For the next six years the French defended the cup on a clay court in Paris, conceding it at last to Great Britain in 1933. France has never since won the cup, and Great Britain has not held it since 1937.

For twenty-seven years after the Second World War the cup was won by either America or Australia until South Africa, in one of the sport's saddest episodes, won it by default in 1974. Today, the competition is more open and unpredictable than ever and the number of nations that have reached the challenge round or final at least once has grown to seventeen. The successful nations are America, Great Britain, Belgium, Australia, Japan, France, Italy, Mexico, Spain, India, Rumania, West Germany, South Africa, Sweden, Czechoslovakia, Chile and Argentina. Up to 1984 America had won the cup twenty-eight times, Australia twenty-five times, Great Britain nine times, France six times, Sweden twice, and South Africa, Italy and Czechoslovakia once each.

The first Davis Cup tie I attended was the 1953 challenge round at Kooyong, in Melbourne, when in a stirring struggle Lew Hoad and Ken Rosewall, both only nineteen years of age, won their last two singles to beat the two-man American team of Victor Seixas and Tony Trabert by three matches to two. The last tie I attended (at the time of writing) was the 1983 final between Australia and Sweden, which was also held at Kooyong. In those thirty years much about the Davis Cup had changed, and yet, as Arthur Ashe has stressed, its essence remained the same. As in 1953, the 1983 matches were played on grass over the Christmas holiday period, and there was again the same pomp and ceremony which contributes so much to the electrifying atmosphere of a big Davis Cup occasion: the national anthems, the presence of prime ministers, heads of state, ambassadors and other dignitaries, and the protocol which requires the umpire to allude not to individuals when calling the score but to nations. The matches, as always, were over five sets; and television interests, so omnipotent in other facets of tennis, had not yet been able to force the abolition of a rest period after the third set or the introduction of the tiebreak. (In 1975 one Davis Cup set between a Canadian and a Colombian at Montreal went to a record forty-six games.)

3

Yet the differences between the circumstances of 1983 and those of thirty years earlier were dramatic enough. For a start, this was a final and not a challenge round. With the scrapping of the challenge round system in 1972 the defending nation no longer could enjoy the privilege of waiting for the other contenders to play off among themselves to determine a challenger, which would then automatically be required to play on the defender's territory. It was a fairer concept, guaranteeing that no nation would monopolize the Davis Cup as America and Australia had done for long periods in the past. Another difference was the absence of temporary stands, which in 1953 enabled a then record number of 17,500 people to watch the spectacle, many of them perched on planks more than a hundred feet above the ground. On the other hand, television swelled the audience for the Australia *v.* Sweden final to millions, both in Australia and Sweden.

In the fifties and sixties neutral referees were the exception rather than the rule, and America and Australia took pride in the fact that they never objected to a national of the home country being the final arbiter of any disputes. Cliff Sproule, an old Davis Cup player, was the referee in 1953, as he was in all the other challenge rounds in Australia in that era. The Americans held him in such respect that they once gave him an award as 'the prince' of referees. In today's less chivalrous and less trusting age, the competing nations in the World Group have little choice: a neutral referee and usually neutral umpires are appointed by the International Tennis Federation to each tie. For the 1983 final, by a happy coincidence, the referee was none other than Victor Seixas, who thus was able to revisit an old battleground.

But perhaps the greatest change of all in thirty years was in the status of the players. Today, they are all wealthy professionals. Up till the advent of open tennis in 1968, and even for several years after that, misguided administrators bled the competition of talent by barring professionals. Perry, Budge, Kramer, Gonzales, Sedgman, Hoad, Rosewall, Cooper . . . all were lost to the game's most glittering showcase when in their prime. Whereas Hoad and Rosewall in 1953 received a few shillings a day to cover their expenses, the winning Australian team of 1983 shared in a $200,000 first prize donated by the giant Nippon Electric Company, whose total sponsorship of the competition exceeded $1 million.

But the financial rewards that NEC has generously made available and which have done so much towards restoring the prestige of the competition following several years of decline are not the main incentive for players to play Davis Cup. The players are more motivated by tradition and the lustre that the competition reflects on all who play in it. For to be a Davis Cup player is to be a member of an elite group of sportsmen. It is the hallmark of a player's standing in his country and an honour to which most young tyros aspire, whether they live in Melbourne or Madras, Stockholm or Santiago. Only a relative few have experienced the thrill of winning the cup and most play every year without the faintest hope of getting very far, but retain their keenness. Tiny Luxembourg, for instance, has entered a team each year since 1947 without winning more than three ties (against Turkey, Ireland and Monaco) in all that time. Yet the annual Davis Cup adventure remains the highlight of the Luxembourg tennis year. 'A good British club team could easily beat Luxembourg,' the English tennis writer, Lance Tingay, once pointed out. 'An Australian club might devour them. One of their players turned out for ten years and never got a set. He must have gone home happy on the only occasion he got as far as 7–5.'

To be part of a national team playing either at home or abroad, where the conditions can be so difficult and the crowds so partisan, gives most players immense satisfaction. Jean Borotra's most treasured memory is of the 'wonderful unity of spirit' developed by the Musketeers, perhaps the most famous of all combinations. Their triumph in Philadelphia in 1927 after many years of endeavour was 'a crowning moment of national pride and emotion'. Millions of Frenchmen felt as elated as Borotra and his team-mates. They literally sang and danced in the streets of Paris.

'Davis Cup was my top thrill,' says Pancho Gonzales, who regrets having not played more than two cup singles before turning pro. 'It's a unique experience,' he recalls. 'Winning tournaments is something that happens if you're good enough. I figure I'd win the tournaments, and I did. But, Davis Cup . . . it's different. You have to be selected, and then you have to deliver on that date. You wait for it, like a fighter waiting for a title fight. And it's not just for yourself, like a tournament. People are depending on you. The umpire doesn't say, 'Game, Gonzales.' He says, 'Game, United

States.' It's altogether different from a tournament, and more difficult. I think back to it a lot.'

One of the greatest exploits in recent Davis Cup history was America's defeat of Rumania in Bucharest in the 1972 final. Because they had to overcome so much adversity, the American players, Stan Smith, Tom Gorman, Erik van Dillen and their captain, Dennis Ralston, ranked the feat above anything they had achieved individually, even Smith's Wimbledon triumph of the same year. 'No victory could have been more satisfying,' said Ralston. 'The court, the crowds, the officials were against us – along with two very good players, Nastase and Tiriac – but we won. We needed tremendous control of ourselves and our games, and Smith, Gorman and van Dillen had just that. Nothing could surpass it. . . .'

The fact that tennis is such a highly individualistic game encouraging players to be self-centred to the point where some seem almost paranoid on occasions explains why many relish the chance to exercise nobler instincts as part of a team. Roy Emerson won more major championships (twenty-eight in singles and doubles) than any man in history and also played on a record number of Australian Davis Cup teams, eight between 1959 and 1967. He was a team man *par excellence*, a single-minded, no-frills competitor who was always superbly fit and a fine sportsman who never made excuses on the few occasions he was beaten. More than one commentator has said that if he were seeking a player he could depend on to win the all-important match in a challenge round he would have chosen Emerson. The lantern-jawed Queenslander doesn't have to think when asked which meant more to him, his swag of titles or his matches for Australia. 'Oh, the Davis Cup, the wonderful team spirit,' he says immediately.

In another era another Australian, Mark Edmondson, rated his part in Australia's 1977 and 1983 Davis Cup triumphs ahead of his upset defeat of John Newcombe in the 1976 Australian Open final. In 1977 Edmondson, as a rookie, beat Vijay Amritraj of India and Onny Parun of New Zealand in the early rounds, but lost his place to Tony Roche in the final. He didn't mind because he thought Roche was the better player. 'But I was the main instigator in winning the first two matches, because I beat Vijay first up and Onny first up. It meant I was really a part of it and that was nice,' says Edmondson. In 1983 he lost his singles place in the semifinal against France to John Fitzgerald, but that didn't detract from his joy at his team's success either.

Most players who have experienced a Wimbledon final and an important Davis Cup tie believe that the tension pervading the latter is far greater. It is something which can destroy the nerves of the steadiest champion and cause sleeplessness, sickness and headaches. It is also often the cause of the upsets in form which are commonplace in the Davis Cup. The normally swashbuckling Fred Perry was afflicted by such a bad case of the jitters in 1932 that he lost a cup match to Daniel Prenn of Germany after leading 5–2 in the fifth set. A year later the American powerhouse Ellsworth Vines, who had destroyed Bunny Austin in the 1932 Wimbledon final for the loss of six games, could gather only six games himself against an inspired Austin in a cup match in Paris. In 1975 Jimmy Connors, one of the most aggressive and determined competitors the game has known, was in his prime. He had beaten Raul Ramirez fairly easily in an early round at Wimbledon, but six months later, in a crucial Davis Cup match in Mexico City, he was affected by nerves and Ramirez turned the tables on him.

Even after three years as a cup player Adrian Quist, who was to engineer an Australian victory in the 1939 challenge round by beating the then Wimbledon champion, Bobby Riggs, on the third day, was so edgy before a tie in Philadelphia that he suffered insomnia night after night. A doctor he consulted advised him to drink several cans of beer before going to bed. 'This,' says Quist, 'was quite a remedy for a sleepless teetotaller. However, it did the trick. It settled my nerves sufficiently to allow me several hours' sleep.' Quist was partly reassured by the legendary Bill Tilden, who told him that he also had never been immune to nervousness. 'Tournament tennis is a wonderful game,' said Tilden, 'but Davis Cup matches are mental torture. Every time I played against those Frenchmen in Davis Cup matches I suffered hell for weeks.' A player walking onto the centre court for his first Davis Cup final, according to Quist, usually experiences a 'muffled tightness' and a dryness of the mouth. Some, he says, quickly throw off these symptoms of anxiety while others succumb and 'simply go through the motions like well-trained seals without ever really getting into the match'.

In 1948 Harold Walton, a carefree British baseliner, was selected to play his first match in a first-round tie against India at Harrogate. He had recently scored tournament victories over both the Indian singles players Sumant Misra and D. K. Bose and was expected to beat at least one of them again. In the days of practice before the tie, however, Walton began to show signs of nerves. His usual happy-go-lucky attitude on and off the court was replaced by one of deadly seriousness. He lost his appetite and his form, and in his matches with Misra and Bose, Walton's usual error-free game fell to pieces. He went down to both of them and left the court a dejected and disappointed man without once having been able to do himself justice.

Walton's compatriot, Tony Mottram, who saved Britain on that occasion, was himself a victim of Davis Cup nerves a few matches later in a contest against Sweden in Stockholm to determine a place in the European Zone final. Both he and Geoffrey Paish had lost their opening singles and desperately needed the doubles to stay in contention. They won the first set against Lennart Bergelin and Torsten Johansson and had two set points against service at 5–4 in the second set when Mottram missed an easy shot at the net. 'Not only did I miss it but I couldn't get it out of my mind,' he recalled years later. 'It stuck there like glue. In a flash the set had gone, so had my concentration, and with it my confidence. The next two sets were nightmares. I couldn't do a thing. The Swedes added to my discomfort by feeding me with every ball while Paish stood by helpless. My play went from bad to worse, and now I couldn't even time the ball correctly. Even my overhead smash, normally the shot I enjoyed the most, cracked wide open. In that nightmare match we went down to disastrous defeat.' Mottram, it should be said, did not often suffer such a jittery lapse. He passed on his fighting qualities to his son, Buster, who became renowned for his bulldog spirit in Davis Cup encounters in the seventies and eighties.

Sometimes, where nerves are concerned, playing before a home crowd is not the advantage it is thought to be. In the famous 1972 final at Bucharest Ilie Nastase went into his match with Stan Smith with the world's acclaim of his recent US Open triumph still ringing in his ears. With the prospect of playing on the clay court that he knew best against a man who was essentially a fast-court player, he had been boasting that America had no hope. But Nastase failed miserably and his defeat was such a devastating blow to his ego that it probably undermined his confidence in big matches for the remainder of his career. 'You want to win so much for the people,' he said, 'that every shot you miss is going like an arrow straight to your heart.' Jaime Fillol of Chile felt much the same way after losing to Corrado Barazzutti of Italy in the crucial opening match of the 1976 final in Santiago. 'In singles you have the whole team on your shoulders when you are out there alone. That can be good or bad, depending on how you react,' said Fillol.

One of the worst attacks of Davis Cup nerves was suffered in an inter-zone final in Brisbane by the late Herbie Flam of America, normally a resourceful competitor and a man who had been good enough to beat Frank Sedgman at Wimbledon. In the nights preceding the final, which was against Belgium, Flam had so much difficulty sleeping that he changed his hotel room four or five times, and then asked his captain, Bill Talbert, for permission to stay in a girlfriend's home. When Talbert expressed fear of a scandal affecting the team, Flam assured him that sex was far from his mind. 'I just want to sleep,' he said. A few days later when Flam still couldn't get much sleep despite the home comforts of suburbia it was decided that he was worrying about his racquets and a phone call was put in to California to order a new batch. Still Flam couldn't sleep, and the occasional glass of port or beer did not ease his stress either. Finally, he was examined by a Brisbane doctor, who found that Flam was probably on the verge of a nervous breakdown. When Talbert broke the news to the overwrought player he was dismayed to see him clench the glass of beer he was holding so tightly that it shattered in his hands. Tranquillizers were prescribed and Talbert resigned himself to naming the veteran Gardnar Mulloy in Flam's place, but at the last moment Flam appeared to get a grip on himself and said he wanted to play.

Flam's first-day match with Jackie Brichant was one of the strangest I have ever seen. Flam often looked confused and disoriented, and it emerged later that he had taken tranquillisers at critical stages. One break up in the fifth set, he said to Talbert, 'Hurry, Cap! Give me another of those pills. I'm not going to make it without one.' By now Talbert's supply had run out, but as he wiped Flam's face he had an idea. 'OK,' said Talbert, 'just open your mouth. I'll toss it down your throat.' He popped a salt tablet into Flam's mouth, Flam swallowed it, and went on to win. However, he lost his next match – against Philippe Washer – and Talbert took no chances with him in the challenge round.

The strain on the captains in very close Davis Cup ties should not be underestimated. In Talbert's time a Davis Cup team could represent a $50,000 investment to a national association. If the team reached the challenge round, that money would be repaid with interest, but if the team failed the stake was lost. Today, national associations have to meet all their players' travelling and living expenses in overseas Davis Cup ties. With television rights for a semifinal or final offering a potential bonanza, there is enormous pressure on a captain to have his players at a physical, mental and psychological peak for the suspenseful three days.

The captain's role distinguishes Davis Cup matches from tournament play, where coaching during the changeovers is explicitly forbidden. It is a role which has grown in importance over the years as the value of captains, particularly when in charge of very young and inexperienced players, has been better appreciated. Some of the best Davis Cup players, such as Gerald Patterson, Réné Lacoste, Lennart Bergelin, Ramanathan Krishnan, Neale Fraser, Jan Kodes, Nikki Pietrangeli and Adriano Panatta, have graduated to their countries' captaincy.

The most famous captain of all has been Harry Hopman, a trim, sandy-haired man whose reputation and composure at all times instilled great confidence in his players. Hopman's record of captaining sixteen successful Australian Davis Cup teams is unlikely ever to be equalled. He had a great advantage in being given complete authority over the best Australian players of the fifties and sixties, and the players knew that without his blessing their tennis future would be limited. Hopman arranged their physical training programmes, supervised their lifestyle and shielded them from the press. Often he appeared to be a martinet, fining them for misdemeanours such as abusing their racquets, getting late to bed, or misbehaving in a restaurant. But they all came to realize how efficient he was at getting them into perfect condition for a Davis Cup match and how reassuring he could be in a crisis.

Hopman rarely left any stone unturned in increasing his team's chances of victory. Whether it be arranging for Malcolm Anderson to win at poker in order to bolster his morale on the eve of a challenge round or spreading suspicions about the propensity to footfault of a challenger, he usually had a trick or two up his sleeve. Mostly, Hopman was unruffled and diplomatic on the court, but in 1969 in Mexico City he seemed deliberately to stir up a volatile crowd by having fierce arguments with the umpire and referee. 'Hopman knows that when I get mad I can't play well,' said Mexico's Rafael Osuna, 'and that's the only reason he did all that out on the court. It was just psychological warfare.' At other times Hopman's attention to detail went generally unnoticed. For instance, while preparing teams in Australia he regularly telephoned the Weather Bureau on arising each morning. Once, before a challenge round at Sydney, he flew his entire team to Brisbane to avoid rain and get in two more days' practice than the opposition. But it was his knowledge of his players that served him best of all. In a challenge round in Cleveland, Australia was down by two matches to one to America when Fred Stolle met Dennis Ralston. The match seesawed and hung in the balance at two sets all, and then Stolle lost his serve to trail 1–2. Hopman felt that he knew Fred sufficiently well to be able to tell him, even at this tense juncture, to hit out confidently to the lines on any ball on which he felt he was in a good enough position to 'go for something'. That Hopman had judged his player's temperament correctly was clear when Stolle immediately broke back for 2 all, hitting two brilliant winners on the final two points of Ralston's service game. He went on to win the match.

The only five American captains to whom Hopman lost in the twenty-one challenge rounds in which he led Australia were Walter Pate (1938), Bill Talbert (1954), Perry Jones (1958), Robert Kelleher (1963) and Donald Dell (1968). The latter, who was one of the most astute captains, presented each of his players in Adelaide with a big team picture inscribed, 'You paid the price – we won. Thanks, Donald.' Dell handed out the mementos on 25 December, the day *before* the 1968 challenge round – a shrewd psychological ploy that Hopman, for once, couldn't match.

The captain's job now has so many ramifications and is so demanding that in some of the leading tennis nations the position is virtually a full-time one. Much of the year for men like Neale Fraser (Australia), Jean-Paul Loth (France), Paul Hutchins (Great Britain) and Hans Olsson (Sweden) is taken up with Davis Cup matters. The modern captain has to be a good organizer, a polished diplomat, an expert in human relations and an authority on all the regulations, as well as being a sound coach and cool tactician. In any one week the captain may have to deal with a temperamental team member, the difficult officials of a host country who won't provide him with the facilities he requires, a pompous ambassador or consul, an unbending referee, stubborn umpires, and scores of wellwishers who want to meet or, if they are groupies, even date his players.

The home-and-away basis on which Davis Cup ties are held involves the captain in a great deal of planning. Climate, for instance, has always exerted a strong influence on Davis Cup results. 'The late R. F. Doherty was nearly prostrated by heat at Newport during his first visit to America,' Wallis Myers wrote in 1913. The Americans, in their turn, never felt quite warm at Wimbledon. Wet grass was anathema to the Frenchmen when they first appeared in Davis Cup matches; the effect on their mercurial temperament was irredeemable. The climate of Christchurch, New Zealand, whatever it may be normally, did not suit the American team which met Australasia on its courts. Larned's rheumatism, contracted as a roughrider in Cuba, returned in full force. Even the victorious Australians were not at their best on strange soil. Belgium undoubtedly missed the comforting ball-grip and foot-grip of a sand court when she met England in the challenge round in 1904.

Today players are much more widely travelled and experienced in most conditions. Nevertheless, all countries attempt to maximize their chances of winning when playing at home by choosing a venue and environment that will either suit their players best or be most difficult for their visitors. When Russia had to play India in 1982 it chose a court in Donetsk, where the temperature never rose above 7 degrees centigrade. Coming from sultry India, Vijay Amritraj and Sashi Menon were so cold that they played both their matches in track suits and wrapped themselves in blankets during the changeovers. 'When it's so cold, the balls compress and become hard,' reported Menon. 'It was almost like hitting wooden balls.' The Indians lost their matches to players ranked far below them.

India herself has chosen some unusual venues. Rather than play Australia on grass, the Indians in 1979 built a makeshift 15,000-seat stadium at the Madras Gymkhana Club. For a month a team of two hundred coolies toiled day and night to erect the structure, which consisted of timber poles and planks tied together by rope, and a roof of dried coconut-tree leaves. The court smelt rather like a farmyard. Layers of fine gravel and clay had been laid over a base of sand and brick, with large amounts of cow dung being mixed with the surface clay to bind it. When rolled and baked under the hot Madras sun, the surface became hard and fairly fast.

In some countries, such as India and Mexico, the hazards for visiting players include the risk of stomach upsets, while an additional problem in Mexico City is the high altitude which can not only impose a physical strain but makes tennis balls more difficult to control in the thin air. In the World Group in the mid-eighties a player may find himself playing in countries as disparate as Paraguay and New Zealand, and on surfaces ranging from grass to cement or even clay indoors, as the French provided for the Americans in Grenoble in 1982. In the European Zones a player may have to adapt to conditions in Lebanon or Israel, Senegal or Morocco.

Has the Davis Cup fulfilled Dwight Davis's hope that it would foster international understanding by throwing together in friendly competition countries that otherwise might have very little contact with each other? By and large it has. Who can measure the goodwill achieved for Australia in America by the succession of excellent sportsmen led by Hopman or put a value on the splendid image of Sweden presented wherever they play by the modest and courageous Swedish teams of the eighties? And what an insight into the French personality tiny Paraguay gained when it was visited by the dashing and flamboyant Yannick Noah and Henri Leconte in 1985!

Of course, the Davis Cup has incited plenty of raucous nationalism and this has led to some of its less attractive features. The first brouhaha occurred during the 1914 challenge round in New York when Norman Brookes became irritated by a noisily partisan crowd as he played Dick Williams; he pointedly stuffed his fingers in his ears, a gesture that only made the turmoil worse. Brookes was not as affected by the crowd's one-sided attitude as much as Williams, who was upset at their teatment of a visitor. Later, the editors of the national tennis magazines in America and Australia, S. W. Merrihew and R. M. Kidston respectively, argued about the uproar in *American Lawn Tennis*. Kidston was affronted by the crowd's disruptive barracking and the cheering of Australasian mistakes. So far as he was concerned, the players were not gladiators and the spectators should not make any untoward noise or disturb play. Merrihew replied that spectators were a part of the modern game. 'The sport that has no gallery can never become a real factor in the national life,' he declared, adding that a match player must either be oblivious of a gallery or spurred on by its presence. Because Brookes and Wilding are generally looked back upon as exemplary sportsmen and gentlemen, it comes as a surprise to read that on this Davis Cup tour at any rate they were not, according to Merrihew, 'good sports'. He wrote: 'We have never in all our experience seen such consistent and persistent questioning of linesmen's decisions. . . . The questioning evidenced itself in words and in looks. Decisions which were correct beyond the possibility of a doubt were questioned in this way and often taken with ill grace. This settled policy, whether premeditated or not, could not and did not escape attention. It predisposed a large portion of the gallery against the visitors and paved the way for trouble.'

Since then nationalism has, if anything, increased, and some Davis Cup galleries have become so obstreperous that the ITF has given referees a discretionary power to penalize a team if, in their opinion, its supporters are unfairly interfering with the play. But considering the divisions in the world and the widely varying political backgrounds of competing nations – encompassing Western democracies, socialist and Marxist states and military dictatorships – there has been remarkably little upheaval. The most violent scenes have been caused by South Africa's participation in the competition (now ended), but on the other hand China and Taiwan, Great Britain and Argentina, India and Pakistan, Israel and Iran, and Viet Nam and Thailand are among the countries that have had difficult political relationships and yet see fit to enter the same tennis competition.

Ugly incidents between players are rare. The worst was caused by Ilie Nastase, perhaps no surprise in view of his record of waywardness in the seventies. In a tie in Bucharest in 1977 his taunts so angered David Lloyd that the Englishman walked off the court during a doubles and a few seconds later looked like becoming embroiled in a fist fight with the Rumanian. Before they could be separated Nastase had tried to tap Lloyd on the head with his racquet, an act which Lloyd interpreted as an assault. Finally, the incensed Englishman was frogmarched off the arena by officials and play was held up for ten minutes before the referee, Jaime Bartroli, got the players back on court and publicly warned Nastase for insulting behaviour. There were more nasty incidents in the match and after it was over the British team argued among themselves as to whether they should immediately fly home as a protest. Common sense prevailed, they stayed, and subsequently had the satisfaction of seeing Nastase suspended from playing Davis Cup for the whole of 1978.

Since Nastase's decline, the worst offender against the spirit of the Davis Cup has been John McEnroe, who has been involved in a number of incidents that would have disgusted Dwight Davis. In the Davis Cup tie in Portland which was preceded by Arthur Ashe's emotional speech dedicated to the traditions of contests between America and Australia McEnroe and his doubles partner, Peter Fleming, incurred two warnings from the Canadian referee for disturbances that broke the Australians' concentration and ended whatever chance they had of saving the match. McEnroe even rebuked his captain for not supporting him and was told by Ashe that his behaviour was disgraceful. Unprecedentedly, the Australian players publicly criticized the Americans, with Phil Dent pointing out the unfortunate reflection on America by the imposition of the disciplinary code and reckoning it a 'pretty poor show'. To work off their feelings of animosity the Australians took potshots at McEnroe's picture with dairy cream – a far cry from the mutual respect displayed by previous Australian and American teams. Three months later, in the final in Cincinnati, McEnroe marred a magnificent winning effort against Argentina by insulting officials and provoking the Argentinians with outrageous behaviour. 'At one stage,' according to Richard Evans, 'Ashe had to order McEnroe back to the baseline as he and [Jose-Luis] Clerc advanced towards each other like gun-fighters in Dodge City.' During the final McEnroe called a middle-aged black linesman 'boy', which must have made Ashe shrivel in embarrassment. Ashe and McEnroe have had little to say to each other since 1981, and it is said that a condition of McEnroe's appearance on the same team as Ashe is that Ashe does not attempt to give him any tactical instructions. The Australian writer, Richard Yallop, reported that at the 1984 Davis Cup tie in Portland it was McEnroe who ordered Ashe to sit down during one unpleasant incident in McEnroe's match with Pat Cash. And in an exhibition match in Seattle shortly before the tie, said

Yallop, McEnroe even made a joke at his captain's expense when a fan yelled out a comment and McEnroe replied, 'That's more than Arthur has said in five years.' Without a doubt, America's number one player is granted far more latitude than his predecessor, Bill Tilden, who was reprimanded and finally suspended in the 1920s for misdemeanours that, by contrast, seem trivial.

In every respect except court demeanour, however, McEnroe's Davis Cup exploits have been as splendid as that of any player in history, and it is America's good fortune that his doubles prowess is probably even better than his singles form. The record shows that although a nation cannot usually win the cup with a one-champion team (Sweden did it only once with Bjorn Borg), it can certainly succeed with one champion and a strong doubles pair. The best teams have been well balanced and without any obvious weakness – for instance, Brookes and Wilding, Tilden and Johnston, the Musketeers, Perry and Austin, Hoad and Rosewall, and Trabert and Seixas. When a team also includes an outstanding doubles line-up – as were the above players, with the possible exception of Perry and Austin, and as also were Smith and Lutz and as are McEnroe and Fleming – it is irresistible.

As for what makes the perfect Davis Cup player, big-match temperament is obviously essential, as is also an intense feeling of patriotism, the adaptability to 'fire' in strange conditions, and the stamina to endure what could be five long advantage sets. The history of the Davis Cup is laced with the names of such illustrious players.

–1–
THE DAUNTLESS
THREE
(1900, USA)

By the end of the nineteenth century lawn tennis was no longer merely a garden party game for well-to-do gentlemen and decorous ladies. It was not quite an international sport either. The championships of the All England Club at Wimbledon had been held since 1877; those of the United States National Lawn Tennis Association at Newport, Rhode Island, since 1881. British players had introduced the game to the Continent and had helped it to take root in the outposts of the Empire, most notably in Australia and New Zealand. But there was no official international competition, although a French *v.* British team match had been played at Paris, and the first Olympic Games at Athens in 1896 included a lawn tennis tournament.

There were, however, private visits by American players to Britain, and by British players to the United States. As early as 1880 a British player, O. E. Woodhouse, won an unofficial American championship at Staten Island Cricket and Baseball Club, astounding the locals by serving the ball over his head. Three years later, William and Ernest Renshaw of Great Britain beat the American brothers, J. S. and C. M. Clark, in a special contest at Wimbledon. In 1884 the American, Dr James Dwight, accompanied by the then American champion, Richard Sears, played at a number of English tournaments. They met success in doubles, but were invariably defeated in singles by the Renshaws. Then, in 1889, E. G. Meers paid a visit to the States and entered the National championship at Newport, where he was narrowly beaten in the final by O. S. Campbell, who in turn played in England in 1892. Most of these exchanges indicated little except that in tennis, as in all else, international rivalry existed and was certain to grow. Those who gave any thought to the question probably assumed that British players were the best in the world, for the 1890s had seen the rise of the brilliant Doherty brothers, Reg and Laurie. The genius of the Dohertys had revived a flagging interest in the game in Britain, where players had become rather academic in perfecting technique at the expense of individuality and vigour. Graceful they may have been; somewhat boring, too.

One American who made regular visits to England was Dr Dwight, president of the USNLTA and the 'father of American lawn tennis'. In a letter to the English LTA in 1897 Dwight said that if England sent three or four leading players to America the USNLTA would pay £40 to each for their steamship passages and £10 each for railway fares. 'I own that I have always had doubts of the propriety of paying expenses of players,' added Dwight, 'but we are willing to go to the extent named.'

As a result of his soundings, the British LTA in that year agreed that it was desirable that a match should be arranged. But there was no immediate follow-up. In the same year, three British players, Harold Mahoney, H. A. Nisbet and the Australian-born Dr Wilberforce Eaves, visited the States. While Mahoney, an Irishman, had won the Wimbledon singles in 1896 and Eaves had been runner-up the year before, all three were now eclipsed by the Dohertys. Yet at Newport, Nisbet beat two of America's best players, Malcolm Whitman and William Larned, while in the challenge round (the title-holder in those days being relieved of the need to play through the tournament) Eaves took Robert Wrenn to five sets. The results did nothing to disturb British complacency.

Over the next three years American standards improved. Whereas English tennis was based on ground stroke play, the athletic Americans rushed to the net. The English certainly volleyed, but they were cautious and volleyed from farther back. 'The Americans,' said Mahoney, 'dart in and kill many a volley which an English player would either let drop, half-volley or volley very weakly.' With their wrist and the palm of their hand solidly behind the racquet handle, the Americans could hit their forehands very hard and impart top spin. Their boyhood games of baseball gave them an advantage too: they had well-developed arm and shoulder muscles which added power to their serves. Above all, they were aggressive. 'The American may be said to make it almost his entire aim to win,' declared the Dohertys. 'He does not care much how the stroke is accomplished so long as it scores, and who shall say this is not correct?' As might be expected in such a competitive society as America, ranking lists had begun as early as 1885, and every good player set great store at being included in the top ten.

American prowess was concentrated on the Atlantic coast, principally in the eastern universities. In the spring of 1899 three Harvard students, Dwight Filley Davis, Holcolme Ward and Malcolm Whitman, and a young man preparing to enter that university, Beals Wright, embarked on the first tennis tour of America along with Wright's father, a well-known former baseballer. Though Davis came from St Louis, Missouri, he had learned the game at Magnolia, a Massachusetts summer resort. He was an idealist as well as a great sportsman, and the stimulus that the tour gave to tennis in the west inspired him. If such a trip could do such good, how beneficial to the game everywhere would be an international competition. After gaining the support of the ever enthusiastic Dr Dwight, he requested Shreve, Crump and Low, silversmiths of Boston, to make up 217 troy ounces of sterling silver into a punchbowl lined with gold.

The trophy, designed so that the upper bowl could revolve on a base, was impressively substantial. Its height varied slightly due to an irregular decoration on the rim of the bowl, but at the highest point it measured 13 inches. The inside diameter of the rim was 17½ inches, while the outside diameter, which also varied because of the decoration, was 18½ inches at the thickest point. The base was 10½ inches in diameter. Decorations were of two kinds. The bowl's top rim and the bottom rim of the base carried very heavy cast-silver decorations of a handsome Georgian design. The same design was effected by hard chasing on the lower part of the bowl and the upper part of the base, merging where the two joined. Inside, the bowl was lightly washed, or plated, with gold, and running round the interior, near the rim, were etched the words 'International Lawn Tennis Challenge Trophy. Presented by Dwight D. F. Davis, 1900'.

On 16 January 1900, James Dwight wrote the following letter to G. R. Mewburn, honorary secretary of the British LTA.

Dear Sir,

I beg to call your attention, as Secretary of the LTA, to an experiment which we are making that will, I hope, increase the interest in lawn tennis. One of our players here has offered us a Cup, to be a sort of International Challenge Cup. I enclose the conditions in a rough form. I trust that we shall both take a deep interest in them for many years to come.

I am very anxious that some of your better players should make us a visit this summer, and I hope that, should they come, your Association will see its way to challenge for the Cup. You can easily understand that we thought it necessary to require the governing Association of a country to make the challenge to prevent a series of stray challenges from players good and bad who might be coming to spend a month here. In yachting, the expense prevents the possibility of too much competition for the right to challenge. In lawn tennis it would be different.

I hope, as I said before, that the scheme will prove a success. It might do a great deal for the game here, and possibly even with you it might be a help. In any case I trust you will do what you can to give us a lead in the matter.

Please accept my sincere sympathy and good wishes in your present troubles! [A reference to the Boer War.] I have eaten your salt too often not to feel very strongly for the anxiety that you all must feel. – With every wish for better times, Believe me, Very truly

Yours,
JAMES DWIGHT,
Pres. USNLT Assoc.

Dwight Davis was then aged twenty. The trophy he donated cost about $1000, equivalent today to perhaps more than $20,000. That did not dismay him. He said a few years later that if he had known how successful his idea would be he would have had the cup made totally in gold. Like most other champions of that era, he came from a family that was comfortably off.

Jingoism was rampant at the turn of the century. The Spanish-American War broke out in 1898 (two leading American players, William Larned and Robert Wrenn, volunteered to fight in Cuba); and the Boer War started in 1899. Even while the first matches for Davis's trophy were played in 1900, a six-nation force was on its way to put down the Boxer Rebellion in China. In spite of these upheavals, Davis believed that sport, and tennis in particular, could help people from different countries understand each other better and cement friendships. In later life he became an urbane American diplomat. He was appointed Secretary of War in 1925 and, subsequently, Governor-General of the Philippines. The Davis Cup, as his trophy was soon called, gave him a distinction he otherwise might have lacked. Visitors were often more interested in talking to him about it than discussing affairs of state, he complained. Privately he was proud of the foresight he had shown.

The LTA, at a meeting on 7 March 1900, acknowledged the competition, which was to be called the International Lawn Tennis Championship, and decided to send a challenge. Dr Dwight drew up draft conditions with the advice of his friend Richard Olney, Secretary of State under President Cleveland. It was proposed that contests should consist of four singles matches between two players of each country and one doubles match. The doubles players would not need to be the same as those who played the singles. All matches would be the best of five sets, and the laws governing the championship of the country where the cup was held would be applicable. An important clause set out the duties of the team captain. His ability to advise and coach his players at the side of the court during changeovers was not specifically mentioned in the first set of rules, but this became accepted practice and was a significant distinction between Davis Cup play and tournament competition in which coaching during matches is not permitted. It was felt that the final regulations should be drafted by the British LTA, a recognition of its status as the senior body. On 25 April Dwight's proposed conditions were published in *Lawn Tennis and Croquet*, and an LTA subcommittee invited suggestions from the public. Then, on 9 July, it was announced that regulations prepared by W. H. Collins, president of the British LTA, had been approved, on all vital points, by the USNLTA. Thus it was Collins who appears to have proposed that the championship should be open to any nation with a recognized lawn tennis association or corresponding organization. The nations originally specified were Australia with New Zealand, the British Isles, British South Africa, Canada, India and the USA. Within the next two years Austria, Belgium, France, Germany, Holland, Sweden, Norway and Switzerland were also specified.

Over the years, the regulations were to be amended many times, though the basic concept remained unchanged.

Only the British Isles challenged in 1900. The Dohertys were unable to make the trip, but the LTA was not greatly concerned, and selected as its representatives Arthur Wentworth Gore, Edmund D. Black and Herbert Roper Barrett. They had to pay some of their expenses themselves and lacked the services of a manager. Though they were not apprehensive at what lay before them, had they known more about the American team of Davis, Whitman and Ward, they would have been.

Davis might have been a genial philanthropist off the court, but he was a pretty tough customer on it. A left-hander, tall, fast and strong, he was the hardest hitter of flat serves in America. He backed these up with steady ground strokes and good volleys. He possessed another weapon, a twist service. This he had been taught by his classmate, Ward, with whom in 1899 he won the intercollegiate and national doubles titles.

Ward was so colour-blind that to him all tennis courts looked brown. He made up for this affliction by continually testing the eyesight of his opponents with sharply twisting serves. It was his relatively short stature that had prompted him to acquire the twist service as an 'equalizer'. It gave him time to get to the net, where he was an adroit volleyer. The American twist came to be a match-winner, especially against those who had never experienced it. In executing the twist (or the kicker, as it is known today), a player arches his back and whips the racquet head upwards and diagonally across the ball from left to right. The ball arcs high over the net and dips sharply. After hitting the court, it swerves towards the receiver's forehand, and rears back towards his backhand.

Whitman, the third American player and the oldest at twenty-three, was the son of a wealthy New England mill owner. For three years, from 1898 to 1900, during which he was holder of the US singles title, he was beaten only four times, whereupon he retired to join the family business. 'He was,' said one commentator, 'a beautiful figure on the courts, a tall, blond, Grecian hero.' Keenly intelligent, his inquiring mind treated the mastery of tennis as an intellectual challenge. Early on, he had decided that what he wanted was an all-court game. Learning from defeat, he relentlessly eradicated weaknesses. His ground strokes were precise, steady and

deceptive, and he rarely wasted an opportunity to finish a point at
the net. Nor did his concentration falter. Ten years after his retirement Whitman could still beat anyone but a ranking player. He gave
some opponents a chance by using a wooden paddle like a pingpong
bat.

Of the more mature British team, Gore was the most celebrated.
At Wimbledon he had been runner-up to Reg Doherty in 1899, and
was to win the first of his three titles in 1901. (His third title came
in 1909, when he was forty-one). Gore, a small, trim man with a
military moustache, was known to his friends as 'Baby'. He relied
almost solely on his forehand and rarely went to the net, but he was
quick on his feet and a good match player. Black was a Scot with
a better rounded game than Gore's, though he was never able to
reach the last eight at Wimbledon. Roper Barrett was a London
solicitor who became an outstanding doubles player. Like Gore,
who was a businessman, his only opportunity to practise was in the
summer evenings after a day's work.

A luncheon was held at the Cannon Street Hotel to say farewell
to Gore and Barrett before they caught the boat train to Liverpool.
(Black, being based in the north, was to rendezvous with them
there.) Collins presented the players with caps of white silk, with
gold embroidery, and bearing the royal standard embroidered in
colours. The LTA requested that as many leading players as possible
should go to Euston railway station at noon on 28 July to give their
representatives 'a hearty send-off'. It may have been surprised by
the response. Tens of thousands lined the route to the station,
and the police assigned to control the crowd thought the occasion
important enough to pin Queen Victoria's jubilee medals to their
tunics. When the players' train departed, the crowd's enthusiasm
knew no bounds, reported a correspondent of *Lawn Tennis and
Croquet*. 'Hats were raised by the men, the ladies waved their
handkerchiefs, and the mob yelled itself hoarse with delight, the
massed bands playing "God Save the Queen" and "Yankee Doodle"
at the same time with brilliant effect.'

The British party arrived at New York on the morning of 4
August, a Saturday. To meet them, there was only the servant of
the American player and USNLTA treasurer, Richard Stevens. 'We
appreciated Mr. Stevens' kindness in sending down his man; it
seemed so friendly and kind and much better than coming himself,'

wrote Roper Barrett years later with apparent sarcasm. Lacking any facilities to practise, 'The Dauntless Three', as they were dubbed by the LTA, decided to visit Niagara, although the matches were scheduled to begin at the Longwood Cricket Club, Boston, in three days' time. They caught a train to Buffalo, crossed to Canada, and made a thorough inspection of the Falls. Then, curiosity satisfied, they made their way back to Boston.

At last they were warmly received. But shocks were in store. The draw for the contest was made by Ward from two straw hats held by Davis and Gore on the clubhouse porch. Outside, next to the two championship courts, there were tables on which were perched the umpires' chairs. On the first day of the tie, which was postponed to the 8th because of rain, Whitman unmercifully attacked Gore's backhand and beat him 6–1, 6–3, 6–2. Black put up stiffer resistance against Davis, but went down in four sets. Davis's first service knocked Black 'all of a heap, as the ball broke at least one yard'. Black vainly hoped that the ball had hit a hole. Both matches were played simultaneously on the adjoining courts and with the heat a stifling 136 degrees Fahrenheit in the sun it was all rather bewildering. After each set the Americans went indoors for a seven-minute rest and rubdown; no doubt a sensible thing to do on a hot day, but a bit unconventional even in those leisurely times. Gore and Black kicked their heels on court.

Next day, Davis and Ward beat Black and Barrett 6–4, 6–4, 6–4. The British pair were reduced to lobbing back the Americans' deliveries. 'Where was Barrett's forehand drive, and where Black's splendid backhand return? Useless, absolutely useless, both of them,' grieved *The Sportsman*. 'Not only did the ball screw, but it rose about 4ft. high in the shape of an egg.'

One reason why in every match the twist services of the Americans were hard to fathom was that they were all different. Davis, being a left-hander, made the ball bound and break differently from Ward, while Whitman, with his Machiavellian reverse twist, was something else again.

The courts added to the visitors' discomfort. 'The ground was abominable . . .' wrote Barrett.

'Picture to yourself a court in England where the grass has been the longest you ever encountered; double the length of that grass and you have the

courts as they were at Longwood at that time. The net was a disgrace to
civilized lawn tennis, held up by guy ropes which were continually sagging,
giving way as much as two or three inches every few games and frequently
requiring adjustment. As for the balls, I hardly like to mention them. They
were awful – soft and mothery – and when served with the American twist
came at you like an animated egg-plum. I do not exaggerate. Neither Beals
Wright nor Holcombe Ward nor Karl Behr can make the balls used at
Wimbledon break as much as these did. They not only swerved in the air,
but, in hitting the ground, broke surely four to five feet. Our team was
altogether taken at a disadvantage. We had never experienced this service
before and it quite nonplussed us.

However, he noted more cheerfully, the spectators were impartial,
and 'the female portion thereof not at all unpleasant to gaze upon'.

Black was also very critical. He alleged that the courts were
covered with worm holes, that the balls squashed flat in the hand,
and that the American officials did not call foot faults though their
players were 'halfway up the court when serving and at the net for
the return of service'.

The British team learned painfully one of the most crucial lessons
of Davis Cup play which was to remain relevant down the years:
that home-court advantage, along with the local environment and
climate, could be all important and warranted a long, careful period
of adaptation.

One American commentator, J. Parmly Paret, a leading player
himself, conceded in *Harper's Weekly* that the American balls were
a shade larger and softer than the British variety. He maintained,
though, that the British failure was one of methods.

The Britishers admit that they had no conception of the skill of the American players before they left home. They came here grossly over-confident,
played for the International Championship with only two days' practice,
and now they have gone home very much disappointed and disgusted.
They were themselves chiefly to blame for their poor showing. Their
objections to the hours of play and the slowness on court of the Americans
seem trivial; they should have adapted themselves to these minor conditions
. . . the inference is plain that at least on our courts, American lawn tennis
players are more skilful than their British cousins.

–2–

THE DOHERTYS
STRIKE BACK

(1901, No contest; 1902, USA;
1903–06, British Isles)

The debacle in a game that they had invented stung British pride and, if nothing else, gave the new competition immediate notoriety. Anxious to reassert their supremacy, the British again challenged in 1901. Britain could draw consolation from the knowledge that her best players had not been involved in the 1900 defeat. Once the Dohertys entered the lists, her fortunes surely would change. Alas, the brothers were not available in 1901. Not wishing to risk another drubbing, the British decided to hold off until they were. At Wimbledon that year, Davis and Ward showed that their Longwood victory was no flash in the pan by reaching the challenge round of the doubles, and were a set all against the Dohertys when rain stopped play. Next day the match was entirely replayed and the Dohertys won the title.

In 1902 the brothers were enlisted with Dr Joshua Pim, under the captaincy of Collins. If Britons were positive the cup would be won, the Dohertys had done much to justify their confidence.

Although of part-Irish decent – and it is remarkable how many of the great players of that period (as in the 1980s!) had Gaelic blood in their veins – the Dohertys were Londoners, from Clapham Park. Reggie Doherty, or 'Big Do', as he was called, was the older by two years, and at 6 feet 1 inch, much the taller. Laurie ('Little Do') had followed him through Westminster School and Cambridge University, where both were unbeaten in inter-varsity matches. An older brother, W.V., who went to Oxford, was also an accomplished player, but gave up the game to concentrate on theological studies.

Reggie won the Wimbledon singles four successive times, from

1897 to 1900, beating his brother in the 1898 challenge round. Laurie won the title five straight times, from 1902 to 1906. Together the brothers won the doubles title eight times and were runners-up twice. Wherever they played in England or on the Continent they were supreme and were universally admired not only for their elegant strokes but for their pleasant personalities, their dark, suave good looks and impeccable sportsmanship. Beautiful women of noble blood patronized them. (When the Dohertys wrote a book on the game in 1903 they gallantly dedicated it to the Grand Duchess Anastasie of Mecklenburg–Schwerin and included a photograph of the fetching young lady on the frontispiece.)

Reggie, a man of grace and careless ease, was the more naturally gifted stroke player. Slower than Laurie, he often appeared to have no need to hurry, his anticipation being so uncanny that the ball seemed attracted to his racquet. Both brothers had shown flair at other ball games in their youth, and at tennis their instinctive coordination was complemented by excellent technique and flawless judgement. Reggie's best shot was his backhand down the line hit with top spin, while Laurie, a quicker man, was famous for his smashing and was probably the better match player. 'Their style was so easy and effortless, and they made the game appear so simple,' said George Hillyard, a contemporary, 'it is probable, indeed almost certain, that the great majority of spectators failed to realize the pace they were getting on the ball, or how exceedingly awkward they were making things for their opponents.'

Reggie's problem was his health. A slender man of 140 pounds, he suffered from chronic dyspepsia and other ailments that undermined his constitution. He often told Hillyard that he didn't know what it was like to feel really well. Finally, doctors advised him not to play long singles matches, and he was to die of heart disease at thirty-six. But whatever his frustrations, Reggie – like Laurie – never failed to be sweet-tempered and courteous. Completely unaffected, they usually carried but one racquet and a pocket handkerchief onto court, and hardly ever took refreshment between sets. Little Do had his shirtsleeves buttoned at the wrist; Big Do liked to let his sleeves flap loosely.

Their team-mate, Dr Pim, was an Irishman, then aged thirty-three. His best playing days were in the early 1890s when he twice won the Wimbledon singles. Once known as 'The Ghost' because of his thinness, he had played little top-class tennis for some years and now his ample silhouette was certainly visible. However, there were doubts about the Dohertys' stamina, and Pim was a hardy character who had experience of American conditions. 'I don't care what *he* does,' Pim was wont to say when reminded of an opponent's skill. 'It's what I do that will decide the result.' Pim sailed from England a week after his team-mates. He had been mysteriously nominated for the contest as 'Mr X' and was otherwise referred to as 'A Famous Player', pseudonyms thought necessary to conform with medical ethics.

The Dohertys were not going to make the same mistake as their predecessors and be underprepared. They entered the Eastern championships at Longwood, hoping to win the doubles. This would enable them later to play the winners of the Western championship for the right to challenge the holders of the national doubles title at Newport. They also entered the Eastern singles, but, anxious to avoid overexertion before the cup matches, both retired after comfortably winning a few rounds. No one appeared to be upset by their blatant use of the tournament for practice. 'The Dohertys availed themselves of an opportunity to become accustomed to the American style of playing and to acquire a familiarity with American turf and balls,' reported the *Boston Globe*. 'Nobody should question the propriety of their withdrawing if it seems policy to do so.' In fact, the brothers delighted American spectators as much as they did their countrymen. 'Wearing the light blue colours of Cambridge University and attired in white clothes,' wrote the *Globe* man, 'they contrasted favourably with the grotesque and dishevelled appearance of some of the American players.'

Quickly adjusting to the Longwood conditions, which had been greatly improved since the visit of The Dauntless Three, the Dohertys won the doubles. In doing so they beat two of the best American pairs and looked in fine form. Collins, however, now made the first big blunder in Davis Cup history. He decided to play Pim and Reggie in the singles, and to reserve Laurie, who had won the singles at Wimbledon only a few weeks before, for the doubles. 'Must be a jolly fine team,' quipped the good-natured Laurie. 'You haven't asked either the Irish or English champion to play!' Collins's rationale was that hot weather might reduce Laurie to 'a rag' if he had to play three matches. He knew the Americans would have a fresh pair for the doubles and did not want to risk having two fatigued men to play them. 'Apart from that,' explained Collins later in reply to English critics, 'the doctor was playing extremely well in practice against the Dohertys, and we saw no reason *before the match* that he would not show the Americans some of his old quality. He was never in better training in his life . . . I don't even think he was over-trained, although he had taken off more than two stone in six weeks.'

For the singles the Americans induced Whitman to come out of retirement and replaced Davis with Larned. The brilliant, free-hitting Larned was then twenty-nine and the reigning US singles title-holder. He was to win the US title six more times – the last occasion in 1911 when he was thirty-eight – and was to be out of the American top ten only once in twenty years (when he fought in Cuba). No man before the advent of Bill Tilden dominated American tennis for so long a period. Best known for his aggressive ground strokes, particularly his backhand, he was not as steady as Whitman, but he was a natural, graceful player and destroyed many a net-rusher with the speed and deception of his passing shots. In addition, he was agile and could volley and smash well.

The matches, which were played in 'terrific heat' at the Crescent Athletic Club, of Bay Ridge, New York, on 6, 7 and 8 August, created immense interest. For the first and only time in Davis Cup history no admission charge was made and crowds of 5000 and 6000 respectively watched the first two days' play. Some fans even went by boat down the Hudson and across the bay. The doubles, oddly, was held on the third day when, although the tie had been decided, 10,000 people attended.

As in 1900, the opening singles were played side by side, Larned met Reggie, while Whitman took on Pim. Both Americans were leading by two sets to love when a thunderstorm caused a postponement. Next morning Whitman lost the third set but came back to take the fourth 6–0. Larned, however, floundered against Reggie, who won in five sets.

In the afternoon of the same day the players returned to the courts for the reverse singles. Larned recovered from his lapse and outdrove Pim for a 6–3, 6–2, 6–3 victory. Now American hopes hinged on Whitman since, if the contest was still alive in the doubles, the Dohertys must be favoured to win. The odds against Reggie were too great. His plucky fightback in the morning had taken toll of his strength and nervous energy. He tried to play Whitman from the net, but the calculating American blocked the ball back to his feet. A 6–1, 7–5, 6–4 win secured the cup.

Finally getting onto court on the third day, Laurie partnered Reggie to a futile four-set win over Davis and Ward.

The Dohertys gained some revenge at the subsequent American championships. In a typical gesture, Laurie forfeited to his brother in the singles semifinals so that Reggie would have a chance to avenge his Davis Cup defeat by Whitman. Reggie duly went on to beat Whitman in the final. But Larned retained his title in the challenge round when Reggie wilted on a very hot day. The brothers again defeated Davis and Ward in the challenge round of the doubles, becoming the first foreign pair to capture the title.

Despite his gaffe, Collins remained captain (being president of the LTA helped) and in 1903 he was determined to play *both* the Dohertys in all matches, come hell or high water. This time it was the Americans whose judgement was astray. Whitman had quit for good and Davis also had retired. As with swimmers and athletes, many American players in those days abandoned their sport while still young to concentrate on careers. Larned virtually picked himself, but the third- and fourth-ranked players, Beals Wright and Holcolme Ward, were passed over in favour of Robert Wrenn. Though 'Battling Bob' had won the US National championship four times, he had not been ranked in the top ten since 1897 when he was number one. He was essentially a bustling volleyer and had been identified with the 'centre theory' – advancing behind a deep shot down the centre to reduce the opponent's angles for a pass.

Collins was keen to make amends. He planned and worked tirelessly to get the Dohertys into peak form and the best possible physical condition. But two days before the matches were scheduled to begin at Longwood he was shocked to learn that Reggie had strained his shoulder while playing in an invitation tournament at Nahant the day before. A doctor made a series of visits to the English camp. He warned that if Reggie played on the first day he might seriously injure his shoulder. On the other hand, if he rested for another twenty-four hours he might be fit for the following day. What a dilemma! Collins had brought to America a third player, the Irishman, Harold Mahoney, for just such an emergency. He

inquired whether he could play Mahoney on the first day and substitute Reggie for him in the second singles. Expressing sympathy,
Larned, the American captain, said that under the rules he could
not. Larned would agree to Mahoney replacing the nominated
Reggie only if he played both singles. Thus Collins had to decide
whether to play Mahoney and risk a fiasco similar to that with Pim,
or concede America a walkover on the first day and hope Reggie
was fit enough to play, *and win*, his remaining matches. He courageously opted for the second course and prayed for a miracle.

Laurie relieved some of the pressure on the first day, 4 August,
by beating Wrenn in straight sets. For the next two days it rained
so hard that no play was possible, and Collins must have felt like
dancing in the deluge. When the rain cleared on the 7th, his patient
was able to partner his brother to a four-set win over Wrenn and
his brother George. Britain was one up with two to play.

The final day was one of drama. Once again, both matches were
played simultaneously, only an umpire's chair between them. Over-
hearing the scores and the cheers or gasps from the adjoining court,
the players were subjected to enormous strain. As Collins was to
point out, the players had 'not only the anxiety of their own match
on their shoulders but could not help following the state of affairs
in the other'.

Both matches went to a fifth set. At one stage Laurie and Larned
were 4 all in the fifth, while Reggie and Wrenn were 3 all. Reggie's
shoulder was troubling him. He could not hit all his shots freely,
and Wrenn, who had come from behind throughout the match, was
fighting hard. As for Laurie, at 4 all he was down 15–40 on his
service. He served and went to the net, and Larned hit a clear
winner. The umpire awarded the point and game to Larned, who
started to change ends. Laurie politely asked the umpire if his serve
had been in. The umpire looked to where a linesman should have
been. There was only an empty chair. Somebody remarked that the
absent official had said earlier that he would have to leave at a certain
time to catch a boat and in the excitement his departure had not
been noticed. Dr Dwight, the referee, was asked for a ruling. He
nobly ordered the point to be replayed. Laurie held service and won
two of the next three games for the match, 6–3, 6–8, 6–0, 2–6, 7–5.
The cup was Britain's.

Little Do was given the greatest ovation that any foreign

sportsman had received in America. 'It was a spontaneous recognition,' said the *Boston Sunday Globe*, 'of the great proficiency, pluck and sportsmanship that had endeared this modest and unassuming British player to all lovers of clean sport.' Minutes later, Reggie had pipped Wrenn 6–4, 3–6, 6–3, 6–8, 6–4. Cheers broke out again.

Laurie left an indelible mark on American tennis, for within a week or so he had relieved Larned of his American title and had retained the National doubles title with Reggie.

For the next three years the trophy was successfully defended at Wimbledon. Laurie was the main means by which the stranglehold was maintained, as Reggie, who now found singles too much of a strain, confined himself to doubles. When Laurie retired he was undefeated in twelve rubbers – the only man ever to escape a loss over a substantial cup career. Reggie's record was eight matches for one loss.

In 1904 the Americans found the task of raising a team (and sufficient funds) too difficult. New York enthusiasts blamed the Boston controllers of the game. There was keen rivalry between the two cities. ('The best thing about Boston is the five o'clock train to New York' was a popular jibe), and the *New York Times* reported that some local players were so aroused that they intended to form a new national body, but the talk came to nothing. Challenges came instead from across the English Channel, where players had become fascinated by the Anglo-American rivalry. France and Belgium, the strongest Continental nations, and Austria wanted to become involved too. Of course, their men would be at a disadvantage because they had little experience of top international play and some were strangers to grass courts which, largely because of the climate, were considered impracticable on the Continent. However, European players would never improve unless they tested themselves against the best, and it was much cheaper to do this in England than in America.

Austria had second thoughts and defaulted to Belgium, who played off against France at Wimbledon in late June for the right to meet the British Isles. France had a versatile player in Max Decugis, who had collected the second of his eight French singles championships in 1904. Decugis was as acquainted with grass courts as with clay, since he had gone to school in England and had won the British junior championship. The Belgians, Paul de Borman and Willie le

Maire de Warzée, were no strangers to grass-court tennis either. Both had played at Wimbledon, where that year de Borman reached the semifinals.

On the first day Belgium suffered a setback when de Borman defaulted to Decugis at 4–6, 3–5 with an injured arm. Le Maire de Warzée levelled matters by easily beating Paul Aymé, but then Decugis and Aymé came from behind to win the doubles in five sets. On the final gripping day Belgium won the last two rubbers, each in five sets, and thus reached the challenge round for what turned out to be the only time in the next eighty years.

De Borman possessed a prodigious top-spin forehand drive which, though awkward for opponents on European hard courts, was less effective on grass. Nevertheless, when the challenge round began on 2 July, he took the first set off Britain's Frank Riseley, who had been runner-up to Laurie Doherty at Wimbledon for the past two years. This was the only set that the Belgians were able to gather in a very one-sided contest. Laurie beat de Borman for the loss of six games, and the doubles was even more of a cakewalk for Laurie and his brother. The British scored a resounding 5–0 victory.

America again looked like being absent in 1905. But with national honour at stake, a public appeal raised the necessary funds, and William J. Clothier, a tall Philadelphian, joined Ward, Larned and Wright on the team, under the captaincy of Paul Dashiel. Dashiel was requested by the selectors to use Ward and Larned in singles, and Ward and Wright in doubles. He did not name either of these combinations in the preliminary matches, and America might have fared better if he had felt strong enough to ignore the instructions in the challenge round also, for over the English summer Wright, a robust, left-handed serve-and-volleyer, emerged as the outstanding American singles player.

In this year Australasia entered the fray. Norman Brookes, a twenty-seven-year-old Melbourne businessman, made his first trip to England accompanied by a New Zealand-born Melbourne friend, Alf Dunlop, and Harry Parker of Sydney, also originally from across the Tasman. They were to join up with yet another New Zealander, the twenty-two-year-old Anthony Wilding, who was studying at Cambridge. The British knew more about Wilding than Brookes, although the ubiquitous Dr Eaves, who had helped Brookes hone his game in Melbourne, had warned of the Australian's prowess.

The Americans were considered the principal threat. According to the foremost English tennis writer of that time, A. Wallis Myers, they were 'trained and tended like racehorses'. Myers was impressed by 'such outward symbols of majesty as black shoes, leather racket-cases and a certain dignified aloofness off the courts'.

Brookes's left-handed serving and volleying quickly commanded British respect. Wright beat him at the Queen's Club tournament, but at Wimbledon the Australian got through to the final. There he was down 2–4 in the fifth set to the new English star, Sidney H. Smith – Smith of Stroud – who had beaten Ward and Larned in earlier rounds and whose forehand was particularly destructive. Brookes, on the brink of defeat, decided to attack it. He so surprised Smith that he broke up his rhythm and ran out the winner. But Little Do was too strong for Brookes in the challenge round.

Before the Davis Cup matches, a dinner to welcome the teams was held at the Café Royal in London. From a witty speech made by W. H. Wilberforce, we can see that by now the glamour of the Dohertys captivated the tennis world. 'It is notorious,' said Wilberforce, 'that both of them have exercised a most extraordinary and, I dare say, excusable fascination over the members of the other sex.' He urged them to 'turn that quality to some useful purpose before it is too late', and added, 'Let them marry and let them rear up a new generation of Dohertys, who shall carry on the traditions, the glorious traditions, of their fathers'.

The qualifying cup contests were held simultaneously at Queen's, Belgium withdrawing because de Borman was indisposed. America, represented by Ward and Clothier in the singles, and by Ward and Wright in the doubles, made quick work of France. Australasia had a slightly harder fight against Austria. In the final round, also played at Queen's, America denied Australasia a single rubber. Wilding, who was still refining his raw talent, had not been expected to beat Wright or Larned, and lost to Larned in straight sets on the first day. But Brookes was already seen as 'a worthy foe for Doherty's steel' and was thought likely to win at least one match. He lost to Wright 12–10, 5–7, 12–10, 6–4 in a spectacular battle of volleys. With his loosely strung racquet, Brookes had fine touch, but Wright's volleys were crisper and more decisive. When Ward and Wright beat Brookes and Dunlop in the doubles, the Americans had won.

The fact that the British Isles then repelled America 5–0 in the challenge round at Wimbledon on 21, 22 and 24 July seemed to indicate a huge margin in British superiority. Such was not the case. Little Do was two sets to love down to Ward in the opening match as the determined New Yorker tore into the net to intercept every return. Ward amassed points with all kinds of volleys – cross-court forehands that zipped away like bullets; stop volleys that fell dead; delicate backhands that grazed the net. For those two sets captain Dalshiel could scarcely hide his glee. Normally, Laurie's tactic against the twist serve was to stand in close and curb the spin. This time he looked helpless and all he could hope was that Ward's pyrotechnics would sputter out. Gradually, and then more quickly, they did. The exhausting service action and the constant net-rushing sapped his energy. The champion allowed him only three games in the last three sets, winning 7–9, 4–6, 6–1, 6–2, 6–0.

Smith's powerful forehand was the decisive factor in his 6–4, 6–4, 5–7, 6–4 win over Larned, and the Dohertys won a seesawing doubles, beating Ward and Wright, 8–6 in the fifth set. Collins, the British captain, had carried a little silver flask filled with 1840 brandy in case his players 'felt faint'. It was not needed. America, however, had played three Davis Cup ties in twelve days, all without the long break at the end of the third set which they were accustomed to. They had needed to be fit and they were.

In the following year, 1906, Wright, who had won the American championship on his return home, was expected to be the linchpin of the American effort, along with Ward. Two lesser players, Raymond Little and Kreigh Collins, were added to the team in case of mishap. And mishap there soon was. On the eve of the team's departure, Wright took part in some exuberant farewells, knowing he had the voyage to England on which to recover. When he awoke in his hotel next morning his mouth was dry and he rang for a bottle of soda water. It arrived unopened. Wright had no bottle opener, so he tried to open the bottle with a toothbrush. The neck of the bottle broke in his right hand. Badly gashed, he called for help and fainted. He received urgent treatment, but on the ship the wound became infected. Within days Wright developed blood poisoning, and in London only expert medical aid saved is life. One of his fingers had to be amputated.

There was no question of the American number one playing and he was replaced by Little. France and Austria had submitted entries but decided to withdraw, and fortunately for America Brookes could not spare the time to make the long trip from Melbourne. In the qualifying tie against Australasia at Newport, in Wales, the first two singles were split. Wilding beat Little in straight sets, but Ward accounted for Les Poidevin, a young Australian who had gone to England to study medicine, hardly dreaming he would ever play at Wimbledon and Lord's (as a member of the Lancashire cricket XI) and in the Davis Cup. Ward and Little comfortably defeated Wilding and Poidevin in the doubles, and in the third singles Wilding pulled up from 3–5 in the fifth set to beat Ward.

The nonchalant New Zealander and his father, together with Wallis Myers, had arranged to travel from England that evening to a tournament at Prague. To meet their schedule they had to catch a train at Newport while the last rubber was in progress. Poidevin and Little were a set all, with Poidevin leading in the third set. Myers arranged for a friend to wire the result to Swindon where their train would stop en route to London. If Poidevin won, Wilding would cancel his trip in order to play in the challenge round.

The cable duly informed them that Little had won in four sets. The Wildings rushed on. Finally, they had twenty minutes to get from Paddington Station to Canon Street. In their haste to load their luggage onto a handsom cab, they knocked down a porter and left some of the baggage behind. But they still missed the connection. Even in those days Davis Cup ties could complicate schedules.

The challenge round was held at Wimbledon on 15, 16 and 18 June, and the British Isles again won 5–0, more convincingly this time. Americans by now had a greater dread of Smith's forehand than any shot of the Dohertys. 'You cannot play Smith from the back of the court,' they used to say. 'Yet if you go to the net he passes you like a knife through butter.' He was in devastating form against Ward and Little. After four Davis Cup matches against America, the only matches he ever played in the competition, Smith had dropped but one set.

Poor Beals Wright watched the rout in anguish. To cheer him up the All England Club presented him with a gold cigarette case. A bottle opener might have been more appropriate.

And so the distinguished reign of the Dohertys came to a close. Many were puzzled why Laurie should decide not to defend either his Wimbledon title or the Davis Cup in 1907 when his powers were undiminished and his country needed him. Perhaps, like Bjorn Borg in a later era, he was tired of the burden that his very excellence had imposed upon him. Now his tennis career was finished. He needed a change and turned to golf. Sadly, he too was to die prematurely, at forty-three. Neither Reggie nor Laurie married, and along with the gallantry and glory there was an element of tragedy in their story. But their example continued to inspire their countrymen. For as *The Times* said of them when Laurie died, they 'played an English game in the spirit in which English men think that games should be played'.

-3-

THE CUP GOES
DOWN UNDER

(1907–11, Australasia)

Norman Brookes and Anthony Wilding were the sons of English migrants. William Brookes arrived in Melbourne from Northampton with £9 in his pocket and became a prosperous businessman. He sent Norman, his youngest son, to the elite Melbourne Grammar School, but denied him the chance of gaining a university degree. Instead, the boy was given a job as a junior clerk at his father's company, the Australian Paper Mills. The fact that he did not make his first visit to England until he was nearly twenty-eight was partly due to old Mr Brookes's insistence that he paid his own way.

Wilding's father, who came from the West Country, was a barrister who acquired a spacious property at Fownhope, near Christchurch. An all-round sportsman, he installed there a tennis court, cricket nets, a bowling green and a swimming pool, and Anthony matured into a very fit young man with his father's love of sport. In 1902 he boarded a freighter packed with 100,000 carcases of frozen mutton on his way to a cramming school in England and thence to Cambridge to study law.

Brookes and Wilding, who became one of the most famous of all cup pairs, were different in many respects. Whereas Wilding was a tall, robust man of 184 pounds, the sallow-skinned Brookes was lean and wiry and suffered from a duodenal ulcer. The gregarious Wilding became intimate friends with statesmen, European aristocrats and royalty, frequently being a house guest in palaces and stately homes. An extrovert, he loved motorbikes and rode them on the Continent, a debonair figure with a silk scarf draped round his neck. Women adored him. Fair-haired and blue-eyed, he was the game's Prince Charming.

Brookes in contrast was reserved and taciturn, his pale blue eyes rarely conveying much emotion. He commanded respect, even awe, rarely affection. 'He was suspicious and cagey,' his wife once said, 'and these characteristics came out in his tennis. He was The Wizard who thought two shots ahead. At every change of ends he planned a little scheme. He was like a general without an army. . . . He saw more in the strategy of the game than he did in the strategy of actual living.'

Even more than Wilding, Norman Brookes had a flair for ball games. It was said that if he had concentrated on cricket, he might have reached Test standard, while at billiards a break of 100 was nothing to him, and at golf he got down to a plus handicap and won national titles. Once, when the Australian croquet championship was held in Melbourne, Brookes invited the winner to his home and converted the family tennis court into a croquet lawn. He had never played the game before, but he soundly beat the champion.

Brookes came to prominence in Australia as an interstate player in 1896, fifteen years after tournament tennis began in that country. Self-taught, his original method was to thump the ball as hard as he could. In 1902 he realized he still had much to learn when Dr Eaves, on a visit from England, ran him to a frazzle in the final of the New South Wales championship with clever serving and volleying. Eaves introduced him to the twist service and encouraged him to temper pace with placement. Constantly experimenting, Brookes changed his style to controlled speed in ground shots and forceful, though subtle, volleying. His serve was baffling and his touch tantalizing. His top-spin forehand was not only more powerful than most others but he could take the ball on the rise so as to get into the net.

Nobody would have guessed at his talent by his appearance. He dressed conservatively, with his shirts buttoned to the throat as well as at the wrists, and he wore a peaked grey tweed cap. One photograph at a Davis Cup practice session shows him wearing a tie! His racquet looked disarming too: it weighed 13½ ounces, was flattened at the top of the rim and had slack strings.

In 1904 the various Australian states formed a national lawn tennis association, and linked up with New Zealand in 1905 to hold Australasian championships and organize joint teams to play for the Davis Cup. That year, when Brookes got permission from his father

39

to take leave from the firm to test his game in England, the new association asked him to represent it in the Davis Cup.

By now Wilding had been persuaded to sacrifice his first love, cricket, in favour of lawn tennis. At Cambridge he became secretary of the Varsity Lawn Tennis Club and was conscious of the Doherty traditions. His own strength was in his ground strokes, which were fast and accurate. He spent many hours hitting balls against a wall to mould a sounder and more orthodox English-style backhand, and played at Wimbledon for the first time in 1904. A year later at Wimbledon, as we have seen, he was overshadowed by Brookes. But clearly he was a young man with a future, and in 1906, when he went home, he won the Australasian singles and doubles.

Brookes meanwhile pondered the lessons of his first visit to England. There were dangers, for instance, in overdependence on the twist service. Players like Smith and Gore, who were fast and had strong forehands, could, once they had got the hang of a delivery, run around an excessively breaking but slower ball and then slam it. Much better to serve a faster ball with not quite so much spin but with good placement. Above all, one needed variety.

At Wimbledon in 1907 Brookes applied his new strategies. Wilding, in the second round, was the only player to push him to five sets. In the final he implacably seized the crown that Little Do had discarded, beating Gore 6–4, 6–2, 6–2. He was the first overseas player and the first left-hander to win the title, and with Wilding he took the doubles to boot.

The successes inflated Australasian expectations for the subsequent cup matches. America was the only other challenger, and both she and the British Isles were weakened. Neither Larned nor Ward was available, and Karl Behr, a Yale man who was ranked fifth, came in to fill the breach. His partner was the persistent Beals Wright.

For the home country there were worse problems in replacing the Dohertys. Smith had played no tournaments all summer and after an attempt to get ready he withdrew, saying his form was too poor. Britain was left with Gore and Barrett, members of the pioneering team seven years earlier. The first was now aged thirty-nine, the other, thirty-three.

The opening match of the elimination round saw Brookes renew his rivalry with Wright. This time he was tactically superior and more accurate. Wright's father noted the way that Brookes, before serving, would shrewdly look over toward Beals and decide where his opponent was expecting the ball to come. Then he would serve. 'It was a nasty serve, fast, twisting, beautifully placed, always coming where his opponent wasn't expecting it. You couldn't do much with it; in fact, you were lucky to get it back at all,' observed George Wright. Brookes won 6–4, 6–4, 6–2.

Wilding had a closer match with the impetuous Behr, an even-time sprinter who threatened to rush him to defeat. Remaining calm, the New Zealander survived in five sets. The doubles was a long, wavering match in which the erratic Behr recovered from a shaky start to give Wright brilliant support. In the end it was Brookes and Wilding who faded and the Americans won 3–6, 12–10, 4–6, 6–2, 6–3.

On the third day Wright gave his country a fighting chance by reversing the result of his first-round Wimbledon defeat by Wilding. Their match was still unfinished when, because of the prospect of failing light, Brookes and Behr commenced the last rubber on another court. Behr's all-out attack, and the noise from the centre court unsettled Brookes, who lost the first set. Then the players were able to move into the centre. Brookes benefited from the changed atmosphere and won 4–6, 6–4, 6–1, 6–2.

The following weekend the challengers were back on court against Gore and Barrett. Gore was a bonny fighter who had been known to revive himself with champagne in long matches. He strove valliantly against Brookes, but not even a magnum of Dom Perignon could have saved him. He lost 5–7, 1–6, 5–7. Barrett led Wilding 6–1, 4–2 when his physical condition began to evaporate. He lost in four sets. Next day Brookes and Wilding went to a 6–3, 6–4 lead in the doubles and the cup looked well within their reach. In the third set, at 5–4, with Brookes serving, they were only a point from victory. The Englishmen dug their heels in. Suddenly, Barrett began to dominate the match with his volleys, and Wilding's game fell away. The defenders won the last three sets 7–5, 6–2, 13–11.

That Wilding still lacked some tactical skill was evident in his next match, against Gore. He tried to play the steady Englishman too much from the baseline. Defying his years, Gore won 3–6, 6–3, 7–5, 6–2. Could Barrett now complete the rearguard action? Brookes quickly gave an answer. He served devilishly, placed the ball to Barrett's maximum embarrassment and won 6–2, 6–0, 6–3. In the

Australian's luggage when he sailed for home a few weeks later were several large pieces of silverware, not least of which was Dwight Davis's trophy. It cost Brookes about £7 10s to get it back to Melbourne, but that didn't bother him at all.

Australasia's triumph had a profound effect on the game world-wide. British superiority in many sports had long been taken for granted, and in lawn tennis it was generally assumed there would be successors to the Dohertys. Now other countries could see wider possibilities for the Davis Cup. Down Under, people who had been only vaguely aware of tennis had their curiosity aroused. More courts were put down and more players attracted to the game.

The cup was to remain in the Antipodes for the next five years. In that period, paradoxically, the competition did not grow despite the initial increased interest, for European nations could not justify the expense of funding teams that might have to travel so far and still be unsuccessful. In any case many players simply would not have been available for selection. A voyage from Britain to Australia and back could take up to twelve weeks. When practice and playing time was added, the trip might last more than three months. For those who had positions in business or the professions, such a journey was impracticable.

After challenges were issued by America and the British Isles in 1908, negotiations between the British and Australasian associations over the staging of the preliminary tie in Australia ended in rancour. Australians were affronted by the British LTA's request for a guarantee of the British team's expenses. It was pointed out that the regulations provided for each visiting team to receive one third of the profits of the preliminary match and one half of the profits from the challenge round. 'Australasia, moreover, never even hinted at receiving any assistance towards sending a team to England,' said an irate John Koch, secretary of the Lawn Tennis Association of Victoria, 'and such a proposal, coming as it did from a country which had held four contests for the cup, and received a large profit therefrom, considerably lowered the prestige which English lawn tennis players and the association which controls the sport on the European Continent had always enjoyed in Australasia.'

The Americans were more accommodating. They offered the British a guarantee of £300 for the match to be played in the United States. Two newcomers to the Davis Cup arena, M. J. G. Ritchie and J. C. Parke, were duly sent away, and fared better than many expected. Ritchie was a handy player of thirty-seven years of age who had reached the final rounds of the Wimbledon singles several times. Parke, an Irish all-rounder, was still improving at tennis at the age of twenty-six since he had begun specializing at the game.

The Americans chose for the singles Larned and Wright, their reigning champion and the runner-up, and for the doubles Fred Alexander and Harold Hackett, who held the doubles crown. Boston was chosen as the venue, and again the bewildering practice of playing the singles side by side was continued. Larned beat Parke 6–3, 6–3, 7–5, but Ritchie surprised Wright 6–1, 6–3, 6–2, mainly by attacking his backhand and keeping him off balance at the back of the court. Wright's basic tactic was to chop the ball and get to the net. Ritchie anticipated Wright's chop shots so well that he took over the net instead. Alexander and Hackett won the doubles in four sets, and on the final day Larned was too steady for Ritchie, while Wright pulled back from 8–10, 3–6, 3–5 to beat Parke, who used the same tactics against him as Ritchie had employed.

The challenge round, at Melbourne on 27, 28 and 30 November, was one of the most thrilling ever held. America relied on a two-man team, Wright and Alexander, who arrived a month early with three supporters. By the time they went home their names had become bywords in Australia for sportsmanship and courage.

Brookes and Wilding approached their task earnestly. The Wizard was so much on top of his game that in the interstate series two weeks before the internationals he beat two of the next best players in Australia, H. A. Parker and Horrie Rice, without conceding a game. 'It's like stealing milk from sick kittens,' commented a spectator. Nevertheless Wilding, who had left Cambridge and hoped to be called to the New Zealand Bar (he never was), set about improving his friend's suspect stamina with a training regimen. They rose every morning at seven o'clock, had a cup of tea, went for a walk and did a little running. At 8.30 they practised strokes, then played up to five sets flat out. After lunch there were three sets of doubles, or special attention was given to a weakness. The programme ended with skipping, running or 'a little game with the wall', followed by a bath and massage. Both were in bed by 10.15.

The challenge round began amid scenes of great excitement. At the Wharehouseman's Ground (now the Albert Ground) seven thousand spectators, many of them watching a tennis match for the first time, packed into stands which extended over the outside footpaths. Some of the best players in the land – men such as Dunlop and Parker – had been given jobs as linesmen. Australia had become a nation only seven years before. Up to then it had been a collection of British colonies and even now the population was well under four million. The Davis Cup was to play a part in binding the young nation together and giving Australians a sense of national identity and pride. The Governor, the Prime Minister and the Chief Justice were among those who saw fit to mark the first Australasian defence with their presence.

Brookes and Alexander walked out arm in arm wearing long overcoats and towels knotted scarflike round their necks. 'The picture as they shed their coats and threw down the towels at the foot of the umpire's chair,' reported an observer, 'was suggestive of a prize fight rather than a tennis bout, for there was a bucket of sawdust, a pail of ice-water, a pair of jugs of barley-water, spare towels, and a small boy in white to wait on each.'

Alexander, who preferred the doubles game, was so nervous at the start that he often foxed the balls himself instead of waiting for the ballboy, and he was soon down 0–4. He continued to hurl himself into the net, and his hard-hitting eventually won him the set. Brookes, who had not lost a set for two years, realized he had a fight on his hands. At 7 all in the second set he was under a lot of pressure, and had to draw on all his resources on a very warm day to win that and then the third set. After Alexander had won the fourth set, the two men slumped on chairs with handkerchiefs over their heads. Wright walked over with a little bottle, which Alexander declined. Wright tossed it to Brookes, who smiled, nodded, and took a swig. Perhaps it helped; he won 5–7, 9–7, 6–2, 4–6, 6–3, and walked off as he had arrived, arm-in-arm with Alexander.

Wright outsmarted Wilding with adroit drops and lobs. Wilding's training was of no avail. The American won 3–6, 7–5, 6–3, 6–1, and it was one rubber all.

The doubles fluctuated. Brookes and Wilding led 6–4, 6–2, 5–4, but again they wilted with victory within grasp and lost the third set, 5–7. Brookes looked spent as the Americans gathered momentum, winning the fourth set at 6–1. Only Wilding's fine play held back the avalanche. Then, in the fifth set, when the defenders were down 0–2, Brookes somehow revived and produced all his brilliance. The home side took the set 6–4, and the gallant Americans leaped the net to congratulate them.

The Brookes *v.* Wright match on the third day was a classic. There was a hot north wind and it was 102 degrees in the shade. Brookes was always vulnerable in extreme heat, but when he led 6–0, 6–3, 4–3 and 40–0, with his serve to follow, he seemed to be out of danger. At that point the physically stronger Wright was heartened by a lucky net cord. He pulled the third set out of the fire, won the fourth set and led 4–1 in the fifth. Brookes now appeared to be fighting a losing battle against disappointment, fatigue and waning concentration. With a supreme effort, he levelled and went on to serve for the match at 6–5. The crowd, who had been yelling at every point, were in uproar. 'I'll take this one instead,' Wright shouted at the stands. He was as good as his word. Brookes, who was trying to ward off exhaustion with sips of brandy, broke through again for 10–9. Again he was kept at bay. At last the lion-hearted Wright won the set, 12–10, and Brookes, ashen and close to collapse, was escorted home.

Wilding had been lying on a bed at the Brookes residence with a novel and an electric fan. He arrived at the ground shortly before it was time for him to play. Alexander less wisely had been at court-side, watching Wright's heroic struggle and emotionally playing every stroke with him. He was a bundle of nerves. To the crowd's delight, Wilding went through him 6–3, 6–4, 6–1.

Enthusiasts hoisted Wilding on to their shoulders. A pressman vaulted the fence, stuffed his copy into his pocket, his pencil into his mouth, grabbed Wilding's foot and led the procession to the clubhouse. The reporter from the *Australasian* noted that Beals Wright appeared in sacque suit and straw hat looking as though he had been out for a quiet stroll. As Wright consoled Alexander and they walked off, there was a call for cheers for America, 'and a response that must have warmed the hearts of as fine a pair of sportsmen as were ever seen in Australia'.

The matches ensured a prosperous future for the game in Australia. Up to now most Australians had regarded lawn tennis as a genteel game for people with money; a 'milk and water' game, as one newspaper put it. The challenge round had shown that it could be a gruelling test of physical fitness, nerve and skill.

But while lawn tennis in Australia and New Zealand was given a tremendous fillip, the rest of the world continued to be inhibited by the difficulty in mounting challenges. In 1909 America offered the British a $2000 guarantee to cover expenses and once more the British team travelled to America for the preliminary round at Germantown. Larned and Clothier were much too strong for Parke and Charles Dixon in the singles, the only set won by the British being in the doubles.

A crisis arose when it was learned that none of the leading Americans was able to make the trip to Sydney for the challenge round. Beals Wright, for instance, did not play all year because he suffered from the prolonged effects of sunstroke Down Under. To prevent a default, two young Californians, Maurice McLoughlin and Melville Long, were pressed into service. McLoughlin, born in Carson City, Nevada, was to be the first public parks player to win the US title (in 1912 and 1913), having been a ballboy in San Francisco when Davis's group played there in 1899. Up to his emergence, most of the champions in all countries were either gentlemen of means or from the upper middle class. There was a widespread belief that you couldn't become a champion unless you had a rich father and gave ten years' undivided attention to developing your game. The champions tended to be members of elite clubs, often had a lawn court at home, and were usually able to travel extensively at their own expense. McLoughlin was from a humbler background and had learned the game on cement in California, where the climate permitted tennis to be played throughout the year. In 1909 he was not yet twenty, but that summer he reached the All-Comers' final at Newport, losing to Clothier. He was a dynamic server and smasher, had a punishing forehand, a deft volley, and never stopped running. His dashing game and meteoric rise, together with his sunny disposition and red hair, captured the American public's imagination. They called him the 'California Comet'.

McLoughlin and Long stayed at the Royal Sydney Golf Club, and impressed their hosts with their demeanour and their equipment – they possessed twelve racquets apiece and seventy tennis shirts between them. But in the challenge round at Sydney on 27, 29 and 30 November, the youngsters could not win a rubber. In stretching

Wilding to 3–6, 8–6, 6–2, 6–3, though, the Comet gave promise of trailblazing to come.

In 1910 there were no Davis Cup matches. America could not raise a sufficiently strong team, and Britain, who selected Charles Dixon, Arthur Lowe and Theodore Mavrogordato, again sought a substantial guarantee before sending players so far to play. The Australasian body did not think the British team looked very exciting and invoked a clause in the agreement giving it the right to disapprove of a team. Britain subsequently suggested that matches between America and herself should be played independently of the Davis Cup, an idea that was not pursued.

South Africa challenged in 1911, then defaulted. Once again the British and Americans had the field to themselves. They met for the first time at the West Side Tennis Club, then situated at 238th Street and Broadway, south of Van Cortlandt Park, New York. Dixon, Arthur Lowe and Arthur Beamish crossed the Atlantic to do battle with Larned, McLoughlin, Tom Bundy and Ray Little. Dixon was unable to capitalize on a lead of 5–2 in the fifth set against Larned, and the Americans scored a fairly easy 4–1 victory, dropping only the doubles.

What seemed to be a strong American team – Larned, Wright and McLoughlin – set off for New Zealand, where the challenge round was scheduled to commence in Christchurch on 29 December, but did not begin until New Year's Day because of rain. Although the venue was chosen in honour of Wilding, who had won the first two of his four Wimbledon singles titles in 1910 and 1911, Wilding was now domiciled in England and did not make the trip home. He rightly believed that Brookes could hold the cup without him.

Australasia brought in Rodney Heath, winner of the first Australasian title in 1905, and Alf Dunlop, and they adjusted better than the Americans to the unseasonal coldness and rain. The thirty-nine-year-old Larned was especially handicapped as he suffered from a bout of rheumatism and should not have played.

Brookes and Heath gave Australasia a tight grip on the tie when they beat Wright and Larned respectively on the first day. Wright, who was thought to be Brookes's *bête noire*, paid for his 1908 win at Melbourne as the Wizard made him scurry to all parts of the court. Brookes and Dunlop added the *coup de grâce* in the doubles.

For Larned, who was confidently expected by Americans to be

47

more than a match for any of the Australians, the whole venture was painful. 'It is my opinion,' wrote F. M. B. Fisher, the referee, 'that Larned's physical condition produced a mental depression that was ultimately disastrous, as his match against Heath revealed. Larned was in an awkward position. He felt that it was largely to him that his nation looked for success; that any hour his ailment might leave him and that a decision on his part not to play might be capable of a construction that was far from being true. So, under pressure, he elected at the eleventh hour to play. . . .'

It was a sad culmination to his career. A few years later, the man who had bestrode American tennis for two decades was an ace of another kind – a US army pilot in the First World War. He retired in 1919 with the rank of lieutenant colonel and in 1921 invented and introduced the steel-framed racquet. But ill health plagued him, and in 1926, while a member of the New York Stock Exchange, he committed suicide.

−4−
GROWTH AND VARIETY

*(1912, British Isles; 1913, USA;
1914, Australasia)*

Australasia's retention of the cup caused some gnashing of teeth. Nobody had anticipated in 1900 that the trophy would remain in so remote a part of the world for so long. Davis's objective of stimulating friendly international rivalry was being frustrated because of the prohibitive cost of sending players Down Under. There had been no matches in 1910, and now there were rumours that America would abandon the competition. Though Larned was reassuring, Wilding conceded in a press interview in London that the presence of the cup in Europe was 'desirable' in order to stir enthusiasm there. Brookes did not share that opinion. For a long time it almost seemed that the cup was one of his personal treasures. It resided in the dining room of his home, on a sideboard, and his wife often filled it with red peonies and used it as a table decoration for dinner parties. The shining silver, reflecting the flickering candles, the vivid blossoms and the polished mahogany, set the room off beautifully.

In January 1912, Harry Waidner of Chicago, secretary of the Western LTA, declared that America should cease to contest the cup unless Australasia agreed to play on American soil. While that was not the view of all American officials, America, after entering the competition in 1912, failed to field a team.

The British Isles and France, the only challengers, played off at Folkestone. Britain again fell back on Gore and Roper Barrett, along with Dixon, while France brought in André Gobert and William Laurentz to support Decugis. France's one win was scored by Gobert, a tall, elegant man whose polished style was flawed by a capricious temperament. He beat Gore in four sets. Decugis lost to

49

Dixon in straight sets and retired to Gore after losing two sets. In the doubles Gobert and Laurentz snatched a set from Gore and Barrett. An interesting aspect to the Gobert–Laurentz combination was that earlier that year, while playing each other in the final of the French covered-court championship, a Gobert service ricocheted off the frame of Laurentz's racquet and struck him in the eye. He suffered a detached retina and lost his sight in that eye. The accident seemed to have a lasting effect on both their careers as singles players, but in doubles they continued to improve with Gobert providing the inspiration Laurentz needed to discard the caution that had crept into his singles game.

It was at Folkestone during the 1912 tie that talks between British and French representatives led in the following year to the formation of the International Lawn Tennis Federation, which was to govern amateur tennis throughout most of the world. The Americans declined to join the body for ten years, mainly because they objected to the ILTF designating Wimbledon as the 'World Championships on Grass'. Americans were also afraid that moves might be made by the federation to replace the Davis Cup as the symbol of international tennis supremacy. In 1923 the USLTA joined the federation after the organization decided to delete the 'World Championships' from its constitution, adopt international playing rules, and recognize the national championships of Australia, England, France and the USA as the four 'big' events. However, the Davis Cup continued to be administered by an organization called the Davis Cup Nations, which met annually during Wimbledon.

Charles Dixon captained the 1912 British team that embarked for Melbourne, his team-mates being James Cecil Parke, Gordon Lowe and Arthur Beamish. While Brookes remained a competitor, the British thought they had little hope of regaining the cup. Dixon was regarded as their best prospect in the singles, even though he was thirty-nine and had never reached the Wimbledon challenge round. A large, hearty man with a walrus moustache, he had not played a Davis Cup match until he was thirty-two years of age. Since then, however, he had gone from strength to strength and had been the architect of the British victory over France. Parke, the likely number two, had a less impressive singles record than Dixon, though he had won a number of titles that year, including the

Wimbledon mixed doubles. He was given no chance of beating Brookes.

The result of the contest – a 3–2 victory for the British Isles – was startling. Parke emerged as one of those players who, in spite of ordinary tournament performances, can play well above themselves when representing their country. A lawyer, he liked to pin two sprigs of shamrock to his tennis shirt, beneath which there beat a big Irish heart. Perhaps he was the most remarkable all-round sportsman ever to play Davis Cup. He played in twenty Rugby Union internationals for Ireland before turning his full attention to tennis. He also played golf for Ireland, was a first-class cricketer, and once represented his home town at chess. As a tennis player, he loathed training but was noted for his speed and fierce driving, his forehand on the run being especially effective.

The matches were again held at Melbourne's Albert Ground, just over the road from Brookes's home. Wilding had won his third successive Wimbledon title that year (he was to win his fourth in 1913), but he had a position with an English firm of wood-pulp merchants and did not want to return home. Brookes, the sole selector, chose Heath and Dunlop as his collaborators. At the Victorian championships, which were held at the Albert Ground shortly before the challenge round, he cagily withdrew Heath and himself from the singles during the early rounds as he wanted to deprive the British of any chance of playing the defenders before the teams met. This may have been a mistake. Parke beat Lowe in the Victorian final, and Brookes subsequently suffered through lack of match play against a top-class back-court player.

The stands were far from full on the first day. People thought the opening match between Brookes and Parke was a foregone conclusion, and the Dixon v. Heath duel was not expected to be much more exciting. Two days earlier Dixon had announced that he would stand down, his form was so bad. His team had had difficulty in dissuading him.

Parke soon shook Australian complacency. Arthur Beamish, in a letter home, explained what happened:

Brookes got to 4–1 in the first set before Parke could gauge the speed of his service or get used to its bound, Brookes at this point, and, in fact, up to the third set, using his straight, fast service without the American twist and hang. When Parke became accustomed to this he hit his returns very fast and firmly all over the court. On the backhand he played a fairly high, slow shot at Brookes's body, waited for the return, which was not punched (Brookes does not punch his slow volleys at all well), and then drove joyously and with the most extraordinary accuracy all over the court, passing Brookes clean at times with the finest cross-court drives.

Of course, Parke revels in slow stuff, not punched out deep and not hit hard, and this Brookes gave him, and often stood watching the drives fly past him while at other times his volleying movements came too late, and put the ball out or in the net. Brookes also gave his opponent angles, and this is what Parke wanted, as he could then go down the line or across the court.

Parke won by 3 sets to 1 [8–6, 6–3, 5–7, 6–2]. In the third set he was 5–1, and 30 all, and at that point tried a very difficult backhand low volley, which hit the tape. Just then Brookes played very well indeed, and went out at 7–5. Parke did not slack off, but Brookes improved, and played all his volleys more keenly, besides anticipating Parke's drives better and getting closer to the net; but he could not keep it up, and relapsed after this set.

This match was interesting, as it showed what a very speedy, hard hitting, and generally good all-round man with no special shots could do against a perfect volleyer and excellent server, not quite up to the mark and apparently not as full of snap and dash as he ought to have been.

Parke's win was the key to a British victory. Dixon beat Heath 5–7, 6–4, 6–4, 6–4, intelligently covering up his own weaknesses while exploiting Heath's. Brookes and Dunlop overcame Parke and Beamish in the doubles, and a much sharper Brookes accounted for Dixon on the final day 6–3, 6–4, 6–4, when seven thousand people were in the stands and others had to be turned away. But everybody believed Parke's ground shots would be too powerful for Heath, and so it turned out to be. He won 6–2, 6–4, 6–4.

One incident reminds us again of the chivalry displayed by players of this period. At the end of an exciting rally Parke hit the ball deep to Heath's backhand and, hearing a cry of 'Out!', stopped playing. Soon he realized that the call had been made by a spectator, not a linesman, and that therefore he had lost the game. Heath urged him to replay the point, but Parke would not hear of it. 'You're a sport, old man,' cried a fan.

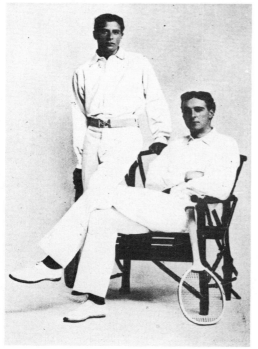

Above left: Dwight Filley Davis: had he known how successful the Cup would be, he would have 'had it made totally in gold'

Above centre: H. Roper Barrett, a London solicitor, could only practise on summer evenings after work

Above right: A. W. Gore, known to his friends as 'Baby'

Left: The Dohertys (left Laurie, right Reg). Their genius had revived a flagging interest in the game in Britain

Ten thousand watch the Dohertys play Davis and Ward at the
Crescent Athletic Club in New York, 1902

The Dohertys in America, 1902. Also seated in the front row are
Holcombe Ward (extreme left), Dwight Davis (extreme right) and
W. H. Collins, the British team manager in the centre

Left: The 1904 Challenge Round: Belgium's W. Lemaire and P. de Borman *v.* the Dohertys

Below: The American Davis Cup team, 1905. Left to right: Holcombe Ward, Beals C. Wright, Paul Dalshields (captain), W. A. Larned and W. J. Clothier

Training at Melbourne, 1908.
Anthony Wilding and a somewhat
overdressed Norman Brookes take a
breather at Brookes's private court

Beals C. Wright and F. B.
Alexander of America

Australia *v.* America, Melbourne, 1908. The players are Brookes
and Wilding (left) and Wright and Alexander

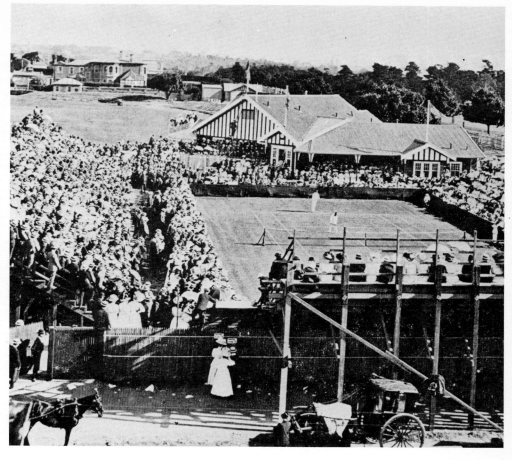

The 1908 Challenge Round between Australasia and
America was held at the Warehouseman's Ground (now
the Albert Ground), Melbourne. Note the stand in the
foreground protruding over the footpath

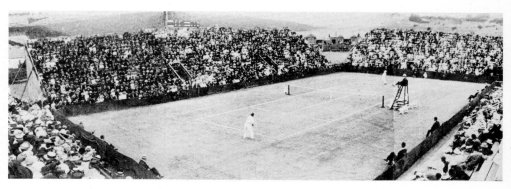

The 1909 Challenge Round at Sydney between Australasia and
America

M. H. Long and M. E. McLoughlin
of America, 1909

Anthony Wilding. Robust and
handsome, he was the game's first
'matinee idol'

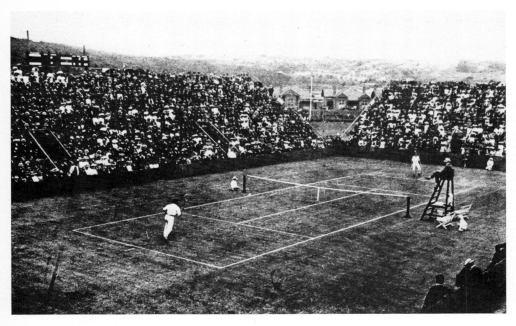

Play in the 1909 Challenge Round, Sydney: Anthony Wilding *v*.
M. E. McLoughlin, alias The Californian Comet

One of the most famous of all Cup
pairs: Anthony Wilding and
Norman Brookes

Norman Brookes, alias The Wizard

Charles Dixon of the British Isles
playing in the 1912 Challenge
Round

M. E. McLoughlin, the American
with the cannonball service

James Cecil Parke's historic victory over McLoughlin: Wimbledon 1913

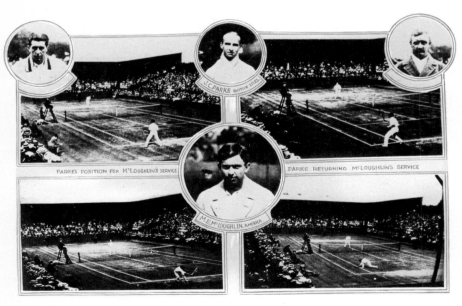

PARKE'S POSITION FOR McLOUGHLIN'S SERVICE

PARKE RETURNING McLOUGHLIN'S SERVICE

J. C. PARKE Britain 1913

M.E.McLOUGHLIN, AMERICA

The 1913 Challenge Round: Britain *v*. America

At the official dinner that night Parke contended that the British had been 'horribly lucky' and he played down his own spectacular success. 'I know that I have never played such a game in my life,' he said, 'and I never hope to play another like it again.' Dixon sounded a sobering note by declaring that the British LTA wanted a change in the rules governing the challenge round. His own view was that the challenge round should be played on the courts of the *challenging* nation, with the proviso that if that nation failed, and then challenged again the following year, the venue should revert to the country of the holder.

Britain's triumph was the shot in the arm that tennis in the Old World needed, and in 1913 the competition assumed new proportions, with seven nations entering – France, Germany, Belgium, America, Australasia, Canada and South Africa.

The Germany *v.* France contest in Wiesbaden on 3, 4 and 5 June was the first occasion on which a Davis Cup tie was played on a surface other than grass; in this case, clay. Though tennis had been played in Germany for about thirty years, it was for much of that time more a social game than a sport. Now, under the patronage of Kaiser Wilhelm and other aristocrats, it was flourishing. For their debut, however, the Germans were without their leading player, Otto Froitzheim, who had hurt his arm. They chose Oscar Kreuzer, F. W. Rahe and Heinrich Kleinschroth. On paper, the French looked stronger, but Gobert had played little tennis since joining the army and needed to get leave. His lack of condition affected him and in the opening match he was outlasted by Kreuzer, 1–6, 6–4, 6–2, 6–3. Rahe did not begin his match with Decugis until 6 p.m., and it had to be postponed at 8.20 p.m. with the score two sets all. Next day the players did not resume until 5 p.m., when Decugis won the necessary two games to tie the score at one rubber all. The doubles followed at 5.30, and looked capable of going to five sets, thus causing another postponement. Fortunately for the inexperienced German officials, Rahe and Kleinschroth beat Decugis and a newcomer, Maurice Germot, 7–5, 6–4, 4–6, 9–7. Overreacting, the officials started proceedings on the third day at 10.30 a.m. As Rahe beat Gobert for the loss of three games, and Decugis defaulted to Kreuzer, play was over by noon!

Australasia was not at full strength for its contest with America at New York on 6, 7 and 9 June. Brookes was too preoccupied with

53

business and family cares to go away, and Wilding was available only if the tie was played in England. Stanley Doust, Horrie Rice and Alan Jones headed for New York, where they met McLoughlin, Hackett and a somewhat unknown quantity named Richard Norris Williams II. Born in Geneva of wealthy American parents, Dick Williams, as he was better known, had begun playing in Switzerland at an early age, coached initially by his father. In 1910, at the age of eighteen, he won the Swiss championship. Two years later father and son boarded the *Titanic* en route for New York. When the ship struck an iceberg in the North Atlantic and sunk, Mr Williams drowned, but young Dick was picked out of the icy water after swimming for over an hour. The ordeal may have reinforced a natural instinct to play tennis with a recklessness that could be breathtaking – or abysmal. There was little margin for safety in Williams's shots. He either thrashed an opponent with sheer brilliance or defeated himself with errors. Not to worry. He was 'a dashing, handsome, glamorous young man and a thrilling performer'.

At last the Americans decided to play cup matches singly, and McLoughlin and Rice met in the opening rubber. The Sydney man, a one-time violinist in a theatre orchestra, was then aged forty – a little chap in knickerbockers and long black socks. A left-hander, famous for his retrieving, he had been overshadowed in his own country by Brookes ('He makes the game extremely restful by playing so many of his strokes well beyond my reach,' the whimsical Horrie once said). The dynamic McLoughlin beat Rice easily 6–1, 6–3, 6–3.

Williams gave his side a 2–0 lead by beating Doust 6–4, 6–4, 1–6, 7–5, but Doust and Jones, both fine volleyers, caused an upset in the doubles, wiping out a two sets to one deficit to topple McLoughlin and Hackett, 9–7 in the fifth set. Doust fought gamely against McLoughlin on the last day to no avail, the American winning 6–4, 6–4, 6–2. And so America qualified to meet Germany at Nottingham, in England, on 10–12 July, while Canada beat South Africa by four rubbers to one at Queen's Club, and was scheduled to play Belgium at Folkestone on the same dates.

That year, McLoughlin reached the challenge round at Wimbledon. If ever he was going to win the title this was the year. He found a perfectly trained Wilding waiting for him. McLoughlin charged to the net from start to finish and came close to taking two of the sets, but Wilding often passed him and won 8–6, 6–3, 10–8. The handsome New Zealander was at the height of his popularity. So great had been the demand for seats that many women swooned in the crush and had to be 'laid out on the court by the roller until they could be removed'.

At Nottingham, it seemed at first that McLoughlin's confidence may have been affected. After Williams had beaten Kreuzer in four sets in the first match, McLoughlin found himself 5–7, 2–6, 0–2 down against Froitzheim. The German was a formidable baseline player, precise, accurate and dour. He had undergone training in the German army, and perhaps as a result lacked some flexibility in his approach to the game. On his day, though, he could beat almost anyone. McLoughlin had to step up his attack before Froitzheim, whose arm injury had kept him idle, tired and lost the last three sets 4–6, 2–6, 2–6. The doubles went to McLoughlin and Hackett after a close four-set tussle with Rahe and Kleinschroth.

The Canadians, R. B. Powell and B. P. Schwengers, beat South Africa 4–1, and Belgium 5–0, but at Wimbledon a week later they were no match for the Americans. And so, after the longest campaign yet waged in the competition, America prepared to take on the British Isles at Wimbledon on 25, 26 and 28 July. The British named their heroes from Melbourne, Parke and Dixon, for the singles, and the Wimbledon champions, Barrett and Dixon, for the doubles.

McLoughlin had beaten Parke comfortably in the All England championships and was thought likely to repeat that performance. Parke, however, played less first-class tennis than most of his contemporaries and had been below form. McLoughlin, on the other hand, had played so much over the summer that he may have lost some of his edge. Parke moreover had learned a few things from his defeat by McLoughlin and had noted also how Wilding had stood in against McLoughlin's service to put pressure on the Californian's volleys. With courage and resourcefulness he now beat McLoughlin 8–10, 7–5, 6–4, 1–6, 7–5. The match revolved around the serving, volleying and smashing of the American, and the Irishman's passing shots and steadiness. In the fifth set Parke led 4–1, but McLoughlin levelled at 5 all, only to lose his next service for the match.

The Dixon *v*. Williams match was just as close. This time, though, it was the American who won, 7–5 in the fifth set. Williams was eighteen years younger than his opponent and, like many American players, preferred to wear spiked shoes or 'steel points', as they were called. The British thought the use of spikes was unfair, as they cut up the court and greatly assisted the volleyer, who is always less affected by poor bounces. Diplomatically, they decided not to make an issue of the matter. Yet one has to feel sympathy for Dixon who, for all his touch and court craft, was inevitably slower than Williams anyway and now found himself at a severe disadvantage.

The doubles was all important. Once again, the match went to five sets, with the veterans stirring British hearts by their gallantry. They led by two sets to one, and lost the fourth set only at 5–7. But Hackett was as steady and guileful as either of the British pair, and McLoughlin's severity overhead and on the volley was decisive. The Americans won, 6–4 in the fifth set.

For the British to have had much chance now, Parke would have needed to play Williams in the third singles. Luckily for America, the draw scheduled Dixon and McLoughlin instead. After putting up some brave resistance in the first set, the weary Englishman succumbed in straight sets, and thus America regained the cup for the first time since 1902. Parke reduced the margin to 3–2 by beating Williams in five sets.

Norman Brookes had noted the events of 1913 with quiet impatience. Early in 1914 he headed for the Continent with his wife and baby daughter, intent on working up his game for another stab at Wimbledon and a challenge for the cup. Wilding, who was as much at home on European clay as English turf, was taking Europe by storm; he beat Brookes twice on the Riviera and in Paris won the World's Hard Court championship. Brookes told inquisitive reporters in England of his plans. 'I've been hearing down in Melbourne that Wilding is unbeatable,' he said. 'I've beaten him in Australia and thought I might here. So I came to see.'

The Brookes magic once more held Wimbledon spellbound. His long preparation had got him into peak form, though he was lucky to survive his All-Comers' final with Froitzheim. After winning the first two sets, Brookes lost the next two. He fortified himself with champagne before beginning the fifth set and won it 8–6, after the

German appeared to suffer from a dubious line call at 6 all. In the challenge round, a confused Wilding could not take a set off his ageing crony. One is left to wonder how many times Brookes would have won Wimbledon had he bothered to enter.

There was one less challenger for the cup in 1914, South Africa having dropped out. The Germans, too, cabled America that they could not raise a team. But Froitzheim's good showing at Wimbledon made them think again. They wanted to play after all, and Brookes, in the euphoria of his triumph, agreed to the American proposal that their earlier default be disregarded. Later, he came to regret his tolerance.

The first-round contests were massacres, with the British Isles beating Belgium by fifteen sets to none at Folkestone, and Australasia trouncing Canada by the same margin in Chicago. France, like Germany, had a bye in the first round, and then could win only the doubles against the British at Wimbledon.

By the time the Australasian and German teams reached the Allegheny Country Club, near Pittsburgh, for their semifinal on 30 and 31 July and 1 August, the German invasion of Belgium was imminent and the First World War was about to begin. When the British writer Wallis Myers arrived at the club he did not discern any untoward hostility among the players. 'Anthony [Wilding] had discovered an American motor which took his fancy, and, between his bouts of training, was sandwiching in some hill-climbing experiments,' he wrote later. 'Brookes and Dunlop were enjoying recreative golf. The members of the German team, Froitzheim and Kreuzer, were, when the hot day was over, in popular demand as dancing partners. Germany might be launching *ultimata* in Europe; there was no sign that her two lawn tennis envoys desired to fight anybody – except with a racquet.'

However, Froitzheim and Kreuzer were both in the army reserve, the former as an officer. They announced they would cease to play the moment war was declared and would return to fight for the Fatherland. They were encouraged by a largely German-descended and pro-German group of American supporters. Brookes and Wilding gave the crowd every opportunity to vent its partisanship by finding fault with almost every aspect of the organization of the tie.

The Wizard was in his most determined mood. The thunderous

applause for Froitzheim's winners, the silence that greeted his own simply made him clench his jaw. He beat Froitzheim 10–8, 6–1, 6–2. Wilding disposed of Kreuzer for the loss of eight games, and he and Brookes conceded only four games in the doubles. Australasia had won, but the remaining matches had to be played. On the last day, 1 August, Germany declared war on Russia. Fearing a last-minute interruption, the president of the club took drastic action; he barred local reporters from the grounds and cut off all telephone communication! Brookes and Wilding won the last two rubbers amid hoots of derision, and departed for Boston 'without a backward look at the German players. . . .'

Within three days Britain and Germany were at war, and before the Australasia *v*. British Isles contest began at Boston on 6 August, one of the British players, Algernon Kingscote, a gunner in the regular army, left for home. In the first singles, Brookes stifled British hopes by avenging his Melbourne defeat by Parke, though only just. The Irishman led 2–6, 6–4, 3–6, 6–1, 5–3, and was within a point of victory when Brookes gambled all by moving to the net behind every shot. Serving at 5–4, 30–15, Parke grazed the net with his racquet as he put away the ball into an open court. Neither Brookes nor the umpire saw the mishap, but Parke reported it and the score was 30 all instead of match point. He did not win another game. Wilding survived a third-set attack of heat exhaustion to defeat Arthur Lowe 6–3, 6–1, 16–14, and combined with Brookes in a 6–0, 6–0, 6–4 rout of Parke and Mavrogordato in the doubles. With the British players anxious to get home, the rest of the programme was abandoned.

The challenge round, held in steamy weather at the West Side Tennis Club's new home at Forest Hills on 13–15 August, featured one of the greatest of all cup clashes, McLoughlin *v*. Brookes. More than 12,000 people attended – the biggest gallery ever to watch a tennis match up to that time. Most of the crowd were more accustomed to baseball and football, and barracked accordingly. As in Pittsburgh, some were of German origin, and all were noisily partisan. To the conservative Brookes, the atmosphere was somewhat vulgar.

McLoughlin went into the match knowing that he almost certainly had to win if America were to keep the cup, because Wilding had beaten Williams 7–5, 6–2, 6–3 in the first rubber. It was nearly four o'clock when he and Brookes went out to play a match that nobody who saw it would ever forget. One spectator was a boy named Al Laney, destined to be one of America's foremost sports writers. McLoughlin's 17–15, 6–3, 6–3 triumph became one of his happiest memories. In his book, *Covering The Court*, he recalls:

My confidence was shaken many times before that terribly long first set was over. Brookes gave the impression he would never yield no matter how many thunderbolts our man might hurl at him, blows one never could have imagined possible with a tennis racket.

About halfway through, and after what seemed an eternity, Brookes, who had served first and thus was forcing McLoughlin to battle for his life every time the American served, was love-40 against the service. You would have to be a teenager again, I suppose, to suffer as I suffered then. But at this crisis, McLoughlin served three balls that Brookes could not even touch with his queer-shaped racket.

Other crises came later, near the end we could not know was near. Brookes again was within a point of winning the set, and each time the answer was the same, an unreturnable service. Was ever a boyhood hero more worthy of worship?

The first set, which established a competition record for length, virtually decided the match. Brookes fought to the last, but thereafter his energy was ebbing.

For the doubles, America chose McLoughlin and Tom Bundy, the national champions. The selectors had sought a stronger partner for McLoughlin and only went along with Bundy because McLoughlin loyally insisted that his friend should play. In the event, it was McLoughlin who was the weaker. He worried about Bundy and did not strike his best form until too late. With the crowd becoming increasingly partisan, Brookes and Wilding won 6–3, 8–6, 9–7. At one stage loud clapping broke out when Wilding was penalized for foot-faulting.

The Wizard now had to grapple with the mercurial Williams, knowing that if he lost, a rampant McLoughlin might possibly sweep through Wilding. The match was played before a capacity crowd that watched dejectedly as the machinelike Brookes won the first two sets 6–1, 6–2. Unexpectedly, Williams won a tight third set 10–8 after Brookes had served for the match at 8–7. All along, the crowd had been disturbing the Australian with its constant yelling and abuse of the court officials. Now, as it shouted raucous applause, he stuffed his fingers in his ears, a gesture that was interpreted as sulking and caused pandemonium. 'Give him a bottle of milk,' cried one man. 'Put him off,' shouted another. Bottles were bowled across the court and some fans jumped over the barriers and were chased by police officers. The defiant Brookes had to be ushered to the side of the court, where he saw his wife beckoning him to follow the deeply distressed Williams, a fine sportsman, into the locker room and change his clothes. He walked off suppressing his rage.

Ten minutes later Mabel Brookes was fearful as her husband returned to face Williams and the exuberant, though unpredictable crowd. She wrote in her memoirs:

As he passed by the Davis Cup, he gave it a little reassuring pat and a twirl which was, I knew, quite unpremeditated. Once more he had regained his poise; there would have to be more than shouting and pop bottles to get him rattled. There was a moment's silence as he passed the cup and came onto the court. Then the crowds recognized that all they had done was yet not enough, and he was returning, unbeaten, for more; and they started to applaud and the noise rose in volume until the cheering voices became a roar. . . . A ballboy handed Norman his discarded racquet and the sound from the gallery lifted almost to hysteria. It was an ovation, a recognition of pure fighting guts. It was also hard on Dick Williams. He played well and doggedly, but the end was in sight.

Brookes won the fourth set 6–3 to reclaim the cup. In the 'dead' rubber McLoughlin beat a Wilding who had half his mind on the war in Europe by three sets to one. The crowd kept barracking to the end, much to the dismay of the visitors. Among the spectators was an Australian tennis writer, R. M. Kidston, who was shocked that such crowd involvement should occur in an amateur game. 'It [lawn tennis] is played primarily and in every way for the competitors,' Kidston complained to *American Lawn Tennis*. 'The spectators are there to look on. They are not there to be pleased at all. It is true they pay for their entrance. But at no time are they supposed to interfere with the progress of the game or to interrupt it. The players are not gladiators in any sense.'

Australians and New Zealanders read of their team's triumph as young men were flocking to join an expeditionary force – another kind of adventure in which national honour was at stake. Reports indicated, claimed the Melbourne *Argus*, 'that volunteers who do not immediately present themselves for medical examination are likely to find themselves amongst cheering crowds along the streets, while the uniform they might have had will be worn by some other enthusiastic youth less given to procrastination.' Within ten months, Captain Tony Wilding was killed by a shell at Neuve Chapelle.

—5—
RETURN OF THE
HEROES
(1919, Australasia)

Wilding was perhaps the best tennis player to perish in the First World War. Powell of South Africa also fell, as did many lesser players of that doomed generation. In England, Laurie Doherty's arduous duties with the anti-aircraft branch of the Royal Navy were believed to have shortened his life. Most of the leading players enlisted and became commissioned officers, some displaying outstanding courage. Lieutenant Colonel Algernon Kingscote of England and Lieutenant Gerald Patterson of Australia, who were to meet in the 1919 challenge round, each won the Military Cross. Colonel Dwight Davis was awarded the Distinguished Service Cross for heroism in France, and Captain Dick Williams the French War Cross at the second battle of the Marne. Major James Parke was wounded twice, and on his return to the game strained his heart and had to take a year off.

By the end of the war many players had lost their prowess. Heath's nerves had deteriorated in his flying sorties over the Western Front, Decugis was past his prime and McLoughlin had lost his fire. The Germans Froitzheim and Kreuzer were interned by the British after the ship taking them home from America was intercepted by a warship. Froitzheim later wrote from 'somewhere in England' to George Hillyard, secretary of the All England Club, asking him to use his influence to get him freed as, he said, it was unsporting to prevent him from fighting for his country. Hillyard declined. For both Froitzheim and Kreuzer the war effectively ended their careers since Germany was barred from international competition when it was over and did not again challenge for the cup until 1927.

There were no contests from 1915 to 1918 and none was originally intended for 1919. But when Belgium issued a challenge to Australasia, France, the British Isles and South Africa decided to do so too. America, which had looked after the cup during the war forwarding it to Australia in 1919, graciously declined to issue a challenge as it had not entered the war until 1917 and had suffered the least of the Allied nations. The Americans were particularly conscious of the losses suffered by Australasia. The war's effect on sport must have extended, in many countries, well into the 1920s, for countless young players had had little or no competition in their youth.

The war did nothing to lessen nationalistic feelings, and it was to nationalism that the Davis Cup owed much of its fame. As with the Olympic Games, millions of people who had little more than an inkling of how the game was played were attracted to the yearly confrontations across a net as one country did battle against another. The Davis Cup ritual that had gradually evolved since 1900 served to heighten public interest. There was, for instance, all the panoply of the draw, with some teams now wearing uniforms and the players' names in envelopes being tensely exchanged by the opposing captains. Often the draw was conducted by a governor, a president or a prime minister. Later, at the courts, there would be a formal opening ceremony amid national flags and to the accompaniment of national anthems. As soon as the matches began, umpires when calling the score never referred to the players' names but to the nations they represented. This was all guaranteed to provoke patriotic fervour.

In the next two decades lawn tennis was to become increasingly popular, and it was the Davis Cup, publicized by the ever expanding popular press and the new phenomenon, radio, that was largely responsible. To be a cup player in any country was a distinction that separated the elite from the ordinary practitioners of the game. Indeed, most players set greater importance in representing their country than in, say, playing at Wimbledon. Yet while much of the idealism remained, some of the traditional values were to change. The Davis Cup helped to make the game a profitable spectator sport, and in the process the concept of amateurism was steadily eroded. Larger stadiums were needed to accommodate the crowds. It was the big names that filled the stadiums, and more and more these stars wanted, one way or another, 'a slice of the action'. With the game's worldwide growth, there was a demand for tennis equipment to be endorsed by the stars. Newspapers meanwhile were only too willing to purchase their views. If the prewar champions had something of the Knights of the Round Table about them, some of the postwar champions were Barons of the Bargaining Table.

In spite of his four years on active service, the twenty-four-year-old Gerald Patterson, who was a nephew of the concert singer Nellie Melba, won Wimbledon in 1919 at his first attempt. He defeated Gobert, Ritchie, Kingscote and the title-holder Brookes (now forty-one) without loss of a set. Brookes, who had spent most of the war as a Red Cross commissioner in the Middle East, was not very disappointed; he viewed Patterson almost as a son and, more importantly, the means by which the cup could be kept Down Under. Kingscote, after all, looked certain to be Britain's main player, and *The Times* was speculating whether English players would ever be masters of the volleying game or if 'the volley calls for a suppleness of joint and muscle denied to us by our damp climate'.

Patterson had developed from being a leading schoolboy player into a big, muscular man who had what was described as 'a battle-axe' type of game. His father, Tom Patterson, was a friend of Brookes, and once a week, when Brookes made up a four at the Patterson home in the Melbourne suburb of Kew, young Gerald was allowed to take the afternoon off from school to act as ballboy. Although he was a right-hander, he tried to copy some of the Wizard's strokes. But he lacked Brookes's magic touch, mainly because his wrist was not as flexible. This deficiency left him with an inferior backhand in particular. He was, though, much stronger physically than Brookes; he had the same kind of indomitable spirit, the same grim demeanour and will to win; and he could be intimidating. Nobody served and smashed with as much power and accuracy as Patterson, and on his day the rest of his game was efficient.

On their way home from Wimbledon, Brookes and his young protégé played in the US Nationals. America had two new players in Bill Johnston and Bill Tilden, neither of whom had contested Wimbledon. Tilden beat Brookes, and Johnston beat Patterson before beating Tilden decisively in the final. But the Australians won the doubles final against Tilden and Vincent Richards. Tilden had never been so impressed by any player as he was by Brookes. 'He is and ever will be the supreme thinker of the tennis game,' he wrote soon afterwards. In 1938 he would continue to describe him as the greatest player he ever met. It was yet too early for anyone to speak in superlatives of Tilden.

When the 1919 competition got under way Decugis and Laurentz of France easily beat Belgium in Brussels, and the British Isles also won the first three rubbers against South Africa at Eastbourne. The South African players, Louis Raymond, George Dodd, H. I. P. Aitkin and Brian Norton, were all ex-soldiers and lacked the experience of their older British opponents, Kingscote, Mavrogordato and Roper Barrett. In fact *no one* could match the experience of Barrett, who was still representing his country nineteen years after his debut in 1900 and who, at the age of forty-five, partnered Kingscote to victory in the doubles.

For the final round at Deauville the British replaced Mavrogordato with Perival Davson, a better hardcourt player, and brought in O. G. N. Turnbull for the doubles. Decugis had hurt his back and so France relied on Gobert and Laurentz. Except for Laurentz's lack of fitness — he apparently had not trained for the tie as he didn't expect to play — France probably would have won. On the first day the tall, fluent-stroking Gobert defeated Davson 7–5, 6–4, 4–6, 6–4, and Laurentz extended Kingscote before the Englishman won 4–6, 6–3, 6–2, 4–6, 6–4. The French pair then lost only one game in the first two sets of the doubles against Barrett and Turnbull. They won the third set 12–10 as Laurentz tired. Another set of twenty-two games in the next day's singles had Laurentz wavering again; he led Davson 4–6, 6–1, 12–10, but lost the next two sets 4–6, 0–6. Gobert's chance of glory faded in the fifth rubber as Kingscote's all-out attack earned him a 6–4, 6–4, 7–5 victory. (Gobert, a terrific hitter, was noted for becoming nervous in difficult circumstances, and Bill Tilden, with typical bluntness, once expressed surprise that a man who was twice decorated for bravery as a flying ace 'had no guts on a tennis court'.)

The challenge round at Double Bay, Sydney, did not commence until 16 January 1920 because of the crowded Australian tournament calendar. British hopes were largely carried by Kingscote, who was assisted by two veterans, Beamish and Arthur Lowe. Brookes was expected to enter the lists, but for the singles he chose J. O. (James) Anderson of Sydney, who had recently beaten him in an interstate match, and Patterson.

Anderson and Patterson had played each other in the final of the

Victorian schoolboys' championships the last time a British team visited Australia, in 1912. That was the beginning of a rivalry in which the honours finally were about even in Australia, although Anderson failed to scale comparable heights abroad. Tall and lean, J. O. had a thin, long face and parted his hair down the middle. He reminded one observer of a greyhound, while another thought he had 'the look of eagles around his eyes'. He certainly had no compunction about savaging 'rabbits'. Whereas Patterson's big guns were overhead, Anderson could destroy an opponent with his rifled forehand. He played the game hard and, later in his career, he lived hard, sometimes helping a friend to empty a bottle of whisky after a match without becoming too much the worse for wear.

In his international debut a nervous Anderson was beaten by Kingscote 7–5, 6–2, 6–4, but Patterson was too powerful for Lowe, though the English baseliner managed to win a set. The doubles was postponed from the Saturday for forty-eight hours because of rain. When the crowd streamed out to the ground again, the match was over in forty-five minutes, Brookes and Patterson annhilating Kingscote and Beamish 6–0, 6–0, 6–2. In this match the Englishmen never recovered from a disastrous first game in which Kingscote was foot-faulted repeatedly. They lost sixteen games before opening their account. Brookes, still lean and flexible, was in such superb form that they had little chance anyway. After the match the referee agreed to Kingscote's request that the foot-fault judge be changed for his next match, while making it clear that he respected the replaced man's competence. The third day's play also had to be postponed because of rain, and when Patterson and Kingscote did get on court the Australian played with an explosiveness appropriate to one who had fought with a howitzer battery. He won 6–4, 6–4, 8–6. Anderson squeezed past Lowe in the final rubber 6–4, 5–7, 6–3, 4–6, 12–10.

Brookes, for ever planning, chose the official dinner as the occasion on which to suggest that the cup should be defended in Australia, and not in New Zealand, as was the understanding. New Zealand had no successor to Wilding worthy of a place in an Australasian team, and to Brookes it was foolish to throw away a home-ground advantage by having the Australians defend the cup in another country. No doubt he realized better than most of his compatriots just how dangerous Johnson and Tilden would be.

Some officials, however, felt he was just a little too hard-headed. Wilding had helped to win the cup in 1914, and a posthumous debt must be repaid to his homeland.

–6–

MORE THAN A
MONARCH

(1920–26, USA)

Although we tend to regard the sporting superstar as a modern phenomenon, it is doubtful if the great athletes of the eighties loom any larger than did those of the twenties, the so-called golden age of sport. Golf had its Walter Hagen and Bobby Jones, baseball its Ty Cobb and Babe Ruth, cricket its Jack Hobbs and the young Don Bradman, boxing its Jack Dempsey, track and field its Paavo Nurmi, swimming its Johnny Weissmuller.

No one dominated his sport more than William Tatum Tilden II, the number-one-ranking player in America for a whole decade, from 1920 to 1929. Tilden equalled the feat of Dick Sears and William Larned in winning the US singles championship seven times, and was five times US doubles champion. He won the Wimbledon singles championship three times and surely would have won it more often had he competed there regularly. In all, Tilden captured seventy important titles before turning professional in 1930.

His Davis Cup record was equally outstanding. He was a member of the American team for eleven years and won seventeen of his twenty-two singles matches. From the time of his debut in 1920 he won sixteen consecutive singles and was not beaten in the competition until 1926 when he went down to Réné Lacoste of France in a 'dead' rubber. Tilden's invincibility was the main reason why America was the champion nation for seven straight years, from 1920 to 1926, a feat that has never been matched and is never likely to be, following abolition of the challenge round in 1972.

It was not his ability alone that made him such a colossus. As John Kieran wrote:

Big Bill was more than a monarch. He was a great artist and a great actor. He combed his dark hair with an air. He strode the courts like a confident conqueror. He rebuked the crowds at tournaments and sent critical officials scurrying to cover. He carved up his opponents as a royal chef would carve meat to the king's taste. He had a fine flair for the dramatic; and, with his vast height and reach and boundless zest and energy over a span of years, he was the most striking and commanding figure the game of tennis had ever put on court.

With such a strong personality, it was no wonder that people either liked or disliked him intensely. The most remarkable aspect of his career was that he was an ordinary player until he reached the age of twenty-seven and won his first American singles title. Sixty years later, Bjorn Borg had won five Wimbledon championships and been retired from the game for one year before reaching that age.

Tilden was the son of a Philadelphia wool and hair merchant, and his mother was a talented pianist. Attracted to tennis as a child, he was by no means exceptional as a junior. Both at school and at the University of Pennsylvania his tennis performances were indifferent, and up to the age of twenty-three his lack of progress was so frustrating that he constantly vowed never to touch a racquet again. He had, however, some natural advantages. He was tall and fast and could move as lightly as a ballet dancer. He was intelligent and was prepared to work hard in acquiring an all-court game. And he possessed a pride and inner confidence which at times bordered on arrogance.

While still a youth Tilden was brash enough to try to teach tennis to others. This may have benefited him more than it did his pupils, for it gave him an early analytical approach to strokes and strategy. He developed an outstanding service and smash, tremendous strength in all other strokes, a mastery of spin and great cunning. A born showman – he went on the stage later in life – Tilden was suspected of prolonging some matches simply to give the gallery entertainment. His strategy might have conveyed a false impression, since he often played to an opponent's strength rather than to his weakness in order that when he did switch to the weakness at a crucial stage, perhaps when the opponent was tiring, his resistance would crumble completely.

Up to 1920, though, Tilden's only major successes were the 1913 US mixed doubles title, for which he gave most of the credit to his partner, Mary K. Browne, and the 1918 clay-court singles title. He did not play in the National singles until he was twenty-three and was then beaten in the first round by Harold Throckmorton. The following year, 1917, he was beaten by Lindley Murray in an early round of the National Patriotic Tournament, which replaced the US Nationals during the two years America was in the war. (Tilden was rejected for military service because of a 'first degree flat foot' and was enlisted in the Medical Corps, based at Pittsburgh.) In 1918 he reached the final of the Patriotic Tournament and lost again to Murray; and the next year, as we noted earlier, he beat his hero, Brookes, in the semifinals of the resumed Nationals but lost to Johnston in the final.

Bill Johnston was the antithesis of Tilden. He was a short, spare man who dethroned his fellow Californian, Maurice McLoughlin, at the 1915 Nationals. Johnston's hair was as sandy as McLoughlin's and he shielded his freckles with a large white cap. They had little else in common apart from their sportsmanship and immense popularity. 'Little Bill', as he was called, did not have a powerful service and was not by instinct a net-rusher, though he had a very good volley. His chief weapon was a Western top-spin forehand drive which, in spite of his lightness, was hit with great pace because of his balance and timing. The Western grip was best suited to the cement courts of California and had drawbacks when used on grass.

Johnston lost his US title to Dick Williams in 1916 and spent the war years in the Navy before regaining the title. He was then only twenty-four and nobody could have imagined that he would never win the championship again. He failed to do so because the 1919 final proved to be a watershed in Tilden's career. Johnston's terrific forehand in that match had exposed the limitations of Tilden's backhand, a defensive chop shot. Tilden was stung by the critics' comments and knew that he had to improve his backhand if he were to realize his ambition. He worked on it all winter on an indoor court, aiming for control and penetration. Hour upon tedious hour the stroke was remoulded. Tilden also added greater variety to his game – to such good effect that Johnston never beat him again in a major tournament. But, though Johnston was five times runner-up to Big Bill for the US championship, he won Wimbledon in 1923, when Tilden did not enter.

Ironically, it was Johnston's strongest shot that, against Tilden, became the chink in his armour. Because of his Western grip, the effort of constantly returning low, sliced shots tired his arm and he lost accuracy. 'I developed my slice drive off both forehand and backhand down to the forehand particularly to shatter Johnston's attack,' Tilden once reminisced. This became one of his most valuable shots, and so the rivalry between the two contributed to America's grip on the Davis Cup.

In 1920, even though Johnston and Tilden had not yet played in the cup competition, America was clearly a force to be reckoned with. Yet Tilden was by no means certain to play when the American team left for Europe; the more experienced Williams was thought to have a stronger claim to the second singles place, and Williams and Charles Garland were the likely doubles pair. Dissatisfied with these assumptions, Tilden was eager to put his new shots to the test. But first there was some drama before the team left. The departure of their ship was so delayed that the players were in danger of missing Wimbledon. An appeal was made to Newton D. Blake, Secretary of War, to place the team on the US Army Transport *Northern Pacific*, scheduled to sail immediately with General March, Chief of Staff, USA, and a special party. Baker was interested in international tennis and granted the request.

There were five other challengers for the cup: the British Isles, Canada, France, Holland and South Africa. Canada and the British Isles drew byes, and the only contest held before Wimbledon was Holland *v.* South Africa at Arnhem. South Africa was weakened by the absence of Brian Norton, who was ill, and the two-man Dutch team of C. J. van Lennep and A. Diemer Kool scored a 3–2 victory over Louis Raymond and Charles Winslow.

At Queen's, Tilden lost to Johnston in the final, but at Wimbledon he overshadowed everyone. Williams must have suspected that he had lost his Davis Cup singles place for ever. In the third round, the remarkable old warhorse Parke, having recovered from his heart trouble, upset Johnston. Watching from the stands, Big Bill noted how the Irishman relished the weighty shots that Johnston fired to the corners of the court, for they enabled Parke to make his famous running drives. In the next round Tilden was not so cooperative;

he hit the ball down the middle of the court to cramp Parke and won easily. He then beat Kingscote, Randolph Lycett and Garland to reach the All-Comers' final, where his opponent was the stocky Japanese, Zenzo Shimizu, whom he had routed at Queen's. Shimizu was a quick learner and gave a better account of himself. Tilden led 6–4, 6–4, 4–4, when he hurt his left knee while chasing a lob. Shimizu exploited the American's reduced mobility and extended the third set to twenty-four games before succumbing.

Tilden's injury raised the possibility of a forfeit in the Wimbledon challenge round as the American team captain, Sam Hardy, did not want him to jeopardize his forthcoming Davis Cup commitments. On the other hand, a forfeit would have disappointed both the British public and Tilden, who had the chance of becoming the first American to win the championship. Big Bill had his knee treated and taped and wanted to play. Hardy nervously concurred. There was no sign of any handicap as Tilden wrested the title from Patterson. Winning the battle of the cannonballs and concentrating on the Australian's vulnerable backhand, he triumphed in four sets.

A few days later at Eastbourne, the Americans, as expected, were too strong for the French. The opening match between Johnston and Gobert was interrupted by rain, and when it was resumed next day the American won 6–3, 8–6, 6–3. Laurentz adopted a 'nothing to lose' policy against Tilden, boldly taking the first set 6–4. Then Tilden cleverly mixed up his game and gave Laurentz slow, heavily cut shots that kept low on the soft, moist grass, and won the next three sets 6–2, 6–1, 6–3. The same four men played the doubles, with the Americans winning 6–2, 6–2, 6–2.

In the second round, America met the British Isles at Wimbledon and Canada defaulted to Holland. British hopes rested with Parke and Kingscote. They lost 5–0 after pluckily taking three of the matches to five sets. The opening match, in which Johnston beat Parke 6–4, 6–4, 2–6, 3–6, 6–2, was the best, though the doubles was also a great fight, with Parke and Kingscote yielding only after leading by two sets to one.

There was no final round as the Dutch retired. The challenge round was scheduled to begin on 30 December in Auckland on a specially prepared court at the Domain Cricket Ground. By now Tilden was the undisputed world champion, for he had added the US championship to his Wimbledon title. He and Johnston were accompanied by Watson Washburn as an emergency. Waiting for them in New Zealand were Brookes, Patterson, Heath and Pat O'Hara Wood.

When Brookes and Tilden walked out to the court for the opening match, a white flag fluttered by the net in remembrance of Anthony Wilding. Brookes doffed his cap as everyone stood for a few moments' silence. Perhaps inspired by thoughts of his dead friend, he played a splendid match and only Tilden's service power and comparative youth pulled him through.

Despite his forty-three years, the Wizard kept pressing his attack at the net, while Tilden was mainly content to stay back. At 5–3 Brookes had a point to take the first set, but Tilden recovered and won the set 10–8. Then one break of service in the tenth game of the second set gave Tilden that set 6–4. Undaunted, Brookes continued to test Tilden with his kicking service. He was passed less often in the third set and from 0–1 he went to 6–1 and 3–0 in the fourth set – nine games in a row.

The interval had partly refreshed Brookes and at last the American was under real pressure. Could the 'old man' win? Tilden raised his game and levelled at 3 all. Though tiring, Brookes made him struggle for every point. But in the seventh game the Australian's innate sense of fairness hurt his chances of winning. He signalled to the umpire that Tilden had been wrongly double-faulted. The umpire refused to change his call and Brookes deliberately hit the next delivery out of court. Tilden held, and Brookes dropped his own service to be down 3–5. Somehow he found the energy to pull up to 4–5. Tilden now went for the kill, slamming Brookes's weakening service back to the veteran's feet. The master's touch could not save him. Tilden clinched the set and the match at 6–4.

Patterson was unable to level the tie. Johnston hammered his backhand and won 6–3, 6–1, 6–1.

The doubles presented the defenders with a faint hope. Brookes was weary and Patterson shaken, but they won the first set. After that, the Americans' returns were so accurate and persistent that the Australians lost command of the net. The result: a 4–6, 6–4, 6–0, 6–4 win to the challengers. The cup was going home. And when finally it arrived at New York it was proudly exhibited in the Fifth Avenue window of Black, Starr and Frost, the official custodians of the trophy. America's victory marked the beginning of a notable era, not only because of the length of her dominance but because the competition spread far and wide in the twenties with the appearance of many new challengers. The expansion reflected the worldwide growth of tennis, though in most countries it continued to be identified with the privileged classes. Some of the leading Davis Cup players of the twenties outside America, Great Britain, France and Australia were Jean Washer of Belgium, Manuel Alonso of Spain, Jhr. C. van Lennep and A. Diemer Kool of Holland, Jan Kozeluh of Czechoslovakia, Baron Hubert de Morpurgo of Italy, and Zenzo Shimizu and Takeiichi Harada of Japan.

In 1921 the trophy was fully inscribed with the names of all the winning teams, and Dwight Davis donated a solid silver tray to accompany it. This was to suffice until 1936, when the tray was also covered with names and Davis presented a circular base for the tray and bowl.

Of the twelve challengers in 1921, Spain, Czechoslovakia, India, Denmark, Japan, Argentina and the Philippines were new to the competition. Rumania and Italy competed for the first time in 1922, and the following year saw entries from Switzerland, Hawaii and Ireland. In 1923, Australia entered separately, its old collaborator playing under the New Zealand flag in 1924, when Hungary, Cuba, China and Mexico were also among the challengers. Sweden, Portugal and Poland tried their luck in 1925.

The expansion made it necessary to put more thought into the organization of matches. In 1923 a system of zoning was introduced, with all the challengers divided into a European or American zone. An inter-zone final was staged to determine the ultimate opponent of the defending nation.

Among those who believed that the competition was becoming too protracted was Tilden. As early as 1921 he was suggesting changes in the format, including the abolition of the challenge round, which he considered gave the defending nation too big an advantage. It was to take fifty-one years for this particular change to be introduced.

In the twenties few officials shared Tilden's opinion. Of course, most countries had little chance of reaching the challenge round, and each year one or two usually retired without playing a match as the difficulties in sending away teams seemed insurmountable. But in Europe there was always some satisfaction in getting through one or two rounds, and to win the zone was to become a notable achievement in itself.

The proliferation of challengers also created a few complications about the eligibility of some players to represent certain countries. In 1921 Randolph Lycett, a superb doubles player, was named in the British team to play Spain. Though born in England, Lycett's family took him to Australia at an early age and he had played most of his tennis there. In 1920, Kingscote, the British captain, urged the LTA not to select Lycett until ascertaining whether Australia objected. Kingscote himself was born in India and had learned the game outside England. About the same time, F. M. B. Fisher, the New Zealand-born player who lived in England, recalled that when Wilding became domiciled in England, 'strenuous efforts' were repeatedly made by the LTA to induce him to play for the British Isles. Under the regulations, a player was not required to represent the country of his birth if he qualified to play for another country by living there for two years, but having been nominated by one country he could never be selected by another. The residential qualification period was extended to three years in 1932.

As it happened, Australia possessed enough good players to be able to relinquish Lycett without hard feelings. But when French newspapers began suggesting that Suzanne Lenglen should be selected in the French team, there was general dismay! The French federation felt obliged to issue an official denial that she was under consideration.

In 1921 Argentina and the Philippines retired and in the first round the British Isles defeated Spain 4–1; Australasia beat Canada 5–0; and Belgium eliminated Czechoslovakia 3–2. The next round brought Australasia and the British Isles against each other, and they played off in Pittsburgh, USA. Lycett was tactfully omitted from the British team, which consisted of Max Woosnam, Gordon Lowe, O. G. N. Turnbull and J. Brian Gilbert. Anderson beat Woosnam in the first match, but Lowe was too steady for the left-handed Jack Hawkes. Australia had found in the outback of New South Wales a fine doubles player in Clarrie Todd, and he and Anderson emerged victorious from a long, hard encounter with Woosnam and Turnbull. On the final day, Anderson settled matters by beating Lowe in four sets.

The two surprise packets of the year were India and Japan. When

India scored an upset 4–1 win over France in Paris, some Frenchmen may well have wondered whether Mademoiselle Lenglen *should* have been playing. Jean Samazeuilh, the new French champion, beat S. M. Jacob in the opening match, but Mohamed Sleem evened the score with a five-set win over Laurentz. In the doubles the Indian pair of L. S. Deane and A. A. Fyzee beat Laurentz and Jacques ('Toto') Brugnon, also in five sets; and Sleem disposed of Samazeuilh 6–1, 6–3, 6–3 in the decider. The contest marked the first cup appearance of Brugnon, who was to be one of the famous 'Four Musketeers'. As he lost the 'dead' singles rubber against Deane, as well as the doubles, his debut was hardly auspicious.

Having received walkovers from the Philippines and Belium, Japan did not play until it met India in Chicago in mid-August. The Japanese players were Shimizu and Ichiya Kumagae, who had modified their primitive technique since leaving Japan several years earlier to study and work overseas. In those days, Japan produced an uncovered soft ball, which had to be hit very hard and with a lot of spin if it was to be controlled. Because of this, Shimizu and Kumagae, like other Japanese, had developed an exaggerated Western grip, which they gradually adapted to conditions outside Japan. The self-taught Kumagae, a left-hander, had only one shot, a looping drive, when he arrived in America. He progressed so quickly that he soon won many tournaments and earned a place in the US rankings.

While Shimizu, who had perfected his game in India, looked more awkward, he was an even better player. As Tilden wrote:

He had not Kumagae's speed. He had much the same unorthodox style, but he had one of the most brilliant subtle brains in tennis history. His choice of shot, his ability to lob his way out of danger, his resource in meeting attack and courage in moments of crisis were, to me, far more impressive than Kumagae's fiery hitting.

Japan was untroubled in beating India 5–0. At Newport she met Australasia, who had beaten Denmark 5–0, with Norman Peach substituting for Hawkes. Japan sensationally won 4–1 to reach the challenge round for the first and only time. Shimizu kept his service low, placed his drives cleverly and denied a bewildered Anderson any pace. He won 6–4, 7–5, 6–4. Hawkes took the first two sets against Kumagae with hard hitting and reached 5–4 in the third set.

Then he became cautious, lost the initiative, and Kumagae snatched the set at 8–6. The Japanese coasted through the next two sets 6–2, 6–3. Though Anderson and Todd kept their unbeaten doubles record intact, the consistency of the Japanese again prevailed in the final two singles.

The challenge round, held at Forest Hills on 2, 3 and 5 September, attracted crowds of up to fourteen thousand. Johnston scored a routine 6–2, 6–4, 6–2 win over Kumugae, but the second match was a thriller. Tilden probably had not fully recovered from an illness he suffered during Wimbledon when he had got out of a nursing-home bed to beat Norton in the challenge round. Now, in addition, he had a boil on his right foot and he flagged in the 100-degree heat. The poker-faced Shimizu won the first two sets 7–5, 6–4 and led 5–3, 30–15 in the third set. His drop shots and lobs had done most of the damage. Tilden had just enough energy to save the third set, at 7–5, with desperate hitting. As he left the court Big Bill comforted himself with the thought that Shimizu must be feeling the strain too.

In the clubhouse Tilden staggered up a flight of stairs to the showers, kicked off his shoes, and stepped under the cold water with his clothes on. 'What can I do for you, Bill?' asked team captain Hardy. 'Undress me,' gasped Tilden.

Sacrificing his suit, Hardy leaped into the shower and pulled Tilden's clothes off. Meanwhile a doctor was called. He lanced the boil on Tilden's foot and removed the pus. When he returned to the court Tilden was revived. Shimizu, however, had not showered or changed his clothes during the rest period and his muscles had stiffened. Early in the fourth set he was beset by cramp and Tilden was able to race through the last two sets with the loss of only three games.

Williams and Washburn won the doubles in four sets, and the concluding singles also went to America. In the final analysis the odds against Shimizu and Kumagae had been simply too great, but they had done their country proud.

Unfortunately, Japan was unable to enter a team in 1922. Kumagae had virtually retired and there was no suitable replacement. Other countries had selection problems; Canada, Hawaii and the Philippines had to default, and the British Isles retired after beating Italy in the second round.

British tennis was to be at a low ebb for most of the twenties. The British climate and the emphasis on cricket in British schools were held to be two of the reasons. The lawn tennis correspondent of *The Times* accepted the problem with resignation, pointing out that 'team spirit is everything' at a British public school and that such an individualistic game as tennis tended to encourage selfishness and would be out of place. 'It is an ideal game for men and women of mature years already imbued with the true spirit of sport, fostered by games of a team character in their school days, but utterly unsuitable for the receptive mind of the schoolboy.'

Perhaps another weakness was the use of inferior technique. According to Tilden, most British players used a Continental backhand grip – for all strokes. 'All over England,' he wrote, 'one saw the same grip and same defects in the game, the weak forehand drive, a lack of hitting power and unwillingness to take the net.'

Rumania's colourful Nicholas Mishu made his debut against India in 1922, when fourteen countries issued challenges (but four of them – Canada, Hawaii, the Philippines and Japan – retired without playing a tie). Mishu specialized in trick shots, and on occasions served with his back to his opponent. Once, when he did this against Tilden, the American caught the ball thinking he was fooling. 'That is my very best serve!' cried the indignant Mishu. None of Mishu's tricks worked against India, and Rumania went down 0–5.

Most of the other early contests were one-sided too. Australasia defeated Belgium and Czechoslovakia, both ties being held in England; Spain beat India, also in England; and France overcame Denmark in Copenhagen. In the latter match two more of the 'Musketeers', Jean Borotra and Henri Cochet, played in the competition for the first time.

France now had to meet Australasia, and the winner would play Spain in the qualifying tie for the challenge round. France wanted to play the matches in England; her opponent preferred America. Acting as arbiter, the USLTA (the 'National' was deleted from the title in 1920) chose Longwood as the venue. Spain also was reluctant to go to America because of the cost and was about to default when the USLTA decided to advance the Spaniards funds. Then France suffered a blow when it seemed that Cochet would not be released from army service. Samazeuilh was named to join Borotra and Gobert, but Cochet at the last moment persuaded his colonel to give him leave and he arrived at the French federation's office just as his replacement was getting into a taxi on the way to the station. Samazeuilh sadly stepped down and Cochet entered the cab instead.

The French appointed a Paris-based American, Allan Muhr, as captain, believing that his knowledge of American and the English language would be invaluable. Unfortunately, Muhr had a fixed idea that Gobert and Cochet would be the best single players, and he discounted Borotra's superior form in practice. Anderson had gone down with influenza, but the French had a tough obstacle to surmount in Patterson, who that year had regained his Wimbledon title at the All England Club's new grounds in Church Road. Admittedly, that performance could have been a little flattering. The Wimbledon challenge round had been abolished, and neither Tilden nor any of the Americans had contested the title. However, the beefy Australian was full of confidence. In the opening match at Longwood he needed to be confident against Gobert, who took the first two sets before Patterson sharpened his net attack. The temperamental Frenchman then allowed a variety of things to unsettle him. He complained about the slipperiness of the court and the bound of the ball, and finally he was foot-faulted and got cramp in his hand before being put out of his agony, 6–3 in the fifth set.

The twenty-year-old Cochet levelled the tie by beating O'Hara Wood in five sets, an ominous sign of growing Gallic strength. His team might still have held a good chance of winning if Cochet and Borotra, who were regular partners, had played the doubles. Instead, Muhr paired Cochet and Gobert, who had never combined before. Patterson and O'Hara Wood were a well-knit and powerful team; even so, Cochet almost carried the French to victory. The Australians won 6–0, 6–8, 4–6, 6–3, 10–8. Next day, O'Hara Wood beat Gobert in four sets to wrap up the tie.

A few days later, at the Germantown Cricket Club, Philadelphia, the same players accounted for Spain's Manuel Alonso and Count Manuel de Gomer 4–1. Spain's one success came on the first day when Alonso, the quickest man of his day and master of the low, angled volley, beat O'Hara Wood in a match that the Australian thought he had won 6–2, 6–3, 2–6, 6–2. O'Hara Wood's weakness that summer was his service; he had torn a shoulder muscle at Wimbledon. Alonso was able to run around the delivery and take it on his strong forehand. During the interval the Australian decided that if he reached match point he would try to surprise his opponent by serving a fast ball down the forehand line. In the fourth set O'Hara Wood held match point at 5–2, 40–30. The first serve was a fault. Alonso moved over to the sideline and Wood put all he could into his second ball down the centre. It was an ace. But as both players went to the net to shake hands and the umpire started to call 'Game, set and match' there was a cry of 'Foot fault!' Wood smiled wryly as he walked back to resume serving. He lost the last two sets 6–8, 1–6.

By the time the challenge round was staged at Forest Hills on 1, 2 and 5 September, Anderson was considered well enough to return to the team. The Americans named Tilden and Johnston for the singles, and brought in Vincent Richards for the doubles. Richards had been labelled a boy wonder since winning the US doubles championship with Tilden at the age of fifteen. A brilliant volleyer, he had now won his third National doubles title with Tilden at the expense of Patterson and O'Hara Wood, reversing their loss in the Nationals by winning 6–4, 6–0, 6–3. There were doubts, though, whether the doubles victory was achieved on merit. Antagonistic feelings had developed between Richards and Tilden that summer. Richards had beaten Tilden in a couple of minor matches during the previous winter and had boasted that he now had his rival's measure. Then, in the final of the National doubles, Tilden had outrageously poached shots, to the extent that he once upstaged Richards completely by virtually shooing him off the court while he put away an easy overhead. As the crowd applauded, an infuriated Richards threatened to hit his partner if he ever showed off like that again. According to Tilden's biographer, Frank Deford, the champion engineered the doubles defeat in the challenge round to humiliate Richards in his Davis Cup debut. 'In the three awful sets, Tilden made only seven earned points, while committing twenty-five errors outright. There was name-calling in the USLTA for months thereafter about the selection of Richards. He was not allowed to play doubles again for the United States for three more years.'

With seventeen entrants and sixteen actual challengers in 1923, it was not only thought necessary to introduce an American and a European zone but to start the competition in Europe in mid-May. Nations situated outside Europe or America could challenge in either zone, but had no choice of ground.

In the European Zone Réné Lacoste, the fourth Musketeer, made his entry at the age of seventeen in France's first-round match against Denmark at Bordeaux, and suffered the team's only defeat. In other first-round European contests, Switzerland beat Czechoslovakia, Ireland (which had achieved Home Rule in the south and therefore competed independently) beat India, and Great Britain (no longer the British Isles) beat Belgium.

The second round saw France succeeding against Ireland, though Borotra surprisingly fell in straight sets to an aristocrat named the Hon. Cecil Campbell, who earlier had taken Cochet to 8–6 in the fifth set. Count de Gomar carried Spain to a 3–2 victory over Great Britain in Manchester; Switzerland beat Argentina; and Holland beat Italy.

Spain reached the zone final by easily defeating Holland, while in Lyons France squeaked through against Switzerland 3–2, after Cochet came within two games of meeting defeat by C. F. Aeschliman. In the final at Deauville, France again just survived after de Gomar and Eduardo Flaquer, who had been runners-up in the doubles at Wimbledon, won a memorable five-set match over Cochet and Brugnon.

Across the Atlantic, Australia and Japan emerged as the American Zone finalists and in Chicago the team from Down Under though without Patterson, who could not spare the time to go to America, set about avenging its 1922 defeat. This time, Anderson did not allow Shimizu to control tactics and beat him 6–0, 6–3, 6–3. Shimizu, however, scored a win over Hawkes before Japan went down.

For the inter-zone final at Longwood, France was weakened by the absence of Borotra and Cochet, who had declared themselves unavailable. Anderson and Hawkes were in good form, and recorded straight-set victories over Lacoste and Brugnon respectively, while in the doubles they defeated the same players 6–8, 6–3, 6–3, 6–8, 9–7.

The challenge round began on 31 August at Forest Hills, where during the year the West Side Tennis Club had erected a 13,500-seat stadium. This development recognized America's growing enthusiasm for the game as a spectator sport, due partly to Tilden's star quality and partly to the number of overseas players who were playing in the States as a result of the Davis Cup.

Anderson retained his form. With a relentless attack of crushing drives he beat Johnston on the first day 4–6, 6–2, 2–6, 7–5, 6–2. It was the first of Johnston's three Davis Cup losses in the eight years he represented his country, and the best win of Anderson's career. The Sydney man also took a set off Tilden, but Hawkes was not strong enough to worry the Americans and lost both his singles in straight sets. The doubles was a tremendous match. Williams was named as Big Bill's partner, though both he and Tilden were left-court players. With Tilden irritated and uncomfortable in the right court the pair did not blend happily. After winning the first set 17–15, they lost the next two 11–13, 2–6. Only Williams's heroic efforts kept the pair in the fray. Terse words were exchanged in the dressing room before the match was resumed. One of the American selectors, Harold Hackett, ordered Tilden, who had been playing from the baseline in exchanging returns with Anderson, to go to the net. With a more coordinated approach, the Americans won the last two sets 6–3, 6–2.

In 1924 there were entries from twenty-three nations, seventeen of them choosing to play in the European Zone. Argentina, not realizing that by entering that zone it would have to play all its matches in Europe, retired. Rumania also pulled out. The French threat to America grew as the Musketeers gained experience. In their national championships that year, Borotra won the singles, and the new pairing of Borotra and Lacoste captured the doubles. Still more impressive, Borotra was triumphant at Wimbledon, where the field included Richards, Williams and Frank Hunter (who incidentally lost to the forty-seven-year-old Brookes in the third round). In the final, Borotra defeated Lacoste.

Using various combinations of players, France swept past Ireland and India and registered her first defeat ever of Great Britain to reach the zone final. Then she met Czechoslovakia, who had beaten New Zealand, Switzerland and Denmark, but who had announced that she would be unable to send a team to America if successful in the final. The French thought that in that case the Czechs should forfeit. However, the match went ahead at Evians-les-Bains, the famous spa town 400 feet above Lake Geneva. It was early August, the height of the season, and perhaps never before had so many millionaires and celebrities attended a cup contest. Among the gallery were the Earl of Derby, the Maharajah Gaekwar of Baroda,

Baron and Baronne de Neuflize, the Duchess of Vendôme, the Duc de Nemours, Prince Louis of Monaco, the Shah of Persia, various Italian, Russian and Spanish princes and numerous financiers and industrialists.

France won 5–0 and so set up another trip to America. There, Australia's Patterson and O'Hara Wood had won the American Zone by trouncing China, Mexico and Japan without dropping a rubber. Against an embarrassed China, the Australians lost only fifteen games in fifteen sets.

In the inter-zone final at Longwood, France selected Borotra and Lacoste for the singles. As they had played together all year, they were expected to play the doubles too. Borotra lost to O'Hara Wood, despite winning two of the first three sets 6–1. Brookes had noticed that Borotra always tried to pass O'Hara Wood down the line and never across court. During the interval he stressed this to O'Hara Wood in the dressing room. His compatriot was then able to anticipate the Wimbledon champion's drives and won the last two sets. On the third day Borotra managed to win only seven games against Patterson. Had Jean played up to his ability, France might well have reached the challenge round for the first time, for Lacoste won both his singles. However, with Brugnon, who replaced Borotra in the doubles, Lacoste lost that rubber.

America's superiority was never more pronounced than in the 1924 challenge round, played at Germantown on 11–13 September. Even without Johnston in the singles, America lost only one set. Johnston's omission in favour of Richards was controversial and was seen by many, including Tilden, as a slight to the Californian. Johnston assumed that he had been named in the team to play singles. He recently had lost carelessly to Richards in an East *v.* West contest, but he regarded that as an exhibition series and was shaken when the selectors apparently attached some significance to the results. Richards had won the first Olympic tennis title in Paris that summer, beating in turn Lacoste, Borotra and Cochet, and was considered a rising world star. He justified the selectors' choice by beating both Patterson and O'Hara Wood in straight sets. Tilden also won simply, and the Australians' tally was confined to one set in the doubles, in which Tilden paired with Johnston.

This challenge round was one of the occasions when Tilden was so confident of his ability to beat his opponents that he toyed with them, prolonging the matches unnecessarily. S. Wallis Merrihew, in *American Lawn Tennis*, wrote:

Throughout the Patterson match, Tilden looked as if he were merely practising strokes, or experimenting with them. He paid comparatively little attention to Patterson's shots. If they were good, as they not infrequently were, he let them go; or, if he could reach them, he would return them with interest. But it was his own shots he was thinking of most of the time, studying them as if he were in a laboratory and they were specimens.

In three sets against O'Hara Wood, Tilden lost four games. He was in no hurry to finish; indeed, he seemed to like long rallies and plenty of them. Although O'Hara Wood won so few games, he played well and appeared to enjoy the match.

Despite Tilden's showmanship, American fans were becoming a bit blasé over their country's succession of easy wins. For four straight years the Australians and Japanese had made little impression, and though the French had youth on their side they had yet to produce their best form in the States.

Yet French officials realized that in Borotra, Brugnon, Cochet and Lacoste they had the raw material with which eventually they could topple America. They sensibly made the most of their opportunity by planning their players' development, and from 1922, as we have seen, the French team came increasingly into prominence. The Musketeers were brilliant individualists and keen rivals. From time to time they did not see eye to eye and even clashed bitterly among themselves. But when playing for France they put their disagreements behind them, placing their country's interest first. Early on, Cochet and Lacoste were handicapped by having to do national service. On the other hand, the well-established indoor season in France helped all the Musketeers to hone their games when many players elsewhere were largely idle.

They were very different in style and personality. Brugnon, who was born in 1895, was the oldest. A quiet, self-effacing man, his chief successes came in doubles, and not until after he had passed the age of thirty. He won two Wimbledon doubles titles with Borotra and two with Cochet, and also won five French and one Australian doubles title. Clever and steady, with superb reflexes and volleying touch, he often created the opening for the spectacular volleys and smashes of his partners.

The next oldest was Borotra, who was born on the French side of the Basque country in 1898. Nicknamed the 'Bounding Basque' because of his spectacular leaps and dives, Borotra was a dynamic athlete whose acrobatic volleys, courage and *joie de vivre* made him a favourite of crowds everywhere. He turned seriously to tennis only after the First World War (in which he won the Croix de Guerre and was twice mentioned in dispatches) and after gaining engineering and law degrees in the immediate postwar years. Borotra was essentially a net-rusher who depended greatly on his speed of eye and foot. Though extremely fit, he had to pace himself in long matches. He added another Wimbledon and another French singles title to those he won in 1924, and also captured the Australian championship, as well as many doubles crowns. The charm of the man may partly be perceived in his custom of presenting a bottle of perfume to his mixed doubles partners as a token of his appreciation. To galleries he displayed the same warmth and generosity of spirit. Borotra was the key figure, the inspiration among the Musketeers, and perhaps the greatest Davis Cup stalwart of all. He continued to play in the competition until he was forty-nine and at Wimbledon he entered the doubles right into his sixties.

Cochet, born at Lyons in 1901, was the most gifted shotmaker of the four. A one-time ballboy at the Lyons club where his father was curator, he played intuitively and with apparent nonchalance. Short, pale and taciturn, his speed and anticipation enabled him successfully to defy all the tenets of good positional play. His hair-trigger reflexes and touch were such that he would reduce the hardest hitters to despair by taking their fiercest shots on the rise. But he was sometimes careless and lazy, and could be beaten by lesser players. Cochet won Wimbledon in 1927 and 1929, the US singles in 1928, and the French title five times between 1922 and 1932.

Réné Lacoste, who was born in Paris in 1905, was the most deliberate and calculating of the Musketeers. The son of a wealthy car manufacturer, he saw a tennis court for the first time at the age of thirteen when on holiday on the Isle of Wight. He developed a passion for the game. Back in Paris he joined several of the leading clubs and, though a thin, rather weakly boy, he practised at every opportunity. He was completely self-made. He built up his physical condition by rigorous training, studied every book on tennis that he could find, and compiled notes on every player who beat him. Lacoste never forgot the reasons for a loss; he would commit to his casebook an analysis of his opponent's strengths and weaknesses, with the methods to be employed in playing him. Thus, the entry under Tilden included the advice: 'Play the ball down the centre of the court in going to the net. . . .'

Lacoste became an all-court player with machinelike strokes and a fine sense of strategy. Like Cochet and the other Musketeers, he used the Continental grip, as opposed to the Eastern grip of Tilden and most of the other leading players. 'I have not the genius of a Tilden, or the physical qualities of a Borotra or of a Cochet,' Lacoste wrote in 1931. 'If I have sometimes succeeded in beating them it is because I have willed with all my force to win, to utilize the means which were within my reach, namely, a meticulous preparation.'

He came to be known as 'The Crocodile,' a pseudonym that was bestowed on him by a Boston sports writer at the time of the 1923 inter-zone final when he learned that the French captain had promised to buy Lacoste a crocodile bag that he coveted if France reached the challenge round. Though Lacoste did not get the bag, the pseudonym stuck. It seemed to suit his austere demeanour on court and his crafty approach to the game. Many years later the crocodile was to become Lacoste's trademark as he established a huge sports clothes empire.

When he was barely nineteen, Lacoste was runner-up to Borotra at Wimbledon. He beat Borotra in the Wimbledon final the following year, 1925, and won the title again in 1928. His other principal successes were the US title in 1926–27, and the French title in 1925, 1927 and 1929.

The Wimbledon victories of Borotra and Lacoste were a warning that America in 1925 could not be complacent. Cochet also was a semifinalist at Wimbledon that year, and the Musketeers picked up a number of other important titles.

Twenty-three nations challenged for the Davis Cup, sixteen in the European Zone. Among them were Austria and Hungary, who, as Germany's allies in the First World War, had been barred from participating since then. France still stood in the way of Germany's readmission.

The Austria *v.* Ireland contest in Vienna produced the most serious incident up to that time. On the first day the match between Ireland's C. F. Scroope and Count Ludwig Salm was stopped by a thunderstorm in the second game of the second set after Scroope had won the first set. Although the Irish captain, S. F. Scroope, had agreed with the Austrian captain the previous day that a postponed match should be recommenced from the point where it had been interrupted, he was now approached by both the Austrian captain and referee with a demand that the match should be replayed from the beginning. According to Scroope, the interview was 'unpleasant'. It was only after he threatened to withdraw his team that the Austrians conceded. Next day, he was again approached by the Austrians. Again, he only won his way by threatening to take his team home.

When the match resumed, Salm beat C. F. Scroope 0–6, 2–6, 6–3, 6–2, 6–3. The other Austrian, P. Brick, overcame L. A. Meldon in straight sets. The doubles went to the Scroope brothers, who nevertheless felt that many bad line decisions favoured the Austrians. At the Irishmen's insistence, a Colonel Sherbrooke from the British Embassy was appointed umpire for the Salm *v.* Meldon singles on the understanding that he would overrule the linesmen's decisions if he deemed that necessary. In fact he did so many times, always in Ireland's favour. As in the opening singles, Salm lost the first two sets. He objected to the colonel, claiming that he made him feel nervous. He wanted him removed. The Austrian captain and referee put the request to S. F. Scroope, who flatly turned it down. But while Sherbrooke remained in the chair, he was no longer permitted to overrule. Salm won the match 8–10, 4–6, 7–5, 8–6, 6–1. In his official report, captain Scroope alleged that the count repeatedly questioned the umpire's decisions; 'called' balls out in such a way that the umpire thought the 'calls' were coming from the linesmen; and spent much time inciting the gallery by addressing them in German.

During the final singles, the provocative Salm took the place of a linesman without referring to the umpire. C. F. Scroope led Brick 7–5, 6–1, 5–7, when darkness forced a postponement, whereupon the Irish decided to default as a protest. They then withdrew from the Austrian international tournament in which they had entered. The Irish LTA subsequently suggested to the Davis Cup Nations that Austria's entry in future should be 'carefully considered', but although an investigation was held no action was taken. 'The matter raises the question,' editorialized *American Lawn Tennis*, 'whether it would not be well to provide a corps of officials for Davis Cup contests held on the Continent, with especial reference to ties held in countries where the traditions of the game are not of such long standing, nor as strong, as they are in, say, those of Western Europe. Had there been an English, or an American, referee at Vienna, matters would almost certainly have been kept under control.'

France's only setback in winning the European Zone this year was a loss by Borotra to Hungary's Bela von Kehrling. France beat in turn Hungary, Italy, Great Britain and Holland. Meanwhile, in the early rounds of the American Zone the star was Takeiichi Harada, who carried Japan to a 3–2 win over Spain and beat Patterson in Japan's vain effort against Australia in Boston.

France went into the inter-zone final at Forest Hills with several advantages. Lacoste had beaten Patterson at the same stage in 1924 and had decisively defeated Anderson at Wimbledon. Moreover, Lacoste and Borotra were the Wimbledon doubles champions. It was a shock therefore when Patterson toppled Lacoste in the first match 6–3, 6–4, 6–2. The Australian served seventeen aces and generally out-hit his opponent. Almost as surprising was Borotra's 6–4, 6–3, 8–6 defeat of Anderson. The sting had gone from J.O.'s forehand and his legs refused to carry him across the court as the vibrant Frenchman harried him.

The doubles was a long, tense duel. Borotra's lively network was having a great influence on the match when, with the French pair leading by two sets to one, he was the victim of a dramatic accident early in the fourth set. From the outset, the French had troubled Hawkes with their returns of service, forcing him to volley upwards. Borotra in particular would intercept with deadly effect, and all Patterson could do was watch helplessly. Finally, Patterson decided to take a chance on Lacoste's next return. He moved across and played a severe volley smash just as Borotra was closing in to the net. The ball struck Borotra on the temple from a range of less than ten feet. He collapsed and lay still. Some people thought he might have been killed. It was two minutes before he regained consciousness and was lifted to a chair. The odds against his continuing seemed so long that when he did rise and took his racquet there was tremendous applause from the stands. This grew louder when the

Frenchman went over to Patterson and gave him a reassuring tap on the shoulder. On the next service of Hawkes to Lacoste, however, there was almost a repetition of the incident, Patterson's smash missing Borotra's head by an inch. Borotra simply smiled, but the gallery roundly booed the Australian.

The Frenchmen lost the fourth set, then led 5–2 in the fifth. Hawkes and Patterson rallied to 5 all, and saved five match points. But Borotra's brilliance could not be contained and the French pair broke Hawkes in the eighteenth game to win 6–4, 3–6, 6–4, 1–6, 10–8.

Incessant rain on the Sunday saturated the court, and on the Monday, Labor Day, the prospect of any play was so remote that only a thousand people turned up. They witnessed a superb display by Borotra, who initially had looked in danger of being hit off the court. After losing the first set 4–6, he began to thrive on Patterson's pace, whipping back the Australian's dreaded first serves even faster than they had arrived. In winning the last three sets 6–4, 6–1, 6–3, his placements were breathtaking. 'France has a right to be proud that it could produce a player capable of rising to such unassailable heights as Borotra achieved in this match,' wrote Allison Danzig in the *New York Times*. 'There must have been many in the gallery who envied captain Decugis his privilege at the end of the match of throwing his arms around his smiling, unaffected team-mate and, in the old French fashion, bestowing a resounding kiss upon his cheek.'

Having reached the challenge round for the first time in twelve attempts, the French were confident of acquitting themselves well. They again relied on Borotra and Lacoste, while America chose Tilden and Johnston for the singles, and Richards and Williams for the doubles. The matches were played on 10–12 September in Philadelphia, where the local officials were a bit put out by the absence of Borotra and Lacoste at the draw. When Decugis subsequently tried to telephone Borotra to tell him he would be playing the first match against Tilden, he received a message that the player did not wish to be disturbed. Jean had decided not to allow himself to be worried over whom he would face!

The match proved to be one of Tilden's greatest, not so much because of his shot-making, which lacked its usual edge, but because of his courage, brains and endurance. On the previous evening he had been ill with ptomaine poisoning, and in the fierce heat on court he felt very weak. He trailed all the way and several times was on the brink of defeat as Borotra maintained an all-out volleying attack. In the end, though, it was the Frenchman who was reduced to utter exhaustion.

Borotra led 6–4, 0–6, 6–2 and 6–5, with his serve to follow. Playing his shots with care and letting loose with lightning drives when given an opening, Big Bill levelled at 6 all. His long legs and court coverage had never stood him in such good stead as he chased Borotra's volleys. The Frenchman dropped the set at 7–9, but broke for 2–0 in the fifth set. Now, however, Borotra was almost sinking to his knees from weariness. He could win only two more games. It was Tilden's skilful lobbing that finished him off. Tilden would chop the ball short to draw Borotra in and then float the ball over his head.

Johnston had an easier match against Lacoste, winning 6–1, 6–1, 6–8, 6–3. The French assault was thwarted when Richards and Williams, exploiting Borotra's stiffness and tiredness, won the doubles 6–4, 6–4, 6–3.

Next day Tilden put in another tremendous effort to beat Lacoste 3–6, 10–12, 8–6, 7–5, 6–2. For much of the match he was dripping wet with perspiration and ice water, which he doused over his head at short intervals. He still wasn't well, and after the first two sets his breathing was laboured. Lacoste had kept him running in the same way that Tilden had sapped the energy of Borotra, and at 3–0 in the third set he looked certain to win. But Tilden would not surrender. He asked the acting US captain, Sam Hardy, to get him some aromatic ammonia. When the bottle came, he drank a quarter of it before Hardy could restrain him. Tilden felt a surge of energy. Playing in his socks, he measured his strokes carefully and mixed them with superb generalship to turn the match around.

With the cup secure, captain Williams wanted to substitute Richards for Johnston in the final rubber to give Richards experience. Tilden strongly objected, believing this would be an insult to the competition. He would never play for America again, he warned, if Johnston were replaced. Johnston played and thrashed the still-weary Borotra 6–1, 6–4, 6–0.

France was far from discouraged. 'The Davis Cup will be ours before 1930,' predicted Decugis when he returned home. 'Tilden is still in a class by himself but he is past thirty. So is Johnston. Cochet and Lacoste are nearer twenty than thirty. They will and must improve.'

The year, 1926, began promisingly, with Lacoste defeating Borotra in the final of the US Indoor championships, and then, in a team match, beating both Tilden and Richards in straight sets. Cochet won the French singles, and at Wimbledon, in the absence of Lacoste, who was ill, Borotra took the singles title, and Cochet and Brugnon the doubles. Twenty-four nations submitted entries for the Davis Cup, a notable absentee being Australia, sidelined by financial problems. In the European Zone, France, captained by Pierre Gillou, did not concede a rubber in beating Denmark, Czechoslovakia, Sweden and Great Britain. Japan easily won the American Zone.

Harada was by now ranked seventh in America. Hitting boldly for the lines, he surprised Lacoste in the inter-zone final at Forest Hills 6–4, 4–6, 6–3, 9–7. Then Cochet lost the first two sets to Tsumio Tawara and just pulled out the third set at 7–5. Finding his rhythm, Cochet won the last two sets easily, and next day with Brugnon he swept through the doubles for the loss of two games. Lacoste ended Japanese hopes by beating Tawara on the third day.

The challenge round, held at Philadelphia on 9–11 September, was not as close as in 1925. Johnston beat Lacoste by the curious score of 6–0, 6–4, 0–6, 6–0, and Tilden dissected Borotra 6–2, 6–3, 6–3. When Williams and Richards dispatched Cochet and Brugnon in the doubles, the tie was over. On the last day, however, Lacoste inflicted upon Tilden his first cup singles defeat 4–6, 6–4, 8–6, 8–6. In the third set, Tilden suffered a similar knee cartilage mishap to the one that almost cost him his Wimbledon match with Shimizu in 1920. After limping off the court at the end of the set he was advised to forfeit, but, with the tie already decided, the American captain, Williams, was out on one of the field courts having a hit and Tilden did not want to scratch without consulting him. Because of Big Bill's stature, his loss, even in a 'dead' rubber, was treated sensationally by the press.

It was only the third match conceded by America in five successive challenge rounds. A week or so later, in the US Nationals, Cochet beat Tilden in the quarter finals; Borotra put out Johnston and Richards; and Lacoste defeated Borotra for the title. How much longer could France be denied the Davis Cup?

—7—

THE MUSKETEERS

(1927–32, France)

In 1927 Bill Tilden decided to carry the fight to the French challengers. Returning to Europe for the first time in six years, accompanied by his doubles partner and best friend in the game, Frank Hunter, he learned painfully he was no longer invincible. In the French championships, after beating Cochet, he lost to Lacoste in the final, 11–9 in the fifth set, double-faulting on match point. At Wimbledon, in the semifinal against Cochet, he failed even more uncharacteristically. Leading 6–2, 6–4 and 5–1, he made a string of errors, losing seventeen straight points. Cochet took the third set 7–5, and the next two 6–4, 6–3. The dapper Frenchman went on to beat Borotra in the final, coming from two sets down for the third time in a row and saving seven match points.

Back in America, Tilden warned the USLTA that the cup could be retained only if careful preparations were made. Even then, the team could need some luck. He wasn't taken seriously.

Twenty-five nations mounted challenges in 1927, twenty-one in the European Zone and four in the American Zone. In the former it was a foregone conclusion that France would defeat all her rivals. This she did despite stiff resistance from the Italians, Baron Humberto de Morpurgo and Giorgio de Stefani, who snatched two rubbers from France in their third-round match at Rome. Most of the French team departed for America a fortnight earlier than in 1926 to ensure a better chance of acclimatization. Australia was again an absentee in the American Zone, and Japan repeated its success of the previous year. This year, though, Japan was no match for France in the inter-zone final in Boston.

In the challenge round, held once more in Philadelphia, the singles

92

players were Tilden and Johnston for America, and Lacoste and Cochet for France. Richards, who would have been a better choice than Johnston, was unavailable, having turned professional at the age of twenty-three. Johnston had played hardly at all during the year and was unimpressive in practice. Moreover, he and Tilden were conceding the challengers a total of nineteen years in age.

On the eve of the draw Lacoste said he hoped to play the first match, and preferably against Johnston. Having been beaten by Johnston in the last two years, he had schemed and trained to take his revenge. Lacoste believed that if Tilden had a hard fight against Cochet on the first day, he would be less able two days later to resist the methods Lacoste intended to employ against him – to keep him on the court as long as possible and wear him down. Lacoste's hopes were fulfilled. He was drawn to play Johnston in the first match and lost only seven games. Little Bill was a shadow of the great player he had been.

To even the scores, Tilden had to produce his best form. Cochet's victories over him – in the US, French and Wimbledon championships – should have given the Frenchman a psychological edge, but here in his home town Tilden was a different proposition. The crowd which so often had wished to see him humbled was moved by the sight of Tilden summoning all his ability, nerve and courage for his country. They cheered him on as never before.

Pacing himself, Tilden won the first set 6–4, and let the second go at 2–6. He won the third set 6–2 and anxiously sought to finish the match in the fourth set as he was concerned about the demands on his stamina over the three days. Cochet was treating his service more and more cavalierly. He stood just inside the baseline and whipped back some of Tilden's hardest serves. At 5–6 Tilden knew a crisis was at hand. He quaffed some spirits of ammonia during the change of ends, then served a love game for 6 all. Cochet was broken to 30 in the next game, and Tilden served another love game, finishing with a cannonball ace. Was it the ammonia?

Johnston's poor form threw the selectors into a quandary. Despite the fact that Tilden and Hunter were a successful pair, having recently won the Wimbledon championship and several other titles, the selectors had nominated Tilden and Johnston for the doubles. The decision infuriated Big Bill. He spent nervous energy he could ill afford to waste arguing on behalf of his friend. Changing their

93

minds with only an hour to spare, the selectors replaced Johnston with Hunter. With Tilden in magnificent form, the Americans beat Borotra and Brugnon 3–6, 6–3, 6–3, 4–6, 6–0. Nevertheless, the French master plan was not affected. The ageing champion had been kept out on the court much longer than he would have wished and he had run back and forth to cope with French lobs. The bickering with officialdom also had taken a toll of his resources. Now he had to contend with a fresh Lacoste, eleven years his junior.

Tilden attacked Lacoste from the start, knowing he had to win quickly if he were to win at all. Lacoste weathered the barrage. Encouraged by his opponent's errors, the Crocodile won the first set 6–4. Tilden made an even bigger effort in the second set. He won it 6–3. But his energy was seeping away. Lacoste persistently played the ball down the middle of the court – a negative but effective tactic. He also prevented Tilden from becoming too grooved in his strokes by varying the length of his shots and returning some fierce drives with soft, looping balls to the backhand. Tilden grew more tired and Lacoste took the last two sets 6–2, 6–2. 'I thought I was playing against a machine,' Tilden was to recall, 'his strokes were so exact and impenetrable.'

It was an emotional moment. The fans forgot their traditional antipathy to the man who had arrogantly ground so many adversaries into the Philadelphia turf. Most of them rose and cheered him, and some cried. Tilden, bewildered, raised his hands above his head like a boxer.

For France, all now depended on Cochet. On Johnston's form of the first day, the American had little chance of beating the Lyonnais. But in a challenge round who could be sure? Watching in the stands in warm sunshine, the normally calm Lacoste was shaking so much that he put on two sweaters and an overcoat.

Cochet won the first set 6–4, Johnston the second by the same margin. Johnston, however, appeared to be distressingly short of breath and was slow. Cochet won the third set easily 6–2. Nobody then realized that Little Bill was suffering from the early stages of tuberculosis. The disease, not diagnozed until a few weeks later when he went to hospital for a check-up, was to end his career.

When the players returned from the locker room for the fourth set, Lacoste occupied the captain's chair, for Gillou the captain was too nervous to stay at courtside any longer! Cochet went to a 5–2 lead and Johnston looked forlorn. 'God bless you, Little Bill,' a woman called down from the stands. Some people began to cry, their hearts wrenched by the tiny, floundering figure. Somehow he rallied. The eighth game went to deuce eight times before Johnston held service. Then he unleashed the kind of drives that had won him his reputation. He took Cochet's service to love. The crowd shouted in excitement. 'My nerves were frayed from the very beginning', Cochet said later, 'and I suddenly felt empty and uncoordinated, incapable of connecting with the ball.' At the change of ends Lacoste quietly offered him some steadying advice. His composure reassured Cochet, who returned to the court and sealed victory.

Lacoste has given us a vivid cameo of what happened next.

Mme. Cochet fainted; Pierre Gillou sprang up like a child; I took off my overcoat and sweaters; Brugnon dropped his pipe; and Borotra – you can imagine him justifying his reputation of 'The Bounding Basque'. Everything after that seemed like a dream. The Davis Cup delivered to our team; a thousand photographs, uniting the players with the French Ambassador and American Minister for War, Dwight Davis, the giver of the cup. The memories of it all seem like a fantasy.

Lacoste capped a glorious tour by beating Johnston and Tilden in defence of his American crown. The Musketeers now ruled Europe, Wimbledon, America, the world, and champagne corks popped continuously as they sailed home. Each night, Cochet, Brugnon, Borotra and Gillou threw themselves into the celebrations. But 'Lacoste, with his serious smile, paid his share of the bottles and retired early to his cabin'. The Crocodile was already plotting the future.

The popularity of the Musketeers and the likelihood that the cup would be successfully defended for several years spurred French officials to provide a more spacious stadium than those existing in the beautiful Stade Français grounds at St Cloud or in the grounds of the Racing Club de France in the Bois de Boulogne. With help from the French Government and civic authorities, they acquired a site just outside the Porte d'Auteuil. A centre court and four outside courts, all of clay, were installed, and a 10,000-seat wooden stand built. The stadium was named after Roland Garros, a French aviator and a prominent rugby player, killed in the war.

For the first time, America, Britain and Australia, all predominantly grass-court nations, were faced with the task of regaining the cup on a far different surface. Moreover, as holders of the trophy, the French were entitled, to some extent, to organize the competition to suit themselves. The first two rounds in 1928 were scheduled for May, before the start of the French championships, and another two rounds were set for June before Wimbledon. The European Zone final, the inter-zone final and the challenge round were all marked down for July.

Australia, New Zealand, Chile, Argentina and the Philippines were among the record number of thirty-two nations which competed in the European Zone. These far-off countries not only fancied their chances of making more progress in Europe than in America, where Tilden was still a force to be reckoned with, but believed it was more economic to enter there, especially if they wanted to give their players the chance to compete at Wimbledon also. Only six nations contested the American Zone, where matches commenced in April.

Australia had a rude – and costly – awakening when her team of Patterson and two young players, Jack Crawford and Harry Hopman, lost to Italy at Genoa in early May. Baron de Morpurgo beat both Patterson and Crawford, and though Patterson defeated de Stefani, who had the unusual style of passing the racquet from one hand to the other to play constant forehands, he and Hopman lost the doubles to de Morpurgo and Placido Gaslini.

An interesting sidelight was the fate of Germany, with the veterans Froitzheim and Klienschroth in her team. Germany had re-entered the competition the previous year when she defeated Portugal but lost to South Africa at Berlin. Froitzheim, Kleinschroth and Rahe of the prewar team had made somewhat sad comebacks. Froitzheim, who was now aged forty-four and the chief of police at Wiesbaden, had a traumatic time in 1928. In Germany's first match, against Greece, he beat one opponent but retired against the other. He did not play when Germany narrowly defeated Spain at Berlin, but in the third round he returned to the nation which had interned him during the war and played Dr Colin Gregory on a wet, soft court at Edgbaston. He was leading 2–1 in the first set when he sprained an ankle. The ankle was bandaged and he resumed playing in great pain. He lost the first set, won the second, then dropped the third 0–6 and retired amid warm applause. Great Britain won the tie 4–1, and Froitzheim never played a cup match again.

In the European Zone semfinals, de Morpurgo's strength was the main factor in Italy's 4–1 defeat of Great Britain at Felixstowe, while Czechoslovakia, aided in the doubles by a newcomer, Roderich Menzel, had a 3–2 win over Holland at Prague. De Morpurgo was again the dominant player in the final which was played in Milan, beating both his opponents in straight sets as Italy won 3–2.

America, in the role of challenger for the first time since 1920, had to begin forging a new team. John Hennessy was selected to play singles against Mexico, and George Lott made his debut against China. America won the American Zone by scoring 5–0 victories over Mexico, China and Japan, with Lott becoming the first player in the competition to beat an opponent (China's P. Kong) 6–0, 6–0, 6–0. W. F. ('Junior') Coen became the youngest to participate when he partnered Tilden in the doubles against China at the age of sixteen.

With their confidence at a peak, the Musketeers collected most of the world's major titles in 1928. Borotra had won the Australian championship, the only Frenchman ever to do so, and Cochet won his second French title, beating Lacoste in the final. A few months later, Cochet was to win the US title, but at Wimbledon he lost in the final to Lacoste. Tilden had continued his mastery of Borotra by beating him at Wimbledon before losing to Lacoste in the semifinals. Cochet and Brugnon won the Wimbledon doubles, and various combinations among the Musketeers annexed other doubles titles. A part of their strength was the ready way in which they always blended together in doubles.

During Wimbledon a storm broke over Tilden's head that was to have international repercussions. He had never enjoyed good relations with the game's rulers in America, who often seemed to be rankled by his image as a superstar. His demand for a cabin to himself when he sailed the Atlantic, and his insistence on having the best hotel accommodation, all at the USLTA's expense, was annoying. So was his habit of telling officials how to pick their teams and his blunt criticism of them when he thought they were wrong. The biggest bone of contention was his flouting of the amateur rules. Unlike most of the great players hitherto, Tilden was never interested in pursuing a career in business or one of the professions. His one significant talent, besides playing tennis, was in writing about it. However, the amateur code prohibited players from writing on tennis since that would mean they were profiting, albeit indirectly, from the game. In Tilden's case it was known that in one year he made about $25,000 from a newspaper syndicate. Tilden argued that he was a *bona fide* writer, and from his many articles and books it is obvious that he was indeed one of the best commentators of his time. In fact, his writings did much to propagate the game worldwide. Nevertheless, to many officials any breach of the amateur code was an evil.

Sometimes it even seemed that officials around the world were trying to outdo each other in their application of the amateur code. In various countries players were suspended for infringements. A typical attitude was expressed by *Australasian Lawn Tennis* when it heard in 1924 that leading players in America were receiving expensive gifts.

If the great players of America or elsewhere are in fact freed from doing anything else than playing lawn tennis by presents of motor cars, then we can allow America to pursue that course without following in its footsteps. The Davis Cup is the finest thing in the greatest game in the world; but greater is the pure spirit of amateurism. We shall follow the spirit of the ancient Greeks – a healthy mind in a healthy body. The mind will not be healthy if we give up amateurism.

While Tilden so far had escaped punishment, the rules in America had been amended once or twice in an effort to clip his wings and he had received several warnings. He finally provoked the USLTA by filing daily newspaper reports during Wimbledon, and was suspended as the US Davis Cup team was preparing to play Italy in the inter-zone final in Paris. The news created a sensation. Joseph Wear, the American captain and chairman of the US Davis Cup committee, who was with the team, immediately resigned from the committee. 'The action of the committee in demanding the withdrawal of Tilden at the last moment,' he cabled home, 'is incomprehensible to competing nations and makes us ridiculous in their eyes.' Tilden dissuaded his team-mates from going on strike.

Even without Tilden, America lost only one rubber against Italy (de Morpurgo beat Hunter), but so much criticism was levelled against the USLTA that some officials thought it would have been better had the team been eliminated so that the matter would have ended then and there. The French were appalled that Tilden would be prevented from playing in their expensive new stadium. 'Beeg Beel' was a huge favourite in Paris and his absence was bound to affect the gate receipts. French officials protested to their government, which then appealed to the American ambassador, Myron Herrick, to intervene with the USLTA. Under pressure from the State Department, the association rescinded its ruling and allowed Tilden to play.

Tilden, anticipating the reprieve, was struggling to find form. In three days of practice with Lott, Hennessy, Hunter and Coen, he failed to win a set. On the day before play started he lost five consecutive sets to Coen. With any other player, doubts might have arisen, but Jospeh Wear knew that Tilden was a notoriously bad practice player and needed time to settle down after so much tension.

Big Bill was drawn to play Lacoste in the first match. A high wind made control difficult, and he was far from impressive as he lost the first set 1–6. Then he stopped trying to hit Lacoste off the court and opted for a more patient and guileful game. He won the next two sets 6–4, 6–4. But Tilden was very tired. During the rest period he was urged by his team-mates to go for a quick win in the fourth set. When he stepped up his attack again, though, he again made errors. Lacoste took the set 6–2. The match came to a crisis in the fifth set when Lacoste was serving at 3–4, 15 all. Lacoste drove deep to the backhand corner and Tilden hit a floating, shoulder-high chop shot. Tilden suddenly realized that Lacoste had come to the net and was going to take the ball on the forehand. He knew that Lacoste invariably hit a short-angle volley off his forehand. Though weary, the American began running to cover such a shot. Sure enough, that was the way Lacoste played. Tilden sprinted almost to the umpire's chair and finished beyond the sideline as he lunged desperately to hit the ball from outside the net post. The ball went down the court and landed in as Tilden crashed into the courtside appendages and fell. Lacoste seemed unnerved. He served a double fault, then missed an easy shot to drop his service. Tilden held for 6–3 and won the match.

The effort was not enough to swing the contest. Cochet beat Hennessy 5–7, 6–8, 7–5, 4–6, 6–2. Two five-set matches had weakened Tilden's resistance, and Cochet beat him in the deciding match

9–7, 8–6, 6–4. Weary and dispirited, he returned home to find the USLTA reconsidering disciplinary action against him. He was suspended for the rest of the season.

Germany, relying mainly on Hans Moldenhauer and Dr Daniel Prenn, was now looming as a tennis power and in 1929 reached the European Zone final. Twenty-four nations, including two newcomers, Monaco and Egypt, entered the European Zone, and five entered the American Zone, a notable absentee being Australia.

Germany defeated Spain, Italy and Czechoslovakia before meeting Great Britain in a dramatic final in Berlin. The British had a new player in twenty-two-year-old H. W. ('Bunny') Austin, who was to play a leading role in his country's tennis revival over the next decade. In many ways, he epitomized the best type of amateur sportsman. The son of a stockbroker, Austin taught himself to handle a racquet at the age of six by hitting a ball against his nursery wall and using a rocking horse in place of a net. As a junior player he had a somewhat weak, cut backhand until he read a book by J. C. Parke and found how to hit the shot more solidly, with his thumb up the back of the handle. He became captain of the Cambridge team and in 1926, while still at university, was invited to play in the Davis Cup, but was dissuaded by his father and his former house master because they felt he was too young. That summer, Austin took little exercise, not realizing that physical fitness quickly declines with inactivity. When he did play a representative match later in the year he was so out of condition that he was thought to have damaged his heart. He was advised by a doctor not to play any sport for four months, and even then no singles for a year. A short, quick-footed man, Austin might be seen in between tournaments in the City of London, bowler-hatted and stiff-collared, on his way to his job at the Stock Exchange.

In 1929 Austin played the deciding fifth match against Prenn. He and Gregory had lost the opening day's singles. Then, against all the odds, Gregory and Ian Collins won the doubles and Gregory allowed Moldenhauer only five games on the third day. It was very hot, and Austin was rarely at his best in such weather. Prenn was a dogged retriever and Austin tried to be patient and rally from the baseline. He won the first set 6–4, but Prenn won the next two 6–2, 6–4, picking up many shots that had looked winners. With a burst of aggression, Austin levelled the scores by taking the fourth set

6–4, and then broke Prenn's first service in the fifth set. At this stage he was utterly worn out. He began clutching his calf muscles and falling on the court. Realizing that Austin had cramp Prenn increased the pressure. The Englishman hobbled around the court as best he could, but at 1–5 he fell once again and had to be carried off as the Berliners expressed their sympathy.

Always imaginative, Austin considered that his mishap was due to the weight of his sweat-soaked flannel trousers. When he got home he asked his tailor in future to cut his pants off just below the knees. And so evolved the fashion of men's tennis shorts!

Tilden, though reinstated, did not feature in the American Zone matches. He played in Europe instead. Without him, America had a brief scare while playing Japan at Washington when Yoshiro Ohta beat John Van Ryn in a rain-interrupted match. There were no other upsets, and the Americans duly made their way to Berlin for the inter-zone final. There, Tilden beat Moldenhauer in straight sets, and Hunter overcame Prenn in five. America had found a fine new doubles team in Wilmer Allison and Van Ryn, who had paired for the first time against Cuba. Since then they had won the Wimbledon title. Now they finished off Germany by beating Moldenhauer and Prenn.

This Berlin interlude apart, it was not one of Tilden's happiest tours. At Roland Garros, where a concrete stand had been built around the centre court, increasing the capacity to 13,000, he lost to Lacoste in the semifinals of the French championships. The Crocodile went on to win the final narrowly against Borotra, who had eliminated Cochet. Illness kept Lacoste out of Wimbledon, where Cochet, who had become Tilden's nemesis, beat the American in the semifinals and then turned the tables on Borotra in the final. Borotra's semifinal victim was Austin, the first Englishman to advance so far for six years.

Still unwell, Lacoste could not play in the challenge round. In fact, he was never to play in the competition again. It was Borotra and Cochet who lined up against Tilden and Lott in the singles, and against Allison and Van Ryn in the doubles. On the first day Borotra conquered Lott in four sets, and Cochet inflicted a humiliating 6–3, 6–1, 6–2 defeat on Tilden. The fact that Tilden was in reasonably good form emphasized the Frenchman's superiority. Allison and Van Ryn gave America a fighting chance by winning the doubles, and hopes were raised higher when Tilden, who always beat Borotra as consistently as he lost to Cochet, stopped the Basque in four sets. But it was too much to expect Lott to beat Cochet, now the world's number one player. Cochet, nevertheless, felt the pressure of the occasion and was nervously prone to error. Lott extended him to 6–1, 3–6, 6–0, 6–3.

As Tilden had announced that the Borotra match would be his last in the competition, the Americans set about rebuilding their team around Lott, Allison, Van Ryn and John Doeg. Like everyone else, they were not overly optimistic that they could make much impact on the Musketeers. Germany had lost Moldenhauer, killed in a car accident on Christmas Day, 1929, and it was to be another two years before she got past the first round.

In 1930, twenty-four nations challenged in the European Zone, and only Canada and Mexico opposed the USA in the American Zone. Australia reappeared, and its team of Crawford, Hopman, Edgar ('Gar') Moon and Jim Willard defeated Switzerland, Ireland and Great Britain before again finding Italy a stumbling block. The match with Italy was played in Milan, where de Stefani was conspicuously absent from the practice courts. He was in the army and it was being said that he might be unable to get away from his military duties in Rome. At three o'clock, the scheduled starting time of the tie, de Stefani could not be seen, though he was drawn to play Hopman in the opening match. At 3.30 Hopman heard that de Stefani had arrived, but did not want to play. A few minutes later, after the players were called onto the court, an announcer informed the gallery that 'de Stefani has been too busy in the army to practise but he is going to fight on the court and do his best for Italy'. The Italian won brilliantly in four sets! Every day for some time he had been practising with Italy's top professional in Rome.

The Italy v. Australia tie also provided an example of the kind of difficulties that could be caused by partisan crowds. At 4 all in the fifth set of the second singles, between de Morpurgo and Crawford, the Italian served a double fault. Despite a noisy protest from the crowd, the linesman would not change his call, and several angry fans climbed into the court area and surrounded him. Fearing violence, the Australian team helped Italian officials to shepherd the linesman to safety and he was replaced. Crawford lost the match, and though Hopman and Willard won the doubles, de Morpurgo gave Italy victory by beating Hopman on the third day.

In the European final at Genoa, Italy narrowly beat Japan, who had entered the zone for the first time. The ever reliable Harada won both his singles and, with Tamio Abe, extended de Morpurgo and de Stefani to five sets in the doubles.

Meanwhile, Tilden had made another assault on the European tournaments and this time fared better. In Paris he beat Borotra but again fell to Cochet in the final. At Wimbledon, however, he was triumphant, winning the title for the third time and at the age of thirty-seven, nine years after his first success. He was helped by the complacency of Cochet, who disliked practice and had been savouring the fruits of his French victory. Wilmer Allison, a rugged Texan, did not possess half the talent of Cochet; he was a net player who had taken an entire season off to work with Mercer Beasley in acquiring better ground strokes. He dispatched Cochet in the quarter finals and then beat Doeg. Tilden, with his bogey-man removed, won a close five-setter against Borotra and swept aside Allison for the crown.

Though Tilden had declared himself unavailable for the 1930 Davis Cup competition, he was enlisted as coach of the American team for the inter-zone final at Roland Garros. He watched anxiously as Allison lost the first two sets to de Stefani 4–6, 7–9, but won the next two 6–4, 8–6. In the last set Allison was down 1–5. Through sheer willpower, he won the set 10–8. Lott led de Morpurgo 3–6, 9–7, 10–8 when darkness stopped play. Next day Lott won the fourth set 6–3, and Allison and Van Ryn beat de Morpurgo and Gaslini in five sets in the doubles. The struggle had been tougher than the final result suggested.

Within twenty-four hours, Joseph Wear, who was back as chairman of the US Davis Cup committee, announced that Tilden would be in the team to play France in five days' time. Allison, who had lost on the last day at Genoa, was thought to be stale, and Tilden after all was the Wimbledon champion. Big Bill accepted the selection 'against my wishes and despite my better judgement'. The French were delighted; they had spent more money installing new permanent facilities at Roland Garros and Tilden's appearance guaranteed a capacity crowd.

To reinforce its player–writer rule, the USLTA had adopted

another rule specifically prohibiting a player from writing, giving interviews or making radio talks while a member of the Davis Cup team. This was waived so that Tilden could write articles in the days preceding the challenge round. He agreed not to comment on the matches themselves.

During practice Tilden wrenched an ankle. When he met Borotra in the first match he was limping. He lost the first set 6–2 and was down 2–5 in the second set, but he was making Borotra run. Suddenly, moving more freely, he won five straight games and then the next two sets. Cochet crushed Lott 6–4, 6–2, 6–2, and America's chances quickly receded when Cochet and Brugnon beat Allison and Van Ryn, the Wimbledon champions. On the third day thousands of fans were turned away from the stadium and some tried to storm the gates. Those inside saw Borotra finally survive Lott's lobs and passing shots to beat him, 8–6 in the fifth set. Cochet, as usual, took care of Tilden, and this time it really was Big Bill's swan song. He had played in eleven successive challenge rounds, and had lost to only two men in singles, Lacoste (twice) and Cochet (three times). Within two months he signed a movie contract which made him a professional.

One who did not begrudge the French their successes was the founder of the competition. Dwight Davis's constant hope was to see the cup circulating among more countries. In 1930 he was serving the American Government in the Philippines, sometimes wistfully recalling his one-time prowess as a tennis player. When he heard that Norman Brookes would be passing through that country he wrote him a rather poignant letter.

Since I have been in Manila I have tried to renew my youth by playing some tennis again and have had great fun doing so. I find that most of the vim, vigor and vitality has disappeared but manage to hobble around the court fairly well and occasionally get a ball back. It has been the best way of getting exercise here and has been a life saver for me. I hope we may have a game while you are here to recall the good old days.

In 1931, the American Zone was divided into two parts, North America and South America, a development that recognized and encouraged the growth of the game in the southern continent. Four countries, Argentina, Paraguay, Uruguay and Chile, entered the South American Zone, with Argentina emerging victorious. The

USA had two young recruits, Frank Shields and Sidney Wood, to assist Allison, Van Ryn and Lott, and they played the major roles in winning the North American Zone and then the inter-zone final against Argentina.

A new British player, Fred Perry, who was to be one of the giants of the game, also appeared this year. Tall, robust and athletic, his background was vastly different from that of Austin. He was the son of a Labour parliamentarian and had gone not to an expensive private school but to Ealing County School. Perry was probably the first leading British player who lacked an old school tie, a fact which, if anything, made him more determined to outshine those who inherited greater privileges.

It was not until he was aged fourteen that Perry began to dabble at the game during his holidays. By then he was already a very good table tennis player. While still in his teens be represented Great Britain at table tennis and won the world championship at Budapest. The indoor game not only helped to sharpen his reflexes but he adapted some of his shots to lawn tennis. As a junior at the Chiswick Park Club, however, he looked far from being a future world-beater until, on the advice of a friend, he learned how to take the ball early. Perry's father greatly encouraged and supported him when the tyro took a year off work at the age of twenty in order to further his game. Soon, Perry had developed his dazzling running forehand, played with a Continental grip. He had the eye of an eagle and catlike agility.

In 1931, when Perry went to Plymouth to play a Davis Cup contest against Monaco, he was twenty-one. He had an uneventful debut. Within three months, he and Austin, supported by Pat Hughes and Charles Kingsley in the doubles, had also beaten Belgium, South Africa and Japan without dropping a rubber. They then had to contend with Czechoslovakia in Prague, always a grim prospect for visitors. Czechoslovakia had defeated Spain, Greece, Italy and Denmark. In the giant Menzel, whose service kicked 'as high as a house', it possessed a very intimidating player. Austin undermined Czech morale by beating Menzel in five sets on the first day, and Great Britain got through by four rubbers to one.

The major tournament season provided little guide to what would happen in the final rounds of the competition. Cochet was not well enough to play in the French championships, and Austin retired with a twisted ankle; Perry was beaten by de Stefani; and Borotra beat the rising Japanese star, Jiro Satoh, in the semifinals. Borotra won the title for the first time in seven years by beating his young compatriot Christian Boussus in the final.

At Wimbledon, Cochet went out in the first round; Austin lost to Shields in a quarter final after having match point; and Perry lost to the nineteen-year-old Sidney Wood in the semifinals. In the other semifinal, Borotra led Shields by two sets to one when the American hurt his ankle. Shields rested it and had it massaged for twelve minutes, then got up and won. The US captain, Gene Dixon, refused to allow him to risk further injury (an indication of how the Davis Cup was regarded as being more important than Wimbledon) and Wood won the final on a default to become the youngest Wimbledon champion this century. With Lott and Van Ryn beating Cochet and Brugnon in the doubles final, the Americans again loomed as the most dangerous challengers for the cup.

But the soft clay of Paris requires a different sort of game than Wimbledon turf, and in the inter-zone final the hurricane hitting of the Americans was less effective. Once more, Austin struck a heavy blow by beating the Wimbledon title-holder 2–6, 6–0, 8–6, 7–5. Shields, making the most of his long reach and volleying ability, beat Perry 10–8, 6–4, 6–2, and the Americans took the doubles to go 2–1 up. Wood, however, fell to Perry 6–3, 8–10, 6–3, 6–3, and in the deciding match Austin avenged his Wimbledon defeat by surprising Shields 8–6, 6–3, 7–5. Perry was never one to be over-awed. 'Your boys seemed very overconfident,' he told George Lott, 'and they are really not that good, you know.' Overconfident or not, it was the first American team to fail to reach the challenge round since 1920.

Having confounded the prophets, the British were now given a chance of winning the cup. They were not quite ready to do so, though they lost to France only after a stiff fight. Austin took the first set from Cochet, led 4–1 in the second set and had two set points. But Cochet beat him 4–6, 11–9, 6–2, 6–4. Perry evened the scores by defeating Borotra 4–6, 10–8, 6–0, 4–6, 6–4, and was so tired at the end that he was rested in the doubles. Cochet and Brugnon beat Hughes and Kingsley in four sets, but Austin then accounted for Borotra 7–5, 6–3, 3–6, 7–5, and it was left to Perry to see if he could prise French hands off the cup. Cochet was still too clever for him. In a rain-protracted match he won 6–4, 1–6, 9–7, 6–3. The man who yet again had saved France was carried off the court as the customary shower of cushions rained down.

The year 1932 saw the rise of two other outstanding players, Ellsworth Vines of America and Baron Gottfried von Cramm of Germany. Vines, a Californian with a cannonball service and a lightning forehand, had risen meteorically to win the US championship in 1931, beating Perry and Lott. A year later, on his first visit to London, the twenty-year-old Vines took Wimbledon by storm. In the final he confined Austin to six games, his ace on match point being so fast that the Englishman did not know on which side of his body the ball passed him.

Vines was to achieve most of his ambitions in tennis before he turned professional in 1933. (He later became a leading professional golfer.) The one dream to remain unfulfilled was the recapture of the Davis Cup. But early in 1932 all looked to be going to plan for America when she swept past Canada, Mexico and Australia to win the North American Zone. Just as easily, she disposed of Brazil, winner of the South American Zone.

Meanwhile, von Cramm proved to be an effective number two to Prenn as Germany defeated India, Austria and Ireland to qualify for another contest with Great Britain. Von Cramm was one of seven sons of a Hanover nobleman who had introduced him to the game on one of the courts on their estates. A classical stylist, he had overcome the handicap of having lost the top joint of his right index finger while feeding pieces of sugar to a horse.

On the same Berlin court on which they had lost two years earlier, the British suffered another agonizing defeat. Austin was experiencing a delayed reaction from the Wimbledon final and lost to Prenn. Perry beat von Cramm, and with Hughes won the doubles. But the final day was a disaster for the British. First, von Cramm beat Austin in four sets. Then an inspired Prenn won the first two sets 6–2, 6–4 against Perry. Fred fought back to take the next two sets 6–3, 6–0 and to lead 5–2 in the fifth set. Prenn saved a match point on his service in the next game and held for 3–5. Serving for the match, Perry surprisingly lost the game and cracked. The gritty German won the set 7–5 to inflict upon Perry the most bitter defeat of his career.

A week later Germany defeated Italy 5–0 in the zone final in

Milan. In the inter-zone final in Paris, however, Vines's power was too much for Prenn and von Cramm. Both the Germans beat Shields, and it was the winning doubles display of Allison and Van Ryn that proved to be crucial.

Because of the form of Vines, the best player in the world on a fast grass court, and the doubles record of Allison and Van Ryn, America was given a good chance of winning the challenge round. Allison, who had done well at Wimbledon, replaced Shields in the singles and was in the mood to cause an upset. French selection problems added to American optimism. Cochet, who had won his fifth French singles title that year, selected himself, but Lacoste had hoped to play and now would not. After competing in the French championships he was taken ill and decided that the strain of playing in the challenge round would be beyond him. As team captain, Lacoste set about persuading Borotra to take his place. The Basque remembered with embarrassment his defeats in the 1931 challenge round and the hurtful criticism they had provoked in the press. His net-rushing style was exhausting on clay and he wanted Lacoste to choose a younger man. Finally, he reluctantly submitted to Lacoste's persuasion.

Having made his commitment, Borotra gave the task of defending the cup all his energy and inspiration. When he walked out onto the court with Vines, thirteen years his junior, for the opening match he may indeed have felt like 'a lamb being led to the slaughter', but he refused to be cowed. President Lebrun was among the crowd who was there to see France fight for her life.

Storming the net, Jean peppered Vines's backhand and forced errors. Vines appeared to lack energy and his eye was hopelessly out. Perhaps he was overly nervous or was put out by the slow court. To the amazement of all, Borotra won in four sets. Cochet won by the same margin against Allison. And even after Allison and Van Ryn had won a marathon doubles against Cochet and Brugnon, the American position looked hopeless.

The lion-hearted Allison had played nine hard sets in two days. On the third day he faced up to Borotra resolutely. He was unwittingly assisted by overzealous groundsmen who had so drenched the clay court that it resembled a quagmire and was unplayable at the scheduled starting time. The French apologized for the 'mistake'; the Americans suspected their opponents were intent on slowing down the court as much as possible to nullify Vines's cannon balls in the last match.

The slow court did not suit the net-rushing Borotra at all. Whereas Allison's lighter footwork skimmed over the surface, Borotra's more muscular assaults were seriously affected. Allison won the first two sets 6–1, 6–3, passing the Frenchman just as he liked on either wing and sometimes, for variation, lobbing with perfect length. Borotra came back strongly to take the next two sets 6–4, 6–2, and then looked the fresher. At the end of a long rally in the fourth game, Allison seemed scarcely able to stand up – three days of hard-fought tennis amid the tension of a challenge round and the moist heat of a Parisian August had brought him to the verge of collapse.

Yet the determined Texan led 5–3, and 40–15 on his service – double match point. The French veteran saved the points and broke Allison's service. In the next game Borotra noticed his big toe was protruding through the canvas of his rope-soled shoe. Already he had changed shoes twice in the match. The Americans wondered if he had been stalling and were loathe to let him hold up play again. Borotra saved a third match point. By his gestures he made it plain that he felt his shoe was handicapping him. The gallery called on the American captain to let their man make adjustments. At last he relented. Soon the fans were laughing as, in mid-court, sucking an orange Borotra sat on the back of a ballboy while two others helped him to change shoes yet again. Allison waited impatiently. To him and his team-mates it seemed blatant gamesmanship.

Borotra lost the next rally and faced his fourth match point. He served into the net. His next delivery was slow and looked a fault too, out by a good four inches. With relief, Allison belted the ball out of court and began walking to the net to shake hands. But there was no call. Allison looked quickly and disbelievingly at the linesman. The man would not change his mind. 'Thieves! Thieves!' cried an American fan. Even many of the French fans booed the decision, for despite their delight in any French victory over America they were proud of the Musketeers' reputation for sportsmanship and did not want to retain the cup unfairly.

The disappointed Allison won only one more point, losing the set 5–7. Never again did he play as well in the Davis Cup. In the final rubber Cochet suffered his first cup defeat since 1927 at the hands of Vines, leaving America to ponder on what might have been. . . .

There were repercussions. The Americans did not approve of the French custom of soaking the court shortly before, and even during, matches. They also thought there were too many attendants at the side of the court at Roland Garros. One attendant guarded an icebox which contained the Dunlop balls. Balls so refrigerated had less air pressure and less bounce (and thus prevented Vines, in particular, from serving his usual profusion of aces).

At a meeting of the Davis Cup Nations in 1933, an American delegate, L. A. Baker, successfully moved that in future only the captains and referee should be allowed on the court in addition to the umpire, linesmen, ballboys and players. Another US proposal was that a court should be prepared at least two hours before a match and that nothing should be done to the surface, except with the consent of the opposing side, until the day's play was concluded, including any rests after the third set. It, too, was carried.

PERRY SUPREME

(1933–36, Great Britain)

If 1932 had looked like being America's year, there were indications in 1933 that, after a long, lean period, Australia's fortunes were beginning to turn. Jack Crawford was the player on whom Australia pinned most of her hopes. A country boy who had learned his tennis on a home-made court on his parents' farm near Albury, Crawford played with a nonchalance similar to Cochet's, making beautiful strokes look easy. Like Cochet, he disliked training and could be careless. He had a moderate service and was relatively slow, but his shots were such that most opponents were too troubled in getting to the ball to have any time to exploit these weaknesses. Crawford's appearance and demeanour were as immaculate as his strokes. His dark hair was always parted in the middle and his sleeves buttoned at the wrist – unless the going got really tough when he neatly folded them at the elbow. A quiet, serene man who suffered from asthma, he might well have belonged to a former era. In long matches he liked to have a pot of tea, with milk and sugar and reserves of hot water, by the umpire's chair.

Early in 1933 Crawford won his third successive Australian title in a field that included Vines and Allison. That season revealed the world-beating potential of a sixteen-year-old Sydney boy, Vivian McGrath, whose double-handed backhand helped him to beat Vines in the quarter finals. Not far behind in ability were two young Adelaide players, Adrian Quist and Don Turnbull.

A record number of thirty-four nations contested the cup in 1933. Australia challenged in the European Zone and, after beating Norway, its team travelled to Paris for the French championships. Perry was expected to be the best foreign contender, but he lost to the Japanese Satoh. Crawford beat Satoh in the semifinals and became the first foreigner to capture the title by toppling Cochet.

When the European ties were resumed, Satoh was instrumental in Japan's 4–1 defeat of Germany, his task made easier by the Nazi's decision to kick Daniel Prenn off the German team. Prenn, who was born in Russia but who had lived in Germany for most of his life, was a victim of Hitler's first Jewish purge. The Prenn affair and the discrimination practised by Germany against all Jewish tennis players was one of the most unfortunate episodes in Davis Cup history. On 12 April, the Berlin correspondent of the London *Times* reported that Prenn's removal was consistent with the Nazi policy of ousting Jews from the public service and professions. He added:

It is a further complication that Dr. Prenn, who has been naturalized in recent years, belongs to that Eastern Jewish stock which enjoys the particular enmity of the Nazis and to which they attribute so many of Germany's troubles.

Also, Germany may well find herself in the second round matched to meet Poland on Polish soil, and to the Nazi mind the idea of a German victory over Poland won through the services of a player of Polish-Jewish origin is intolerable. One needs to be familiar with the tone of bitter and sometimes derisory contempt and dislike in which the average Nazi refers to the Poles, and especially to the Polish Jews, to fully appreciate the situation.

There is certainly much irony in this incident for those who remember the tremendous ovations given to Dr. Prenn, one of the dourest fighters who ever trod a lawn tennis court, when, by beating, against all expectations, Gregory and Austin in 1929, and Austin and Perry in 1932, he put Germany into the finals . . . of the Davis Cup competition.

The German LTA submitted to the Nazi order and ruled that 'non-Aryans' not only were debarred from representing Germany but could not serve on tennis committees. All Jewish members of the German LTA committee resigned. The effect on Prenn and other champions who hitherto had been national heroes can be imagined, Prenn fled to England. Frau Nelly Neppach, the German women's champion of 1925, committed suicide.

One wonders why at least some of the nations did not move to have Germany disqualified from the competition. The only public protest, however, came from Perry and Austin in a letter to *The Times* published on 15 April. Expressing their dismay, they wrote:

We have always valued our participation in international sport because we believed it to be a great opportunity for the promotion of better international understanding and because it was a human activity that contained no distinction of race, class or creed. For this reason, if for no other, we view with great misgivings any action which may well undermine all that is most valuable in international competitions.

Bunny Austin, at this time, spent a great deal of energy as a public speaker urging measures to be taken against the growing threat of war.

Japan, who had beaten Hungary and Ireland, as well as Germany, was joined in the semifinals of the European Zone by Australia, Great Britain and Czechoslovakia. This was the fourth consecutive year that Japan had reached the semifinals, and in Satoh, who had succeeded Harada as Japan's champion, she had one of the most dangerous players in the world. Orthodox and intelligent, Satoh could patiently outmanoeuvre an opponent from the baseline, then speedily go in to the net on a short ball and put away a winner.

The Australians in their second match had beaten South Africa; Great Britain had scored wins over Spain, Finland and Italy; and Czechoslovakia had defeated Monaco and Greece. In Paris, Australia won the first three rubbers against Japan, with young McGrath's double-hander surprising Satoh. The British disposed of the Czechs at Eastbourne.

British hopes received a jolt at the Wimbledon championships when Perry lost on the second day to Norman Farquharson and Austin went out to Satoh. 'Why can't we win our own championships?' complained British critics, writing off their team in the Davis Cup. In the Wimbledon semifinals Crawford beat Satoh for the second time within a month, and Vines accounted for Cochet for the third time in twelve months. The title – and third leg of the Grand Slam – went to Crawford, who magnificently beat Vines, 6–4 in the fifth set.

To freshen up its players, Britain decided to send them to Eastbourne for a break. Perry was allowed to go to Brighton instead as his band-leader friend Jack Hylton was playing there. A week listening to dance music helped him to forget his recent failure and he returned to Wimbledon for the European final in better spirits.

Ironically, it was Crawford's successes of the past few weeks (as well as McGrath's inexperience) which told against Australia. Though Crawford was still in good touch, he was tired. After beating Austin on the first day he felt so exhausted that he asked to be relieved of playing in the doubles. Otherwise, he said, he would be too tired for his second singles. Perry beat McGrath, and paired with Hughes to defeat Quist and Turnbull in the doubles. When Austin out-generalled McGrath on the third day, Britain had won.

Perry had hurt his shoulder in the doubles and stayed in London for treatment while his team-mates went to Paris to prepare for the inter-zone final against America. When he turned up later, his shoulder was still tender. Dan Maskell, the professional, gave him half an hour of smashing at lobs in the belief that the sooner Perry overcame the psychological hazard associated with his injury, the better his confidence would be.

The tie was virtually decided in the first match, Austin v. Vines. After his thrashing by the 6-foot 4 American at Wimbledon the previous year, the 5-foot 8 Austin seemed to have an impossible mission. Wearing a jockey cap and tying a wet handkerchief around his neck, he waited nervously for Vines to fire his bullets. The first serve sped towards him. He swung his racquet, aiming at a cross-court drive, and struck the ball perfectly for a winner! Vines was unsettled. Thereafter, the American's best shots missed by a fraction or else came back. Hardly making an error, Austin amazingly went to a 6–1, 6–1 lead. In the third set Vines gained more accuracy, but Austin remained calm. Games went with service until the Englishman, at 5–4, held a match point. He drove to Vines's backhand, advanced to the net and fluffed a volley which nevertheless fell dead.

Perry beat Allison in straight sets; Lott and Van Ryn won the doubles; and Austin fittingly scored the winning point by defeating Allison in four sets on the last day.

For Vines there was a miserable anticlimax. He had been distracted by a professional contract that Tilden's agents were offering him, and was worried by his Wimbledon and Paris form. Against Perry in the final rubber he twisted an ankle, but did not retire for fear of being thought a quitter. Match point down, Vines collapsed with pain and fatigue and was carried off the court semiconscious.

Before the challenge round, the British had two days of golf. Their confidence was high, for no longer was Borotra available to play singles and Lacoste had recruited nineteen-year-old André Merlin. It was a tall order to expect a youngster to beat seasoned players in his first challenge round. Sure enough, Merlin lost to Austin in straight sets. Perry pushed France closer to the abyss by outlasting Cochet in five sets. Cochet, the man who had saved his country so many times, was actually booed by some of his disappointed compatriots as the end drew near. Yet the Lyonnais made Perry pay a price, and when Perry reached the dressing room, he passed out. Alarm swept through the British camp. Fred soon came to, but was so dazed he could not remember who had won. A doctor thought his condition might have been caused by mental strain.

Roper Barrett, the British captain, told his players to keep the collapse a secret and pulled Perry out of the doubles. As expected, Borotra and Brugnon beat Hughes and Harold Lee. There was still no need for British concern so long as Perry regained fitness. That evening, he and Austin went out to practise. In five minutes Barrett had seen enough to call a halt. Perry's nerves were frayed; it would be wiser for Maskell to practise with Austin, and for the masseurs to work on Perry. He was sent to bed early. But though he slept soundly, he was still shaky in the morning.

The President of the Republic was among the fifteen thousand Frenchmen who flocked to Roland Garros that day. All cheered themselves hoarse as Cochet, in his last appearance for France, fought back from two sets to one down to beat Austin, 6–4 in the fifth set. Now it was all up to Merlin and Perry. The youngster was not aware of the doubts about his opponent's fitness. That was just as well for Perry for Merlin was positive and aggressive enough as it was.

Encouraged by the frenzied crowd, Merlin threw caution to the winds. He chased every shot and hit winners from every angle. His inspired hitting gave him the first set at 6–4 and he was twice within a point of winning the second set. On one of these set points he went up for an easy smash, and mishit it. The tension of the match had given him cramp in his racquet hand! Perry scraped through the crisis and took the set at 8–6. With one set in his keeping he felt better. Merlin, on the other hand, looked deflated. Sensing the change, the crowd could no longer lift the lad. Perry won the last two sets 6–2, 7–5. The cup had changed hands.

When the presentation was made, Perry was prostrate in the dressing room. He soon recovered and by the time the team reached Dover on the ferry he was his ebullient self again. At Dover there was a message of congratulations from the King, and later when the Golden Arrow pulled into Victoria railway station in London thousands of people jostled to give the party a welcome. There was a burst of cheering as the Davis Cup was sighted in the window of a carriage, and after the players alighted, Perry and Austin were carried away on the shoulders of their friends. Suzanne Lenglen was among the crowd. She had seen the team depart from Paris and then flown across to Croydon and driven to Victoria to greet the players on their arrival. As the crowd began to disperse, the cup was placed on a barrow with a few suitcases and wheeled down the platform, closely watched by LTA officials. It was an especially proud moment for Roper Barrett for whom the saga had begun thirty-three years before.

Great Britain held the cup until 1937 and might have held it longer except that Perry turned professional. In a four-year span he won Wimbledon and the US championships three times, the French and Australian championships each once, as well as all eight of his challenge-round singles. He became increasingly flamboyant. Off the court he flaunted a lordly, though unlit, pipe; and on the court he joked with ballboys, chatted with spectators and dazzled everyone with his athleticism and tricky shots. When Perry walked out to play in his crisp white flannels and matching white blazer, thousands of female hearts missed a beat.

The burgeoning of Perry coincided with the gradual decline of Crawford, who had failed to achieve the Grand Slam when Perry beat him in the 1933 US final. In January 1934 the Englishman invaded Crawford's own territory, relieved him of his Australian crown and, with Hughes, won the doubles championship as well.

By 1934 the number of countries that had at some time played in the competition had increased to forty-one. The Philippines first played in 1926, Greece and Yugoslavia in 1927, Chile, Finland and Norway in 1928, Monaco and Egypt in 1929, Paraguay and Uruguay in 1931, and Brazil in 1932. The entries had reached such

The Musketeers of France, 1927–1932: 'Toto' Brugnon and Jean Borotra

Henri Cochet

René Lacoste

H. W. 'Bunny' Austin played a
leading role in Britain's revival in
the 1930s

Bill Tilden. The rules were
amended in America to clip his
wings

Above: Australia's 1936 team in America. (Left to right): Adrian
Quist, Vivian McGrath, Jack Crawford and Cliff Sproule

Opposite: Fred Perry endured mixed fortunes in the Davis Cup

1936: Spain meets Germany in Barcelona. (Left to right): Maier,
Von Cramm, Henkel and Blanc

The unexpected winners of the Cup in 1939: Australia's Jack
Crawford, Adrian Quist, John Bromwich and Harry Hopman

Above: Ken McGregor smashes towards Tony Trabert in the 1951
Challenge Round doubles. The other players are Frank Sedgman
and Ted Shroeder

Opposite: The 1939 Challenge Round doubles. Jack Kramer (left
foreground) plays a low volley to Adrian Quist and John
Bromwich. Kramer's partner, Joe Hunt, was killed in the Second
World War

Sedgman (right) beats Seixas,
Sydney 1951

Frank Sedgman, Harry Hopman
and Ken McGregor in 1952

Lew Hoad spreadeagled on the Kooyong Centre Court during his
1953 match with Tony Trabert. Moments later Harry Hopman
threw a towel over his head to break the tension

Vic Seixas scored a rare victory over
his tormentor Ken Rosewall in the
1954 Challenge Round in Sydney

Alex Olmedo

'Hop' collects the famous trophy from the Governor-General of
Australia, Sir William Slim, in 1957

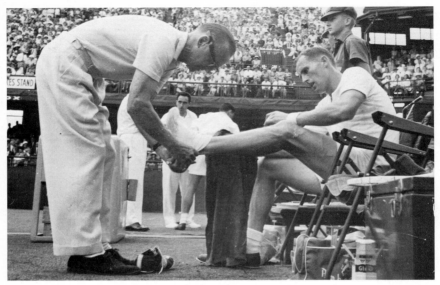

Top: Harry Hopman helps Neale Fraser change into spiked shoes in
the 1962 Challenge Round against Mexico at Brisbane

Bottom: Australia's Neale Fraser (left) and Malcolm Anderson lost a
marathon doubles to Ham Richardson and Alex Olmedo at
Brisbane, 1958

proportions that eighteen nations, including a newcomer, Estonia, were required to play in a qualifying competition in the late northern summer of 1933. The four qualifiers to emerge were Italy, Switzerland, Austria and Germany. Before the 1934 French championships began, Switzerland beat India, and Austria was eliminated by France.

Perry was expected to be the main threat to Crawford's French title, but he twisted his ankle in a match with de Stefani and, for the second time in Paris, he lost to the Italian. When Crawford reached the final it was von Cramm who faced him. He lost to the German after holding a match point in the fourth set.

Von Cramm's ability could not save Germany against France in the Davis Cup quarter finals, even though he won his singles against Merlin and Christian Boussus. In the other quarter finals Czechoslovakia beat India 4–1; Italy beat Switzerland 5–0, and Australia beat Japan 4–1. A tragedy had befallen Japan. Increasingly, Satoh had been expected to surpass the feats of Kumagae, Shenzo and Harada, but the strain of competing for months on end in lands whose cultures were alien to him had become too much. In the spring of 1934 he was unwell and unhappy. He did not want to leave his fiancée for yet another campaign in Europe. For the glory of his country he was persuaded to go. As his ship sailed out of Singapore, Satoh's depression deepened. He flung himself into the sea and drowned.

Japan continued to produce remarkably clever players. In the contest with Australia at Eastbourne on grass – a surface that greatly favoured Australia – Jiro Yamagashi led McGrath 6–2, 5–3, and the Australian survived only by a drastic change of tactics. Whereas he had been repeatedly trying to hit winners, he concentrated instead on keeping a good length and playing to Yamagashi's backhand. He won nine games in a row to take control of the match.

In the seminfinals the Czechs beat Italy 3–2 at Milan, with de Stefani winning both his singles, while Australia overcame France at Paris by the same margin. Cochet, now a professional, would have been proud of Merlin, who defeated both Crawford and McGrath. The fact that Boussus's two singles and the doubles went to five sets indicated the closeness of the tie. Borotra and Brugnon had beaten two Australian pairs in winning the French championship a week earlier. Learning from that experience, the Australians changed their formation to Crawford and Quist, who won the first two sets and virtually the tie. The days were past when the French veterans could come back from such a deficit.

When Australia beat Czechoslovakia in the zone final at Prague, the margin was again 3–2. Menzel won both his singles, and McGrath was faced with having to defeat Ladislav Hecht in the fifth rubber. He lost the first set, but remained calm and won 3–6, 6–2, 6–1, 7–5.

Only two ties were played in the North American Zone, the USA making a clean sweep of both Canada and Mexico. Led by Frank Shields and Sidney Wood, the Americans then made an assault on Wimbledon, where their one success was the victory of George Lott and Lester Stoefen in the doubles. In the men's singles Perry heartened post-Depression Britain by becoming the first native-born champion to succeed since A. W. Gore in 1909. His victim in the final was Crawford.

For all his fine touch, Crawford was not physically equipped to battle his way through three hard matches in a Davis Cup tie. In the inter-zone final at Wimbledon he won his opening match against Shields in straight sets, while McGrath shook the fluent but somewhat overconfident Wood by beating him in four sets and putting Australia in a strong position. Lott and Stoefen, as expected, won the doubles against Crawford and Quist. There was a feeling among some critics that Crawford should have been rested and that Turnbull should have partnered Quist in a match that the Australians had little chance of winning.

The moment of truth for 'Gentleman Jack' came when he faced Wood. It was a wet day and Wood's great backhand won him many points as he took the first set 6–3. Crawford was about to serve for the second set at 7–6 when a few spots of rain drove the players off the court. When they returned, the Australian's touch had deserted him and he lost the second set 7–9. Rain then caused an overnight postponement. Next day Crawford bravely attempted to win three straight sets. He won two, each at 6–4, and held Wood for the first four games of the fifth set. But in the end Wood's speed and service power gave him an edge and he took the last set 6–2. Shields wrapped up victory by beating McGrath in straight sets.

In the challenge round on 28, 30 and 31 July – the first to be held at the 'new' Wimbledon – the Americans again found themselves two matches down. Wood led Perry by two sets to one, but the

Englishman kept improving. Shields had a bad day against Austin, losing in straight sets. The dependable Lott and Stoefen won the doubles and then, in the decisive rubber, Perry wore down Shields 6–4, 4–6, 6–2, 15–13.

In late 1934 fourteen nations played in European qualifying rounds from which Holland, Poland, Yugoslavia and Germany passed into the 1935 competition proper. The eight quarter finalists were South Africa, Poland, Czechoslovakia, Japan, Australia, France, Germany and Italy. Assisted by a young recruit, Henner Henkel, von Cramm emerged as the dominant player on the Continent, defeating de Stefani, Crawford, McGrath and Menzel in guiding Germany into the inter-zone final.

Inevitably, Germany's opponent there was America, who had a new player in John Donald Budge, a redheaded, freckle-faced Californian of nineteen who came from a Scottish-Irish family of modest circumstances. Don's father had played soccer for the famous Glasgow Rangers and the lad was good at many sports. The one he liked least was tennis. When he was eleven he quit playing with his brother Lloyd on the local courts at Oakland and did not play again for four years. Then, encouraged by Lloyd, he entered his first tennis tournament, the Californian State boys' championship, and, with a coolness that became his hallmark, won it. Thereafter, he rose rapidly through the junior and senior ranks and when he took his first trip east he was immediately seen as a successor to the Californian aces McLoughlin, Johnston and Vines. Budge was not then a volleyer or an abnormally hard hitter. His big shot was an exquisite backhand.

He gained his chance on the American team after Lott and Stoefen had turned professional and Shields and Wood had asked to be passed over. Up to then, Budge had used a Western grip. He soon became aware of the limitations of such a grip on grass, and Walter Pate, who captained the American team in the zone matches at Mexico City, advised him to switch to an Eastern grip. Don found that this worked perfectly for him.

In Mexico City, Budge won all his matches against China and Mexico. At that stage, however, he was considered too immature to play against Germany. Just how raw a traveller he was may be discerned from an incident that occured when the US team arrived in England. Budge was still in his pyjamas and sleepy-eyed when an official knocked on his cabin door and said, 'Let me see your visa.'

Young Don was puzzled and irritated that anyone should arouse him so early. Then he thought he understood what the man wanted. He became even angrier.

'Oh, you mean my vizor,' he said sharply.

'Listen, young man,' snapped the official, 'I've been in this business for twenty years and it's visa.'

'I don't care how long you've been in the business, mister,' said Don, unabashed. 'Out in California everybody wears eyeshades, and we call 'em vizors.'

Budge earned a singles place against Germany when, a week or so before the final, he put Bunny Austin out of Wimbledon. The title again went to Perry, the first champion since Tilden to win it two years in a row. In Paris, Perry had beaten Crawford and von Cramm on successive days to capture his first French crown, and he repeated those wins at Wimbledon.

Budge's temperatment became legendary. On the eve of his match with Henkel he went to bed at ten o'clock and fell into a sound sleep. At 2 a.m. he awoke, went out to the hall and noticed the light was on in Wilmer Allison's room. Putting his head around the door, he asked, 'What are you doing up at this hour?'

'What are *you* doing?' Allison replied.

'I'm just going down to the bathroom to get a drink,' said Budge, yawning sleepily. 'Don't know what woke me up. I was sure sleeping beautifully.'

The match-hardened Texan shook his head in wonder. 'You haven't got any nerves at all,' he complained. 'I wish to heaven I could go to sleep before a match. It's still the same after all these years. . . .'

Budge laid the foundation for America's victory by beating Henkel 7–5, 11–9, 6–8, 6–1. Von Cramm levelled by beating Allison in straight sets, but then the great combination of Allison and Van Ryn squeezed past von Cramm and Kay Lund in the doubles, 8–6 in the fifth set, after the Germans had lost five match points. On one of those points, both von Cramm and Lund lunged to reach a shot down the middle, and Lund returned it for a winner. The umpire announced, 'Game, set and match to Germany.' But the baron lifted his hand in protest, saying that the ball had tipped his racquet and that the point should go to the Americans.

In the locker room afterwards, von Cramm was reprimanded for letting down the German people and his team-mates. He was called a disgrace to his country. 'Let me get something straight right now,' replied an outraged von Cramm. 'When I chose tennis as a young man, I chose it because it was a gentleman's game and that's the way I've played it ever since I picked up my first racquet. Do you think that I would sleep tonight knowing that the ball had touched my racquet without my saying so? Never, because I would be violating every principle that I think this game stands for. On the contrary, I don't think I'm letting the German people down. As a matter of fact, I think I'm doing them credit, and until I'm asked to resign, this is the way I'll continue to play.'

Allison put his country in the challenge round by beating Henkel 6–1, 7–5, 11–9, and Budge made the margin 4–1 by impressively beating von Cramm in the 'dead' rubber.

Don Budge was still no match for Perry. He lost to both Perry and Austin in the challenge round, as did Allison. The resounding 5–0 triumph of the British emphasized their superiority. It was during the Perry v. Budge match that an incident occurred which reflected the happy natures of these two tennis giants. The score was one set all when a piece of paper fluttered down towards the court as Budge sent up a lob. Lobbing was not one of Don's strengths and his lob was not particularly good, but as his opponent prepared to smash he was distracted by the paper and missed an easy shot. Perry waited for the paper to come within reach, caught it, studied it and began to laugh. When Budge walked to the net, Fred showed him the paper and said, 'For God's sake, laugh!' Budge complied. The gallery, intrigued, chuckled too. The paper, however, was completely blank. Perry was simply having a bit of fun with the crowd amidst the tension of a challenge round.

It was Australia's turn to blood a new singles player in 1936. Adrian Karl Quist had eased his way into the competition as a doubles player and he was to become an outstanding exponent of the tandem game. He and Crawford had won the Wimbledon doubles titles in 1935, and he was to win it with John Bromwich no less than fifteen years later. Quist held the Australian doubles title continuously from 1936 to 1950, the first two years with

Turnbull, the rest of the time with Bromwich. Short, though solid, he was the son of a leading cricketer who had sent him to a gymansium when the boy's physique looked likely to rule out a sporting career. The training helped Quist to develop the power and speed that he displayed in an excellent all-round game. In the 1936 Australian championships he won the singles title from Crawford and thus ousted McGrath from his place as a regular singles player in the Australian team.

Australia decided to avoid the hazards of playing on European clay by entering the North American Zone, and in late May she defeated the USA in Philadelphia. Budge, who had benefited immensely from his 1935 trip, won his two singles, though he had to save a match point against Crawford, but Allison lost to both Crawford and Quist. The crucial rubber was the doubles, in which Crawford and Quist best Budge and Gene Mako 4–6, 2–6, 6–4, 7–5, 6–4.

In Europe the qualifying competition was scrapped. It had not been popular. Nobody could be expected to be interested in next year's qualifying events at the same time as the challenge round was held, and the participating players had felt a sense of inferiority. Now, in 1936, sixteen nations completed two rounds before the start of the French championships.

An upset was caused at Zagreb when the home side, Yugoslavia, won the last two matches to beat Czechoslovakia, the previous year's European finalist, 3–2. Rivalry between these two countries was always intense, and the Czechs strongly objected to the behaviour of the partisan gallery. A few months later the Czech delegate to the Davis Cup Nations, Dr J. Gerke, proposed that contests should be controlled by neutral referees. When spectators interrupted a match, said Gerke, the referee should have the power to declare it void and direct it to be replayed with different court officials. Moreover, he wanted the referee to be able to clear the stands if necessary, and have a match replayed in an empty stadium. The South African delegate mildly protested that the Davis Cup had been instituted to promote goodwill among nations, and the meeting, while conceding that international animosities could lead to wild behaviour in the stands, did not accept the Czech proposal. 'The spirit of the players all over the world is the same,' said Gerke, 'but some education of the spectators is necessary.'

Von Cramm, regarded as the world's second best amateur player, beat Perry in the 1936 French championship final and later carried Germany into the inter-zone final in the cup. Despite Australia's elimination of America, Germany was generally expected to win the encounter. At Wimbledon the Australians had fared badly, while von Cramm had been runner-up to Perry for the second successive year. Henkel, too, had come on and was now one of Europe's most consistent players.

In the first match of the inter-zone final, played on Wimbledon's court one, Crawford led Henkel 6–2, 6–2, when the German retired, feeling the effects of a recent chill. Quist initially handled the gusty conditions better than von Cramm in what became a thrilling second match. He took the first set at 6–4. In the opening game of the second set the Australian wrenched his right ankle and was soon down 1–5. He saved four set points before losing the set 4–6. But he won the next set by the same score.

After the interval Quist played with his ankle strapped and matched the German's powerful drives. However, he lost the fourth set, again by 4–6, and slumped to 3–5 in the fifth set as swirling dust tested the patience of both players. Quist saved two match points in the ninth game. Then von Cramm served and saw three more match points slip by. Quist levelled at 5 all, went ahead, and in the sixteenth game had three match points himself, with von Cramm trailing 0–40 on service. The baron saved the game, once with a drive that hit the top of the tape and dropped dead. Finally, in the twentieth game, the German needed another astonishing five match points before putting Quist away.

For 'stubborn stamina and heroic courage, the match had seldom been equalled,' wrote Wallis Myers. He added, 'Quist's services frequently beat von Cramm, as also did his forehand drives deep to the corners. No short lob could live against the power of his smash. Despite his ankle injury, Quist was a happy fighter, living up to his renown as Australia's champion. He might have won in three sets had he been fit.'

Quist could not play in the doubles because he was on crutches. McGrath was an admirable substitute, and he and Crawford beat von Cramm and Henkel in four sets. The rules allowed Australia to replace Quist with McGrath for the remaining singles. With

McGrath punishing Henkel's comparatively weak second serve, another four-set win resulted.

And so the Australians returned to Wimbledon on 25 July to play in the challenge round for the first time in twelve years. Quist was still a bit stiff and sore. He did better than most people expected in taking a set off Perry. Austin then dealt with the fading Crawford, running as much as was necessary in returning Crawford's smooth ground strokes and usually having the last shot. He won 4–6, 6–3, 6–1, 6–1. Crawford and Quist beat Hughes and Charles Tuckey in a tight four-set doubles; and Quist brought the tie to life by out-hitting Austin to make the score 2–2. But Crawford could not cope with Perry's murderous attack in the last match. The Englishman's weighty drives, his speed and volleying gave him a 6–2, 6–3, 6–3 victory in his final Davis Cup appearance.

Perry thus helped Great Britain to repeat the performance of the Dohertys in winning four straight challenge rounds. A few weeks later he won his third US title in a five-set final against Budge and at the end of the summer he turned professional. His departure was a loss from which British tennis never recovered in the next fifty years.

—9—

BUDGE
BEATS THE BARON

(1937–38, USA)

Don Budge's greatness was as much the result of his eagerness to learn and to adjust his technique as to his natural talent. Despite his rapid success as a tennis player, he knew that he could be much better if he applied lessons intelligently. Having changed his grip from Western to Eastern, he realized on his first trip to Europe that he must develop his volleying. He had a strong serve and forceful ground strokes (though his forehand could give him problems), but they were not fully exploited because he neglected opportunities to add the final thrust at the net.

The man who influenced him most was Fred Perry. The Englishman's own game had been transformed when he mastered the art of taking the ball on the rise. With one flowing movement, Perry was able to take the ball early and get into position for the volley. He was quick on his feet and had a quick eye, good balance and coordination – important attributes in perfecting his dynamic style. Perry showed Budge how to make the running drive so as to get to the net quickly, and in 1936 he helped him on various occasions in the United States. Budge adapted Perry's technique to his backhand drive, his stronger side, and learned from his doubles partner, Gene Mako, how to make a high drive-volley on the forehand.

Two defeats by Brian 'Bitsy' Grant, one in the 1935 US championships, made Budge even more determined to change his tactics. Grant was then essentially a retriever, yet, for all his heavy artillery, Budge could not finish him off because he lacked a good enough volley.

By 1937 the two contenders for Perry's mantle were Budge and von Cramm. Budge had beaten the German, and had scored wins over Perry (in the Pacific Southwest championship at Los Angeles), Austin, his fellow countrymen Bobby Riggs and Frank Parker, and the Australians Crawford and Quist. Nevertheless, there were some who considered von Cramm the more accomplished player and thought he might capture the cup for the Fatherland.

The 1937 challengers in the American Zone were the USA, Australia, Japan and Mexico. Australia beat Mexico 5–0 in Mexico City, with eighteen-year-old John Bromwich playing the fifth rubber against Esteban Reyes. America, using Budge and Parker for the singles and Budge and Mako for the doubles, defeated Japan 5–0 in San Francisco. Bitsy Grant was preferred to Parker for the zone final at Forest Hills and did not drop a set to either Crawford or Bromwich (Quist being indisposed). Budge also won his singles handsomely and, with Mako, beat Crawford and McGrath in the doubles.

Twenty nations entered the European Zone, with Germany, Italy, Belgium, Sweden, Yugoslavia, South Africa, Czechoslovakia and France reaching the quarter finals. The German federation, which had become increasingly autocratic, ordered von Cramm not to defend his French singles title as his team-mate Henkel was thought likely to win in his absence and this would increase his confidence and stature. The German plan was fulfilled: Henkel beat Austin in the final, and won the doubles with von Cramm.

When the cup competition was resumed, Germany beat Italy 4–1 in Milan, Belgium beat Sweden 3–2 in Brussels, Yugoslavia beat South Africa 4–1 in Zagreb, and Czechoslovakia beat France 4–1 in Prague. Von Cramm and Henkel for Germany, and Menzel and Hecht for Czechoslovakia then easily defeated Belgium and Yugoslavia respectively to qualify for the European final.

At Wimbledon the Europeans could make little impression on the Americans. The only set Budge lost in the singles was to Parker in the semifinals. In the singles final he beat von Cramm 6–3, 6–4, 6–2, and he partnered Mako to victory over Hughes and Tuckey in the doubles final. He also won the mixed doubles with Alice Marble, becoming the first man to score a Wimbledon triple.

As a three-time runner-up at Wimbledon, von Cramm was entitled to feel jaded when he returned to Berlin for the cup contest with the Czechs. He lost the first two sets to Menzel, who was booed by the crowd for stalling, but won the next three. Henkel beat Hecht in straight sets and the Germans clinched a place in the inter-zone final for the third successive year with a four-set win in the doubles.

Throughout the summer the American squad of Budge, Mako, Grant, Parker and Wayne Sabin, with Walter Pate as captain–manager, had rented an apartment at Fulham overlooking the River Thames. Pate was one of the first captains to foster the concept of a tennis team as a tight-knit unit, and for weeks the Americans were virtually isolated in their apartment except for dinner visits by movie actor Paul Lukas, a tennis buff who was friendly with Budge and Mako. Aware of the distractions that London offered, Pate realized how difficult it would be to control the players if they stayed in hotels. One former American player had been in the habit of going to dog races in London until the early hours, while another, Frank Shields, 'used to stay up all night drinking and chasing dames', according to Jack Kramer. (Shields was the handsomest man to play any sport, said Kramer. His granddaughter is the actress Brooke Shields.)

'We lived together, ate together, and planned together,' Pate once wrote. 'The sole idea was to let nothing interfere with the training programme. There were no theaters or movies. Every night after dinner, before going back to the flat, we stopped at the [Hurlingham] Club's 18-hole putting course with short, tricky holes. Putting became just as much a part of the routine as eating, and we rarely missed an evening.'

Pate caused a mild surprise by nominating Grant, instead of Parker, for the second singles spot against Germany. The diminutive Bitsy had flopped at Wimbledon, but on that occasion he had been weakened by a bout of influenza and Pate was mindful that he had beaten Henkel the year before. The contest was played at Wimbledon as the political climate worsened. A German triumph would bolster Hitler's fascist philosophies; and, to add to the tension for the Americans, Bill Tilden had been coaching the German team.

On the first day Grant lost to von Cramm in straight sets, and Budge slaughtered Henkel. The second day belonged to Mako, who was famous for his catlike reflexes. He was the best player on the court as he and Budge defeated the German pair 4–6, 7–5, 8–6, 6–4. The Germans led 5–3 in the second set, had two set points in the third set and were 4–1 in the fourth, but were handicapped by

Henkel's soft second serve. Henkel's morale wasn't improved by Mako's ability to volley clean winners from several smashes hit directly at him.

On the third day the German captain, Kleinschroth, foiled Pate's selection of Grant by instructing Henkel to go to the net more often than he usually did. Henkel beat the American in four sets. All now hung on the final match, which was to become one of the greatest in Davis Cup annals. Before he went out to the court, von Cramm was asked to take a long-distance call from Hitler, who urged him to win for the Fatherland. As he picked up his racquets the baron looked pale and serious. Budge had beaten him in the Queen's and Wimbledon finals. But that Budge was going to have a much tougher fight this time became obvious in the first set. The American led 5–4, but von Cramm took the set 7–5. The German won the second set 8–6; Budge took the third set 6–4; and, after the rest period, he won the fourth set 6–2 to level the score.

In the fifth set von Cramm played the tennis of his life, opening up a 4–1 lead. Pate up to now had made several suggestions to Budge during the change of ends. Now, in this crisis, he was afraid to say anything in case he upset his player. He patted him on the back and said, 'Don, I still think you will win this match.'

'Don't worry, Cap. I won't let you down,' replied Budge. 'I'll win this one if it kills me.'

Budge knew that he had to take more chances to get to the net, for von Cramm was out-hitting him from the back of the court. The German's length was so good that Budge had no obvious openings to get in. Finally, Budge forced himself to react more adventurously to any ball that came high over the net. Even if it was deep, he would step in and volley it from far back in the court. He needed to make those volleys perfectly or he would be passed on the next shot. He kept moving in, desperately, and pulled up to 4 all. Von Cramm twice led again until Budge broke through at 6 all. Budge then had 40–15 on his own service, but the German got to deuce. Von Cramm saved, in all, five match points before succumbing at 8.45 p.m. in semidarkness. Not one spectator had left the stands, and as excited as anyone was Bill Tilden. So animated was he in his support of von Cramm that the American columnist Ed Sullivan, who was sitting nearby, became enraged. Sullivan leaped up and began to remove his coat, shouting, 'Why, you dirty son of a bitch!' Sullivan's companions, Paul Lukas and comedian Jack Benny, restrained him. (Despite his allegiance to the German team, however, Tilden was one of the first to congratulate Budge and told him the match was the greatest he had ever seen.)

The closing stages of the epic were well described by Allison Danzig in the book *Budge on Tennis*:

The brilliance of the tennis was almost unbelievable, with the big preponderance of the points being earned rather than won on errors. The gallery, enraptured by the scintillating display to a degree that it forgot its allegiance to the Baron, looked on spellbound as two great players, taking their inspiration from each other, worked miracles of redemption and riposte in rallies of breakneck pace that ranged all over the court. Shots that would have stood out vividly in the average match were commonplace in the cascade of electrifying strokes that stemmed from the racquets of two superb fighters until the onlookers were fairly surfeited with brilliance. In game after game they sustained their amazing virtuosity without the slightest deviation or faltering on either side.

Gradually, inch by inch, Budge picked up, and the suspense was almost unbearable. Once, only a stroke stood between him and defeat. Captain Pate does not know how he lived through that moment. At last, it was over and von Cramm, with the fine sportsmanship which won his every rival to him, came forward with a sunny smile to shake the hand of his opponent. He had lost the most important match of his life – a match that would have put his country in the position to win the Davis Cup for the first time in the 37 years of its history – and he took his defeat as nobly as he had played.

As Budge ran forward to the net and saw that smile, which hid a disappointment that must have been cruel, he thought, as he confided afterwards to Captain Pate, 'Gottfried, you certainly have got more out of the game than any player who has won everything.'

Everybody sensed that the fate of the cup had been decided since, without Perry, British superiority had evaporated. Only four days after the inter-zone final ended, the Americans returned to Wimbledon on 24 July to play Great Britain, and Parker replaced Grant in the singles. Parker, a stylish back-court player, was twenty-one. Coached by Mercer Beasley, he had been the junior champion of America in 1932 and was considered a future world champion. With an opening flurry of resistance, Austin beat him in straight sets. Charles Hare extended Budge to 15–13 in the first set, but then crumbled so completely that he won only three games in the next two sets. Hughes and Tuckey put up a creditable showing in the doubles, losing 12–10 in the fourth set, and the final two rubbers were won decisively by Budge and Parker. When the American team sailed home on the S. S. *Manhattan* the cup nestled on one of the twin beds in Pate's cabin. Later, New York turned on a ticker-tape reception.

Within a few weeks, von Cramm and Henkel had some small consolation when they scored a straight sets win over Budge and Mako in the final of the American doubles championship at Long-wood. However, von Cramm lost another five-set match to Budge in the singles final at Forest Hills. The rivals met yet again in the final of the Pacific Southwest championship with the same result.

At about this time Budge declined a $50,000 offer to turn professional. Many people thought that he was unwise. An injury or the emergence of a new star might well affect his market value in the future, and he could be risking the chance to gain financial security for life. Budge acknowledged this. At the same time he was conscious of an obligation to amateur tennis. In 1938 the USLTA would be staging the Davis Cup challenge round for the first time in eleven years, and he felt duty bound to ensure the defence was successful. His decision turned out to be fortuitious, for in 1938 he was to become the first man to achieve the Grand Slam.

It was Allison Danzig who first applied the term 'Grand Slam' to tennis, taking the expression from the card game bridge. Danzig was Budge's friend and ghosted his autobiography. Together, they chose the championships of Great Britain, America, France and Australia as constituting the Grand Slam because these were the only nations that had won the Davis Cup (though Australia's successes had been shared by New Zealand). Entries for the Australian championship were usually far inferior to those in the other major championships. That it was elevated to the status of the others was simply because of Australia's Davis Cup background – and the whim of Budge and Danzig.

The Australian championship was the first leg of the Slam; Budge beat Bromwich in the final after the Australian had eliminated von Cramm in the semifinals. The trip had serious repercussions for von Cramm. He had refused to become a Nazi, and while in Australia he publicly criticized the Hitler regime. On his return home he was arrested and charged with homosexual activities involving a German Jew, who was alleged to have extorted money from him. Convicted at a private hearing, von Cramm was sentenced to a year's imprisonment. There were suggestions that the charge was politically concocted and that Henkel had informed against him. Whatever the truth, the Nazis almost certainly would not have taken action had von Cramm beaten Budge in their cup encounter. He would then have been too big a national hero and too much needed for a possible challenge round in Berlin. Following the banishment of Prenn, the persecution of von Cramm should have outraged the tennis world. Instead many people adopted the Nazi line. Wimbledon, for instance, let it be known that it would not accept his entry. One who *was* angry at the Nazis was Don Budge. As a reprisal, he cancelled a promise to compete in Germany during 1938.

To replace von Cramm, Germany recruited George von Metaxa, a Greek-born Austrian who had played for Austria the previous year. Since then the Nazis had cowed Austria into subservience, and von Metaxa and his Davis Cup team-mate, Hans Redl, had become German nationals. In 1939, after the cession of Sudeten territory to Germany, Menzel found himself in the German team too. He welcomed the change because he was pro-German. Not so Menzel's team-mate, Ladislav Hecht; he was a Jew and was exiled. Normally, players had to stand out of the competition for three years if they wished to play for another country. In the political circumstances the Davis Cup Nations amended Regulation 33 so that it read:

If a player shall have represented a Nation and such Nation shall be absorbed, in whole or in part, by another Nation, he shall, if belonging to the whole or part absorbed, be deemed for the purpose of these Regulations not to have previously represented any Nation.

Ever since 1924 there had been proposals that the Davis Cup should be contested in alternate years. The growth of the competition caused problems for many countries. There was the cost of financing teams for what might be up to six months of the year and the difficulty of players making themselves available over that period. The burden could be particularly great on countries outside Europe, such as Australia and South Africa. Whenever Australia, for instance, failed to reach the challenge round, its Davis Cup campaign usually incurred a severe financial loss that the LTA could ill afford. Some critics felt the competition was damaging the cause of amateurism, since it was almost impossible for young men to establish themselves in a career when they were required to give so much time to representing their country. The temptation for them to find ways of living off the game was increasing. Other critics believed athletes would physically harm themselves if they played too hard and too often. Sports medicine was unheard of in those days and the durability and resilience of the well-trained athlete was greatly underestimated.

In the 1930s agitation for a biennial competition stepped up. The British view, as expressed by R. J. McNair to a meeting of the Davis Cup Nations in 1934, was that international sport was attracting too much ballyhoo. A certain section of the press was giving the public an exaggerated idea of the importance of sport, he said, and *bone fide* amateurism was suffering. Another British delegate, H. H. Monckton, went further:

It cannot be argued that everything is right in the state of lawn tennis because great galleries are being obtained for the Davis Cup. It is not good to encourage the public too much to come to these spectacles. There is too much idea of money in connection with the game . . . not only . . . of the players making money but of associations making large sums of money which they are just as well without. They do not require great riches.

Such sentiments make strange reading half a century on.

By 1938 the move to introduce a biennial competition had become very strong. About forty nations were now competing for the Davis Cup, and with the proliferation of tournaments around the world there had been formed 'a continuous chain of events almost all the year round'. The more conservative administrators were alarmed by the commercialism which these developments had made possible. America, however, strongly resisted the would-be reformers. The USLTA thought people would be less interested in the Davis Cup if matches were held only every other year, and some players, it said, would have their chances of gaining international honours greatly reduced. Moreover, more professional exhibitions might spring up to fill the vacuum. The Americans put their case in a letter to all the nations and threatened to withdraw the Davis Cup from competition if the proposed change was made. They won the day.

But various suggestions to alleviate the congestion of matches continued to be made over many years. In the late thirties, Norman Brookes even proposed that a similarly organized women's team competition could be conducted in alternate years to the Davis Cup. (It was to be 1963 before the Federation Cup was established for women.)

Perhaps the Americans, better than others, realized just how much the Davis Cup had become the lifeblood of tennis. Even the British did not seem to appreciate sometimes how the competition had stimulated the Wimbledon championships. Before the inception of the Davis Cup, Wimbledon was confined mainly to British players, and a few from nearby countries or of independent means. Later, players from many far-flung countries were able to play at Wimbledon because their national associations sent them there in teams as part of their Davis Cup arrangements. The associations would have been less willing to finance individuals. The championships of America, France and Australia also benefited when those countries staged the challenge round, as invariably there were then more top-class overseas players among the entries.

Seventeen nations contested the European Zone in 1938. Great Britain paid the price for not having groomed players to fill the shoes of Perry and Austin and lost to Yugoslavia in Zagreb in the second round. This was not such a bad loss, since Yugoslavia had four very good players in Franjo Puncec, Drago Mitic, Josip Pallada and Franjo Kukuljevic. They had beaten Czechoslovakia in the first round and were to reach the zone final. The victory over Czechoslovakia was highly controversial, for in the decisive fifth match in Zagreb between Mitic and F. Cejnar the Czech was ordered by his captain to stop playing when the score was two sets all and 2–1 to Mitic in the fifth set. The captain believed he had reached an agreement with the Yugoslavs before the start of play that the match would be postponed at 7 p.m. whatever the score. The umpire awarded the match to Yugoslavia on a forfeit and Czechoslovakia's subsequent protest was dismissed.

Yugoslavia's opponents in the zone final in Berlin were the new combination of Henkel and von Metaxa, who had steered Germany past Norway, Hungary and France. Henkel lost the opening match to Puncec; von Metaxa just managed to square the series by beating

Pallada, 12–10 in the fifth set; the German team won the doubles; and Henkel scored over Pallada on the last day.

Without Perry or von Cramm to test him, Budge was in full flight that summer. He conceded only nine games to Menzel in the French final and four games to Austin in the Wimbledon final. At Wimbledon he was the triple champion again.

Meanwhile, Australia's cup team emerged victorious from the group of four nations in the American Zone, though it only narrowly beat Japan in Montreal, where Bromwich lost both his singles. In the inter-zone final at Longwood, Henkel and von Metaxa were unable to reproduce their European form and failed to take a set from Quist and Bromwich.

For the challenge round at Germantown, over the American Labor Day weekend, the Australians relied on Quist and Bromwich again, while America chose Budge and Riggs for the singles and Budge and Mako for the doubles. Robert Larrimore Riggs was a small, cocky young Californian, the youngest in a family of six boys and a girl, from whom he had learned the game. At a critical period in his development he was befriended by Dr Esther Bartosh, then the third-ranking woman player in Los Angeles, who coached him after school. Riggs became an excellent all-court player, a keen competitor and a cagey tactician. He won the US junior title in 1937 and was ranked number two in America behind Budge. But the American selectors initially seemed loath to play him in the Davis Cup, perhaps because of his size or his cheekiness.

On a rain-sodden court Riggs virtually assured America of victory when in the key match he defeated Quist 4–6, 6–0, 8–6, 6–1 after Budge predictably had beaten Bromwich in the opening rubber. Quist had been expected to win, but his fear of being foot-faulted destroyed his concentration. He had been foot-faulted in the American doubles championship, and friends and officials had warned him that he risked being penalized again in the challenge round if he did not alter his service action. In the first set against Riggs he was able to play an aggressive net-attacking game. Then a foot fault upset his equilibrium. He became more tentative and Riggs was quick to seize the initiative.

Quist and Bromwich repeated their Australian championship win over Budge and Mako to reduce the leeway, and then Budge faced Quist in the fourth rubber. Budge led 5–4 when Quist was foot faulted. He was called on three consecutive services, yet despite two double faults he won the game. However, Quist continued to be penalized and the match became a nightmare for him. He became so rattled that he won only four more games, Budge winning 8–6, 6–1, 6–2. Budge was embarrassed and the crowd, believing the foot-fault judge was unfairly ruining what had promised to be a good match, noisily expressed its disapproval. The boos turned to applause when the Australian captain, Harry Hopman, asked the central umpire to inform the crowd that he concurred with the legality of the foot-fault decision. Even when standing two feet behind the baseline, Quist occasionally was foot-faulted because he jumped in striking at the ball, and the foot-fault rule at that time required the server to maintain contact with the ground. And so, in somewhat unfortunate circumstances, America retained the cup.

The subsequent American championships confirmed Budge's status as one of the very greatest of the game's immortals. In the final he beat the unseeded Mako to complete the Grand Slam, and two months later turned professional. The fact that the signing of the pro contract was done in Walter Pate's New York law office and in the presence of the USLTA president, Holcome Ward, reflected the affection and esteem in which Budge was held. On the other hand, he was only twenty-three years of age, and it was sad that one so young and talented should be lost to the Davis Cup. The trend of the year's leading amateur to turn professional in order to play the previous amateurs who had turned professional before him was now well established. It was to be thirty years before the sport was sensibly rationalized to avoid the constant fragmentation.

QUIST HANGS IN

(1939, Australia)

The Americans knew that without Don Budge their chances of retaining the cup were greatly reduced and that Australia in particular presented a threat. Naturally, the 1939 challenge round would be held on a grass court, the Australians' best surface, and in Adrian Quist they had a talented and experienced player and a proven fighter. Quist moreover was no longer the number one Australian. After being runner-up for the Australian championship in the previous two years, first to McGrath and then to Budge, young John Bromwich beat Quist comprehensively in the 1939 final. Together, the two formed a doubles pair that was superior to any combination the Americans could muster.

Bromwich was perhaps the most unorthodox champion Australia ever produced. He played with a left-handed forehand, had a double-handed backhand, and served with his right hand. Relying on length and touch, he developed pinpoint accuracy and could destroy powerful hitters with his perfectly controlled drives, delicate lobs, drop shots and dinks. His tenacity and perfectionism sometimes led to bizarre incidents. In a championship match at Adelaide, Bromwich was leading 6–0, 6–0, 5–0, and had his opponent 15–40 down on service when the unlucky adversary served and volleyed the return at an angle, forcing Bromwich well off court. Bromwich scampered across and, with a breathtaking recovery, sent up a two-handed cross-court lob that hit the baseline chalk – but just wide of the sideline. When he heard the call of 'Out' Bromwich stopped in his tracks, grimaced and scratched his chest nervously. 'I'll *never* win this,' he groaned, 'if I keep making mistakes like that!'

Despite this fanatical streak, he was the gentlest of men off the court and modest to a fault.

The American defence was considered certain to be in the hands of Riggs and Parker, with Mako playing in the doubles with a partner yet to be decided.

The increasing inevitability of war in Europe did not deter twenty-six nations from entering the competition, twenty of them in the European Zone. Yugoslavia had become one of the strongest European teams. Its number one player, Puncec, was very solid and lost only to Josef Asboth of Hungary as Yugoslavia won the European Zone for the first time, beating Belgium in the semifinals and Germany in the final in Zagreb. Germany had called on Henkel, Menzel, von Metaxa and R. Goepfert. In the semifinals they inflicted on the British team of Charles Hare, Ronald Shayes, Frank Wilde and Laurie Shaffi the worst defeat in British tennis history. Germany did not drop a set or more than fifteen games in the first three matches. The British had one valid excuse. Hare hurt his back while playing Menzel and retired when trailing 0–6, 1–6.

In an earlier contest, against Poland, von Metaxa found himself on the opposite side of the net to his former Austrian team-mate, Count Adam Baworowski, who had switched to Poland.

In the American Zone, Australia beat Mexico, the Philippines and Cuba without losing a set. The inter-zone final, played at Longwood, appeared to boost the host country's hopes of retaining the cup, for Puncec beat Bromwich 6–2, 8–6, 0–6, 6–2 in the opening rubber. The Australians easily won the next three rubbers to set up their appearance in the challenge round.

If anything seemed certain about this contest, which was held at the Merion Cricket Club, Philadelphia, on 2, 4 and 5 September, it was that Riggs would win both his singles. That year he had succeeded Budge as the world's top player, reaching both the French and Wimbledon singles finals. At Paris he was beaten by his fellow countryman Don McNeill, but he was triumphant at Wimbledon. Self-doubt was never one of Rigg's failings. A compulsive gambler, he was said to have won more than £50,000 from English bookmakers by backing himself to win the singles, doubles and mixed doubles. In the singles final he trailed by two sets to one before rallying to beat his doubles partner, Elwood Cooke. He and Cooke beat Hare and Wilde in the men's doubles final, and he won the mixed doubles with Alice Marble.

As the challenge round approached, speculation over the Americans' doubles pair grew. In August the final of the American doubles championship was an all-Australian affair, Quist and Bromwich beating Crawford and Hopman. However, two young Americans, Welby van Horn and Jack Kramer, attracted attention by giving Quist and Bromwich a tough fight in the quarter finals. At that stage, Walter Pate still favoured the combination of Mako and twenty-year-old Joe Hunt, a midshipman at the US Naval Academy, who was considered to be the coming star in American tennis. Providentially, in a practice match, van Horn and Kramer split four sets with this pair and were invited by Pate to go to Philadelphia as sparring partners. The rookies thereupon complicated the selection by trouncing Mako and Hunt in practice. Riggs's solution was that he and Parker should play the doubles as well as the singles. Pate wasn't happy with that idea since both Riggs and Parker were rather small and lacked big serves. So Pate tried Riggs with Mako. Van Horn and Kramer beat them more easily than they had Hunt and Mako! The final phase in the evolution of the American pair is described in Kramer's book, *The Game*, written with Frank Deford:

In all of this it never occurred to anybody to play the two kids who were winning. Welby was playing so well that he kept on winning after Merion and went all the way to the singles finals at Forest Hills before Riggs beat him (and Hunt, the sixth seed, needed five sets to beat me). But Welby was only nineteen and I had just turned eighteen, and nobody dared play such young unknowns in a challenge round. The possibility went out the window anyway the next day when Welby came down with one of his asthma attacks.

Pate had figured that it was time to try Parker and Riggs together, so he made a pick-up team of Hunt and Kramer and threw us against the stars. On bad grass with our big serves, Joe and I knocked Riggs and Parker right off the court. Pate was desperate now, and he tried pairing Riggs and Mako again. Hunt and I whipped them as badly as van Horn and I had a couple of days before.

At last I came into the picture. While it was inconceivable that two teenagers play together, one could be tolerated. Hunt was an established, ranked player. So just before the deadline, I was officially named to the team, and when the time came, Pate nominated Hunt and me to play doubles. This wasn't fair to Welby; like most Davis Cup captains, Pate could make a wrong move at the last minute out of desperation.

Kramer, a Californian high-school student, thus became the youngest player to play in a challenge round, a record that stood for twenty-nine years, until it was broken by an Australian, John Alexander.

On the day of the draw, Hitler launched his *Blitzkrieg* against Poland. As in 1914, the shadow of war hung over the Australian team, and when the draw was made at the club people listened to the latest newsflashes on radios or grabbed newspaper extras. Captain Hopman and Quist had enlisted in the 6th Battalion Machine Gun Corps of Melbourne earlier in the year and believed they would be required to return home immediately war was declared. Dwight Davis meanwhile had made hurried apologies for not attending the draw. Instead, he sailed for England to bring back members of his family, who were somewhere in Europe.

The draw pitted the two number one players, Riggs and Bromwich, against each other in the opening match, with Parker and Quist to follow. According to Kramer, the Americans thought Parker would win, but, 'to help matters along', Quist, a golf buff, received an invitation to play a round at one of Philadelphia's finest courses the day before the event. Quist thought a break in beautiful country would take his mind off the depressing situation in Europe. Kramer suggests it might also have taken the edge off his game.

Riggs beat Bromwich 6–4, 6–0, 7–5, and Parker beat Quist 6–3, 2–6, 6–4, 1–6, 7–5. No nation had ever recovered from a two-match deficit to win a challenge round and Australia's prospects were bleak. The recently knighted Sir Norman Brookes was considered to be whistling in the dark when he said that Quist and Bromwich would 'find themselves' now that they were the underdogs and had everything to gain and nothing to lose. Next day, Sunday, 3 September, Great Britain and the British Commonwealth declared war on Germany. The Australians received the solemn news before they went out to play the doubles. They got off to a faltering start and dropped the first set to Kramer and Hunt 5–7. Gradually, they wrested the attacking position away from their young opponents, winning the next three sets 6–2, 7–5, 6–2. 'Look here,' Bromwich said to his older partner afterwards, 'this tie isn't over yet. If you beat Riggs, I reckon I can win the last one.' It was a big 'if' because Riggs had conquered Quist in the 1938 challenge round, when Quist had suffered trauma over his foot faults. Now Riggs was the Wimbledon champion. Quist had rectified his foot-fault problem in a practice session under the trained eye of Norman Brookes at Brookes's holiday home, but he realized he would need to play above his normal level to have any chance of success.

A crowd of 7500 turned up on Labor Day confidently expecting Riggs to seal victory. Many had only half their minds on the tennis. They were talking among themselves in the stands of the air raids in Poland, the torpedoing of the British ship *Athenia*, the French bombardment from the Maginot Line and other war news. Quist was soon to rivet their attention to the tennis court.

Half an hour before the match, according to R. S. Whitington in *An Illustrated History of Australian Tennis*, Quist formed a plan.

He sought a secluded court on the outskirts of the club to perform some self-ordained and self-conceived practice, a kind of practice he had not indulged in previously. He had taken Fred Perry with him to that hideaway and he asked him to serve to him for ten minutes. During those minutes Adrian kept hitting for the sidelines harder than he had ever hit. Then he moved to the main court of the Merion Cricket Club feeling more confident that he had ever felt.

Quist's workout paid off. Never before had his ground strokes functioned so splendidly, his powerful flat forehand being a match-winner. After losing the first game, he amazed everyone by capturing ten games in succession. Riggs had no counter to Quist's fast, deep drives and hit raggedly from both sides. The American's volleying suffered too as he played rash approach shots against Quist's unvarying good length.

In the second set Riggs tried to break the Australian's rhythm with drop shots, but neither they nor his lobs availed. Quist continued to slam deep drives and follow up with sharp volleys and ruthless smashes. The score went to 6–1, 4–0. Then, holding 40–15 on Riggs's service, the strain began to tell. Quist fell into errors and Riggs held his serve.

Heartened, Riggs got more speed and length on his shots. He

fought up to 3–4 as the crowd cheered him on. Quist conserved his energy for his service. Though down 15–30, he went to 5–3. He was fading, however. Riggs won the ninth game quickly and looked likely to level at 5 all. But again Quist had been saving himself. After Hopman did his best to freshen him, he took the tenth game to love for the set, the American making his task easier by returning service weakly on the first two points.

These were costly errors. Riggs might well have won the match if he had levelled at one set all. The third set was gripping. Quist seemed ready to concede it when he was down 0–2, but he struck back after noticing that Riggs was also tiring and making mistakes. They grimly traded shots until Quist finally wilted from fatigue and lost the set 3–6.

After the rest period Riggs continued in the ascendancy. He was now as confident and skilful as ever. His shots were perfectly timed; he opened up the court and hit clever drop volleys; and his backhand lobs made Quist hesitate to go to the net. From 3–2, Quist lost four games straight and looked tired and dispirited.

When Riggs then took the first game of the fifth set from 0–30 with two volleys and a smash, the cup seemed safe. Quist, though, still had something in reserve. Somehow he began to produce the same brand of tennis that he had shown at the start. The American charge faltered. Thrown onto the defensive, Riggs lost his smoothness. His volleying touch deserted him, his lobs fell shorter, and he erred by attacking Quist's deadly forehand, which repeatedly fired shots past him. Quist took five games in a row before his opponent braced himself. At 5–2 Quist had a match point. Riggs chopped a backhand into mid-court and went to the net. It would have been easy for Quist to have made a passing shot either down the line or across the court, but with the pressure so intense, he lobbed. Momentarily, it appeared a perfect shot, but it missed the line by an inch. Quist winced. Riggs gained enough confidence to win the next two games. The score stood at 5–4 in Australia's favour. 'I recall sitting down by the umpire's chair,' Quist recalled later, 'with Harry squeezing lots of ice water down the back of my neck and also handing me the inevitable towel. We both felt the need for quiet.'

Quist knew that if he was going to win, it was now or never. He simply wouldn't have the strength to hold off the younger and more gifted Riggs in front of the volatile American crowd if the score got to 5 all. He reminded himself of Bromwich's words after the doubles and of how long it had taken Australia to find such an opportunity. He steeled himself for a maximum effort. Making sure he served deeply, he took the first two points with aggressive forehand volleys. He lost the next point but won the fourth with a smash – 40–15. Suddenly, he felt a slight pain in his midriff. He had strained a stomach muscle! Somehow, he must keep attacking. Riggs saved one of the match points. On the next, he overhit his return as Quist ran to the net. The Australian had won 6–1, 6–4, 3–6, 3–6, 6–4.

Bromwich had spent the first part of the match on a masseur's table listening to the scores by radio or trying to judge them by the reactions of the crowd. Early in the fifth set Fred Perry said to him, 'Come on, let's practise – Adrian has it won.' They went out to a nearby court and began hitting. Bromwich heard the umpire call '5–1 Australia'. As Riggs fought back, Brom found himself sweating more and more. After Quist lost a match point, the suspense was too much. Brom looked at Perry and they instinctively dropped their racquets and raced for the centre court, clearing fences in their stride. They arrived to see Quist win his service and the match.

Strangely enough, the Parker v. Bromwich match, though the deciding one, was almost anticlimactic. As good as his word, Bromwich won it 6–0, 6–3, 6–1. According to Hopman, this was the finest match of Bromwich's career. He hit almost every ball to Parker's forehand, which finally broke down. Not that the match was over quickly. Many of the rallies lasted more than a minute, but Parker could not win the points. He had not expected Riggs would lose and the strain was tremendous.

'As the winning players gathered around the cup, which apparently everyone but themselves had thought was sure to remain here after the opening day's matches,' wrote Allison Danzig in the *New York Times*, 'they were as happy as a lot of schoolboys. The fact that all of them might be carrying guns within a few months did not enter into their thoughts for the moment. That scrap could wait for a little while.'

In fact, the team remained in the States for the American championships. Bromwich fared the best: he reached the semifinals and was beaten by van Horn. Riggs consoled himself for his loss to

Quist – perhaps the most hurtful of his career – by winning the title. The Australians returned home keenly aware that their exploit had been completely overshadowed by the outbreak of war. (One news agency man had been told in the middle of the matches to stop filing – 'London doesn't want any more, even the result.') But the satisfaction of being the first team to capture the cup for Australia as a separate nation in the competition was hardly diminished and they had not lost any friends. If the cup had to go, as apparently it did, editorialized the *New York Times*. 'there is no custody in which we would be happier to see it than in that of the Australians. . . . It is in excellent hands.'

—11—

JACK KRAMER
AND THE BIG GAME

(1946–49 USA)

For six years there was no competition for the cup and the trophy remained in a bank vault in Melbourne. Some famous players gave their lives in the war, most notably Joe Hunt, who was killed in a training flight, and Henner Henkel, who died at Stalingrad. No nation's cup players were more hit by tragedy than was Germany's in little more than a decade – Moldenhauer, killed in a car crash; Prenn, barred and exiled; von Cramm, disgraced; and now Henkel, a war casualty. Of the players whose careers were worst affected, Bromwich probably suffered the most. In 1946, when the competition resumed, he became twenty-eight years old. Not only did he contract malaria while serving in the army in New Guinea, but he had also put on weight and was slower than before the war.

Some Davis Cup giants did not emerge from the war altogether untouched. Borotra, once loved almost as much in England as in his own country, was refused entry to Wimbledon in 1946 because he had been Minister of Sport in the puppet Vichy Government. (However, he had been imprisoned by the Nazis after trying to escape to North Africa.) Meanwhile Perry disappointed some of his British admirers by remaining in America, where he pursued his career as a professional. Austin also went to America, where he continued his work for the religious movement known as Moral Rearmament and later joined the US Air Force. Some members of the British tennis establishment resented both Austin's absence from England and his involvement with Moral Rearmament, and his membership of the All England Club was cancelled and not renewed until 1984, when he was seventy-seven. Of all the prewar stars, perhaps von Cramm's fate was the most dramatic. After resisting

Herman Goering's efforts to make him join the Nazi party he was sent to the Russian front as a private, though he was a reserve officer in the German Army. At Stalingrad he led two hundred German soldiers to an escape route and held off Soviet troops with a machine gun long enough for his men to get back to the German lines. Von Cramm finally got back and was awarded the Iron Cross for bravery.

The leading players of America were the least handicapped by the war. America did not enter the worldwide conflict until attacked by the Japanese in December 1941, and the National championships were conducted each year without interruption. Many players who were to be prominent after the war served in the armed forces. Frank Parker was an army sergeant, Jack Kramer went into the Coast Guard, and Ted Schroeder served in the Navy. Most of the top players, however, had access to tennis courts throughout the war and were able to obtain leave to contest the Nationals. The most notable exception was Schroeder, who, after beating Parker in the final of the 1942 championships, played little tennis until he was discharged from the Navy in December 1945.

Dwight Davis died in November 1945. Shortly before his death he entertained Sir Norman Brookes at his home in Washington. They sat and reminisced and speculated about the resumption of the competition. According to Mabel Brookes,

Dwight was dying, and knew it; but the old reserve maintained; life and death, the two imposters, just like triumph and disaster, must be treated just the same, so he sat calm and discussed the future of the game he loved. 'Don't keep the cup too long, Norman,' he said, 'it is meant to travel; its appearance in any country brings a flock of exterior implications very beneficial to sporting unity in the tennis world, and the tennis world is a big world. If I had known of its coming significance, it would have been cast in gold.'

Twenty nations issued challenges to Australia in 1946 – fifteen in the European Zone, four in the American Zone, and one (New Zealand) in a new Pacific section of the American Zone. Nine countries defeated in the war were expelled from the ILTF and debarred from participating. Among the talented young players who made their debut were Jaroslav Drobny of Czechoslovakia, Lennart Bergelin and Torsten Johansson of Sweden, and Philippe Washer of

Belgium. Bergelin and Washer helped to take their countries into the semifinals, alongside Yugoslavia and France.

The French called upon four prewar players, Yvon Petra, Marcel Bernard, Bernard Destremau and Pierre Pellizza. They easily beat a weak British team in the first round and then accounted for Switzerland. Petra, who was born in Indo-China, was lucky to be playing tennis as he had badly damaged his left knee while serving as a machine gunner. A sympathetic German medical officer in a prisoner-of-war camp operated on the knee just in time to prevent a permanent disability and later arranged for Petra's release. In the contest with Yugoslavia in Paris, Petra and Bernard won their first two singles against Mitic and Puncec respectively, but they were replaced by Destremau and Pellizza for the doubles, and Mitic and Puncec lived to fight another day by winning that match 8–10, 8–6, 6–3, 5–7, 10–8. Mitic then beat Bernard, and Puncec won the tie for his country by beating Petra, 6–0 in the fifth set. This was one of the closest contests on record as every match went to five sets. It was remarkable for another aspect. The 6-foot 5 Petra was so stung by criticism in the French press that he played above himself in the subsequent Wimbledon championships and won the first postwar title from an eighth seeding.

The other European semifinal was won by Sweden, who beat Belgium 4–1 in Stockholm. Sweden and Yugoslavia had a very close struggle in the final, played at Varberg. On the first day Pallada beat Bergelin in three sets and Mitic beat Johansson in five after being two sets down. The same players contested the doubles, Sweden narrowly averting defeat in the fourth set to win the fifth. On the third day Johansson evened the tie by beating Pallada in straight sets, and Bergelin then recovered from being two sets down to Mitic to win 10–8 in the fifth set and make Sweden the European Zone winner for the first time. Across the Atlantic, meanwhile, the USA, represented by Frank Parker, Bill Talbert and Gardnar Mulloy (Riggs had turned professional in 1941), enjoyed a cakewalk, beating the Philippines and Mexico without dropping a set. A New Zealand default put America into the inter-zone final.

By now Jack Kramer was regarded as America's best singles player, though he seemed to be jinxed in the US Nationals, which he had not yet won. The champion of the last two years was Parker. Kramer was twenty-five years old at the end of the war, a tall, wide-shouldered man with a crew cut. His second great love was gambling, but on a tennis court you would not have guessed that. He played what was known as 'the big game', based on power and relentless aggression, and he had all the shots to make this style devastating. Just as important was Kramer's intelligence. He had thought about tennis through his long stints of coast-guard duty and, more than anyone before, except possibly Lacoste, he realized the value of playing exactly the right shot at every stage of a match. He called his approach to the game 'percentage tennis'.

Kramer's jinx followed him to Wimbledon. He had a badly blistered hand and wore a glove when he played Drobny in the fourth round and lost. The top seed was Dinny Pails of Australia, who had taken Bromwich to five sets in the Australian final in January. As in 1938 and 1939, Bromwich did not go to Wimbledon, absences that may well have cost him his chance of winning the crown. Pails, an unknown quantity outside Australia, had reached the age of twenty-five without ever having met a foreign player in competition. He was a baseliner, largely self-taught, and had a backhand weakness. Petra beat him in the quarter finals and it was Pails's travelling companion, the unseeded Geoff Brown, who faced Petra in the final.

Kramer began to achieve his destiny at the American championships, where he conceded but one set. His unexpected opponent in the final was a fellow Californian, Tom Brown, who defeated Parker and Mulloy. Brown extended Kramer to 9–7 in the first set and lost the third set 6–0, but he did enough to ensure a place in the Davis Cup squad bound for Australia. First, however, America had to contend with Sweden in the inter-zone final at Forest Hills. Kramer and Parker won the singles, and Talbert and Mulloy the doubles.

Before the squad headed for Melbourne it was joined by Schroeder, who in recent years had played less tennis than the others. He was a Stanford graduate and in his job as a sales engineer in commercial refrigeration he was trying to make up for the lost war years. Schroeder's long-term ambitions in tennis were limited. Usually he didn't trouble to make the trip east to play in the Nationals and he was to compete at Wimbledon only once (in 1949, when he won). Regarded as a bit of a character, he often had a corn-cob pipe in his mouth and walked with a rolling gait which, according to one writer, 'made him look as though he had just got off a horse'. He was also Kramer's closest Californian buddy, and Kramer, who was taken to four sets by Schroeder in the 1946 Pacific Southwest championships, respected his fighting qualities above those of anyone else. Kramer told the US Davis Cup committee that unless Schroeder made the trip Down Under he wouldn't be going either.

There was bitter rivalry in the US team. While Kramer was certain to be given a singles berth, Walter Pate, the captain, indicated that the other singles place was open. Parker was considered the most likely man to fill it despite his bad loss to Bromwich in 1939.

Before the squad departed, Kramer learned that Parker's wife would be travelling with the party on full expenses. Sometimes in the past the wives of players had been barred from travelling with cup teams. The Australian rule was that wives could not even be in the same overseas country as their husbands. Apart from the additional expense that they incurred, it was thought that wives militated against team spirit since naturally they would wish to have their husbands to themselves for much of the time abroad. On this occasion, when Kramer found that special consideration was being given to the Parkers, he insisted that an equivalent amount of expenses be set aside for his wife and Schroeder's wife, even though they were unable to make the trip. Jack argued that his wife was going to have to live off the nominal $75 a week he received from the company that employed him, while Schroeder was not going to be paid by his company at all. The USLTA's mention of the amateur rules had no effect on Kramer's attitude. He was even then a tough, pragmatic businessman. Finally, some wealthy patrons contributed money equal to Mrs Parker's expenses for the Kramers and the Schroeders.

Pate's team was the first cup team to fly to Australia. Before, players had travelled Down Under by ship, usually stopping off and playing exhibitions at one or two countries en route and taking about a month for the journey. Pate's players 'sped' to Australia in four days in a propeller-driven aircraft.

Australians eagerly looked forward to the challenge round, the first to be held in their country for more than a quarter of a century. During the war America had supplanted Great Britain as Australia's most important ally, but although the relationship between the two countries was friendly the Australians always had a tremendous desire 'to beat the Yanks'. In 1946 they thought they had the players to do this, even if Kramer was as good as he was made out to be. Bromwich and Pails should at least win one rubber each, thought the Aussies, while the old firm of Bromwich and Quist ought to wrap up the doubles.

The Victorian championships, which preceded the challenge round, did not lessen their optimism. Kramer and Parker played in only the doubles, and though Schroeder beat Pails in the singles semifinals, he lost in straight sets to Bromwich in the final. In the doubles, Kramer and Schroeder lost to Bromwich and the hard-hitting Colin Long, who went on to beat Talbert and Mulloy in the title round. The latter match created a stir, with Talbert and Mulloy protesting several times at Bromwich's habit of dropping the second ball when his first service was good. The Americans claimed that the bouncing ball was distracting, especially when it fell on the court and not behind the baseline. The umpire ruled against them and next day some newspapers speculated that the Americans were conducting nerve warfare. The controversy fizzled out when Schroeder raised no objection to Bromwich's action during or after the singles final.

The US captain named Kramer, Parker, Schroeder and Mulloy as his team, thus ruling out the reigning American doubles champions, Talbert and Mulloy, for the doubles. Mulloy believed he should be in the doubles line-up, and Parker was sure he ought to be selected for the singles. At a team meeting Parker said he had been led to believe he would play. Denying this, Pate called for each player's opinion. Kramer strongly urged the selection of Schroeder. He said Schroeder was in better form than the other players and had the net-attacking game to beat Bromwich and Pails, whereas Parker lacked the big game. 'But the main thing is that Frankie doesn't ever upset anybody,' added Kramer bluntly. 'He doesn't get upset himself either. He just plays the same level every match. Here, that's not good enough. Schroed plays over his head in big matches.' Talbert, Brown and Mulloy all supported Schroeder, and he was chosen.

The news gave Australians a pleasant surprise. One newspaper headline said: 'Pate Gives Cup Away'. In the Melbourne *Sun* R. E. Schlesinger changed his forecast from a 3–2 to 4–1 victory for the home team.

For the first time, temporary stands were erected at Kooyong

Stadium, and fourteen thousand people filled them on the opening day, 26 December. The day was hot and still when Bromwich and Schroeder walked out onto the same court on which they had played the Victorian final. Though nervous, Schroeder was a rugged, resourceful man and he was confident of doing better. He planned to rally from the baseline, waiting for an opportunity to attack, and then to give his net-assault everything he had. Before the match began, Sir Norman Brookes, standing in the middle of the arena, spoke in memory of Dwight Davis. The founder of the competition would have been gratified by the colourful scene.

Bromwich was in good touch. He won the first set 6–3 and Schroeder knew he had to put him under more pressure. In the second set the American approached the net on shots down the middle of the court. Bromwich tried to forestall him by putting up lobs. Schroeder smashed them away and took the set 6–1.

If the crowd was slightly shaken by this reverse, worse was to follow. After losing the first two games of the third set, Schroeder took the next six games in a row. Now, he was serving and volleying ruthlessly, and Bromwich, labouring to make his double-handed shots, was floundering.

The stands buzzed during the rest period. On the resumption, Bromwich lifted Australian hopes by hitting a succession of great passing shots. He won the fourth set so easily, 6–0, that the crisis seemed over. But Schroeder, who had wanted to serve first in the fifth set, thrived in these situations. He broke Bromwich's first service in the fifth set and went to a 5–3 lead. Every effort Bromwich made to get back into the match was determinedly rebuffed. A sharply angled backhand on match point gave the Australian no hope, and Schroeder jubilantly tossed his racquet high in the air. As expected, Kramer outgunned Pails 8–6, 6–2, 9–7. The cup was as good as won.

After the Victorian championships the Australian captain, Gerald Patterson, had decided to split the Bromwich–Long doubles combination in order to bring in Quist. This was a mistake. Though Bromwich and Quist had never lost a cup match, Quist was not in good form. Like Bromwich, he was slower than before the war. Any hope Australia had of fighting back, as in 1939, soon vanished. Kramer and Schroeder blitzed Quist and powered their way to a 6–2, 7–5, 6–4 victory.

In the remaining singles Kramer beat Bromwich in straight sets, and Mulloy, substituting for Schroeder, overcame Pails by the same margin, with Talbert fulfilling an old ambition by assuming the umpire's job.

There was much emotion during the presentation of the cup. Besides being a contemporary, Joe Hunt had been a friend of Kramer and Schroeder. He and Schroeder had yarned on warships about how one day they would take the cup back to America. When Schroeder went to the Kooyong microphone, he said, 'Joe, the Dog-Faced Boy, wherever you are, I wish you were here today. We owe a lot to you.' The remark mystified the crowd, but Australians were only too well aware that the cup would be leaving their country. Hundreds jumped over a stadium wall to take one last look at the gleaming silver. Soon it was packed for its first airborne journey.

The defeat was the worst ever inflicted on a defending nation. It sent shockwaves through Australian tennis. 'I do not belong to the Jeremiahs who believe that it will take Australia ten years to regain the Davis Cup,' said R. G. Menzies, then the Federal Opposition leader, but others were less complacent, realizing that Australia would have to produce a new type of attacking player to match the style of Kramer and Schroeder. As Kramer said, 'Tennis today is a serve and volley game. If you don't come in on your second serve, your opponent will come in and force *you* into errors.'

The Americans' superiority in physical fitness was another important lesson. Besides staying too much on the baseline, both Bromwich and Pails were overweight, perhaps, in the case of Pails, because officials held old-fashioned views about diet. In his book, *Set Points*, Pails wrote:

They made me eat three big meals a day; steak or chops and eggs for breakfast, more steak or chops for lunch and a large dinner at night. I preferred a salad in the middle of the day. But could I have a salad? Not on your life! Plaintively I'd order a salad and the bosses would countermand my order. I must have a thumping big piece of steak or a chop. They told me that I had to keep up my strength; that if I didn't eat up big and be a good boy I would not last the distance in a hard singles contest. So I ploughed my way through the steak, gnawed at my chops and longed for my salad. My waistline was expanding and I could do nothing about it. I would play a practice set and when I thought nobody was looking, would

151

sneak away for a run on my own in an attempt to reduce my weight. If I was detected I was led back to the court for another set. Then I would waddle back to the hotel for another whopping meal.

Mervyn Weston, who wrote for the Melbourne *Argus*, believed that most of the Australian players were not temperamentally suited to hard training and did not know the meaning of fitness. Weston was particularly critical of Bromwich, whose example influenced the New South Wales group of players. Bromwich, said Weston, was wrong in claiming that the only way of acquiring condition for tennis was by playing tennis. Recalling how, a generation before, Vivian McGrath had faded at an age when most players were reaching their peak, Weston suggested that the physical demands imposed by a double-handed style might preclude a long career. He doubted whether either Bromwich or Geoff Brown would go any further.

The discarded Australian captain, Harry Hopman, now a tennnis writer for the Melbourne *Herald*, agreed with Weston. He knew that a more spartan approach was needed and he was planning several years ahead. The genesis of the Australian dominance of the 1950s lay in the ruins of 1946, when Hopman concluded that a player's potential could best be achieved if speed, strength and stamina were scientifically added to natural talent. Fortunately, he knew of a young Melbourne lad willing to work as hard in a gymnasium as he did chasing balls on the court. A lad named Frank Sedgman. . . .

The late 1940s set the pattern for the next two decades. Not until 1960 did a nation other than America or Australia play off in the challenge round. America and Australia, with Great Britain, were the strongholds of grass-court tennis, and since the defending nation always had the right to choose the surface on which it played, the odds were stacked against other challengers. Nevertheless, more and more countries wished to take part in the competition. By 1959, Luxembourg, Pakistan, Turkey, Israel, the British West Indies, Ceylon (now Sri Lanka), Burma, Malaysia, Lebanon, Venezuela, Thailand, Korea, Iran and Colombia would be Davis Cup nations. They were to be followed by Indonesia, Ecuador, Morocco, USSR,

Rhodesia (now Zimbabwe), Bulgaria, Vietnam, Peru, Hong Kong and Bolivia. By 1971, sixty-five nations had contested the cup.

Twenty-two countries challenged in 1947, the teams including such fresh blood as Great Britain's Tony Mottram and South Africa's Eric Sturgess. The two-man team of Drobny and Cernik gave Czechoslovakia its first triumph in the European Zone with wins over Sweden, Switzerland, New Zealand, France and Yugoslavia. Sweden, the next strongest team in Europe, was unlucky to draw the Czechs in the first round. Both Bergelin and Johansson beat Cernik, but each lost to Drobny; and they dropped the doubles too. France called on the forty-eight-year-old Borotra for the doubles in its match with Czechoslovakia; he and Petra lost in three hard sets after Drobny had beaten Destremau, and Cernik had beaten Bernard. The political climate in Europe still affected the competition: Czeslaw Spychala and Ignacy Tloczynski of Poland, nominated by their country to play Great Britain in Warsaw, preferred to remain exiled in Britain.

Kramer swept all before him in the Wimbledon singles, and with Bob Falkenburg also won the doubles. While he was in the American team, America looked impregnable.

Australia, who challenged in the American Zone, played both of her preliminary contests in Montreal; first against Canada, whom she defeated 5–0, and then against Czechoslovakia in the inter-zone final. Bromwich was in fine form. He dropped only three games against Cernik on the first day, and, with Long, only six games in the doubles. Pails lost to Drobny, but Bromwich beat Drobny in straight sets to clinch victory.

In the challenge round at Forest Hills the Schroeder *v.* Bromwich match was again the crucial rubber. Kramer overwhelmed Pails 6–2, 6–1, 6–2 before Schroeder snuffed out what little hope Australia had by beating Bromwich 6–4, 5–7, 6–3, 6–3. In the fourth set Schroeder complained of cramp in his right arm and a masseur was called to the court to treat him. During a changeover, while he was having his arm massaged, Schroeder called to Bromwich, 'Let me know when you are ready to resume, John, and I will be ready.' However, the masseur's intervention broke a rule of the competition, a fact that Fred Perry, who was doing a radio commentary, noted and passed on to the US captain, Alrick Man, after the match. Man was mortified, as was the referee, Dr Russell Davenport. They immediately went to the Australian captain, Roy Cowling, and asked him to accept a default. Cowling replied that Australia would never consent to winning on a technicality. So far as Cowling was concerned, Schroeder had won fairly.

Next day Davenport made another attempt to give Australia the match. Other members of the American Davis Cup committee had expressed concern at the violation of the rule which had been proposed by America in 1933. Davenport had spent a sleepless night worrying over the incident. 'I have been refereeing national championships and other important tournaments for fifteen years,' he told the press, 'but this is my first Davis Cup tie. I am dreadfully sorry about the whole thing and wish Mr Cowling would accept the default.' Cowling would not hear of it.

Bromwich and Long beat Kramer and Schroeder in the doubles, and Pails only narrowly failed to level the scores when he and Schroeder battled for a then record seventy-one games in the fourth rubber. The court had become slippery, and Schroeder at one stage played in his socks, then in his bare feet, and finally in spiked shoes. He won the first two sets 6–3, 8–6 after saving five set points in the second set. Pails won the next two sets 6–4, 11–9, and had a match point in the fifth set before losing it 8–10. Once again there was controversy. One of the linesmen thought the Australians received a raw deal, and after the match he immediately wrote a letter to Brian Fuller, president of the New South Wales LTA, claiming that Schroeder had 'stalled' at every opportunity. The linesman, a United Nations official, added that during the match he had told Cowling that Schroeder was deliberately wasting time, but Cowling had taken no action.

Kramer turned professional after winning the 1947 American doubles championship with Schroeder and successfully defending the US singles title. While his departure opened up the amateur game to new contenders for the number one position, it did not seriously damage America's Davis Cup prospects. Only Australia was seen as a threat, and Australia was not promoting younger players well enough. When Quist returned to form and beat Bromwich in a five-set Australian championship final he ensured his place in the LTAA overseas team and was made captain-manager. He was, however, nearly thirty-five and his best years in singles were behind him. Others in the team were Bill Sidwell and Geoff Brown of Sydney, and Colin Long of Melbourne. Pails had turned professional and Bromwich ruled himself out by declaring he would travel only by ship (as he had done with Brown in 1947, joining the other team members in Europe). Without Bromwich, the LTAA felt it could not afford to include the twenty-year-old Sedgman, as tournaments would not be prepared to pay as much to the association for the team's appearances.

Twenty-nine nations filed entries in the 1948 competition, twenty-five in the European Zone, and four in the American. The congestion of matches in Europe still caused concern, and France suggested one remedy might be to reject the entry of any country whose players were not of a sufficiently high standard. America opposed the idea. No one could tell when a small country would produce an outstanding player, said Russell Kingman, instancing Ecuador's Pancho Segura.

Czechoslovakia and Sweden were consolidating and proved themselves the strongest of the twenty-five nations that challenged in the European Zone. After Italy, Rumania, Hungary and Austria, four of the wartime Axis powers, were readmitted to the competition. Sweden had little to spare against Hungary in Budapest, where Josef Asboth, the French title-holder of 1947, beat both Bergelin and Johannson. The Czechs had to struggle to squeeze past Belgium and Italy. Czechoslovakia won the zone final against Sweden in Prague when Drobny and Cernik captured the first three rubbers for the loss of only one set.

A remarkable comeback to Davis Cup play in this year was made by Hans Redl, who first played for Austria in 1937, and then for Germany in 1938 and 1939. From 1948 to 1955 Redl again played for Austria. Now he had lost his left arm while on active service. Because of his disability, the rules of tennis were amended to permit a player with only one arm to use the racquet to toss the ball. Redl rested the ball on his racquet and flipped it into the air.

Americans dominated the singles events at Paris and Wimbledon, Parker beating Drobny in the Roland Garros final, and the lanky Bob Falkenburg surviving three match points to deny Bromwich the Wimbledon crown. On one of those points the unlucky Australian deliberately allowed a ball to pass him, thinking it was going out, and was dismayed to see it fall in. Bromwich, who had travelled to England privately, understood that if he won Wimbledon he would be added to the Davis Cup team. Whereas most Australians thought he would bolster the team, the LTAA declined to take any action. Harry Pitt, the association's vice-president, said, 'Unfortunately the question has been settled by the fact that Bromwich was beaten!' The LTAA's inflexibility was particularly silly as Bromwich had won the Wimbledon doubles final with Sedgman against two possible cup defenders, Mulloy and Tom Brown. The youngster Sedgman was making his first overseas trip on a fund raised by readers of the Melbourne *Herald* and organized by Hopman.

Australia's path to the challenge round was difficult. She defeated Cuba comfortably in Havana, but in the rarefied atmosphere of Mexico City Quist went down in straight sets to Armando Vega, and Sidwell was taken to 7–5 in the fifth set by the same player before Australia won 4–1. The inter-zone final at Boston further exposed Australian weaknesses. While Quist beat Cernik, and Sidwell beat Drobny, the Czechs grabbed the doubles from Long and Geoff Brown. On the third day Quist led Drobny 8–6, 6–3 and had a match point at 10–9 in the third set. He lost that chance, and Drobny took the last three sets 18–16, 6–3, 7–5, with Quist, towards the end, too tired to chase shots beyond his reach. Sidwell led Cernik 7–5, 3–1 when darkness caused an overnight postponement and next day Sidwell completed a straight sets victory.

Australian morale could not be restored before the challenge round, to be held at Forest Hills on 4–6 September, and the Americans knew it. They entrusted Parker with a singles role for the first time since 1939. He showed his gratitude by beating both Sidwell and Quist in straight sets. Schroeder gave Sidwell only four games and, although he dropped a set to Quist, he won the last two sets against him 6–0, 6–0. Sir Norman Brookes was in hospital in Melbourne (not from shock) and said from his bed, 'I can't understand Quist's disastrous showing: it is beyond me.' The closest match was the doubles in which Talbert and Mulloy beat Sidwell and Long 8–6, 9–7, 2–6, 7–5.

The Australian press lambasted the LTAA for failing to groom new players. 'It will not be enough to seek younger players,' wrote the *Sydney Morning Herald*'s sports editor. 'Younger administrators who will think of the present and the future rather than the faded glories of the past would inject new life and hope into the game.'

There now flashed across the scene – only too briefly – the sleek and swarthy form of Richard (Pancho) Gonzales. The 6-foot 3 Californian son of Mexican parents, he had been introduced to the game by some of his friends who played on public courts in Los Angeles. Later he came under the notice of Perry T. Jones, the czar of Californian tennis, who invited Gonzales into the Los Angeles Tennis Club, where he could play with better players. Gonzales possessed the kind of talent that makes fluent, speedy shots look effortless, but was rebellious and at that time lacked self-discipline. By not attending school regularly he disappointed Jones, who believed that this gave him an unfair advantage over those juniors who were more conscientious. Jones barred him from tournaments, and Pancho went into the Navy for eighteen months. The break from tennis sharpened his keenness to return to the game. After settling his differences with Jones, he began playing tournaments again at the age of nineteen. In the following year, 1948, Jones sent him across America. He won the Western and clay-court championships and was seeded eighth for the Nationals. Until that summer Gonzales had never seen a grass court. Yet at Forest Hills he upset Parker, who was fresh from his Davis Cup triumphs, and then beat Drobny to reach the final. There, his opponent was the smooth-stroking baseliner Eric Sturgess, who also fell before Pancho's powerful barrage.

Frank Sedgman was seven months older than Gonzales. He had begun playing tennis with his parents when he was eight years old. Four years later his speed and never-say-die spirit attracted the attention of Hopman. Later still, Sedgman's willingness to build up his stamina and physique in gymnasium training made him an ideal protégé. Australia's 1946 debacle underlined the lessons Hopman drummed into the boy: to rush the net behind his service and to hit boldly for the lines when returning serve.

Right through the junior ranks, and then in senior company, Sedgman never ceased trying to improve his technique, strategy and physical condition. According to his mentor, he 'set an example of fitness through training, of splendidly modest court demeanour, of willingness to practise and maintain a virile, attacking, net-rushing type of game that became standard for young and ambitious players to follow.' In January 1949 Sedgman began to assume the responsibility for Australia's revival when he won the Australian championship, beating Sidwell, Quist and Bromwich in turn.

Neither Gonzales nor Sedgman made any real impact at Paris and Wimbledon in 1949. It was the more seasoned Parker and Schroeder who triumphed. Parker retained his French title by beating Budge Patty, an American living in Europe, in the final, and at Wimbledon Schroeder won three five-set matches in a row – over Sedgman, Sturgess and Drobny – to become the champion. Gonzales lost to Geoff Brown in the fourth round.

In this year there were twenty-four entries in the European Zone and four in the American Zone. The former zone produced a number of upsets. In Paris, Bernard toppled Drobny as France beat Czechoslovakia 3–2, and in Zagreb, Yugoslavia beat Sweden, with Bergelin losing to both Mitic and Pallada. France had another narrow win in her semifinal against Hungary in Budapest, where Asboth beat first Bernard, then Robert Abdesselam, while in Rome Italy conquered Yugoslavia 4–1.

The zone final, played between France and Italy at Paris, was another thriller. Gianni Cucelli, the Italian's number one, had represented his country before the war. He was actually born with the name Kucel, but under pressure from the Fascist authorities, who did not think this sounded Italian enough, he changed it to Cucelli. A chunky little man, he had a pug nose as a result of a short career as a professional boxer, and displayed plenty of fighting spirit on a tennis court, dashing at the ball with a wide range of shots that were sometimes ungainly but often effective. Against Abdesselam he was down 1–6, 6–8, 0–4, but bounced off the ropes to win, 6–2 in the fifth set. In the second rubber, Marcello del Bello was distracted at match point by the shout of a spectator and lost, 8–10 in the fifth set, to Bernard. The Italians won the doubles in five sets, but Abdesselam levelled the scores by beating del Bello. In the decisive match, Cucelli was down 8–6, 3–6, 4–6 at the intermission. When he returned he launched a furious onslaught and won the last two sets 6–0, 6–1.

Bromwich was back in the Australian team, the LTAA having agreed to send him, Sedgman and Sidwell to Europe and thence to America by ship. In America the team beat Canada and Mexico to qualify for the inter-zone final at the Westchester Country Club, Rye. Cliff Sproule, the manager, chose Sedgman and Sidwell as his singles players after Bromwich had told him his own form did not warrant his selection. On the first day only one singles could be completed because of a downpour which saturated the court, Sidwell beating Cucelli in four sets. When the teams returned to the club next day they found that vandals had dug up parts of the court with a garden fork and had ground their heels into other parts. The culprits were believed to be irate spectators who had not been refunded ticket money when rain cut the previous day's programme short. As the court was unplayable, another had to be used.

Soon there was more drama. Sproule announced that he would substitute Sidwell for Sedgman in the doubles if Sedgman had a long, tiring match against del Bello in the second singles. The Italians protested that this would be unfair because they would be obliged to use del Bello in the doubles whatever happened in the singles. The American referee, Leven Richards, ruled that either team could have an overnight postponement of the doubles if it wished. The wrangle ended tamely when Sedgman beat del Bello in straight sets. He returned to the court with Bromwich, and they beat Cucelli and del Bello in the doubles.

Before the challenge round, Australia was heartened to see two of its pairs in the final of the American doubles championship. Bromwich and Sidwell eliminated Gonzales and Parker and Talbert and Mulloy, before beating Sedgman and a Sidney youngster named George Worthington to win the title. A week later, at Forest Hills, Australia's doubles prowess was not enough. Gonzales beat Sedgman 6–4, 6–3, 6–3, and Schroeder beat Sidwell 6–1, 5–7, 4–6, 6–2, 6–3. Bromwich and Sidwell came from behind to win a marathon doubles against Talbert and Mulloy 3–6, 4–6, 10–8, 9–7, 9–7, with Sidwell starring. But Schroeder was too tough and experienced for Sedgman on the last day, winning 6–4, 6–3, 6–3, and Gonzales made the tally 4–1 with a simple win over Sidwell. The American citadel was still secure.

DAWN OF THE HOPMAN ERA

(1950–52, Australia)

The year 1950 marked the beginning of Australia's golden era of sport. Over the next two decades Australia would win the Davis Cup fifteen times, with America breaking the sequence in three years, only to see Australia regain the trophy at her first attempt. Other sports in Australia in the fifties and sixties rivalled tennis in the number of world champions produced, and the reasons for such an upsurge of sporting excellence in a country so remote and still possessing a relatively small population are still not clearly identified. A favourable climate and a high standard of living, a traditional love of sport, and a desire to express national pride through sporting achievements were probably the main factors. Nor should it be forgotten that the Old World was slowly recovering from the ravages of war. All over the world, over the next twenty years, there would be a growing investment in sporting facilities and coaching techniques, and international competition in all sports would intensify to the benefit of standards generally.

As opposed to the situation in most countries, tennis was a very egalitarian game in Australia. No other country had a higher ratio of courts to population, and at clubs and in the public parks tennis could be played at negligible cost. There were two other important reasons why Australia was ready to begin its long period of dominance. As we have seen, Harry Hopman, working from a Melbourne base, had been emphasizing the big game and the need for players to attain perfect physical condition. Sedgman was his protégé, and by 1950 Hopman also had around him other young players, including Ken McGregor, Mervyn Rose and Don Candy. Australia had not won a challenge round singles for four straight years, and it was thought to be time for a new approach. Hopman, who had been captain in 1938–39 but who had concentrated on establishing himself as a sportswriter in the immediate postwar years, was in a strong position to reclaim the captaincy.

He was completely dedicated. He had played for Australia in 1928, 1930 and 1932, his greatest talent being as a doubles player (though he once beat Don Budge in the final of a Californian tournament). In doubles he won the Australian championship with Crawford in 1929 and 1930 and was twice runner-up for the French title, while in mixed doubles he and his first wife Nell, who died in 1967, won the Australian championship in 1936–37 and were runners-up at Wimbledon in 1935. Hopman was also four times Australian squash champion.

An indefatigable worker, he would finish his daily duties at the Melbourne *Herald* soon after lunch and devote his afternoon to tennis. Then, at home in the evenings, he would catch up with his filing and correspondence. In 1950 he was in his forty-fourth year. He had no children and no other interests except punting on racehorses. As his wife was similarly committed to the game, the time they could give to developing tennis players (without any financial return) was considerable.

The other reason that Australia's fortunes abruptly turned was that Pancho Gonzales became a professional late in 1949 after winning his second US championship with a brilliant five-set victory over Schroeder. With hindsight, Gonzales may often have wished that he had stayed amateur longer. He was only twenty-one, had never won Wimbledon and had played in only one challenge round. Thus the division of professionals and amateurs enabled Australia to gain a grip on the cup, for in 1950 Kramer was only twenty-eight and Riggs thirty-two, and a team of Kramer, Gonzales, Riggs and Schroeder surely would have held the cup for a few more years. And who can tell if the young Australians who followed Sedgman – Lew Hoad, Ken Rosewall, Ashley Cooper, Neale Fraser *et al.* – would have blossomed so quickly if they had been obliged to make their way, from the start, against those who had turned pro?

Ken McGregor came under notice when, at the age of twenty and unseeded, he beat the top seed, Drobny, in the second round of the 1950 Australian championships and went on to be runner-up to Sedgman. McGregor and Candy were South Australians who had moved to improve their tennis. In the case of the 6-foot 3 McGregor, the Australian code of football was his first love and he was reluctant to sacrifice his involvement in that game. McGregor's father had been a champion footballer, and young Ken, with his height, agility, balance, courage and kicking ability, looked like being just as good. When McGregor senior learned from Hopman, however, that his son had tremendous potential as a tennis player, he encouraged the lad to leave home and pursue a career with a racquet.

The youngster needed to be carefully developed. In Hopman's words, 'It took big occasions and a terrific amount of work to put the fine edge on McGregor's touch.' Nevertheless, Hopman knew that if he could get him properly primed and motivated, the big fellow held the key to a Davis Cup victory.

The Australian team selected early in 1950 comprised Sedgman, McGregor, Rose, Worthington, the old hand John Bromwich, and Hopman as captain. Most people thought that the younger players, with experience, might be ready to regain the cup in 1952.

Twenty-two nations, including two from Asia – the Philippines and Pakistan – challenged in the European Zone. Germany and Japan were reaffiliated with the ILTF in 1950. Their exclusion had seemed to contradict the message given by Trygve Lie, secretary general of the United Nations, when making the 1948 draw: 'If the nations of the world could settle their differences in the same spirit that prevails in the Davis Cup competition, there would be no need to fear serious conflict among them.'

Japan's entry had been opposed in the late 1940s by Australia, whose Prime Minister informed the LTAA that many people who had lost relatives in the war would not like to see their country play Japan in a sporting contest. Ironically, it would be a Japanese company that thirty years later rehabilitated a declining Davis Cup competition with the injection of millions of sponsorship dollars.

In 1950 the emergence of Kurt Nielsen and Torben Ulrich lifted Denmark's stock. They carried their country into the European Zone final with wins over Egypt, France and Italy. Ulrich was a rare example of a son following his father's footsteps in the competition. Einer Ulrich represented Denmark from 1924 to 1938, and Torben's cup career was to stretch from 1948 to 1977. Jorgen Ulrich, another of Einer's sons, was also to play for his country, from 1955 to 1971. When Torben played his last cup match, the family had been involved in eighty ties and 226 rubbers, a remarkable family record in international sport.

Denmark's opponents in the final were Sweden, strengthened by a rising star, Sven Davidson. While Bergelin and Johansson played the bulk of the singles in Sweden's matches against the Netherlands, Norway, the Philippines and Poland, Davidson took over Bergelin's singles spot in the final in Båstad and beat Nielsen in four sets. Johansson defeated Ulrich, also in four sets, and Bergelin and Davidson won the doubles.

Meanwhile, the French championship was won by Budge Patty, who beat Drobny in five sets. The Australians had a bad tournament. Bromwich was beaten by Talbert in an early round, leaving Hopman convinced that McGregor would be a preferable player in the challenge round. He thereupon told McGregor that a singles place would be his if he could find his best form. Sedgman missed the French championships because he had injured a wrist while skylarking and he was still not fully fit at Queen's, where Bromwich won the title. But Sedgman surprisingly battled his way to the Wimbledon final with plucky wins over Art Larsen and Drobny. The cool and elegant Budge Patty beat him in four sets for the championship. Bromwich lost in Wimbledon's first week to Victor Seixas, but he and Quist went on to score a memorable triumph in the doubles.

Australia opened its American campaign in Montreal, where Sedgman and McGregor were nominated to play the Canadians Brendan Bracken and Lorne Main on a grass court. They did not drop a set. The next tie was against Mexico in Mexico City. Aware of the problems of acclimatization, Hopman changed his schedule to permit twelve days of preparation. Bromwich was retained for the singles since he had better control of the ball in the thin atmosphere. Australia won 4–1, with McGregor losing a 'dead' rubber to Gustavo Palafox.

The inter-zone final between Sweden and Australia was held on a grass court at Rye. Since McGregor had failed to impress with his practice form, Hopman felt he had no choice but to select Bromwich in the singles. He was sure anyway that Bromwich would win against Johansson because the Swede was not fast enough at the net to worry him. One Bromwich victory would probably ensure the team's passage into the challenge round, and with the tour's financial success depending on that, a gamble with McGregor did not seem justified. However, the Americans were misled by the choice of Bromwich, reasoning that if McGregor were going to play in the challenge round, he would have been given the experience of playing the Swedes.

The star of the final was neither Sedgman nor Bromwich but the blond 6-foot 3 Bergelin, whose fluent style and sweet timing of the ball reflected his immense natural talent. Introduced to tennis by his father, who was a good player, Bergelin had benefited as a teenager in the latter part of the war by practising with von Cramm in Stockholm. He caused a sensation at the 1948 Wimbledon when he beat, almost casually, the number one seed, Frank Parker, with a borrowed racquet. But overall his happy-go-lucky character often appeared to deny him the consistency and mental toughness to take full advantage of his talent.

Bergelin played at his graceful best in going to a two sets to one lead against Sedgman in the opening rubber. At the end of the third set rain held up play for almost an hour, and when Sedgman returned to the court he was wearing spikes. Bergelin promptly lost control of the match and won only one game in the fourth set. In the fifth set Sedgman broke Bergelin's service to lead 2–1. The Swede then lost the first point of the fourth game, whereupon he discarded his shoes and socks. This helped him to stem the avalanche of winners engulfing him on the slippery court. With better footing, Bergelin resumed serving at his best and hitting his forehand brilliantly. Sedgman could win only one more game.

Bromwich easily accounted for Johansson 6–2, 6–3, 6–0, and he and Sedgman beat Bergelin and Davidson in the doubles 6–1, 7–5, 7–5. On the third day Bergelin again excelled himself by beating Bromwich 6–3, 6–2, 1–6, 7–9, 6–3. The Australian appeared to have the match in his grasp when he pulled up from 2–4 in the fourth set and led 3–2, with his service to follow, in the fifth. But Bergelin ran over the top of him with an onslaught of serves, forehand drives and volleys. The winner was carried off the court on the shoulders of his countrymen to the strains of a patriotic Swedish song.

In the decisive match Sedgman had some anxious moments against Johansson when he trailed 2–3 and 0–40 on his service in the first set. After extricating himself, he was never in danger and won 6–4, 7–5, 6–3.

While Australia's struggle raised American hopes, some Americans thought the youthful vigour of the challengers was ominous. Allison Danzig expressed a popular view:

No one would begrudge the Australians victory, they have been such good sports in taking a licking from the Americans in the past few challenge rounds, travelling some ten thousand miles annually to receive same. What is agitating the high brass of the G.H.Q. at 120 Broadway [then home of the USLTA] is that if we do lose the cup, we can kiss it goodbye for a long spell. In Frank Sedgman, Kenneth McGregor, George Worthington and Mervyn Rose the Anzacs have the best group of rising young players mustered by any nation since the Four Musketeers of France began their long climb in 1921. . . .

America suffered two blows before the challenge round began. Patty, who had spent most of his career outside America, but who wanted to show American fans the kind of form that had won him his French and Wimbledon titles, sprained an ankle. Then Talbot and Mulloy lost the US doubles championship to Sedgman and Bromwich, the fourth successive time they had lost to Australian pairs in major events. In response to these setbacks, the American selectors named Schroeder and Tom Brown for the singles, and chose a new pair, Mulloy and Schroeder, for the doubles.

Unexpectedly, at the draw, Hopman named McGregor for the singles, along with Sedgman. In a practice session two days earlier, McGregor had suddenly hit top form. He was serving powerfully and accurately, and playing his volleys and overheads with great confidence.

America banked heavily on Schroeder winning both his singles. Ted had never been beaten in a cup singles and recently had won the Newport grass-court tournament. Brown, who was believed to have a good chance of winning at least one singles, was a Californian with a hard-hitting 'slam-bang' style. A finalist at both Forest Hills and Wimbledon, his only regular circuit play was from 1946 to 1948 during his vacations from law school.

The fate of the cup was virtually decided on the first day at Forest Hills. Sedgman beat Brown 6–0, 8–6, 9–7, his speed and anticipation being too much for the American in the early stages. Schroeder was confidently expected to equalize, but McGregor caught him, and indeed the whole tennis world, off-guard by winning 13–11, 6–3, 6–4.

Before the first match, Hopman had watched Schroeder and McGregor warming up on separate courts. 'Look, Mac,' he told McGregor, 'Ted's passing strokes are weak. Go for your life all the way. Force him and he'll make as many errors as you, or more, trying to pass you.'

Schroeder soon realized he was in for a fight. Six times he was within a stroke of losing the first set and had to struggle to save himself. Unleashing all his power, McGregor frequently aced him and applied constant pressure with his aggressive volleying. Finally, with a set point in the twenty-fourth game, the lanky Australian varied his pattern. He had been returning to Schroeder's backhand, with the idea of volleying the next shot to the American's feet. This time he hit to the forehand, and Schroeder, wrong-footed, dived back the other way too late.

The long battle for the first set took the sting out of Schroeder's game. He kept fighting for points, but McGregor could not be subdued. According to Hopman,

Every superlative used in describing McGregor's tennis that day was well earned. He was simply *terrific*. His temperament for a comparatively inexperienced player left nothing to be desired and his fitness in standing up to the nervous strain of such a close fight against a dour and determined opponent in a vital match was superb.

Sedgman and Bromwich sealed victory in the doubles 4–6, 6–4, 6–2, 4–6, 6–4. On the third day the stunned crowd saw Sedgman widen the Australian margin to 4–0 by inflicting a second loss on Schroeder. McGregor, after winning the first two sets against Brown, 11–9, 10–8, lost the next three 9–11, 1–6, 4–6.

The result greatly increased the game's popularity in Australia. Thousands turned out to view the cup and watch the players in exhibition matches at various centres over the next few months. Everyone wanted to know more about the conquering heroes. As Sedgman's somewhat bewildered father, a carpenter, told a reporter, 'You'd think we had had a royal baby or quads or something. All this talking about Frank makes us feel like kings.' A delighted LTAA began making early plans to defend the cup in Sydney.

Twenty-six nations challenged in 1951 when the most interesting occurrence in the early rounds was von Cramm's reappearance. In guiding Germany to the European final in his forty-second year, he beat such players as Mitic, Nielsen, Ulrich, Washer, Jackie Brichant and Cucelli. He was to continue playing in the competition for another two years. In the 1951 final in Båstad, however, the two-man Swedish team of Bergelin and Davidson was too strong for Germany and did not lose a match.

The Americans, knowing their team needed reinforcing, must have thought a strong recruit was ready at hand with the success of big-hitting Dick Savitt. Then ranked seventh in the States, Savitt was invited to tour Australia with the reigning American champion, Art Larsen, in the summer of 1950–51 and beat both Sedgman and McGregor in the Australian championships. Six months later he was the Wimbledon champion, again beating McGregor in a major final, and this time mixing his solid baseline game with effective forays to the net.

At Forest Hills Savitt had a painful leg infection and lost to Seixas. Sedgman beat Larsen in a semifinal, and Seixas in the final, becoming the first Australian to capture the American title. Just as memorable, he and McGregor completed the Grand Slam of doubles titles, the only pair ever to do so.

Savitt played four cup singles without dropping a set as America swept past Japan, Mexico and Canada in the American Zone. When Dick was included in the squad to go to Australia, it was generally assumed that he would be America's trump and that the other most likely singles player would be the rapidly improving Tony Trabert. Seixas was included as a back-up player; eighteen-year-old Hamilton Richardson was put in for experience; and at the last moment an out-of-form Schroeder was added because of his fighting qualities and the belief that the Australian tournaments would sharpen his game and toughen his condition. Unluckily for Savitt, he soon fell out with both his captain, Frank Shields, and Jack Kramer, the team's semi-official coach and trainer. Shields and Kramer instituted rigorous training methods, similar to the Australians'. These were foreign to all Savitt's instincts, and unavailingly he asked permission to prepare in his own way, simply by playing tennis. Required to jog and do exercises, he failed to pick up form and became increasingly disgruntled. When he missed selection for the inter-zone final against Sweden at Melbourne, he realized he had little chance of playing in the challenge round. His brooding suspicion that his Jewish background was responsible for his omission added to the undercurrent of tension in the team.

Sweden fared badly against the Americans, with Bergelin as mediocre as he had been brilliant the previous year. He had got off to a poor start in the New South Wales championships and was unsettled by a shoulder injury. He lost in straight sets to both Schroeder and Trabert, as did Davidson. The only set won by the Swedes was in the doubles.

As became the case throughout the fifties and sixties, the New South Wales and Victorian championships could make or break a player's claims to selection for the challenge round. In this year the New South Wales championship was won by Seixas, who downed Trabert, Sedgman and Rose, and the Victorian title was won by Sedgman, who defeated Trabert, Seixas and Savitt. As the New South Wales champion and a Victorian semifinalist, Seixas thus placed himself strongly in line for selection.

A Philadelphian, Vic Seixas was something of a late developer. He had been a leading junior, but after serving as a pilot in the South Pacific during the war he was ranked no higher than eighth in America in 1950, when he was aged twenty-seven. A fierce competitor, he played a persistent net-storming game and had a fine top-spin lob. His backhand was a weakness against the best players.

Shortly before the challenge round an Associated Press correspondent, Gayle Talbot, claimed that Hopman was trying to brand Seixas as a habitual foot-faulter.

If he can worry Seixas and at the same time cast several seeds of doubt into the minds of potential foot-fault judges, he will have struck a considerable blow for his country.

As full-time writer for the Melbourne *Herald*, good old Harry has been in a fine spot to conduct his preliminary campaign.

To put it mildly, members of the American team think Harry is hitting below the belt.

Hopman certainly recalled the part that foot faults played in destroying Quist's confidence in 1938, and he admitted having taken a movie film of Seixas playing Sedgman in Melbourne. The film showed, he said, that Seixas did foot-fault. Kramer meanwhile was writing for a Sydney newspaper and referred several times to the 'strain' that Sedgman would be under in having to win both his singles and help win the doubles. He, too, may have been applying psychological pressure.

Hopman soon had other trouble. He learned that the Australian selectors were favouring Rose rather than McGregor for the singles. Sir Norman Brookes in particular had a soft spot for left-handers, and Rose had looked a more complete player than McGregor when losing a close match to Seixas in the Sydney final. That match was played in the same arena as the one scheduled for the challenge round. Left-handers usually did well there because the prevailing breeze assisted their service. Rose had consolidated his form at Melbourne, where he pushed Savitt to five hard sets. McGregor had been unimpressive in both tournaments. But Hopman knew that Rose's backhand weakness could be exploited by good net-rushers, and he felt that McGregor was improving each day in practice. He pleaded with the selectors, telling them he was willing to publicize his part in having Rose replaced, and so accepting the responsibility. Hopman persuaded two of the selectors, but the other two remained adamant, even though Harry kept arguing his case up to ten minutes before the draw. (The fifth selector, Roy Cowling, had died a few weeks earlier.)

When the names of the singles players, Sedgman and Rose, Schroeder and Seixas, were announced at the Australia Hotel on Christmas Day, there was a moment of complete silence. Then a burst of clapping overcame the tension.

This was the first challenge round held in Sydney since January 1910, and it set an Australian pattern. Temporary stands increased the seating capacity at White City to 15,300, and hundreds of people attended the practice sessions. Davis Cup news dominated the front pages, as well as the sports and social pages, of Australian newspapers, and by the time the event started the nation was in a state of feverish excitement.

For Seixas and Rose, who were drawn to play first, it was their Davis Cup debut. Both were very nervous, but Seixas was the quicker to settle down. As Hopman feared, his relentless attack broke Rose's confidence in his backhand, and the American won 6–2, 6–4, 9–7.

Sedgman showed that he was equal to the strain by playing some of his best tennis to defeat Schroeder 6–4, 6–3, 4–6, 6–4. Both players hit boldly for the lines with their volleys and passing shots, the decisive factors being Sedgman's speed and greater precision.

The next question to be answered was how McGregor would shape up in the doubles. He had been bitterly disappointed by his omission from the singles, especially as he had worked hard to reach peak form just as the selectors turned towards Rose. After the first day's matches McGregor was so emotionally churned up he could not concentrate enough to practise. He went for a run instead. If there were any doubts about his morale, he soon dispelled them. He opened the doubles with an ace! He continued to serve brilliantly, and with Sedgman devastating in every department of the game, they outmanoeuvred Schroeder and Trabert to win 6–2, 9–7, 6–3. Schroeder was the weakest player. Perhaps his unimpressive display was a reaction to his tough singles. Or perhaps he was simply over the hill.

America now had little chance, for Sedgman was a clear favourite to beat Seixas in the fifth rubber. Nevertheless, Schroeder wanted to give Seixas the opportunity to pull America out of the fire. Ted was depressed by his showing in the doubles and knew he would not beat Rose if his touch did not improve. This would be his last important match and his pride made him desperately want to win. He went to Kramer's room during the evening and asked him to play cards. Both men realized they were near the end of the road as players; Schroeder had lost some of his enthusiasm and Kramer was beginning to be afflicted with arthritis. During a game of gin rummy which lasted till 4 a.m. they indulged in some nostalgic memories of the heights each had scaled. Then Schroeder suggested they went for a walk. They strolled around Sydney until sunrise, returned to the hotel and had breakfast. Schroeder then began to get ready to play.

Despite his lack of sleep, he beat Rose 6–4, 13–11, 7–5. Only Schroeder's nervous energy allowed him to play so well, for Rose made him fight for every point. Ted never eased up for a moment. In the front row of the stands Kramer was seen to be gesticulating. It may have been the excitement or possibly he was waving advice to his pal. Hopman conferred with referee Sproule. They both thought Jack was passing handsignals to Schroeder. Sproule walked across and told Jack that under the rules only the team captains could give advice to the players, and he would have to keep his hands behind the railings out of sight. Kramer sat back and kept his hands still.

Sedgman watched much of the Rose match and when it ended Frank's shirt was saturated from sweat brought on by tension. Yet in the dressing room, after he changed clothes, he lay down on the couch and fell asleep! His nap lasted five minutes.

The atmosphere when Sedgman and Seixas walked out for the final match was electric. All round Australia activity ceased as people listened intently to radio commentary. Seixas served the first ball to Sedgman's forehand and Sedgman slammed it for a winner. But Seixas kept coming forward, troubling Sedgman by dropping his volleys short. 'Next time you dash in for a short volley,' Hopman told his protégé, 'don't try to hit the cover off the ball, but try to touch it back just over the net to Vic's feet and move in to crowd him.' Hopman recalled in his book *Aces and Places*:

I could say such a thing to Sedgman . . . and know he had the adaptability to try it. He did, and it worked. It got him out of a lot of bother in the next few games, and until Seixas realized that his short volleys, which the fast Sedgman could reach, were boomeranging back at him. Sedgman played magnificently as he countered everything Seixas tried, got on top and then maintained the pressure until he had won 6–4, 6–2, 6–2, and kept the cup in Australia.

Hopman believed that Savitt's omission from this challenge round was as much an error as the passing over of McGregor. Savitt's baseline game, according to Hopman, would have had a better chance of upsetting Sedgman than the net-rushing style of Schroeder and Seixas.

Within a few weeks McGregor gained consolation in his home town by beating Savitt and Sedgman to win the Australian championship, while Savitt won the 1952 US indoor championship. But Dick was severely criticized by Shields for his alleged lack of cooperation and never fully recovered from the rebuff he suffered. He retired before the end of 1952, 'almost hounded from the game'.

The challenge round turned Sedgman into one of Australia's greatest national heroes, and suggestions that he would turn professional filled the country with gloom. Guests at the teams' dinner vigorously applauded when Frank announced that he hoped to play for Australia again. Next day newspapers carried stories of moves to 'keep him for Australian tennis'. One businessman was reported to be ready 'to sit down with others interested to work out a plan whereby Sedgman would be partly compensated for his sacrifice'. Eventually, a public subscription fund raised £5473 10s 3d as a wedding gift for Sedgman and his wife, and Frank was helped to acquire a petrol station as well as an interest in a business making straws.

Twelve months later, when Sedgman and McGregor seemed certain to accept professional offers after the 1952 challenge round, they were tempted to stay 'amateur' with opportunities to work for an insurance company at salaries rising to £5000 and to purchase a string of petrol stations at a very low interest rate. The LTAA attracted to itself charges of hypocrisy by becoming involved in these plans. It was influenced by the fact that the 1951 challenge round had yielded £23,510 (almost three times as much as the 1946 profit) and by the improved gate receipts at the various state championships. In addition, boys and girls all over the continent were learning to play tennis and the game was flourishing as never before. With so much at stake, the LTAA was keen to retain the services of its stars.

Sedgman's biggest year was 1952. He reached all of the Big Four finals, in singles and doubles, though it was not until Wimbledon that he proved irresistible. There, he dropped only two sets, and beat Drobny in the final. He also retained his men's doubles title with McGregor and won the mixed with Doris Hart, becoming one of only three men to achieve the triple. At Forest Hills Sedgman easily defended his US singles championship, but at Longwood he and McGregor were denied a second Grand Slam of doubles titles when beaten by the scratch pair of Seixas and Rose.

In 1952 twenty-two nations challenged in the European Zone, and seedings were used for the first time. Belgium, France, Italy and Denmark went through to the semi-finals. A notable match was that between Yugoslavia and Great Britain on the red clay of the Partizana Stadium at Belgrade. Disaster faced the British at the end of the first day, for although the score stood at one match all, Geoffrey Paish, in his match against Josip Pallada, had taken two heavy falls, knocking himself unconscious in the first, and then seriously twisting his right ankle in the second. Not only would he be unable to play the second singles but he was also out of the doubles. The British captain, Dr Colin Gregory, had been nominated in the team as a playing member. He had to make the very difficult decision whether to put himself alongside Tony Mottram in the doubles or bring in the raw, inexperienced Roger Becker. Gregory was forty-eight years old, but inspite of his age he courageously accepted the responsibility to play himself. He knew that if he played badly there would be a storm of criticism when he returned home. In a sense it was the most important match of his life. Mottram and Gregory won it 'in five nervy sets,' according to Mottram, 'with Gregory hitting his old form of twenty years previously in the fourth and fifth sets'. The British players were as much relieved for their captain as for the victory. He was believed to have been the oldest man ever to win a Davis Cup rubber. The following day Mottram beat Pallada in straight sets for the decisive point.

France lost a close contest to Belgium at Paris, while Italy, which had been reinforced by the unorthodox and cunning Fausto ('The Spider') Gardini, had an easier win over Denmark at Milan. In the European final at Milan, Gardini beat both Washer and Brichant; while the veterans, Cucelli and del Bello, won the crucial doubles for Italy.

There were only four challengers besides the USA in the American Zone, and, using a wide range of players, the States disposed of Japan, Cuba and Canada to line up another visit Down Under.

Two inter-zone finals were played in Australia. In the first, at Brisbane, Italy defeated India, sole challenger to the new Eastern Zone, by three rubbers to two. As usual where Italy was involved, there was plenty of drama. It centred around the excitable Gardini. Despite his odd strokes, he was a tremendous match player, seemingly unbeatable in cup matches on his native soil. In the opening match Gardini was foot-faulted fourteen times for jumping over the line when playing Naresh Kumar, but his strong forehand enabled him to win in four sets. Big-serving Sumant ('Tiny') Misra, a tall, strongly built man, evened the score with a 7–5, 6–4, 6–1 win over del Bello. In the doubles Misra and Kumar won the first two sets 6–1, 6–1, but Misra suffered a hernia in the second set and the Italians won the third set 6–2. Although Misra had the injury strapped during the interval, he was still badly handicapped. He and

Kumar lost the last two sets 2–6, 11–13, after holding three match points in the fifth set.

Misra defied medical advice that he should not play in the final singles and put up a gritty performance against Gardini. Despite another seventeen foot faults, the Italian won 8–6, 8–6, 1–6, 6–4. At the end the two players had the crowd roaring with laughter when they jumped the net simultaneously, hands outstretched in midair but making no contact. They were acting out a cartoon in the programme which had amused them so much that they had agreed, whatever the result, to finish the match that way!

America had sent to Australia the team of Seixas, Trabert, Richardson and Straight Clark. If they were not expected to regain the cup they at any rate were thought to be much too accomplished for Italy. However, in the inter-zone final in Sydney, Gardini shook American complacency when he led Seixas 7–5, 6–3, 3–6, 5–2 and held several match points. With great courage, the Italian followed his unimpressive flat service to the net and from the most difficult positions ingeniously drove-volleyed Seixas's sliced backhand return for winners. Seixas was so surprised by the temerity of his gangling opponent that not until it was almost too late did he get his own attack flowing properly. He pulled out the fourth set at 8–6 and won the fifth 6–3. Another sixteen foot-faults hurt Gardini's chances, but he did not complain.

Trabert easily swept aside the rotund Cucelli, and he and Seixas just as comfortably beat Cucelli and del Bello in the doubles.

The victory over Italy showed that Trabert, who was on leave from the Navy, was approaching good form. Seixas left little doubt about the calibre of *his* game by beating Sedgman in the final of the Victorian championship. America therefore could not be underestimated. The husky, freckle-faced Trabert was only twenty-two years old and was as aggressive as Seixas. A former basketball star from the University of Cincinnati, Tony had a weighty attack without the back-court weakness that was occasionally evident in Seixas's game.

The challenge round was scheduled for Adelaide, where 13,000 of the 15,500 seats at Memorial Drive were temporary. Australia named Sedgman, McGregor, Rose and, for the experience of savouring the atmosphere, eighteen-year-old Lewis Hoad. Sedgman had agreed to join Kramer's professional troupe immediately after the event, using his own market value to obtain the best possible deal for McGregor. Great secrecy was observed to ensure that their amateur status was not infringed before the matches were completed.

Sedgman beat Seixas in the opening singles 6–3, 6–4, 6–3. Both served, volleyed and smashed at their best, but Sedgman was more aggressive with his returns of service. The selectors no longer under-estimated McGregor's temperament. He was preferred to Rose for the second singles and once again he killed American hopes stone dead. Serving powerfully and maintaining a nonstop net attack, McGregor wore down the rugged Trabert, whose lack of match play became increasingly evident. The day was very hot and humid, and Trabert was close to collapse when the match ended 11–9, 6–4, 6–1.

Seixas and Trabert played solidly in the doubles, but Sedgman and McGregor won 6–3, 6–4, 1–6, 6–3. The cup was still Australia's. Sedgman completed three years of cup play without a loss in singles or doubles by beating Trabert 7–5, 6–4, 10–8, but McGregor went down to Seixas.

Next night Sedgman and McGregor informed Sir Norman Brookes of their decision to turn pro. He thought they were making a mistake. He told them they would benefit more from the prestige of being amateurs and picking up opportunities in the business world. Certainly, they could make quick money as professionals, but in the long run the prominence and popularity they had achieved in Australia, said Sir Norman, might be of greater value to them. The fact was there was an immense gulf between the one-time champion and his modern counterparts. Brookes was from a privi-leged class that had never needed to be concerned about financial security. For him professionalism was tainted. They were from typical working-class families and were trained for little else but tennis. They thanked him for his advice and departed.

—13—

TWO BABIES AND
A FOX

(1953, Australia; 1954, USA;
1955–56, Australia)

When Sedgman and McGregor turned professional, Sir Norman Brookes said despairingly to Hopman, 'What will we do?'

'Cheer up,' said Hopman. 'Give me the boys for twelve months and everything will be all right.'

The boys were now eighteen-year-olds Lew Hoad and Ken Rosewall, already known as the 'Sydney twins'. They had come triumphantly through the junior ranks from the age of ten, with Rosewall initially the better because of his back-court accuracy but with Hoad's big hitting later giving him an edge.

The game had known few more rugged characters than Hoad, who built up his physique with a variety of sports and exercises at the Glebe Boys' Club. Hoad had the arms and wrists of an axeman and the cool daring of a high trapeze artist. When he was concentrating fully he could hit winners from any part of the court. Flicked top-spin passing shots, severe backhand smashes, bulletlike volleys – he played them all with apparent nonchalance. Rosewall, at five feet seven, was smaller, less muscular and less flamboyant in his style, but was equally fast and, because of his dedication and consistency, he could be just as demoralizing.

Both the 'twins' left school at fourteen to join sporting goods companies. Some critics were to draw a contrast between their limited schooling and the desire of most young American players to obtain a college education. The *New York World Telegram* called Hoad and Rosewall 'machine-tooled stars, home financed and developed'. They were, however, from a far different social background than most of the leading Americans. Hoad's father was a tramwayman and Lew would have left school early whether he had possessed sporting talent or not. Ken's parents owned a small suburban shop.

With funds generated by the feats of Sedgman and McGregor, the LTAA included Hoad and Rosewall in its 1952 overseas team. Among their achievements that year was Rosewall's defeat of Seixas and Hoad's elimination of Larsen in the American championships. Then, in January 1953, Rosewall denied Rose the opportunity of stepping into Sedgman's shoes by beating him in the final of the Australian championships.

Touring in a team managed by Hopman, Hoad and Rosewall quickly hit form in the Italian championships, where they beat Drobny and Patty in the doubles final. In Paris, Rosewall got through to the singles final and beat Seixas, who had eliminated Hoad. The French doubles title also fell to the youngsters.

At Wimbledon, Rosewall was seeded number one, a well-deserved honour but one which along with all the attention he was getting as an 'infant prodigy', put him under much nervous strain. In the quarter finals, Nielsen beat a tense Rosewall, and Seixas overcame a careless Hoad and went on to win the championship, a good omen for America's Davis Cup prospects. But Hoad and Rosewall were again unbeatable in the doubles.

The American section of the tour did not go as well for the 'twins'. Though Hoad won the Eastern grass-court title at Orange, he and Rosewall lost to Seixas and Trabert in the American doubles championship at Longwood, where the title eventually went to the new combination of Rose and Rex Hartwig. At Forest Hills, Trabert ousted Rosewell, Seixas again had the better of Hoad, and Trabert beat Seixas in the final. America could look forward to its coming Davis Cup campaign with confidence.

Of the twenty-nine nations that played in the 1953 competition, twenty-two entered the European Zone. Nielsen and Washer were the outstanding European players, neither losing a match up to the final. Washer was something of a throwback to an earlier era as he was the managing director of a steel company, a millionaire, and a gifted sportsman who represented his country at golf, squash and tennis as well as being a leading skier. He won a hard five-set match against Gardini in the Belgium v. Italy semifinal in Brussels. Italy's new player, little Beppe Merlo, levelled the tie by beating Jackie Brichant, 10–8 in the fifth set, and Cucelli and del Bello won the doubles to put Italy in front. On the last day Washer accounted for Merlo, and Brichant snatched victory for Belgium by beating Gardini 6–2, 7–5, 4–6, 9–7. In the zone final against Denmark in Copenhagen, Washer and Brichant each beat Torben Ulrich, and they also won the doubles. Nielsen beat Washer to preserve his unbeaten record, but by then the tie had been decided.

The new American captain was Bill Talbert, the first diabetic to become a topline player. After his team had met little resistance in the American Zone he took them to Australia, where the reality was somewhat harsher. Hoad won the Queensland, New South Wales and Victorian championships and in the space of a few weeks became markedly more controlled and menacing. Rosewall was only slightly less formidable. Though he had fallen in love and was having a problem concentrating on tennis, he tested Hoad in the Sydney and Melbourne finals. Seixas was unimpressive, losing early to Worthington in Melbourne, and Trabert lost there to Hartwig in straight sets.

The Belgians faced a daunting prospect in flying to Australia to play the final rounds of the competition on grass after having played thus far on clay. In Perth, they met India, from the Eastern Zone, and won all five matches. On the Indian team was sixteen-year-old Ramanathan Krishnan, a subtle strokemaker who pressed Brichant to five sets in a debut that stamped him as a class player of the future. The Belgium v. USA tie was staged in Brisbane, which in those days was at least ten hours' flight from Perth. When the Belgians arrived, Washer had a shoulder injury which affected his morale, and, after so many solid performances during the year, his 6–4, 6–2, 6–4 defeat by Trabert was disappointing. Brichant had not played as well as Washer up till now, but his team-mate's loss seemed to galvanize him. Using Seixas's own bustling tactics, he beat the American 6–3, 11–9, 2–6, 6–1. When Seixas won the third set, Brichant was expected to fade. But after dropping his serve early in that set, he threw other games to save energy in the tropical sun and his reinvigorated net attack and top-spin passing shots were too much for the Wimbledon champion.

Vic's timing was poor, his confidence low. Talbert did not want to risk him in the doubles, and at the eleventh hour decided to partner Trabert himself. He put young Ham Richardson in the captain's chair so that Seixas could take a complete day off. For

Talbert, the extreme heat was a special danger because of his diabetes and at thirty-five his reflexes were slower than in his prime. But he was a master of doubles play and in Trabert, his protégé, with whom he had won the 1950 French doubles title, he had a partner who could make the most of the openings he created. Moreover, he knew Washer was off form. It was an open secret that the Belgian was so worried about his shoulder that he had threatened not to play unless given a pain-killing injection. Talbert and Trabert won the match 6–3, 6–2, 4–6, 9–7, and on the final day Trabert overpowered Brichant in the decisive rubber.

The challenge round, held at Kooyong just after Christmas, was probably the best ever played in Australia. There was keen human interest in the youthfulness of Hoad and Rosewall, who at the age of nineteen were about to make their cup debut against two mature players who between them held the Wimbledon and US championships. For America, much depended on Seixas. He had beaten Hoad six straight times without loss, yet often had been mastered by Rosewall. If he could regain form, America had a very good chance of victory. The doubles was thought likely to be critical. Australia possessed the Wimbledon champions in Hoad and Rosewall, and a strong reserve combination in Rose and Hartwig, but Seixas and Trabert were an outstanding pair too.

When Seixas and Hoad appeared on the centre court for the opening match a world record crowd of 17,500 craned forward to see them. Many were seated in temporary stands, and as everyone stood for the national anthems, radio commentators in the top row thought they saw the stands move. The anthems were never played again for fear that movement in the structure might cause a panic.

Hoad looked completely relaxed as he gave Seixas a 6–4, 6–2, 6–3 pasting. He served strongly and hit many of his ground strokes so low over the net and so aggressively towards the lines that Seixas was continually off balance.

Australian jubilation was short-lived. In the next match Trabert dispatched a nervous Rosewell 6–3, 6–4, 6–4. Rosewall had two weaknesses. His service lacked pace and his second delivery could be soft and short. Against most opponents his back-court game was so solid it more than atoned for this deficiency, but against a top-class net-rusher, especially on grass, his forehand was suspect. With cool deliberation, Trabert successfully worked on both the chinks in Rosewall's armour, capturing his opponent's first three service games to go to 5–0. Though Ken got back to 3–5, Trabert won the set and never relaxed his grip.

His decisive win cast the Australians into gloom. The selectors, however, had a contingency plan. They had discussed the possibility of Rosewall failing so badly in the first singles that his confidence would be affected for his subsequent matches. In those days 'Muscles', as he was nicknamed, appeared much more frail than he actually was. On the rare occasions that he took a beating he could look such a dejected lad that his tough spirit was underestimated. The selectors themselves were deceived. On 21 December they had watched Hoad and Hartwig, both normally right-court players, beat Sedgman and McGregor in a secret trial at Royal South Yarra Lawn Tennis Club. After Rosewall's defeat, the selectors recalled that match. Hopman argued against splitting Hoad and Rosewall, fearing that Rosewell might lose confidence for his second singles if the selectors showed loss of faith in him. Hopman spoke to some of the selectors, argued his case and later told Rosewell he would be playing the doubles. He was wrong. Only the selectors from Rosewell's home state voted for him. The others, including Brookes, wanted him replaced.

Rex Hartwig hailed from the country town of Culcairn, and like most Australian country boys had struggled for recognition in his junior days. Starved of opportunities and often overlooked for representative teams, he had left home to board in Melbourne and had finally established himself as an international by sheer brilliance. His ground strokes were perfectly timed, his volleys crisp and accurate, and he was known as 'Wrecker' because of his demolition ability. But the years of disappointments had left him with a temperamental flaw. On the biggest occasions in singles he could go off the boil, clutching defeat from the jaws of victory.

After practising with Rosewall on the morning of the challenge round doubles, Hartwig planned to catch a tram and go home for lunch with his wife. Abruptly, he was told that in two hours he would be playing for Australia. He was understandably nervous, though not especially at the prospect of playing in the left court, for he had a very good backhand.

The selectors' gamble might have come off if Hoad and Hartwig had been given more notice and had practised together more often.

Fausto Gardini in action on the first day of hostilities in Milan,
England *v*. Italy, July 1962

India reached the Challenge Round for the first time in 1966.
Posing after the draw at Kooyong are (left to right): Fred Stolle,
Roy Emerson, John Newcombe, Tony Roche, Harry Hopman,
Raj Khanna (Indian captain), Ramanathan Krishnan, Jaideep
Mukerjea, Premjit Lall and Shiv Misra

Roy Emerson. With Ken Fletcher in 1964 he had led a players' revolt which threatened to smash the Australian tennis machine

Jack Kramer as administrator: a force to be reckoned with

August 1969, the Great Britain *v*. Rumania inter-zone final. Ion Tiriac in play against Mark Cox

Mexico's Rafael Osuna: fast, clever, crafty and capable of
pressurizing linesmen

Stan Smith and Bob Lutz: a top Davis Cup combination

Buster Mottram, seen here with his captain, Paul Hutchins, was
one of Great Britain's most dependable players in the 1970s

A young challenger from Sweden

Victory at last. Borg jumps for joy
as Sweden win the Davis Cup for
the first time, in 1975

Bjorn Borg surrounded by some of the thousand policemen drafted
in to prevent violence when Sweden played Chile in 1975

Ilie Nastase: a spot of bother

Raul Ramirez of Mexico, ecstatic after beating Jimmy Connors in a North American zone match in 1976

Great Britain *v*. Italy at Wimbledon 1976. Adriano Panatta in full flight

Like many other great Davis Cup players, Nicola Pietrangeli
(right) became his country's team captain when his playing days
were over. Here he advises Panatta

1908: jubilation sweeps Buenos Aires. Argentina has just beaten the
United States

Top: In the 1980s John McEnroe established himself as one of the greatest Cup players of all time

Bottom: The odd couple: Arthur Ashe and John McEnroe have often had a strained relationship on the US team

Eighteen months later they were to become the Wimbledon champions. Seixas and Trabert made sure the scratch pair did *not* settle down by using a 'scissor' cross-over system against them. Talbert and Mulloy, with the help of the American coach, Mercer Beasley, had developed the system years before. When the Americans were serving, the American at the net would turn his back to his opponents and indicate by a signal to the server whether he intended to cross over or remain in his own court. Thus, the server always knew what his partner was going to do, whereas their opponents had to overcome the psychological hazard of not knowing when the net man was going to dart sideways and poach the ball. An angry Hopman thought Seixas and Trabert went 'close to the border of poor sportsmanship' in holding up the game while the net man made the signal. They certainly prevented the Australians from gaining any coordination and rhythm and they won 6–2, 6–4, 6–4. Perhaps they would have won anyway, for they played with great purpose and understanding.

The defeat created an atmosphere of crisis in Australia, with the selectors taking the unprecedented step of calling a press conference to explain the doubles switch. They were not forgiven. Newspapers highlighted the terrific task now confronting Hoad and Rosewall. 'All Australia Looks to the Tennis Twins', pronounced the Melbourne *Argus* in a front-page headline. Telegrams poured into Kooyong. 'Australian mothers are behind you,' said one message to Rosewall. 'Rats to the selectors,' declared another.

Rosewall's father, who had watched the first two days' play, had to return home. Gerald Patterson thought it might help Ken if his mother could watch him play Seixas, and so he persuaded the International Lawn Tennis Club of Australia to pay her return airfare from Sydney. Hoad, as usual, was phlegmatic, apparently unaffected by nerves. The odds, however, were heavily in America's favour, since only twice had a team come back from 1–2 in a challenge round to win. Lacoste and Cochet had done it in 1927, and Quist and Bromwich in 1939. They had been very seasoned players, whereas Hoad and Rosewall were the youngest and most inexperienced defenders in history.

Trabert and Hoad began by attacking each other with every heavy shot in their armoury, trying to break the other's will. They served thunderbolts and returned the ball with great pace and accuracy.

From the outset there was some needle in the match, for Trabert accused Hoad of serving before he was ready.

Games went with service and the tension mounted. Eleven times Hoad was down game point on service. Each time he got out of trouble. Finally, at 11–12, Trabert was down 30–40. He served to Hoad's backhand and Hoad chipped his return short, forcing Trabert to volley upward. Hoad raced in and Trabert instinctively moved to his left to cover his backhand. Hoad just had enough time to check his shot. He clipped his volley wide of Trabert's forehand for a clean winner.

The crowd's thunderous applause was echoed by groups clustered around radio sets throughout the continent. Outside the stadium, in Glenferrie Road, a tram conductor clambered onto the top of a stationary tram, making sure he avoided the electrified pole. He saw the scoreboard and shouted the news to the passengers.

The Americans hoped Hoad would suffer a letdown, and Trabert took greater risks in trying to hustle him. Time after time, as Trabert charged to the net, Hoad's heavily topped cross-court forehand left the big man standing. Light rain started to fall. It soon made the court slippery and Trabert, the heavier of the two, was most affected. At 1–4 he asked for permission to put on spiked shoes. Referee Cliff Sproule agreed. Hoad was not used to playing in spikes and did not want to wear them. He went to 5–3, but slumped to 15–40 on service. He pulled out two aces, a semi-ace and yet one more ace to win the set.

But Trabert was beginning to look more assured and Hoad more insecure on the damp court. In the third set Lew twice fell heavily and when he was trailing 1–4 he reluctantly agreed with Hopman that he should wear spikes also. He had never practised in spikes and looked uncomfortable. After dropping his serve a second time, he lost the third set 2–6.

The new trend continued after the interval. Trabert could see that his opponent was unhappy playing in spikes. Hoad was unable to slide into his shots and his form had become patchy. At each change of ends Hopman encouraged him to persevere, giving him tips on how to adapt. 'It'll come to you, just keep going.' Trabert now was repeatedly going to the net behind sliced returns that kept low on the wet turf, and Hoad made errors in trying to pass him. When Tony won the fourth set at 6–4 he was clearly on top.

Although it was still raining, the crowd barely noticed how wet they were getting. I recall my notebook becoming sodden, the ink blurring almost illegibly across each page. Neither team asked for a postponement. The Americans thought they had the momentum; the recapturing of the cup seemed but one set away. And as for Hoad, he was gradually getting used to the rain, the slippery court and the wet, heavy balls. Hoad was to serve first in the fifth set, an important advantage. Hopman impressed on him the need to chip the ball to Trabert's feet or wide of Trabert to make him lunge, as this would add to his tiredness.

For most of the fifth set Trabert appeared the most likely winner. He certainly held his service more easily. In the second game Hoad tried to pass him with a backhand down the line. Trabert intercepted the ball and angled it short across court. Hoad made a dash, slipped and fell heavily face down. For a few moments he did not move. Hopman jumped up, grabbing the towel on his lap. As Lew looked up, Hopman threw the towel over his head and said, 'Come on, Musclebound, you can't lie there for ever.' Lew smiled, climbed to his feet and brushed himself down. The tension was broken.

However, in his next service game he was down 30–40. Trabert narrowly missed taking the game with a backhand return which might have decided the match. As in the first set, games went with service . . . 2 all, 3 all, 4 all. In the eighth game Hoad broke a string. The mishap to his favourite racquet might have disturbed him, but was turned to good account. 'The dry and tighter strings in a new racquet will give you an advantage on the wet court,' Hopman told Hoad. Suddenly, Lew was able to impart more pace to his shots.

The score went to 5 all. Trabert had lost only eight points in five service games and still had the edge. But Hoad never stopped aiming for the lines. At 5–6, and after three hours of gut-wrenching suspense, Trabert served again. Hoad's first return was a blinding winner. On the second point, he hit a cross-court backhand which Trabert volleyed up the line. Hoad played a top-spin forehand across court, just over the net. Trabert volleyed it up. Instead of moving in to volley, Hoad stepped back and slammed the ball at Trabert, who got his racquet to it but hit it out. Love–30. Trabert slammed down a cannonball. A fault was called, and the crowd gasped with relief. As Trabert wound up to serve his kicker, Hoad moved and Trabert took his eye off the ball. Tony followed the ball to the net,

183

only to see Hoad angle it sharply across court. The acute angle and the slice on the ball were too much for Trabert – but the serve was called a fault anyway! Most of the drenched gallery did not hear the call and cheered the return. The American imagined they were cheering his double fault. For a few moments he stood with his hands on his hips glaring into the stands. Now he had three match points against him. He served at threequarter pace. Hoad had enough time to move in and take the ball on the rise. He chipped it low and wide of the incoming Trabert, who made a vain attempt to half-volley it back. The ball went into the net. At last the match was over and the stands erupted into prolonged applause. As Hoad walked to the dressing room a man yelled at Prime Minister Robert Menzies, 'Give him a knighthood, Bob – Bradman didn't ever do anything like that!'

Trabert's tears were as much due to frustration as to sorrow. The misunderstanding over the double fault rankled with him. Interviewed by Ted Schroeder on radio, he criticized the crowd for applauding his mistake. 'I disagree with you, boy,' said Schroeder, trying to comfort his countryman. 'I know these people and I don't think a thought like that would enter their minds.'

Rosewall and Seixas had spent an edgy afternoon. Ken had gone for a car drive oblivious of the score until he returned to Kooyong when Hoad was two sets up. Then came Trabert's recovery and all the uncertainty of how the match would finish. When it did finish, the two captains and the referee agreed that the court was too wet for further play and the last match was postponed till next day.

That night the players attended a dinner at Government House. The Davis Cup ball, customary in those days, followed as scheduled, with Rosewall an absentee. For Australia, all now depended on how well he held his nerve. The tension was felt across the nation and work stopped in many offices as the staff gathered around radios. In Sydney police were needed to control crowds flowing onto the roads outside shops and hotels where the broadcast could be heard. It was soon obvious that Rosewall was in command of himself. Seixas adopted the same tactics as Trabert, attacking his forehand and trying to rush him into errors. Ken was steady and produced brilliant passing shots. Concentrating on Seixas's backhand, he took the first set 6–2.

Vic gained the upper hand in the second set. He won it by the same margin, often standing two yards inside the baseline to receive service. In the third set the match tilted Australia's way when three doubtful line calls against the American rattled him, and Rosewell won the set 6–3. He gave Seixas only one more chance to get back into the match – when he was serving for the cup at 5–4 in the fourth set and was down 15–40. He saved one break point, and then Seixas missed a volley that would have made the score 5 all. A greatly relieved Rosewall added the final points for victory.

The roar of applause that rang around Kooyong was deafening, and at least a thousand seat cushions were flung simultaneously into the air and onto the court. It had been an emotional four days, summed up best by Trabert during the closing ceremony. 'I have been playing tennis since I was six years old,' said Tony, 'but this is the first time I have been beaten by two babies and an old fox.'

The immaturity of Hoad and Rosewall was underlined in 1954, when their form was below people's expectations. They failed to win any of the world's major singles titles, though Rosewall was runner-up to Drobny at Wimbledon. Hoad missed the Australian championships because he had to do national service, and a spider bite that he suffered while in the army added to his difficulties. Even more distracting, both the 'twins' were bitten by love. Seixas and Trabert, on the other hand, were close to their peak all year. Trabert won the French championship, and Seixas the American. Their Davis Cup defeat rankled with them and they badly wanted to square accounts.

Mostly, it was the same established players who dominated the European Zone. Davidson carried Sweden through to a 3–2 semifinal victory over Belgium, while the Algerian-born Paul Remy performed a similar role for France against Denmark. Sweden won the final in Paris 5–0, each match being reasonably close. In the American Zone, the USA won three rounds for the loss of one rubber, Seixas's defeat by Gustavo Palafox in Mexico City.

America again took Richardson and another young player, Mike Green, along with Seixas and Trabert to Australia. There, the lead-up tournaments revealed problems in the Australian team, with Hoad's flashes of temper providing the main cause for concern. After he had whacked a ball out of the Kooyong stadium, his mother complained that he had been subjected to too much discipline and needed more time to relax.

Sweden was no match for America in the inter-zone final in Brisbane. The only close match was the five sets Seixas took to beat Bergelin. 'To me,' wrote Adrian Quist in the Sydney *Morning Herald*, 'it seems a great pity that neither the Americans nor the Australians are ever pressed to reach the challenge round. The Davis Cup has become an issue between Australia and the United States.'

The challenge round was scheduled for Sydney, and there was enormous public interest. Almost 16,000 temporary seats were erected at White City, increasing total capacity to 25,578 (a Davis Cup record which still stands). Even so, £90,000 had to be returned to disappointed applicants for tickets. On Boxing Day more than five thousand people paid to watch the final practice sessions and remained for the draw. There was a murmur when Trabert's name was read out first. A roar followed as Hoad's name was announced next. The challenge round was to open with a rematch of the 1953 epic.

Monday, 27 December was warm and gusty, and Trabert realized that Hoad's powerful first serve would be less accurate in the windy arena. Trabert decided to reduce the speed of his own first delivery to make sure of getting it in. Both players twice broke service in the early games, and tension mounted. With Trabert leading 5–4, and Hoad 40–15 up on service, a repetion of the long first-set struggle in 1953 looked likely. But suddenly Hoad faltered. Trabert broke his service to take the first set 6–4.

Cutting down his errors, Hoad won the second set 6–2. Then the match swung again. The Australian's form was erratic, with brilliant shots being followed by simple errors. Down 3–5 in the third set, he fought back and bludgeoned his way to 5 all. Later, he broke through again to go to 7–6. The match was within his grip. He served two aces and reached set point. It was the most important point of the match. Hoad served and went in. Tony hit a backhand return and went in too. Hoad thumped a forehand volley. It flew straight at Tony, who stuck out his racquet and weakly knocked the ball back with a two-handed shot. Caught by surprise, Lew dumped his return just outside the line. The reprieve encouraged Tony, and eventually the set was his 12–10. In the fourth set he maintained his momentum. One break of service gave him the set and the match.

The win removed some of the pressure on Seixas. His plan, as usual, was to attack Rosewell's forehand. But he was determined not to rush his returns. He would make certain of hitting a hard, deep shot before moving to the net. The strategy succeeded, for Vic made fewer errors and achieved a safer net position for his volleys. An increasingly anxious Rosewall, on the other hand, tried to make his first serve more severe and failed to get it in very often. Seixas won the first set 8–6 and had a break point at 5 all in the second set. Then a doubtful line call went against him. He was upset and dropped the set 8–6. But soon Seixas was again playing systematically to Rosewell's forehand. He drove deep or wide before making his charge to the net. Ken's forehand could not cope and he lost the next two sets 6–4, 6–3.

To hold the cup, Australia would now have to reproduce its 1939 feat. The selectors pondered whether to replace Hoad and Rosewall with Wimbledon champions Rose and Hartwig in the doubles. They decided not to. To drop the 'twins' would only be denying them match play and possibly hurting their morale. But when they returned to the court, the strain was obvious. Seixas and Trabert, much the more confident, played a steady, though bustling, type of game, letting their opponents make the errors. They again resorted to signals and confusing cross-overs, but more sparingly than in 1953. Hoad and Rosewall slumped to 2–6, 4–6, 4–5 and 0–40. They gamely saved four match points before conceding the match – and the cup – at 8–10.

Hopman's programme for 1955 was geared towards recapturing the trophy. For a start, he wanted to scrap the Hoad and Rosewall pairing and give Hoad and Hartwig a better chance of developing as a combination. Seixas and Trabert were not being put under sufficient pressure by Rosewall's service. Whereas strong servers often had Seixas in trouble on his backhand side, against Rosewall he could chip low backhand returns and quickly move in alongside Trabert, camped on the net. Other flaws in the Hoad–Rosewall team at this time were its lack of variety and the failure of both players to worry the Americans with their interceptions. The Hoad–Hartwig combination clicked almost instantly in practice matches, with Hartwig taking over the right court.

Hopman had other young players, such as Neale Fraser, Ashley Cooper, Roy Emerson and Malcolm Anderson, in his overseas team, as well as the more experienced Mervyn Rose. No risks were taken with staleness, and the squad skipped the Italian and French championships. The year belonged to Trabert, who won the French, Wimbledon and American championships. In all, he was successful in sixteen of the eighteen tournaments that he entered.

Two days before Wimbledon, and just before he played Rosewall in the Queen's Club final, Hoad was secretly married to Jenny Staley, a member of the LTAA touring women's team. They were soon to be separated because the LTAA made it clear that the rule forbidding wives from being in the same continent as their husbands during a Davis Cup contest would not be relaxed. At Wimbledon Hoad lost to Patty, and Rosewall was beaten by Nielsen, who lost to Trabert in the final. However, Hoad and his best man, Hartwig, won the doubles.

In 1955, thirty-four countries challenged for the cup, and because of the overcrowding a system was introduced whereby a nation could be required to stand down for a year if its standards were assessed as weak. There were many new faces in the teams, among them Robert Haillet of France, Nicola Pietrangeli and Orlando Sirola of Italy. Ulf Schmidt of Sweden, Gordon Forbes and Abe Segal of South Africa, Billy Knight of Great Britain, Luis Ayala of Chile, and Bob Falkenburg, the American winner of the 1948 Wimbledon title, who played for his adopted country, Brazil. The four countries to reach the European Zone semifinals were Italy, Great Britain, Sweden and Chile, with Italy winning the zone by beating Sweden 4–1 at Milan. Australia challenged in the American Zone and beat Mexico, Brazil and Canada before sailing through two inter-zone finals against Japan, the Eastern Zone winner, and Italy. Hoad's form since Wimbledon had been indifferent, and Hartwig had a chance to grab a singles berth in the challenge round. But though he beat Japan's Kosei Kamo and Atsushi Miyagi, his court demeanour told against him.

America was not very confident of staving off Australia's challenge at Forest Hills. For Seixas, who had been beaten by Gil Shea at Wimbledon, the years were beginning to take their toll. And while Trabert was certainly the game's number one amateur, a shoulder injury that he suffered four weeks before the challenge round affected his preparation. For their part, Hoad and Rosewall were concentrating better than in 1954. After reading an issue of *Sports Illustrated*. Hoad was especially keen to get to grips with Trabert. . . .

Possibly Rosewall has improved a little bit [said Trabert], but Hoad has been fairly disappointing. I think it stems from the fact that they were exceptional as young kids. Everyone thought they were sort of cute, sort of phenomenal. They had no reason to get choked up in a match because they were not expected to win often. When they did win, it was great. But after they had won a few tournaments and were expected to win more often, they suddenly felt the pressure the other big players had felt all along. They haven't been able to carry this pressure too well!

The draw was made by the US Secretary of State, John Foster Dulles, a tennis buff who had watched McLoughlin beat Brookes at New York in 1914. Hopman asked him how long he could stay in New York and was informed 'only the first two days'.

'Well, sir, you won't miss anything,' quipped Hopman.

The draw gave Australia exactly what it wanted. Rosewall met Seixas in the first match and beat him 6–3, 10–8, 4–6, 6–2. No longer was Rosewall content to remain on the baseline and foil Seixas with passing shots and lobs. He had begun to develop a net-attacking game, based on a penetrating first volley. Seixas fought tenaciously, but at thirty-two years of age the narrow loss of the second set left him with too big a task.

American stocks sunk further when Hoad beat Trabert 4–6, 6–3, 6–3, 8–6. While neither player was at his best, Hoad produced the more punishing game. Trabert's serving and volleying lacked its usual sting and he had no inspiration off the ground. A blister on his racquet hand added to the American's problems.

In the best match of the series, Hoad and Hartwig beat Seixas and Trabert 12–14, 6–4, 6–3, 3–6, 7–5, with Hartwig the outstanding player. The nervous novice of 1953 was in such great touch that not even the scissors movement could shake him. Australia completed a clean sweep by picking up the final day's singles, Richardson substituting for Trabert in the final rubber. It was America's worst defeat in a challenge round since 1935, but Trabert had some consolation. After the ensuing American championships, in which he beat Hoad in the semifinals and Rosewall in the final, he was rewarded with a contract from Jack Kramer.

By recruiting Trabert, Kramer scuttled the American team. Seixas was past his best, and the younger players, Herb Flam, Ham Richardson, Barry MacKay, Sam Giammalva and Mike Green, were not in the class of Hoad and Rosewall. Kramer also tried to sign the 'twins' so that he could arrange a Kramer–Trabert v. Hoad–Rosewall tour, and he almost succeeded. Hopman, who joined the discussions, believed Hoad should accept Kramer's offer because he would be more suited to professional tennis than a business career. Hopman was equally sure that Rosewall's temperament and style would make it difficult for him to survive in the pro atmosphere (an ironic misconception in view of Rosewall's subsequent long career) and that he had the potential to do well in business. A position with a tinned milk company was duly found for Ken and this, together with his continued 'work' for Slazenger, 'saved him for amateur tennis'. Hoad, whose salary from Dunlop had been boosted, also rejected Kramer's offer and in frustration Kramer built his tour round Trabert, Gonzales, Segura and Hartwig.

Australia watched these manoeuvrings with less apprehension than she had regarded the loss of Sedgman and McGregor, for the obvious replacements for Hoad and Rosewall – all of them employed by sporting goods companies and thus part of the official system – were making rapid progress.

Now, the 'twins' resumed their doubles partnership. With Trabert and Hartwig out of the picture, they were easily the best pair in the world, winning the Australian, Wimbledon and American titles. Hoad's defeat of Rosewall in the 1956 Australian singles championship inspired him to attempt Don Budge's feet of achieving the Grand Slam. He beat Sven Davidson in the French final, Rosewall in the Wimbledon final, and also won the Italian and German titles. He was an overwhelming favourite to win at Forest Hills, but in a brilliant final he was thwarted by Rosewall.

Twenty-two nations challenged for the cup in 1956. Australia's superiority was so clear-cut that most teams must have regarded their mission as futile. Yet, if anything, European rivalry had grown. The last eight in Europe, in their order of meeting, were Denmark, Italy, Germany, France, Belgium, Sweden, Great Britain and Chile.

In Bologna, Pietrangeli, in beating both Nielsen and Ulrich, and sharing in a doubles win with Sirola, made sure of an Italian victory. France comfortably defeated Germany, while Sweden won the first three rubbers against Belgium, though Davidson was taken to a fifth set by Brichant. Great Britain, at Bristol, beat Chile 3–2, mainly because of her doubles strength since Billy Knight and Roger Becker both lost to Ayala. But nobody expected the British to survive against the Swedes in Stockholm, and they were duly humbled.

In Paris the French caused a sensation by winning both the singles against Italy on the opening day. The talented young Pierre Darmon defeated Pietrangeli, 6–3 in the fifth set, and the top-spin control of Paul Remy confounded Merlo in four sets. Pietrangeli and Sirola gave Italy breathing space by beating Remy and the veteran Bernard in the doubles; and Pietrangeli and Merlo showed improved singles form on the third day to give their country a 3–2 victory. Italy then had a fairly straightforward win over Sweden in Båstad, with Pietrangeli beating Davidson, and Merlo getting the better of Schmidt on the first day, and Pietrangeli and Sirola again proving too strong in the doubles.

India's victory over Japan in the final round of the Eastern Zone rested on the doubles. In 1955, Atsushi Miyagi and Kosei Kamo had become the first Japanese pair to win the US doubles championship, but in Tokyo they went down to Kumar and Krishnan in straight sets. Meanwhile, in the American Zone the USA had little trouble, though Mexico kept the final round alive into the third day when, at Rye, Mario Llamas and Francisco Contreras beat Giammalva and MacKay 11–13, 6–4, 1–6, 8–6, 6–3. This was the first rubber ever won by Mexico on American soil.

Italy opted to play her inter-zone final in America rather than Australia. It was an understandable decision as it avoided a long journey to the other side of the world in the middle of winter. Yet with more match play on grass – as they would have had in Australia – they might have reached the challenge round. As it was, they had little more than a week's practice at Forest Hills, and had not played on grass for almost three months since Wimbledon, whereas the Americans in that time had hardly been off the surface. Richardson beat Pietrangeli 6–3, 6–2, 6–3, and Seixas beat Sirola 6–3, 11–9, 6–4. The same players contested the doubles, with a four-set victory going to the Americans.

The Italians' shortsightedness became more apparent when it was announced that America's number one player, Richardson, would not be making the trip to Australia. He had been unsuccessfully negotiating with the selectors to have his wife accompany him at the USLTA's expense, and decided to return to Oxford University, where his studies as a Rhodes Scholar had been jeopardized by his many absences to play tournaments. Seixas, who had begun to form a good doubles partnership with Richardson, was now the only experienced cup player available to America.

The American squad of Seixas, Flam, Giammalva and the youngsters Mike Green and Myron Franks headed for Australia in what was destined to be one of the more pedestrian seasons Down Under. This was as much due to the staging of the Olympic Games at Melbourne, which overshadowed all other events, as to the inevitability of another Australian triumph.

There was some speculation that the twenty-year-old Ashley Cooper, who defeated Anderson, Rosewall and Hoad to win the Queensland championship, would deprive Rosewall of his challenge-round place. Rosewall was under particular strain because it was an open secret that he would turn professional as soon as the challenge round was over. He ended Cooper's chances by beating him in Sydney and Adelaide, and winning the New South Wales, South Australian and Victorian championships.

The challenge round was staged in Adelaide, where crowds of eighteen thousand attended each day. Hoad predictably outgunned Flam, an unusual touch player with a good tactical brain, 6–2, 6–3, 6–3. Seixas, though over the hill and facing his most consistent tormentor, put up a brave showing against Rosewall, who nevertheless beat him 6–2, 7–5, 6–3. American hopes briefly flickered when the virtual scratch pair of Seixas and Giammalva lost only one game in the first set against Hoad and Rosewall in the doubles, but they quickly died as the Australians got on top and won 1–6, 6–1, 7–5, 6–4.

Rosewall was determined to accept Kramer's offer and, on Kramer's behalf, made a last-minute effort in the locker room to persuade Hoad to join him. Lew turned him down. He wanted another year of amateur tennis, another chance to secure the Grand Slam. Lew's ambition was thwarted by Neale Fraser, who toppled him in the semifinals of the Australian championship. When Cooper then beat Fraser to become the new Australian champion, Hopman could afford a contented smile. Partly as a tribute to Harry, the Davis Cup Nations had decided earlier in the year that henceforth the winning captains' names, as well as the players', should be inscribed on the trophy, and he was confident of filling his fair piece of space over the next decade.

Gonzales meanwhile had crushed Trabert in their pro tour by seventy-four matches to twenty-four, and he was to outplay Rosewall by fifty matches to twenty-six. How America missed him in the Davis Cup!

—14—

AMERICA
CALLS ON THE CHIEF

(1957, Australia; 1958, USA)

Hoad's defeat in the 1957 Australian championships, followed by his second-round loss in Paris to Neil Gibson, convinced him he should join Rosewall in the professional ranks. The back injury which would cut short his competitive career was beginning to worry him and he had a family to support. In April Kramer offered Hoad a $100,000 contract to turn professional after Wimbledon, with a $25,000 bonus if he retained his title. He accepted the bait.

Hoad's logical successor in the Australian team was Cooper, who was less endowed with natural talent than many others but was dedicated and intelligent. Cooper was the son of a schoolteacher. His father had taught him the game but wanted him to continue his academic studies, at which Cooper excelled, and become a doctor. Father and son came to a compromise: Ashley would have two years in which to establish himself as a leading player. If he failed, he would go to university. Cooper had heavy legs and relatively cumbersome footwork, which affected his general mobility and his ability to play low volleys. He became a fitness fanatic, trimmed the surplus weight off his thighs, quickened his court movements, and lowered his resting pulse rate to forty-eight. Despite his fitness, he could take only five games off Hoad in the 1957 Wimbledon final.

There were some thrilling Davis Cup encounters this year. Among the twenty-four entrants in the European Zone were the outsiders, Mexico, New Zealand, South Africa and Chile. Five countries entered the Eastern Zone, and seven, including Israel, the American Zone.

Great Britain had two fine players in Bobby Wilson and Mike

Davies. They seemed likely to give their country its best results since the war. In Paris, in the third round, Davies beat Darmon, and Wilson overcame Haillet to put Britain two up. France reduced the deficit by winning the doubles, mainly through the agency of the determined Remy. Then Darmon beat Wilson, 7–5 in the fifth set, and the scene was set for a gripping climax featuring Davies and Haillet. The Frenchman won the first two sets 8–6, 7–5, but Davies kept attacking the net at every opportunity, forcing Haillet to make good shots if he was to win the points. The Welshman never let up with his serving, volleying or smashing, and at last the pressure told on Haillet. Davies won the last sets 6–4, 6–1, 6–4. With a shout of joy, the Welshman leaped the net to console his opponent as fifteen thousand Frenchmen sighed in disappointment.

In the same round, Brichant and Washer of Belgium came from 1–2 down to beat Mexico at the Royal Leopold Club. They then met Great Britain at the same venue. Again, the Belgians were down 1–2. On the third day Washer beat Wilson 3–6, 6–4, 6–4, 6–0, but a British victory looked safely in hand when Davies, the hero of Paris, led 6–1, 6–4 against Brichant. Using a racquet strung more loosely than usual for slow-court play, Davies commanded most of the long rallies, and by again choosing the right ball on which to go to the net he worked himself into an apparently impregnable position. He led 2–0 in the third set, but Brichant recovered and won that set 6–3. Davies also led 3–0 in the fourth set when an inspired burst by Brichant gave him twelve of the next fifteen games. The last two sets were thus the Belgian's, 6–4, 6–2. At the crunch it was Brichant's passing shots and lobs that saved him. A weary Davies could neither pick the direction of the balls that went by him nor anticipate those passing over his head.

On the other side of the draw Italy was too strong for Sweden in Milan, and went to Brussels to play the final. The battling Belgians once more trailed 1–2 after the doubles. Then Brichant beat Merlo 6–8, 7–5, 6–8, 7–5, 6–1. Pietrangeli took a two sets to one lead over Washer, but the Belgian led 2–1 in the fourth set when play was called off because of bad light. Next day Washer won the last two sets 7–5, 6–2 to complete a notable series of Belgian fightbacks.

A more jarring note in Europe was Ireland's default to Hungary. There had been a good deal of civil strife in Hungary following the abortive 1956 revolution, and the Irish players felt that as family men they could not risk injury or death by going to that country. They were unsuccessful in trying to get the tie transferred to Ireland or a neutral country. At the subsequent Davis Cup Nations meeting Ireland wanted the rules changed to cover such contingencies. A majority of delegates felt that politics should not interfere with sport and voted against the Irish motion. The episode foreshadowed the coming political problems over South Africa.

In the Eastern Zone, the smallest man in the competition, Felicisimo Ampon, played the role of a giantkiller as the Philippines defeated India and Japan in Manila. Little more than 5 feet in height and weighing less than 132 pounds, he had been beaten 6–0, 6–0, 6–0 by Frankie Parker in his Davis Cup debut in 1946, but had played many fine matches against some of the world's best players since then.

Any doubts about the composition of the defending team were swept away when the unseeded Malcolm Anderson beat Cooper in the final of the American championship with a brilliant display of free hitting. The son of a Queensland cattle farmer, the rangy Anderson virtually put paid to Rose's hopes of ever forcing his way back into the Australian team as a singles player.

America had used a variety of players in winning the American Zone, and Talbert took to Australia a makeshift team that included Seixas and Mulloy, both past their best, a talented but edgy Flam, and a raw college player, MacKay. The team would have been much stronger had Richardson and Savitt made themselves available. Richardson stepped down because he was not permitted to take his wife, and Savitt remained sour about the events of 1951.

The first inter-zone final in Adelaide did not test the Americans. They defeated the Philippines 5–0. The second inter-zone final, against Belgium in Brisbane, was a different matter. America won largely because Brichant could not cope with the tropical heat and played far beneath his European form.

Talbert's chief problem was in selecting his second singles player. The old warrior, Seixas, now thirty-four, was first choice, but Herbie Flam, the second-ranked American, seemed reluctant to accept the responsibility of representing his country. Because of Flam's attitude, Talbert felt he had no option but to nominate the forty-four-year-old Mulloy. As the team was leaving its hotel to attend the draw, Flam announced that he would like to play. 'You mean that?' replied Talbert. 'That's the first positive statement you have made since we arrived here. All right, you will play,' said Talbert. He thereupon replaced Mulloy's name with that of Flam on the slip of paper he was carrying. Mulloy, who had already left for the draw thinking he was to play the singles, did not learn until the last moment of his replacement.

On the first day Seixas beat Washer 6–0, 6–3, 6–4 and Flam edged out Brichant 6–3, 3–6, 1–6, 6–3, 6–3. The latter match was highly dramatic as both men wilted in the heat, with Flam early on seeming to suffer most. Strained and unsteady, Herbie sometimes staggered like a punchdrunk boxer. Twice he fell and groped for the spectacles that he wore only when playing. Once, befuddled, he began to change ends before a game was finished. Talbert plied him with salt tablets and wrapped wet towels round his neck, and in the last two sets Flam's clever changes of pace got the better of a very distressed Brichant.

Belgium came back into the running when Washer and Brichant defeated Seixas and Mulloy 7–5, 6–3, 4–6, 6–3. Though Mulloy fought all the way, he knew by the end that he no longer possessed the split-second reflexes that high-pressure doubles demands. As for Talbert, he realized that he had to find another pair for the challenge round – if America got that far.

On the third day Flam was little more than a shambling wreck. He had been so sick with worry overnight that he needed medication, and Washer, playing calmly and purposefully, won 6–2, 6–3, 0–6, 6–3. It was left to Seixas to try to pull the tie out of the fire as he faced the man who had beaten him on the same court four years earlier. Vic and Jackie had a terrific first set, which Seixas won at 10–8. Bonny fighter though he was, the Belgian then succumbed to the heat. Feeling that the odds against him were too great, he won only one game in the next two sets. How different from his tremendous recoveries in Europe!

For the challenge round in Melbourne, Talbert replaced Flam with MacKay. Like Trabert, the tall, heavy economics graduate came from Talbert's home city of Cincinnati, and captain and player had a good rapport. MacKay was inexperienced, but he was a fighter and possessed a blistering service. His serving would have been more effective still but for his tendency to double-fault.

The first match, Cooper *v.* Seixas, went to five sets and, had Cooper lost his nerve, Seixas might well have won. Cooper resolutely maintained his serve-and-volley pressure throughout the fifth set and one break of service was enough to give him the match 3–6, 7–5, 6–1, 1–6, 6–3. The second match also went to five sets. MacKay's twenty double faults were the difference between victory and defeat, Anderson winning 6–3, 7–5, 3–6, 7–9, 6–3. For the doubles, Hopman paired Anderson and Rose. The guileful left-hander made a splendid return to Davis Cup play as Seixas and MacKay went down 6–4, 6–4, 8–6. The Americans consoled themselves by winning the last two rubbers to reduce the Australian margin to 3–2.

Most of the big tennis events of 1958 emphasized Australia's apparent superiority. Cooper won the Australian, Wimbledon and American championships, with Fraser runner-up at Wimbledon, and Anderson at the other two tournaments. The championships of Italy and France were won by Rose.

In America there were rumblings of discontent at the succession of Davis Cup failures. These erupted into a revolt when the Eastern leadership of the USLTA was deposed and replaced by a combination of Middle Western, Far Western and Southern officials. Among their first acts was the sacking of Talbert as cup captain in favour of Perry T. Jones, the seventy-year-old Californian administrator who had never been a leading player and had never seen a challenge round. Jones, who had been a father figure to such players as Kramer, Schroeder and Gonzales, announced that Kramer would take over the coaching of the 1958 team. A Peruvian named Alejandro (Alex) Olmedo, a student at the University of Southern California, was Jones's latest protégé. Olmedo had won the US Intercollegiate singles and doubles championships in 1956 and was to win them again in 1958, as well as the National doubles championship with Richardson.

Olmedo's selection in the US team met with some criticism because he was not an American citizen (and so not liable to the military draft). Nor, at that time, did he have any intention of changing his status. There was no doubt, though, that he was eligible to play for America under the rule allowing a nation to name a player who had been a resident for three years and who had not represented any other country. In 1930 John Doeg, who was born in Mexico, had qualified to play for America under the same rule. American objections to Olmedo's inclusion might have been stronger had anyone suspected he would play a leading role in the cup campaign. He figured in none of the ties in the American Zone and was expected, at the most, to play only in the doubles in Australia. The main burden of America's challenge appeared to rest with Richardson and MacKay.

Thirty-six nations issued challenges in this year. Great Britain, with Becker and Knight helping out Davies and Wilson at Scarborough, scored an impressive 5–0 win over Germany, whose Willie Bungert was a rising star. The French, at home, beat Sweden, but in the semifinals were no match for the British on Manchester turf. Italy's Pietrangeli and Sirola formed the strongest European team, and in the final in Milan they accounted for Davies and Knight after Pietrangeli had lost his opening match with the Welshman.

There was growing resentment among some of the nations at the way the competition was being dominated by two countries. Most tennis around the world was not played on grass, yet until some nation could break the American–Australian monopoly of the challenge round and win the cup, the destiny of the trophy looked like always being determined on grass on which the big-serving Americans and Australians were supreme. As Sirola put it, 'Australia and America don't care who wins the Davis Cup, just so long as it is one of them. They're getting all the money between them and don't care about us.' Sirola might have been even more cynical if he had realized how much money was involved. In seven challenge rounds in Australia between 1951 and 1958, Australia and America split more than £370,000.

In 1958 Argentina wanted to play the American Zone final in Buenos Aires, where the matches would have stimulated great public interest. America insisted on the final being played at Rye, and duly won it 5–0. 'We have no choice about where we play and we have no choice of the surface we can use,' complained the Argentian player Enrique Morea. 'We are forced into long trips and are given little consideration on expenses.' Like other critics, he could not see why so many of the key contests should be played on grass when most of the world's players played all their tennis on clay.

The Italians also were disgruntled when required by Australia to play the first inter-zone final, against the Philippines, in Sydney and then to travel to the other side of the continent to play America in Perth. They argued that if they won in Sydney (as they did) they would have only a few days in Perth to acclimatize. Their objections were overruled and they did not produce their best form. Pietrangeli took the first set against Olmedo 7–5 and led 8–7 and 30–0 on his service in the second set. But when Olmedo saved the second set at 10–8, the Italian lost heart and won only one more game. Richardson beat Sirola in straight sets, and he and Olmedo won the doubles 7–9, 6–4, 13–11, 7–5.

The use of Olmedo against Italy suggested he might play in the challenge round in Brisbane. As his selection became more likely, so did the acrimony surrounding the American team become increasingly bitter. Kramer was the target for much of the vitriol. Besides being the US coach, he remained very much a private promoter. He had fallen out with Australian officials, who were angry at his clear intention to keep waving his chequebook in front of their players. Kramer was reported to have said that he could destroy the entire Davis Cup structure by signing up all the world's leading amateurs, a boast that Basil Reay, the ILTF secretary, described as 'disgusting'. The czar of pro tennis was also arguing with officials over his troupe's coming tour of Australia, and it seemed that it would be banned from playing in any of the main stadiums. To make matters more difficult, Kramer had signed Cooper and Anderson to join the troupe after the challenge round. When he indiscreetly told a reporter that they were favourites to retain the cup for Australia, he infuriated Richardson. Ham accused Kramer – unjustly – of trying to fix the matches to ensure a Cooper–Anderson triumph. Gradually, the American number one had realized from the rumours that were circulating that Kramer did not want him to play in the singles. Like Talbert, Richardson was a diabetic, and Kramer believed that he was not strong enough to endure a three-day ordeal in the heat and humidity of Brisbane. In addition, Richardson's second service lacked overspin, said Kramer, and Cooper and Anderson would play havoc with it. Richardson had not done his cause any good by losing to Bob Mark in the third round of the New South Wales championships and resting during the Victorian titles.

In fact, Kramer's preference was for Earl Buchhalz, rather than

Olmedo, but Jones was keen to play the Peruvian. In America, *Sports Illustrated* said that Kramer's position was untenable.

It has become the vogue recently for men to take up conflicting interests and to defend that act with the assertion that everybody knows they are honest. There is an older tradition which seems to us better: to avoid conflicts of interest so that one's acts don't need defending.

Two days before the challenge round Richardson discovered that Olmedo and MacKay would definitely play the singles and that he would be confined to the doubles. He was outraged. He and his wife packed their suitcases, ready to fly home. Then he went to the races instead of practising with the rest of the team.

Richardson's background made his anger understandable. He had first won notice when he was seventeen by putting the reigning champion, Patty, out of the 1950 Wimbledon tournament. He had been associated with American teams since 1951, yet for one reason or another had never played in a challenge round. This time, said Richardson, he and the Louisiana senator who employed him as a research assistant had agreed that he should go to Australia only after the USLTA told the senator that without him America's chances were hopeless. The association had been so grateful, said Ham, it had even permitted him to take his wife on the trip.

Less than forty-eight hours before the matches were scheduled to begin the American team could hardly have been in more disarray. From his hotel room Richardson issued a long typewritten press statement in which he accused Jones of being unfair and discourteous, but said he would do his best in the doubles 'for my country and not Mr Jones'. On another floor of the hotel Jones also called a press conference. He read a statement defending his actions, which had been prepared by Kramer's publicity man.

The least agitated of all was Olmedo, otherwise known as 'The Chief' because of his Inca blood. Few people knew much about him or gave him much chance of winning. Olmedo was one of eleven children in a poor family, and had been discovered in Peru by an American coach, Stanley Singer, who, with George Harten, president of the Peruvian LTA, collected funds to get him to Los Angeles. He arrived there at the age of seventeen not knowing any English and with only a few dollars in his pocket. Alex was befriended first by a sports shop owner, who found him a cheap apartment and introduced him to night school, and then by Jones, who arranged for his enrolment at college. Periodically, however, the Chief was trailed by FBI agents who suspected him of being an illegal Mexican migrant. In time Jones groomed him to the stage where he was ready to play in a challenge round. 'I had no desire to be a US citizen,' Olmedo recalled years later, 'but this [America] was my home. I was playing with guys I'd grown up with in tennis, and I sure wanted to win for the US, and for Peru, too, to show that a Peruvian could play very good.'

It was an odd event. On paper the Americans looked outclassed against the world's top two amateurs, who had the astute Hopman to guide them through any rough patches. On the other hand, Olmedo and MacKay were relaxed and had nothing to lose, whereas both Cooper and Anderson had part of their minds on Kramer's contracts. Cooper, in addition, had a further reason to be distracted as he was to be married to a former Miss Australia at the end of the week.

A crowd of 17,880 turned out to watch Brisbane's first challenge round. They were amazed to see Olmedo beat Anderson in the opening match 8–6, 2–6, 9–7, 8–6. Anderson's ability to make his usual brilliant shots was affected by nerves. Though he hit more winners than Olmedo, who had very ordinary ground strokes, he committed more mistakes. Overnight rain had made the court spongy and slippery, and both players used spikes, Olmedo for the first time in his life. The Peruvian was very nimble and had a fine, feathery touch and instinctive court craft. As Olmedo piled up points, captain Jones often led the applause, jumping excitedly to his feet and gesticulating.

Cooper made the score one match all by beating MacKay 4–6, 6–3, 6–2, 6–4. He too was nervous, but he benefited from MacKay's decision not to use spikes until the fourth set.

The successful duo of Anderson and Rose was no longer intact. Rose had been suspended by the LTAA for accepting unauthorized expense money in Europe and had turned professional. His place alongside Anderson was taken by Fraser, who had waited almost as long as Richardson to get a challenge-round match. The doubles was remarkable in that Richardson did not seem to be affected in the slightest by his deep anger and disappointment. If anything, his row with Jones made him produce his best. The Australians won the first two sets 12–10, 6–3, but Richardson and Olmedo took the third 16–14 when a jittery Anderson dropped his serve in the thirtieth game. During the interval Gonzales, who was broadcasting from a position at the top of the temporary stands, took the trouble to visit the American locker room and suggest that the tandem formation (in which the server and the man at the net stand on the same side of the court) be used on some of the important points when Fraser was receiving service. Up to then Fraser had been the best player on the court. But Fraser's backhand down the line was his weakest shot, and by introducing an element of uncertainty and sometimes preventing him from using his cross-court backhand, American tactics over the last two sets tipped the match their way, 6–3, 7–5. Even so, the struggle was fairly even until 5 all in the fifth set. Then, with Anderson serving, the Americans caught the Queens-lander with a series of well-placed returns to his feet, and volleyed winners as he scrambled the ball up. That gave them the vital breakthrough and they sealed victory after four hours eight minutes and eighty-two games – the longest doubles match in terms of the number of games in challenge-round history.

The Australians had their backs to the wall. Cooper was still expected to be too sound for Olmedo, but nobody was game to predict the result of the Anderson *v*. MacKay match. To everyone's surprise, the copper-skinned Olmedo, with hardly a singles title to his credit, beat the Wimbledon, American and Australian champion 6–3, 4–6, 6–4, 8–6 to give America the cup. He did it by simply outsteadying his opponent, who was nervous and lost confidence in his second serve. Sometimes Cooper was so shaky he would halt in his service swing and catch the ball. The Chief, it seemed, had been well briefed by Kramer and Gonzales. He moved in on Cooper's second delivery, pushing the ball down the line and following it to the net. Then he confused the Australian by carefully and deliber-ately steering his volleys past him.

When it was over, Olmedo smiled broadly at Jones. 'Well, we did it, Captain,' he said, and they hugged each other. Suddenly, Olmedo broke away from his benefactor, buried his head in a towel and sobbed.

Many Americans seemed embarrassed by the victory. Arthur Daley in the *New York Times* said the only decent thing America could do was send the trophy to Peru and hold the next challenge round in Lima. 'A sportsminded nation of 171 million persons can't even find three players good enough to wrest the cup from Australia with a population of 9,640,000. So a foreigner is recruited to do the job that this country can't do by itself,' wrote Daley. The United Press correspondent Oscar Fraley also felt the victory damaged America's reputation for sportsmanship. He wrote: 'The score should read, Alex Olmedo of Peru, 2½ points; Australia, 2 points; United States, ½ point.'

There were no such recriminations in Peru. The country rejoiced in Olmedo's glory. Washington was happy too, and the State Department paid for a trip home by the Chief, accompanied by the Davis Cup.

THE LATINS
BREAK THROUGH

(1959–62, Australia)

With Olmedo and MacKay likely to improve, and Cooper and Anderson out of the way, America could be excused for feeling complacent. Olmedo soon showed he was no flash in the pan by winning the Australian championship and the US indoor title. In July he became the Wimbledon champion with a straight sets win over Rod Laver in the final. The little Queenslander had beaten MacKay in the semifinals after MacKay had eliminated Fraser.

Fraser was Hopman's most experienced player as the Australian captain rebuilt his team. The Melbourne left-hander had been on the team since 1955 without ever getting a game until he played in the 1958 doubles. The son of a licensing court judge, he had been, for most of his career, 'always the bridesmaid, never the bride', overshadowed first by Hoad and Rosewall, both of whom were slightly younger, and then by the also younger Cooper and Anderson. Far from discouraging him, the continual frustration only made Fraser more resolute and appreciative of success when it duly arrived in his twenty-sixth year. His main weapon was a viciously swinging and kicking service which could be devastating on grass.

Laver was then still under twenty-one years of age. He had grown from being a scrawny and sickly child on his parents' cattle farm at Gladstone into a wiry and highly aggressive, though small, tennis player sardonically nicknamed 'Rocket', and in 1959 he became the Australian singles and doubles champion. With his ability to hit winners from all parts of the court, Laver had more talent than any of the other members of the Australian squad – Fraser, Roy Emerson, Bob Mark, Ken Fletcher and Martin Mulligan – but it is worth noting that initially they were all considered pretty ordinary by the somewhat spoiled Australian public.

Forty-two nations issued challenges in 1959. In Europe, Poland, a semifinalist of 1958, lost its opening tie to Brazil, and in the third round Great Britain just squeezed past Chile at Bournemouth when Wilson beat Patricio Rodriguez on the third day. In the semifinals Italy was too strong for France, and Britain lost 3–2 to Spain in Barcelona, where Manuel Santana beat Davies in five sets in the last match. In the final in Milan, Italy won the first three rubbers.

After Wimbledon the Australians gave themselves three weeks in which to adapt to Mexico City's altitude. They had a nasty shock when Fraser was stricken by appendicitis pains, and for two days it was touch and go whether he would need an operation. Gradually the pains disappeared and he was given a medical clearance. In the opening match his fighting spirit saw him through to a five-set win over Antonio Palafox. Laver lost to Mario Llamas; Fraser and Emerson, the Wimbledon champions, won the doubles; and Laver clinched victory by narrowly beating Palafox.

Australia overcame Canada and Cuba, her other opponents in the American Zone, more easily and then beat Italy 4–1 in the first inter-zone final at Germantown, with Emerson losing a 'dead' rubber to Pietrangeli. The following week, at Longwood, Australia beat India, winner of the Eastern Zone, but only after the artistic Krishnan had bamboozled Laver in the first match.

In approaching the challenge round, scheduled for Forest Hills from 28 to 30 August, America's principal concern was to decide on a doubles pair. With Richardson, Seixas and Savitt unavailable, the selectors opted for Olmedo and the eighteen-year-old Buchhalz. The two played together successfully at Merion and Orange, and led Fraser and Emerson in the final of the Nationals by two sets to one, losing only at 7–5 in the fifth set.

The flamboyant Perry Jones moved his players into Manhattan's swish Waldorf Astoria, saying they deserved nothing but the best. He predicted a 5–0 whitewash. Hopman more cautiously suggested a 3–2 victory for Australia, believing Olmedo must be favoured to win two singles. 'Hopman,' wrote New York sports columnist James A. Burchard, 'is trying to whistle his way past a graveyard – a graveyard that soon may be loaded with fallen Down Under tennis players.'

In the opening match on a very hot and humid day Fraser shook the tennis world by beating Olmedo 8–6, 6–8, 6–4, 8–6. He had developed a new spin service and Olmedo could make nothing of it. Neale was also able to cover up his usual backhand weakness, and his returns in the fourth set were so effective they prevented Olmedo from pulling up.

MacKay avenged his five-set Wimbledon loss to Laver by blasting him off the court 7–5, 6–4, 6–1 with powerful serving. In the doubles it was again Fraser's service that did much of the damage. He and Emerson beat Olmedo and Buchhalz 7–5, 7–5, 6–4, with Emerson's returns and interceptions reminding Jones of Zorro ('He struck and stabbed us silly!').

Olmedo regained some of his best form in his duel with Laver. In the longest four-set challenge-round match to that time, he won 9–7, 4–6, 10–8, 12–10 in three hours twenty minutes. Laver could well have won, for in each of the three sets that he lost, his inexperience allowed Olmedo to save set points.

MacKay and Fraser did not step onto the horseshoe-shaped arena for the deciding match until close to six o'clock and realized there was little chance of a finish that night. Fraser took the first set at 8–6, and MacKay the second 6–3 before the postponement was called. Next day, MacKay's twenty-fourth birthday, a further delay was caused by rain. Then, after a few games, both players put on spiked shoes. Fraser scrambled out of early trouble and won the third set 6–2, after MacKay had floundered in a morass of double faults. More double faults plagued MacKay in the fourth set. He held service to 4–5, and was then down 30–40, match point. Slamming a serve to Fraser's backhand, the 'Bear' charged to the net. Fraser lobbed. Despite his height, MacKay could not reach the ball. He spun round and rushed back to the baseline, frantically flicking at the ball as it was about to bounce for the second time. The ball flew out of court, and Fraser, who had been mesmerized as he watched the American, shouted, 'You beauty!', flinging his racquet high in the air. After only eight months in America, the cup faced another journey.

Fraser confirmed his mastery of Olmedo by beating him in the final of the US championship, and when Alex departed for the pro ranks his record had lost some of its gloss. Fraser, too, was offered a contract by Kramer. He was enjoying his amateur successes too much to accept it, and when he won the Wimbledon championship the following year, beating Laver in the final, his Cinderella story was complete.

The year 1960 marked the first time since 1904 that a nation outside the so-called Big Four reached the challenge round. Italy was clearly the strongest European tennis power, and in this year the Italians won their zone for the seventh time since 1948. Their past efforts had always ended in anticlimax when they took on the Australians or Americans on grass. Now they had Drobny as team manager and his guidance helped them do better.

In Pietrangeli, who won his second French title in 1960, Italy possessed the best clay-court performer and one of the most gifted players in the world. With his flowing ground strokes and fine touch, he played an elegant, unhurried game. Some observers thought he should have hurried a little more, for the charming Nicky, who came from a prosperous Turin family, was probably too easygoing to train hard, and sometimes on a court he could look lackadaisical. The 6-foot 3, 224-pound Sirola came from a very different background. He was born of humble parents in Fiume, his father being a Hungarian, and his mother a Slav. As a teenager, Sirola fought with the Yugoslav partisans in the Second World War, spent a brief spell in a concentration camp, and was then a slave labourer. After the war, somewhat incongruously, he worked for a knitting firm, and it wasn't until he was twenty-four that he turned to tennis seriously. Relaxed and humorous, he used to say that even the biggest matches held no tension for him. 'I have known the ultimate fear; I am a father,' said Orlando. 'Playing in a challenge round cannot be more frightening than becoming a father.' Despite their different make-ups, Pietrangeli and Sirola were an excellent doubles pair and in twenty-four cup matches had yet to be beaten.

The European Zone was so crowded in 1960 that New Zealand could not be found a place and had to switch to the American Zone. As it turned out, there would have been room after all, for the scheduled Turkey v. Brazil contest never got to court, Turkey being preoccupied by a revolution.

A significant result was Sweden's 3–2 win against the previous year's finalist, Spain, in Stockholm in the second round. The elegant Andres Gimeno beat both Jan Erik Lundquist and Ulf Schmidt, but his team-mate, Manuel Santana, yielded both his singles, and the tie turned on the doubles in which Lundquist and Schmidt beat Gimeno and Juan Arilla. Belgium beat Brazil 3–2, with Washer playing his 100th and last rubber. When Belgium met Great Britain in the next round, Washer, who was losing interest in tennis, was absent playing golf!

In the quarter finals Chile's great warrior Luis Ayala gave Italy a fright in Turin by winning both his singles, France routed Denmark, Sweden put out Germany and Britain disposed of the weakened Belgians. For the semifinals, Sweden brought back its old stalwart Davidson in place of the injured Schmidt, and he and Lundquist won the first three rubbers against France in Båstad. Britain chose Wimbledon as the venue for its clash with Italy, but was not greatly assisted by the surface. Pietrangeli beat Wilson, Sirola outsteadied Davies in five sets and the Italians inevitably won the doubles.

Sweden and Italy thus met in the final for the third time in six years. On this occasion, in Båstad, Lundquist beat Sirola in the opening match, only to see Pietrangeli level with a four-set win over Schmidt. The Italians won a tight five-set doubles; and on the third day Sirola secured the winning point against Schmidt.

America was regrouping under a new captain, David Freed of Salt Lake City. He had in his squad Tut Bartzen (as assistant), MacKay, Buchhalz and two youngsters, Chuck McKinley and Dennis Ralston. After crushing Canada, they travelled to Mexico City, where they drank only bottled water and Mrs Freed did all the cooking in an attempt to avoid stomach upsets. Mexico thought she might beat the visitors because of the emergence of Rafael Osuna, a fast, clever, all-court player with an effervescent personality, who had won the Wimbledon doubles title with Ralston only a few weeks before. Osuna justified their hopes. He outplayed MacKay (aided by the American's twenty-one double faults) and was swept by an excited crowd to the locker room amid cries of 'Olé!' Buchhalz dropped the first set to Llamas but took the next three. The doubles was a tense affair, with MacKay and Buchhalz coming from behind to win 2–6, 6–4, 7–9, 6–4, 7–5. Buchhalz broke a blood vessel in his leg during the doubles, and that night he went to MacKay's room to tell him to make sure of winning next day. 'If it goes to a fifth match,' said Buchhalz, 'I'll never win with this leg.' MacKay was used to pressure. Keeping his serve under better control, he rushed the net against the deliberate Llamas and won the vital rubber 6–2, 6–4, 1–6, 12–10.

Before the Americans flew to Australia, Fraser and Emerson had defended their US doubles title, and Fraser had won his second successive US singles title, with Laver runner-up. The trio looked too strong for any challenger.

In Brisbane, America inevitably overpowered the Philippines, winner of the Eastern Zone, but the second inter-zone final, against Italy in Perth, was rather more sensational. The first two singles were close: Buchhalz beat Sirola 6–8, 7–5, 11–9, 6–2, and, in a match that stretched over two days, MacKay defeated Pietrangeli 8–6, 3–6, 8–10, 8–6, 13–11 after saving eight match points. Pietrangeli wept at losing such a cliffhanger, but the Italians did not give up. They got back into the contest by beating the eager, though youthfully unstable, Buchhalz and McKinley 3–6, 10–8, 6–4, 6–8, 6–4. The Americans had a service break in the fifth set when, with Buchhalz serving at 3–2 and the score deuce, McKinley hit the net with his racquet in putting away a 'sitter'. They lost that game and never regained the initiative. After the last point McKinley, who always played with the intensity of a firecracker, vented his frustration by hurling his racquet out of the arena. It landed amongst a group of Italian fans, who had to be pacified by the diplomatic Sirola before they stopped berating the Americans. Chuck was later suspended by the USLTA over the incident.

Italian morale was so high that Pietrangeli and Sirola could hardly wait to play the last two singles. Pietrangeli beat Buchhalz in yet another five-set match, and then the two biggest men in the game confronted each other. Pounding down his serves from nine feet above the ground, Sirola played the match of his life to beat MacKay 9–7, 6–3, 8–6. Italy at last had broken the Australian–American monopoly, and America was out of the challenge round for the first time since 1936. All the nations which entered the competition each year without any hope of winning more than one or two rounds drew encouragement from Italy's success. One day they too might unearth a couple of champions who could take them into a challenge round. . . .

Alas, in Sydney the Italians were outclassed. Fraser was not fully fit, having irritated a bursa behind his left knee. Nevertheless, he was too accomplished for Sirola, winning in four sets. Laver's brilliance gave him a straight-sets victory over Pietrangeli, and in the doubles the Italians' unbeaten record was ended by Fraser and Emerson. Laver's defeat of Sirola made the tally 4–0, but Pietrangeli reduced the margin by beating Fraser.

In 1961 Italy remained Europe's strongest nation, Spain having been weakened by the defection of Gimeno to the pro ranks. However, both Pietrangeli and Sirola were beaten by Brichant before Italy overcame Belgium. Another upset in the early rounds was Bobby Wilson's loss to Austria's Franz Saiko. Against Germany in Munich, Sirola fell to both Willie Bungert and Christian Kuhnke and the decisive fifth rubber had to be postponed overnight with Pietrangeli and Bungert 3 all in the fifth set. When the match was resumed Bungert immediately broke the Italian but then lost the next three games.

In the European final in Milan, Lundquist got Sweden off to a good start by defeating Pietrangeli, and Schmidt led Fausto Gardini, whom Italy had chosen in place of the injured Sirola, 4–6, 6–4, 6–1, 3–1, when the Swede pulled a muscle and won only one more game. Italy eventually sealed a 4–1 victory.

Neale Frasser's leg injury worsened and he failed in all but one of the singles events that he entered in 1961. Since it was Laver who won the Wimbledon crown, and Emerson who succeeded at Kooyong and Forest Hills, Australia did not have anything to worry about. But a cloud hung over Fraser's career as he underwent surgery in Melbourne.

David Freed had expressed regret in 1960 that America was required to play the Philippines in Brisbane because the attendance was poor, whereas the same tie held in Manila might have attracted several thousands. Now, the regulations were changed to permit the staging of inter-zone finals on a home-and-away basis, and ironically, it was the USA who suffered most over the next few years. America had lost MacKay and Buchhalz to Kramer's troupe, but won her zone after surviving another torrid battle with Mexico, this time in Cleveland. It was Ralston's turn to be suspended; he was accused of misconduct during his losing doubles with McKinley against Osuna and Palafox.

In the first inter-zone final in Delhi, America beat India, after both McKinley and Whitney Reed had lost to Krishnan. McKinley subsequently returned home to his university studies and was replaced for the second inter-zone final by Jon Douglas. In the opening match in Rome, Gardini easily won the first two sets against Douglas and led 5–2 in the third set, but somehow Douglas saved that set. After the interval Gardini became affected by cramp and fatigue, and the match slipped away from him. The second match was postponed because of fading light at 4 all in the third set, with Reed leading by two sets to love. In the morning Pietrangeli took control and won in five sets. Reed and Donald Dell picked up only four games in the doubles, and Pietrangeli made sure of Italy's second successive challenge-round appearance with a convincing win over Douglas.

Since Gardini declined to go to Australia unless guaranteed a singles berth, the party consisted of Pietrangeli, Sirola, Sergio Tacchini, Sergio Jacobini and team manager Drobny. It is interesting to note that although Tacchini was then little known outside Europe he was to become in another twenty years one of the best known names in the international clothing business. Laver was certain to play for Australia, but the second singles player was unknown up till the draw. Though Fraser struggled grimly to hold on to his place, he was still not fully fit, and Emerson, who did better in the Australian tournaments, could not be denied. At Kooyong, in a one-sided challenge round, Emerson was at his fleet-footed best as he whipped Pietrangeli 8–6, 6–4, 6–0. Laver beat Sirola just as quickly, and the doubles went to the Wimbledon champions Fraser and Emerson.

For the first time since the war no temporary seating had been needed at Kooyong, and the twelve thousand fans who paid to watch the matches were disappointed by what they thought were the Italians' listless endeavours. The fans underestimated the calibre of their own players, for a line-up of Laver and Emerson, with Fraser and Fred Stolle in reserve, ranked with some of the best teams of all times. But perhaps too the very efficiency of Australia's tennis machine was beginning to dampen public interest. No other country exploited the amateur rules so effectively as Australia in this period. Since 1935, for instance, the ILTF had had a rule limiting a player to receiving travelling and other expenses for a maximum of eight weeks in any year unless he was travelling as a member of an official national team. The leading Australians invariably made their tours

– and long tours they were – as members of the Australian national team. Such tours were financed by Davis Cup profits, and because tournaments around the world were eager to secure the Australians' appearance, they readily reimbursed the LTAA. At the same time, virtually every top Australian was employed by a sporting goods company. Apart from learning to string racquets, all a player was expected to do was win tennis matches and promote the companies' products by playing exhibitions when in Australia. Hoad had joined the Dunlop company at fourteen, received all the equipment he required, and had two afternoons off each week to practise with Adrian Quist, a Dunlop director. Laver, who went straight to Dunlop from secondary school, admitted that 'from the age of fifteen I was a tennis pro. I didn't sign a contract until much later, but obviously I was a pro.'

The Americans by contrast were more conscientious in observing the spirit of the amateur rules. Most, as we noted earlier, came from a different social class than the Australians, and both they and the US administrators thought a college education should take precedence over a game. It wasn't until after America had received repeated drubbings, and after the conservative Eastern control of the USLTA was broken, that American officials adopted a more permissive attitude to 'shamateurism'.

The challenge-round format, and the influence that grass played in the closing stages of the competition, also favoured Australia in the fifties and sixties. In 1960 there was a significant change in the rules. America persuaded the Davis Cup Nations to include cement as one of the approved surfaces in the competition. Some nations doubted the wisdom of the change and abstained from voting. Australia was not one of them and voted for the proposal. As a result of the change, Davis Cup ties could be staged on America's West Coast, where cement courts were predominant and the game was very popular.

The year 1962 is best remembered for Laver's Grand Slam. He beat Emerson in three of the big finals and Martin Mulligan in the fourth. The year was also notable for the rise of Mexico as a Davis Cup force.

In Europe the highlight of the first round was Germany's defeat of Spain in Madrid, but Santana was handicapped by a high temperature which partly accounted for his losses to Bungert and Ingo Buding. One of the new personalities of the European Zone was a young South African, Clifford Drysdale, making his first overseas tour. With his penetrating double-handed backhand, Drysdale helped South Africa beat France and Germany and so reach the semifinals. He followed up his Berlin win over Bungert by beating Schmidt in Båstad, but that was the only rubber Sweden conceded to the Springboks. The other European semifinal was between Great Britain and Italy in Milan, the British winning only three sets. Sweden took extreme measures to win the final, luring Drobny away from the Italians and persuading its players to stay home during Wimbledon and work on their clay-court games. This approach was successful. Italy made a promising start when Gardini defeated Schmidt, but Pietrangeli was devoid of confidence and the Swedes won 4–1.

America's new captain, Bob Kelleher, a Californian lawyer, led the USA to a 5–0 win over Canada, and then took his team to Mexico City in early August. Kelleher chose McKinley and Douglas for the singles, and McKinley and Ralston for the doubles. After McKinley beat Osuna, Douglas lost to Palafox, and America's plans went further awry in the doubles. Osuna completed a stirring Mexican victory by beating Douglas, 6–1 in the fifth set. It was the first time that any country other than Australia had defeated the States in the American Zone, and there were joyous scenes at the Chapultepec Club, with Osuna being carried off the court shoulder-high while sobbing with emotion.

Sweden went to Mexico for the inter-zone final. As a curfew of 5.30 p.m. was agreed to, the Osuna v. Schmidt match on the first day had to be postponed when Schmidt held a commanding lead after Lundquist had beaten Palafox. On the resumption Schmidt lost. Mexico won the doubles to go 2–1 up, and Schmidt beat Palafox in the fourth match. In the clincher, Osuna's crafty all-court play held out Lundquist in five sets and once again the emotional Rafael was in tears. The Mexicans also beat Yugoslavia, who had challenged in the American Zone, and then set off for India. There, the Mexicans won 4–1.

Mexico had never won the American Zone before. Now, by reaching the challenge round, it gave a shot in the arm to tennis in the whole of Latin America. Osuna was not only the reigning US singles champion but he and Palafox also held the US doubles title, so they were considered to have an outside chance. Their colourful personalities, allied to their feline quickness of foot and graceful movements, with a corresponding speed of thought, made them attractive to watch. In Brisbane, however, Australia possessed too much firepower. To add to the visitors' grass-court difficulties, rain made the court slippery, and the Mexicans had to borrow spiked shoes to which they were unaccustomed. Fraser, restored to a singles berth, beat Palafox in four tight sets. Laver, who was on the verge of turning professional, soundly beat Osuna. Emerson and Laver had surprisingly little trouble in the doubles; and in the remaining singles Laver and Fraser completed a 5–0 sweep in front of the smallest crowd (7360) to watch a challenge round in Australia since the war.

-16-

NEW CHALLENGERS
TO THE FORE

(1963, USA; 1964–67, Australia)

No sooner had the 1962 challenge round ended than Laver threw in his lot with the pros and Fraser announced his retirement. The main responsibility for keeping the cup in Australia was assumed by the twenty-six-year-old Roy Emerson, who, like Laver, was a Queensland farmer's son. A member of the Australian squad since the age of seventeen, Emerson in his early years was a very flat hitter of the ball with defects in his service action and forehand. In 1958 he wisely withdrew from the Australian touring team in order to work on his weaknesses. He not only gained more control over his shots, but in time his constant involvement in doubles enabled him to develop top spin.

At school Emerson had been a track star, and he became the fastest and most athletic man ever to represent his country. Nobody pressed a net attack more persistently than Roy, whose speed and strength in covering the court also made him sound in defence with firm passing shots and controlled lobs. By 1963 he had been playing Davis Cup for four years, and he was to spearhead the Australian effort for another five years. When at last he stepped down he had played in nine successive challenge rounds (as opposed to Tilden's eleven), winning eleven out of twelve singles matches and four out of six doubles. Resisting frequent pro offers, Emerson also won more Grand Slam tournaments than any of his contemporaries – two Wimbledon, two American, two French and six Australian championships, apart from numerous doubles titles.

There were forty-eight challengers for the cup in 1963. America, under Bob Kelleher, was able to field its strongest team for years, but faced a difficult draw. Her first opponent was Iran, who, though challenging in the American Zone, received a pleasant surprise when America offered to play the tie in Iran in order to promote the game there. Another confrontation with Mexico followed, this time on a cement court at the Los Angeles Tennis Club. Nominating McKinley and Ralston, captain Kelleher was dismayed to see Osuna beat McKinley in five sets. Even more upsetting was that a large section of the American gallery loudly supported the Mexican, who, being a student at the University of Southern California, was regarded as a local boy. Ralston evened the score with a strong display against Palafox, and he and McKinley gained a grip on the tie in the doubles by beating Osuna and Palafox, the reigning Wimbledon and US champions, 6–1, 6–3, 8–6. Ralston settled the issue with a surprisingly easy win over Osuna. A 5–0 whitewash of Venezuela subsequently put America into the inter-zone finals.

Europe witnessed a resurgence by Great Britain, whose well-balanced team of Billy Knight, Michael Sangster, Bobby Wilson and Roger Taylor made the most of a home-ground advantage in its last three contests, beating Russia at Eastbourne, Spain in Bristol, and, in the zone final, Sweden on court one at Wimbledon. The British thought they would have a good chance against the Americans if they played them on a clay court at Bournemouth, rather than on a grass court. Their hopes rose further when Kelleher nominated Frank Froehling instead of Ralston for the second singles berth. Anticipation turned to sharp disappointment, for Froehling beat both Knight and Sangster, storming back from 4–6, 0–5 against the former. McKinley also won both his singles, and, with Ralston, beat Wilson and Sangster in the doubles.

There remained but one other hurdle before the Americans reached the challenge round. This was cleared on a rubble court in Bombay, where they comfortably beat India, winner of the Eastern Zone.

All year the Americans had been beset with medical problems. Ralston had nearly lost an eye in a fluke accident in England, and McKinley had suffered dysentery in India. Now, McKinley, who was the Wimbledon champion and the mainstay of the team, was troubled by a back injury, and Froehling needed surgery on an abscess on his bottom. No fewer than twenty-six physicians had been consulted along the way, and the Americans' medical experiences suggested that the addition of a doctor to the team would be a sound investment. But it would be more than a decade before this occurred and few other nations possessed the resources to follow America's lead. Meanwhile, Froehling's operation ruled him out of consideration for the challenge round, while McKinley's ailment denied him vital tournament toughening.

The Australians' problems were not so painful. They had to decide on who should assist Emerson. Fraser made a comeback and was chosen for the doubles, but was not thought to be up to playing singles. The selectors also passed over Fred Stolle, who had lost to McKinley at Wimbledon. They eventually selected John Newcombe, a tall, husky nineteen-year-old who had looked impressive in beating Ralston in the recent South Australian final. The challenge round was to be held in the same arena.

Newcombe was tense and nervous when he opened the defence against Ralston on Boxing Day. Ralston's fluent strokes gave him the first two sets 6–4, 6–1, but gradually Newcombe relaxed and, just as he was looking out of the match, he began to hit more freely and won the next two sets 6–3, 6–4. Games followed service in the fifth set until the eighth game when Ralston broke for 5–3. He then jumped to 40–0, triple match point. Newcombe fought off two of the points and a shaky Ralston double-faulted twice before dropping his service. There was an anxious changeover. But the Californian got his nerves under control and, with some penetrating ground shots, he won the fifth set 7–5.

The second match was almost as close. At one set all, McKinley served for 5–1 in the third set. Suddenly, Emerson hit an irresistible streak. He won nine of the next ten games to take the third set and lead 3–0 in the fourth. McKinley came back with explosive tennis, pulling up to 5 all. but Emerson usually had a superior shot to call on when he needed one most and he triumphed 6–3, 4–6, 7–5, 7–5.

As a pair, Fraser and Emerson were undefeated in three challenge rounds. Fraser, though, had lost some of his sharpness and his backhand crumbled under the Americans' attack. He had no effective counter to their low, spinning returns and he was vulnerable to their top-spin lobs. Only Emerson's lionhearted efforts averted a blitz. The Americans won 6–3, 4–6, 11–9, 11–9 and knew the cup was within their grasp.

On the third day Emerson sustained his brilliance. Ralston wilted and Emerson won 6–2, 6–3, 3–6, 6–2, leaving McKinley and

Newcombe to determine the cup's fate. They each won a set and for a while it seemed that Newcombe was getting on top. Standing five inches taller than the chunky 5-foot 8 McKinley, the dentist's son from Sydney pasted big serves all around him and boldly stroked for the lines. He went to 4–1 in the third set but McKinley held firm and responded with a blaze of placements. He was, according to the American writer, Bud Collins, 'a firebird swooping and swirling about the court in a frenzy of shotmaking'. McKinley broke back and won the third set 9–7. Now, blasting Newcombe's backhand, he allowed him only two games in the fourth set as he wrested the cup from Australia. It was a sweet moment for Chuck, the first American since Malcolm Whitman beat Reggie Doherty in 1903 to succeed when the outcome of a challenge round depended on the final rubber. What better way could there have been to atone for his tantrum in Perth four years earlier?

America had high hopes of keeping the cup for a long time, especially after a players' revolt early in 1964 threatened to smash the Australian tennis machine. The revolt was led by Roy Emerson and Ken Fletcher, who breached an LTAA ruling that they must not travel abroad before 31 March. Instead, they were expected to play in country exhibition matches, as were all the leading Australians. Emerson and Fletcher defiantly went off to America and the Caribbean, where they could make good money (by amateur standards) on the tournament circuit. The LTAA promptly suspended them from the Davis Cup team. Other players, including Fred Stolle, Bob Hewitt, Martin Mulligan and several women players, followed the rebels' example and were similarly banned from representing their country. The revolt was the first sign that the Australian system, based on the LTAA's complete control of the players, was breaking down. Emerson and Stolle were now employed by cigarette companies, not sporting goods firms, and they were married men who regarded themselves as independent citizens free to play wherever they desired and possessing as much right to benefit from under-the-lap payments as any other nation's 'shamateurs'.

The episode caused shockwaves around the tennis world and brought heaps of criticism on to the head of the LTAA president, Norman Strange, a retired bureaucrat, who stubbornly defended the ban. Hopman more sensibly worked for a settlement of the quarrel. When Emerson and Stolle met in the Wimbledon final, with Emerson winning in four sets, the pressure on the LTAA to make concessions was irresistible. If the association did not bend, Australia might as well pull out of the Davis Cup. Encouraged by their captain, Emerson and Stolle made formal apologies and were hastily reinstated. Fletcher, Mulligan and Hewitt, not being so valued, were consigned to the wilderness. Subsequently, Mulligan became residentially qualified to play for Italy, and Hewitt for South Africa.

Forty-six nations challenged for the cup in 1964, thirty-two of them in the European Zone, where an early surprise was the defeat of Spain by Denmark. Germany beat Denmark in Munich and was joined in the semifinals by Sweden (who defeated Italy), Great Britain and France. Sweden then defeated Germany, while France eliminated Great Britain, and in the zone final in Båstad the Swedes were again triumphant.

The USLTA had scheduled the challenge round for Cleveland, Ohio, where an enterprising promoter intended to lay a clay court on a school playground and surround it with temporary stands. It was to be the first time a challenge round in America was to be held away from the East and on a surface other than grass.

When the plans were made, Mexico appeared to be the likely challenger. The scenario changed after the Australians settled their differences. Hopman's men quickly disposed of Canada and hurried to Mexico City. There, Emerson beat Palafox in straight sets, but Stolle, in a jittery singles debut, lost by the same margin to Osuna. For the doubles, Hopman had to consider replacing the unhappy Stolle with either of the youngsters John Newcombe or Tony Roche, and did not make up his mind until shortly before the match. Stolle was retained. With the ever dependable Emerson at his side, Fred, it was hoped, would recover his confidence and touch. Hopman's intuition proved right. Stolle was the star of a marathon struggle against Osuna and Palafox which the Australians won 18–16, 7–9, 7–9, 6–4, 10–8. For the Mexicans, to lose such a long match which they had often looked like winning was demoralizing, and on the third day both Stolle and Emerson won their singles in straight sets. The weekend ended on a sour note, with Hopman publicly accusing the gallery of being too loudly pro-Mexico and castigating Osuna for pressuring and bullying the linesmen. Francisco Contreras, the Mexican captain, defended both his player and the crowd, admitting the crowd was noisy 'because that is the way Mexicans are', but maintaining they were not unfair to the Australians. His comments were endorsed by the Chilean referee.

When Australia won the American Zone by easily defeating Chile, and Emerson beat Stolle in the final of the US Nationals a fortnight prior to the challenge round, Cleveland had a bigger spectacle to offer and sold out its 7000-seat makeshift stadium. The event was advertised as 'The 1964 Davis Cup World Finals' because the local people did not understand what a challenge round was. Despite their unfamiliarity with big tennis the challenge round became the first anywhere to earn more than a quarter of a million dollars. That was about the only consolation for the USLTA, for Australia, after being 1–2 down, regained the cup.

Captained by Vic Seixas, the Americans banked on beating Stolle twice and taking the doubles. They failed by a hair's breadth. McKinley scored a four-set win over Stolle, but Emerson countered by overwhelming Ralston. Then McKinley and Ralston edged Emerson and Stolle out of the doubles, 6–4 in the fifth set. The key match, between Ralston and Stolle, was delayed by rain. Ralston was eager to reverse his recent five-set loss on Forest Hills grass to the former Sydney bank officer, and waited impatiently until the weather cleared. He lost the first two sets 5–7, 3–6, but won the next two 6–3, 11–9, and when he produced a slashing backhand placement to break for 2–1 in the fifth set, the simmering crowd reached a fever pitch of excitement. Stolle coolly levelled at 2 all and the score went with service to 4–5. Then, with Ralston serving, the Australian took the set and match with a string of splendid returns.

The last match had to be postponed to the following day. When it got under way McKinley gave the crowd something to cheer by initially out-hitting Emerson. Roy was undeterred. In the second set he began to streak to the net like an unleashed greyhound. Volleying and smashing with great severity, he won 3–6, 6–2, 6–4, 6–4. Back in Melbourne, Australia's prodigal sons were totally forgiven.

American fortunes now sank to a low ebb. For three years the USA failed to reach the challenge round, losing to Spain in 1965, to Brazil in 1966, and to Ecuador in 1967. The losses to Spain and

Brazil were in inter-zone finals and provided further proof of how the introduction of the home-and-away concept for the finals had given smaller nations a much better chance. There was no doubt, too, international standards were becoming more even, though the number of players (and not merely from America and Australia) who had turned professional and were therefore lost to the Davis Cup was an indictment of the narrow-mindedness and hypocrisy of many of the game's rulers. Various attempts to open up tennis in the early sixties proved abortive.

George MacCall, the new US captain, had more than his share of problems. To begin with, he lacked the services in singles play of McKinley, who had entered a stockbroking company and had to curtail his tennis. MacCall also for a while had to do without Ralston, whom he suspended for the tie with Canada as a matter of discipline. Ralston had disobeyed MacCall's orders to pair in doubles with Richardson in the Houston tournament, where the American combination was scheduled to meet the Mexican pair of Osuna and Palafox in what would have been a Davis Cup preview. Following his Houston singles defeat by Richardson, Ralston flew home to Bakersfield, defaulting the doubles and greatly annoying his captain. To aggravate the situation, the tie with Canada had been scheduled for Bakersfield to honour Ralston. His place was filled by a young man destined to leave an indelible mark on the competition, Arthur Ashe, the first Negro to represent his country in men's tennis. Ashe came from a modest background in Richmond, Virginia, and owed his tennis education to a tennis-playing Negro doctor who thought it was as important to develop in his protégé a wise philosophy and a pleasant court demeanour as an aggressive playing style. Ashe would become not only an outstanding representative of his race but a fine ambassador for his country. Against Canada, he won both his singles as America coasted to a 5–0 victory.

Ashe was retained as a singles player when Ralston returned for the tie with Mexico, a contest that was originally scheduled for Mexico City, where the Mexicans would have enjoyed an enormous advantage in the thin atmosphere and in front of their own crowd. After receiving a $20,000 guarantee from a group of Texan enthusiasts, Mexican officials almost risked a public lynching by agreeing to shift the venue to Dallas. In making the deal, the Texans hoped that eighteen-year-old Cliff Richey, son of a Dallas tennis pro, would be playing for America. They were disappointed. MacCall dropped the Texan because he objected to Cliff's frequent telephone calls to his father during the team's European tour. George Richey had a strong influence over his son, and MacCall felt his authority was being undermined.

The Mexicans were pleased when Osuna was drawn to play the rookie Ashe in the opening match on an asphalt composition court. Ashe surprised them with his brilliant service and flashing backhands. He took Osuna apart 6–2, 6–3, 9–7. Ralston beat Palafox 6–2, 6–3, 6–2, but he and Richardson lost the doubles. It was Ashe who wrapped up victory on the third day by dispatching Palafox 6–1, 6–4, 6–4.

Of the forty-two nations who entered the competition in 1965 twenty-nine were in the European Zone. Spain proved to be the strongest, beating South Africa in the final. Santana, the one-time Madrid ballboy who carved his first racquet out of wood, did not drop a set in any of his singles and was clearly the best player in Europe. He had won the French championship in 1964, and he was to win the US title in 1965 and Wimbledon the following year. He not only possessed the most flexible and dangerous forehand in the world, but could play the net game with touch and artistry. His natural charm and good spirits won galleries everywhere.

When the Americans flew to Spain, it was Santana they feared most. They knew they would have their work cut out on a slow clay court in Barcelona, yet they may have made their task even harder by dropping Ashe. Froehling, whose form had been unimpressive all year, was preferred after he had beaten Ashe in a series of practice matches and appeared to be coping better with the clay court.

America got off to a disastrous start when Juan Gisbert beat Ralston 3–6, 8–6, 6–1, 6–3. Leading 4–1 in the second set, Ralston looked well in command but then he became tight and cautious. When Santana outmanoeuvred Froehling 6–1, 6–4, 6–4, the largest crowd ever to watch a match in Spain – five thousand – flung cushions onto the court and broke into song. Ralston and Clark Graebner, pairing for the first time, quietened the stands when they took an unexpected 6–4, 6–4 lead over Santana and Jose Luis Arilla. The Spaniards captured the next two sets 6–3, 6–4, but seemed well beaten when the Americans went to a 5–2 lead in the fifth set. At this stage, Santana turned on one of his inspired bursts of hitting and he and Arilla pulled out the set 11–9. Within seconds the Spanish fans were chairing their heroes around the enclosure. Later, a grateful General Franco, the Spanish dictator, rewarded Santana and Gisbert with the Gold Medal of Spain. Arilla received the Silver Medal.

Barcelona next played host to India, the Eastern Zone winner, and Spain won 3–2, with Santana overcoming Krishnan 6–3, 6–3, 6–3 in the first match of the third day to clinch matters. Spain thus became the ninth nation to reach the challenge round. By the time its team arrived in Sydney Santana had proved his ability on grass by winning at Forest Hills, so he was given a good chance to win both his Davis Cup singles.

Manuel lived up to his reputation by helping to provide one of the finest cup matches ever held in Australia, but he lost and with his defeat went Spain's only hope of winning the cup. The vital match was the first one, Santana *v*. Stolle. It might have ended differently if Santana had played in lead-up tournaments in Australia. He relied instead solely on a long practice period at White City and was not match-hardened on grass. As Adrian Quist wrote in the official programme. 'Practice sessions are necessary, but they do not provide that nervous tension which is so essential to every champion and enables him to give his best under the toughest conditions.' Santana won a tense and fluctuating first set 12–10, and the second set more easily 6–3. Stolle never looked like cracking. With tremendous determination, Fred, whose timing generated terrific pace, lifted his whole game and won the third set 6–1 in eleven minutes. After that, Santana was never the same player. Even his famous forehand lost its sting as the Australian continued to attack him determinedly. Stolle had suffered many disappointments in his career. At Wimbledon in 1965 he had been runner-up for the third consecutive year, but this challenge round almost made up for all of that. He won the last two sets 6–4, 7–5 to complete the longest opening singles in any challenge round.

In the next match Gisbert was outclassed. Emerson trounced him 6–3, 6–2, 6–3. The Spanish captain, Jaime Bartroli, could only ponder how badly Spain had been hurt by Andres Gimeno's loss to the professional ranks. Feeling safe, Hopman swung the Wimbledon champions, Newcombe and Roche, into the doubles, and in 114-degree heat they defeated Arilla and Santana 6–3, 4–6, 7–5, 6–2. In the remaining singles Santana inflicted on Emerson his first challenge-round defeat, but Stolle was too strong for Gisbert.

In 1966, in another move to cope with the growing number of nations that wished to participate, the European Zone was split into two sections, each containing sixteen nations and each ranking as a zone for inter-zone finals. Zone A would play the American Zone winner; the winner of Zone B the Eastern Zone winner. The non-European nations which chose to play in Europe were Brazil, the United Arab Republic, Canada, Israel, New Zealand, Morocco and South Africa. The total number of challengers was forty-seven.

Brazil, represented mainly by Edison Mandarino and Thomas Koch, caused havoc in Section A. She defeated Denmark, Spain, Poland, France and, in the inter-zone final, America. In the second round against Spain in Barcelona the Brazilians began slowly; Gisbert beat Koch in four sets and Santana held Mandarino comfortably 7–5, 7–5, 6–4. However, Spain was in trouble as Santana had injured his shoulder and could not play in the doubles. Arilla and Gisbert went down to Koch and Mandarino 3–6, 6–2, 7–5, 5–7, 6–4. Next day Santana had to serve underarm because of the pain in his shoulder. Koch battered him 7–5, 6–1, 6–1. The deciding match developed into a gripping battle. Mandarino's strong backhand gave him an early edge, but the plucky Gisbert won a long third set and led in the fourth. Three fine lobs helped to turn the scales again and Mandarino evened at two sets all, then struggled to 5–4 in the fifth set. At that stage the match was postponed overnight because of darkness. On the resumption, Gisbert won the first seven points to hold 0–40 at 5 all. Attacking in desperation, Mandarino turned impending defeat into a 7–5, 3–6, 9–11, 8–6, 8–6 triumph. The courageous Brazilian maintained his form in the subsequent clashes with Poland and France, emerging unbeaten.

Competition was just as close in Section B. In the second round, Hungary's Istvan Gulyas, who was to be runner-up to Roche in the French championship, defeated Britain's Sangster 4–6, 6–3, 6–4, 2–6, 7–5 in the opening singles in Budapest. But after a succession of hard matches Gulyas found Taylor too physically strong in the crucial fifth match. Britain subsequently lost to West Germany, who went on to beat South Africa in the section final. Meanwhile, America had a clear win in the American Zone, where a significant development was the good showing in Cleveland of two young Mexicans, Joaquin Loyo-Mayo and Marcelo Lara, heirs apparent to Osuna and Palafox. In the Eastern Zone, India's Krishnan, Mukerjea and Premjit Lall were a class above all their opposition.

The real sensations occurred in the inter-zone finals. MacCall took the American team to Porto Alegre, accompanied by Pancho Gonzales as coach, and chose Ralston and Richey as his singles players to meet Brazil on a clay court. Though the choice of Richey over Ashe was controversial, Richey was the American clay-court champion and had earned his selection by beating both Mandarino and Koch while winning the Argentine championship a week earlier. Fans at the Club Leopoldina Juvenil were packed close to the court and were all patriotic and vociferous Brazilians. They added to the pressure on the Americans. Still, after two days' play the visitors appeared to have matters well in hand. While an overtense Richey had lost to Mandarino 5–7, 6–3, 7–5, 6–3, suffering cramp in the fourth set, Ralston had dominated Koch 6–4, 6–4, 6–0, and Ralston and Ashe had put their country in front with a 7–5, 6–4, 4–6, 6–2 doubles win over Koch and Mandarino. On the third day, the tension again affected Richey and as a result he suffered cramp for a second time. Losing confidence against the controlled stroke-making of Koch, he went down 6–1, 7–5, 6–1. Ralston, who had been runner-up to Santana at Wimbledon a few months earlier, was expected to rush Mandarino into errors in the final encounter. The partisan gallery boosted Mandarino's spirits, but irritated Ralston, who was not noted for turning the other cheek, and once more tension undermined American chances. Ralston led 6–4, 4–6, 6–4 and broke Mandarino's first service in the fourth set. However, most of the points were long and after two and a half hours on court Ralston was tiring. He immediately lost his own service and struggled to 3 all. Mandarino's murderous forehand now took its toll. Worried by his opponent's passing shots, drop shots and top-spin lobs, the American unwisely tried to match him from the back of the court. Mandarino responded by seizing nine of the last eleven games to take the fourth and fifth sets 6–4, 6–1.

In the second inter-zone final, at Calcutta, India took charge when, on the first day, Krishnan and Mukerjea outsteadied Bungert and Buding respectively. The Germans won the doubles, but

Bungert, who was as much rattled by the Indian crowds as Ralston was by the Brazilian, lost his vital singles to Mukerjea in four sets.

India again chose Calcutta grass as the playing surface for its clash with Brazil, believing the Brazilians would be less comfortable than on clay. Serving powerfully, the left-handed Koch did his best to disprove this theory by trouncing a nervous Mukerjea 6–2, 6–3, 6–2. The ambling and deceptively casual-looking Krishnan levelled by defeating Mandarino 5–7, 6–2, 6–3, 6–2. In the doubles India sprung a surprise by nominating Krishnan and Mukerjea instead of the usual duo of Mukerjea and Lall. By putting the maximum pressure on Mandarino's service, they won in five sets. There could be no questioning, however, of Mandarino's temperament after his cliffhanging wins over Gisbert and Ralston, and he again showed his courage in overcoming Mukerjea, who had a service break at 6–5 in the first set, and two breaks in the fifth set. Each time Mandarino came back with great backhand passing shots. He finally won 9–7, 3–6, 6–4, 4–6, 7–5. Krishnan opened tentatively against Koch, who went to 6–3, 3–1 before the Indian found his touch and saved the second set at 6–4. Maintaining his momentum, Krishnan went to 4–2 in the third set, but after a desperate struggle Koch won that set 12–10, at which stage failing light stopped play. When the match was resumed next day, Koch confidently reached 5–2 in the fourth set and was only two points from victory. Krishnan held service for 3–5 and broke back with fine passing shots down the lines after Koch had again stood within two points of putting Brazil into the challenge round. From then on Krishnan played almost faultlessly. He won the last two sets 7–5, 6–2, and it was India who gained the right to challenge Australia.

The defenders had hardly considered the possibility of playing India. During the year about eleven thousand fans had bought tickets for Kooyong certain that America would get through, but they turned up anyway, hoping the Indians would put up a fight. Alas, the hero of Calcutta looked out of his element on the faster Australian turf as the lean, hard-hitting Stolle, in his last challenge round before turning professional, exposed his limitations. Krishnan's exquisite touch was of no avail. He tried to resist Stolle's power from the back of the court and was swept away 6–3, 6–2, 6–4. In the second match Mukerjea played more aggressively against Emerson, but was only briefly in the match and was beaten 7–5,

6–4, 6–2. Nobody gave the Indians any chance in the doubles against Newcombe and Roche. To the gallery's delight, Mukerjea and Krishnan achieved a plucky win, 4–6, 7–5, 6–4, 6–4. India's respite was short-lived, for Krishnan's graceful strokes were no answer to Emerson's athleticism and the Queenslander went to a 6–0, 6–2, 5–2 lead before the Madras man could make any impression. Emerson wound up the third set 10–8, and the Davis Cup was repacked and driven back to its vault.

While America's repeated failure in the mid-sixties was a bitter pill for enthusiasts in the USA, it acted as a tonic to smaller nations, particularly in South America. In 1967 came the most surprising American reverse of all, a humiliating defeat by tiny Ecuador in Guayaquil. It happened on clay, the surface on which America had lost in recent years in Rome, Mexico City, Barcelona and Porto Alegre. With the game's growth – forty-seven countries challenged for the cup in 1967 – choice of ground had often become crucial.

When the Davis Cup Nations met during this year some made an unsuccessful attempt to have grass courts outlawed from the competition. Czechoslovakia claimed that Britain, America, Australia and India were the only nations that could play on either clay or grass in their own countries. To all other nations, grass was an alien surface, and they were therefore denied the advantage of basing their choice of court on their opponents' known weaknesses. A sympathetic Jean Borotra said it had taken many years for the Musketeers to adapt their games to grass courts. However, Bob Kelleher pointed out that although the USA was a grass-court nation, it had chosen grass for only one tie in fourteen years. Although the Czech move failed, some important changes were made in this period. In 1965 asphalt was included in the list of approved surfaces, and in 1967 the use of floodlighting was permitted as a concession to tropical countries where playing and viewing was more suitable in the evenings.

America's loss to Ecuador was especially unexpected after America had beaten Mexico 4–1 in Mexico City. For the latter contest Osuna trained diligently and his hard work was rewarded as he scampered to a five-set win over Richey. Ashe, who was on leave from the army, came to his country's rescue, bombarding young Marcelo Lara with aces and placements to win the second match in straight sets. The doubles went to Graebner and Marty Riessen over Osuna and Loyo-Mayo, and then Ashe, still in fine form, provided the clincher with another straight-sets win, at the expense of Osuna.

When the Americans travelled to Ecuador they did not know their opponents, Francisco Guzman and Miguel Olvera, until introduced to them. Their ignorance was understandable. Guzman, son of a wealthy banker, was rarely seen at major events; and though Olvera, who came from a poor family, was more prominent in the tennis world, he recently had been kept out of the game by tuberculosis. Richey's 6–2, 2–6, 8–6, 6–4 defeat of Guzman in the first match gave no hint of the drama to come. The court was very slow, however, and Ashe lacked patience against Olvera. Their match was spread over two days and when Olvera won in four sets Danny Carrera, Ecuador's captain, showed a certain degree of impatience, too; he attempted to leap the net to embrace Olvera, tripped and broke an ankle.

The crisis deepened for America in the doubles. Graebner and Riessen, an experienced clay-court pair, sped to 6–0, 5–2, but Guzman and Olvera dug their heels in and turned the match around to such an extent that they scored a stunning victory, 8–6 in the fifth set. Now Ashe and Richey had to win the remaining singles. Ashe won the first and third sets against Guzman 6–0, but Guzman's consistency and slow-balling kept him in the match. Ashe held a break point for 3–1 in the fifth set. He lost it. Guzman took the set at 6–3 for a sensational Ecuadorian triumph. For a few moments an ecstatic Carrera looked as though he might try to clear the net again, on one leg! The unfortunate George MacCall had failed in three attempts to get his country into the challenge round. A good sportsman, he graciously made a contribution to the fund to take the winners to Spain for their inter-zone final.

Spain won European Zone A with 3–2 wins over Rumania and Great Britain, and, in the final, a 4–1 win over Russia, who in the first round had upset Germany when Alex Metreveli beat Bungert in five sets in the decisive fifth rubber. In Bucharest Spain was 1–2 down against Rumania when Gisbert upset Ilie Nastase 6–3, 4–6, 9–7, 6–4 and Santana beat Ion Tiriac 6–2, 8–6, 7–5. Santana was the mainstay of the team at Eastbourne, beating Britain's Sangster and Wilson and saving four match points against the former. He and

229

Arilla beat Sangster and Wilson in the doubles. In the other European Zone, South Africa, after a close call against the Netherlands in the first round, blitzed its way through Monaco and France into the final, with the expatriate Australian Hewitt unbeatable in singles and doubles. At Durban, in the first Davis Cup contest ever held in South Africa, Brazil's Koch and Mandarino failed to show their form of the previous year and lost their singles to Hewitt and Drysdale. They also lost the doubles to a pair destined for greatness, Hewitt and Frew McMillan.

Nations such as Italy and Sweden, who had dominated the European Zone in past years, were fading, and Italy, for instance, could not win a rubber against Brazil. Pietrangeli was nearing the end of his distinguished career and so far the Italians had resisted the temptation to invite the Australian-born Martin Mulligan, now resident in Rome and a three-time Italian champion, to join them in their campaigns.

Both of the first two inter-zone finals were staged in Barcelona. For the Ecuadorians their clash with Spain was an anticlimax and they lost 5–0. South Africa also scored a 5–0 victory at India's expense and loomed as a likely challenge-round contender until Hewitt slipped and broke an ankle in the doubles. His injury put him out of the final with Spain in Johannesburg, where twenty-one-year-old Ray Moore was named as a replacement. On the opening day, Moore was no match for Santana, but Drysdale easily beat the Spanish junior, Manuel Orantes. Spain took a 2–1 lead when Santana and Arilla beat the patchwork team of Drysdale and McMillan. On the third day Moore wore down Orantes in five sets, and once more Spain's fate rested with Santana. He won the first two sets against Drysdale 6–3, 6–3, then tired and lost some power and accuracy as Drysdale climbed back into the match, winning the third set 6–3. Heavy rain washed out further play that day, a Saturday. With the match poised on a knife edge, the players had the whole of Sunday to reflect on the position. On the Monday the match was over in twenty minutes, a cool and confident Santana taking the fourth set 6–2.

Spain's hopes of reversing the result of her first challenge-round appearance lay in Santana winning both his singles and also the doubles with Arilla. Orantes, though the Wimbledon junior champion and a battler, was out of his depth. Unfortunately for Santana,

Emerson was still smarting over his defeat by him in a 'dead' rubber two years earlier. The event was held before a Brisbane crowd of 6500 and Emerson intended to end his Davis Cup career on a high note. Santana served badly and was out of touch. After struggling to 4–5 in the first set, he won only another two games. Newcombe, the reigning Wimbledon and US champion, overwhelmed Orantes 6–3, 6–3, 6–2. Spain's plight worsened when Arilla had to be scratched from the doubles because of a pulled leg muscle. Santana and Orantes had little hope of beating Newcombe and Roche, and won only sixteen points in their opponents' fifteen service games. On the last day Santana gained Spain's only point by beating Newcombe, who was reported to be suffering from a stomach upset and could not cope with the 105-degree heat. Emerson predictably downed Orantes. Australia had won the cup for the fifteenth time in eighteen years, but Emerson, Newcombe and Roche were about to turn professional and the end of Australian supremacy was near.

THE CUP IN CRISIS
(1968–72, USA)

Between 1968 and 1972 the Davis Cup became devalued and was in danger of becoming irrelevant. Paradoxically, it was the advent of open tennis – a development which most observers for many years had seen as necessary and inevitable – that damaged the competition. This was because in the early years of open tennis the Davis Cup Nations cautiously decided to confine the competition to 'amateurs'. Eastern European countries were opposed to open tennis and they and other countries lacking star players saw perhaps an advantage in keeping the top professionals out. There were countries, too, which were afraid private promoters, such as World Championship Tennis and the National Tennis League, would exercise undue influence over the competition if professionals whom they had under contract were allowed to compete.

America was one of the countries that in 1968 wanted the Davis Cup open to all players. L. A. Baker, an American delegate, told a meeting of the nations that the Davis family did not wish the competition to become second rate. It was their intention, he said, that countries with strong teams should visit those with weaker teams, and thus help to lift standards worldwide.

At the inception of open tennis, the distinction between amateurs and professionals was still blurred. The ILTF recognized four classifications: (1) Amateurs, who would not accept prize money; (2) Teaching professionals, who could compete with amateurs only in open events; (3) 'Contract pros', who signed guaranteed contracts with independent promoters; (4) 'Registered players', who could take prize money in open tournaments but still accepted the authority of their national associations and were eligible for 'amateur' events. The latter category was to contain, in the main, the rank-and-file tournament players. Some were very good, but generally their names lacked the lustre of the Rosewalls and Lavers. The Davis Cup Nations allowed registered players to participate in the competition, realizing that, if they did not, many countries would be unable to enter credible teams and the way would be open for a rival competition to be established. However, by continuing to bar the contract pros – who were now free to compete in open tournaments such as Wimbledon and Forest Hills – the nations unwittingly reduced the stature of the Davis Cup in the eyes of the public. 'Only tennis,' commented one cynic, 'could take its premier event, the challenge round, and transform it into the Runner-up Bowl.'

After three years in the wilderness, America was able to put together a strong squad in Arthur Ashe, Clark Graebner, Charles Pasarell, Stan Smith, Bob Lutz and Jim Osborne. Their young captain, Donald Dell, skilfully improved their fitness, team spirit and confidence. In another decade Dell's organizational flair would make him a prosperous players' agent and one of the most influential men in the game.

In early rounds, America dismissed the British Caribbean, Mexico and Ecuador without conceding a match. The defeat of Ecuador not only avenged America's loss in 1967, but because it occurred indoors at Charlotte, North Carolina, and on a synthetic surface called Supreme Court, marked the first time such facilities had been used for the Davis Cup. For Guzman and Olvera, the court was too fast and their opponents too forceful.

In Europe the two most successful nations were Spain and West Germany. Gisbert was proving to be a handy backstop to Santana, and in the first round of Section A, against the Netherlands in Valencia, when Tom Okker beat Santana in five sets, it was Gisbert in the fifth match who ensured a Spanish victory. Spain then beat Sweden, Britain and, in the sectional final, Italy who was now using Mulligan (or Martino Mulligano, as he was known to Italians), along with the veteran Pietrangeli.

Sweden made history by playing her first-round tie with Rhodesia on a private court at Bandol, in the south of France. Like South Africa, Rhodesia always trod a precarious path in the competition because some countries saw her as a symbol of white supremacy, especially after her unilateral declaration of independence from the

British Commonwealth. In 1965, the USSR defaulted to the Rhodesians rather than play them. Now the Swedish police informed tennis authorities that the Rhodesia contest could not be successfully staged anywhere in Sweden because of the likelihood of civil disturbances. Sweden proposed a walkover to the Rhodesian captain, but he declined to accept it. Finally, the contest was secretly set for Bandol. The French federation was not informed to save it embarrassment and, after only one day's practice on a court composed of rough asphalt, the tie was completed.

In Section B, Bungert of Germany skipped most of the major tournaments to save himself for Davis Cup play and performed superbly. Germany defeated Switzerland, Turkey, Czechoslovakia and South Africa, with the unbeaten Bungert scoring decisive wins over such capable players as Jan Kodes, Bob Hewitt and Ray Moore. (South Africa had received a third-round walkover from Rumania, who refused to play the tie as a protest against the South African Government's apartheid policy.)

For the first inter-zone final, Spain travelled to Cleveland. The opening match on an asphalt court saw Santana take on Graebner, who had beaten him at Wimbledon. With his broad chest and black-rimmed glasses, Graebner was thought to resemble the comic-strip hero, Clark Kent, and was nicknamed 'Superman' by his team-mates. However, Santana quickly brought him down to earth in front of his home-town crowd, winning 6–2, 6–3, 6–3. Ashe stormed through Gisbert, who then had to fill in for the injured Arilla in the doubles. Dell surprisingly nominated Graebner and Pasarell instead of Smith and Lutz, and they won a tight match against Santana and Gisbert 11–13, 17–15, 7–5, 6–2. Graebner ended Spain's hopes by beating Gisbert in straight sets and Ashe rounded off the victory by overcoming Santana 11–13, 7–5, 6–3, 13–15, 6–4, a score which broke the record set in the 1958 challenge round doubles as the longest cup match.

The European Zone B winner, West Germany, played the Asian champion, India, in the second inter-zone final in Munich. Bungert's continued good form – he beat both Krishnan and Lall – could not avert an Indian victory.

When America and India met in San Juan, Puerto Rico, for the right to play in the challenge round, the honours on the first day were even. Ashe beat Lall in four sets and Krishnan outfoxed

Graebner by the same margin. Any hope the Indians held that Krishnan and Mukerjea could reproduce the form that had surprised Newcombe and Roche was soon dispelled. Smith and Lutz gave them only seven games. On the third day Ashe was equally ruthless with Krishnan. America could begin making plans to revisit Adelaide.

It was obvious that the Americans had a stronger line-up than Australia, who was to rely on the new Australian amateur champion, Bill Bowrey, left-hander Ray Ruffels, and the youngsters John Alexander and Phil Dent, all Sydney men. Neither team had a player with challenge-round experience. 'Sure,' said Dell, 'we're the favourites, and we should be. But coming down to Australia to play against Australians under Harry Hopman is a tough proposition because of the unknown. We don't know quite what to expect.'

There was some uncertainty as to which Americans would play. Dell was disappointed with Graebner's form and attitude in the Queensland championships, and ten days before the challenge round he named Pasarell in the team in his place. Under a new rule, a captain had five days in which to make one change to his team if he so wished. Graebner asked for a chance to redeem himself. He played a series of four matches against Pasarell, won three of them, and Pasarell had to step down.

For four sets in the first match of the challenge round there was nothing between Graebner and Bowrey. First one man surged, then the other. Bowrey won the first and fourth sets 10–8 and 6–3, Graebner the other two 6–4, 8–6. The match turned on the first game of the fifth set when Graebner was down 15–40 on service. Bowrey returned one serve wide and then lost a volleying duel. Graebner held service and was soon leading 5–0. He won the set 6–1 to put America one up. Ruffels served and volleyed well against Ashe, but Ashe was now the world's most dominant amateur and when he found his range he rode over the Australian 6–8, 7–5, 6–3, 6–3.

Hopman made one of his rare mistakes in selecting his doubles combination. The Australian champions, Allan Stone and Dick Crealy, were not in the team. Ruffels and Bowrey regularly partnered each other, as did Dent and Alexander. Hopman put together Ruffels and Alexander, saving a tired Bowrey for the third day. At seventeen years and five months, Alexander became the youngest player ever to play in a challenge round. He had a fierce serve and great potential, but Smith and Lutz, the US titleholders, were too solid to be bothered by a scratch pair and they won 6–4, 6–4, 6–2. The cup's long stay Down Under was over and after four sterile American years more than one American team member shed tears. In the fourth rubber Graebner beat Ruffels after again trailing two sets to one. 'Clark grew in stature not by winning but by *how* he won,' said Dell. Bowrey reduced the Americans' winning margin to 4–1 by scoring over Ashe.

While nothing could mar America's elation, the fact was that barely sixteen thousand people watched the matches over the three days and not once were the stands full. Even with a rematch of the old foes, there was something seriously wrong with the Davis Cup.

In 1969, the year in which Laver performed his second Grand Slam, the ILTF scrapped the 'registered player' concept, and at a meeting of the Davis Cup Nations another attempt was made to open up the competition. Robert Abdesselam of France asked how the competition could retain its standing when fifteen of the world's best twenty players, including Laver, were barred from playing in it. Though Australia, America and Britain supported the move, it failed to gain the necessary two thirds majority. America warned the smaller nations that if they continued to vote against admission of the contract pros, they might suffer financially. Up to now the smaller nations had been assisted by what was known as the Special Travelling Expenses (STE) Fund, to which the more successful countries paid a percentage of their Davis Cup profits. If the competition lost public support, said Bob Kelleher, the fund would dry up and those dependent upon it might be unable to finance teams. The American team, under Dell's leadership, did their best to combat humbug in their own country. They called themselves 'independent pros', instead of 'players', as the USLTA preferred, and refused to play in tournaments that offered expenses and guarantees rather than prize money.

America had no difficulty in retaining the trophy, winning the challenge round 5–0 at Cleveland against the colourful two-men Rumanian team of Ilie Nastase and Ion Tiriac. As was often the case, the earlier rounds were more sensational than the climax. Australia, challenging in the American Zone, lost its opening tie when humbled in Mexico City. This was the first time since 1928 that Australia had lost so early and the first time since 1937 that it failed to reach the challenge round. An era had certainly ended. The sparkling Osuna brought about the Aussies' downfall by beating Ruffels in the opening rubber and Bowrey in the fifth, decisive, rubber. Tragically, Osuna was killed soon afterwards when a plane on which he was travelling plunged into a mountain near Monterey. His death crippled Mexican tennis, and it was Brazil – who beat Mexico in São Paulo – who won the American Zone. India won the Eastern Zone, thwarting Japan in the final for the fifth successive year.

In Europe, the upset winner in Section A was Great Britain, whose players were paid cash bonuses by a tobacco firm for every tie won – a portent of the commercial influences to come. The British knocked out Switzerland, Ireland, West Germany and South Africa. The tie with Germany saw the record for the length of a match broken yet again when Bungert and Christian Kuhnke took ninety-five games to beat Mark Cox and Peter Curtis in the doubles. Cox's five-set victory over Bungert in the fifth rubber got Britain through.

There were more political problems over South Africa's participation. Poland and Czechoslovakia defaulted to the Springboks, and at Bristol demonstrators interrupted play several times during the Britain v. South Africa tie. A big surprise in this contest was the defeat of Hewitt and McMillan, the 1967 Wimbledon champions, by Cox and Curtis. Britain subsequently won her inter-zone final against Brazil at Wimbledon when Mandarino, for a change, lost a vital fifth rubber, this time to Cox.

In Section B, Rumania narrowly beat the United Arab Republic, for whom Ismail El Shafei won both his singles. She then pushed past Israel, Spain (who were without the injured Santana) and the USSR. In Bucharest, in their inter-zone final with India, the Rumanians were again fortunate in that Krishnan was absent, and they took the first three rubbers. When Nastase and Tiriac arrived in London on the last phase of their journey to the challenge round, they had Hopman with them as coach. Tiriac complained that he could not play on grass, but with classical clay-court tennis he managed to beat Cox 6–4, 6–4, 6–3 in the opening match at Wimbledon. After Graham Stilwell levelled by beating Nastase in four sets an edgy

Cox refused to play doubles with Curtis. Britain's captain, Headley Baxter, therefore paired Stilwell with Cox, a combination that was doomed to failure against the seasoned Nastase–Tiriac team. Undeterred, the dependable Stilwell trounced Tiriac in perhaps the best British performance for twenty years, but, after a promising start, an over anxious Cox faded against Nastase, and Rumania, a country of merely 3500 players who never before had won more than two rounds in a season, became America's unlikely challenger on a cement court in Cleveland.

The thirty-year-old Tiriac was a veteran of thirty-six cup matches, a hulking and menacing gamesman who reminded some people of Count Dracula and who certainly knew how to exploit an opponent's weaknesses. Nastase, aged twenty-three, was a gifted and attractive strokemaker, not then the controversial figure he would become. He had shown his potential by defeating Smith in the second round of the US Open. Had Graebner not been injured, that result might have put the tall, blond Californian out of the running for a singles berth in the challenge round.

Nastase's game was a little off in the first match, however, and Ashe beat him 6–2, 15–13, 7–5. The Rumanian tried to play safe, hitting cross-court as he would on slow clay. It was the wrong strategy on a surface which had been painted lengthways and buffed for speed. Ashe made sure there were no rallies as he attacked the net with cool efficiency. In the second match, Tiriac tried to intimidate the umpire, linesmen and even the referee, one Philippe Chatrier of Paris. He met his match in the impassive Smith, who declined to be distracted. With a mixture of lobs, passing shots and some mediocre hacking, Tiriac scrambled to a 2–1 lead. Annoyed with his performance, Smith half-apologized to his team-mates when he got to the locker room. 'I'm letting you guys down,' he muttered, shaking his head. 'No, Stan,' Dell replied, 'if you lose you're not letting anyone down but yourself.' He advised Smith to concentrate on getting his first serve in. Tiriac meanwhile was fuming in the Rumanian locker room because he could not get any hot water for a shower, the facilities at Roxboro Junior High School (the adapted venue) not being very reliable. He had to go back out cold on a raw, windy day and promptly lost his serve to 15 in the first game. More determined, and assisted by a backhand that grew sharper with every game, Smith denied Tiriac much chance to regain the initiative. He won the last two sets without dropping a serve. Smith and Lutz snuffed out any lingering Rumanian hopes by winning the doubles in straight sets. For the first time since 1947, an American team had successfully defended the cup the year after capturing it.

For several years South Africa's participation in the competition had caused difficulties in some countries, and when the South African Government refused Ashe a visa to enable him to play in a Johannesburg tournament the problem came to a head. At an extraordinary general meeting of the Davis Cup Nations in 1970 America proposed the establishment of a special committee with power to reject the challenge of any nation whose entry could endanger the competition. But some countries were reluctant to throw South Africa out. The Springboks had been competing for the cup since 1913 and had produced several outstanding players, such as Brian Norton, Eric Sturgess, Abe Segal and Cliff Drysdale. The Belgian delegate probably expressed the views of many when he said the nations should not set themselves up as judges of the internal politics of any country. If they did, he said, there were numerous countries which would no longer agree to play each other. The South African delegate, B. L. S. Franklin, pointed out that no player had ever been refused a visa to play a Davis Cup match in South Africa. Having accepted Ashe's tournament entry, the South African Lawn Tennis Union had tried to facilitate his visit, said Franklin, and the decision to deny him a visa was beyond its control. Many countries sympathized with the South African LTU's predicament. Yet, as Ben Barnett of Australia said, it was theoretically possible for South Africa, through a series of defaults, to become the champion nation without striking a ball. Moreover, if this occurred, South Africa would be responsible for organizing the competition the following year. The special committee was duly set up and by a two thirds majority decided that South Africa should not play in the competition. As it was already scheduled to play Belgium in the 1970 draw, Belgium was given a bye. Rhodesia withdrew from the competition voluntarily.

Of the remaining fifty-one challengers, Rumania was again favoured to reach the challenge round. However, it squandered a 2–1 lead against Yugoslavia in Maribor when on the last day Nicki Spear beat Nastase 7–5, 8–6, 6–2 and Zeljko Frenulovic wore down

Tiriac 1–6, 5–7, 6–4, 6–4, 6–0. Rumania's departure followed the first-round defeat of Great Britain by Austria in chilly Edinburgh. Never before had the British lost to Austria, but Cox and Stilwell were now contract pros and unavailable, and in the decisive fifth rubber a young Scot, John Clifton, was outclassed by the left-handed Hans Kary. The section final was won by Spain over Yugo-slavia 4–1.

In Zone B, where West Germany was triumphant, Bungert and Kuhnke were dubbed 'weekend players' and 'the last of the amateurs'. Bungert was a wealthy sporting goods merchant in Düsseldorf, and Kuhnke a tall, scholarly Cologne lawyer. Germany swept through Denmark, Egypt and Belgium, but the final in Düsseldorf became difficult when USSR's Metreveli beat Kuhnke to level the score at 1–1. Bungert and Buding lost the first two sets of the doubles to Metreveli and Serge Likhachev, and at 1–2 in the third set their chance appeared gone. They rallied to win the match, 7–5 in the fifth set. Kuhnke added the decisive point by subduing Vladimir Korotkov in four sets.

Stripped of its great champions, Australia suffered another blow when Hopman settled in America. His wife had died, he had failed in a bid to become president of the LTAA, and a brief career on the Melbourne Stock Exchange ended in disappointment. At sixty-four, Harry had seen many of the players he had groomed become wealthy men, yet the game had not given him any financial security. Also, it sometimes seemed that his country did not fully appreciate him, even though he had led it to success in sixteen out of twenty challenge rounds dating back to 1938. Sportsmen with lesser records had been knighted. Hopman soon established himself as one of the leading coaches in America and at least two of his protégés, John McEnroe and Vitas Gerulaitis, were to be instrumental in denying his home country the Davis Cup. He was replaced as the Australian captain by Neale Fraser, the only Australian champion of the past twenty years to remain an amateur. Fraser had a rough introduction to the cares of captaincy. His team lost in India, where Premjit Lall beat Dick Crealy for the winning point.

Brazil won the American Zone for the second successive year, hanging on through three 3–2 contests, the closest being with Chile when Koch outlasted Jaime Fillol, 8–6 in the fifth set of the fifth match. In the zone final against Canada, Mandarino blitzed John

Sharpe, an expatriate Australian, 6–1, 6–0, 6–2 in the fifth match. Brazil then played host to Spain in São Paulo. Orantes scored a splendid win over Koch; Santana pipped Manderino, 6–4 in the fifth set; and Santana and Gisbert took the doubles.

Even more impressively, the Germans blasted India 5–0 on a grass court in Poona. The ease of the victory convinced the Germans that they could defeat the Spanish on a fast surface and in fifty-five hours they laid an asphalt court in a Düsseldorf football stadium. It cost them $15,000 and was to be pulled up after the tie, but it was effective. Not only did the German players like the court but the Spaniards, who were peeved by the manoeuvre, did not. The Germans had a big incentive, for to reach the challenge round would mean the fulfilment of a long dream. Six times between 1929 and 1938 German teams had stood on the brink of performing the feat, with von Cramm and Henkel going the closest in 1937 when von Cramm led Budge 4–1 in the fifth set of the fifth match of their epic inter-zone battle. The 1970 German team was captained by Ferdinand Henkel. 'My brother couldn't quite get to the challenge round as a player,' he said, 'but at least I can take the Henkel name there.'

Thanks largely to Kuhnke's serving and volleying, he did. Orantes drew first blood, beating Bungert in straight sets. Santana was expected to be too classy for the aloof, aristocratic-looking Kuhnke. The match was even up to 10 all in the third set, Santana having failed to convert two set points. Then the German left-hander, a year the younger at thirty-one, hit a streak, winning eight of the last ten games to take the match 6–4, 6–8, 12–10, 6–2. Kuhnke and Bungert won the doubles and Kuhnke achieved further glory by beating Orantes 6–3, 6–3, 7–5.

But the Germans had done their dash. Though the challenge round was also played on an asphalt court – again in Cleveland – the visitors looked listless and inflexible and had no answer to the Americans' aggression. For the first time, the USA wrapped up a challenge round in nine sets. With Hopman filling the unaccustomed role of referee ('looking like a ghost at a discredited feast', according to one observer), Ashe led off with a 6–2, 10–8, 6–2 win over Bungert, demoralizing the German with his sizzling serve. The new US captain, Ed Turville, and coach Ralston had faced a quandary in deciding who should support Ashe, eventually opting for Richey

241

over Smith, hero of the previous challenge round. As Richey felt he should have played in 1968 he was out to prove something, particularly after Fred Stolle, the German coach, announced that Cliff's temperament was suspect and his choice 'as good as loading the cup on the plane for Germany'. With wolfish ferocity, Richey ripped through Kuhnke 6–3, 6–4, 6–2, and then glared at Stolle, who, Cliff claimed later, 'looked a little green'. Smith and Lutz added to the Germans' discomfort by outvolleying them 6–3, 7–5, 6–4 in the doubles. The rout continued on the third day with Richey confining Bungert to fifteen games and Ashe beating Kuhnke in a five-set, eighty-six-game marathon.

The days of the challenge round were drawing to a close. More countries felt that the defending nation held too great an advantage in being required to play only the final round and then having the choice of ground while all the other teams played themselves to a frazzle here, there and everywhere. In 1970 a committee was established to consider changes to the format. The following year its recommendation that the challenge round be abolished was accepted. From 1972 the defending nation would have to play through the draw and the venue for the final round would be decided on the same home-and-away basis as for the other ties. The change was a tremendous victory for the smaller nations and virtually guaranteed that no country would dominate for year after year as America and Australia had done. In addition, it was made possible for all ties in future to be played indoors and on a synthetic surface, a recognition of the changing face of tennis the world over as television and commercial interests exerted a greater influence.

The year 1971 was notable for another string of victories by Rumania, and Japan's 3–2 defeat of Australia in Tokyo. The key element in the latter result was the unknown Toshiro Sakai's win over Colin Dibley, reputedly the world's fastest server, on a slow clay court. Rumania became the most successful of the fifty challengers when she beat the Netherlands, Israel, Yugoslavia and West Germany to win European Zone B, then overcame the Eastern Zone winner, India, and the American Zone winner, Brazil, who had eliminated Czechoslovakia, winner of European Zone A.

There was the usual amount of drama in the early rounds. On a grim, damp weekend in Prague the Czechoslovakia v. USSR contest was marked by political undertones. Two years earlier Russia had crushed the Czech reform movement and ousted the Czechs' liberal Prime Minister, Alexander Dubček, and now the Czech people craved a victory over their oppressors. 'It is politics, not sport,' complained Czechoslovakia's Jan Kodes after losing to Metreveli in the rain. 'The people want us to win so much we try too hard.' Metreveli's win made the score 1–1. He and Likhachev won the first two sets of the doubles before Kodes and big Jan Kukal hit back to take that match in five sets. Kodes then won the clincher over Korotkov. The Czechs had another close call against Spain, only winning 3–2 when Frantisek Pala thrashed Gisbert 6–0, 6–1, 6–1 in the last match. However, they never recovered from first-day reverses against Brazil in Porto Alegre, where Koch dumped Kodes and Mandarino topped Pala. In Zone B the ample figure of Pietrangeli was again on view after a year's absence from the competition, but at thirty-seven he could not save Italy from defeat by Yugoslavia.

Rumania's defeat of Brazil in São Paulo showed that Tiriac and Nastase were fighting fit. Down 1–2 after the doubles, they defied a hostile crowd and emerged triumphant when Nastase brought down Koch, and a fierce Tiriac seized the first ten games against Mandarino, beating him 6–0, 6–2, 6–4. With Ashe and Lutz now contract pros, the Rumanians thought they had a good chance of upsetting America. Their hopes rose further when they heard that the challenge round would be held on a clay court at Charlotte, North Carolina. A disgusted Richey quit the US team grumbling that 'Turville and the USLTA have let down their players by giving up the advantage of a fast court'. Turville and coach Ralston caused another surprise when they picked the twenty-nine-year-old Froehling – ranked eighteenth in America – over Graebner as Richey's replacement. This was a bold gamble. Turville was 'counting on Froehling's qualities as a fighter in any situation', qualities he had shown in America's defeat of Britain at Bournemouth in 1963. But Froehling had not played a cup match for six years and until a year earlier had been immersed in business.

Smith, the reigning US Open champion, got America off to a good start by beating Nastase 7–5, 6–3, 6–1. The match was decided in the first set when Nastase brilliantly pulled up from 0–5, to 5 all and had Smith down 0–40 on service in the eleventh game. Smith resolutely saved that game, took Nastaste's next service, and seemingly broke his spirit.

Tiriac looked like levelling when he quickly won the first two sets against Froehling and had seven chances to break him early in the third set. The tall, spiderish American escaped from 15–40 in the first game and from 0–40 in the third before he began to turn the match around. Froehling's fortunes changed when he ditched his baseline strategy and went on the offensive. He volleyed his way to two sets all, and in the fifth set it was Tiriac's turn to fight. The Rumanian saved a match point and got to 6 all, when dusk forced a postponement. Next day Froehling nervously opened with two double faults. But Tiriac was just as jittery. Frank held his service, and at match point in Tiriac's next service game he ran around his backhand, as he had done throughout the match, and clubbed a forehand winner.

Tiriac and Nastase were too strong for the new doubles pair of Smith and Erik van Dillen, but Tiriac could not withstand Smith's net attack in the fourth rubber and lost the last eight games in an 8–6, 6–3, 6–0 debacle. Nastase's defeat of Froehling in the remaining singles suggested the contest had swung on the Tiriac v. Froehling match.

Thus the last challenge round ended as had the first with an American victory, her twenty-third. Australia had won twenty-two challenge rounds, Britain nine and France six. None of the other sixty-one nations had got a look in, and it was no wonder that they viewed the scrapping of the challenge round with little regret.

That America was able to retain the cup when the new-style competition got under way was due to a fine team effort under the leadership of a new captain, Ralston. The chief threat to America was again posed by Rumania, and America tactfully surrendered her choice of ground to permit Bucharest to stage the contest. When the two countries met in October, Nastase had succeeded Smith as the US Open champion and this fact, along with the home-ground advantage, was expected to tip the scales Rumania's way. But despite much dubious line-calling the Americans' grip on the cup did not loosen.

After two years of exclusion South Africa was one of the fifty-five nations whose entries were accepted. The Springboks had been

Top: Chaos at Portland, Oregon, in 1981. John McEnroe has
something to say to the referee, US team captain Arthur Ashe
remonstrates with Peter Fleming (out of shot), the Canadian
umpire tries to catch Ashe's attention, Australian team captain
Neale Fraser wants to know what's going on, and the net-cord
judge hopes it is just a bad dream

Bottom: More chaos. US team captain Tony Trabert had a violent
confrontation with anti-apartheid demonstrators when America
played South Africa

France's Yannick Noah and Henri Leconte playing on a specially
laid indoor court at Grenoble in 1982

The triumphant 1982 US team. (Left to right): Peter Fleming, Eliot
Teltscher, Gene Mayer, John McEnroe, Arthur Ashe

Pat Cash became Australia's youngest Davis Cup singles player in
1983

First day of the electric confrontation between Sweden and the
USA, December 1984. McEnroe goes down in more ways than
one

Henrik Sundström, moments after the Swedish Cup victory

The moment of Swedish victory. Anders Järryd takes to the air.
Kneeling is his doubles partner, Stefan Edberg

Top: Post–victory celebrations for the Swedes. McEnroe consoles himself chatting to Mats Wilander and Henrik Sundström. Edberg and Järryd are in the background

Bottom: The Swedish victors with the biggest trophy in the game

Top: A not-so-happy American Cup line-up in Gothenburg, Sweden

Bottom: The NEC's sponsorship has ensured the Cup's future

Philippe Chatrier

allowed to stage the Federation Cup, the women's team competition in Johannesburg, and surprisingly won the trophy. However, the Davis Cup Nations had second thoughts about letting them play for the Davis Cup and they were defaulted.

France followed Britain's example in providing her players with a financial incentive to play in the competition. Whereas a sponsor was paying bonuses to the British players, the French federation began paying its men a percentage of the gate money when matches made a profit. The two countries met in the first round of European zone B in Paris, with France winning 3–2. France then lost by the same margin and at the same venue to Spain, who went on to win the zone. A first-round contest in Båstad attracted some interest because a lad named Bjorn Borg, aged fifteen years and ten months, beat New Zealand's Onny Parun, 6–4 in the fifth set. (Borg was not the youngest cup player; that distinction goes to Haroon Rahim of Pakistan, who was fifteen years and 140 days when he played against Viet Nam in 1965.)

In Zone A Rumania beat Switzerland, Iran, Italy and Russia. The Italian tie in Bucharest marked the last appearance of Pietrangeli. His record of having played 164 rubbers (110 singles, 54 doubles) since 1954 still stands. Rumania's closest tie was against Russia in Tbilisi, where Nastase beat Metreveli in the decisive fifth match.

Neale Fraser was still having a wretched time trying to fill Hopman's shoes. He recruited the thirty-seven-year-old Mal Anderson, who played his first cup matches for fourteen years and helped Australia successfully negotiate the Eastern Zone. But Fraser's men were beaten 4–1 at Bucharest in an inter-zone final.

Though Ralston named a six-man squad of Smith, van Dillen, Tom Gorman, Harold Solomon, Brian Gottfried and Eddie Dibbs, the latter two were ineligible to play because of their status as contract pros. The Americans swept past the Commonwealth Caribbean, Mexico and Chile before facing their first serious test, Spain, in Barcelona. Ralston had painful memories of the city, for it was there in 1965 that he had lost to Gisbert during America's defeat of that year. This time, Spain brought in the thirty-five-year-old Andres Gimeno, the French Open champion, as a substitute for the injured Orantes, and American stock dipped when he whipped Smith, still tired after his Wimbledon triumph, in straight sets. Now it was the nineteen-year-old college boy Solomon who faced

Gisbert. He won the first two sets 9–7, 7–5, but he was then exhausted and Gisbert took the third set 6–0. Fortunately, nightfall saved the tiring Solomon, and next day he out-rallied Gisbert for the last two sets 6–1, 6–4. Smith and van Dillen dropped only one set to Gisbert and Gimeno, but Gimeno then disposed of Solomon, and Gisbert gave the visitors some anxious moments before falling to Smith 11–9, 10–8, 6–4. This was the first American victory on the European continent for forty years.

The excitement engendered by the American visit to Bucharest justified the abolition of the challenge round. Communist Rumania went down with cup fever. Crowds appeared daily to view the Davis Cup while it was exhibited in a hall on Boulevard Magheru. Posters of Nastase and Tiriac were displayed all over the city, bakeries sold huge cakes made in the same shape as the cup, and the stands at the Progresul Club were enlarged to extend seating capacity from 2400 to 7200. Nastase knew the club's clay courts like the back of his hand, so none of his countrymen doubted him when he said, 'It is impossible for the Americans to beat us in Bucharest. We should be ten-to-one favourites.'

There was a less acceptable cause for the tension. It was rumoured that the assassins of the 1972 Munich Olympics would strike at the US team. Though the rumour was thought to be false, two members of the US squad, Solomon and Gottfried, were Jewish and nobody could be absolutely sure. Both teams were put under constant armed guard.

Surprisingly, Ralston replaced the clay-court specialist Solomon with Gorman for the singles. Gorman was in good form and, being older, might have a better chance of coping with Rumanian games-manship. It didn't work out that way.

Smith had beaten Nastase in the Wimbledon final in five sets. Here on alien clay he trimmed him in the opening match 11–9, 6–2, 6–3. The gallery expected too much of their national hero and the importance of the occasion destroyed him. Gorman dampened the local fans' spirits further by outplaying Tiriac for two sets. Tom rallied patiently until presented with a short ball, when he would hit a forcing shot and follow up with an angled volley that kept Tiriac lurching and diving. He led 6–4, 6–2 and 3–2 with his serve to follow. But Tiriac broke back and the crowd gave him more and more vocal support. The Rumanians recalled Tiriac's five-set comeback against Italy's Adriano Panatta a few months earlier. Then Tiriac had held on till it was dark and pulled Panatta down next day. Could he do that again? The crowd helped their straining player by cheering him until ordered to desist by the umpire and the neutral referee, Enrique Morea. During the din, while they chanted his name, Tiriac took breathers. Sometimes he brazenly rested for up to a minute. Sometimes he even sat down on the dais under a linesman's chair and received an encouraging pat from the linesman.

Gorman's volleys lost some of their sting and accuracy. Tiriac hauled himself into the match and won the third set. Tom needed the interval to regroup, but he had lost his momentum, whereas Tiriac grew in confidence and cleverly varied his pace. Tiriac took the fourth set, and forged into the lead in the fifth set as several bad calls unnerved Gorman still more. With the crowd bellowing encouragement, the resourceful Rumanian won the last five games of the match.

Tiriac and Nastase felt they could repeat their 1971 drubbing of Smith and van Dillen – if van Dillen played. Ralston almost dropped him after noting how he was shouting uncontrollably from the stands during the singles. Ralston knew the situation demanded coolness. He got an assurance from van Dillen that he would keep a tight rein on his emotions during the doubles before retaining him. It was the right decision. Van Dillen's volleying was outstanding as he and Smith stunned Tiriac and Nastase 6–2, 6–0, 6–3 in what was clearly the pivotal match.

Tiriac, who had described himself as 'the best player in the world who can't play tennis', began awesomely against Smith. In winning the first set 6–4 he shrewdly mixed drives with floaters and kept Smith unbalanced with unexpected forays to the net. He also blatantly stalled when he needed a rest. Smith was being hurt by repeated bad calls. He stiffened his guardsman's shoulders and fought back. From 2 all in the second set, the American won eight straight games to go to 4–1 in the third. Tiriac broke back, and some of the line calls became ludicrous. With Ion serving at 3–5, one of his deliveries a foot long was allowed to stand. 'I knew I had to hit everything as though it was good,' Smith recalled later. At set point he fired a service return down the line for a clear winner, but the linesman made a late call of fault. Stan smiled wryly at the official's improved eyesight! Tiriac served again, and the ball

247

plopped into the net. 'That,' thought Smith, 'is justice at last. No way they can reclaim that one from Ion!'

But Tiriac was far from finished. He played marvellously in the fourth set, and Smith, normally the most phlegmatic of players, became embroiled with the officials. 'I started to believe they weren't going to let me win . . . no matter how well I played.' Ralston did his best to calm him. Tiriac won the fourth set 6–2, but Smith opened the fifth set with an ace. It was the start of an avalanche of big shots that buried Tiriac. With power and touch, the American won the set 6–0 in twenty minutes. Despite their disappointment, the Rumanian fans realized they had witnessed one of the great cup performances and gave him the applause he deserved. Nastase narrowed America's winning margin by beating Gorman, but the cup could be freighted home.

–18–

REFORM AND REACTION

(1973, Australia; 1974, South Africa;
1975, Sweden)

The year 1973 was one of the most controversial in the history of tennis. By now many officials were worried about the future of the Davis Cup. A number of leading players were either unable or unwilling to play in the competition and it no longer represented a true test of international tennis strength. Once the premier tennis event in the world, it was being increasingly overshadowed by the bonanza that had been created by open tennis. For some the quest for loot clearly took precedence over patriotism.

America, supported by France, urged that play in each zone should be confined to one venue during one week of the year. After this move failed, France proposed that the twenty-four strongest teams should compete in a 'final phase' at one venue over two weeks. Then, it was said, a company such as American Express might sponsor the event, thus guaranteeing the participation of all the top players. Jack Kramer, who supported the French proposal, warned that without some such change a new competition might be launched. Those who favoured the change thought it would overcome the old problem of overcrowding. Players no longer would be called on to give up four or five weeks of the year to represent their country for little or no financial return. The traditionalists arguing against the change believed the Davis Cup would lose much of its value if nations were denied the stimulus of staging contests on their own courts. These critics claimed that few countries possessed the facilities to accommodate twenty-four contests at one time and that fans in the smaller countries might never have the chance to see a Davis Cup match again. Moreover, the population of the host nation could not be expected to be vitally interested in

watching contests between other nations on its soil. The traditionalists won the day.

A belated decision to admit the contract pros was more effective in
reviving public interest. It led indirectly, however, to the notorious
players' boycott of Wimbledon. Nikki Pilic, who had turned
professional with WCT in 1967, was now eligible to play for Yugoslavia and his federation selected him for the tie with New Zealand
in Zagreb. When Pilic declined to play and Yugoslavia lost a tie it
expected to win, the federation suspended him for nine months.
Pilic appealed to an ILTF emergency committee and in the meantime
was permitted to play in the French Open, where he finished runner-
up to Nastase. The committee reduced the suspension to one month,
but this meant that Pilic would still be unable to play at Wimbledon.
Pilic wanted to play and the recently formed Association of Tennis
Professionals supported him by imposing a players' boycott. The
unfortunate chain of events did no great harm to Wimbledon, where
Kodes, a Czech, beat Metreveli, a Russian, in the final. What it
mainly showed was that the somewhat feudal old days when countries could dictate to their players were gone for ever.

There was another break from tradition in 1973 when the
responsibility for the overall running of the Davis Cup each year
was shifted from the defending nation. In future the administration
would be in the hands of a committee of management elected from
among the competing nations. This was a logical sequel to the
abolition of the challenge round.

The easing of the ban on contract pros gave Australia a chance
to relive some golden memories. In Wayne Reid the Australian
association had a young president adept at enlisting commercial
sponsors. To get Australia's commercially backed challenge under
way, Reid and Neale Fraser recruited two former stalwarts, Malcolm
Anderson, who was thirty-eight, and John Newcombe, who was
twenty-nine and in his prime. Later in the year they added thirty-
nine-year-old Ken Rosewall and thirty-five-year-old Rod Laver.
This Dad's Army formed one of the oldest teams on record – and
one of the best.

The Australian campaign almost ended disastrously in Madras, in
southern India, on a Sunday in April before a ball had been struck
in the Eastern Zone final. Having beaten Japan at Tokyo (where
Newcombe lost a 'dead' rubber to Toshiro Sakai), the Australians

had just arrived in Madras when they were informed by the police of a death threat to them made by a Pakistani terrorist group called Black December. The group was said to be trying to force the Indian Government to release some ninety thousand Pakistani prisoners-of-war. Only a few days before, it had blown up an airline office.

Fraser called an immediate meeting of the players – Newcombe, Anderson, Geoff Masters, Bob Giltinan and John Cooper – and the two writers travelling with the squad, Peter Stone and myself, to discuss whether to stay in Madras or leave immediately. The person most at risk was thought to be Newcombe because of his international fame. Both he and Anderson were married and had children, and Masters, who was then single, nobly suggested that he and the other bachelors should stay and play the matches while Newcombe and Anderson departed. What finally determined everyone to stay was the personal guarantee of safety by the Madras assistant commissioner of police. Drastic emergency measures were enforced. All the Australians were moved onto one floor of their hotel, and when Wayne Reid, his wife and an LTAA councillor, John Heathcote, subsequently arrived they were allocated rooms on the same floor. The players were confined to the hotel except for visits to the courts, when they were accompanied by a van full of armed police. Police with machine guns guarded the visitors day and night, checked all their meals and intercepted every letter or package addressed to them. In charge of the operation was one of the best sharp-shooters in the Madras police force. Dressed in civilian clothes, he was never far from the players' sides, whether at the hotel or the courts. The sharpshooter always carried a sun hat. Inside it was concealed his revolver.

After so much suspense, the matches were an anticlimax. However, one glance around the temporary stadium – built from wood, nails and rope around a cow-dung court in just ten days – at the scores of armed police on the lookout for possible assassins quickly dissolved any complacency. Newcombe crushed Anand Amritraj 6–2, 6–1, 6–0. Anderson was in even better form, beating the more talented Vijay Amritraj 6–1, 6–2, 6–1. Then Newcombe and Masters added the decisive point by defeating Vijay and Premjit Lall in the doubles 4–6, 6–2, 7–5, 6–3. The Australians felt a lot easier when they left Madras, but even in Calcutta, where a connecting flight was made to Hong Kong, a dozen soldiers, all armed with machine guns, surrounded their plane until it took off.

Meanwhile, America started inauspiciously in Mexico City when Tom Gorman succumbed in the opening match to the deft touch of Raul Ramirez. The patient baseliner Solomon saved his country by beating both Ramirez and Joaquin Loyo-Mayo. Gorman and van Dillen won the doubles. America's next opponent was Chile, which had scored an upset win over Argentina in Buenos Aires, with Pat Cornejo beating Guillermo Vilas in five sets. At the unlikely venue of Little Rock, Arkansas, Fillol and Cornejo put up stout resistance in the singles before losing to Gorman and Smith respectively. There followed a doubles match of a record 122 games which took six hours and ten minutes (spread over two days) to complete. Smith and van Dillen wore down Fillol and Cornejo 7–9, 37–39, 8–6, 6–1, 6–3.

In European Zone A, Rumania was weakened by Tiriac's temporary retirement from cup play and only narrowly beat the Netherlands, which could now call on the fleet-footed Tom Okker. In the zone final in Bucharest, Russia led Rumania 2–1. Then Nastase whipped Metreveli, and his new team-mate, Toma Ovici, beat Teimura Kakuliya.

In Zone B the young Bjorn Borg collected only four games against Orantes as Sweden went down to Spain in Båstad. But Spain failed against Italy, who had found a dogged young player in Corrado Barazzutti. He beat both Santana and Jose Higueras, and in the final in Prague he raised Italian hopes by beating Kodes in the opening match.

Gardini, the former player who was now the Italian captain, may have been of too excitable a temperament to perform the role. According to the referee's report from Prague, 'he incessantly incited his players without any reason, thus disturbing not only his own players but the Czech players too. Any time the ball was close to the lines,' added the referee, 'he jumped out of his chair and onto the court, shouting and gesticulating, every time pointing to a wrong mark.' Gardini received a warning from the committee of management. But the Czechs recovered to beat Italy and so earn a trip to Australia for an inter-zone final.

By the time the Czechs arrived in Australia, Laver and Rosewall were in the Australian team, after an absence of eleven years in

Rod's case and seventeen years in Ken's. Laver's form that year had been poor until he returned home and captured the inaugural Australian indoor title at Sydney with wins over Newcombe and Rosewall. The prospect of again playing Davis Cup enlivened him.

Kooyong was packed to capacity for the first time in years when in the opening match Laver toppled Kodes 6–3, 7–5, 7–5. But Jiri Hrebec, the Czechs' number two, shook Newcombe in the second match 6–4, 8–10, 6–4, 7–5. In the doubles Rosewall returned to the court where he had made his debut twenty years earlier and with Laver beat Kodes and Vladimir Zednik 6–4, 14–12, 7–9, 8–6. On the third day Laver put Australia into the final with a 4–6, 6–3, 6–4, 4–6, 6–4 win over the gallant Hrebec. Awaiting her old foe was America, who once more beat Rumania, this time at Alamo, California. Rumania's only point was gained by Nastase with a 6–2, 6–4, 6–2 win over Marty Riessen, another of the comeback pros.

Before the final, which was held indoors for the first time before a disappointing crowd in Cleveland, captain Ralston had to make a difficult decision. He badly needed reinforcements. Ashe would have been an obvious one, but Ashe hadn't realized he would be eligible and had made a commitment to play in South Africa, where a government anxious to see its team readmitted to the Davis Cup had granted him a visa. America had a younger star, Jimmy Connors. Connors had said he wasn't 'ready' when invited to play in the early ties. Now he volunteered for the final, but Ralston turned him down saying he preferred to stick with those who were 'part of the team during the early hard work'. Fraser also had a problem. He had to decide which of his great players to disappoint. After much deliberation he nominated Newcombe and Laver for the singles and doubles, leaving Rosewall and Anderson 'on the bench'.

The final resulted in a 5–0 whitewash for Australia, an abrupt end to America's record streak of seventeen cup wins stretching over five years and 231 days. However, the contest was far from one-sided and the first day provided some of the best tennis ever. Newcombe put Australia one up by beating Smith in a repetition of their 1971 Wimbledon final 6–1, 3–6, 6–3, 3–6, 6–4. He served and returned splendidly and was very sharp at the net. But Smith improved as the match progressed and led 3–1 in the fifth set. Though Smith held a break point for 4–1, Newcombe held service and fought his way to 5–4. In the next game Smith made three volleying errors and went match point down. A serve and volley saved him, but Newcombe reached match point again with a backhand that clipped the net cord. Gambling with a bold second serve down the middle, Stan served a double fault.

Laver overhauled Gorman 8–10, 8–6, 6–8, 6–3, 6–1. Although Gorman produced the finest tennis of his career for the first three sets, Laver had been through such crises many times before. He kept hitting out. When the tide turned, Tom was swamped.

While everyone expected a fresh Rosewall to be named for the doubles, Fraser resisted a sentimental instinct to name him. Newcombe and Laver had better serves and were fit and confident after their singles. Also, they formed the ideal right-handed/left-handed combination. Fraser's judgment proved correct: Newcombe and Laver destroyed Smith and Erik van Dillen 6–1, 6–2, 6–4. They bombarded van Dillen, whose 'freshness' was, if anything, a disadvantage. Against two champions who now had their eye in Erik found his best shots coming back harder than he had hit them. He was overwhelmed. There was no holding the Australians. Newcombe swept aside Gorman 6–2, 6–1, 6–3; Laver subdued Smith 6–3, 6–4, 3–6, 6–2.

For their cup efforts over the year the Americans were reported to have been paid $15,000 each, while the Australians received $1000 apiece per match up to the final, when they were paid an unrevealed sum, believed to have been $3000. If the rewards might have surprised Dwight Davis, he at least would have been grateful that the great players were coming back.

But the events of 1974 would have appalled him. In this year South Africa became the fifth nation to win the cup. Davis would have been pleased to see another nation break through, though not in these circumstances. For there was no final. South Africa was given a hollow victory by India, who defaulted as a protest against apartheid.

The readmission of South Africa indicated a certain degree of naiveté by some of the Davis Cup Nations. To be fair, they were concerned at keeping politics out of sport and were worried at what might happen if the game in some countries could be penalized because of government policies in those countries. The South

African LTU was perceived to be a non-racial body and the South African championships in 1973 had featured a number of non-white players, including Ashe. Yet, with a significant number of countries intent on having nothing to do with South African sport, the ILTF courted disaster by letting South Africa return. The readmission was conditional on South Africa entering the South Section of the American Zone, as it was expected fewer problems would occur there. (The American Zone was first divided into two sections in 1931, but not until the late 1960s did the south section regularly function.) Nevertheless, Argentina defaulted to South Africa, and Chile agreed to play the Springboks only in Colombia. A less publicized default was that by Sri Lanka, who objected to playing Taiwan.

The two giants, America and Australia, both failed early, and their elimination helped to make the embarrassing outcome more inevitable. America's defeat in Colombia was its earliest loss ever. Because of scheduling difficulties, and Connors' continued lack of cooperation, Ralston was again denied the services of America's best players. Since Connors won the Australian, Wimbledon and US championships his absence particularly diminished the Davis Cup. No American before him had ever treated the competition with such apparent disdain. Ralston took away a second-string line-up of Solomon, van Dillen and Pasarell, who were not strong enough to master the altitude of Bogotá (8660 feet) and the clay-court skill of Jairo Velasco and Ivan Molina. The Colombians won each of their singles against Solomon and van Dillen, with Pasarell and van Dillen salvaging a little pride by taking the doubles.

When Australia played the Eastern Zone final against India in Calcutta, it also was without its stars. Newcombe and Laver were in Dallas at the WCT finals and Rosewall was playing in World Team Tennis. Fraser chose John Alexander and Bob Giltinan for the singles, and paired Colin Dibley with Alexander for the doubles. Alexander beat Vijay Amritraj 14–12, 17–15, 6–8, 6–2 and Jasjit Singh 8–6, 6–4, 6–3, but Giltinan lost to Singh 9–11, 11–9, 10–12, 6–8 and to Amritraj 1–6, 7–5, 4–6, 4–6. The critical doubles went to the Amritraj brothers 17–15, 6–8, 6–3, 16–18, 6–4. (The total number of games, 327, is the greatest ever played in any tie.) For India, the triumph brought great joy. For Australia, such a jolt so soon after the exhilaration of Cleveland showed how capricious fate could be in the 1970s.

Russia emerged as winner of European Zone B when she beat Czechoslovakia 3–2 in Donetsk. The Czechs led 2–1, but Metreveli came from two sets to one down to beat Kodes, 7–5 in the fifth set, and Kakuliya won in five sets against Pala. The Soviets could not repeat their rearguard action in the inter-zone final in Poona. After the Amritraj brothers had given India a 2–1 lead by winning the doubles, Anand scored the clincher against Kakuliya on the third day.

In Zone A, Italy fared better than for more than a decade, squeezing past Sweden and Rumania. The Italians not only possessed a dynamic new player in Adriano Panatta but in him and Paolo Bertolucci they usually held an edge in doubles. A major factor in South Africa's success was that it, too, had an outstanding doubles pair in Hewitt and McMillan. The pair wrapped up the American Zone final against Colombia's Molina and Velasco after Moore and Hewitt had won the first two singles. Next, South Africa won its inter-zone final by beating the Italians 4–1 on cement in Johannesburg. The visitors sprung a surprise by bringing in Tony Zugarelli but he lost to Hewitt in five sets. Moore beat Panatta in four sets, and Hewitt and McMillan defeated Panatta and Bertolucci 7–5, 6–4, 10–8 to assure themselves (though they did not then know it) of the cup.

Anxious letters and telegrams were written and dispatched when it became clear that India would refuse to play South Africa. Although they had the choice of ground, the South Africans offered to play the final anywhere, but were firmly rebuffed by the Indian Government. The Indian LTA pointed out that India could become the first Asian country to win the cup. Still the government would not relent and all negotiations came to nothing. Instead, India demanded the expulsion of South Africa, and South Africa the expulsion of India. Dwight Davis's ideals were forgotten.

The Davis Cup Nations continued to allow South Africa to compete in 1975, a two thirds majority being needed to vote her out of the competition. South Africa again entered the American Zone and reached the zone final as Mexico and Colombia both regretfully gave walkovers. The tennis world breathed a sigh of relief when the South Africans, without Hewitt and Drysdale, went down to Chile in Santiago.

Mexico's forfeit was especially tragic as she had achieved one of her greatest feats by beating America in the second round. The architect of her 3–2 victory on a cement court at the Palm Springs Racquet Club was the dashing twenty-one-year-old Ramirez, who not only beat Stan Smith and Roscoe Tanner in the singles but shared in a doubles win with the little-known Vicente Zarazua over the makeshift team of Bob Lutz and Dick Stockton. Jimmy Connors had again declined to play and spent that weekend winning a $100,000 challenge match against Rod Laver in Las Vegas. Despite his absence, the USA had looked a stronger and better balanced side than Mexico. Ralston, however, made one of his rare blunders, splitting the strong Smith–Lutz combination because Smith had seemed tired after falling in four sets to the lively, precise volleying of Ramirez. The tally on that first day was 1–1, as Tanner had easily beaten Roberto Chavez. Ralston paired Stockton with Lutz. Both were left-court players and had never combined before. They led 6–4, 3–6, 8–6, and 4–1, 40–15 on Zarazua's serve in the fourth set. Then they became tentative. When the pressure was on, the better teamwork of the Mexicans earned them the last two sets 6–4, 6–4. The doubles win gave Mexico the edge. Though Tanner fired left-handed rockets at Ramirez in the fourth rubber, the confident Raul could not be intimated. Exploiting Tanner's lapses, he won 7–5, 7–9, 6–4, 6–2. It was the first time America had been beaten on its own soil by one of its continental neighbours.

American fans were frustrated by their teams' continued humiliation, and the fact that two Americans, Ashe and Connors, subsequently fought out the Wimbledon final underlined the Davis Cup's problems. On the other hand, the American defeat opened up the competition and several countries now realized they had a good chance of winning. The two that eventually reached the title round, Sweden and Czechoslovakia, had never got there before.

Sweden's victory was a personal triumph for the nineteen-year-old Borg, who had twice won the French Open and was beginning to take the world by storm. It added to the tennis mania that was sweeping Sweden and helped to prime Bjorn for his long Wimbledon reign, which began the following year. He won all his twelve singles as Sweden came through European Zone A by beating

Poland 4–1 in Warsaw; Germany 3–2 in Berlin; Russia 3–2 in Riga; Spain 3–2 in Barcelona; Chile 4–1 in Båstad; and finally the Czechs 3–2 indoors in Stockholm. Since Borg had won all his six singles in 1974 as well as his last match of 1973, his streak stretched to nineteen wins, breaking Tilden's run of sixteen wins between 1920 and 1926.

Borg received solid support from Birger Andersson, a clay-court scrambler who was barely ranked among the world's top hundred players but who possessed a fine Davis Cup temperament. It was Andersson who, when the score stood at 2–2, pluckily notched the winning point against Germany and Spain with wins over Karl Meiler and Jose Higueras respectively.

The Sweden v. Chile inter-zone final was ruined by Swedish opponents of the Chilean military junta which in 1973 had violently overturned the Marxist, but democratically elected, Allende government. A death threat was even directed at Chile's Fillol, a University of Miami graduate and one of eight children of a retired government lawyer who was sacked under the Allende regime. Alarmed by adverse newspaper reports and news of the virulent posters appearing in Stockholm, Chile requested that the tie be played on neutral ground. At an emergency meeting in New York between the committee of management and Swedish and Chilean players and officials, the Swedes promised their opponents full protection. Cornejo said he wasn't afraid of physical violence, but he felt there was going to be an unpleasant atmosphere in Sweden and he did not see why police protection should be necessary for a player in a Davis Cup tie. While the committee of management was sympathetic to the Chileans, it ruled that the tie must proceed in Sweden. The matches were duly staged in Båstad almost in private and under heavy guard on a court besieged by protesters.

Besides the large contingent of police and troops that were posted to Båstad, armed boats patrolled the harbour, aircraft hovered overhead, and huge nets around the stadium protected the players from projectiles hurled by demonstrators, who chanted and set off fire crackers nearby. In the circumstances, the Chileans performed well. Cornejo took the first set from Borg before losing in four sets and Fillol levelled by beating Andersson. The doubles went to Borg and Ove Bengston in four sets. Then Andersson added a 6–3, 14–12, 6–1 win over Cornejo.

For Czechoslovakia, in Zone B, Kodes was the rock on which success was founded. He won six successive singles in Prague as the Czechs pushed aside Hungary 4–1, France 3–2, and, in the inter-zone final, Australia 3–1. France had beaten Italy after being 1–2 down in Paris, Patrice Dominguez upsetting Panatta, and François Jauffret beating Barazzutti, 6–3 in the fifth set. Against the Czechs, the script was changed: Jauffret lost to Kodes rather easily in the fifth set.

Australia had again harnessed Newcombe and Rosewall for its Eastern Zone ties against Japan and New Zealand, but neither they nor Laver accepted Fraser's invitation to Prague. On the slow clay of Stvanice Stadium, Kodes looped enough backhands past Alexander to win 6–4, 2–6, 7–5, 6–4. But the most damaging blow for the visitors came when Jiri Hrebec beat Roche. The unpredictable Czech was down 3–6, 4–6, and 0–40 in the first game of the third set when he unleashed a torrent of winners. Urged on by Kodes, the inspired Jiri won the last three sets 6–1, 6–3, 6–3. Alexander and Phil Dent were too accomplished for Pala and Zednik, but Roche had no answer to the sturdy Kodes and so the Czechs began planning for Stockholm.

For the first all-European final since 1933, on a fast, tiled court at the Kungliga Tennishallen, the Swedish captain, Lennart Bergelin, replaced Birger Andersson with Bengtson, a serve-and-volley player who was ranked even lower than Birger but who knew the court well. It was a sound move. For although the lanky Bengtson lost both his singles, he was perfectly tuned for the crucial doubles. Borg obliterated Hrebec in the opener, winning 6–1, 6–3, 6–0. Kodes, grim and uncompromising, worked hard to beat the bearded Bengtson 4–6, 6–2, 7–5, 6–4 to level. Though Borg and Bengtson were not a top-class doubles pair, they both had good serves, and they were helped by a selection gaffe by the Czech captain, Anton Bolardt.

Kodes and Hrebec had done moderately well together and were now adjusted to the conditions. However, Bolardt nominated Kodes and Zednik, and Zednik, looking slow and clumsy, never got into the match. He double-faulted three times in losing the opening game, and also dropped his serve in the second and third sets. The Swedes won 6–4, 6–4, 6–4.

With their backs to the wall, the Czechs were cheered on by a small group of supporters. Slowly, the cheers drew a reaction from the normally undemonstrative Swedish fans. As the Borg *v.* Kodes match got under way there were cries of '*Heja* (Come on) *Borg*', and every Swedish point was applauded. Up to now Bjorn had never won a big event in Stockholm. Only a fortnight earlier he had been massacred here by Nastase in the Masters final. But he was determined not to let his country down. Kodes, serving poorly, trailed 2–4 in the first set, resolutely pulled up to 4–4 and had two game points for 5–4. It was a testing time for Borg. He blasted everything in sight, both at the baseline and at the net, and flattened Kodes 6–4, 6–2, 6–2. Hrebec beat Bengtson in the anticlimactic last rubber.

Sweden, a country of eight million people, had joined the elite club of Davis Cup winners and the Swedes were ecstatic. Supporters grabbed Borg and began flinging him towards the ceiling. Bergelin came in for the same treatment, and later, at the official dinner, the man who had masterminded the victory was the recipient of a special gift. Bengtson revealed that the superstitious Bergelin had worn the same pair of long johns through all seven Davis Cup ties – even in the heat of Barcelona. He ceremoniously presented his captain with six more sets of long underwear to mark the occasion.

—19—

ITALY'S
LUCK CHANGES

(1976, Italy; 1977, Australia)

Politics continued to plague the Davis Cup in 1976–77, so much so that the competition was threatened with extinction. In 1976 Mexico, who had beaten the USA for the second year in succession, again refused to play South Africa in a semifinal of the American Zone. Ireland would not allow its team to play against Rhodesia, and Rhodesia, realizing its next opponent, Egypt, would adopt a similar line, withdrew voluntarily. Later, Russia refused to play Chile in an inter-zone final, and in November was suspended for one year by the committee of management, the first time such a sanction had been invoked.

The problem in penalizing countries that wanted nothing to do with South Africa was that they claimed they were simply following United Nations policy which strongly discouraged sporting contacts with 'racist South African sports bodies'. South Africa after all had been out of the Olympic Games since 1960 and the Mexicans could argue that they were only being consistent. The other side of the argument was that any nation which realized it would be unable to play against any of the countries that had entered should withdraw before the competition began. Some officials were becoming increasingly convinced that the Davis Cup's only hope of survival was for a commercial sponsor to come to its aid. But no company wanted to be associated with an event from which countries arbitrarily withdrew for political reasons. There was not even a guarantee any more that a final would be held.

A crisis arose when America, reacting angrily to Mexico's default, threatened to withdraw from the 1977 competition unless a rule was introduced to suspend automatically any country which defaulted

261

for a political reason. The 1976 annual general meeting of the Davis
Cup Nations during Wimbledon narrowly failed to obtain the
necessary two thirds majority to pass the American resolution, and
the USTA announced it would resign from the competition. Britain
and France then declared that they also would not play in 1977. The
cup, said Joe Carrico, chairman of the US Davis Cup committee,
was slowly being destroyed. Rather than share in its destruction,
America had decided that it did not wish to participate any longer.
'Governments are making decisions as to who will play whom
at tennis,' added Carrico. 'That is repugnant to us and frankly
unacceptable. The players just want to play each other.' Most of the
other nations were shocked by this drastic turn of events. At an
informal meeting at Monte Carlo in July, Pablo Llorens of Spain
moved that 1977 be regarded as a 'neutral year' in which every nation
considered the future course of the competition. In the meantime,
America, France and Britain should reconsider their decision. Brian
Tobin of Australia supported Llorens. 'America, France and Britain
have made their point,' said Tobin, 'and other countries must now
give full and final consideration to what action should be taken
in 1977.' The Spanish motion was successful and the 'Big Three'
relented.

Russia, Czechoslovakia and Hungary aggravated the situation a
few weeks later by withdrawing from the Federation Cup, which
was to be held in Philadelphia, in protest against the participation of
South Africa and Rhodesia. The ILTF's committee of management,
pointing out that all three countries had known that South Africa
and Rhodesia were in the competition when they entered, suspended
them from the 1977 Federation Cup and ordered each to pay $10,000
for the damage and inconvenience they had caused. The Philippines
were also fined $2500 for having withdrawn from a Plate event.

No sooner had the ILTF dealt with that problem than Russia
disturbed the Davis Cup Nations' neutral year compromise by
declining to play Chile in a semifinal. Announcing their decision,
the Russians cabled:

USSR Lawn Tennis Federation declares its refusal to participate in Davis
Cup tie against Chilean terrorists. The whole world knows bloody terror
still going on in Chile. Human rights violated. USSR Lawn Tennis Federation expresses indignation at appalling crimes committed by Chilean junta.

Deciding that the Russians had 'endangered the competition', the Davis Cup Nations' committee of management gained a two thirds majority for a move to suspend them for a year. It was blatantly obvious that the USSR had withdrawn because of a naked political decision, said the committee chairman, W. Harcourt Woods. The Russian cable had been 'much more the language of politicians than of sportsmen' and the committee had felt the government of the USSR was trying to spoil the competition for a political purpose.

In June 1977 the Davis Cup Nations were reminded by the committee of management that four nations had withdrawn in 1975, seven in 1976, and four during the first few months of 1977. (One of the latest was Kenya, which objected to New Zealand's rugby contacts with the Springboks and was suspended from the 1978 competition.) Whatever the reasons for nations withdrawing, said the committee, the result was always that the competition suffered. At a time when tennis could easily outstrip all other sports in public interest, the Davis Cup was dying. The committee proposed that 'every nation who enters the competition must play until defeated by a better team'. Those who failed to honour this obligation must not be allowed to compete the following year. The proposal was carried by forty votes to twelve.

Apart from politics, the chief features of these two troubled years were the rise of Italy and the continued misfortunes of America. Dennis Ralston bore the brunt of the blame for America's 1975 defeat by Mexico and was replaced as captain by Tony Trabert. Ralston was out of favour with Jimmy Connors; as much as anything, it seemed, because Ralston was a client of Donald Dell, with whom Bill Riordan, Connors' manager, was continually feuding. Though Trabert was able to attract Connors to the 1976 team, he erred in not also enlisting Ashe for the team's visit to Mexico City in December 1975. Trabert realized that Ashe was a better player on fast surfaces than on clay and would have had to fly straight from Stockholm, where he had been playing in the Grand Prix Masters. But Mexicans well remembered Ashe's defeat of Osuna on Mexican clay in the 1967 tie and his experience would have been invaluable. Trabert compounded the error by substituting Gottfried for the tireless retriever Solomon in the second singles. Like Connors, Gottfried had never experienced Davis Cup singles pressure, and Mexico City was no place for a cup baptism. On the opening day Connors squeaked by Marcelo Lara in a five-set marathon, but Gottfried lost to Ramirez, his usual doubles partner. Though Gottfried had beaten Ramirez five times that year, Raul was a hardened cup campaigner, and in the difficult Mexico City conditions he took his friend apart 6–1, 6–4, 6–2. Trabert was expected to name Connors and Gottfried as his doubles pair. As Connors had jammed a thumb during the singles, Trabert went with van Dillen and Stockton, who lost in four sets to Ramirez and Lara.

The fourth rubber was a searching test of Gottfried's nerve. Against Lara he saved two match points in the fourth set and bravely won, 6–1 in the fifth. Now the outcome was up to Connors and Ramirez. Their Wimbledon quarter final that year had resulted in a straight sets win for the American but, as leading sports writer Bud Collins pointed out, nobody was screaming 'Me-hee-co!' in London. Connors ripped through the first set 6–2, his two-fisted backhand creating havoc. Ramirez steadied and drew strength from the crowd. From 3 all in the second set he won six straight games and took the second and third sets at 6–3. The fourth set was postponed because of darkness when the Mexican was down 2–3 with his service to come. When the match was resumed, Connors went to 4–3 and held a break point, but put a forehand return into the net. In his next service game he nervously double-faulted on break point. Ramirez moved in for the kill, clinching the set 6–4, to give Mexico victory. 'Connors,' wrote Collins, 'discovered what he'd been missing amidst the Davis Cup fervor and pressure, even though he'd lost his first major case in this court. So had others such as Laver, Rosewall, Budge, Newcombe, Kramer, Sedgman, Lacoste. It made them all the more determined.' Jimmy reacted differently. He was not to play in the Davis Cup again until 1981.

There were two ironies about the victory. One was that Mexico had almost lost in the previous round to an inspired team of second-rate Canadians while Ramirez had been engaged at the Masters. In the decisive fifth match of that contest in Mexico City Lara beat Rejean Genois, 7–5 in the fifth set. The other irony was that it was Mexico's last hurrah before she defaulted to South Africa.

A record fifty-eight nations had entered for the competition in 1976. Italy, captained by Pietrangeli, took over from Sweden as the strongest team in Europe. In Panatta, who won the Italian and

French titles this year, the Italians had a truly heroic champion who thrived on desperate situations. (In the Italian Open he survived no fewer than eleven match points against Kim Warwick.) Panatta's game was an attractive mixture of artistry and clout, while his countryman Barazzutti was steadier but no less determined.

Italy scored easy wins over Poland, Yugoslavia, Sweden and Britain, the Swedes being handicapped at Rome by the absence of Borg, who had strained his abdominal muscles at Wimbledon. Russia was impressive in Zone A, with Metreveli in great form as he beat such players as Orantes of Spain and Taroczy of Hungary. The Soviets would have had a good chance of reaching the final had they not defaulted.

Chile reached the final by winning twice at home – against Argentina and South Africa. Fillol and Cornejo each lost to Vilas, but each beat Ricardo Cano and they also won the doubles. In the zone final the South Africans went to a 2–1 lead and, with Russia certain to default, had visions of reaching the ultimate round for a second time. Cornejo and Fillol thought otherwise. The former beat Moore 5–7, 6–2, 10–8, 7–5, and Fillol downed Bernie Mitton 7–5, 6–3, 4–6, 6–2.

Meanwhile, in mid-October Pietrangeli steered his side to an immensely satisfying 3–2 win over Australia at the Foro Italica. Pietrangeli, who had been a member of the two Italian teams that had lost in the challenge round to Australia, called on all his experience to assist Panatta, Barazzutti, Bertolucci and the back-up man, Antonio Zugarelli. Australia turned up in Rome by a roundabout route, its Eastern Zone final against New Zealand in Brisbane in February having been halted by a cyclone, with Australia 2–1 ahead and Newcombe about to play Brian Fairlie. Because of the players' tournament commitments, the final could not be completed in Brisbane and the Newcombe v. Fairlie match was deferred for four months until it was played in Nottingham, England, as a pipe-opener to a Connors v. Nastase tournament final. Recovering from an arm injury, Newcombe then took three and a half hours to beat Fairlie 8–6, 5–7, 11–9, 6–3, by which time the weather had deteriorated so much that the tournament final could not be completed!

The tie in Rome was the thirty-two-year-old Newcombe's last. He fell to Barazzutti's cagey baseline play after an aggressive Alexander had beaten Panatta, also in three sets. With Roche, with whom he had won five Wimbledon titles, Newcombe also lost the doubles in straight sets to Panatta and the bouncy and often brilliant Bertolucci. Alexander, storming the net once again, kept his country in the fight with a five-set win over Barazzutti. For a couple of sets Newcombe seemed likely to get the better of Panatta. He won the first set 7–5, lost the next 6–8, and was 2 all in the third set when darkness stopped play. When play recommenced, Panatta broke for 3–2, saved a break point with a typical diving volley and launched a bold attack that won him the last two sets 6–4, 6–2. Towards the end the Roman crowd, so often criticized for its partisanship, began chanting 'New-combe, New-combe', so anxious were they to see an old favourite live up to his reputation.

Before the first final ever to be staged in South America took place the Italians, as well as the Chileans, had to withstand political taunts. They were called 'fascists' by Italian leftists and were the subject of a debate in the Chamber of Deputies. For a while it seemed that Chile, like South Africa, might win the cup on a forfeit. Fortunately, the Italian Government did not intervene and Pietrangeli's men set off for Santiago shortly before Christmas.

The final was a tremendous boost to tennis in South America and in Chile in particular. About 6500 fans went to the Estadio Nacional, where a patriot wearing flamboyant headgear in Chile's national colours led the cheers and the chanting with his trumpet. 'Chee . . . lay! Chee-Chee-Chee . . . lay-lay-lay! Viva Chee-lay!' The chants swept over the court. 'Not too many people in Chile know much about tennis,' explained Fillol, 'but everybody knows we are playing for the world championship.'

The vigorous support was not enough. Captain Luis Ayala knew his side would have to beat Barazzutti twice to have any chance, and from the moment the wiry Italian overcame Fillol in the first match, the contest was as good as over. Both players were jittery and made many unforced errors. Barazzutti held up the better and won 7–5, 4–6, 7–5, 6–1. With the pressure eased, Panatta was too powerful for Cornejo, winning 6–3, 6–1, 6–3. Panatta and Bertolucci then took the doubles 3–6, 6–2, 9–7, 6–3, and, fifty-four years after issuing its first challenge, Italy was the champion nation. All the Italians on the court and in the stands hugged each other in joy. Pietrangeli and Mario Belardinelli, Italy's national coach, were hoisted skyward as they clutched the cup, and then Pietrangeli ran with it around the arena. His players followed him jubilantly waving little Italian flags. Many of the Italian officials wept.

On the third day Panatta increased the lead to 4–0 by beating Fillol in four sets, his tenth singles win in eleven cup matches over the year. Cornejo, however, was unable to play the last match. He had awoken at 4 a.m. with severe chest pains and thought he was dying. His first reaction was to put on his tennis clothes since he was determined to quit the world in the uniform in which he had represented his country. He was rushed to hospital, where he was found to be suffering from acute pericarditis, an inflammation of the membranes around the heart. Belus Prajoux took his place on the court and beat the Italian substitute, Zugarelli.

Latin countries continued to have a great influence on the cup's destiny in 1977. Italy made a spirited defence of the trophy and America once more was surprised by a South American nation, Argentina. In spite of the wealth of talent in his country, Trabert found that he could not rely on having the right combination precisely when he needed it. In the early rounds, as America beat Venezuela, Mexico and South Africa, Trabert was able to use Vitas Gerulaitis, Tanner and Ashe, but the team that lost to Argentina in Buenos Aires was not the strongest for an encounter on clay.

Tanner was given the chance to exact revenge on Ramirez when America met Mexico in Tucson, Arizona, and again looked shaky when he was down 1–5, 15–40. From then on his serves and volleys began to zip off the cement court and he won 7–5, 6–4, 6–4. Ashe put away Roberto Chavez 6–4, 6–4, 6–4; and Smith and Lutz also recorded a straight sets victory. The American tie with South Africa at Newport Beach, California, resulted in the ugliest scenes ever enacted at a tennis match in the States. Tanner and Gottfried put their country two up on the first day with clear-cut wins over Byron Bertram and Ray Moore respectively. Disturbances first erupted in the doubles between Smith and Lutz and McMillan and Bertram when anti-apartheid protestors ran onto the court and emptied a carton of motor oil over it. Trabert jumped from his captain's chair and struck two of the interlopers with a racquet. 'My instinct,' he said later, 'was to protect myself and my players. Who knows what these guys were up to?' The oil was cleaned up and the Americans won the match. Next day there were more ructions, and as the protestors tried to display a banner on the court, Trabert again went after them with his racquet.

Trabert knew the Buenos Aires assignment was going to be tough. This was Guillermo Vilas's best year; he won the French and US Open titles and was compiling a record streak of fifty wins in the Grand Prix. The so-called 'Bull of the Pampas' was particularly intimidating on his home courts. On the other hand, Ricardo Cano, the Argentinian number two, was hardly known, and the Americans were far superior at doubles. The results from two earlier rounds, though, should have provided a warning. In the decisive fifth match in São Paulo, Cano beat Carlos Kirmayr of Brazil 5–7, 6–2, 6–0, 6–0, and in the clincher against Chile in Buenos Aires he thwarted Fillol 6–4, 6–4, 6–4. Trabert intended to use the machinelike clay-court experts Harold Solomon and Eddie Dibbs for the singles, but Solomon was ill and Dibbs declined Trabert's invitation, saying he had other commitments. The captain settled for Gottfried and Stockton.

American hopes were shattered in the first match when Cano, the world's 121st-ranked player, upset Stockton 3–6, 6–4, 8–6, 6–4. Stockton had chances; in fact the match fluctuated so much that there were twenty breaks of service in all. But Cano, a touch player, usually produced a passing shot when he needed one most. Vilas allowed Gottfried only six games, and the tie was virtually over. Though Sherwood Stewart and Fred McNair delayed the Argentinian victory by winning the doubles, Stockton predictably went down to Vilas. Hundreds of flags were waved by excited fans and the stadium reverberated with exuberant sounds from horns and drums.

Argentina loomed as Australia's main hurdle after Fraser's men had won the Eastern Zone. The star of the zonal matches was the burly Mark Edmondson, a one-time janitor from Gosford who had leaped from obscurity to win the 1976 Australian Open, beating Rosewall and Newcombe in the process. Edmondson gave his country perfect starts by outgunning Vijay Amritraj of India in the opening match in Perth, and repeating that form against the dour Onny Parun of New Zealand in Auckland. In both contests Alexander added the second singles point, and he and Dent won the doubles.

Australia had never played farther south in the American continent than Mexico City. None of the Australian players had ever visited Buenos Aires and none could remember seeing Cano play. So captain Fraser decided to do some detective work. He interviewed Trabert on the subjects of tennis in Buenos Aires and Ricardo Cano. He learned that Cano had a sound service, a rolled forehand and a backhand which he chipped but which he could also hit with top spin across court. Fraser tracked Cano to the Canadian Open at Toronto and watched him play. The following week Cano was scheduled to play at Boston. Fraser went to Boston only to find that Cano had made a last-minute change of plans and was playing in a round-robin event at Westchester Country Club, near New York. The Australian captain hurried to Westchester and, in order to avoid conveying any impression that he was worried by Cano, he and his companion entered the grounds incognito, paying at the gate to sit in the public stands. They wore hats and dark glasses. A few days later Fraser studied Cano again at the US Open. At last he knew all he wanted to know.

The tie opened with Vilas playing Dent. The Australian also had enjoyed a good year, reaching the semifinals at Rome and Paris, and the quarter finals at Wimbledon. He upset Vilas's rhythm by varying his game, but Vilas had too much faith in his strength and heavy top spin to be greatly shaken and he won 6–2, 4–6, 7–5, 6–3. Cano was under more pressure than in his previous cup matches because of the crowd's expectations. With Fraser aware of every facet of his game and advising Alexander accordingly, Ricardo had nowhere to hide. Alexander pulverized him 6–3, 6–0, 6–0. The demolition was so complete that it made Dent, who had to play Cano in the critical fourth rubber, supremely confident.

But Australian strategy almost went awry in the doubles when Vilas and Cano adopted a ploy that unsettled Alexander and Dent. When the Argentinians served, the net man positioned himself on the centre line two yards back from the net. By prearrangement with the server, he would dart to the left or right as soon as the ball was struck while the server raced in to cover the open space. Alexander and Dent won the first set 6–2, lost the next 4–6, and just tipped Vilas and Cano out of the third 9–7. The Australians were watching their opponents more than the ball and playing more defensively than usual. Vilas and Cano won the fourth set 6–4, and the Australians were relieved to walk off the court when an over-

THE STORY OF THE DAVIS CUP

night postponement was called at 2 all in the fifth. Next morning the Argentinians could not win another game.

Dent had an hour's rest before playing Cano. Though edgy, he was clearly a class above Cano and he beat him 6–4, 6–4, 6–3 to put Australia into the final. Vilas did his best to console the crowd by overcoming Alexander in the 'dead' rubber.

The strongest teams in Europe were Italy, Spain, France and Rumania, with Sweden crippled by Borg's decision to bypass the competition. The fact that both Borg and Connors for several years apparently put the amassing of tournament riches above the opportunity of representing their countries was to remain a blot on their records. With Tiriac pairing with Nastase in doubles, Rumania looked a threat to any team. Rumanian victories in Zone A were achieved over Belgium, Czechoslovakia and Britain (whose complaints about Nastase's misbehaviour led to his suspension from cup play in 1978). Further success seemed likely at Roland Garros, where the mercurial but moody Nastase led Jauffret 6–3, 6–0 and had a break in the third set. However, Jauffret pulled off a splendid recovery to win, 6–1 in the fifth set. It was the crucial point in France's 3–2 triumph. Italy reached the European final when Barazzutti beat Orantes of Spain 7–5, 7–5, 6–1 to establish a 3–1 lead in Barcelona. Italy met stout resistance from France, with Dominguez and Jauffret each going down in five sets to Panatta and Barazzutti respectively and together losing the doubles in four sets.

There was some irony in Australia's selection (predictable though it was) of a grass court at Sydney for the final. That year the ILTF had deleted the 'Lawn' from its title – so becoming the ITF – in recognition of the decline in grass-court tennis. Captain Fraser had a trump up his sleeve. He brought back Roche into the Australian team as a singles player. As Newcombe's doubles partner, Tony had played his part in Australia's victories from 1965 to 1967 before turning professional in 1968, but he had never played singles for his country, and, what with his frequent injuries, it had become increasingly improbable that he ever would. Now, at the age of thirty-two, he was asked to make his singles debut in a final. He was an ideal choice, for the prevailing breezes at White City favoured left-handers and he always had played well there.

Sure enough, the craggy-faced Sydney player laid the foundation for an Australian victory by producing the form that took him to the 1968 Wimbledon final. He beat Panatta 6–3, 6–4, 6–4 in the first match. Tony gave a perfect exhibition of intelligent serving, relying on spin and swing rather than power and following up his awkward deliveries with deep volleys that gave Panatta scant opportunity to attack.

It was a tall order to expect Barazzutti to strike back against Alexander. He had played only six previous matches on grass and lost them all. Yet he kept Alexander at full stretch and even won a few points by daringly going to the net behind his 'powder puff' service. Alexander finally won 6–4, 8–6, 4–6, 6–2.

The doubles seemed certain to go Australia's way, but Panatta and Bertolucci did not think so. Playing with flair and resolution, they had the Wimbledon finalists Alexander and Dent struggling for points. Bertolucci was omnipotent. He flicked deceptive ground shots and intercepted brilliantly. Panatta provided the muscle and they won 6–4, 6–4, 7–5.

A strong wind troubled Alexander and Panatta in the next match, a duel between two powerful and courageous men, one stolid and phlegmatic by temperament, the other, Panatta, inspirational and adventurous. After Panatta had adjusted his game to the wind and led 4–6, 6–4, 6–2, his top spin looked to be the match-winning factor. Italian migrants in the crowd played bells and klaxon horns and chanted 'Italia, Italia' to encourage him. Then, when Panatta broke through for a 2–1 lead in the fifth set, an Italian supporter leaped to his feet and gave a rendition of the song, 'It's Now or Never'. Alexander had led 3–0 and 4–1 in the fourth set, but only just managed to win it 8–6 after Panatta served for the match at 6–5 only to double-fault at 30 all. The fifth set seesawed as Panatta immediately lost his 2–1 (and 40–15) lead, and then dropped a further three games, only to surge back when Alexander served for the match at 5–3. The score went to 5 all. Neither man now showed any sign of cracking. But Alexander, serving first, was able to apply a bit more pressure to the Italian's service. Also, he used the lob cleverly. Panatta had little margin for error with his smashing and missed a few overheads that proved costly. At the end, after nearly four hours' play, Alexander's ability to scramble and rally helped to wear Panatta down. When Alexander went to 40-love on Panatta's serve in the twentieth game, Panatta flung himself around the court in a valiant bid to avert defeat. He saved one match point, but

Alexander took the set at 9–7 with a winning volley. The cup once more was Australia's.

–20–

McENROE
TO THE RESCUE

(1978–79, USA; 1980, Czechoslovakia; 1981–82, USA;
1983, Australia)

The fact that only six thousand people attended the exciting last day of the 1977 final – less than a quarter of the crowd that had packed White City for the 1954 challenge round – indicated that, in some countries at any rate, the competition was still ailing. America's failure since 1973 to reach the final was another symptom. Nobody could expect the American public to remain greatly interested in the Davis Cup if Connors, their number one player, declined to play for his country and, as a result, American fortunes languished. Borg meanwhile also became less inclined in the eighties to play for Sweden. Scheduling difficulties and the spiralling amounts of money being offered to players to play in tournaments and exhibitions were threatening the cup's future.

The man who, more than anyone else, saved the competition in the late seventies and early eighties was John Patrick McEnroe, an extremely gifted and fiery New Yorker who burst on the tennis world in 1977 when, as an eighteen-year-old qualifier, he reached the Wimbledon semifinals at his first attempt. Nobody like McEnroe had been seen before. His tempestuous outbursts rocked the tennis establishment and helped to prompt officials into compiling a code of conduct. The left-hander was seen by some not only as a tennis genius, with an amazing touch and an innate sense of strategy, but as a reckless maverick whose behaviour, if copied by others, could destroy many of the game's most cherished values.

The paradox was that McEnroe, who was dubbed 'Superbrat' early in his career, was in some ways a traditionalist at heart. He dearly wanted to play Davis Cup and let it be known that whenever and wherever his country wanted him he would answer the call.

273

Perhaps his early coaching by Hopman at the Port Washington Tennis Academy had something to do with this outlook and perhaps too he was influenced by the exploits of his childhood hero Laver. But perhaps it was simply his natural instinct to be eager to play for his country, an attitude which even in an increasingly cynical and mercenary age should still be considered the norm. Whatever the basis for McEnroe's enthusiasm, he pumped fresh life into the competition and by 1984, when he was the best player in the world, his regular participation helped to give the Davis Cup the status that its tradition and dimensions deserved. With McEnroe playing even in the early rounds, and public interest restored, the circumstances were right for a multinational company to sponsor the Davis Cup to the tune of millions of dollars.

McEnroe dominated the new-style competition almost as much as Tilden had conquered all rivals in the twenties and in 1983 he surpassed Vic Seixas's American record of forty wins in singles and doubles. But because the format had been so drastically changed, McEnroe was exposed to difficulties in foreign lands that Tilden rarely experienced. America won the cup in four years out of six, from 1978 to 1983, losing on clay, McEnroe's least favoured surface, in Buenos Aires in 1980 and 1983. The hopes of most other countries often seemed to depend on McEnroe losing in South America.

He made his debut in 1978 in a doubles match against Chile. American officials dreaded that Santiago would be another South American graveyard, as Chile previously had put out Argentina in Buenos Aires and the Americans had only five days after the US Open in which to prepare for the tie. Chile had a tricky player in Hans Gildemeister, who hit double-handed shots from both sides of his body. He had won the key match against Vilas. But both he and Fillol failed against Solomon and Gottfried respectively. Gottfried and McEnroe wrapped up victory with a four-set win over Fillol and Prajoux.

South Africa was still permitted to enter a team in the American Zone and, in protest, Canada, the Commonwealth Caribbean, Mexico and Venezuela withdrew their entries, leaving fifty countries in the competition. There was further inconvenience when Colombia felt obliged to switch her home tie with South Africa to Johannesburg; and when America played, and beat, the Springboks in Nashville, Tennessee, there were again anti-apartheid demonstrations. Despite the political problems, the competition was still growing. Taiwan had joined the Davis Cup Nations in 1972, and, reflecting the growth of the game in Africa, there followed Nigeria (1974), Kenya (1975) and Algeria (1976). Tunisia was accepted into the competition in 1982, and then Senegal and Singapore in 1984, making the total number of countries that had participated seventy-two.

In 1978 an important change in the administration occurred when the Davis Cup Nations ceased to exist as an autonomous body, and complete responsibility for the cup was assumed by the International Tennis Federation. The change was largely engineered by Philippe Chatrier, who was increasingly stamping his dynamic personality on both the Davis Cup and the ITF, of which, in 1977, he had become president. Chatrier realized that it would be easier to attract a sponsor to the competition if the ITF was in control of the negotiations.

If 1978 was notable for McEnroe's debut it was also remarkable for a sudden, unexpected revival by Great Britain, who played in the final round for the first time since 1937. The British themselves were unprepared for their success, for earlier that year they had appointed a committee to inquire into the sad state of British tennis! Paul Hutchins, the British team manager since 1975, was an energetic leader and had built a new team round Christopher (Buster) Mottram, whose father had once represented Britain, and John Lloyd. In Zone A, Britain swept through Monaco and Austria, then scored convincing victories over France in Paris, and Czechoslovakia at Eastbourne. On the first day of the latter two contests, Mottram disposed of two rising stars in Yannick Noah and Ivan Lendl. Lloyd was just as valuable as he battled to five-set wins over Eric Deblecker and Jiri Hrebec.

Few gave the British much hope of surviving their semifinal with Australia in an indoor arena at the Crystal Palace in London. Australia, which had come through the Eastern Zone without conceding a match, could again count on Roche and Alexander, the heroes of 1977, along with Geoff Masters and Ross Case, the Wimbledon doubles champions of 1977. What happened shook everyone. Mottram, departing from his usual baseline game, took the attack to Roche and beat him 8–6, 3–6, 7–5, 6–4. While Tony's touch made him the classier player, Buster, ten years his junior, wore him down. Lloyd lost the first ten points against Alexander before mastering his nerves. He then concentrated on the Australian's backhand. After winning the first set 7–5, Lloyd unleashed a breathtaking onslaught to hit the Australian off the court 6–2, 6–2. In the doubles, the star was John Lloyd's brother, David, well supported by Cox. They overcame Masters and Case 8–6, 3–6, 6–4, 6–3. Captain Fraser was flabbergasted. 'I would have bet my house and all my possessions,' he said, 'against a 0–3 reversal after two days.'

So would have the Americans, who had reached the final with a semifinal 3–2 win over Sweden at Gothenburg. They were so certain they would be travelling to Australia that they did not have an American site chosen for a final against Britain and eventually had to opt for an outdoor desert location: the Mission Hills Country Club at Rancho Mirage, near Palm Springs, California.

America had not used McEnroe against Sweden, an omission that meant that Borg and McEnroe, the two giants of their era, were destined never to meet in the Davis Cup. Sweden had relied on Borg to drag them through close contests in Zone B against Yugoslavia, Spain and, to a lesser extent, Hungary, who had upended Italy. In planning the visit to Gothenburg, Trabert knew Borg was almost certain to win both his singles and that the doubles would be vital. Stockton, who was going to partner Smith, suffered a back injury and could not play. Smith's regular partner, Lutz, had another commitment which he did not feel like breaking as he thought Trabert had shown a cavalier attitude towards him. At the eleventh hour Lutz was persuaded to change his mind. It was as well for America that he did. Borg beat Ashe in straight sets, Gerulaitis levelled by dismissing Kjell Johansson, also in straight sets, and Smith and Lutz just tipped out Borg and Bengtson, 6–3 in the fifth set, after trailing by two sets to one and being a break down in the fourth set. The long experience of Smith and Lutz as a pair was the decisive factor in this win. It enabled them to move and poach better and turn the match around. Ashe added the clincher by easily beating Johansson on the third day.

For the final, Trabert decided to replace Ashe and Gerulaitis with McEnroe and Gottfried. Over the year, Trabert had underlined the depth of American talent by using nine different players. It was a difficult decision to drop the old stalwart Ashe, now thirty-five, but the nineteen-year-old McEnroe had recently won his first US Open crown and obviously had a superior claim. He was the youngest American to play in the final round since Kramer in 1939.

The British arrived at Palm Springs fairly confident, hoping the draw would pit Mottram against Gottfried in the opening singles as they felt Buster could win this match and so put McEnroe under more pressure in the second match. However, the draw gave Lloyd the first match against McEnroe, and playing McEnroe outdoors on cement was a vastly different proposition from meeting Alexander indoors on a carpet court. McEnroe's mixture of spin and pace was too much for the Englishman, who won only five games. 'I've never been made to look like an idiot on the court before,' said Lloyd. 'Not by Borg, not by Connors, not by anyone until I played McEnroe today.'

Mottram enhanced his reputation as a tough Davis Cup competitor in the second singles. After Gottfried won the first two sets 6–4, 6–2, the third set became a dour struggle as the sun set behind the nearby mountains and the temperature fell. Mottram fended off a match point in the thirteenth game and held on to win the set 10–8. With bulldog spirit, he continued to fight desperately under floodlights in the chilly evening atmosphere and won the last two sets 6–4, 6–3.

The British thought they could still succeed if they captured the doubles and so piled more pressure on the inexperienced McEnroe in the fourth rubber. They were unfortunate to find Smith and Lutz at their best. The Americans gave a polished display in beating Cox and David Lloyd 6–2, 6–2, 6–3. Next day Mottram's courage was of no avail. McEnroe brilliantly dissected him 6–2, 6–2, 6–1. By conceding only ten games in his two matches he had beaten Bill Johnston's record of losing the fewest number of games in the final round. Johnston lost eleven games in the 1922 challenge round when he beat Anderson 6–1, 6–2, 6–3, and Patterson 6–2, 6–2, 6–1. It was an impressive omen that the curly-haired youngster with the ambition to join the game's immortals should set a new standard in his first final.

McEnroe was again the dominant player in 1979 as America dropped only two matches in four ties in retaining the cup. His personal record was intimidating: in his first two years he did not concede a set in singles or doubles. America began by thrashing

Colombia 5–0 indoors at Cleveland, with McEnroe and Stockton winning both their singles, and McEnroe's regular doubles partner, Peter Fleming, making his debut on the second day. Next came the American Zone final against Argentina on the weekend following the US Open at which McEnroe had defended his title in the final against Gerulaitis. At Memphis, again indoors, Gerulaitis allowed Jose-Luis Clerc only seven games and McEnroe was no more generous to Vilas, but the near-veterans Smith and Lutz were fully extended by Clerc and Vilas, who held a match point in the third set and lost, 6–1 in the fifth.

The competition was more even in Europe. In Zone A, Italy eliminated Poland 4–1, Hungary 3–2, and Great Britain 4–1, with the gritty Barazzutti, 'Il Soldatino' (The Little Soldier), saving the side whenever the more glamorous Panatta faltered. After Panatta lost to Wojtek Fibak in Warsaw, it was Barazzutti who levelled by beating Henryk Drzmalski. Then Barazzutti filled the unfamiliar role of doubles partner to Panatta, whose usual collaborator and soulmate Bertolucci was off form. Despite his indifferent volleying, Barazzutti played well enough for the Italians to win, and capped a great performance by downing Fibak in the decisive match. For the tie with Hungary, Italy reverted to the Panatta–Bertolucci combination, but they lost, and again it was Barazzutti who came up with the clincher by beating Peter Szoke for the loss of six games. In the zone final in Rome, Panatta lost to Mottram, Barazzutti beat John Lloyd, and a new pair, Barazzutti and Zugarelli, outrallied Cox and David Lloyd. This time Panatta added the decisive point with a win over John Lloyd.

In Zone B, Czechoslovakia blended the youthful vigour of Lendl and Tomas Smid with the experience of the hardy Kodes. They beat the French in Paris, with Lendl, on the first day, getting the better of Noah, and Smid, a fine competitor, coming from two sets down to stop Gilles Moretton. Kodes and Smid beat Noah and Moretton in the doubles. The zone final in Prague was against Sweden, who had the all-conquering Borg back in her team. Lendl and Smid feasted on Johansson; Kodes and Smid won the doubles; and Borg was powerless to stop a 3–2 defeat.

The inter-zone semifinal between Italy and Czechoslovakia opened at the Foro Italico with two of the most tenacious players, Barazzutti and Smid, facing each other. Smid emerged the victor,

7–5 in the fifth set. Now it was Panatta's turn to fill the breach. He did so handsomely, exchanging sets with Lendl before wiping him out, 6–0, 6–0, in the third and fourth sets. Panatta and Bertolucci, back in favour, ended the run of Kodes and Smid in four sets, and in a gruelling struggle with Lendl, Barazzutti put Italy into the final for the third time in four years by winning 4–6, 6–1, 6–2, 3–6, 7–5.

In the Eastern Zone, Australia returned to Madras, scene of its scary tie with India in 1973. Again there was suspense, though this time fortunately it was confined to tennis. As the Australians practised on a makeshift cow-dung court at the Gymkhana Club, scores of coolies erected bamboo stands around them. The structure looked fragile, as did the visitors as, one by one, they went down with stomach upsets, always a hazard for sportsmen in the subcontinent. India chose Vijay Amritraj and Sashi Menon for the singles, and Vijay and Anand Amritraj for the doubles. Australia went with Alexander and Case in the singles, and Case and Masters in the doubles. For India, Vijay ('Victorious Nectar') was the key.

The acrobatic Case beat Menon, and the ever resolute Alexander curbed Vijay, whose flashy brilliance was marred by defects in technique. ('He ought to go to church more,' said an Indian commentator. 'It would help him to bend his knees.') Australian stock soared, but then came the day of reckoning. Masters was unwell, and it was touch and go whether he could play the doubles. He took the court and wilted in the withering heat. The Amritraj boys won in four sets. Next day a rampant Amritraj put paid to Case in straight sets, and Menon won the first two sets against Alexander 8–6, 6–3. Australia was reeling. Alexander had been sick for more than a week and had been treated with drugs. He was drained of strength. Menon, who was ranked far below him, was serving, volleying and smashing as though his life depended on the result. The turning point came in the first game of the third set when Alexander, looking groggy, nevertheless saved five break points as service went to deuce eleven times. He hung in, won the third and fourth sets 6–3, 6–3, but slumped to 1–3 in the fifth. It was 5.52 p.m., eight minutes before the agreed curfew time. The crowd in the rickety stands were in a frenzy, urging Menon on. Alexander held for 2–3 and called on his last reserves of energy in an attempt to get to 3 all before the postponement. He succeeded. In the morning it was all over in four games, 6–4 to Alexander.

America played Australia in Sydney, with Gerulaitis supporting McEnroe in the singles, and Edmondson, a strong grass-court player, replacing Case in the Australian line-up. The contest was notable for Gerulaitis's dramatic escape from defeat by Edmondson in the rain-interrupted opening match. Serving and volleying decisively, Edmondson won the first two sets 8–6, 16–14. On the damp, windy court he went to 8–7, 40–0 on Gerulaitis's service in the third set – triple match point. Though serving poorly, Vitas kept charging in. He played two winning volleys and Edmondson netted a backhand. Disappointment and anxiety affected the Australian's game, and Gerulaitis's speed and fitness helped the American get on top. Vitas was ranked fifth in the world, sixty-eight places above his opponent, and his experience was an important factor. After more than six hours, including three hours of rain delays, he was the winner, having taken the last three sets 10–8, 6–3, 6–3.

McEnroe cut down the valiant Alexander 9–7, 6–2, 9–7, but Alexander and Dent coped with the tricky wind better than Smith and Lutz, handing them their first cup defeat in eleven matches. Gerulaitis snuffed out Australia's flickering hopes by beating Alexander on the last day.

The odds were stacked heavily America's way in the final. Italy had tragically lost its captain, Umberto Bergamo, in a car smash in October, and when they got to America the players were distracted by an emotional argument over whether or not the new captain should sit on the court or Bergamo's memory be honoured by an empty chair. The Italians also felt they could not contain their opponents on the fast indoor carpet at San Francisco's Civic Auditorium, and they were right. The debacle was the biggest in history; Italy did not win a set. As if Italy's task wasn't hard enough, Barazzutti twisted an ankle in the opening match against Gerulaitis and had to default. McEnroe cleaned up Panatta and Zugarelli; Gerulaitis also trounced Panatta; and Smith and Lutz beat Panatta and Bertolucci to make their overall record 12–1. A sponsor, Congoleum, was paying the American team $50,000 per tie, and in this year it was pretty easy money.

But in 1980, after surviving an awkward tie in Mexico City, America suffered its second defeat in Buenos Aires, and the battle for the trophy by the remaining teams immediately became much more open. Fifty-one nations had set out on the quest, but not South Africa, who at last was barred.

Vilas and Clerc were keen to avenge their loss to America in Memphis in 1979 and had a big advantage in playing on slow clay in front of their local fans. Vilas beat Gottfried 7–5, 6–4, 6–3, and Clerc wrecked McEnroe's proud record of having won all eleven of his cup singles without losing a set by beating him 6–3, 6–2, 4–6, 11–9 in a six and a half hour struggle that ran over two days. Argentine rested its two stars in the doubles, and McEnroe and Fleming kept the tie alive by easily beating Cano and Alejandro Gattiker. But in another grinding match, which lasted four and a half hours, Vilas overcame McEnroe 6–4, 4–6, 6–3, 2–6, 6–4. The Bull of the Pampas was carried around the arena by supporters while flags were waved and drums beaten.

Argentina would have had a good chance of winning the trophy except that Vilas and Clerc began bickering with their national association over playing fees and other matters and at one point threatened to go on strike. When their next opponents, the Czechs, arrived to play them in the inter-zone semifinal, they were in a less positive mood than they had been against America. The Czechs had benefited from two strokes of luck in winning Section B of the European Zone. Noah could not play against them because of injury when France visited Prague, and Nastase was again under suspension (for poor behaviour against Great Britain at Bristol) when the Czechs visited Bucharest. Team captain Bolardt, who first captained Czechoslovakia in 1967, had his own selection problem in Buenos Aires, because Smid was recovering from a back injury. Bolardt decided to save him for the doubles, and use Lendl and the less experienced Slozil for the singles. It was Lendl's tie. After Slozil had lost to Clerc, the rangy young man from Ostrava scored one of his finest wins by beating Vilas 7–5, 8–6, 9–7. He and Smid then beat Clerc and Vilas in the doubles 6–2, 6–4, 6–3, and he followed up by outlasting Clerc 6–1, 7–5, 6–8, 6–2. Czechoslovakia was thus in the final for the second time, and with a much better prospect of winning than in 1975. It was a well-deserved reward for methodical planning, solid teamwork and what was generally regarded as the world's best national training scheme for young players.

Italy became the other finalist. She played only two contests in European Zone A, beating Switzerland 5–0, and Sweden, who were without Borg, the five-time Wimbledon champion, 4–1. The Italians then faced a restructured Australian team built around Peter McNamera and Paul McNamee, who had just won the Wimbledon doubles title. Unlike most of their Australian contemporaries, the two Macs enjoyed playing on clay, but they were not well enough equipped to win in Rome. McNamee won the opening set before petering out against Panatta; McNamara beat Barazzutti in four sets despite the attempts of some spectators to distract him by throwing coins onto the court; and a strenuous doubles went to Panatta and Bertolucci 2–6, 9–7, 9–7, 2–6, 6–4. Panatta gave Italy an unbeatable lead by downing a weary McNamara 6–1, 7–5, 6–4.

The Italians had mixed feelings about reaching the final round for the sixth time since 1960. Not one of their finals had been at home, and on this occasion, instead of playing on a clay court in sunny Buenos Aires, as they had anticipated, they were required to travel to chilly Prague and perform in a converted ice-hockey stadium. Fortunately, two thousand of their supporters decided to go to Prague too and, though outnumbered five to one by Czech fans, they nevertheless managed to make most of the noise. Public interest was such that the Czech Tennis Federation reported 300,000 applications for tickets.

It must have been the rowdiest and most bizarre final ever. Officials had draped large banners across the rafters of the stadium exhorting 'Sport for Peace and Friendship among Nations' and pledging 'The Future Successes of the Czechoslovakian Socialist Republic'. Even if they could have understood the Czech words, the Italian fans would not have tempered their singing, clapping, jeering and hooting. They had much to shout about in the first match, Smid v. Panatta, which Italy had to win if she was to emerge triumphant. Panatta raised their hopes by winning the first two sets. Smid had suffered stomach cramps overnight and had visited a hospital. The trouble may only have been nervousness, for Smid grew stronger as the match progressed. Panatta, on the other hand, appeared to tire and lose concentration, complaining regularly about line decisions. The Italian fans invariably caused a bedlam when they thought the umpire and linesmen were being biased, and finally play was halted for forty-five minutes at 3 all in the fifth set after the arrest of an Italian spectator. According to the Czech police, the man (who turned out to be a lawyer and the brother of a prominent communist politician in Italy) had been ejected from the hall for breaking a no-smoking rule. His friends denied this and said he had been cheering for his team 'in a normal manner'. Led by Paolo Galgani, president of the Italian Tennis Federation, the Italian contingent would not allow play to continue until the offender was returned to his seat. The hiatus did nothing for Panatta's declining spirits and he went down 3–6, 3–6, 6–3, 6–4, 6–4.

Lendl defeated Barazzutti 4–6, 6–1, 6–1, 6–2, and Czechoslovakia became the eighth nation to win the cup (and the first from Eastern Europe) when Smid and Lendl beat Panatta and Bertolucci 3–6, 6–3, 3–6, 6–3, 6–4. The Czechs received only token congratulations from Panatta, Barazzutti and Bertolucci, who declined to attend the closing ceremony in protest against what they considered shabby treatment by court officials. However, the Italian journalist Rino Tommasi put the controversial umpiring decisions into perspective when he said, 'There were only a few mistakes, but the right ones. The Czechs knew when to steal and what to steal. You cannot say we were robbed; we had our pockets picked by experts.'

The year 1981 proved momentous. Nippon Electric Company, a multinational organization specializing in the manufacture of tele-communications systems and electronic equipment, agreed to sponsor the Davis Cup to the tune of $1,000,000 a year; and once again the competition's format was modified. Two of the ITF's objectives were to simplify the Davis Cup and make it less cumbersome and time-consuming. Many people around the world were confused by a competition which stretched over sixteen months, with the preliminary rounds being played in the last four months of the previous year.

Henceforth, the event would be divided into two separate competitions, and each round up to the finals would be played during weeks specified by the ITF. The sixteen strongest tennis nations would participate in a World Group. The other nations would compete in zonal competitions as hitherto. Linking the two competitions would be a promotion and relegation system. Those nations which lost in the first round of the World Group would be required to play off to determine four nations to be relegated to the zonal competition. Meanwhile, the winners of the European A and B, American and Eastern Zones would be promoted to the World

Group. Thus only the sixteen nations in the World Group had the chance of winning the trophy in the immediate year, while the nations in the zones struggled for the right to contest the trophy in the following year.

The generous sponsorship by NEC, which already had agreed to support the Federation Cup financially, permitted incentives to be offered to all participating nations. The champion nation, for instance, would receive $200,000, the runner-up $100,000, and even the losers of the first-round play-offs would each get $20,000 to console them in their disappointment. 'All this,' said Philippe Chatrier, in announcing the agreement, 'should reinforce the event and help us to assure its future. The Davis Cup is the oldest multi-nation event in sport. We have done well to preserve its traditions for so long in a tennis world that has changed so tremendously in the last twelve years. The new arrangement with NEC will help us to maintain its position in the forefront of the sport.'

In its first year the format showed how flexible and stimulating the competition could be. Among the World Group, Argentina had to travel to West Germany, Sweden to Japan, and Australia to France for contests which under the old competition would have been unlikely to occur. Appropriately, in the centenary year of the USTA, the cup was won by America, who beat Mexico, Czechoslovakia, Australia and Argentina, a succession of victories leaving no doubt at all about American superiority. This was the year in which McEnroe dethroned Borg in a gripping Wimbledon final. He won every cup match he played except the one immediately following that final – against Lendl at the new US National Tennis Centre at Flushing Meadow.

Without McEnroe, America probably would have progressed no further than the Californian resort of La Costa, scene of her tussle with Mexico. Arthur Ashe, whose playing career had been curtailed by a serious heart condition, had succeeded Trabert as captain. He nominated Tanner to back up McEnroe in singles, and handed the doubles assignment to Stewart and Riessen. Tanner lost in five sets to the always dangerous Ramirez, but McEnroe predictably squared accounts by beating the seventeen-year-old schoolboy Jorge Lozano. Then America was in trouble as Ramirez lifted Lozano to a five-set doubles victory over the ageing Stewart–Riessen combination.

Tanner had too much experience for Lozano, though, and McEnroe hammered Ramirez.

America was joined in the quarter finals by Czechoslovakia, Australia, Sweden, New Zealand, Great Britain, Rumania and Argentina. McNamara was the hero of Australia's 3–2 win over France indoors in Lyon, beating both Noah and Pascal Portes. Mottram performed a similar role for the British against Italy at Brighton, where he grafted his way to a four-set win over Panatta. Barazzutti levelled by beating Richard Lewis, but Panatta and Berto-lucci were upset by the little-known Andrew Jarrett and Jonathan Smith. Though Panatta kept Italy in the fight on the final day, Mottram destroyed Barazzutti. The West Germany v. Argentina tie also went to the fifth match after Clerc had lost to both Uli Pinner and Rolf Gehring in Munich. Vilas saved his team by beating Pinner.

For America's match with Czechoslovakia Connors made a reappearance – his only cup engagement of the year – and gave a glimpse of how strong America would have been at full strength. Suffering an obvious letdown, McEnroe bewildered a record Amer-ican crowd of 17,445 by losing in straight sets to Lendl, who whipped heavy ground shots past him with relative ease. Connors had little difficulty against an off-form Smid, and in the doubles the old firm of Smith and Lutz gave an impeccable display in outclassing Lendl and Smid. McEnroe was back to near his best in beating Smid, and Connors mopped up with a 7–5, 6–4 win in his shortened 'dead' rubber with Lendl.

Australia scored a 3–1 win over a young Swedish side in Båstad, with McNamara and McNamee losing to Anders Jarryd and Hans Simonsson in the doubles, but registering singles victories over Mats Wilander which would look very impressive in years to come. However, Wilander was only sixteen at the time! Australia's other point came via McNamee's defeat of Per Hjertquist, the remaining match being abandoned. For Britain, Mottram was again the trump, coming from two sets down to thwart New Zealand's Chris Lewis indoors at Christchurch after Britain's Richard Lewis, who had also been two sets down, had beaten Russell Simpson in the opening match. Jarrett and Smith scored another solid win in the doubles. The British run was abruptly stopped by Argentina (who had beaten Rumania), and Hutchins's men returned from Buenos Aires without winning a set. It had taken Argentina twenty-five attempts to reach the final round.

The other semifinal, between America and Australia on an indoor carpet in Portland, Oregon, was marked by high drama. McNamee was having problems with his back and could not play, and twenty-year old John Fitzgerald was favoured to take his place in the singles when he collapsed on the practice court and was at first thought to have suffered a heart attack. Doctors in the intensive care unit of a nearby hospital could find nothing seriously wrong with him but he was ruled out of playing, and Edmondson joined McNamara as Australia's singles players against McEnroe and Tanner.

The two American left-handers dominated the opening singles with their serving. Edmondson could hardly get his racquet on to McEnroe's deceptive deliveries, and an edgy McNamara tended to be intimidated by the meteoric serves of Tanner. However, after trailing by two sets to love, McNamara took Tanner to a fifth set and then broke his serve in the first game. On the changeover Ashe advised Tanner to loosen up and swing more freely on his returns. Tanner responded by standing in and hitting three winners to break back. He won the fifth set 6–2.

With an American victory seemingly inevitable, McEnroe and Fleming should have been fairly relaxed facing the scratch pair of McNamara and Dent in the doubles. Instead, they were tense and irritable and, when two sets up, became involved in several heated incidents with the Canadian umpire. After verbally abusing the umpire, McEnroe was given a formal warning by the referee, who was also a Canadian. Such behaviour in a Davis Cup tie would have been unthinkable in the old days, but, as in the Grand Prix, a penalty system was now deemed necessary and the referee had drastic powers. There was another dispute in the fifth game of the third set. Play was delayed for five minutes while McEnroe and Fleming berated the umpire and also Ashe when he tried to intervene. At the end of the game another official warning was announced. Under the rules a third breach would have brought instant disqualification, but Ashe revealed later that he might have defaulted his players personally rather than let that happen. After the Americans had won 8–6, 6–4, 8–6, an embarrassed Ashe apologized to the Australian team.

The USTA chose Cincinnati's Riverfront Coliseum as the venue for the final. Either because no cup match had been held in the city before, or because the tickets were overpriced, only a small number of the 17,000 seats were sold on the eve of the contest, whereupon a local businessman decided to save Cincinnati's reputation by buying 10,000 tickets and giving them to his staff and business friends. With a concern for his country's reputation, Ashe repeated to McEnroe and Fleming the warning he issued at Portland; he would pull them off the court rather then have them disqualified by the referee.

McEnroe atoned for his 1980 loss to Vilas by opening with an easy straight-sets win against his fellow left-hander. Tanner won the first set against the fast-improving Clerc, now the world's fifth-ranked player, but lost in four. The doubles was a bad-tempered match which several times threatened to explode into fisticuffs. McEnroe and Clerc in particular traded insults and more than once Ashe and the US trainer, Bill Norris, jumped between them for fear that blows might be swung. The two Argentinians, who frankly disliked each other, surprised everybody with the quality of their play. Vilas actually served for the match at 7–6 in the fifth set, but, as so often happened, McEnroe produced his best shots in the crisis and, helped by a Clerc volleying error, the Americans broke back to love. After nearly five hours it was over; a 6–3, 4–6, 6–4, 4–6, 11–9 win to America.

McEnroe stretched the American lead to a decisive 3–1 with a tenacious 7–5, 5–7, 6–3, 3–6, 6–3 win over Clerc, whose form might have been too good for anyone else in the world. The Argentinian served for the first set at 5–4, saved three set points in the second set, led 3–1 in the third, and dominated the fourth with his forceful serve and backhand. But in the fifth set McEnroe lifted his percentage of first serves and confined Clerc to four points against service. When he had won he had more than one reason to jump ecstatically into his captain's arms, for he had completed a rare feat, winning the Wimbledon and US singles and doubles titles and both his singles and the doubles in the Davis Cup final. Only one man had ever done that before – Don Budge.

Brazil, South Korea, Japan and Switzerland were relegated at the end of 1981, their places being taken by Spain and the USSR, winners of the European Zones, Chile, winner of the American Zone, and India, winner of the Eastern Zone. Thirty-seven nations had taken part in the zonal competition, making a total of fifty-three in the whole event, and most agreed that the new format was a success. They were even more satisfied the following year, when fifty-eight nations entered teams, many exciting clashes occurred, and spectators totalled 344,322, a 32 per cent increase on 1981. It was again America's year. Even without Connors, who won the Wimbledon and US Open championships, Ashe's squad was too strong at home for India and Sweden, and for Australia and France away, though there were anxious moments.

A feature of the new-style Davis Cup was that the leading teams of one year could quickly come a cropper in the next, such was the quality of the opposition and the importance of the draw. Thus, Argentina, without Clerc, who was feuding with his association and still disliked Vilas, lost in the first round to France in Buenos Aires. Vilas won both his singles, but Noah and Thierry Tulasne both beat Cano, and Noah and Moretton won the doubles. In other first-round contests that were not decided before the last rubber, Italy beat Great Britain in Rome, New Zealand defeated Spain in Christchurch, and Australia squeezed past Mexico in Mexico City. The men whose nerve stood the test in these exciting encounters were Panatta, Simpson and Edmondson respectively. Simpson's match with Angel Gimenez was the closest; he was down two sets to love before winning, 6–1 in the fifth set. But the most astonishing result was Edmondson's determined 6–1, 6–4, 6–2 win over Ramirez, perhaps the finest performance of his career. Mexico had given the second singles role to another schoolboy, Francisco Maciel, who lost to both Edmondson and McNamara. Ramirez had been too solid for McNamara, and he and Lozano had won what seemed likely to be the all-important doubles against Alexander and Dent. With his black beard and his cap and his ruthless mien making him look like a reincarnated Cortes, the swarthy Edmondson blanketed Ramirez's artistry with controlled aggression. In other first-round matches Chile beat Rumania 3–2; Sweden ousted the USSR 4–1; and Czechoslovakia whitewashed West Germany.

In the second round (or quarter finals), America defeated Sweden 3–2 indoors in St Louis, Australia had little difficulty in disposing of Chile 4–1 on grass in Brisbane, New Zealand surprised Italy 3–2 in Cervia, and France knocked out Czechoslovakia 3–1 in Paris.

The St Louis tie was distinguished by some dogged resistance by Mats Wilander, who that year had become the youngest winner

ever of the French championship. McEnroe, still recovering from
the loss of his Wimbledon crown five days earlier, beat Anders
Jerryd in the opening match, while Wilander outsteadied Eliot
Teltscher, a wiry Californian who had made his debut against India.
When McEnroe and Fleming flattened Jarryd and Hans Simonsson
in the doubles, America looked well in command. Teltscher,
however, had strained his back and Gottfried, who was permitted
to play in his place, lost in straight sets to Jarryd. That left McEnroe
and young Wilander to decide the issue. McEnroe was in one of his
most turbulent moods. His temper cost him a penalty point (just as
it had in the tie with India) and his disputes with line officials were
so unpleasant that several of the officials considered withdrawing in
protest. Frustration was the main cause of his misbehaviour. He led
9–7, 6–2 and had four break points for a 5–2 lead in the third set,
but Wilander, who was as phlegmatic as McEnroe was excitable,
stubbornly kept him at bay and levelled at 4 all. The Swede's deep
ground strokes began to stop McEnroe from getting to the net, and
Mats finally won the third set 17–15 when McEnroe double faulted.
Wilander won the fourth set 6–3. Then he was down 0–2 in the
fifth set, but struck back and held to 6 all. McEnroe pulled out two
aces in winning the thirteenth game and finished off Wilander in the
next game after six hours and thirty-two minutes of play.

The Czechs confidently expected to stage the final against America
in Prague. Their plans went awry in Paris, where the doubles success
of Noah and young Henri Leconte against the more highly rated
Smid and Slozil gave France a 2–1 lead. Lendl had unhappy
memories of Roland Garros, where at the French Open he had been
heralded as the natural successor to the retired Borg but had lost to
Wilander. They were not improved by his five-set loss on the third
day to Noah, which put France into the semifinals. The defeat was
particularly galling as Lendl had missed Wimbledon to concentrate
on the Davis Cup.

France's next opponent, New Zealand, had pulled off one of the
greatest upsets of the year by eliminating Italy on Italian clay, with
Chris Lewis beating both Barazzutti and Panatta, and Simpson also
beating Barazzutti. The Kiwis showed this victory was no fluke
when they journeyed to Aix-en-Provence. Lewis and Simpson lost
both their opening singles, but then beat Noah and Leconte in the
doubles and Lewis made the score 2–2 by outplaying the nineteen-

year-old Tulasne. Simpson, though, was no match for the athletic Noah.

For their semifinal with America, the Australians departed from local tradition and selected an indoor venue, Perth's Entertainment Centre. They also did something else which might have had Norman Brookes spinning in his grave; they imported a synthetic court from France. McNamara had played impeccably on such a court at Lyon the previous year and was thought likely to do well on the surface again. (Ironically, an accident on the same type of court in 1983 wrecked McNamara's right knee and his career.) The Australians hoped that the long trip to Perth might tire McEnroe and that the court would not be to his liking. They were soon disillusioned. Even though McEnroe's flight was delayed and he arrived at Perth with only enough time for a day's practice, he found the court suited him perfectly and he beat McNamara in four sets. One jarring note was McEnroe's running verbal battle with officials, which brought him two warnings and a reproval from his captain. After the match McEnroe publicly rebuked Ashe by saying he should have supported him in the arguments, adding, 'Arthur and I do not agree on the conduct which should be shown in Davis Cup matches.'

Ashe brought in the ambidextrous and tricky, but accident-prone, Gene Mayer for the second match and his angled drives, lobs and drop shots were too baffling for the old warrior Alexander. Mayer too was critical of his captain, whom he considered remiss for having overlooked him for previous ties. As he watched McEnroe and Fleming reverse the result of the 1982 Wimbledon doubles final by beating McNamara and McNamee, Ashe may have mused that the open era had done nothing to enhance the respect shown to US Davis Cup captains.

Much poignancy surrounded the final, which the French staged in November in the 15,000-seat Palais des Sports at Grenoble. It was the first time for forty-nine years that the ultimate round of the competition had been held in France, and there was much nostalgia concerning the Musketeers. In recent years the French federation had invested millions of francs in raising the standards of its players. The primary objective was to recapture the glory won originally by the Musketeers. So thorough was the French coaching system that Noah as a schoolboy was brought from his home in the Cameroons (where he had been spotted by Ashe, who mentioned his potential to Philippe Chatrier) and carefully developed by the federation. Leconte and Tulasne also were products of the elaborate system.

Like the Australians, the French wanted to gain the maximum advantage from the choice of court. Though the season dictated an indoor venue, they none the less decided to play on clay. Statistics disclosed that sixteen of America's forty cup defeats had occurred on clay, mostly in South America. McEnroe in particular usually looked uncomfortable at Roland Garros and had won only one clay-court tournament in his life. Noah and Leconte, on the other hand, grew up on clay. It cost the French $50,000 to construct the temporary clay court in the Palais des Sports, but with the final a sellout and a certain high-rating spectacle for television, the cost was irrelevant.

France's best hope was for Noah to win both his singles and for Leconte to beat Mayer, an outcome that looked more probable if Noah drew Mayer in the first match. He drew McEnroe. The opening set of 111 minutes had the crowd frantic with excitement. Six times Noah held points to break McEnroe's service, but every time he was in danger McEnroe would respond with vicious serves or stinging volleys. In all, he was to serve sixteen aces to Noah's thirteen, figures which suggest the conditions were not as slow as the French had desired, possibly because of the altitude of Grenoble and the fast American ball that was used.

McEnroe had held only one break point until, leading 11–10, he forced his way to deuce, clipped a winning backhand volley, and won the set with a superb lob. Most of the crowd groaned. Noah's chance seemed gone. For the next two sets Yannick played like a man possessed. The most impressive athlete in the game, he served ferociously, volleyed with flair, hit top-spin lobs and angled passes, and generally rampaged with touch and power. McEnroe lost those sets 6–1, 6–3 as the chanting fans sometimes held up play for minutes at a time. He was relieved to retreat to the peace of the locker room for a fifteen-minute interval. When McEnroe returned to the court he was a different player. He had switched to a tighter racquet midway through the third set, and now he regained control by taking the ball earlier and hitting harder. As he put it, the break gave him the chance 'to get my head back together'. Despite some attempts by sections of the crowd to distract him, he won the final two sets 6–2, 6–3.

Leconte, a nineteen-year-old left-hander, knew only one way to play. His speedy arm propelled the ball like a bullet. Sometimes his hurricane hitting was devastating, but almost as often he was rash and erratic and opponents battened down until the storm blew out. Mayer took the first two sets 6–2, 6–2 and was too experienced to panic when a Leconte onslaught earned him the third set at 9–7. In the fourth set, double faults made Leconte vulnerable. Mayer seized on this weakness to win the set 6–4.

The French retained the same players for the doubles, and fought to the end. But they were impotent against McEnroe's expertise and lost 6–3, 6–4, 9–7. McEnroe, said Ashe, was the greatest doubles player he had ever seen, and Fleming modestly estimated his partner was '95 per cent of the team'. On the last day Noah overwhelmed a listless Mayer 6–1, 6–0 in an abbreviated match. McEnroe dispatched Leconte.

In beating Wilander and Noah, McEnroe had played in two of the year's longest matches, but not *the* longest. That dubious honour belonged to Harry Fritz of Canada and Jorge Andrew of Venezuela, who played in a record 100-game marathon in Caracas that went to Fritz 16–14, 11–9, 9–11, 4–6, 11–9. Canada subsequently reached the American Zone final, losing to the new Paraguayan combination of Victor Pecci and a Puerto Rican import, Francisco Gonzalez. Paraguay was joined in the World Group by Indonesia, Denmark and Ireland, while Mexico, India, Spain and West Germany were demoted.

In 1983, after America had again lost in Buenos Aires – its third defeat there in seven years – Argentina became the early favourite. It did so because in another first-round tie its South American neighbour Paraguay caused an even bigger shock by upsetting Czechoslovakia in Asunción. McEnroe, never short of an opinion, thought it 'outrageous' that two such strong teams as America and Argentina should clash so early in the competition. The fact was that Argentina had lost in the first round in 1982 and therefore lacked a seeding. (In 1984, however, there was a change in the seeding rules. Whereas previously the eight nations to win their first round matches were seeded in the following year, in future only the four semifinalists would be automatically seeded with four other nations nominated by the committee of management. The committee thus gave itself the means to ensure inappropriate first-round matches did not recur.) Despite his criticism, McEnroe typically looked forward to the tie as a challenge, hoping to atone for his earlier defeats in Argentina. Unfortunately a shoulder injury affected his preparation and he went down to Clerc and Vilas, though whether he could have beaten them on slow clay even if fully fit was doubtful. Vilas beat Gene Mayer in the first match in straight sets, and Clerc then went to a two sets lead over McEnroe, who was nettled by the noisily partisan crowd. Fighting hard, McEnroe pulled up to two sets all, but slumped to 2–5 in the fifth set when darkness forced a postponement. He recovered to 5-all in the morning, saving three match points in the process, but Clerc, who was said to have slept badly, pulled himself together to win his serve for 6–5 and with three great returns reached match point again, forcing a backhand error to clinch it.

Two hours later McEnroe was back on court and with Fleming beat Vilas and Clerc in a surprisingly long doubles. At that stage he had played more than nine hours of tension-packed tennis in two days and was tired. Vilas, prolonging the rallies as much as he could, beat him in the decisive match 6–4, 6–0, 6–1.

Paraguay's 3–2 win over Czechoslovakia was perhaps not as big an upset as the respective rankings of the players suggested. By winning the Italian title and giving Borg a good match in the French final, Pecci had shown he was capable of playing a very good brand of tennis, and he and Gonzalez were developing into a dangerous doubles pair. The main surprise was the form of Gonzalez, a good-looking giant who, like McEnroe, was born at Wiesbaden, where his father too was serving in the US Army. Believing the Czechs would prefer to play on clay, the Paraguayans gambled by staging the tie indoors on a fast wooden court. Gonzalez lost to Lendl in the first rubber, and Pecci then beat Smid. For the doubles, the Czechs probably erred in nominating Lendl and Smid instead of Smid and Slozil; they went down in straight sets. Smid battled gamely in the first match next day, but the court did not suit him. Gonzalez won 6–3, 12–10, 3–6, 6–3 and was carried off shoulder-high by happy Paraguayans, none of whom would have remembered Paraguay's unheralded entry into the competition back in 1931.

In the other first-round contests France beat the USSR 4–1 in Moscow, Australia beat Britain 4–1 in Adelaide, Rumania beat Chile 5–0 in Timisoara, Sweden beat Indonesia 5–0 in Lomma-Bjarred, New Zealand beat Denmark 5–0 in Christchurch, and Italy beat Ireland 3–2 in Reggio Calabria. The most interesting of these wins were those scored by Australia and Italy.

Australia named a new star, Patrick Cash, a powerfully built seventeen-year-old who became the youngest player to play singles for his country since Vivian McGrath in 1931. Only two months before, Cash had become the youngest player ever to win a Grand Prix tournament, the Victorian Open. He possessed a rugged all-court game, with no obvious weaknesses, but his outstanding attributes were his will to win and his speed and athleticism. Cash had to fight all the way to overcome a determined John Lloyd in the opening match against Britain. He lost the first set 5–7 and at 4 all in the second set was down 0–40 on service, but averted the crisis with some brilliant serving. He won the second and third sets 7–5, 6–3, suffered a letdown in the fourth set, which he lost 1–6, and was down a break at 1–2 in the fifth. With great courage, Cash set about regaining his mastery of a man who, though he had slipped down the rankings since he had helped to rout Australia in 1978, was a very experienced cup player and was playing more confidently than for a long time. With a mixture of audacity, opportunism and good fortune, Cash finally won the fifth set 7–5. It was only the second five-set match of his life. His win took some of the pressure off McNamee, who completely dominated a lacklustre Mottram 6–3, 6–2, 6–2. Mottram's display was so disappointing that captain Hutchins discarded any idea of playing him in the doubles. He nominated John Lloyd and Andrew Jarrett. They had no answer to the lively McNamee's interceptions as he and Edmondson won in four sets.

Italy's difficulties against Ireland were the result of blooding Adriano Panatta's younger brother, Claudio, whose inexperience was evident as he lost to both Sean Sorensen and Matt Doyle, a Californian of Irish descent who had claimed Irish citizenship, after winning the first set 6–1 in each match. Adriano Panatta and Berto-lucci won the critical doubles, and in the fifth rubber Barazzutti, who earlier had beaten Doyle, was too accurate for Sorensen, winning 6–0, 6–3, 6–3.

The quarter finals indicated that Australia would have at least as good a chance as Argentina of winning the cup, mainly because of home-ground advantage but also because of the worry Vilas was suffering over a possible year's suspension from tournament play for having allegedly received illegal appearance money in Rotterdam. In July the Vilas controversy had not yet reached a peak and he was in a ruthless mood in Rome as he crushed Adriano Panatta, once more reinstated as a singles player. Clerc also won, though much less quickly, and the Italians were crushed 5–0.

Noah of France was also in trouble with the authorities and under suspension for having walked out of a World Cup match. France was without him for the testing encounter with Paraguay at Marseilles and chose the youngsters Leconte and Tulasne. A slow court nullified Gonzalez's superior volleying ability and Tulasne beat him in straight sets. The unpredictable Leconte hit some sensational returns to win the first set against Pecci, hardly got a ball into play in losing the second set, then overwhelmed the big South American in the next two sets. France was up 2–0, but the contest was far from over. Pecci and Gonzalez had too much skill for Leconte and Moretton in the doubles, and Pecci was too strong for Tulasne in the fourth rubber. Now the score was 2–2 and, with Leconte taking on Gonzelez, anything could happen. A break of service in each of the first two sets gave Henri those sets 6–4, 6–4. In the third set he served for the tie at 5–4 and had five match points. On two of them he served double faults and on two others he made nervous forehand errors. Gonzalez made the score 5 all, but Leconte came back strongly to break him to 15 and served out the match with a love game, finishing with an ace. Several million French fans, watching on television, unclenched their fists.

The New Zealanders elected to play Sweden on grass at Eastbourne rather than make the long journey home after Wimbledon. Chris Lewis was the man of the moment, having just lost in the Wimbledon final to McEnroe. As Simpson was also a seasoned grass-court player, New Zealand had reason to be confident of beating a Swedish squad whose average age was under twenty and whose grass-court experience was inferior. However, by winning 3–2 the Swedes demonstrated they were going to be a considerable force for some time to come on *any* surface. The key match was Wilander *v.* Lewis on the first day. Simpson had beaten a nervous

Henrik Sundstrom 9–7, 10–8, 6–4, and Wilander needed to win if his country were to have a chance. Assisted by Lewis's thirteen foot faults, he curbed the speedy Kiwi with the steadiness of his ground strokes, winning 6–4, 7–5, 6–8, 10–8. Jarryd and Simonsson won the doubles, but Lewis recorded a five-set win over Sundstrom to make the score 2–2. In the last match Wilander's ground strokes were again the main factor as he beat Simpson 6–3, 6–3, 6–2.

The Australia v. Rumania tie in Brisbane was uneventful except for the misbehaviour once again of Nastase. His antics failed to distract Edmondson or Cash in the singles or Edmondson and McNamee in the doubles, and the Australians romped to a 5–0 victory.

Australia was now in the fortunate position of being able to play at home on grass against France, and, if successful in that tie, to play also at home against either Sweden or Czechoslovakia. That was a tremendous advantage and made up for the fact that not one of her players was ranked among the world's top thirty, whereas all the leading players of the three other nations were.

The Australia v. France semifinal at Sydney belonged to John Fitzgerald, nicknamed 'The Cockaleechie Kid' after the outback hamlet in South Australia from which he hailed. He lacked the natural talent of many other players and had been up and down in the rankings, but on a given week he could be inspired and win a tournament. Although Fitzgerald had not played in the previous rounds, his form had recently improved and, backing a hunch, captain Fraser nominated him with Cash for the singles, ahead of Edmondson and McNamee. France's players, Noah and Leconte, virtually picked themselves. Noah did not like to play on grass, but he had an aggressive type of game that could be adapted to the surface, and his French Open triumph in June had given him a new confidence.

Apart from the court surface, Australia had one psychological advantage. A few days before the tie, the Australian players lost some sleep but gained much in inspiration by watching on television the Australian yacht *Australia II* become the first foreign vessel ever to capture the America's Cup at Newport, Rhode Island. Recovering from a seemingly hopeless position in the series of races, the *Australia II* crew provided a striking example for the cup team.

Noah struck first, beating Cash 6–4, 10–8, 6–3. He was lithe and agile and made the most of Cash's serving lapses. Australia's prospects looked grim when Leconte won the first set against Fitzgerland and gained a break in the second set. Fitzgerald was in danger of being swept away by a whirlwind as Henri served rockets and fired winners from all parts of the court *à la* Laver. Gradually, Fitzgerald worked his way into the match. He won the second set and saved two set points in the third. He finally frustrated Leconte through sheer willpower, determined volleying and a string of backhand passes, winning 4–6, 10–8, 9–7, 6–2. The doubles was expected to be Australia's and so it turned out to be, though Noah's performance was poorer than anticipated and not a good omen for his coming match with Fitzgerald. The latter had benefited from a day's rest in which to recharge his batteries and began to play Noah very positively. He needed to keep his nerve in the crucial first set, for three times he lost his service, the most undependable part of his game, but each time as Noah served for the set he was thwarted. Fitzgerald won the set 13–11, and though Noah won the second set at 6–4, the resolute Australian had the confidence and the shots to win the next two sets 6–3, 6–4, sometimes orchestrating the crowd's support with his pumping fists.

Sweden had an easier entry into the final, winning the first three matches at Stockholm in straight sets. Argentina had little hope after Wilander beat Vilas in the first match. Vilas by now was finding it hard to concentrate on tennis and Wilander was superior all round. Jarryd beat Clerc just as comfortably, and with Simonsson won the doubles.

The final was held over the Christmas holiday period and Australians were reminded of the halcyon challenge-round days. Kooyong Stadium was sold out. By now Sweden was a clear favourite, despite the court surface. Wilander had beaten McEnroe and Lendl in capturing the Australian Open on the same court a few weeks before, and Joakim Nystrom had won the New South Wales title after that. Even in the doubles the Swedes looked formidable, for Jarryd and Simonsson were the French champions and Wimbledon semifinalists. Fraser faced problems in raising the morale of the out-of-form Australians. Cash's on-court demeanour had landed him in trouble several times during the year and he was irritable during the practice sessions. After he had bounced his racquet into the Kooyong stands, Fraser sent him to the dressing room and seriously considered disciplining him. 'I went home that night thinking we couldn't have Cash in the team,' he admitted later. He had a long heart-to-heart talk with Cash and that cleared the air. As for Fitzgerald, he had achieved nothing since the semifinal with France and his confidence was seeping away. Fraser arranged for the psychologist who had helped the *Australia II* crew to talk to Fitzgerald and lift him. Another master stroke was to invite John Bertrand, the *Australia II* skipper, into the Australian dressing room.

The draw favoured Australia because it left Wilander and Fitzgerald playing the last match. If the final was still alive, Wilander's strength would be invaluable at the end, but there was a risk that Mats would be unable to influence events as much as the Swedes wanted him to. And so it transpired. He played the first match against Cash and won 6–3, 4–6, 9–7, 6–3. The tennis was not of a high standard, with Cash serving sixteen double faults and making many mistakes in going for outright winners. A tense Wilander was not as accurate as usual, but was certainly the steadier.

Nystrom, who also possessed a double-handed backhand and played a similar game to Wilander, was preferred to Jarryd on the strength of his Sydney win and Jarryd's indifferent form. It was a mistake. He had played only one previous cup match and had a vulnerable service on grass which had not been exposed in Sydney. Fitzgerald's instructions were to chip and charge whenever the opportunity presented itself. He raced in to the net like a greyhound chasing a hare. The first two sets went to the Australian 6–4, 6–2. Then Nystrom pluckily came back from 0–2 to win the third set 6–4. For a few games the match was in the balance; Fitzgerald's service got ragged and Nystrom's double-hander gave him a slight edge. But Fitzgerald kept rushing the net and would not be denied. He won the fourth set 6–4.

The unbeaten team of Edmondson and McNamee put Australia 2–1 up with a 6–4, 6–4, 6–2 win over Jarryd and Simonsson. The Swedes made the mistake of standing too deep to receive service and were put on the defensive by the Australians' slice and spin. The match marked the end of the Swedish partnership.

Nystrom now had to bear the full burden of saving Sweden. Cash had lost to him in Sydney, but he decided to play a more disciplined game this time. He took pains to get his first service in consistently; to stand in on Nystrom's second serve and play deep approach shots;

and to rush and crowd his opponent. He also did not intend to attempt anything overly ambitious or to feed Nystrom's passing shots by hitting too much top spin. The tactics worked perfectly. Nystrom's service failed and Cash controlled the net. The unhappy Swede won only two of the last twenty points as Cash whipped him 6–4, 6–1, 6–1. From his seat nearby Wilander watched in frustration. His subsequent 6–8, 6–0, 6–1 win over Fitzgerald was little consolation.

For captain Fraser, the 1983 competition had represented the greatest challenge of his life. It was indeed remarkable that Australia had won the cup with a group of such relatively lowly ranked players, one of them a teenager playing his first year in the competition. But such happenings were now always possible and Dwight Davis, who had always wanted to see an even and unpredictable competition, would have approved. There was even the spectacle of the mighty USA playing off against Ireland in Dublin to avoid relegation and that could only be good for the game.

SWEDISH RHAPSODY

(1984, Sweden)

The Australians had only two months in which to savour their triumph before being required to begin their defence. Again, the luck of the draw gave them an early advantage and they comfortably beat Yugoslavia at Perth, then Italy at Brisbane. But the prospect of a semifinal clash with the USA in America was sobering.

Arthur Ashe had mixed feelings when Jimmy Connors, who had often rebuffed his country's captain, volunteer for Cup duty. Perhaps influenced by his new adviser, Donald Dell, and realizing that at thirty-two years of age his career record was conspicuously weakened by the absence of his name on the famous old trophy, Connors lined up with McEnroe and the unbeaten doubles combination of McEnroe–Fleming to form what Ashe considered was the strongest team he had ever led, and what some thought might be the strongest team ever. Whether in retrospect that was true is extremely doubtful, for Connors in particular proved to be vulnerable and American hopes were to end in ruins shortly before Christmas in the cold, sombre Swedish city of Gothenburg. Something else was threatened by the events of Gothenburg: Dwight Davis's ideals, to which Ashe had once expressed his emotional attachment, seemed to be mocked by the behaviour of some of the American players. So much so that US administrators, under prodding from the Press and sponsors, began to take measures to restore a more sportsmanlike spirit in their team.

Great Britain, the other of the competition's founding nations, had different problems. In 1984 it was one of four countries relegated from the World Group – the others being Rumania, New Zealand and Denmark – after play-offs with Yugoslavia, West Germany,

Ecuador and India respectively. Meanwhile, Spain, Chile, the USSR and Japan gained promotion by winning their respective zones.

The first round of the World Group produced only one surprise as Paraguay crossed the Pacific to do battle with New Zealand, a seeded nation, at Christchurch and won the first three rubbers. Ashe took his superstars to Bucharest, but, with Nastase now an increasingly rotund veteran, there was no chance of a repetition of the drama that occurred in the 1972 final and the Americans won 5–0. Sweden beat Ecuador 4–1 at Norrokopin; France won by the same margin against India at New Delhi; Czechoslovakia, even without Lendl, who had been suspended by his country for having played in southern Africa, did not lose a match against Denmark at Hradec Kralove; and Argentina eliminated West Germany 4–1 at Stuttgart. The most exciting first-round tie was that between Great Britain and Italy at Telford, the third meeting between the countries in four years. Barazzutti, beaten in the crucial fifth rubber by Mottram three years earlier, this time had the satisfaction of clinching victory in the fifth rubber against Colin Dowdeswell. Though born in London, Dowdeswell previously had represented Rhodesia. Replacing Mottram, who was ill, he found his first appearance for Britain nerve-wracking.

The quarter finals, held after Wimbledon, went as expected, but there was more than one match of significance. A wrist injury to Wilander gave Henrik Sundstrom his first opportunity to play for Sweden since losing both his singles to New Zealand the year before, and he made the most of it. He beat Pecci in the opening match, and then, after Jarryd had beaten Gonzalez but had lost the doubles with his new young partner, Stefan Edberg, Sundstrom sealed victory for his country by soundly defeating Gonzalez 6–3, 6–1, 6–2. The confidence Sundstrom derived from these encounters was to be of great value in Sweden's coming matches with Czechoslovakia and America. Lendl, by contrast, when his twelve months' suspension was completed and he returned to the Czech team at Hradec Kralove, was shaken by France's Leconte. With brilliant hitting, Leconte won their opening match in straight sets. Another French youngster, Guy Forget, who was substituting for the injured Noah, raised French hopes when he then led Smid by two sets to one. Smid weathered the crisis and, with Slozil, put his country in the lead by beating Leconte and Pascal Portes in five sets in the doubles, whereupon Lendl won the decisive rubber against Forget.

America again turned the tables on Argentina, winning all five matches at Atlanta. Twice before, McEnroe had lost to Clerc in cup matches. This time he crushed him 6–4, 6–0, 6–2. But with his successful Wimbledon campaign only just concluded he found it hard to maintain his concentration in the doubles. The scratch pair of Clerc and Jaite (a replacement for the injured Vilas) took McEnroe and Fleming to four sets, and a tetchy McEnroe could not resist taunting the small contingent of Argentinian fans and exchanging insults with Clerc over the net.

Australia was not willing to concede the cup without a fight and optimistically travelled to Portland, Oregon, for its semifinal. The mood was mainly due to the continued improvement of young Cash, who had reached the semifinals of both Wimbledon and the US Open and, in the long term at any rate, looked a possible challenger to McEnroe's supremacy. Captain Fraser hoped that Cash would be pitted against Connors on the first day. The draw ordained otherwise, and Cash met McEnroe in the opening match. From the moment the public address system began to relay commercial jingles during the change of ends proclaiming McEnroe as the world's number one little went the Australians' way. Fraser had the jingles stopped, but he couldn't stop his player's tendency to waste break-points. McEnroe won the first set 6–3 and at 3 all in the second set staged one of his familiar stand-up protests which eventually led to the referee overruling the Canadian umpire in the American's favour. Cash promptly lost his composure and then his concentration. He won only two more games in the match and was warned by the umpire in the third set for verbal abuse. Fitzgerald, a heroic figure on grass the previous year, had no answer to Connnors' raking drives in the second match, and the contest was all over when the hitherto invincible Edmondson and McNamee went down in straight sets to McEnroe and Fleming. Cash's 6–4, 6–2 defeat of Connors in the 'dead' fifth rubber was all the Australians could salvage from the wreckage.

Czechoslovakia meanwhile allowed winning opportunities to slip away in its semifinal with Sweden at Bastad. After Wilander had beaten Smid 7–5, 7–5, 6–2 in the opening rubber, Sundstrom found himself trailing 4–6, 3–6, 0–3 and 0–40 to Lendl. Many fans streamed out of the stadium convinced that Lendl, who had won the French championship a few months earlier, was going to overpower Sundstrom just as he did, eventually, McEnroe in the final of that event. They underestimated their player's doggedness. At the French Open, Sundstrom had tenaciously clawed his way back into his match with Hans Gildemeister after being down 2–6, 0–6, 1–5 to win in five sets. The memory of that feat stood him in good stead. He picked up his game and won six games in a row against Lendl, who became increasingly nervous and lost control of the proceedings. Indeed, the Czech could win only one game in each of the last two sets. The doubles provided another astonishing comeback when Jarryd and Edberg recovered from being two sets down to beat Smid and Slozil 2–6, 5–7, 6–1, 10–8, 6–2. Then the Swedish team went on to complete a morale-boosting 5–0 whitewash.

Sweden thus reached its third Davis Cup final and, following the French example, immediately began making arrangements to play America on a specially laid indoor clay court at Gothenburg. It was to be America's fifty-fourth appearance in the final round, and because of the superior rankings of McEnroe and Connors, and the awesome doubles record of McEnroe and Fleming, many observers thought the Americans would be too strong for the less experienced Swedes, whose eldest player, at twenty-three, was Jarryd.

Yet however formidable as individuals, the Americans lacked the poise and team spirit of their opponents. To the amazement of the world, they lost nine of the first ten sets that were played in suffering one of their most humiliating defeats for many years. To Richard Evans, Ashe's men formed 'the most uptight and least harmonious Davis Cup team' he had known and Ashe was 'quite unable to exert any authority over two millionaire superstars who would have no compunction in threatening to walk off the team if Ashe started to lay down the law'. One part of the problem was that McEnroe and Connors intensely disliked each other. The pair made uncomfortable teammates, especially, according to Evans, when Connors was 'snapping at junior members of the team, absenting himself from the bench while his colleagues sweated it out on court, and risking disqualification as a result of his inability to accept defeat in a civilized manner'.

The Scandinavium Stadium was packed with 12,000 people when Wilander dispatched Connors 6–1, 6–3, 6–3. Like McEnroe,

Connors had not arrived at Gothenburg until four days before the final began and was under-prepared. Wilander, on the other hand, was still sharp and buoyant following his recent Australian Open victory and he put the net game he had been obliged to develop in Melbourne to good effect. He hit deep ground strokes, varying his pace to prevent Connors getting his own ground strokes too grooved. Connors became more and more disgruntled. He received a code of conduct warning in the first set, and in the third set was docked a penalty point for an audible obscenity. Because of another outburst, he lost a whole game to give Wilander a 5–3 lead. At the end of the match Connors abused the British umpire so savagely that the referee, Alan Mills, spent a troubled twenty-four hours pondering whether to disqualify him from his remaining singles. There were unconfirmed reports that the American contingent applied great pressure to Mills, though there is no suggestion that its attitude influenced him in his ultimate decision to accept Connors' apology and fine him $2000 for the incidents which occurred during the match. Mills did make allowance, though, for the stress Connors might have been under because of the imminent arrival of his second child. For his leniency the unfortunate referee received almost as severe a lashing in some British newspapers as Connors himself.

McEnroe was expected to even the scores by beating Sundstrom. He had lost only two matches throughout the year and even a clay court seemed unlikely to dim his brilliance. But, as a result of suspension and injury, McEnroe had not played competitively for six weeks. Against Sundstrom's heavily topped forehands he did not time the ball very well. It was obvious he was in trouble when the determined Sundstrom took the tense and exhausting first set 13–11. A single break of serve gave the second set to the Swede at 6–4, and though he trailed 1–3 in the third set a succession of great backhand shots destroyed the tiring American's last hope and he won that set 6–3.

By now American morale was at a low ebb. Despite their unbroken run of fifteen Davis Cup victories, McEnroe and Fleming were in no mood to stem the confident doubles attack of Jarryd and Edberg, to whom they had lost in a semifinal of the US Open. The Swedes won 7–5, 5–7, 6–2, 7–5, with the nineteen-year-old Edberg the most dominant player, ripping the American defence apart with the speed and precision of his backhand volley as he poached on returns. Edberg also returned serve strongly and never dropped his own service. Jarryd played the steadying role – when steadying was needed.

On the last day McEnroe derived little consolation in beating Wilander, and Jimmy Arias, substituting for Connors, went down to the all-conquering Sundstrom.

There were repercussions to the uglier incidents at Gothenburg, which were only the latest chapter in a regrettable history of misconduct by American cup players, particularly McEnroe. The American team's sponsor, the Louisiana Pacific Corporation, threatened to withdraw its $300,000 backing of the team unless team members behaved more civilly in future. 'True, our team shines if one were to consider only the skills of the game,' said Harry Merlo, the corporation's president, in a letter to Gordon Jorgensen, chairman of the USTA Davis Cup committee. 'But we fail badly when it comes to living up to minimum standards on the court during awards ceremonies and at other official Davis Cup events.' Merlo, like the USTA president, Hunter Delatour, had been embarrassed by Connors' rudeness and McEnroe's earlier gracelessness in criticizing the hosts over the dates of the final and the facilities. He cited in his letter such demeanours as abusive language and gestures, abuse of racquets and balls, and courtside excessiveness. Such irresponsible and immature behaviour should not be tolerated, he said, and he proposed a code of conduct requiring each player to agree to conduct himself in a manner which reflected well on his team and country and to treat with respect those individuals he came into contact with as a team member. While Merlo and his company reserved their main criticism for the American team, they were also annoyed at the earlier behaviour of Australia's Pat Cash in apparently wilfully damaging his hotel room at Portland. They released a picture of the room with a hole in the wall, and this was published in *World Tennis* with the caption: 'The big smash. Everyone knew about Pat Cash's temper but this hotel room wall couldn't fight back during the US–Australia Davis Cup series.' The Australian team paid $300 damages to the hotel.

In response to the damage being done to America's reputation for sportsmanship, the USTA introduced new guidelines which those selected for Davis Cup assignments in future would be required to sign. The players would have to show 'courtesy and civility towards competitors, officials and spectators at all times'. Yet, judging by the scornful reaction of Connors and McEnroe to Harry Merlo's letter (they were each sent copies), the situation was far from resolved, and it almost seemed that to them the fine ideals espoused by Dwight Davis when he put up his trophy in 1900 appeared to mean nothing.

RESULTS
YEAR BY YEAR

Abbreviations: d. = defeated; def. = defaulted; ret. = retired; unfin. = unfinished

1900: USA

CHALLENGE ROUND
USA d. British Isles 3–0, Boston: D. F. Davis d. E. D. Black 4–6, 6–2, 6–4, 6–4; M. D. Whitman d. A. W. Gore 6–1, 6–3, 6–2; Davis–H. Ward d. Black–H. R. Barrett 6–4, 6–4, 6–4; Davis v. Gore 9–7, 9–9 unfin.

1901: NO CONTEST

1902: USA

CHALLENGE ROUND
USA d. British Isles 3–2, New York: M. D. Whitman d. Dr J. Pim 6–1, 6–1, 1–6, 6–0; W. A. Larned lost to R. F. Doherty 6–3, 6–2, 3–6, 4–6, 4–6; D. F. Davis–H. Ward lost to R. F. & H. L. Doherty 6–3, 8–10, 3–6, 4–6; Larned d. Pim 6–3, 6–2, 6–3; Whitman d. R. F. Doherty 6–1, 7–5, 6–4.

1903: BRITISH ISLES

CHALLENGE ROUND
British Isles d. USA 4–1, Boston: R. F. Doherty lost to W. A. Larned def.; H. L. Doherty d. R. D. Wrenn 6–0, 6–3 6–4; R. F. & H. L.

Doherty d. R. D. & G. L. Wrenn 7–5, 9–7, 2–6, 6–3; H. L. Doherty d. Larned 6–3, 6–8, 6–0, 2–6, 7–5; R. F. Doherty d. R. D. Wrenn 6–4, 3–6, 6–3, 6–8, 6–4.

1904: BRITISH ISLES

FIRST ROUND
Belgium d. Austria def.

SECOND ROUND
Belgium d. France 3–2, London: P. de Borman lost to M. Decugis 4–6, 3–5, ret.; W. Lemaire d. P. Ayme 6–1, 6–0, 6–1; Lemaire–de Borman lost to Decugis–Ayme 7–5, 4–6, 6–0, 4–6, 2–6; de Borman d. Ayme 6–1, 6–3, 2–6, 1–6, 6–3; Lemaire d. Decugis 5–7, 8–6, 0–6, 6–4, 6–2.

CHALLENGE ROUND
British Isles d. Belgium 5–0, London: F. L. Riseley d. W. Lemaire 6–1, 6–4, 6–2; H. L. Doherty d. P. de Borman 6–4, 6–1, 6–1; R. F. & H. L. Doherty d. de Borman–Lemaire 6–0, 6–1, 6–3; H. L. Doherty d. Lemaire def.; Riseley d. de Borman 4–6, 6–2, 8–6, 7–5.

1905: BRITISH ISLES

FIRST ROUND
USA d. Belgium def.

SECOND ROUND
USA d. France 5–0, London: H. Ward d. M. Germot 6–2, 6–2, 6–1; W. J. Clothier d. M. Decugis 6–3, 6–4, 6–4; Ward–B. C. Wright d. Germot–Decugis 6–2, 6–2, 6–2; Ward d. Decugis 6–2, 6–2, 6–1; Clothier d. Germot 6–3, 5–7, 6–1, 6–3. **Australasia d. Austria 5–0, London:** N. E. Brookes d. R. Kinzel 6–0, 6–1, 6–2; A. F. Wilding d. C. von Wessely 4–6, 6–3, 7–5, 6–1; Brookes–A. W. Dunlop d. Kinzel–von Wessely 9–7, 6–2, 7–5; Brookes d. von Wessely 6–0, 6–2, 6–2; Wilding d. Kinzel 6–3, 4–6, 6–2, 6–4.

FINAL ROUND
USA d. Australasia 5–0, London: B. C. Wright d. N. E. Brookes 12–10, 5–7, 12–10, 6–4; W. A. Larned d. A. F. Wilding 6–3, 6–2, 6–4;

Wright–H. Ward d. Brookes–A. W. Dunlop 6–4, 7–5, 5–7, 6–2; Wright d. Wilding 6–3, 6–3; Larned d. Brookes 14–12, 6–0, 6–3.

CHALLENGE ROUND
British Isles d. USA 5–0, London: H. L. Doherty d. H. Ward 7–9, 4–6, 6–1, 6–2, 6–0; S. H. Smith d. W. A. Larned 6–4, 6–4, 5–7, 6–4; R. F. & H. L. Doherty d. Ward–B. C. Wright 8–10, 6–2, 6–2, 4–6, 8–6; H. L. Doherty d. Larned 6–4, 2–6, 6–8, 6–4, 6–2; Smith d. W. J. Clothier 6–1, 6–4, 6–3.

1906: BRITISH ISLES

FIRST ROUND
Australasia d. Austria def.; USA d. France def.

SECOND ROUND
USA d. Australasia 3–2, Newport (Wales): H. Ward d. L. O. S. Poidevin 6–2, 6–4, 7–5; R. D. Little lost to A. F. Wilding 2–6, 6–8, 1–6; Ward–Little d. Wilding–Poidevin 7–5, 6–2, 6–4; Ward lost to Wilding 3–6, 6–3, 6–0, 4–6, 6–8; Little d. Poidevin 6–2, 1–6, 7–5, 6–2.

CHALLENGE ROUND
British Isles d. USA 5–0, London: S. H. Smith d. R. D. Little 6–4, 6–4, 6–1; H. L. Doherty d. H. Ward 6–2, 8–6, 6–3; R. F. & H. L. Doherty d. Ward–Little 3–6, 11–9, 9–7, 6–1; Smith d. Ward 6–1, 6–0, 6–4; H. L. Doherty d. Little 3–6, 6–3, 6–8, 6–1, 6–3.

1907: AUSTRALASIA

FIRST ROUND
Australasia d. USA 3–2, London: N. E. Brookes d. B. C. Wright 6–4, 6–4, 6–2; A. F. Wilding d. K. H. Behr 1–6, 6–3, 3–6, 7–5, 6–3; Brookes–Wilding lost to Wright–Behr 6–3, 10–12, 6–4, 2–6, 3–6; Brookes d. Behr 4–6, 6–4, 6–1, 6–2; Wilding lost to Wright 8–6, 3–6, 3–6, 5–7.

CHALLENGE ROUND
Australasia d. British Isles 3–2, London: N. E. Brookes d. A. W. Gore 7–5, 6–1, 7–5; A. F. Wilding d. H. R. Barrett 1–6, 6–4, 6–3, 7–5; Brookes–Wilding lost to Gore–Barrett 6–3, 6–4, 5–7, 2–6, 11–13; Brookes d. Barrett 6–2, 6–0, 6–3; Wilding lost to Gore 6–3, 3–6, 5–7, 2–6.

1908: AUSTRALASIA

FIRST ROUND

USA d. British Isles 4–1, Boston: W. A. Larned d. J. C. Parke 6–3, 6–3, 7–5; B. C. Wright lost to M. J. G. Ritchie 1–6, 3–6, 2–6; F. B. Alexander–H. H. Hackett d. Ritchie–Parke 6–3, 2–6, 7–5, 6–1; Larned d. Ritchie 4–6, 6–3, 6–2, 6–3; Wright d. Parke 8–10, 3–6, 6–4, 7–5, 6–2.

CHALLENGE ROUND

Australasia d. USA 3–2, Melbourne: N. E. Brookes d. F. B. Alexander 5–7, 9–7, 6–2, 4–6, 6–3; A. F. Wilding lost to B. C. Wright 6–3, 5–7, 3–6, 1–6; Brookes–Wilding d. Wright–Alexander 6–4, 6–2, 5–7, 2–6, 6–4; Brookes lost to Wright 6–0, 6–3, 5–7, 2–6, 10–12; Wilding d. Alexander 6–3, 6–4, 6–1.

1909: AUSTRALASIA

FIRST ROUND

USA d. British Isles 5–0, Philadelphia: W. A. Larned d. C. P. Dixon 6–3, 6–2, 6–0; W. J. Clothier d. J. C. Parke 6–4, 6–3, 8–6; H. H. Hackett–R. D. Little d. Parke–W. C. Crawley 3–6, 6–4, 6–4, 4–6, 8–6; Larned d. Parke 6–3, 6–2, 6–3; Clothier d. Dixon 6–3, 6–1, 6–4.

CHALLENGE ROUND

Australasia d. USA 5–0, Sydney: N. E. Brookes d. M. E. McLoughlin 6–2, 6–2, 6–4; A. F. Wilding d. M. H. Long 6–2, 7–5, 6–1; Brookes–Wilding d. McLoughlin–Long 12–10, 9–7, 6–3; Brookes d. Long 6–4, 7–5, 8–6; Wilding d. McLoughlin 3–6, 8–6, 6–2, 6–3.

1910: NO CONTEST

1911: AUSTRALASIA

FIRST ROUND

USA d. South Africa def.

FINAL ROUND

USA d. British Isles 4–1, New York: W. A. Larned d. C. P. Dixon 6–3, 2–6, 6–3, 3–6, 7–5; M. E. McLoughlin d. A. H. Lowe 7–5, 6–1,

4–6, 4–6, 6–3; R. D. Little–T. C. Bundy lost to Dixon–A. E. Beamish 3–6, 5–7, 4–6; Larned d. Lowe 6–3, 1–6, 7–5, 6–1; McLoughlin d. Dixon 8–6, 3–6, 6–3, 6–2.

CHALLENGE ROUND
Australasia d. USA 5–0, Christchurch: N. E. Brookes d. B. C. Wright 6–4, 2–6, 6–3, 6–3; R. W. Heath d. W. A. Larned 2–6, 6–1, 7–5, 6–2; Brookes–A. W. Dunlop d. Wright–M. E. McLoughlin 6–4, 5–7, 7–5, 6–4; Brookes d. McLoughlin 6–4, 3–6, 4–6, 6–3, 6–4; Heath d. Wright def.

1912: BRITISH ISLES

FIRST ROUND
British Isles d. France 4–1, Folkestone: C. P. Dixon d. M. Decugis 6–3, 6–2, 6–4; A. W. Gore lost to A. H. Gobert 4–6, 6–4, 3–6, 3–6; Dixon–H. R. Barrett d. Gobert–W. H. Laurentz 3–6, 6–4, 6–1, 6–1; Dixon d. Gobert 4–6, 6–4, 6–2, 6–3; Gore d. Decugis 6–3, 6–0 ret.

SECOND ROUND
British Isles d. USA def.

CHALLENGE ROUND
British Isles d. Australasia 3–2, Melbourne: J. C. Parke d. N. E. Brookes 8–6, 6–3, 5–7, 6–2; C. P. Dixon d. R. W. Heath 5–7, 6–4, 6–4, 6–4; Parke–A. E. Beamish lost to Brookes–A. W. Dunlop 4–6, 1–6, 5–7; Parke d. Heath 6–2, 6–4, 6–4; Dixon lost to Brookes 2–6, 4–6, 4–6.

1913: USA

FIRST ROUND
Germany d. France 4–1, Wiesbaden: O. Kreuzer d. A. H. Gobert 1–6, 6–4, 6–2, 6–3; F. W. Rahe lost to M. Decugis 6–2, 4–6, 6–2, 6–8, 5–7; Rahe–H. Kleinschroth d. Decugis–M. Germot 7–5, 6–4, 4–6, 9–7; Kreuzer d. Decugis def.; Rahe d. Gobert 6–1, 6–1, 6–1. **USA d. Australasia 4–1, New York:** M. E. McLoughlin d. H. Rice 6–1, 6–3, 6–3; R. N. Williams d. S. N. Doust 6–4, 6–4, 1–6, 7–5; McLoughlin–H. H. Hackett lost to Doust–A. B. Jones 6–2, 2–6, 7–5, 2–6, 7–9; McLoughlin d. Doust 6–4, 6–4, 6–2; Williams d. Rice 1–6, 4–6, 9–7, 6–1, 6–2. **Canada d. South Africa 4–1, London:** R. B. Powell d. R. F. Le Sueur 6–3, 6–4, 4–6, 3–6,

7–5; B. P. Schwengers lost to V. R. Gauntlett 9–11, 3–6, 0–6; Powell–Schwengers d. Gauntlett–Le Sueur 7–5, 6–3, 3–6, 6–3; Powell d. Gauntlett def.; Schwengers d. Le Sueur 6–3, 6–3, 6–3.

SECOND ROUND
USA d. Germany 5–0, Nottingham: R. N. Williams d. O. Kreuzer 7–5, 6–4, 4–6, 6–1; M. E. McLoughlin d. O. Froitzheim 5–7, 2–6, 6–4, 6–2, 6–2; McLoughlin–H. H. Hackett d. F. W. Rahe–H. Kleinschroth 6–4, 2–6, 6–3, 8–6; Williams d. Froitzheim 5–7, 6–1, 6–3, 6–1; W. F. Johnson d. O. Kreuzer 7–5, 6–4, 5–7, 6–4.   **Canada d. Belgium 5–0, Folkestone:** R. B. Powell d. P. de Borman 6–2, 6–1, 6–1; B. P. Schwengers d. A. G. Watson 6–4, 6–1, 6–0; Schwengers–Powell d. Watson–W. H. Du Vivier 6–2, 6–2, 6–2; Schwengers d. de Borman 4–6, 6–4, 6–2, 6–2; Powell d. Watson def.

FINAL ROUND
USA d. Canada 3–0, London: R. N. Williams d. B. P. Schwengers 6–4, 6–2, 6–4; M. E. McLoughlin d. R. B. Powell 10–8, 6–1, 6–4; McLoughlin–H. H. Hackett d. Powell–Schwengers 6–3, 6–3, 12–10.

CHALLENGE ROUND
USA d. British Isles 3–2, London: M. E. McLoughlin lost to J. C. Parke 10–8, 5–7, 4–6, 6–1, 5–7; R. N. Williams d. C. P. Dixon 8–6, 3–6, 6–2, 1–6, 7–5; H. H. Hackett–McLoughlin d. H. R. Barrett–Dixon 5–7, 6–1, 2–6, 7–5, 6–4; McLoughlin d. Dixon 8–6, 6–3, 6–2; Williams lost to Parke 2–6, 7–5, 7–5, 4–6, 2–6.

1914: AUSTRALASIA

FIRST ROUND
British Isles d. Belgium 5–0, Folkestone: J. C. Parke d. A. G. Watson 6–2, 6–2, 6–3; T. M. Mavrogordato d. P. de Borman 6–1, 6–3, 8–6; H. R. Barrett–Mavrogordato d. Watson–W. H. du Vivier 6–1, 6–2, 6–2; Parke d. de Borman 6–4, 6–3, 6–0; Mavrogordato d. Watson 6–1, 6–0, 6–3.   **Australasia d. Canada 5–0, Chicago:** N. E. Brookes d. B. P. Schwengers 6–2, 6–3, 6–2; A. F. Wilding d. R. B. Powell 6–1, 6–2, 6–2; Brookes–Wilding d. Schwengers–Powell 6–4, 6–3, 6–4; Brookes d. Powell 6–0, 6–1, 6–3; Wilding d. Schwengers 7–5, 6–3, 6–1.

SECOND ROUND
British Isles d. France 4–1, London: T. M. Mavrogordato d. M. Germot 4–6, 7–5, 9–7, 6–2; J. C. Parke d. M. Decugis 6–2, 4–6, 3–6,

6–3, 6–3; H. R. Barrett–Mavrogordato lost to Decugis–Germot 3–6, 7–5,
5–7, 4–6; Parke d. Germot 7–5, 6–1, 6–3; Mavrogordato d. Decugis 6–1,
7–5, 7–5. **Australasia d. Germany 5–0, Pittsburgh:** N. E. Brookes
d. D. Froitzheim 10–8, 6–1, 6–2; A. F. Wilding d. O. Kreuzer 6–2, 6–2,
6–4; Brookes–Wilding d. Froitzheim–Kreuzer 6–1, 6–1, 6–2; Brookes d.
Kreuzer 6–4, 6–2, 6–8, 6–2; Wilding d. Froitzheim 6–3, 6–4, 6–2.

FINAL ROUND
Australasia d. British Isles 3–0, Boston: N. E. Brookes d. J. C. Parke
6–2, 4–6, 6–3, 1–6, 7–5; A. F. Wilding d. A. H. Lowe 6–3, 6–1, 16–14;
Brookes–Wilding d. Parke–T. M. Mavrogordato 6–1, 6–0, 6–4.

CHALLENGE ROUND
Australasia d. USA 3–2, New York: A. F. Wilding d. R. N. Williams
7–5, 6–2, 6–3; N. E. Brookes lost to M. E. McLoughlin 15–17, 3–6,
3–6; Brookes–Wilding d. McLoughlin–T. C. Bundy 6–3, 8–6, 9–7;
Brookes d. Williams 6–1, 6–2, 8–10, 6–3; Wilding lost to McLoughlin
2–6, 3–6, 6–2, 2–6.

1915–18: NO CONTESTS

1919: AUSTRALASIA

FIRST ROUND
France d. Belgium 3–0, Brussels: M. Decugis d. P. de Borman 6–2,
6–3, 6–4; W. H. Laurentz d. M. Lammens 5–7, 6–3, 6–4, 6–2;
Decugis–Laurentz d. de Borman–Lammens 6–3, 7–5, 6–2. **British Isles
d. South Africa 4–1, Eastbourne:** T. M. Mavrogordato d. B. Raymond
1–6, 7–5, 2–6, 8–6, 6–1; A. R. F. Kingscote d. G. H. Dodd 6–3, 6–3,
6–2; H. R. Barrett–Kingscote d. Dodd–H. I. P. Aitken 7–5, 9–7, 6–4;
Kingscote d. Raymond 1–6, 6–0, 6–4, 6–1; Mavrogordato lost to Dodd
7–9, 5–7, 6–3, 6–4, 5–7.

FINAL ROUND
British Isles d. France 3–2, Deauville: P. M. Davson lost to A. H.
Gobert 5–7, 4–6, 6–4, 4–6; A. R. F. Kingscote d. W. H. Laurentz 4–6,
6–3, 6–2, 4–6, 6–4; H. R. Barrett–O. G. N. Turnbull lost to
Gobert–Laurentz 0–6, 1–6, 10–12; Kingscote d. Gobert 6–4, 6–4, 7–5;
Davson d. Laurentz 6–4, 1–6, 10–12, 6–4, 6–0.

CHALLENGE ROUND
Australasia d. British Isles 4–1, Sydney: J. O. Anderson lost to A. R.
F. Kingscote 5–7, 2–6, 4–6; G. L. Patterson d. A. H. Lowe 6–4, 6–3,
2–6, 6–3; N. E. Brookes–Patterson d. Kingscote–A. E. Beamish 6–0,
6–0, 6–2; Patterson d. Kingscote 6–4, 6–4, 8–6; Anderson d. Lowe 6–4,
5–7, 6–3, 4–6, 12–10.

1920: USA

FIRST ROUND
Holland d. South Africa 3–2, Arnhem: C. van Lennep lost to C. L.
Winslow 3–6, 4–6, 4–6; A. D. Kool d. L. B. Raymond 6–3, 6–3, 7–5;
van Lennep–Kool d. Winslow–Raymond 6–2, 7–5, 6–4; van Lennep d.
Raymond 4–6, 6–4, 6–4, 3–6, 6–3; Kool lost to Winslow 3–6, 2–6,
5–7.   **USA d. France 3–0, Eastbourne:** W. M. Johnston d. A. H.
Gobert 6–3, 8–6, 6–3; W. T. Tilden d. W. H. Laurentz 4–6, 6–2, 6–1,
6–3; Johnston–Tilden d. Gobert–Laurentz 6–2, 6–3, 6–2.

SECOND ROUND
Holland d. Canada def.; USA d. British Isles 5–0, London: W. M.
Johnston d. J. C. Parke 6–4, 6–4, 2–6, 3–6, 6–2; W. T. Tilden d. A. R.
F. Kingscote 4–6, 6–1, 6–3, 6–1; Johnston–Tilden d. Parke–Kingscote
8–6, 4–6, 4–6, 6–3, 6–2; Johnston d. Kingscote 6–4, 4–6, 3–6, 6–4, 7–5;
Tilden d. Parke 6–2, 6–3, 7–5.

FINAL ROUND
USA d. Holland def.

CHALLENGE ROUND
USA d. Australasia 5–0, Auckland: W. T. Tilden d. N. E. Brookes
10–8, 6–4, 1–6, 6–4; W. M. Johnston d. G. L. Patterson 6–3, 6–1, 6–1;
Tilden–Johnston d. Brookes–Patterson 4–6, 6–4, 6–0, 6–4; Tilden d.
Patterson 5–7, 6–2, 6–3, 6–3; Johnston d. Brookes 5–7, 7–5, 6–3, 6–3.

1921: USA

FIRST ROUND
British Isles d. Spain 4–1, London: F. G. Lowe d. M. de Gomar 6–3,
4–6, 6–1, 6–0; R. Lycett d. M. Alonso 6–4, 6–2, 6–4; Lycett–M.
Woosnam d. Alonso–de Gomar 2–6, 9–7, 6–2, 6–2; Lowe lost to Alonso

6–8, 1–6, 6–8; Lycett d. de Gomar 6–1, 6–8, 7–9, 6–3, 6–2. **Belgium d. Czechoslovakia 3–2, Prague:** J. Washer d. K. Ardelt 4–6, 7–5, 7–5, 6–3; M. Lammens lost to L. Zemla 2–6, 4–6, 2–6; Washer–Lammens d. Zemla–J. Just 4–6, 3–6, 8–6, 6–4, 6–0; Washer lost to Zemla 6–3, 3–6, 7–9, 6–2, 2–6; Lammens d. Ardelt 6–3, 6–2, 4–6, 6–1. **Australasia d. Canada 5–0, Toronto:** J. O. Anderson d. E. H. Laframboise 4–6, 7–5, 6–0, 6–2; J. B. Hawkes d. P. Bennett 8–6, 6–4, 6–4; Anderson–C. V. Todd d. Bennett–G. D. Holmes 6–2, 6–3, 6–1; Anderson d. Bennett 6–3, 6–0, 6–2; Todd d. Laframboise 6–2, 6–3, 6–8, 6–2. **Japan d. Philippines def.**

SECOND ROUND

Denmark d. Argentina def.; Australasia d. British Isles 3–2, Pittsburgh: J. O. Anderson d. M. Woosnam 6–4, 6–2, 6–4; J. B. Hawkes lost to F. G. Lowe 4–6, 4–6, 1–6; Anderson–C. V. Todd d. Woosnam–O. G. N. Turnbull 4–6, 9–7, 4–6, 6–2, 6–4; Anderson d. Lowe 6–2, 6–3, 3–6, 6–2; Hawkes lost to Woosnam 3–6, 6–0, 9–7, 3–6, 3–6. **Japan d. Belgium def.; India d. France 4–1, Paris:** M. Sleem d. W. H. Laurentz 4–6, 6–2, 3–6, 6–2, 6–0; S. M. Jacob lost to J. Samazeuilh 3–6, 6–8, 5–7; L. S. Deane–A. A. Fyzee d. Laurentz–J. Brugnon 6–1, 2–6, 5–7, 6–2, 6–4; Sleem d. Samazeuilh 6–1, 6–3, 6–3; Deane d. Brugnon 6–3, 4–6, 7–5, 4–6, 8–6.

THIRD ROUND

Australasia d. Denmark 5–0, Cleveland: J. O. Anderson d. V. Ingerslev 6–0, 6–1, 7–5; N. Peach d. E. Tegner 7–5, 6–2, 6–4; Anderson–C. V. Todd d. Tegner–P. Henriksen 6–3, 6–3, 6–2; Anderson d. Tegner 6–0, 6–2, 6–1; Peach d. Ingerslev 3–6, 6–2, 6–0, 3–6, 6–2. **Japan d. India 5–0, Chicago:** Z. Shimizu d. M. Sleem 7–5, 2–6, 6–0, 6–2; I. Kumagae d. A. H. Fyzee 3–6, 6–3 6–3, 9–7; Shimizu–Kumagae d. Fyzee–L. S. Deane 6–1, 6–1, 2–6, 2–6, 6–0; Shimizu d. Fyzee 6–2, 6–1, 9–7; Kumagae d. Sleem 9–7, 6–1, 6–1.

FINAL ROUND

Japan d. Australasia 4–1, Newport: Z. Shimizu d. J. O. Anderson 6–4, 7–5, 6–4; I. Kumagae d. J. B. Hawkes 3–6, 2–6, 8–6, 6–2, 6–3; Shimizu–Kumagae lost to Anderson–C. V. Todd 6–4, 4–6, 6–8, 0–6; Shimizu d. Hawkes 4–6, 6–2, 6–3, 6–2; Kumagae d. Anderson 3–6, 6–4, 2–6, 7–5, 6–2.

CHALLENGE ROUND

USA d. Japan 5–0, New York: W. M. Johnston d. I. Kumagae 6–2, 6–4, 6–2; W. T. Tilden d. Z. Shimizu 5–7, 4–6, 7–5, 6–2, 6–1; R. N. Williams–W. Washburn d. Shimizu–Kumagae 6–2, 7–5, 4–6, 7–5; Tilden d. Kumagae 9–7, 6–4, 6–1; Johnston d. Shimizu 6–3, 5–7, 6–2, 6–4.

1922: USA

FIRST ROUND

France d. Canada def.; India d. Rumania 5–0, Beckenham: A. A. Fyzee d. N. Mishu 3–6, 5–7, 6–4, 6–4, 6–0; A. H. Fyzee d. M. Stern 6–0, 6–1, 6–1; A. H. Fyzee–C. Ramaswami d. Mishu–Stern 6–2, 6–4, 6–0; A. A. Fyzee d. Stern 6–2, 6–2, 6–1; A. H. Fyzee d. Mishu 4–6, 6–1, 6–1, 7–5. **Italy d. Japan def.; Australasia d. Belgium 4–0, Scarborough:** G. L. Patterson d. J. Washer 6–3, 6–4, 6–4; J. O. Anderson d. A. G. Watson 6–2, 6–1, 6–2; Anderson–P. O'Hara Wood d. Washer–Watson 6–1, 6–2, 4–6, 7–9, 7–5; Anderson d. Washer 6–4, 6–3, 6–2. **Czechoslovakia d. Hawaii def.; Spain d. Philippines def.**

SECOND ROUND

France d. Denmark 4–1, Copenhagen: J. Borotra d. E. Tegner 6–0, 3–6, 6–4, 1–6, 6–4; J. Couiteas lost to V. Ingerslev 6–8, 3–6, 1–6; H. Cochet–Borotra d. Tegner–E. Worm 3–6, 6–2, 2–6, 10–8, 6–2; Borotra d. Ingerslev 6–3, 6–2, 6–4; Cochet d. Tegner 7–5, 6–2, 9–7. **Australasia d. Czechoslovakia 5–0, Roehampton:** G. L. Patterson d. F. Rohrer 6–1, 6–3, 3–6, 6–2; J. O. Anderson d. K. Ardelt 7–5, 6–4, 6–4; Patterson–R. C. Wertheim d. Ardelt–Rohrer 9–7, 6–0, 6–3; Patterson d. Ardelt 6–3, 6–2, 2–6, 6–2; Anderson d. Rohrer 4–6, 6–4, 6–3, 6–0. **Spain d. India 4–1, Bristol:** M. Alonso d. A. H. Fyzee 6–1, 6–2, 6–2; M. de Gomar d. A. A. Fyzee 6–1, 6–3, 3–6, 6–3; de Gomar–E. Flaquer lost to A. H. Fyzee–C. Ramaswami 6–3, 5–7, 9–11, 10–8, 4–6; Alonso d. A. A. Fyzee 6–3, 6–4, 0–6, 6–4; de Gomar d. A. H. Fyzee 1–6, 6–2, 6–3, 3–6, 6–1. **British Isles d. Italy 4–0, Roehampton:** A. R. F. Kingscote d. C. Colombo 7–5, 6–4, 6–1; F. G. Lowe d. B. di Robecco 6–1, 6–3, 6–1; Kingscote–F. L. Riseley d. di Robecco–Colombo 6–1, 6–4, 6–0; Kingscote lost to di Robecco def.; Lowe d. Colombo 6–1, 6–2, 6–0.

THIRD ROUND

Spain d. British Isles def.; Australasia d. France 4–1, Boston: G. L. Patterson d. A. H. Gobert 4–6, 3–6, 6–3, 6–4, 6–3; P. O'Hara Wood lost to H. Cochet 4–6, 6–3, 0–6, 9–7, 3–6; Patterson–O'Hara Wood d.

Gobert–Cochet 6–0, 6–8, 4–6, 6–3, 10–8; Patterson d. Cochet 6–2, 2–6, 6–4, 6–2; O'Hara Wood d. Gobert 2–6, 6–2, 6–1, 6–4.

FINAL ROUND

Australasia d. Spain 4–1, Philadelphia: G. L. Patterson d. M. de Gomar 6–3, 8–6, 6–4; P. O'Hara Wood lost to M. Alonso 6–2, 6–3, 2–6, 6–8, 1–6; Patterson–O'Hara Wood d. Alonso–de Gomar 6–3, 6–3, 6–4; Patterson d. Alonso 8–6, 6–2, 6–2; O'Hara Wood d. de Gomar 6–8, 3–6, 6–0, 6–4, 6–1.

CHALLENGE ROUND

USA d. Australasia 4–1, New York: W. T. Tilden d. G. L. Patterson 7–5, 10–8, 6–0; W. M. Johnston d. J. O. Anderson 6–1, 6–2, 6–3; Tilden–V. Richards lost to Patterson–P. O'Hara Wood 4–6, 0–6, 3–6; Tilden d. Anderson 6–4, 5–7, 3–6, 6–4, 6–2; Johnston d. Patterson 6–2, 6–2, 6–1.

1923: USA
European Zone

FIRST ROUND

France d. Denmark 4–1, Bordeaux: H. Cochet d. E. Tegner 6–1, 6–4, 1–6, 5–7, 6–4; R. Lacoste lost to H. Larsen 4–6, 4–6, 6–2, 8–6, 6–8; Cochet–Samazeuilh d. Tegner–E. Worm 6–1, 7–5, 6–3; Cochet d. Worm 6–3, 8–6, 6–1; Samazeuilh d. Tegner 5–7, 6–1, 1–6, 8–6, 6–4. **Spain d. Rumania def.; Great Britain d. Belgium 3–2, Brussels:** R. Lycett d. A. G. Watson 6–2, 8–6, 6–2; J. B. Gilbert lost to J. Washer 2–6, 6–4, 2–6, 3–6; Lycett–L. A. Godfree d. Washer–Watson 6–1, 6–4, 6–1; Lycett lost to Washer 1–6, 3–6, 4–6; Gilbert d. Watson 6–1, 6–4, 6–1. **Switzerland d. Czechoslovakia 3–2, Territet:** C. F. Aeschliman d. L. Zemla 7–5, 6–2, 8–10, 6–3; C. Martin d. F. Rohrer 2–6, 6–3, 6–3, 6–8, 6–2; G. A. Sautter–M. A. Ferrier lost to Zemla–Rohrer 6–4, 4–6, 5–7, 6–8; Aeschliman d. Rohrer 4–6, 7–5, 13–11, 3–6, 6–0; Martin lost to Zemla 4–6, 6–3, 3–6, 4–6. **Ireland d. India 3–2, Dublin:** C. Campbell lost to S. M. Jacob 2–6, 2–6, 3–6; E. D. McCrea d. A. H. Fyzee 7–5, 9–7, 2–6, 6–3; S. F. Scroope–L. A. Meldon lost to L. S. Deane–Fyzee 6–0, 3–6, 6–8, 6–4, 6–8; Campbell d. Fyzee 6–4, 7–5, 6–2; McCrea d. Jacob 6–4, 6–2, 6–4.

SECOND ROUND

Holland d. Italy 5–0, Noordwijk: C. van Lennep d. H. L. de Morpurgo 6–1, 0–6, 6–3, 6–2; A. D. Kool d. C. Colombo 6–2, 6–1, 5–7, 6–4; van

317

Lennep–Kool d. de Morpurgo–B. di Robecco 6–4, 6–4, 6–3; van Lennep d. Colombo 6–2, 3–6, 6–2, 6–3; Kool d. de Morpurgo 7–5, 5–7, 3–6, 6–4, 6–4. **Switzerland d. Argentina 4–1, Geneva:** C. Martin d. C. Caminos 8–6, 6–4, 6–3; C. F. Aeschliman d. R. R. Boyd 8–6, 4–6, 6–4, 6–4; Aeschliman–G. A. Sautter d. A. J. Villegas–W. Robson 4–6, 6–3, 9–7, 6–3; Martin lost to Boyd 3–6, 1–6, 9–7, 6–4, 5–7; Aeschliman d. Caminos 6–3, 7–5, 6–3. **Spain d. Great Britain 3–2, Manchester:** E. Flaquer lost to R. Lycett 0–6, 1–6, 1–6; M. de Gomar d. J. D. P. Wheatley 4–6, 10–8, 6–1, 6–2; Flaquer–de Gomar d. Lycett–L. A. Godfree 6–2, 6–3, 4–6, 6–3. Flaquer lost to Wheatley 6–0, 6–4, 3–6, 1–6, 9–11; de Gomar d. Lycett 6–4, 6–1, 7–5. **France d. Ireland 4–1, Dublin:** H. Cochet d. E. D. McCrea 6–1, 6–3, 13–11; J. Borotra lost to C. Campbell 1–6, 5–7, 0–6; J. Brugnon–R. Lacoste d. Campbell–S. F. Scroope 6–2, 6–3, 14–12; Cochet d. Campbell 0–6, 7–5, 4–6, 10–8, 8–6; Borotra d. McCrea 7–5, 1–6, 5–7, 6–0, 6–2.

THIRD ROUND

Spain d. Holland 5–0, Eastbourne: M. de Gomar d. C. van Lennep 6–4, 6–3, 6–3; E. Flaquer d. M. van der Feen 4–6, 6–2, 6–3, 6–0; de Gomar–Flaquer d. H. Timmer–C. Bryan 6–4, 6–3, 6–2; de Gomar d. van der Feen 6–3, 6–0, 7–5; Flaquer d. van Lennep 5–7, 6–3, 8–6, 6–1. **France d. Switzerland 3–2, Lyons:** P. Blanchy d. C. F. Aeschliman 6–4, 6–2, 6–4; H. Cochet lost to C. Martin 6–4, 4–6, 6–3, 1–6, 3–6; Blanchy–J. Samazeuilh lost to Aeschliman–G. A. Sautter 10–8, 6–3, 2–6, 4–6, 4–6; Blanchy d. Martin 7–5, 6–3, 6–2; Cochet d. Aeschliman 1–6, 6–3, 6–3, 5–7, 6–4.

FINAL ROUND

France d. Spain 3–2, Deauville: R. Lacoste d. M. de Gomar 6–3, 6–4, 5–7, 6–4; P. Blanchy d. E. Flaquer 6–1, 6–2, 3–6, 6–1; H. Cochet–J. Brugnon lost to de Gomar–Flaquer 4–6, 6–8, 13–11, 6–1, 4–6; Lacoste d. Flaquer 6–1, 6–3, 6–2; Blanchy lost to de Gomar 3–6, 6–2, 2–6, 2–6.

American Zone

FIRST ROUND

Japan d. Canada 5–0, Montreal: Z. Shimizu d. W. F. Crocker 3–6, 9–7, 6–1, 8–6; M. Fukuda d. W. L. Rennie 6–2, 6–0, 6–0; Shimizu–S. Kashio d. Crocker–J. A. Wright 6–1, 6–2, 6–2; Shimizu d. Rennie 6–2, 6–3, 6–0; Fukuda d. Crocker 6–2, 6–3, 6–2. **Australia d. Hawaii 4–1, Orange:** J. O. Anderson d. B. Detrick 6–1, 6–3, 6–3; J. B. Hawkes d.

W. N. Eklund 6–2, 6–1, 6–4; Anderson–Hawkes d. Detrick–Eklund 6–0, 8–6, 7–5; Hawkes d. Detrick 6–3, 6–1, 6–1; R. E. Schlesinger lost to Eklund 4–6, 6–4, 1–6, 4–6.

FINAL ROUND

Australia d. Japan 4–1, Chicago: J. O. Anderson d. Z. Shimizu 6–0, 6–3, 6–3; J. B. Hawkes d. M. Fukuda 6–3, 6–4, 6–3; Anderson–Hawkes d. Shimizu–S. Kashio 6–1, 6–2, 6–2; Hawkes lost to Shimizu 4–6, 6–3, 6–2, 1–6, 4–6; Anderson d. Fukuda 6–1, 3–6, 6–2, 6–1.

INTER-ZONE FINAL

Australia d. France 4–1, Boston: J. O. Anderson d. R. Lacoste 7–5, 6–3, 6–4; J. B. Hawkes d. J. Brugnon 6–2, 6–1, 7–5; Anderson–Hawkes d. Brugnon–Lacoste 6–8, 6–3, 6–3, 6–8, 9–7; Anderson d. P. Hirsch 7–5, 6–2, 6–0; I. D. McInnes lost to Lacoste 2–6, 1–6, 2–6.

CHALLENGE ROUND

USA d. Australia 4–1, New York: W. T. Tilden d. J. B. Hawkes 6–4, 6–2, 6–1; W. M. Johnston lost to J. O. Anderson 6–4, 2–6, 6–2, 5–7, 2–6; Tilden–R. N. Williams d. Anderson–Hawkes 17–15, 11–13, 2–6, 6–3, 6–2; Tilden d. Anderson 6–2, 6–3, 1–6, 7–5; Johnston d. Hawkes 6–0, 6–2, 6–1.

1924: USA
European Zone

FIRST ROUND

Great Britain d. Belgium 3–2, Torquay: A. R. F. Kingscote d. A. G. Watson 7–5, 6–2, 6–3; J. B. Gilbert lost to J. Washer 3–6, 9–7, 6–2, 4–6, 6–8; M. Woosnam–L. A. Godfree d. Washer–Watson 6–4, 8–6, 6–4; Kingscote lost to Washer 3–6, 3–6, 3–6; Gilbert d. Watson 6–4, 6–3, 6–1.

SECOND ROUND

India d. Holland 4–1, Arnhem: S. M. Jacob d. C. van Lennep 0–6, 3–6, 6–2, 7–5, 9–7; M. Sleem d. H. Timmer 6–0, 6–2, 6–2; Jacob–S. M. Hadi lost to van Lennep–Timmer 4–6, 6–4, 6–3, 2–6, 4–6; Jacob d. Timmer 3–6, 8–6, 6–3, 2–6, 6–1; Sleem d. van Lennep 6–3, 6–3, 7–5. **France d. Ireland 5–0, Dublin:** J. Couiteas d. E. D. McCrea 6–3, 8–6, 3–6, 4–6, 7–5; R. Lacoste d. H. S. V. Dillon 6–1, 6–2, 6–2; Lacoste–J. Brugnon d. L. A. Meldon–Dillon 8–6, 6–1, 6–2; Couiteas d.

Dillon 4–6, 1–6, 6–2, 11–9, 6–2; Lacoste d. McCrea 6–1, 6–3,
6–1. **South Africa d. Argentina def.; Great Britain d. Spain 3–2,
Birmingham:** J. D. P. Wheatley d. E. Flaquer 6–3, 1–6, 8–6, 6–1; J. G.
Gilbert lost to M. Alonso 2–6, 7–9, 6–3, 6–4, 4–6; M. Woosnam–L. A.
Godfree d. M. Alonso–Flaquer 6–1, 6–4, 6–8, 6–2; Wheatley lost to
Alonso 3–6, 7–9, 6–2, 4–6; Gilbert d. J. M. Alonso 6–0, 6–4,
6–0. **Denmark d. Hungary 3–2, Copenhagen:** A. Petersen d. E.
Takacs 6–2, 6–3, 6–3; E. Ulrich lost to B. Kehrling 8–10, 0–6, 4–6;
Ulrich–B. Thalbitzer d. Kehrling–E. Peteri 7–5, 7–5, 1–6, 5–7, 7–5;
Petersen lost to Kehrling 2–6, 4–6, 3–6; Ulrich d. Takacs 6–0, 4–6, 6–2,
6–3. **Italy d. Rumania def.; Switzerland d. Austria 4–1, Vienna:**
C. F. Aeschliman d. P. Brick 6–2, 6–3, 6–3; C. Martin lost to L. Salm
6–8, 4–6, 2–6; Aeschliman–G. A. Sautter d. L. & O. Salm 2–6, 6–3,
6–4, 6–4; Aeschliman d. L. Salm 7–5, 8–6, 7–5; Martin d. Brick 6–2, 3–6,
6–8, 7–5, 6–2. **Czechoslovakia d. New Zealand 4–0, Prague:** F.
Rohrer d. F. M. B. Fisher 3–6, 6–0, 6–4, 0–6, 6–4; L. Zemla d. J. C.
Peacock 7–5, 6–4, 7–5; Zemla–J. Kozeluh d. Peacock–Fisher 4–6, 6–3,
6–8, 6–2, 7–5; Rohrer d. Peacock 6–2, 7–5, 6–3.

THIRD ROUND

Czechoslovakia d. Switzerland 4–1, Prague: F. Rohrer d. C. Martin
2–6, 6–2, 6–3, 8–6; L. Zemla lost to C. F. Aeschliman 3–6, 6–8, 6–4,
6–1, 1–6; Zemla–J. Kozeluh d. Aeschliman–G. A. Sautter 6–2, 6–3, 6–2;
Rohrer d. Aeschliman 2–6, 4–6, 7–5, 6–2, 6–4; Zemla d. Martin 6–2, 6–2,
6–2. **Great Britain d. South Africa 4–1, Scarborough:** J. D. P.
Wheatley d. P. D. B. Spence 6–4, 6–3, 6–3; J. B. Gilbert d. L. B.
Raymond 6–1, 4–6, 6–2, 3–6, 8–6; M. Woosnam–L. A. Godfree lost to
Spence–Raymond 9–11, 5–7, 4–6; Wheatley d. I. Richardson 6–3, 6–4,
6–4; Gilbert d. Spence 4–6, 6–1, 6–1, 6–1. **Denmark d. Italy 3–2,
Copenhagen:** E. Tegner d. C. Colombo 6–0, 8–6, 3–6, 6–4; A. Petersen
lost to H. L. de Morpurgo 5–7, 2–6, 2–6; Tegner–E. Ulrich d. de
Morpurgo–Colombo 7–5, 7–5, 4–6, 6–0; Tegner lost to de Morpurgo
3–6, 1–6, 3–6; Petersen d. Colombo 6–2, 6–3, 6–4. **France d. India
4–0, Paris:** R. Lacoste d. M. Sleem 4–6, 6–4, 6–2, 6–4; H. Cochet d.
S. M. Jacob 6–4, 4–6, 6–4, 6–2; Cochet–J. Brugnon d. A. H. Fyzee–S.
M. Hadi 6–1, 6–4, 7–5; Cochet d. Sleem 6–4, 0–6, 6–4, 2–6, 6–0.

FOURTH ROUND

Czechoslovakia d. Denmark 3–2, Copenhagen: L. Zemla d. A.
Petersen 6–2, 7–5, 7–5; F. Rohrer d. E. Worm 6–4, 3–6, 3–6, 6–3, 10–8;
Zemla–J. Kozeluh d. Worm–E. Ulrich 6–1, 6–3, 6–1; Zemla lost to Worm
2–6, 6–3, 4–6, 8–10; Rohrer lost to Petersen 6–3, 3–6, 5–7, 0–6. **France**

d. Great Britain 4–1, Eastbourne: H. Cochet d. A. R. F. Kingscote 3–6, 6–4, 4–6, 6–3, 6–3; R. Lacoste d. J. B. Gilbert 6–4, 7–5, 6–3; J. Borotra–J. Brugnon d. M. Woosnam– L. A. Godfree 6–4, 4–6, 6–3, 6–1; Cochet lost to Gilbert 7–5, 6–1, 7–9, 6–8, 2–6; Lacoste d. Kingscote 8–6, 3–6, 3–6, 6–2, 6–4.

FINAL ROUND

France d. Czechoslovakia 5–0, Evian-Les-Baines: R. Lacoste d. P. Macenauer 6–2, 10–8, 6–4; H. Cochet d. L. Zemla 6–1, 8–6, 6–4; Cochet–J. Brugnon d. Zemla–J. Kozeluh 7–5, 3–6, 6–4, 6–4; Lacoste d. Zemla 6–3, 6–2, 6–2; Cochet d. Macenauer 6–4, 3–6, 7–5, 3–6, 6–2.

American Zone

FIRST ROUND

Canada d. Cuba 3–2, Ottawa: J. A. Wright lost to R. Paris 8–10, 6–3, 6–2, 0–6, 3–6; W. F. Crocker d. I. Zayas 6–1, 6–2, 6–2; Wright–Crocker d. G. S. Villalba–V. Banet 7–5, 7–5, 6–2; Wright lost to Banet 6–4, 4–6, 0–6, 6–3, 4–6; Crocker d. Paris 6–3, 7–5, 6–3. **Australia d. China 5–0, New York:** G. L. Patterson d. W. L. Wei 6–1, 6–2, 6–2; P. O'Hara Wood d. P. Kong 6–0, 6–1, 6–2; Patterson–O'Hara Wood d. Wei–C. K. Huang 6–1, 6–2, 6–0; Patterson d. Kong 6–0, 6–0, 6–2; O'Hara Wood d. Wei 6–0, 6–0, 6–2.

SECOND ROUND

Japan d. Canada 4–1, Montreal: S. Okamoto d. J. A. Wright 8–6, 6–4, 7–5; Z. Shimizu d. W. F. Crocker 4–6, 7–5, 6–4, 0–6, 6–1; Okamoto–T. Harada lost to Crocker–Wright 5–7, 4–6, 3–6; Okamoto d. Crocker 6–2, 9–7, 4–6, 6–2; Shimizu d. Wright 4–6, 6–3, 6–4, 6–0. **Australia d. Mexico 5–0, Baltimore:** G. L. Patterson d. M. Llano 6–0, 6–1, 6–2; P. O'Hara Wood d. I. de la Borbolla 6–3, 6–0, 9–7; Patterson–O'Hara Wood d. de la Borbolla–F. Gerdes 6–4, 6–4, 6–0; Patterson d. de la Borbolla 6–2, 6–2, 6–1; O'Hara Wood d. Gerdes 6–1, 6–2, 6–1.

FINAL ROUND

Australia d. Japan 5–0, Providence: G. L. Patterson d. Z. Shimizu 7–5, 11–9, 6–4; P. O'Hara Wood d. S. Okamoto 6–4, 2–6, 6–4, 2–6, 6–1; Patterson–O'Hara Wood d. Okamoto–T. Harada 7–5, 6–2, 6–4; Patterson d. Okamoto 7–5, 6–1, 6–4; O'Hara Wood d. Shimizu 6–4, 6–4, 6–2.

INTER-ZONE FINAL
Australia d. France 3–2, Boston: G. L. Patterson lost to R. Lacoste
3–6, 2–6, 8–10; P. O'Hara Wood d. J. Borotra 1–6, 6–4, 1–6, 6–4, 6–2;
Patterson–O'Hara Wood d. Lacoste–J. Brugnon 6–4, 6–4, 6–2; Patterson
d. Borotra 6–3, 6–1, 6–3; O'Hara Wood lost to Lacoste 10–8, 1–6, 1–6,
5–7.

CHALLENGE ROUND
USA d. Australia 5–0, Philadelphia: W. T. Tilden d. G. L. Patterson
6–4, 6–2, 6–2; V. Richards d. P. O'Hara Wood 6–3, 6–2, 6–4; Tilden–W.
M. Johnston d. Patterson–O'Hara Wood 5–7, 6–3, 6–4, 6–1; Tilden d.
O'Hara Wood 6–2, 6–1, 6–1; Richards d. Patterson 6–3, 7–5, 6–4.

1925: USA
European Zone

FIRST ROUND
Holland d. Czechoslovakia 3–2, Noordwijk: A. D. Kool lost to P.
Macenauer 6–3, 3–6, 2–6, 1–6; H. Timmer d. J. Kozeluh 6–3, 6–4, 6–2;
C. van Lennep–Kool d. L. Zemla–Kozeluh 6–3, 6–1, 8–6; Kool lost to
Kozeluh 6–3, 3–6, 6–3, 1–6, 1–6; Timmer d. Macenauer 6–1, 6–2,
6–2. **Sweden d. Switzerland 3–2, Berne:** S. Malmstrom d. C. F.
Aeschliman 6–3, 6–3, 7–9, 6–3; M. Wallenberg d. C. Martin 6–1, 6–3,
6–3; Wallenberg–Malmstrom lost to Aeschliman–Martin 6–3, 5–7, 5–7,
5–7; Malmstrom d. Martin 6–1, 6–2, 6–1; Wallenberg lost to Aeschliman
3–6, 3–6, 7–5, 4–6. **India d. Belgium 3–2, Brussels:** S. M. Jacob d. J.
Washer 6–4, 4–6, 6–3, 5–7, 6–4; E. B. Andrea d. A. G. Watson 6–0,
6–3, 6–0; S. M. Hadi–J. M. Lal lost to Washer–Watson 6–4, 6–2, 4–6,
5–7, 3–6; Jacob d. Watson 6–3, 6–1, 6–3; Andrea lost to Washer 5–7,
1–6, 1–6. **Austria d. Ireland 4–1, Vienna:** L. Salm d. C. F. Scroope
0–6, 2–6, 6–3, 6–2, 6–3; P. Brick d. L. A. Meldon 6–4, 6–2, 6–4;
Salm–Brick lost to S. F. & C. F. Scroope 1–6, 4–6, 6–0, 5–7; Salm d.
Meldon 8–10, 4–6, 7–5, 8–6, 6–1; Brick d. C. F. Scroope 5–7, 1–6, 7–5
ret. **France d. Hungary 4–1, Budapest:** J. Borotra d. E. Takacs 6–2,
6–2, 6–1; R. Lacoste d. B. Kehrling 6–3, 6–3, 6–3; Borotra–Lacoste d.
Kehrling–A. Kelemen 6–4, 6–2, 8–10, 6–3; Borotra lost to Kehrling 8–6,
1–6, 4–6, 2–6; P. Feret d. Takacs 6–1, 6–0, 6–2. **Italy d. Portugal
4–1, Lisbon:** C. Serventi d. J. de Verda 5–7, 6–1, 6–8, 6–4 ret.; H. L.
de Morpurgo d. A. Casanovas 6–0, 6–1, 6–2; de Morpurgo–P. Gaslini
d. F. de Vasconcellos–Casanovas 6–3, 6–1, 3–6, 9–7; Serventi lost to
Casanovas 4–6, 6–4, 2–6, 6–4, 6–8; de Morpurgo d. de Verda 6–2, 6–1,

6–8, 6–2. **Denmark d. Rumania 4–1, Roehampton:** E. Worm lost to N. Mishu 3–6, 3–6, 7–5, 3–6; E. Ulrich d. Dr Luppu 6–1, 6–2, 8–6; Ulrich–P. Henriksen d. Mishu–Luppu 7–5, 6–0, 6–1; Worm d. Luppu 6–2, 6–2, 6–4; Ulrich d. Mishu 7–5, 6–1, 6–2. **Great Britain d. Poland 5–0, Warsaw:** F. G. Lowe d. M. Szwede 6–0, 6–1, 6–1; J. D. P. Wheatley d. A. Foerster 6–1, 6–2, 6–1; C. H. Kingsley–L. A. Godfree d. M. Kuchar–K. Steinert 6–4, 6–2, 6–2; Lowe d. Foerster 6–0, 6–0, 6–0; Wheatley d. Szwede 6–2, 6–0, 6–0.

SECOND ROUND

Great Britain d. Denmark 3–0, Copenhagen: J. D. P. Wheatley d. A. Petersen 4–6, 6–4, 1–6, 6–2, 6–2; J. B. Gilbert d. E. Ulrich 6–1, 9–11, 3–6, 6–4, 6–2; C. H. Kingsley–L. A. Godfree d. Ulrich–E. Worm 7–5, 7–5, 6–2. **Holland d. Sweden 5–0, Noordwijk:** H. Timmer d. C. E. von Braun 7–5, 6–1, 6–0; A. D. Kool d. M. Wallenberg 6–2, 4–6, 6–3, 6–0; Kool–C. van Lennep d. Wallenberg–von Braun 3–6, 6–1, 6–4, 9–7; Timmer d. Wallenberg 6–1, 6–4, 6–2; Kool d. von Braun 8–6, 6–1, 6–2. **India d. Austria 4–0, Vienna:** S. M. Jacob d. P. Brick 8–6, 6–1, 6–1; E. B. Andrea d. L. Salm 6–4, 6–2, 8–6; J. M. Lal–A. H. Fyzee d. Salm–O. Relly 6–0, 6–3, 6–1; Jacob d. Salm 6–4, 6–4, 7–5; Brick v. Andrea 2–6, 7–5, 6–4, 2–3 unfin. **France d. Italy 5–0, Paris:** R. Lacoste d. H. L. de Morpurgo 6–0, 6–2, 2–6, 6–0; J. Borotra d. C. Colombo 6–4, 6–1, 6–1; Lacoste–J. Brugnon d. de Morpurgo–Colombo 6–1, 6–1, 6–1; Borotra d. de Morpurgo 6–1, 2–6, 12–10, 6–1; P. Feret d. Colombo 8–6, 3–6, 1–6, 6–2, 6–3.

THIRD ROUND

Holland d. India 4–1, Noordwijk: A. D. Kool d. J. M. Lal 3–6, 6–3, 6–4, 6–1; C. van Lennep lost to A. H. Fyzee 1–6, 4–6, 11–9, 6–3, 4–6; Kool–van Lennep d. Fyzee–S. M. Hadi 6–4, 6–2, 6–3; Kool d. Fyzee 7–5, 6–1, 6–4; van Lennep d. Lal 6–2, 6–4, 7–5. **France d. Great Britain 4–0, Eastbourne:** R. Lacoste d. O. G. N. Turnbull 3–6, 6–1, 7–5, 6–2; J. Borotra d. G. R. O. Crole-Rees 6–4, 10–8, 4–6, 6–0; Lacoste–J. Brugnon d. L. A. Godfree–J. D. P. Wheatley 6–4, 6–4, 6–3; Lacoste d. Crole-Rees 6–2, 6–4, 6–2.

FINAL ROUND

France d. Holland 4–0, Noordwijk: R. Lacoste d. H. Timmer 5–7, 7–5, 6–2, 6–2; J. Borotra d. A. D. Kool 6–2, 6–4, 10–8; Lacoste–J. Brugnon d. Kool–C. van Lennep 6–2, 6–3, 6–8, 6–4; Lacoste d. Kool 6–4, 6–4, 6–1.

American Zone

FIRST ROUND
Spain d. Cuba 5–0, Havana: M. Alonso d. V. Banet 6–4, 6–1, 6–1; E. Flaquer d. R. Paris 6–3, 6–3, 6–2; M. & J. M. Alonso d. Paris–R. Chacon 8–6, 6–4, 8–6; M. Alonso d. Paris 6–1, 6–0, 6–3; Flaquer d. Banet 6–1, 6–0, 6–0.

SECOND ROUND
Japan d. China def.; Spain d. Mexico 5–0, Mexico City: M. Alonso d. C. M. Butlin 6–2, 6–1, 6–2; E. Flaquer d. I. de la Borbolla 6–2, 6–4, 6–2; M. & J. M. Alonso d. de la Borbolla–Butlin 6–4, 6–2, 7–5; M. Alonso d. de la Borbolla 6–4, 6–4, 6–2; Flaquer d. Butlin 10–12, 6–4, 6–1, 7–5. **Australia d. Hawaii def.; Canada d. New Zealand def.**

THIRD ROUND
Japan d. Spain 3–2, Baltimore: T. Harada d. E. Flaquer 6–2, 6–4, 6–0; Z. Shimizu lost to M. Alonso 5–7, 0–6, 6–3, 3–6; Harada–Shimizu d. M. & J. M. Alonso 6–2, 6–3, 2–6, 8–10, 6–3; Harada d. M. Alonso 2–6, 6–4, 6–3, 6–4; Shimizu lost to Flaquer 6–3, 0–6, 3–6, 4–6. **Australia d. Canada 5–0, Montreal:** J. O. Anderson d. W. F. Crocker 6–1, 6–3, 6–2; G. L. Patterson d. J. A. Wright 5–7, 3–6, 6–3, 6–1, 6–3; Patterson–J. B. Hawkes d. Crocker–Wright 6–0, 6–2, 6–4; Anderson d. Wright 6–2, 6–4, 6–1; Patterson d. Crocker 6–4, 11–9, 6–4.

FINAL ROUND
Australia d. Japan 4–1, Boston: G. L. Patterson d. Z. Shimizu 6–1, 6–4, 6–2; J. O. Anderson d. T. Harada 6–4, 3–6, 6–3, 6–1; Patterson–J. B. Hawkes d. Shimizu–Harada 6–1, 6–2, 9–7; Patterson lost to Harada 2–6, 6–3, 1–6, 5–7; Hawkes d. M. Fukuda 6–1, 6–3, 6–0.

INTER-ZONE FINAL
France d. Australia 3–1, New York: R. Lacoste lost to G. L. Patterson 3–6, 4–6, 2–6; J. Borotra d. J. O. Anderson 6–4, 6–3, 8–6; Lacoste–Borotra d. Patterson–J. B. Hawkes 6–4, 3–6, 6–4, 1–6, 10–8; Borotra d. Patterson 4–6, 6–4, 6–1, 6–3.

CHALLENGE ROUND
USA d. France 5–0, Philadelphia: W. T. Tilden d. J. Borotra 4–6, 6–0, 2–6, 9–7, 6–4; W. M. Johnston d. R. Lacoste 6–1, 6–1, 6–8, 6–3; V. Richards– R. N. Williams d. Lacoste–Borotra 6–4, 6–4, 6–3; Tilden d. Lacoste 3–6, 10–12, 8–6, 7–5, 6–2; Johnston d. Borotra 6–1, 6–4, 6–0.

1926: USA
European Zone

FIRST ROUND

Italy d. Rumania 5–0, Bucharest: H. L. de Morpurgo d. N. Mishu
6–2, 6–1, 6–3; C. Serventi d. A. San Galli 6–2, 6–2, 6–1; de Morpurgo–
Serventi d. Mishu–San Galli 6–3, 6–3, 7–5; de Morpurgo d. San Galli
6–1, 6–1, 6–2; Serventi d. Mishu 2–6, 6–3, 6–1, 0–1 ret. **Holland d.
Belgium 3–2, Noordwijk:** C. van Lennep lost to J. Washer 6–4, 3–6,
6–8, 6–3, 2–6; H. Timmer d. A. Laloux 6–1, 6–0, 6–1; van Lennep–A.
D. Kool d. Washer–G. Francois 0–6, 8–10, 6–3, 6–2, 7–5; van Lennep d.
Laloux 6–0, 6–0, 6–2; Timmer lost to Washer 1–6, 3–6, 5–7. **South
Africa d. Portugal 4–1, Sutton:** P. D. B. Spence d. A. Casanovas 6–1,
6–1, 6–4; J. J. Lezard lost to J. de Verda 3–6, 2–6, 1–6; Spence–Lezard
d. de Verda–F. Vasconcellos 6–1, 6–4, 6–2; Spence d. de Verda 6–1, 2–6,
6–2, 6–2; Lezard d. Casanovas 6–4, 6–1, 6–2.

SECOND ROUND

Argentina d. Hungary 3–2, Barcelona: W. Robson lost to B. Kehrling
3–6, 6–3, 3–6, 2–6; E. M. Obarrio d. E. Takacs 6–0, 6–4, 6–0;
Obarrio–Robson d. Kehrling–K. Kirchmayer 6–2, 6–4, 6–3; Robson d.
Takacs 6–4, 6–1, 6–1; Obarrio lost to Kehrling 3–6, 5–7, 4–6. **Great
Britain d. Poland 5–0, Harrogate:** O. G. N. Turnbull d. E. Kleinadel
6–1, 7–5, 6–0; J. D. P. Wheatley d. S. Czetwertynski 6–4, 6–3, 6–4; G.
R. O. Crole-Rees–C. H. Kingsley d. Kleinadel–K. Steinert 7–5, 6–4, 6–3;
Turnbull d. Czetwertynski 6–0, 6–2, 7–5; Wheatley d. Kleinadel 6–2, 6–4,
6–1. **Spain d. Ireland 3–2, Dublin:** F. Sindreu d. E. A. McGuire 6–3,
6–2, 6–3; A. Juanico lost to L. A. Meldon 1–6, 4–6, 4–6; Sindreu–Juanico
lost to Meldon–B. Haughton 4–6, 6–8, 3–6; Sindreu d. Meldon 6–1, 6–1,
6–2; Juanico d. McGuire 6–4, 7–5, 2–6, 6–4. **Sweden d. Switzerland
3–2, Malmo:** M. Wallenberg d. C. F. Aeschliman 6–4, 4–6, 6–2, 6–1; S.
Malmstrom d. E. Wuarin 6–4, 6–1, 6–2; Wallenberg–Malstrom lost to
Aeschliman–Wuarin 6–4, 2–6, 4–6, 6–4, 4–6; Wallenberg d. Wuarin 4–6,
6–1, 6–1, 6–1; Malmstrom lost to Aeschliman 6–1, 2–6, 2–6, 6–4,
3–6. **France d. Denmark 5–0, Copenhagen:** R. Lacoste d. A. Petersen
6–4, 7–5, 6–1; H. Cochet d. E. Ulrich 6–2, 6–3, 2–6, 6–0; Cochet–J.
Brugnon d. Ulrich–P. Henriksen 4–6, 6–3, 4–6, 7–5, 6–0; Brugnon d.
Ulrich 6–1, 6–2, 6–8, 3–6, 6–1; Cochet d. Petersen 3–6, 6–2, 3–6, 7–5,
6–4. **Czechoslovakia d. India 4–1, Prague:** P. Macenauer lost to A.
A. Fyzee 4–6, 6–4, 7–9, 0–6; J. Kozeluh d. A. H. Fyzee 6–1, 6–3, 6–1;
Kozeluh–L. Zemla d. A. H. Fyzee–S. W. Bobb 6–2, 6–3, 6–1; Macenauer
d. A. H. Fyzee 6–2, 7–5, 5–7, 6–0; Kozeluh d. A. A. Fyzee 6–3, 6–2,

7–5. **Italy d. Holland 3–2, Rome:** C. Serventi lost to H. Timmer 4–6, 2–6, 4–6; H. L. de Morpurgo d. C. van Lennep 6–3, 6–3, 6–4; de Morpurgo–Serventi d. Timmer–C. Bryan 6–3, 6–4, 6–3; de Morpurgo d. Timmer 6–4, 6–2, 6–3; Serventi lost to van Lennep 3–6, 6–3, 1–6, 4–6. **South Africa d. Austria def.**

THIRD ROUND

France d. Czechoslovakia 3–0, Prague: R. Lacoste d. J. Kozeluh 7–5, 5–7, 6–3, 6–8, 6–3; H. Cochet d. P. Macenauer 6–3, 6–4, 6–3; Lacoste–J. Brugnon d. Kozeluh–L. Zemla 6–2, 3–6, 6–8, 6–2, 7–5. **Great Britain d. Italy 3–2, Rome:** J. D. P. Wheatley d. C. Serventi 5–7, 6–4, 6–1, 6–3; O. G. N. Turnbull lost to H. L. de Morpurgo 6–4, 2–6, 6–4, 4–6, 2–6; G. R. O. Crole-Rees–C. H. Kingsley d. de Morpurgo–Serventi 3–6, 6–8, 6–4, 6–3, 6–3; Wheatley lost to de Morpurgo 2–6, 3–6, 2–3 ret.; Turnbull d. Serventi 3–6, 6–1, 6–1, 6–2. **Spain d. Argentina 3–1, Barcelona:** E. Flaquer d. E. Obarrio 4–6, 5–7, 6–0, 6–0, 6–2; F. Sindreu lost to W. Robson 6–4, 5–7, 7–5, 4–6, 2–6; Flaquer–R. Morales d. Obarrio–Robson 6–4, 9–7, 6–3; Sindreu d. Obarrio 5–7, 6–1, 7–5, 4–6, 6–3. **Sweden d. South Africa 3–1, London:** I. Garell lost to P. D. B. Spence 4–6, 4–6, 6–8; L. Malmstrom d. G. R. Sherwell 8–6, 6–3, 6–4; Malmstrom–Garell d. Spence–J. J. Lezard 6–2, 8–6, 8–6; Malmstrom d. Spence 8–6, 6–3, 6–1.

FOURTH ROUND

Great Britain d. Spain 4–1, Barcelona: J. C. Gregory d. E. Flaquer 6–3, 6–0, 6–2; C. H. Kingsley d. F. Sindreu 7–5, 2–6, 7–5, 3–6, 6–3; Kingsley–G. R. O. Crole-Rees d. Flaquer–R. Morales 11–9, 6–4, 6–2; Gregory d. Sindreu 2–6, 6–4, 6–2, 6–3; H. K. Lester lost to Morales 3–6, 2–6, 2–6. **France d. Sweden 5–0, Stockholm:** H. Cochet d. M. Wallenberg 6–3, 6–3, 6–3; J. Borotra d. S. Malmstrom 3–6, 2–6, 8–6, 6–3, 6–3; Borotra–J. Brugnon d. Wallenberg–Malmstrom 6–4, 6–1, 6–1; Cochet d. Malmstrom 6–4, 5–7, 6–4, 4–6, 6–3; Borotra d. Wallenberg 6–8, 6–4, 6–2, 6–1.

FINAL ROUND

France d. Great Britain 5–0, Cabourg: H. Cochet d. J. C. Gregory 7–5, 4–6, 7–9, 7–5, 6–0; R. Lacoste d. O. G. N. Turnbull 6–4, 6–4, 6–4; J. Borotra–J. Brugnon d. G. R. O. Crole-Rees–C. H. Kingsley 6–2, 6–0, 6–3; P. Landry d. Gregory 6–3, 6–2, 6–1; Brugnon d. Turnbull 4–6, 1–6, 6–2, 6–4, 6–0.

American Zone

FIRST ROUND

Japan d. Mexico 4–1, Mexico City: T. Harada d. A. Unda 6–2, 6–4, 6–4; T. Toba d. M. Llano 6–1, 5–7, 6–3, 6–4; Harada–S. Tawara d. C. M. Butlin–Llano 6–0, 9–7, 6–4; Toba lost to Butlin 2–6, 3–6, 1–6; Tawara d. M. Lozano 6–1, 6–3, 6–4.

SECOND ROUND

Japan d. Philippines 5–0, San Francisco: S. Tawara d. G. Aragon 8–6, 6–1, 8–6; T. Harada d. F. Aragon 6–0, 6–4, 6–3; Harada–Tawara d. G. & F. Aragon 6–3, 1–6, 5–7, 6–2, 6–2; Harada d. G. Aragon 6–2, 6–3, 7–5; Tawara d. F. Aragon 6–2, 8–6, 4–6, 1–6, 7–5. **Cuba d. Canada 3–2, Havana:** R. Paris d. J. A. Wright 2–6, 6–4, 2–6, 6–3, 6–4; V. Banet lost to W. F. Crocker 4–6, 4–6, 1–6; Paris–R. Chacon d. Wright–Crocker 8–6, 3–6, 6–8, 8–6, 6–2; Banet lost to Wright 4–6, 5–7, 2–6; Paris d. Crocker 6–4, 6–2, 6–4.

FINAL ROUND

Japan d. Cuba 5–0, Montreal: T. Harada d. R. Paris 7–5, 6–0, 6–3; S. Tawara d. V. Banet 9–7, 6–1, 6–2; Harada–Tawara d. Paris–R. Chacon 6–4, 6–3, 6–2; Tawara d. Paris 6–2, 6–0, 6–2; T. Toba d. Banet 6–2, 6–2, 6–2.

INTER-ZONE FINAL

France d. Japan 3–2, New York: H. Cochet d. S. Tawara 1–6, 4–6, 7–5, 6–3, 6–2; R. Lacoste lost to T. Harada 4–6, 6–4, 3–6, 7–9; Cochet–J. Brugnon d. Harada–Tawara 6–0, 6–0, 6–2; Lacoste d. Tawara 6–1, 6–3, 6–2; Cochet lost to Harada 1–6, 3–6, 6–0, 4–6.

CHALLENGE ROUND

USA d. France 4–1, Philadelphia: W. M. Johnston d. R. Lacoste 6–0, 6–4, 0–6, 6–0; W. T. Tilden d. J. Borotra 6–2, 6–3, 6–3; R. N. Williams–V. Richards d. H. Cochet–J. Brugnon 6–4, 6–4, 6–2; Johnston d. Borotra 8–6, 6–4, 9–7; Tilden lost to Lacoste 6–4, 4–6, 6–8, 6–8.

1927: FRANCE
European Zone

FIRST ROUND

India d. Spain 3–2, Barcelona: K. Prasada d. E. Flaquer 6–2, 6–2, 6–3; A. H. Fyzee lost to A. Juanico 6–3, 3–6, 6–3, 4–6, 1–6; Prasada–Fyzee

d. Flaquer–R. Morales 0–6, 6–3, 6–3, 6–3; Prasada d. Juanico 11–9, 6–4, 6–3; Fyzee lost to Flaquer 5–7, 0–6, 2–6.   **Great Britain d. Sweden 4–1, Birmingham:** C. H. Kingsley d. I. Garell 6–2, 6–1, 7–5; E. Higgs d. S. Malmstrom 3–6, 6–3, 6–0, 3–6, 6–2; L. A. Godfree–J. C. Gregory d. Malmstrom–H. Muller 4–6, 6–3, 6–1, 6–1; Kingsley lost to Malmstrom 4–6, 2–6, 3–6; Higgs d. Garell 8–6, 8–6, 3–6, 9–7.   **Denmark d. Holland 4–1, Copenhagen:** E. Ulrich d. H. Timmer 6–0, 1–6, 6–4, 7–5; A. Petersen d. C. Bryan 6–2, 6–1, 1–6, 3–6, 6–1; P. Henriksen–Ulrich d. Timmer–C. van Lennep 6–1, 3–6, 6–3, 6–4; Ulrich d. Bryan 6–1, 6–3, 6–0; Petersen lost to Timmer 3–6, 4–6, 6–4, 6–8.   **Switzerland d. Austria 3–2, Basle:** C. F. Aeschliman d. F. Matejka 4–6, 6–1, 6–1, 6–3; J. Wuarin d. H. W. Artens 6–1, 6–0, 6–4; Aeschliman–M. A. Ferrier d. L. Salm–Artens 10–8, 6–4, 6–8, 6–2; Wuarin lost to Matejka 3–6, 2–6, 4–6; Aeschliman lost to Artens 5–7, 1–6, 1–6.   **South Africa d. Ireland 5–0, Dublin:** J. Condon d. C. Campbell 3–6, 2–6, 6–3, 6–3, 6–4; P. D. B. Spence d. A. St J. Mahony 6–2, 6–3, 8–6; L. B. Raymond–Condon d. L. A. Meldon–Mahony 6–3, 6–2, 7–5; Condon d. Mahony 6–0, 8–6, 6–1; Spence d. Meldon 6–3, 6–1, 4–6, 3–6, 6–4.

SECOND ROUND
Czechoslovakia d. Greece 4–1, Prague: J. Kozeluh d. K. Zachos 6–0, 6–1, 6–1; M. Gottlieb lost to A. J. Zerlendi 5–7, 7–5, 6–4, 7–9, 2–6; Kozeluh–M. Zemla d. Zerlendi–Zachos 6–2, 6–3, 6–4; F. Soyka d. Zachos 6–4, 6–3, 6–2; Kozeluh d. Zerlendi 6–2, 6–1, 6–3.   **Belgium d. Poland 5–0, Brussels:** J. Washer d. E. Kleinadel 6–0, 6–0, 6–1; W. H. Botsford d. S. Czetwertynski 6–2, 7–5, 4–6, 6–2; Washer–Botsford d. Kleinadel–G. Stolarow 8–6, 9–7, 6–1; Washer d. Czetwertynski 6–2, 6–2, 6–2; Botsford d. Kleinadel 6–3, 9–7, 6–2.   **Germany d. Portugal 5–0, Lisbon:** G. W. Demasius d. J. de Verda 4–6, 6–0, 6–3, 6–3; H. Moldenhauer d. A. Casanovas 6–2, 6–2, 6–4; Demasius–Moldenhauer d. de Verda–Casanovas 6–4, 3–6, 6–1, 6–2; F. W. Rahe d. Casanovas 6–4, 6–4, 1–6, 6–3; Moldenhauer d. de Verda 6–8, 6–3, 5–7, 6–2, 6–1.   **India d. Yugoslavia 3–0, Zagreb:** K. Prasada d. G. Dungyersky 6–2, 7–5, 6–2; A. H. Fyzee d. D. Balas 6–4, 6–2, 6–1; Prasada–Fyzee d. Dungyersky–Balas 6–1, 6–2, 6–4.   **Denmark d. Great Britain 3–2, Harrogate:** E. Ulrich d. J. C. Gregory, 6–0, 6–3, 3–6, 3–6, 6–2; E. Worm lost to E. Higgs 3–6, 4–6, 10–8, 8–10; Ulrich–Worm d. L. A. Godfree–J. C. Godfrey 6–4, 1–6, 6–2, 7–5; Worm lost to Gregory 8–6, 4–6, 8–10, 4–6; Ulrich d. Higgs 1–6, 3–6, 6–2, 6–2, 6–4.   **South Africa d. Switzerland 5–0, Montreux:** J. Condon d. J. Wuarin 6–0, 6–2, 2–6, 7–5; P. D. B. Spence d. C. F. Aeschliman 6–4, 6–4, 9–7; Spence–L. B. Raymond d. Aeschliman–M. A. Ferrier 6–2, 9–7, 6–4; Condon d.

Aeschliman 6–4, 6–4, 6–2; Spence d. Wuarin 6–1, 8–6, 6–2. **Italy d.**
Hungary 3–2, Budapest: H. L. de Morpurgo d. B. Kehrling 5–7, 6–4,
6–4, 5–7, 6–1; G. de Stefani lost to E. Takacs 6–2, 6–1, 4–6, 3–6, 4–6; de
Morpurgo–de Stefani d. Kehrling–E. Peteri 6–3, 7–5, 8–6; de Morpurgo
d. Takacs 6–2, 6–1, 7–5; C. Serventi lost to Kehrling 2–6, 1–6,
4–6. **France d. Rumania 4–1, Paris:** J. Borotra d. G. Poulieff 6–1,
6–2, 6–2; R. Lacoste d. N. Mishu 6–3, 6–2, 6–2; Borotra–J. Brugnon d.
Mishu–Poulieff 6–4, 6–1, 8–6; Lacoste lost to Poulieff def.; Borotra d.
Mishu 6–4, 2–6, 6–4, 7–5.

THIRD ROUND

Denmark d. India 5–0, Copenhagen: A. Petersen d. K. Prasada 6–4,
6–4, 6–3; E. Ulrich d. A. H. Fyzee 1–6, 6–3, 9–7, 11–9; P.
Henriksen–Ulrich d. Prasada–Fyzee 6–2, 6–2, 6–3; Ulrich d. Prasada 6–4,
7–5, 6–4; Petersen d. Fyzee 6–0, 6–2, 6–4. **Czechoslovakia d. Belgium**
4–1, Prague: J. Kozeluh d. J. Washer 2–6, 3–6, 7–5, 8–6, 6–0; F. Rohrer
d. W. H. Botsford 6–2, 6–3, 4–6, 6–4; Kozeluh–L. Zemla d.
Washer–Botsford 8–6, 10–8, 6–4; Kozeluh d. Botsford 6–3, 6–2, 6–4;
Rohrer lost to Washer 4–6, 5–7, 3–6. **South Africa d. Germany 4–1,**
Berlin: P. D. B. Spence d. O. Froitzheim 2–6, 6–4, 6–3, 4–6, 7–5; L. B.
Raymond d. H. Landmann 7–5, 8–6, 6–2; J. Condon–Raymond d.
Landmann–H. Kleinschroth 7–5, 6–4, 9–11, 6–3; Spence d. Landmann
6–3, 6–8, 6–4, 1–6, 6–2; Condon lost to H. Moldenhauer 6–4, 3–6, 3–6,
6–3, 4–6. **France d. Italy 3–2, Rome:** R. Lacoste d. H. L. de Morpurgo
2–6, 6–0, 6–2, 0–6, 6–1; H. Cochet d. G. de Stefani 6–1, 6–3, 6–3;
Cochet–J. Brugnon lost to de Morpurgo–de Stefani 4–6, 4–6, 4–6; Cochet
lost to de Morpurgo 5–7, 7–5, 1–6, 5–7; Lacoste d. de Stefani 6–3, 6–8,
6–1, 6–3.

FOURTH ROUND

Denmark d. Czechoslovakia 3–2, Prague: A. Petersen d. F. Rohrer
7–5, 6–1, 4–6, 8–10, 6–3; E. Ulrich lost to J. Kozeluh 6–0, 1–6, 5–7,
4–6; Petersen–Ulrich d. L. Zemla–Kozeluh 3–6, 4–6, 8–6, 7–5, 9–7;
Petersen lost to Kozeluh 4–6, 10–12, 3–6; Ulrich d. F. Rohrer 6–4, 6–4,
10–8. **France d. South Africa 5–0, Eastbourne:** H. Cochet d. J.
Condon 6–0, 8–10, 6–2, 7–5; R. Lacoste d. L. B. Raymond 6–2, 6–2,
6–1; J. Borotra–J. Brugnon d. Condon–Raymond 7–5, 6–4, 8–6; Brugnon
d. P. D. B. Spence 6–2, 6–3, 6–4; Lacoste d. Condon 7–5, 6–3, 6–1.

FINAL ROUND

France d. Denmark 3–0, Copenhagen: H. Cochet d. E. Ulrich 9–7,
9–7, 6–4; J. Borotra d. A. Petersen 6–8, 6–2, 6–1, 6–0; Borotra–J. Brugnon
d. Ulrich–Petersen 6–4, 6–0, 6–3.

American Zone

FIRST ROUND
Japan d. Mexico 4–1, St. Louis: Y. Ohta d. R. G. Kinsey 2–6, 1–6, 6–4, 6–1, 6–2; T. Harada d. A. Unda 6–2, 6–3, 6–3; Harada–Z. Shimizu lost to Kinsey–C. M. Butlin 5–7, 2–6, 6–2, 6–3, 3–6; Ohta d. Unda 6–1, 4–6, 6–3, 6–4; Harada d. Kinsey 9–7, 6–0, 0–6, 6–1. **Canada d. Cuba 3–2, Toronto:** J. A. Wright d. V. Banet 2–6, 6–2, 6–4, 4–6, 6–4; W. F. Crocker d. R. Paris 6–4, 8–6, 6–4; Crocker–Wright d. Paris–R. Chacon 6–0, 6–3, 6–0; G. Nunns lost to Banet 3–6, 2–6, 7–5, 3–6; Wright lost to Paris 6–1, 6–2, 5–7, 5–7, 4–6.

FINAL ROUND
Japan d. Canada 3–2, Montreal: T. Harada d. W. F. Crocker 7–5, 6–0, 6–4; Y. Ohta lost to J. A. Wright 3–6, 4–6, 4–6; Harada–T. Toba d. Wright–Crocker 6–3, 4–6, 7–5, 3–6, 10–8; Harada lost to Wright 3–6, 3–6, 6–8; Ohta d. Crocker 6–4, 3–6, 10–8, 6–3.

INTER-ZONE FINAL
France d. Japan 5–0, Boston: H. Cochet d. Y. Ohta 6–0, 6–3, 6–2; R. Lacoste d. T. Harada 6–1, 6–1, 6–2; J. Brugnon–Cochet d. Harada–T. Toba 9–7, 6–1, 6–2; Cochet d. Harada def.; Lacoste d. Ohta def.

CHALLENGE ROUND
France d. USA 3–2, Philadelphia: R. Lacoste d. W. M. Johnston 6–3, 6–2, 6–2; H. Cochet lost to W. T. Tilden 4–6, 6–2, 2–6, 6–8; J. Borotra–J. Brugnon lost to Tilden–F. T. Hunter 6–3, 3–6, 3–6, 6–4, 0–6; Lacoste d. Tilden 6–3, 4–6, 6–3, 6–2; Cochet d. Johnston 6–4, 4–6, 6–2, 6–4.

1928: FRANCE
European Zone

FIRST ROUND
Italy d. Australia 4–1, Genoa: H. L. de Morpurgo d. J. H. Crawford 7–5, 6–3, 6–2; G. de Stefani lost to G. L. Patterson 1–6, 3–6, 3–6; de Morpurgo–P. Gaslini d. Patterson–H. C. Hopman 6–3, 6–4, 1–6, 1–6, 6–2; de Morpurgo d. Patterson 1–6, 6–4, 6–3, 2–6, 6–1; de Stefani d. Hopman 7–5, 8–6, 10–8. **Rumania d. Belgium 5–0, Bucharest:** N. Mishu d. M. Iweins d'Eeckhoutte 6–3, 8–6, 3–6, 6–3 and d. A. Ewbank 6–4, 6–1, 6–4; G. Luppu d. Ewbank 6–3, 7–9, 7–5, 7–9, 6–3 and d. d'Eeckhoutte 3–6, 4–6, 6–4, 6–4, 6–0; Mishu–L. Dorner d. Ewbank–A.

Lacroix 6–4, 4–6, 6–2, 7–5. **Germany d. Greece 4–1, Munich:** O. Froitzheim d. M. Balli 3–6, 6–3, 6–1, 9–7 and lost to A. J. Zerlendi def.; Dr Buss d. Zerlendi 7–5, 6–4, 4–6, 6–2 and d. Balli 6–1, 6–4, 6–4; H. Kleinschroth–C. Bergmann d. Balli–Zerlendi 6–1, 6–3, 6–4. **Spain d. Chile 3–2, Barcelona:** N. F. Sindreu d. D. I. Torralva 6–3, 6–2, 3–6, 6–3 and d. L. Torralva 6–4, 7–5, 6–4; A. Juanico lost to L. Torralva 4–6, 2–6, 2–6 and d. D. I. Torralva 6–4, 4–6, 6–3, 3–6, 6–1; E. Flaquer–R. Morales lost to D. I. Torralva–L. Torralva 6–4, 2–6, 3–6, 9–7, 2–6. **Finland d. Yugoslavia 4–1, Zagreb:** A. Grahn d. A. Popovic 6–2, 6–2, 6–2 and d. F. Schaffers 6–2, 6–0, 6–1; B. Grotenfelt d. A. Popovic 6–4, 1–6, 6–3, 7–5 and lost to Schaffers 3–6, 6–2, 7–9, 5–7; Grahn–Grotenfelt d. Popovic–Schaffers 6–2, 6–2, 8–6. **Great Britain d. Argentina 4–1, Torquay:** J. C. Gregory d. W. Robson 10–12, 13–11, 6–3, 8–6 and d. R. Boyd 6–4, 11–9, 6–2; E. Higgs lost to Boyd 3–6, 6–4, 3–6, 3–6 and d. Robson 7–5, 6–2, 2–6, 7–5; G. R. O. Crole-Rees–C. G. Eames d. Robson–Boyd 6–4, 6–1, 9–11, 1–6, 7–5. **Hungary d. Norway 5–0, Christiana:** B. von Kehrling d. R. Christoffersen 6–1, 6–3, 6–1 and d. T. Torkildsen 7–5, 3–6, 6–3, 6–1; I. de Takacs d. Torkildsen 7–5, 7–9, 6–4, 1–6, 6–2 and d. Christoffersen 6–1, 6–1, 6–2; von Kehrling–Dr Peteri d. Torkildsen–Christoffersen 6–2, 6–2, 4–6, 6–0. **Holland d. Ireland 5–0, Dublin:** H. Timmer d. D. F. Scroope 6–2, 6–2, 6–2 and d. C. H. D. O'Callaghan 6–1, 6–2, 6–0; A. Diemer Kool d. O'Callaghan 6–2, 5–7, 6–1, 6–2 and d. Scroope 3–6, 6–3, 5–7, 6–1, 6–1; Timmer–Diemer Kool d. O'Callaghan–Scroope 6–4, 8–6, 8–6. **Denmark d. Poland 5–0, Warsaw:** E. Ulrich d. G. Stolarow 3–6, 6–4, 6–0, 6–4, and d. P. Warminski 6–4, 6–4, 8–6; A. Petersen d. Warminski 6–2, 3–6, 6–4, 6–2, and d. Stolarow 6–1, 6–0, 6–2; Ulrich–Petersen d. G. & M. Stolarow 6–1, 6–3, 6–4. **Austria d. Philippines 3–0, Vienna:** H. W. Artens d. Aragon 6–3, 6–3, 6–3; F. Matejka d. Ingayo 6–2, 6–2, 6–4; Artens–L. Salm d. Aragon–Ingayo 6–2, 11–13, 6–0, 6–3.

SECOND ROUND

India d. Switzerland 3–2, Zurich: M. Sleem d. C. F. Aeschliman 6–3, 9–7, 6–2, and d. J. Wuarin 6–1, 6–1, 6–4; E. V. Bobb d. Wuarin 6–3, 6–1, 7–9, 6–3, and lost to Aeschliman 4–6, 6–1, 4–6, 2–6; A. M. D. Pitt–H. L. Soni lost to Aeschliman–M. Ferrier 6–4, 10–8, 3–6, 4–6, 1–6. **Italy d. Rumania 5–0, Rome:** H. L. de Morpurgo d. Dr Luppu 6–2, 6–2, 6–2, and d. L. Dorner def.; G. de Stefani d. Dorner 6–3, 6–2, 6–2, and d. Luppu 3–6, 6–4, 6–4, 5–7, 9–7; de Morpurgo–P. Gaslini d. Luppu–Dorner 6–2, 6–4, 4–6, 3–6, 6–4. **Germany d. Spain 3–2, Berlin:** H. Moldenhauer d. E. Flaquer 6–4, 3–6, 7–5, 6–3, and lost to

331

N. F. Sindreu 4–6, 1–6, 7–5, 6–1, 3–6; D. Prenn d. Sindreu 5–7, 6–2,
2–6, 6–3, 6–4, and d. Flaquer 4–6, 6–3, 6–2, 6–4; K. Bergmann–H.
Kleinschroth lost to Flaquer–R. Morales 5–7, 3–6, 6–2, 9–7, 1–6.   **Great
Britain d. Finland 5–0, Helsingfors:** J. C. Gregory d. A. Grahn 6–0,
1–6, 6–1, 6–1, and d. R. Granholm 6–2, 6–1, 6–2; E. Higgs d. B.
Grotenfelt 6–2, 6–1, 2–6, 6–0, and d. Grahn 4–6, 6–1, 6–4, 6–4; G. R.
O. Crole-Rees–C. G. Eames d. Grahn–Grotenfelt 6–3, 6–2, 6–2.   **Holland
d. Hungary 3–2, Noordwijk:** H. Timmer d. I. de Takacs 6–2, 6–0,
6–1, and d. B. von Kehrling 6–3, 6–4, 6–3; A. Diemer Kool lost to von
Kehrling 5–7, 6–4, 6–2, 1–6, 1–1 ret.; D. Koopman lost to de Takacs
4–6, 2–6, 5–7; Timmer–Koopman d. von Kehrling–Dr Peteri 1–6, 6–4,
6–2, 7–5.   **Austria d. Denmark 4–1, Copenhagen:** H. W. Artens d.
A. Petersen 6–4, 6–2, 7–5, and d. E. Ulrich 6–4, 6–4, 3–6, 9–7; F.
Matejka d. Ulrich 6–1, 6–2, 6–2, and d. Petersen 8–6, 6–2, 5–7, 2–6, 6–3;
Artens–L. Salm lost to Ulrich–P. Henriksen 6–8, 0–6,
9–11.   **Czechoslovakia d. Sweden 4–1, Stockholm:** J. Kozeluh d. O
Garell 8–6, 6–0, 6–1; P. Macenauer lost to S. Malmstrom 8–10, 6–1,
5–7, 3–6; R. Menzel d. Malmstrom 6–3, 6–3, 3–6, 7–5, and d. Garell 6–2,
6–0, 5–7, 8–6; Kozeluh–Macenauer d. Malmstrom–Wennergren 6–0, 6–2,
6–4.   **New Zealand d. Portugal 4–1, Lisbon:** E. D. Andrews d. A.
Pinta Coelho 6–3, 6–4, 6–0, and d. J. de Verda 6–4, 6–3, 6–1; R. R. T.
Young lost to de Verda 2–6, 2–6, 2–6, and d. Pinto Coelho 4–6, 6–1,
6–3, 6–0; Andrews–Young d. de Verda–F. de Vasconcellos 5–7, 6–4,
6–2, 6–2.

THIRD ROUND

Italy d. India 4–1, Turin: H. L. de Morpurgo d. M. Sleem 6–3, 6–3,
6–1, and d. E. V. Bobb 6–2, 6–4, 6–4; G. de Stefani d. Bobb 6–4, 6–1,
6–3, and lost to Sleem 4–6, 6–8, 6–4, 3–6; de Morpurgo–de Stefani d.
Sleem–Bobb 6–3, 6–3, 3–6, 6–3.   **Great Britain d. Germany 4–1,
Birmingham:** E. Higgs d. H. Moldenhauer 6–4, 4–6, 6–2, 0–6, 6–4, and
lost to D. Prenn 6–3, 1–6, 5–7, 6–2, 3–6; J. C. Gregory d. O. Froitzheim
6–4, 4–6, 6–0 def., and d. Moldenhauer 2–6, 6–4, 3–6, 6–1, 6–2; G. R.
O. Crole-Rees–C. G. Eames d. H. Kleinschroth–Prenn 7–5, 6–2,
6–4.   **Holland d. Austria 3–0, The Hague:** H. Timmer d. F. Matejka
2–6, 5–7, 6–0, 6–3, 6–4; A. Diemer Kool d. H. W. Artens 6–3, 4–6,
6–3, 3–6, 6–0: Timmer–Diemer Kool d. Metejka–Artens 6–2, 6–3,
6–0.   **Czechoslovakia d. New Zealand def.**

FOURTH ROUND

Italy d. Great Britain 4–1, Felixstowe: H. L. de Morpurgo d. E. Higgs
7–5, 6–4, 7–5, and d. J. C. Gregory 6–0, 6–1, 6–2; G. de Stefani d.

Gregory 3–6, 6–3, 6–3, 6–2, and lost to Higgs 1–6, 6–3, 3–6, 7–5, 2–6;
de Morpurgo–P. Gaslini d. G. R. O. Crole-Rees–C. G. Eames 6–4,
3–6, 4–6, 9–7, 7–5. **Czechoslavakia d. Holland 3–2, Prague:** J.
Kozeluh d. C. J. van Lennep 6–2, 6–0, 6–2, and lost to H. Timmer 3–6,
6–1, 1–6, 4–6; P. Macenauer d. Timmer 6–2, 0–6, 6–0, 6–4, and d. van
Lennep 6–2, 6–2, 6–2; Kozeluh–R.Menzel lost to Timmer–van Lennep
3–6, 6–3, 2–6, 4–6.

FINAL ROUND

Italy d. Czechoslovakia 3–2, Milan: H. L. de Morpurgo d. P.
Macenauer 6–3, 6–3, 6–4, and d. J. Kozeluh 6–1, 6–2, 6–0; P. Gaslini
d. Macenauer 0–6, 6–4, 6–4, 6–3, and lost to Kozeluh 1–6, 7–9, 6–3, 4–6;
de Morpurgo–Gaslini lost to Kozeluh–Macenauer 6–8, 6–4, 4–6, 4–6.

American Zone

FIRST ROUND

Japan d. Cuba 3–0, Havana: Y. Ohta d. R. Paris 6–1, 6–1, 6–3; T. Toba
d. V. Banet 6–1, 6–2, 6–1; Toba–T. Abe d. Paris–Banet 6–3, 6–3, 4–6,
9–7. **USA d. Mexico 3–0, Mexico City:** W. T. Tilden d. R. G. Kinsey
6–1, 6–2, 6–4; J. F. Hennessey d. R. Tapia 6–2, 9–7, 6–1; Tilden–A.
Jones d. Kinsey–A. Unda 6–2, 4–6, 6–3, 6–3.

SECOND ROUND

Japan d. Canada 3–1, Montreal: T. Toba lost to W. Crocker 0–6, 2–6,
6–4, 3–6, and d. J. Wright 7–9, 3–6, 6–3, 6–0, 6–4; Y. Ohta d. Wright
4–6, 6–4, 1–6, 6–4, 6–1; Toba–T. Abe d. Wright–A. Ham 5–7, 2–6, 6–3,
6–4, 10–8. **USA d. China 5–0, Kansas City:** G. M. Lott d. P. Kong
6–0, 6–0, 6–0, and d. G. Lum 6–3, 6–2, 6–0; J. F. Hennessey d. Lum
6–3, 6–4, 6–0, and d. Kong 6–1, 6–0, 6–1; W. T. Tilden–W. F. Coen
d. Kong–Lum 6–2, 6–1, 6–3.

FINAL ROUND

USA d. Japan 5–0, Chicago: W. T. Tilden d. Y. Ohta 6–8, 6–3, 6–1,
6–0, and d. T. Abe 6–2, 6–3, 6–0; J. F. Hennessey d. Ohta 8–6, 6–3,
6–3; W. F. Coen d. Abe 7–9, 6–2, 6–4, 7–5; Tilden–G. M. Lott d. Abe–
T. Toba 6–1, 10–8, 6–2.

INTER–ZONE FINAL

USA d. Italy 4–1, Paris: F. T. Hunter d. P. Gaslini 6–1, 6–1, 6–0, and
lost to H. L. de Morpurgo 4–6, 8–6, 3–6, 6–3, 3–6; J. F. Hennessey d.

de Morpurgo 6–4, 7–5, 6–2, and d. Gaslini 7–5, 6–3, 6–4; Hennessey–G. M. Lott d. de Morpurgo–Gaslini 6–2, 6–3, 6–1.

CHALLENGE ROUND
France d. USA 4–1, Paris: R. Lacoste lost to W. T. Tilden 6–1, 4–6, 4–6, 6–2, 3–6; H. Cochet d. J. F. Hennessey 5–7, 9–7, 6–3, 6–0; Cochet–J. Borotra d. Tilden–F. T. Hunter 6–4, 6–8, 7–5, 4–6, 6–2; Cochet d. Tilden 9–7, 8–6, 6–4; Lacoste d. Hennessey 4–6, 6–1, 7–5, 6–3.

1929: FRANCE
European Zone

FIRST ROUND
Czechoslovakia d. Austria 3–2, Vienna: J. Kozeluh d. H. W. Artens 6–4, 6–3, 8–10, 6–4, and lost to F. Matejka 3–6, 5–7, 1–6; R. Menzel d. Artens 6–3, 6–4, 6–2, and lost to Matejka 8–10, 3–6, 1–6; Kozeluh–P. Macenauer d. Matejka–Artens 6–4, 7–5, 6–2. **Belgium d. Rumania 4–1, Brussels:** A. Lacroix d. N. Mishu 6–2, 6–4, 3–6, 6–3, and d. Dr Luppu 8–6, 6–4, 6–3; A. Ewbank d. Luppu 6–2, 4–6, 6–2, 6–4, and lost to Mishu 2–6, 4–6, 8–6, 3–6; Lacroix–Ewbank d. Luppu–Dorner 7–5, 6–2, 6–1. **Denmark d. Chile 4–1, Copenhagen:** P. Henriksen d. L. Torralva 8–6, 7–5, 7–5, and d. D. I. Torralva 5–7, 7–5, 6–4, 6–4; E. Ulrich d. D. I. Torralva 6–2, 6–4, 7–5, and lost to L. Torralva 5–7, 4–6, 6–8; Ulrich–Henriksen d. L. & D. I. Torralva 6–2, 6–3, 6–4. **Greece d. Yugoslavia 4–1, Athens:** A. J. Zerlendi d. K. Friedrich 6–3, 6–0, 6–2, and d. Sefer 6–4, 7–5, 6–4; C. Efstratoiades d. Sefer 6–2, 7–5, 3–6, 6–3, and lost to Friedrich 1–6, 3–6, 4–6; Zerlendi–K. Georgiades d. Sefer–Friedrich 6–3, 6–3, 6–3. **Hungary d. Norway 4–1, Oslo:** B. von Kehrling d. J. Neilsen 11–9, 1–6, 6–2, 6–2, and d. T. Torkildsen 6–1, 6–2, 6–1; I. de Takacs d. Neilsen 6–1, 6–1, 7–5, and lost to Torkildsen 6–1, 1–6, 1–6, 2–6; von Kehrling–Dr. Peteri d. Neilsen–Torkildsen 6–4, 6–4, 6–1. **Monaco d. Switzerland 3–2, Monte Carlo:** R. Gallepe d. J. Wuarin 6–3, 6–8, 6–4, 6–4, and lost to C. F. Aeschliman 7–5, 3–6, 5–7, 6–3, 5–7; V. Landau d. Wuarin 4–6, 6–3, 6–2, 6–2, and lost to Aeschliman 2–6, 1–6, 2–6. Gallepe–Landau d. Aeschliman–Wuarin 4–6, 6–4, 6–4, 3–6, 8–6. **Egypt d. Finland 4–1, Helsingfors:** J. Grandguillot d. A. Grahn 1–6, 6–4, 6–2, 5–7, 6–4, and d. R. Granholm 2–6, 3–6, 6–3, 7–5, 6–2; L. Wahid d. Grahn 3–6, 6–0, 6–2, 6–3, and lost to Granholm 4–6, 4–6, 3–6; Grandguillot–N. Zahar d. Grahn–B. Grotenfelt 7–5, 6–2, 6–3.

SECOND ROUND

Germany d. Spain 4–1, Barcelona: H. Moldenhauer d. E. Maier 6–1, 6–2, 6–3 and d. Tejada 6–0, 6–2, 6–3; D. Prenn d. N. F. Sindreu 6–3, 5–7, 6–4, 4–6, 6–4; H. Kleinschroth lost to Maier 5–7, 3–6, def.; Moldenhauer–Prenn d. Maier–Tejada 6–3, 1–6, 7–5, 6–1. **Italy d. Ireland 5–0, Dublin:** H. L. de Morpurgo d. G. L. Rogers 8–6, 6–1, 5–7, 6–2, and d. E. A. McGuire 6–0, 5–7, 6–4, 6–2; G. de Stefani d. McGuire 6–4, 4–6, 8–6, 4–6, 8–6, and Rogers 4–6, 7–5, 6–2, 7–5; de Morpurgo–A. del Bono d. Rogers–N. G. Holmes 6–4, 7–5, 7–5. **Czechoslovakia d. Belgium 4–1, Prague:** R. Menzel d. A. Lacroix 6–3, 6–1, 6–1, and d. A. Ewbank def.; J. Kozeluh d. Ewbank 7–5, 12–10, 6–4; J. Malacek lost to Lacroix 3–6, 6–3, 0–1, def.; Kozeluh–P. Macenauer d. Lacroix–Ewbank 6–2, 6–3, 6–4. **Denmark d. Greece 4–1, Copenhagen:** P. Henriksen d. A. J. Zerlendi 6–0, 7–5, 6–4, and d. G. Zafiropoulo 6–4, 6–4, 6–1; E. Ulrich d. Zafiropoulo 6–3, 6–4, 6–2, and lost to Zerlendi 6–3, 6–8, 5–7, 15–17; Henriksen–Ulrich d. Zerlendi–Zafiropoulo 6–2, 6–4, 6–3. **Hungary d. Monaco 3–2, Budapest:** I. de Takacs d. R. Gallepe 6–3, 1–6, 9–7, 8–6, and lost to V. Landau 3–6, 2–6, 3–6; B. von Kehrling d. Landau 6–4, 6–4, 6–2, and d. Gallepe 6–0, 6–3, 6–1; von Kehrling–Dr Peteri lost to Gallepe–Landau 4–6, 6–3, 2–6, 8–10. **Holland d. Egypt 4–1, The Hague:** A. Diemer Kool d. N. Zahar 2–6, 8–6, 6–2, 6–1; and lost to J. Grandguillot 2–6, 6–1, 10–8, 4–6, 1–6; H. Timmer d. L. Wahid 3–6, 6–2, 6–1, 6–2 and d. Grandguillot 7–5, 6–0, 3–6, 6–2; Diemer Kool–Timmer d. Zahar–R. Danon 9–7, 6–8, 6–4, 6–1. **South Africa d. Sweden 5–0, Saltsjobaden:** L. Raymond d. S. Malmstrom 6–2, 6–3, 6–2 and d. K. Ostberg 7–5, 6–0, 6–0; C. J. J. Robbins d. Ostberg 6–2, 6–1, 6–1 and d. Malmstrom 6–8, 10–8, 9–7, 6–4; Raymond–N. G. Farquharson d. Ostberg–H. Muller 8–6, 6–2, 6–2. **Great Britain d. Poland 5–0, Warsaw:** H. W. Austin d. A. Tarnowski 6–1, 6–1, 6–1, and d. M. Stolarow 6–1, 11–9, 7–5; G. P. Hughes d. Tarnowski 6–1, 6–0, 7–5, and d. Stolarow 7–5, 6–1, 6–2; G. R. O. Crole-Rees–C. G. Eames d. J. Loth–Stolarow 6–1, 6–4, 6–3.

THIRD ROUND

Germany d. Italy 3–2, Hamburg: H. Landmann d. G. de Stefani 3–6, 6–4, 6–3, 3–6, 6–3 and lost to H. L. de Morpurgo 4–6, 0–6, 5–7; H. Moldenhauer d. de Morpurgo 5–7, 6–3, 6–3, 3–6, 6–2 and d. de. Stefani 6–3, 3–6, 5–7 6–4, 6–3; Moldenhauer–D. Prenn lost to de Morpurgo–A. del Bono 6–8, 3–6, 3–6. **Czechoslovakia d. Denmark 4–1, Copenhagen:** J. Kozeluh d. P. Henriksen 5–7, 6–2, 6–2, 6–4 and lost to E. Ulrich 6–4, 7–5, 1–6, 2–6, 2–6; R. Menzel d. Henriksen 9–7, 6–2, 6–3, and d. Ulrich 7–5, 7–5, 6–2; Kozeluh–P. Macenauer d. Henriksen–Ulrich 6–1, 4–6, 6–4, 6–2. **Hungary d. Holland 3–2, Budapest:** B. von Kehrling d. H. Timmer 8–6, 6–3, 3–6, 6–3, and d. A. Diemer Kool 6–2, 6–1, 6–2; I. de Takacs d. Timmer 5–7, 7–5, 6–8, 6–1, 6–4 and lost to Diemer Kool 2–6, 2–6, 4–6; von Kehrling–de Takacs lost to Timmer–Diemer Kool 6–1, 2–6, 6–4, 3–6, 2–6. **Great Britain d. South Africa 5–0, Bournemouth:** H. W. Austin d. L. Raymond 8–6, 6–1, 2–6, 6–3 and d. C. J. J. Robbins 6–0, 6–4, 6–1; J. C. Gregory d. Raymond 6–4, 6–1, 6–2 and d. Robbins 6–1, 6–1, 6–4; Gregory–I. G. Collins d. Raymond–N. G. Farquharson 2–6, 6–3, 6–2, 6–1.

FOURTH ROUND

Great Britain d. Hungary 3–2, Budapest: J. C. Gregory d. I. de Takacs 6–1, 6–0, 6–3 and lost to B. von Kehrling 7–5, 5–7, 7–5, 2–6, 3–6; H. W. Austin d. de Takacs 6–4, 6–2, 6–2 and lost to von Kehrling 6–3, 4–6, 2–6, 2–6; Gregory–I. G. Collins d. von Kehrling–K. Aschner 6–2, 4–6, 6–2, 6–3. **Germany d. Czechoslovakia 3–1, Prague:** H. Moldenhauer d. P. Macenaur 6–3, 6–4, 8–6 and d. R. Menzel 6–4, 8–6, 6–4; H. Landmann lost to Menzel 3–6, 3–6, 6–3, 6–0, 4–6; Moldenhauer–D. Prenn d. J. Kozeluh–Macenauer 6–2, 6–2, 6–3.

FINAL ROUND

Germany d. Great Britain 3–2, Berlin: D. Prenn d. J. C. Gregory 6–3, 6–3, 6–2; H. Moldenhauer d. H. W. Austin 6–4, 6–2, 6–3; H. Kleinschroth–H. Landmann lost to Gregory–I. G. Collins 4–6, 2–6, 0–6; Moldenhauer lost to Gregory 0–6, 2–6, 3–6; Prenn d. Austin 4–6, 6–2, 6–4, 4–6, 5–1 def.

American Zone

FIRST ROUND

USA d. Canada 5–0, Montreal: J. van Ryn d. W. F. Crocker 9–7, 6–2, 6–3 and d. J. Wright 6–1, 6–0, 6–1; J. F. Hennessey d. Wright 6–3, 4–6, 6–1, 7–5; W. L. Allison d. Crocker 2–6, 6–4, 9–7, 4–6, 6–2; van Ryn–Hennessy d. Wright–A. Ham 6–1, 6–1, 1–6, 6–2.

SECOND ROUND

USA d. Japan 4–1, Washington: J. van Ryn d. T. Abe 6–2, 4–6, 6–3, 6–2 and lost to Y. Ohta 4–6, 7–5, 6–2, 4–6, 5–7; J. F. Hennessy d. Abe 8–6, 6–1, 3–6, 6–1 and d. Ohta 6–2, 6–2, 6–3; van Ryn–Hennessey d. Ohta–Abe 6–3, 6–4, 6–2. **Cuba d. Mexico 3–1, Havana:** V. Banet

d. I. de la Borbolla 6–2, 6–3, 8–6; G. Vollmer d. de la Borbolla 6–3, 6–3, 8–6 and d. R. Tapia 6–2, 6–3, 6–1; R. Morales–G. Upmann lost to R. Kinsey–A. Unda 2–6, 12–10, 4–6, 3–6.

FINAL ROUND

USA d. Cuba 5–0, Detroit: J. F. Hennessey d. R. Morales 6–0, 6–3, 6–4; J. van Ryn d. G. Vollmer 6–0, 6–1, 6–1; W. L. Allison d. Vollmer 6–3, 6–2, 7–5; G. M. Lott d. G. Upmann 6–4, 6–3, 6–3; van Ryn–Allison d. Morales–Upmann 6–2, 6–0, 6–1.

INTER-ZONE FINAL

USA d. Germany 5–0, Berlin: W. T. Tilden d. H. Moldenhauer 6–2, 6–4, 6–4; F. T. Hunter d. D. Prenn 3–6, 6–3, 6–4, 6–3; J. van Ryn–W. L. Allison d. Moldenhauer–Prenn 9–11, 6–2, 6–4, 6–3; Tilden d. Prenn 6–1, 6–4, 6–1; Hunter d. Moldenhauer 6–3, 1–6, 6–4, 4–6, 6–1.

CHALLENGE ROUND

France d. USA 3–2, Paris: H. Cochet d. W. T. Tilden 6–3, 6–1, 6–2; J. Borotra d. G. M. Lott 6–1, 3–6, 6–4, 7–5; Cochet–Borotra lost to W. L. Allison–J. van Ryn 1–6, 6–8, 4–6; Borotra lost to Tilden 6–4, 1–6, 4–6, 5–7; Cochet d. Lott 6–1, 3–6, 6–0, 6–3.

1930: FRANCE
European Zone

FIRST ROUND

India d. Greece 3–2, Athens: J. Charanjiva d. O. Garangiotis 7–5, 1–6, 6–2, 6–4 and lost to A. J. Zerlendi 4–6, 2–6, 6–3, 4–6; H. L. Soni d. Garangiotis 11–9, 6–4, 5–7, 6–4 and lost to Zerlendi 3–6, 6–4, 5–7, 1–6; Charanjiva–Soni d. M. Balli–Garangiotis 6–2, 3–6, 6–1, 9–7. **Japan d. Hungary 4–0, Budapest:** Y. Ohta d. I. de Takacs 6–1, 6–4, 6–0; Ohta v. B. von Kehrling 6–4, 4–6, 5–7, 6–6 unfin.; T. Harada d. von Kehrling 2–6, 6–3, 8–6, 6–2; H. Satoh d. de Takacs 6–4, 6–3, 6–3; Harada–T. Abe d. von Kehrling–K. Aschner 6–2, 6–2, 3–6, 6–4. **Yugoslavia d. Sweden 3–0, Belgrade:** K. Friedrich d. H. Ramberg 6–3, 1–6, 6–4, 5–7, 6–4; F. Schaffers d. J. Soederstrom 4–6, 6–3, 6–1, 6–0 and d. Ramberg 6–0, 3–1, def.; Schaffers–I. Radovic d. Ramberg–Soederstrom 6–3, 6–1, 5–7, 6–2. **Spain d. Belgium 4–1, Antwerp:** E. Maier d. A. Lacroix 3–6, 6–1, 2–6, 6–2, 6–3 and d. A. Ewbank 6–2, 6–1, 6–1; A. Juanico lost to Ewbank 3–6, 5–7, 6–2, 6–2, 1–6 and d. Lacroix 6–3, 6–3, 7–5; Maier–Saprissa d. Ewbank–L. de Borman 6–1, 4–6, 1–6, 8–6,

337

6–3. **Australia d. Switzerland 5–0, Zurich:** J. H. Crawford d. C. F. Aeschliman 6–0, 6–3, 6–1 and d. H. Chiesa 6–4, 10–8, 6–3; E. F. Moon d. Chiesa 3–6, 6–2, 6–1, 6–1 and d. Aeschliman 3–6, 6–1, 6–4, 6–3; J. Willard–H. C. Hopman d. J. Wuarin–Aeschliman 2–6, 6–4, 6–2,

6–3. **Ireland d. Monaco 4–1, Dublin:** G. L. Rogers d. V. Landau 6–1, 6–4, 6–2 and d. R. Gallepe 2–6, 8–6, 6–2, 11–9; E. A. McGuire lost to Gallepe 2–6, 5–7, 5–7 and d. Landau 13–11, 0–6, 2–6, 6–4, 6–1; Rogers–V. Allman Smith d. Gallepe–Landau 6–1, 6–1, 6–4. **Poland d. Rumania 3–2, Warsaw:** M. Stolarow lost to N. Mishu 3–6, 6–4, 4–6, 1–6 and d. G. Poulieff 3–6, 6–1, 6–2, 7–9, 6–3; I. Tloczynski d. Poulieff 6–3, 7–5, 6–4 and d. Mishu 6–3, 7–9, 7–5, 4–6, 6–0; M. & G. Stolarow lost to Mishu–Poulieff 6–1, 2–6, 3–6, 5–7. **Great Britain d. Germany 3–2, London:** H. W. Austin lost to H. Landmann 3–6, 6–8, 7–5, 6–4, 4–6 and d. D. Prenn 6–3, 6–4, 7–5; H. G. N. Lee lost to Prenn 4–6, 9–7, 3–6, 2–6 and d. Landmann 5–7, 6–3, 6–2, 6–3; J. C. Gregory–I. G. Collins d. H. Kleinschroth–W. Dessart 6–2, 6–4, 6–3.

SECOND ROUND

Czechoslovakia d. Denmark 3–2, Prague: J. Kozeluh lost to E. Ulrich 6–0, 2–6, 5–7, 6–3, 5–7 and d. E. Worm 7–5, 6–2, 10–8; R. Menzel d. Worm 6–2, 6–2, 4–6, 6–2 and d. Ulrich 6–2, 6–2, 6–1; Menzel–F. von Rohrer lost to Ulrich–Worm 3–6, 6–1, 4–6, 6–4, 7–9. **Holland d. Finland 4–1, Amsterdam:** H. Timmer d. B. Grotenfelt 6–1, 6–1, 6–0 and d. A. Grahn 6–1, 6–3, 6–2; A. Diemer Kool lost to Grahn 6–8, 6–8, 4–6 and d. Grotenfelt 6–2, 6–0, 6–0; Timmer–Diemer Kool d. Grahn–R. Granholm 6–4, 6–1, 6–2. **Japan d. India 5–0, London:** T. Harada d. J. Charanjiva 6–3, 6–3, 6–1; Y. Ohta d. A. Madan Mohan 6–2, 7–5, 6–4 and d. H. L. Soni 6–1, 6–4, 6–0; H. Satoh d. Madan Mohan 10–8, 6–1, 6–2; Harada–T. Abe d. Charenjiva–Soni 5–7, 4–6, 6–2, 6–2, 6–2. **Spain d. Yugoslavia 3–0, Zagreb:** E. Maier d. F. Schaffers 6–3, 6–4, 6–3; A. Juanico d. K. Friedrich 6–0, 6–1, 6–3; Maier–Juanico d. Freidrich–Schaffers 6–0, 6–1, 6–3. **Australia d. Ireland 4–1, Dublin:** J. H. Crawford d. E. A. McGuire 6–1, 6–2, 6–4 and lost to G. L. Rogers 3–6, 6–3, 5–7, 6–2, 3–6; E. F. Moon d. Rogers 4–6, 2–6, 6–3, 6–2, 12–10 and d. McGuire 6–2, 7–5, 3–6, 8–6; J. Willard–H. C. Hopman d. Rogers–V. Allman Smith 6–4, 6–2, 6–2. **Great Britain d. Poland 5–0, Torquay:** H. G. N. Lee d. I. Tloczynski 6–1, 6–4, 6–2 and d. M. Stolarow 6–4, 6–2, 8–6; N. Sharpe d. Stolarow 6–3, 6–4, 6–1 and d. Tloczynski 6–2, 6–1, 6–1; J. C. Gregory–I. G. Collins d. Tloczynski–P. Warminski 6–0, 6–0, 6–0. **Austria d. Norway 4–0, Oslo:** H. W. Artens d. T. Torkildsen 6–4, 6–3, 6–4 and d. J. Nielsen 0–6, 6–1, 6–1, 7–5; F. Matejka d. Nielsen 6–2, 6–1, 6–0; Artens–Matejka d. Nielsen–R.

Christofferson 6–2, 6–4, 6–3. **Italy d. Egypt 5–0, Rome:** H. L. de Morpurgo d. L. Wahid 6–1, 6–4, 6–2 and d. J. Grandguillot 6–4, 6–1, 6–2; G. de Stefani d. Grandguillot 6–2, 6–1, 6–2 and d. Riches 6–0, 6–2, 6–0; de Morpurgo–P. Gaslini d. N. Zahar–Riches 5–7, 8–6, 6–1, 3–6, 7–5.

THIRD ROUND

Czechoslovakia d. Holland 3–2, Scheveningen: J. Kozeluh lost to H. Timmer 1–6, 3–6, 1–6 and d. A. Diemer Kool 6–4, 4–6, 6–3, 6–3; R. Menzel d. Diemer Kool 6–3, 6–3, 6–2 and lost to Timmer 6–8, 0–6, 6–4, 5–7; Kozeluh–Menzel d. Timmer–Diemer Kool 7–9, 6–2, 6–1, 3–6, 6–4. **Japan d. Spain 4–1, Barcelona:** Y. Ohta d. A. Juanico 6–1, 3–6, 6–2, 6–2 and d. E. Maier 6–1, 6–1, 6–1; T. Harada d. Maier 3–6, 6–2, 6–0, 6–4 and d. Juanico 6–0, 6–3, 6–3; Harada–T. Abe lost to Maier–F. Sindreu 6–2, 4–6, 4–6, 4–6. **Australia d. Great Britain 4–1, Eastbourne:** J. H. Crawford d. H. G. N. Lee 3–6, 6–2, 4–6, 6–2, 6–2 and d. J. C. Gregory 6–2, 7–5, 6–8, 6–3; H. C. Hopman d. Gregory 8–6, 6–4, 9–7 and d. Lee 6–3, 4–6, 7–9, 6–2, 6–4; Crawford–Hopman lost to Gregory–I. G. Collins 6–8, 8–10, 2–6. **Italy d. Austria 3–2, Vienna:** H. L. de Morpurgo d. F. Matejka 6–2, 6–2, 6–3 and d. H. W. Artens 6–2, 6–2, 6–2; P. Gaslini lost to Artens 6–8, 2–6, 2–6 and lost to Matejka 3–6, 4–6, 5–7; de Morpurgo–Gaslini d. Artens–Matejka 9–11, 8–6, 6–1, 1–6, 6–4.

FOURTH ROUND

Japan d. Czechoslovakia 3–2, Prague: T. Harada lost to R. Menzel 11–9, 3–6, 5–7, 1–6 and d. J. Kozeluh 6–2, 6–3, 6–3; Y. Ohta d. Kozeluh 6–4, 4–6, 6–4, 7–5 and lost to Menzel 2–6, 6–4, 3–6, 3–6; Harada–T. Abe d. Kozeluh–Menzel 1–6, 7–5, 8–6, 9–7. **Italy d. Australia 3–2, Milan:** H. L. de Morpurgo d. J. H. Crawford 5–7, 6–2, 6–4, 3–6, 6–4 and d. H. C. Hopman 8–6, 2–6, 6–4, 1–6, 6–1; G. de Stefani d. Hopman 6–3, 3–6, 7–5, 6–2 and lost to Crawford 4–6, 3–6, 2–6; de Morpurgo–P. Gaslini lost to Hopman–J. Willard 7–9, 7–9, 6–4, 4–6.

FINAL ROUND

Italy d. Japan 3–2, Genoa: H. L. de Morpurgo d. Y. Ohta 6–0, 6–2, 6–1 and lost to T. Harada 4–6, 3–6, 5–7; G. de Stefani lost to Harada 2–6, 5–7, 5–7 and d. Ohta 6–3, 6–4, 4–6, 6–4; de Morpurgo–de Stefani d. Harada–T. Abe 8–6, 9–7, 6–8, 2–6, 6–1.

American Zone

FIRST ROUND

USA d. Canada 5–0, Philadelphia: J. van Ryn d. J. Wright 6–2, 6–2, 3–6, 6–2; G. M. Lott d. M. Rainville 6–2, 6–2, 8–6; J. H. Doeg d. Wright 6–2, 6–3, 6–2; W. Allison d. Rainville 6–2, 6–2, 7–5; van Ryn–Allison d. Wright–W. Crocker 6–0, 6–4, 6–2. **Mexico d. Cuba def.**

FINAL ROUND

USA d. Mexico 5–0, Washington: W. L. Allison d. R. Tapia 6–3, 3–6, 6–8, 6–2, 7–5; G. M. Lott d. I. de la Borbolla 6–0, 6–0, 6–0; J. H. Doeg d. F. Sendel 6–1, 6–0, 6–2; J. van Ryn d. Tapia 6–2, 6–3, 6–1; van Ryn–Allison d. M. Llano–A. Unda 6–0, 6–1, 6–3.

INTER-ZONE FINAL

USA d. Italy 4–1, Paris: W. L. Allison d. G. de Stefani 4–6, 7–9, 6–4, 8–6, 10–8 and lost to H. L. de Morpurgo 5–7, 2–6, 7–5, 4–6; G. M. Lott d. de Morpurgo 3–6, 9–7, 10–8, 6–3 and d. de Stefani 6–3, 6–1, 6–3; Allison–J. van Ryn d. de Morpurgo–P. Gaslini 5–7, 6–2, 6–4, 1–6, 6–3.

CHALLENGE ROUND

France d. USA 4–1, Paris: J. Borotra lost to W. T. Tilden 6–2, 5–7, 4–6, 5–7; H. Cochet d. G. M. Lott 6–4, 6–2, 6–2; Cochet–J. Brugnon d. W. L. Allison–J. van Ryn 6–3, 7–5, 1–6, 6–2; Borotra d. Lott 5–7, 6–3, 2–6, 6–2, 8–6; Cochet d. Tilden 4–6, 6–3, 6–1, 7–5.

1931: FRANCE
European Zone

FIRST ROUND

Great Britain d. Monaco 5–0, Plymouth: H. W. Austin d. V. Landau 6–0, 6–0, 6–1 and d. R. Gallepe 6–0, 6–1, 6–2; F. J. Perry d. Gallepe 6–3, 6–2, 7–5; C. H. Kingsley d. Landau 6–0, 6–1, 6–4; Kingsley–G. P. Hughes d. Gallepe–Landau 6–0, 6–2, 6–0. **South Africa d. Germany 5–0, Dusseldorf:** V. G. Kirby d. Dr Buss 1–6, 6–1, 6–2, 6–3 and d. E. Nourney 4–6, 6–3, 6–4, 6–3; L. Raymond d. Nourney 3–6, 6–3, 4–6, 6–4, 7–5 and d. Buss 4–6, 6–3, 7–5, 8–6; Kirby–N. G. Farquharson d. Nourney–W. Dessart 6–2, 6–3, 6–3. **Ireland d. Switzerland 5–0, Montreux:** G. L. Rogers d. C. F. Aeschliman 6–2, 7–5, 6–2 and d. H. C. Fisher 6–1, 2–6, 6–2, 8–6; E. A. McGuire d. Fisher 6–4, 7–5, 7–5 and d. Aeschliman 5–7, 7–5, 2–6, 8–6, 6–2; Rogers–C. F. Scroope d.

Aeschliman–Fisher 6–3, 5–7, 13–11, 6–2. **Greece d. Austria 3–2, Athens:** A. J. Zerlendi d. H. W. Artens 1–6, 6–3, 1–6, 6–2, 8–6 and lost to F. Matejka 3–6, 2–6, 8–6, 3–6; O. Garangiotis d. Matejka 8–6, 3–6, 7–5, 1–6, 6–4 and d. Artens 6–1, 2–6, 6–4, 6–8, 6–2; M. Balli–K. Georgiades lost to Artens–M. Haberl 7–5, 3–6, 4–6, 4–6.
Czechoslovakia d. Spain 3–2, Prague: R. Menzel d. E. G. Maier 6–3, 6–2, 6–3 and d. M. Alonso 6–8, 6–2, 6–1, 6–3; L. Hecht d. Alonso 6–3, 4–6, 7–5, 0–6, 6–1 and lost to Maier 6–4, 3–6, 4–6, 4–6; Menzel–F. von Rohrer lost to Alonso–Maier 1–6, 7–9, 1–6. **Italy d. Hungary 4–1, Budapest:** H. L. de Morpurgo d. I. de Takacs 6–3, 8–6, 6–1 and lost to B. von Kehrling 3–6, 3–6, 4–6; G. de Stefani d. de Takacs 6–3, 6–3, 6–3 and d. von Kehrling 6–2, 4–6, 6–2, 4–6, 6–2; de Morpurgo–A. del Bono d. von Kehrling–E. Gabrowitz 8–6, 3–6, 7–5, 7–5.

SECOND ROUND

Japan d. Yugoslavia 5–0, Zagreb: J. Satoh d. F. Kukuljevic 6–3, 6–3, 6–2 and d. F. Schaffers 7–5, 6–3, 6–0; H. Satoh d. Schaffers 6–3, 6–4, 7–5 and d. Kukuljevic 6–3, 6–2, 3–6, 5–7, 6–2; J. Satoh–M. Kawachi d. Schaffers–Kukuljevic 9–7, 3–6, 9–7, 6–3. **Egypt d. Finland 4–1, Helsinki:** J. Grandguillot d. A. Grahn 3–6, 7–5, 7–5, 6–2 and d. B. Grotenfelt 3–6, 6–1, 6–4, 6–2; L. Wahid d. Grotenfelt 6–3, 2–6, 6–4, 6–4 and lost to Grahn 6–8, 3–6, 8–6, 3–6; Grandguillot–A. Shukri d. Grahn–Grotenfelt 6–4, 2–6, 6–4, 3–6, 7–5. **Great Britain d. Belgium 5–0, Brussels:** H. W. Austin d. A. Lacroix 6–4, 6–4, 6–4 and d. L. de Borman 6–0, 6–1, 6–0; F. J. Perry d. de Borman 6–2, 6–0, 6–2 and d. Lacroix 8–6, 6–4, 7–5; G. P. Hughes–Perry d. de Borman–Lacroix 6–1, 6–4, 6–2. **South Africa d. Ireland 4–1, Dublin:** P. D. B. Spence d. E. A. McGuire 6–3, 6–4, 6–2 and lost to G. L. Rogers 4–6, 2–6, 6–4, 6–4, 4–6; V. G. Kirby d. McGuire 4–6, 6–3, 7–5, 7–5 and d. Rogers 3–6, 7–5, 10–8, 6–2; Spence– N. G. Farquharson d. Rogers–C. F. Scroope 1–6, 6–1, 7–5, 2–6, 6–3. **Czechoslovakia d. Greece 4–1, Athens:** R. Menzel d. A. J. Zerlendi 6–2, 6–2, 6–1 and d. O. Garangiotis 6–1, 6–3, 6–1; L. Hecht d. Zerlendi 6–2, 6–4, 3–6, 6–4 and lost to Garangiotis 6–1, 6–8, 2–6, 9–11; Menzel–F. Marsalek d. M. Balli–G. Nicholaides 6–2, 6–2, 6–4. **Italy d. Holland 3–0, Turin:** H. L. de Morpurgo d. Knappert 6–3, 6–1, 6–1; G. de Stefani d. I. van der Heide 6–3, 6–3, 6–3; de Morpurgo–A. del Bono d. van der Heide–Knappert 2–6, 6–2, 6–4, 6–1. **Denmark d. Rumania 5–0, Copenhagen:** E. Ulrich d. N. Mishu 6–4, 6–4, 9–7 and d. C. Bunea 6–1, 6–1, 6–0; P. Henriksen d. Bunea 6–0, 6–2, 6–3 and d. Mishu 4–6, 6–1, 6–4, 4–6, 6–1; Ulrich–Henriksen d. Mishu–Bunea 6–4, 6–2, 6–3. **Poland d. Norway 3–0, Oslo:** J. Hebda d. J. Nielsen 6–1, 6–1, 6–2; I. Tloczynski d. T. Torkildsen 6–2,

6–1, 7–5; M. Stolarow–Tloczynski d. R. Christoffersen–O. Fagerstroem 6–2, 6–2, 5–7, 6–2.

THIRD ROUND

Japan d. Egypt 5–0, Paris: J. Satoh d. P. Grandguillot 6–0, 6–1, 6–0; H. Satoh d. L. Wahid 6–4, 2–6, 6–1, 6–8, 6–1 and d. A. Shukri 6–0, 6–1, 6–2; M. Kawachi d. Wahid 6–3, 4–6, 8–6, 3–6, 6–2; J. Satoh–Kawachi d. Wahid–Shukri 6–2, 6–2, 6–1.   **Great Britain d. South Africa 5–0, Eastbourne:** H. W. Austin d. V. G. Kirby 6–2, 6–8. 2–6, 10–8, 6–3 and d. N. G. Farquharson 6–2, 5–7, 6–2, 6–3; F. J. Perry d. Farquharson 6–2, 6–3, 6–3 and d. Kirby 3–6, 6–4, 6–1, 6–4; Perry–G. P. Hughes d. Farquharson–P. D. B. Spence 8–6, 6–4, 6–3.   **Czechoslovakia d. Italy 3–0, Prague:** R. Menzel d. H. L. de Morpurgo 6–3, 6–3, 4–6, 6–2; L. Hecht d. G. de Stefani 6–4, 7–5, 3–6, 8–6; Menzel–F. Marsalek d. de Morpurgo–A. del Bono 6–3, 6–4, 6–1.   **Denmark d. Poland 3–2, Copenhagen:** E. Ulrich d. J. Hebda 6–2, 6–4, 6–3 and lost to I. Tloczynski 6–8, 1–6, 6–3, 8–6, 2–6; P. Henriksen d. Hebda 6–3, 6–1, 6–2 and lost to Tloczynski 2–6, 6–4, 3–6, 2–6; Ulrich–Henriksen d. M. Stolarow–Tloczynski 6–4, 7–9, 3–6, 6–3, 6–4.

FOURTH ROUND

Great Britain d. Japan 5–0, Eastbourne: H. W. Austin d. H. Satoh 0–6, 6–2, 6–4, 6–1 and d. M. Kawachi 6–1, 0–6, 8–6, 6–2; F. J. Perry d. J. Satoh 6–1, 4–6, 7–5, 7–5 and d. H. Satoh 6–2, 6–3, 4–6, 6–2; Perry–G. P. Hughes d. J. Satoh–Kawachi 6–4, 6–4, 8–6.   **Czechoslovakia d. Denmark 5–0, Copenhagen:** R. Menzel d. E. Ulrich 6–3, 6–2, 7–5 and d. E. Worm 3–6, 6–2, 6–4, 6–1; L. Hecht d. Ulrich 6–3, 6–2, 6–2 and d. P. Henriksen 6–8, 6–0, 3–6, 6–2, 11–9; Menzel–F. Marsalek d. Ulrich–Worm 9–7, 1–6, 6–3, 6–0.

FINAL ROUND

Great Britain d. Czechoslovakia 4–1, Prague: H. W. Austin d. R. Menzel 3–6, 6–2, 6–8, 6–3, 6–3 and lost to L. Hecht 2–6, 5–7, 4–6; F. J. Perry d. Hecht 6–1, 8–6, 6–3 and d. Menzel 7–5, 6–3, 7–5; Perry–G. P. Hughes d. Menzel–F. Marsalek 6–4, 4–6, 6–4, 6–2.

North American Zone

FIRST ROUND

USA d. Mexico 5–0, Mexico City: W. L. Allison d. A. Unda 6–3, 6–1, 6–3; F. X. Shields d. R. Tapia 6–4, 6–4, 6–2; Shields–S. B. Wood d.

Tapia–M. Llano 6–3, 6–3, 6–4; Shields d. J. Acosta 6–3, 6–0, 6–3; Allison d. Tapia 6–4, 6–3, 6–2.

FINAL ROUND

USA d. Canada 4–1, Montreal: F. X. Shields d. J. Wright 8–6, 6–2, 6–2; S. B. Wood lost to M. Rainville 6–4, 4–6, 3–6, 6–2, 4–6; Shields–Wood d. Wright–Rainville 8–6, 6–4, 6–2; Wood d. Wright 8–6, 6–3, 6–4; Shields d. Rainville 6–1, 6–4, 6–1.

South American Zone

FIRST ROUND

Argentina d. Paraguay 5–0, Asunción: L. del Castillo d. A. Cusmanich 6–3, 6–0, 6–2 and d. H. R. Walters 6–0, 6–0, 6–1; A. Zappa d. A. Portaluppi 6–1, 6–1, 6–1 and d. I. Ubaldi 6–2, 6–0, 6–1; W. Robson–A. R. Sissener d. Cusmanich–L. Sosa 6–0, 6–3, 6–0.

SECOND ROUND

Argentina d. Uruguay 5–0, Buenos Aires: L. del Castillo d. J. C. da Silva 6–1, 6–2, 6–0 and d. C. E. Gainza 6–0, 6–0, 6–1; R. Boyd d. E. Stanham 6–2, 6–1, 6–3 and d. E. Hernandez 6–0, 6–0, 6–1; W. Robson–A. Zappa d. da Silva–Stanham 6–1, 6–2, 6–1. **Chile d. Brazil def.**

FINAL ROUND

Argentina d. Chile 3–0, Santiago: A. Zappa d. E. Schronherr 2–6, 6–2, 6–0, 6–0; W. Robson d. L. Page 6–2, 6–2, 6–4; Zappa–L. del Castillo d. R. Conrads–H. Muller 6–1, 6–0, 6–0.

AMERICAN INTER–ZONE FINAL

USA d. Argentina 5–0, Washington: F. X. Shields d. W. Robson 3–6, 6–2, 6–2, 6–2; S. B. Wood d. R. Boyd 6–4, 6–1, 6–2; Shields–Wood d. A. Zappa–L. del Castillo 6–4, 8–6, 2–6, 6–2; Shields d. Boyd 6–2, 6–2, 6–2; C. S. Sutter d. Robson 3–6, 6–4, 6–3, 6–3.

INTER–ZONE FINAL

Great Britain d. USA 3–2, Paris: H. W. Austin d. S. B. Wood 2–6, 6–0, 8–6, 7–5; F. J. Perry lost to F. X. Shields 8–10, 4–6, 2–6; G. P. Hughes–Perry lost to G. M. Lott–J. van Ryn 1–6, 3–6, 6–4, 3–6; Perry d. Wood 6–3, 8–10, 6–3, 6–3; Austin d. Shields 8–6, 6–3, 7–5.

343

CHALLENGE ROUND

France d. Great Britain 3–2, Paris: H. Cochet d. H. W. Austin 3–6, 11–9, 6–2, 6–4; J. Borotra lost to F. J. Perry 6–4, 8–10, 0–6, 6–4, 4–6; Cochet–J. Brugnon d. G. P. Hughes–C. H. Kingsley 6–1, 5–7, 6–3, 8–6; Borotra lost to Austin 5–7, 3–6, 6–3, 5–7; Cochet d. Perry 6–4, 1–6, 9–7, 6–3.

1932: FRANCE
European Zone

FIRST ROUND

Hungary d. Finland 5–0, Budapest: B. von Kehrling d. A. Biaudet 6–1, 6–2, 6–2 and d. B. Grotenfelt 6–0, 6–3, 6–4; E. Gabrowitz d. Grotenfelt 6–0, 6–2, 6–1 and d. Biaudet 6–1, 6–1, 6–1; von Kehrling–Gabrowitz d. Biaudet–Grotenfelt 6–4, 6–3, 6–3. **Germany d. India 5–0, Berlin:** D. Prenn d. A. Madan Mohan 6–2, 7–5, 6–1 and d. J. Charanjiva 6–3, 6–1, 6–2; G. von Cramm d. Charanjiva 6–2, 6–0, 6–1 and d. Madan Mohan 6–3, 8–6, 6–3; W. Dessart–E. Nourney d. Charanjiva–H. Prasada 6–4, 2–6, 3–6, 6–2, 6–3. **Austria d. Czechoslovakia 3–2, Prague:** H. W. Artens d. L. Hecht 2–6, 6–3, 7–5, 6–1 and lost to R. Menzel 2–6, 1–6, 7–5, 4–6; F. Matejka d. Menzel 6–3, 6–3, 3–6, 2–6, 6–4 and d. Hecht 6–4, 6–4, 8–6; Artens–H. Kinzel lost to Menzel–F. Marsalek 2–6, 1–6, 1–6. **Monaco d. Norway 5–0, Oslo:** R. Gallepe d. R. Hagen 6–3, 6–4, 6–8, 6–1 and d. J. Haanes 6–1, 6–1, 6–0; V. Landau d. T. Torkildsen 7–5, 6–2, 6–2 and d. Hagen 6–1, 6–4, 6–0; Gallepe–Landau d. Haanes–F. T. Smith 6–1, 6–3, 6–1. **Switzerland d. Belgium 5–0, Brussels:** C. F. Aeschliman d. A. Lacroix 7–5, 6–3, 6–0 and d. M. Tweins D'Eeckhoutte 6–3, 6–2, 6–2; H. C. Fisher d. D'Eeckhoutte 6–1, 6–1, 6–2 and d. G. van Zuylen 8–6, 6–1, 8–6; Aeschliman–Fisher d. Lacroix–L. de Borman 6–1, 6–1, 6–4. **Italy d. Egypt 3–2, Genoa:** G. de Stefani d. P. Grandguillot 9–7, 6–1, 6–4 and d. L. Wahid 7–5, 6–4, 6–1; O. de Minerbi d. Wahid 6–3, 8–6, 6–8, 6–3 and lost to P. Grandguillot 6–1, 6–3, 1–6, 4–6, 3–6; A. del Bono–A. Sertorio lost to J. & P. Grandguillot 2–6, 3–6, 7–5, 4–6.

SECOND ROUND

Great Britain d. Rumania 5–0, Torquay: F. J. Perry d. N. Mishu 6–0, 6–1, 6–1 and d. G. Poulieff 6–1, 6–2, 6–1; H. F. David d. Poulieff 7–5, 7–5, 6–1 and d. Mishu 4–6, 6–0, 8–6, 3–6, 6–4; Perry–G. P. Hughes d. Mishu–Poulieff 6–0, 6–1, 6–1. **Poland d. Holland 4–1, Warsaw:** I. Tloczynski d. H. Timmer 7–5, 6–3, 6–4 and d. T. Hughan 6–3, 6–4, 6–2;

344

M. Stolarow d. Timmer 6–4, 6–2, 5–7, 4–6, 6–4 and d. Hughan 6–8, 6–2, 5–7, 6–0, 6–0; Tloczynski–G. Stolarow lost to O. Koopman–Hughan 6–3, 15–17, 6–3, 3–6, 5–7. **Ireland d. Hungary 4–1, Dublin:** G. L. Rogers d. E. Gabrowitz 7–5, 3–6, 6–4, 7–5 and d. B. von Kehrling 6–0, 6–3, 6–3; E. A. McGuire lost to von Kehrling 3–6, 2–6, 4–6 and d. Gabrowitz 6–1, 8–6, 6–2; Rogers–McGuire d. von Kehrling–Gabrowitz 4–6, 7–5, 6–4, 6–3. **Germany d. Austria 3–2, Vienna:** D. Prenn d. F. W. Matejka 6–2, 10–8, 6–1 and lost to H. W. Artens 4–6, 2–6, 3–6; G. von Cramm d. Artens 6–2, 6–0, 6–4 and d. Matejka 6–2, 2–6, 6–3, 5–7, 8–6; W. Dessart–von Cramm lost to Matejka–Artens 3–6, 5–7, 4–6. **Switzerland d. Monaco 3–2, Lucerne:** C. F. Aeschliman lost to R. Gallepe 4–6, 6–4, 6–3, 2–6, 3–6 and lost to V. Landau 2–6, 7–9, 6–8; H. C. Fisher d. Landau 6–0, 6–2, 4–6, 6–4 and d. Gallepe 6–1, 6–1, 6–2; Aeschliman–Fisher d. Gallepe–Landau 2–6, 6–2, 2–6, 7–5, 6–1. **Italy d. Spain 4–1, Rome:** G. de Stefani d. E. Maier 6–1, 6–4, 6–0 and d. A. Juanico 6–0, 6–1, 6–2; G. Palmieri d. Juanico 6–0, 6–1, 6–2 and d. Maier 2–6, 6–0, 6–2, 5–2 def.; A. del Bono–O. de Minerbi lost to Maier–J. Tajada 7–5, 2–6, 2–6, 4–6. **Denmark d. Yugoslavia 4–1, Copenhagen:** P. Henriksen d. F. Schaffers 4–6, 0–6, 6–2, 13–11, 6–1 and lost to F. Kukuljevic 6–4, 6–8, 3–6, 3–6; E. Ulrich d. Kukuljevic 6–3, 7–5, 6–2 and d. Schaffers 3–6, 7–5, 6–4, 11–9; Ulrich–Henriksen d. Kukuljevic–Schaffers 6–3, 5–7, 6–4, 6–4. **Japan d. Greece 5–0, Athens:** J. Satoh d. M. Balli 6–0, 6–3, 6–3 and d. O. Garangiotis 6–4, 12–10 6–3; T. Kuwabara d. Garangiotis 4–6, 5–7, 7–5, 6–1, 10–8 and d. G. Nicholaides 6–3, 6–3, 6–3; R. Miki–Satoh d. Balli–I. Georgiades 6–2, 3–6, 6–4, 6–2.

THIRD ROUND

Great Britain d. Poland 4–1, Warsaw: F. J. Perry d. I. Tloczynski 7–5, 8–6, 6–2 and d. M. Stolarow 6–3, 7–5, 6–4; H. G. N. Lee lost to Tloczynski 4–6, 4–6, 6–2, 5–7 and d. Stolarow 6–4, 6–3, 6–3; Perry–G. P. Hughes d. L. Hebda–P. Warminski 6–0, 6–2, 6–0. **Germany d. Ireland 4–1, Berlin:** D. Prenn d. E. A. McGuire 6–1, 6–1, 6–1 and d. G. L. Rogers 6–2, 7–5, 6–2; G. von Cramm lost to Rogers 4–6, 8–10, 6–4, 7–5, 4–6 and d. McGuire 6–2, 6–4, 6–2; Prenn–von Cramm d. Rogers–McGuire 6–4, 6–3, 3–6, 8–6. **Italy d. Switzerland 3–2, Montreux:** G. de Stefani d. C. F. Aeschliman 6–4, 7–5, 8–6 and lost to H. C. Fisher 6–3, 6–0, 7–9, 6–8, 6–8; G. Palmieri lost to Fisher 8–6, 4–6, 6–1, 1–6, 3–6 and d. Aeschliman 6–3, 6–1, 7–5; Palmieri–A. Sertorio d. Fisher–Aeschliman 3–6, 6–4, 6–4, 6–4. **Japan d. Denmark 5–0, Copenhagen:** J. Satoh d. Jacobsen 6–1, 6–2, 6–4 and d. E. Ulrich 4–6, 6–3, 7–5, 7–5; T. Kuwabara d. Ulrich 6–4, 6–2, 6–0 and d. Jacobsen

5–7, 2–6, 6–3, 6–0, 6–1; Satoh–R. Miki d. Ulrich–P. Henriksen 6–3, 4–6, 6–2, 6–2.

FOURTH ROUND

Germany d. Great Britain 3–2, Berlin: D. Prenn d. H. W. Austin 6–0, 8–10, 6–2, 6–3 and d. F. J. Perry 6–2, 6–4, 3–6, 0–6, 7–5; G. von Cramm lost to Perry 1–6, 2–6, 3–6 and d. Austin 5–7, 6–2, 6–3, 6–2; Prenn–W. Dessart lost to G. P. Hughes–Perry 3–6, 4–6, 4–6.   **Italy d. Japan 3–2, Milan:** G. de Stefani d. J. Satoh 6–3, 6–4, 6–4 and d. T. Kuwabara 6–2, 6–2, 6–4; G. Palmieri lost to Kuwabara 0–6, 2–6, 6–1, 3–6 and d. Satoh 4–6, 4–6, 6–1, 6–1, 6–2; Palmieri–A. Sertorio lost to Satoh–R. Miki 4–6, 4–6, 3–6.

FINAL ROUND

Germany d. Italy 5–0, Milan: D. Prenn d. G. de Stefani 6–1, 6–4, 1–6, 6–2; G. von Cramm d. G. Palmieri 6–3, 6–4, 6–0 and d. A. del Bono 8–6, 6–3, 3–6, 6–1; G. Jaenecke d. Palmieri 6–3, 0–6, 6–1, 2–6, 6–1; Prenn–von Cramm d. de Stefani–del Bono 6–3, 6–3, 6–2.

North American Zone

FIRST ROUND

USA d. Canada 5–0, Washington: H. E. Vines d. J. Wright 8–6, 3–6, 6–4, 4–6, 6–2; W. L. Allison d. M. Rainville 6–2, 6–4, 6–2; Allison–J. van Ryn d. Rainville–Wright 6–2, 6–1, 6–2; Vines d. Rainville 6–3, 6–3, 6–4; F. X. Shields d. Wright 8–6, 6–1, 8–10, 6–1.

SECOND ROUND

USA d. Mexico 5–0, New Orleans: H. E. Vines d. A. Unda 6–1, 6–2, 6–4; W. Allison d. R. Tapia 6–2, 6–3, 6–4; Allison–J. van Ryn d. Unda–Tapia 6–1, 6–2, 3–6, 9–7; Vines d. Tapia 6–4, 5–7, 10–12, 8–6, 6–3; F. X. Shileds d. E. Mestre 6–0, 6–1, 6–0.   **Australia d. Cuba 5–0, Havana:** J. H. Crawford d. R. Morales 6–3, 6–1, 7–5; C. Sproule d. G. Vollmer 6–1, 6–1, 6–4; H. C. Hopman d. Vollmer 6–2, 6–1, 4–6, 6–1 and d. Morales 6–2, 6–2, 6–4; Crawford–Hopman d. Vollmer–Morales 4–6, 6–4, 8–6, 6–4.

FINAL ROUND

USA d. Australia 5–0, Philadelphia: H. E. Vines d. J. H. Crawford 6–2, 6–4, 2–6, 6–4; F. X. Shields d. H. C. Hopman 6–4, 6–1, 6–2; W. Allison–J. van Ryn d. Crawford–Hopman 6–0, 6–4, 5–7, 7–5; Shields d.

Crawford 6–4, 7–5, 4–6, 3–6, 6–2; Vines d. Hopman 6–2, 9–11, 6–4, 6–4.

South American Zone won by Brazil.
Chile and Paraguay withdrew.

AMERICAN INTER-ZONE FINAL
USA d. Brazil 5–0, New York: W. Allison d. N. Cruz 6–3, 6–2, 6–3; F. X. Shields d. R. Pernambuco 6–1, 6–3, 0–6, 6–4; Allison–J. van Ryn d. Pernambuco–I. Simoni 6–1, 6–1, 6–2; van Ryn d. Simoni 6–2, 6–0, 6–0; Allison d. Pernambuco 6–1, 6–2, 6–0.

INTER-ZONE FINAL
USA d. Germany 3–2, Paris: F. X. Shields lost to G. von Cramm 5–7, 7–5, 4–6, 6–8; H. E. Vines d. D. Prenn 6–3, 6–3, 0–6, 6–4; W. Allison–J. van Ryn d. Prenn–von Cramm 6–3, 6–4, 6–1; Vines d. von Cramm 3–6, 6–3, 9–7, 6–3; Shields lost to Prenn 1–6, 0–6, 8–6, 2–6.

CHALLENGE ROUND
France d. USA 3–2, Paris: J. Borotra d. H. E. Vines 6–4, 6–2, 3–6, 6–4; H. Cochet d. W. Allison 5–7, 7–5, 7–5, 6–2; Cochet–J. Brugnon lost to Allison–J. van Ryn 3–6, 13–11, 5–7, 6–4, 4–6; Borotra d. Allison 1–6, 3–6, 6–4, 6–2, 7–5; Cochet lost to Vines 6–4, 6–0, 5–7, 6–8, 2–6.

1933: GREAT BRITAIN
European Zone

FIRST ROUND
Great Britain d. Spain 4–1, Barcelona: F. J. Perry d. E. Maier 7–5, 7–5, 6–2 and d. N. F. Sindreu 6–1, 6–3, 6–0; H. W. Austin d. Maier 8–6, 7–5, 6–1 and d. Sindreu 6–0, 6–3, 6–2; Perry–G. P. Hughes lost to Maier–A. Durall 3–6, 1–6, 6–1, 6–4, 3–6. **Austria d. Belgium 3–2, Brussels:** H. W. Artens d. L. de Borman 4–6, 6–2, 6–4, 7–5 and lost to A. Lacroix 2–6, 2–6, 4–6; F. Matejka d. de Borman 2–6, 6–4, 6–0, 3–6, 6–3 and d. Lacroix 6–3, 6–4, 6–2; R. Kinzel–A. Bawarowski lost to Lacroix–de Borman 4–6, 3–6, 1–6. **Italy d. Yugoslavia 4–1, Florence:** H. L. de Morpurgo d. F. Puncec 9–7, 6–3, 6–4 and d. F. Kukuljevic 7–5, 6–3, 6–4; G. de Stefani d. Kukuljevic 6–4, 6–0, 3–6, 6–2 and d. J. Pallada 6–1, 6–2, 6–2; de Morpurgo–A. Rado lost to Kukuljevic–Pallada 14–12, 3–6, 6–1, 4–6, 3–6. **Germany d. Egypt**

5–0, Wiesbaden: G. von Cramm d. L. Wahid 6–3, 6–4, 6–2 and d. A. Bogdagli 6–2, 6–2, 6–2; E. Nourney d. Bogdagli 8–6, 6–1, 6–1 and d. Wahid 5–7, 8–6, 6–2, 9–7; von Cramm–G. Jaenecke d. Wahid–A. Shukri 4–6, 6–4, 8–6, 6–4. **Holland d. Poland 3–2, The Hague:** H. Timmer d. J. Hebda 6–3, 6–2, 6–2 and d. I. Tloczynski 6–1, 3–6, 6–4, 3–6, 6–2; T. Hughan lost to Tloczynski 1–6, 2–6, 4–6 and lost to Hebda 3–6, 1–6, 3–6; Timmer–A. Diemer Kool d. Tloczynski–Hebda 3–6, 6–1, 6–2, 6–3. **Ireland d. Denmark 3–2, Copenhagen:** G. L. Rogers d. E. Ulrich 8–6, 6–2, 6–2 and d. A. Jacobsen 6–1, 6–3, 6–4; T. G. McVeagh lost to Jacobsen 6–3, 6–2, 4–6, 6–8, 3–6 and lost to Ulrich 2–6, 3–6, 3–6; Rogers–E. A. McGuire d. Ulrich–P. Henriksen 4–6, 6–1, 8–6, 6–4. **Japan d. Hungary 5–0, Budapest:** J. Satoh d. E. Gabrowitz 6–4, 6–2, 6–3 and d. B. von Kehrling 6–4, 6–4, 9–7; R. Nunoi d. von Kehrling 4–6, 8–6, 6–3, 6–1 and d. Gabrowitz 3–6, 1–6, 6–3, 9–7, 6–4; Satoh–Nunoi d. Gabrowitz–Count Zichy 6–0, 6–1, 6–2. **Finland d. India def.**

SECOND ROUND
Greece d. Rumania 4–1, Athens: G. Nicholaides d. T. Rety 7–5, 6–1, 6–3 and d. G. Poulieff 6–2, 1–6, 6–2, 6–2; L. Stalios d. Poulieff 6–2, 4–6, 6–3, 7–5; S. Xydis d. A. Botez 4–6, 6–3, 6–4, 6–1; Xydis–Stalios lost to Poulieff–Rety 3–6, 2–6, 6–3, 5–7. **Czechoslovakia d. Monaco 5–0, Prague:** R. Menzel d. V. Landau 6–2, 6–2, 6–4 and d. R. Gallepe 6–3, 6–2, 6–1; J. Siba d. Gallepe 6–1, 6–2, 6–1 and d. Landau 3–6, 9–7, 6–4, 6–1; Menzel–F. Marsalek d. Landau–Gallepe 6–1, 6–4, 8–6. **Great Britain d. Finland 5–0, London:** F. J. Perry d. B. Grotenfelt 6–0, 6–3, 6–1 and d. A. Grahn 6–1, 6–2, 6–4; H. W. Austin d. Grahn 6–0, 6–2, 6–2 and d. Grotenfelt 6–0, 6–1, 6–4; Perry–G. P. Hughes d. Grahn–Grotenfelt 6–1, 6–1, 6–3. **Italy d. Austria 4–1, Genoa:** H. L. de Morpurgo d. H. W. Artens 4–6, 7–5, 6–3, 6–3 and lost to F. Matejka 3–6, 6–3, 6–3, 3–6, 3–6; G. de Stefani d. Artens 7–5, 6–2, 6–0 and d. Matejka 6–3, 6–3, 4–6, 6–2; A. Rado–V. Taroni d. Matejka–Artens 6–3, 4–6, 4–6, 6–2, 7–5. **Germany d. Holland 4–1, Berlin:** G. von Cramm d. H. Timmer 6–2, 6–3, 1–6, 6–4 and d. G. Leembruggen 6–3, 6–2, 6–3; F. Kuhlmann d. Leembruggen 6–3, 6–3, 6–1 and lost to Timmer 2–6, 1–6, 2–6; von Cramm–E. Nourney d. Timmer–O. Koopman 6–3, 6–1, 1–6, 8–6. **Japan d. Ireland 5–0, Dublin:** J. Satoh d. E. A. McGuire 6–2, 6–2, 6–2 and d. G. L. Rogers 6–1, 6–3, 6–1; R. Nunoi d. Rogers 7–5, 6–3, 7–5 and d. McGuire 4–6, 3–6, 6–4, 6–3, 6–3; Satoh–Nunoi d. Rogers–McGuire 6–3, 8–6, 3–6, 6–2. **Australia d. Norway 5–0, Oslo:** J. H. Crawford d. J. Haanes 6–1, 6–3, 6–3; V. B. McGrath d. F. T. Smith 6–1, 6–1, 6–3 and d. Haanes 7–5, 7–5, 6–2; A. K. Quist d.

Smith 7–5, 4–6, 6–1, 6–0; Crawford–D. P. Turnbull d. R. Hagen–Haanes 6–2, 6–3, 6–1. **South Africa d. Switzerland 4–1, Basle:** V. G. Kirby d. H. C. Fisher 5–7, 6–4, 0–6, 7–5, 6–3; C. J. J. Robbins d. M. Ellmer 6–1, 6–1, 5–7, 6–3, and d. Fisher 8–10, 3–6, 6–1, 6–4, 6–4; J. Condon lost to Ellmer 4–6, 6–4, 4–6, 2–6; Kirby–N. G. Farquharson d. Fisher–W. Steiner 6–4, 6–3, 6–2.

THIRD ROUND

Czechoslovakia d. Greece 5–0, Prague: R. Menzel d. L. Stalios 6–2, 6–4, 9–7 and d. G. Nicholaides 6–1, 6–2, 4–6, 6–0; J. Siba d. Stalios 6–3, 6–1, 3–6, 8–6 and d. Nicholaides 6–3, 3–6, 6–2, 6–1; Menzel–F. Marsalek d. Nicholaides–Xydis 6–1, 6–1, 6–1. **Great Britain d. Italy 4–1, Eastbourne:** F. J. Perry d. H. L. de Morpurgo 6–4, 7–5, 6–4 and lost to G. de Stefani 7–5, 4–6, 4–6, 4–6; H. W. Austin d. de Stefani 6–2, 7–5, 7–5 and d. de Morpurgo 6–4, 6–3, 6–2; Perry–G. P. Hughes d. A. Rado–V. Taroni 6–1, 6–4, 9–7. **Japan d. Germany 4–1, Berlin:** J. Satoh d. G. von Cramm 6–3, 2–6, 6–3, 6–4 and d. G. Jaenecke 6–2, 6–2, 6–2; R. Nunoi d. Jaenecke 6–2, 4–6, 6–3, 6–2 and lost to von Cramm 6–3, 2–6, 5–7, 7–5, 3–6; Satoh–Nunoi d. von Cramm–E. Nourney 6–2, 6–3, 3–6, 6–1. **Australia d. South Africa 3–2, London:** J. H. Crawford d. V. G. Kirby 8–6, 6–1, 6–3 and d. C. J. J. Robbins 6–4, 6–1, 6–0; V. B. McGrath d. Robbins 7–5, 6–4, 4–6, 10–8 and lost to Kirby 8–6, 0–6, 4–6, 2–6; Crawford–McGrath lost to Kirby–N. G. Farquharson 4–6, 4–6, 4–6.

FOURTH ROUND

Great Britain d. Czechoslovakia 5–0, Eastbourne: F. J. Perry d. R. Menzel 6–1, 6–4, 6–3 and d. L. Hecht 6–2, 6–2, 6–2; H. W. Austin d. Hecht 6–1, 11–9, 6–4 and d. Menzel 3–6, 9–7, 6–0, 6–1; Perry–G. P. Hughes d. Menzel–F. Marsalek 6–3, 6–4, 6–4. **Australia d. Japan 3–2, Paris:** J. H. Crawford d. R. Nunoi 6–2, 4–6, 6–3, 4–6, 7–5 and lost to J. Satoh 6–3, 3–6, 1–6, 6–1, 2–6; V. B. McGrath d. Satoh 9–7, 1–6, 4–6, 6–4, 7–5 and lost to Nunoi 4–6, 4–6, 8–6, 5–7; Crawford–A. K. Quist d. Satoh–Nunoi 7–5, 7–9, 6–3, 3–6, 6–3.

FINAL ROUND

Great Britain d. Australia 3–2, London: H. W. Austin d. V. B. McGrath 6–4, 7–5, 6–3 and lost to J. H. Crawford 6–4, 2–6, 2–6, 3–6; F. J. Perry d. McGrath 6–2, 6–4, 6–2; H. G. N. Lee lost to Crawford 6–8, 5–7, 4–6; G. P. Hughes–Perry d. D. P. Turnbull–A. K. Quist 7–5, 6–4, 3–6, 6–3.

North American Zone

FIRST ROUND

Canada d. Cuba 4–1, Hot Springs: J. Wright d. R. Morales 8–6, 2–6,
6–1, 6–2 and d. L. Nodarse 6–1, 6–2, 6–1; G. Nunns d. Morales 8–6,
6–2, 6–4 and d. Nodarse 6–1, 6–2, 6–0; Wright–M. Rainville lost to
Morales–A. Randin 6–4, 6–0, 4–6, 8–10, 4–6.   **USA d. Mexico 5–0,
Mexico City:** W. L. Allison d. R. Tapia 4–6, 6–3, 6–4, 6–4; C. S. Sutter
d. E. Reyes 6–1, 6–0, 6–1; G. M. Lott–J. van Ryn d. E. Mestre–A.
Unda 6–0, 6–1, 7–5; Sutter d. Tapia 6–1, 3–6, 7–5, 2–6, 6–1; Allison d.
Mestre 6–0, 9–7, 6–2.

FINAL ROUND

USA d. Canada 5–0, Montreal: W. L. Allison d. J. Wright 6–2, 7–5,
6–2; H. E. Vines d. G. Nunns 6–3, 6–1, 6–3; G. M. Lott–J. van Ryn
d. M. Rainville–Wright 6–1, 6–3, 6–3; Allison d. Nunns 6–4, 8–6, 6–4;
Vines d. Wright 7–5, 6–3, 7–5.

South American Zone

FIRST ROUND

Brazil and Peru both withdrew.

SECOND ROUND

Chile d. Uruguay 5–0, Montevideo: E. Deik d. E. Hernandez 6–2,
6–1, 6–0 and d. E. Stanham 6–2, 6–2, 6–2; S. Deik d. Stanham 5–7, 6–0,
6–3, 6–3; E. Schronherr d. J. Galceran 6–2, 6–2, 6–3; Schronherr–S. Deik
d. Stanham–J. C. da Silva 6–4, 8–6, 6–3.

FINAL ROUND

Argentina d. Chile 4–0, Buenos Aires: A. H. Cattaruzza d. E. Deik
6–2, 6–8, 6–3, 3–6, 6–2 and v. S. Deik 6–1, 2–6, 6–6 unfin.; W. Robson
d. S. Deik 6–1, 6–3, 6–1 and d. E. Deik 6–1, 6–1, 7–9, 6–2; A. Zappa–L.
del Castillo d. E. Schronherr–S. Deik 6–4, 6–2, 6–3.

AMERICAN INTER-ZONE ROUND

USA d. Argentina 4–0, Washington: H. E. Vines d. A. Zappa 6–2,
6–3, 6–4; W. L. Allison d. A. H. Cattaruzza 6–2, 6–4, 6–3; G. M. Lott–J.
van Ryn d. Zappa–G. Echeverria 6–1, 6–4, 6–1; Vines d. Cattaruzza 7–5,
6–1, 5–7, 6–1; Allison v. Zappa 6–2, 6–1, 2–2 unfin.

INTER-ZONE FINAL
Great Britain d. USA 4–1, Paris: H. W. Austin d. H. E. Vines 6–1, 6–1, 6–4; F. J. Perry d. W. L. Allison 6–1, 7–5, 6–4; Perry–G. P. Hughes lost to G. M. Lott–J. van Ryn 6–8, 4–6, 1–6; Austin d. Allison 6–2, 7–9, 6–3, 6–4; Perry d. Vines 1–6, 6–0, 4–6, 7–5, 7–6 def.

CHALLENGE ROUND
Great Britain d. France 3–2, Paris: H. W. Austin d. A. Merlin 6–3, 6–4, 6–0; F. J. Perry d. H. Cochet 8–10, 6–4, 8–6, 3–6, 6–1; H. G. N. Lee–G. P. Hughes lost to J. Borotra–J. Brugnon 3–6, 6–8, 2–6; Austin lost to Cochet 7–5, 4–6, 6–4, 4–6, 4–6; Perry d. Merlin 4–6, 8–6, 6–2, 7–5.

1934: GREAT BRITAIN
European Zone

FIRST QUALIFYING ROUND
Belgium d. Hungary 3–2, Brussels: A. Lacroix d. B. von Kehrling 6–1, 7–5, 6–2 and d. E. Gabrowitz 6–4, 6–4, 6–2; L. de Borman lost to Gabrowitz 0–6, 5–7, 2–6 and lost to von Kehrling 5–7, 3–6, 4–6; Lacroix–de Borman d. von Kehrling–Gabrowitz 2–6, 6–1, 7–5, 3–6, 6–4.

SECOND QUALIFYING ROUND
Holland d. Rumania 4–1, Amsterdam: H. Timmer d. G. Poulieff 6–0, 6–0, 6–3 and d. A. Cantacuzene 6–1, 6–1, 6–1; W. Karsten d. Cantacuzene 6–2, 10–8, 0–6, 8–6 and lost to Poulieff 3–6, 6–2, 8–6, 6–8, 4–6; Timmer–G. W. Scheurleer d. Poulieff–Cantacuzene 6–3, 6–3, 6–0. **Italy d. Poland 3–2, Warsaw:** G. de Stefani d. I. Tloczynski 6–3, 2–6, 6–2, 7–5 and d. J. Hebda 6–2, 6–3, 0–6, 4–6, 6–2; E. Sertorio lost to Tloczynski 2–6, 6–4, 3–6, 4–6 and lost to Hebda 5–7, 0–6, 0–6; Sertorio–V. Taroni d. Hebda–E. Wittmann 6–2, 6–2, 3–6, 2–6, 6–4. **Switzerland d. Monaco 4–1, Monaco:** H. C. Fisher d. R. Gallepe 6–3, 6–3, 6–1 and d. V. Landau 6–2, 6–1, 6–3; M. Ellmer d. Landau 6–2, 6–3, 6–2 and d. G. Medecin 6–1, 6–2, 6–1; C. F. Aeschliman–W. Steiner lost to Gallepe–Landau 4–6, 6–3, 3–6, 4–6. **Belgium d. Sweden 3–2, Stockholm:** A. Lacroix d. C. Ostberg 7–5, 6–3, 2–6, 5–7, 8–6 and d. C. Ramberg 6–3, 6–4, 6–3; G. van Zuylen lost to Ostberg 3–6, 4–6, 8–10 and lost to Ramberg 2–6, 4–6, 3–6; Lacroix–L. de Borman d. Ostberg–Ramberg 5–7, 7–5, 7–5, 6–2. **Yugoslavia d. Norway 3–0, Oslo:** F. Puncec d. J. Haanes 6–1, 6–0, 3–6, 6–4; F. Kukuljevic d.

F. T. Smith 6–1, 6–1, 6–1; Kukuljevic–Puncec d. Haanes–R. Hagen 6–3, 6–4, 6–2. **Austria d. Spain 5–0, Vienna:** H. W. Artens d. E. Maier 7–9, 6–3, 2–6, 7–5, 6–2 and d. A. Suque 6–3, 4–6, 6–4, 4–6, 6–4; F. Matejka d. Suque 6–0, 6–3, 9–7; and d. A. Durall 6–3, 6–1, 8–10, 6–3; W. Brosch–G. von Metaxa d. Maier–Durall 6–8, 6–4, 6–4, 2–6, 6–3. **Denmark d. Greece 4–1, Copenhagen:** A. Jacobsen d. L. Stalios 4–6, 6–3, 3–6, 6–2, 6–4 and d. S. Xydis 6–1, 6–3, 6–3; E. Ulrich d. Stalios 6–4, 6–1, 6–3 and lost to Xydis 6–4, 4–6, 12–10, 4–6, 1–6; Jacobsen–Ulrich d. Stalios–Xydis 7–5, 4–6, 6–3, 7–5. **Germany d. Ireland 4–1, Dublin:** G. von Cramm d. G. L. Rogers 6–1, 6–4, 6–4 and d. E. A. McGuire 6–4, 6–4, 6–2; E. Nourney d. McGuire 6–1, 1–6, 6–4, 6–3; F. Frenz lost to T. G. McVeagh 4–6, 3–6, 4–6; von Cramm–Nourney d. McGuire–McVeagh 5–7, 6–2, 6–3, 6–4.

THIRD QUALIFYING ROUND
Italy d. Holland 3–2, Rotterdam: G. de Stefani d. H. Timmer 11–9, 5–7, 4–6, 6–2, 6–2 and d. W. Karsten 6–3, 6–2, 6–1; A. Rado d. Karsten 6–1, 6–3, 6–1 and lost to Timmer 7–5, 1–6, 1–6, 1–6; V. Taroni–F. Quintavalle lost to O. Koopman–G. Scheurleer 4–6, 1–6, 6–2, 3–6. **Switzerland d. Belgium 3–2, Montreux:** H. C. Fisher d. A. Lacroix 6–2, 3–6, 6–2, 6–2 and d. C. Naeyaert 6–2, 6–2, 6–3; M. Ellmer d. Naeyaert 6–2, 3–6, 7–5, 7–5 and lost to Lacroix 6–3, 6–0, 0–6, 3–6, 2–6; Fisher–C. F. Aeschliman lost to Lacroix–L. de Borman 4–6, 3–6, 4–6. **Austria d. Yugoslavia 4–1, Zagreb:** H. W. Artens d. F. Puncec 7–5, 8–6, 6–1 and d. F. Kukuljevic 6–3, 6–2, 4–6, 3–6, 6–0; F. Matejka d. Puncec 6–4, 6–1, 6–4 and d. Kukuljevic 8–6, 7–5, 6–4; Artens–G. von Metaxa lost to Puncec–Kukuljevic 2–6, 6–0, 4–6, 5–7. **Germany d. Denmark 5–0, Leipzig:** F. Frenz d. E. Ulrich 6–4, 7–5, 0–6, 6–3 and d. A. Jacobsen 0–6, 3–6, 7–5, 6–3, 6–3; G. von Cramm d. Jacobsen 2–6, 6–3, 6–3, 12–10 and d. Ulrich 6–3, 6–4, 6–3; von Cramm–E. Nourney d. Ulrich–P. Henriksen 6–3, 8–6, 7–5.

FIRST ROUND
Switzerland d. India 5–0, Lucerne: H. C. Fisher d. M. Bhandari 6–1, 6–2, 7–5 and d. M. Sleem 6–4, 6–2, 6–4; M. Ellmer d. Sleem 1–6, 6–2, 6–3, 6–0 and d. Bhandari 6–0, 6–2, 6–2 Fisher–W. Steiner d. Bhandari–A. E. Browne 6–3, 6–0, 6–1. **France d. Austria 5–0, Paris:** C. Boussus d. F. Matejka 6–1, 6–1, 6–4 and d. G. von Metaxa 7–5, 6–3, 6–3; A. Merlin d. von Metaxa 4–6, 8–6, 6–2, 6–2 and d. Matejka 6–3, 3–6, 6–2, 6–2; J. Borotra–J. Brugnon d. H. W. Artens–von Metaxa 4–6, 6–3, 6–3, 6–4.

SECOND ROUND

Czechoslovakia d. New Zealand 4–1, Prague: R. Menzel d. C. E. Malfroy 6–2, 6–0, 6–1 and d. E. D. Andrews 6–1, 6–3, 6–3; L. Hecht d. Andrews 6–1, 6–1, 6–0 and d. Malfroy 6–4, 6–1, 4–6, 6–1; Menzel–Hecht lost to Malfroy–A. C. Stedman 5–7, 4–6, 5–7. **Italy d. Switzerland 5–0, Rome:** G. de Stefani d. H. C. Fisher 6–3, 6–2, 6–3 and d. M. Ellmer 6–3, 6–3, 6–3; A. Rado d. Ellmer 6–4, 6–2, 6–4 and d. Fisher 6–1, 6–0, 11–9; V. Taroni–F. Quintavalle d. C. F. Aeschliman–W. Steiner 0–6, 0–6, 6–3, 6–3, 6–4. **France d. Germany 3–2, Paris:** C. Boussus d. E. Nourney 6–1, 6–2, 6–2 and lost to G. von Cramm 1–6, 0–6, 6–0, 4–6; A. Merlin d. Nourney 6–4, 7–5, 6–2 and lost to von Cramm 1–6, 9–7, 2–6, 5–7; J. Borotra–J. Brugnon d. von Cramm–H. Denker 5–7, 6–2, 6–4, 10–8. **Australia d. Japan 4–1, Eastbourne:** J. H. Crawford d. J. Fujikura 6–3, 6–3, 11–9; V. B. McGrath d. J. Yamagishi 2–6, 7–5, 6–2, 6–4 and lost to Fujikura 4–6, 7–5, 2–6, 6–8; D. P. Turnbull d. Yamagishi 6–4, 7–5, 9–7; Crawford–A. K. Quist d. Yamagishi–H. Nishimura 6–1, 6–0, 4–6, 9–7.

THIRD ROUND

Czechoslovakia d. Italy 3–2, Milan: R. Menzel d. A. Rado 6–1, 6–2, 10–8 and lost to G. de Stefani 6–0, 5–7, 2–6, 7–5, 3–6; L. Hecht d. Rado 6–2, 8–6, 6–2 and lost to de Stefani 3–6, 5–7, 6–1, 2–6; Menzel–F. Marsalek d. F. Quintavalle–Rado 6–8, 6–3, 6–0, 6–4. **Australia d. France 3–2, Paris:** J. H. Crawford d. C. Boussus 2–6, 6–2, 4–6, 6–4, 6–0 and lost to A. Merlin 6–4, 4–6, 4–6, 2–6; V. B. McGrath d. Boussus 6–3, 0–6, 6–8, 6–2, 6–2 and lost to Merlin 6–4, 2–6, 3–6, 0–6; Crawford–A. K. Quist d. J. Borotra–J. Brugnon 6–3, 6–4, 5–7, 4–6, 6–3.

FINAL ROUND

Australia d. Czechoslovakia 3–2, Prague: J. H. Crawford d. L. Hecht 6–4, 6–2, 6–2 and lost to R. Menzel 4–6, 4–6, 6–2, 6–8; V. B. McGrath d. Hecht 3–6, 6–2, 6–1, 7–5 and lost to Menzel 8–10, 2–6, 6–8; Crawford–A. K. Quist d. Menzel–Hecht 6–4, 6–3, 6–4.

North American Zone

FIRST ROUND

USA d. Canada 5–0, Wilmington: L. R. Stoefen d. M. Rainville 6–1, 7–5, 6–1; F. X. Shields d. W. Martin 6–2, 6–3, 9–7; G. M. Lott–J. van Ryn d. Martin–Rainville 6–0, 6–4, 6–0; Stoefen d. G. Nunns 6–4, 6–2, 6–3; Shields d. M. Laird Watt 6–1, 6–3, 6–4.

FINAL ROUND
USA d. Mexico 5–0, Baltimore: S. B. Wood d. E. Reyes 6–3, 6–2, 6–2; L. R. Stoefen d. R. Tapia 6–2, 6–3, 6–1; G. M. Lott–Stoefen d. Tapia–E. Mestre 6–4, 6–4, 6–4; F. X. Shields d. A. Roldan 6–2, 6–1, 6–2; Wood d. Tapia 6–4, 9–7, 6–0.

South American Zone

FIRST ROUND
Brazil d. Peru def.

AMERICAN INTER-ZONE FINAL
USA d. Brazil def.

INTER-ZONE FINAL
USA d. Australia 3–2, London: F. X. Shields lost to J. H. Crawford 1–6, 2–6, 10–12; S. B. Wood lost to V. B. McGrath 5–7, 4–6, 6–1, 7–9; G. M. Lott–L. R. Stoefen d. Crawford–A. K. Quist 6–4, 6–4, 2–6, 6–4; Wood d. Crawford 6–3, 9–7, 4–6, 4–6, 6–2; Shields d. McGrath 6–4, 6–2, 6–4.

CHALLENGE ROUND
Great Britain d. USA 4–1, London: H. W. Austin d. F. X. Shields 6–4, 6–4, 6–1; F. J. Perry d. S. B. Wood 6–1, 4–6, 5–7, 6–0, 6–3; G. P. Hughes–H. G. N. Lee lost to G. M. Lott–L. R. Stoefen 5–7, 0–6, 6–4, 7–9; Perry d. Shields 6–4, 4–6, 6–2, 15–13; Austin d. Wood 6–4, 6–0, 6–8, 6–3.

1935: GREAT BRITAIN
European Zone

FIRST QUALIFYING ROUND
Poland d. Belgium 4–1, Warsaw: J. Hebda d. C. Naeyaert 0–6, 6–3, 6–2, 8–6 and d. A. Lacroix 6–0, 6–4, 6–4; I. Tloczynski d. Lacroix 6–3, 6–3, 10–8 and d. Naeyaert 6–4, 10–8, 8–6; Tloczynski–M. Stolarow lost to Lacroix–L. de Borman 2–6, 4–6, 6–4, 2–6.

SECOND QUALIFYING ROUND
Sweden d. Ireland 3–2, Stockholm: C. Ostberg lost to G. L. Rogers 4–6, 6–1, 3–6, 5–7 and d. T. G. McVeagh 6–3, 6–3, 4–6, 6–3; K.

Schroder d. McVeagh 6–3, 6–2, 6–2, and lost to Rogers 1–6, 4–6, 4–6; Ostberg–Schroder d. Rogers–E. A. McGuire 5–7, 6–2, 6–2, 6–3. **Holland d. Monaco 4–1, Amsterdam:** H. Timmer d. V. Landau 6–4, 6–1, 6–4 and d. R. Gallepe 5–7, 6–2, 6–3, 6–4; J. H. Knottenbelt d. Gallepe 6–3, 4–6, 6–1, 2–6, 6–4 and d. Landau 2–6, 6–2, 5–7, 8–6, 7–5; Timmer–O. Koopman lost to Landau–Gallepe 4–6, 3–6, 5–7. **Poland d. Estonia 5–0, Warsaw:** I. Tlocyznski d. H. Pukk 6–4, 6–4, 6–3 and d. R. Lassen 6–3, 6–2, 6–2; K. Tarlowski d. Lassen 6–2, 6–4, 2–6, 6–4 and d. Pukk 6–3, 6–4, 6–1; Tloczynski–E. Wittmann d. Lassen–Pukk 6–3, 6–8, 6–4, 1–6, 6–4. **Hungary d. Norway 3–2, Budapest:** E. Gabrowitz d. J. H. Haanes 6–2, 6–4, 9–11, 6–3 and d. F. T. Smith 6–3, 7–5, 6–4; F. Straub d. Smith 5–7, 5–7, 6–1, 6–4, 6–2 and lost to Haanes 2–6, 3–6, 3–6; Count Zichy–E. Ferenczy lost to Haanes–Smith 6–3, 4–6, 6–4, 4–6, 3–6. **Germany d. Rumania 5–0, Berlin:** G. von Cramm d. A. Hamburger 6–1, 6–2, 6–3 and d. O. Schmidt 7–5, 6–4, 6–1; H. Henkel d. Schmidt 6–1, 6–1, 6–0 and d. Hamburger 6–2, 6–3, 6–3; von Cramm–Henkel d. Hamburger–Schmidt 6–1, 6–2, 6–2. **Greece d. Austria def.; Yugoslavia d. Spain def.; Denmark d. Switzerland def.**

THIRD QUALIFYING ROUND

Holland d. Sweden 3–2, Stockholm: H. Timmer d. C. Ostberg 6–1, 6–3, 6–1 and d. K. Schroder 6–0, 6–4, 6–3; J. H. Knottenbelt lost to Schroder 1–6, 5–7, 0–6 and lost to Ostberg 1–6, 1–6, 4–6; Timmer–O. Koopman d. Ostberg–Schroder 6–4, 6–1, 6–1. **Poland d. Greece 3–0, Warsaw:** I. Tloczynski d. K. Zachos 6–1, 6–0, 6–2; J. Hebda d. L. Stalios 6–3, 6–0, 7–5; K. Tarlowski–W. Bratek d. Stalios–Zachos 7–5, 6–1, 6–1. **Yugoslavia d. Hungary 3–2, Budapest:** F. Puncec d. E. Gabrowitz 3–6, 6–1, 7–5, 6–3; and d. F. Straub 6–3, 6–4, 7–5; J. Pallada lost to Straub 0–6, 1–6, 4–6; F. Schaffers lost to Gabrowitz 4–6, 4–6, 2–5 def.; Puncec–Schaffers d. Gabrowitz–Count Zichy 6–4, 6–4, 6–3. **Germany d. Denmark 5–0, Copenhagen:** G. von Cramm d. E. Ulrich 6–3, 6–1, 6–2 and d. A. Jacobsen 6–2, 6–2, 6–0; H. Henkel. d. Jacobsen 13–11, 6–3, 6–2 and d. Ulrich 6–2, 6–4, 6–1; von Cramm–H. Denker d. Jacobsen–Ulrich 8–6, 6–3, 7–5.

FIRST ROUND

Czechoslovakia d. Yugoslavia 4–1, Prague: R. Menzel d. F. Puncec 6–3, 6–1, 6–1 and d. J. Pallada 6–0, 6–1, 6–1; J. Caska lost to Pallada 2–6, 3–6, 3–6 and d. Puncec 6–4, 6–1, 4–6, 6–0; Menzel–L. Hecht d. F. Kukuljevic–Puncec 4–6, 4–6, 6–2, 8–6, 6–2. **Japan d. Holland 5–0, Scheveningen:** J. Yamagishi d. T. Hughan 6–4, 6–3, 6–1 and d. D. Teshmacher 6–1, 6–4, 6–3; N. Nishimura d. H. Timmer 7–5, 2–6, 7–5,

6–4 and d. Hughan 6–3, 4–6, 6–3, 9–11, 6–2; Yamagishi–Nishimura d. Hughan–O. Koopman 6–4, 6–0, 6–3. **Australia d. New Zealand 3–0, Eastbourne:** J. H. Crawford d. E. D. Andrews 6–4, 6–4, 7–5 and v. A. C. Stedman 14–12, 17–15, 4–3 unfin.; V. B. McGrath d. Stedman 6–3, 6–2, 8–6; Crawford–A. H. Quist d. Stedman–C. E. Malfroy 6–3, 4–6, 6–1, 6–4.

SECOND ROUND
South Africa d. Poland 3–2, Warsaw: N. G. Farquharson d. J. Hebda 6–4, 7–5, 4–6, 0–6, 8–6 and d. K. Tarlowski 3–6, 6–1, 7–5, 6–3; V. G. Kirby lost to Tarlowski 9–7, 6–8, 4–6, 2–6 and lost to Hebda 6–4, 4–6, 6–4, 1–6, 2–6; Farquharson–Kirby d. I. Tloczynski–Hebda 6–3, 6–2, 6–2. **Czechoslovakia d. Japan 4–1, Prague:** R. Menzel d. H. Nishimura 6–2, 6–3, 8–6; J. Caska d. J. Yamagishi 6–1, 8–6, 6–3 and d. Nishimura 6–2, 6–3, 6–8, 6–4; L. Hecht lost to Yamagishi 1–6, 4–6, 4–6; Menzel–F. Malecek d. Yamagishi–Nishimura 2–6, 6–2, 6–2, 6–1. **Australia d. France 3–2, Paris:** J. H. Crawford d. A. Merlin 6–4, 4–6, 6–3, 6–3 and d. C. Boussus 2–6, 6–4, 6–4, 3–6, 9–7; V. B. McGrath lost to Boussus 4–6, 6–4, 6–8, 1–6 and lost to Merlin 4–6, 7–5, 3–6, 4–6; Crawford–A. K. Quist d. J. Borotra–M. Bernard 6–3, 4–6, 10–8, 6–4. **Germany d. Italy 4–1, Berlin:** G. von Cramm d. S. Mangold 6–0, 6–4, 6–4 and d. G. de Stefani 6–3, 6–4, 5–7, 6–1; H. Henkel lost to de Stefani 1–6, 3–6, 4–6 and d. Mangold 6–1, 6–8, 6–4, 6–4; von Cramm–H. Denker d. F. Quintavalle–V. Taroni 4–6, 6–3, 2–6, 6–3, 6–1.

THIRD ROUND
Czechoslovakia d. South Africa 5–0, Prague: R. Menzel d. N. G. Farquharson 6–2, 5–7, 6–3, 6–2; J. Caska d. M. Bertram 6–2, 6–4, 6–1 and d. Farquharson 6–4, 6–2, 6–0; F. Malecek d. Bertram 6–1, 2–6, 6–3, 3–6, 6–2; Menzel–Malecek d. Farquharson–V. G. Kirby 9–11, 6–4, 6–2, 6–1. **Germany d. Australia 4–1, Berlin:** G. von Cramm d. J. H. Crawford 6–3, 7–5, 6–2 and d. V. B. McGrath 6–3, 4–6, 6–3, 4–6, 6–2; H. Henkel d. McGrath 4–6, 6–2, 6–0, 6–2 and d. Crawford 2–6, 6–3, 9–7, 4–6, 6–4; K. Lund–H. Denker lost to Crawford–A. K. Quist 1–6, 9–11, 3–6.

FINAL ROUND
Germany d. Czechoslovakia 4–1, Prague: G. von Cramm d. R. Menzel 6–2, 6–4, 3–6, 5–7, 6–1 and d. J. Caska 6–2, 6–4, 6–2; H. Henkel lost to Menzel 5–7, 1–6, 6–4, 6–2, 4–6 and d. Caska 2–6, 7–5, 6–4, 6–0; von Cramm–K. Lund d. Menzel–F. Malecek 6–3, 9–7, 6–4.

North American Zone

FIRST ROUND

USA d. China 5–0, Mexico City: B. M. Grant d. G. Cheng 4–6, 6–3,
6–2, 6–2; J. D. Budge d. Kho Sin Kie 6–2, 6–1, 6–8, 6–2; Budge–C. G.
Mako d. Cheng–Kie 7–5, 6–2, 6–1; Budge d. Cheng 6–4, 6–2, 6–1; Grant
d. Kie 6–1, 6–4, 6–3. **Mexico d. Cuba 5–0, Mexico City:** E. Reyes
d. A. Randin 6–2, 6–0, 6–3 and d. J. Etcheverry 8–6, 6–1, 6–3; D.
Hernandez d. L. Nodarse 5–7, 6–3, 4–6, 8–6, 6–2 and d. J. Aguero 6–3,
7–5, 3–6, 7–5; A. Unda–J. Llano d. Randin–Aguero 6–4, 6–1, 6–3.

FINAL ROUND

USA d. Mexico 4–1, Mexico City: B. M. Grant d. E. Reyes 6–2, 6–3,
6–3; J. D. Budge d. D. Hernandez 6–4, 6–3, 6–4; Budge–C. G. Mako
d. A. Unda–J. Llano 6–0, 6–2, 6–3; Grant d. Hernandez 6–1, 6–3, 6–0;
Mako lost to Reyes 6–1, 3–6, 6–8, 6–4, 2–0 def.

South American Zone

FIRST ROUND

Brazil d. Uruguay 3–2, Montevideo: S. L. Campos d. M. Harreguy
4–6, 7–5, 3–6, 6–4, 6–1 and lost to P. de Leon 4–6, 0–6, 4–6; I. Simone
lost to de Leon 2–6, 2–6, 8–6, 1–6 and d. Harreguy 7–5, 6–4, 6–4;
Simone–T. de Freitas d. M. Cat–E. Stanham 7–5, 4–6, 6–1, 8–6.

AMERICAN INTER-ZONE FINAL

USA d. Brazil def.

INTER-ZONE FINAL

USA d. Germany 4–1, London: J. D. Budge d. H. Henkel 7–5, 11–9,
6–8, 6–1; W. L. Allison lost to G. von Cramm 6–8, 3–6, 4–6; Allison–J.
van Ryn d. von Cramm–K. Lund 3–6, 6–3, 5–7, 9–7, 8–6; Allison d.
Henkel 6–1, 7–5, 11–9; Budge d. von Cramm 0–6, 9–7, 8–6, 6–3.

CHALLENGE ROUND

Great Britain d. USA 5–0, London: H. W. Austin d. W. L. Allison
6–2, 2–6, 4–6, 6–3, 7–5; F. J. Perry d. J. D. Budge 6–0, 6–8, 6–3, 6–4;
G. P. Hughes–C. R. D. Tuckey d. Allison–J. van Ryn 6–2, 1–6, 6–8,
6–3, 6–3; Austin d. Budge 6–2, 6–4, 6–8, 7–5; Perry d. Allison 4–6,
6–4, 7–5, 6–3.

1936: GREAT BRITAIN
European Zone

FIRST ROUND

Holland d. Monaco 3–2, Monte Carlo: H. Timmer d. R. Gallepe 6–3, 6–2, 6–1 and d. V. Landau 6–2, 6–3, 8–6; T. Hughan d. Landau 6–3, 5–7, 6–2, 6–1 and lost to Gallepe 2–6, 4–6, 3–6; Hughan–W. Karsten lost to Landau–Gallepe 4–6, 5–7, 6–3, 5–7. **France d. China 5–0, Paris:** C. Boussus d. Kho Sin Kie 6–0, 6–0, 6–1 and d. G. Cheng 6–0, 6–0, 6–2; B. Destremau d. Cheng 6–1, 6–3, 6–8, 6–3 and d. Kho Sin Kie 6–3, 6–2, 4–6, 6–2; J. Borotra–M. Bernard d. Kho Sin Kie–G. Lum 6–1, 6–3, 4–6, 6–2. **Germany d. Spain 4–1, Barcelona:** G. von Cramm d. M. Alonso 6–3, 6–4, 6–3 and lost to E. Maier 3–6, 2–6, 1–6; H. Henkel d. Maier 6–4, 7–5, 8–6 and d. Alonso 6–2, 6–3, 6–4; von Cramm–K. Lund d. Maier–J. M. Blanc 6–3, 6–3, 9–7.

SECOND ROUND

Belgium d. Norway 3–2, Oslo: A. Lacroix d. F. Jenssen 7–5, 6–2, 6–4 and d. J. Haanes 4–6, 6–3, 6–0, 6–2; P. Geelhand lost to Jenssen 6–8, 6–4, 2–6, 4–6; J. van den Eynde lost to Haanes 4–6, 6–2, 6–8, 2–6; Lacroix–L. de Borman d. Haanes–Jenssen 6–4, 6–2, 7–9, 6–3. **Austria d. Poland 3–2, Vienna:** A. Bawarowski d. I. Tloczynski 6–4, 6–3, 6–3 and lost to J. Hebda 0–6, 6–2, 6–4, 1–6, 5–7; G. von Metaxa d. Tloczynski 6–4, 6–8, 3–6, 7–5, 6–3 and lost to Hebda 4–6, 5–7, 4–6; Bawarowski–von Metaxa d. Hebda–K. Tarlowski 6–1, 6–2, 6–4. **Yugoslavia d. Czechoslovakia 3–2, Zagreb:** F. Puncec d. J. Siba 6–1, 6–2, 2–6, 6–0 and d. L. Hecht 6–3, 4–6, 1–6, 6–4, 6–2; J. Pallada d. Siba 6–3, 6–2, 6–4 and lost to Hecht 6–8, 1–6, 6–2, 2–6; Puncec–F. Kukuljevic lost to Hecht–F. Malacek 6–4, 7–9, 6–2, 3–6, 4–6. **France d. Holland 4–1, The Hague:** C. Boussus d. T. Hughan 3–6, 10–8, 6–2, 6–0 and lost to H. Timmer 3–6, 3–6, 1–6; B. Destremau d. Hughan 6–4, 3–6, 3–6, 6–4, 6–1 and d. Timmer 0–6, 6–1, 6–3, 6–2; J. Borotra–M. Bernard d. Timmer–W. Karsten 6–1, 6–3, 6–8, 6–2. **Germany d. Hungary 5–0, Dusseldorf:** G. von Cramm d. E. Gabrowitz 6–3, 6–2, 6–3 and d. G. Dallos 6–1, 7–5, 6–3; H. Henkel d. Dallos 6–1, 6–1, 6–2 and d. Gabrowitz 8–6, 6–3, 7–5; von Cramm–K. Lund d. E. Ferenczy–E. Gabory 6–3, 7–5, 6–0. **Argentina d. Greece 4–1, Athens:** L. del Castillo d. G. Nicholaides 6–4, 6–0, 6–1 and d. L. Stalios 6–2, 6–4, 9–7; A. Zappa d. Nicholaides 6–3, 6–1, 5–7, 6–1 and lost to Stalios 4–6, 3–6, 4–6; Zappa–del Castillo d. Stalios–Nicholaides 4–6, 6–1, 6–1, 6–2. **Ireland d. Sweden 4–1, Dublin:** G. L. Rogers d. K. Schroder 9–7, 2–6, 1–6, 6–3, 6–4 and d. C. Ostberg 0–6, 6–2, 6–4, 6–3; T. G.

McVeagh d. Ostberg 6–4, 6–4, 6–4 and d. Schroder 2–6, 7–5, 6–3, 6–3; Rogers–McVeagh lost to Schroder–Ostberg 6–3, 2–6, 7–9, 5–7. **Switzerland d. Denmark 5–0, Montreux:** H. C. Fisher d. N. K. Koerner 6–2, 6–1, 6–0 and d. H. Plougmann 6–0, 7–5, 4–6, 6–8, 6–1; M. Ellmer d. Plougmann 6–1, 6–4, 6–1 and d. Koerner 6–3, 6–0, 3–6, 6–0; H. Steiner–B. Maneff d. E. Ulrich–Plougmann 6–1, 6–3, 11–9.

THIRD ROUND

Austria d. Belgium 4–1, Vienna: A. Bawarowski d. J. van den Eynde 6–3, 3–6, 4–6, 6–3, 6–2 and d. A. Lacroix 6–4, 6–3, 11–9; G. von Metaxa d. Lacroix 3–6, 6–3, 6–4, 2–6, 6–3 and d. van den Eynde 6–3, 4–6, 6–3, 6–2; Bawarowski–von Metaxa lost to Lacroix–L. de Borman 6–2, 6–8, 5–7, 3–6. **Yugoslavia d. France 3–2, Paris:** F. Puncec d. C. Boussus 3–6, 6–1, 4–6, 7–5, 6–1 and lost to B. Destremau 6–3, 2–6, 5–7, 6–0, 7–9; J. Pallada d. Boussus 6–2, 2–6, 6–3, 6–2 and d. Destremau 6–1, 1–6, 8–6, 6–4; D. Mitic–F. Kukuljevic lost to J. Borotra–M. Bernard 6–8, 5–7, 6–4, 6–3, 2–6. **Germany d. Argentina 4–1, Berlin:** G. von Cramm d. L. del Castillo 6–0, 4–6, 6–4, 6–1; H. Henkel d. A. Zappa 6–1, 6–1, 6–3 and d. del Castillo 6–0, 6–1, 6–1; H. Denker lost to Zappa 6–3, 0–6, 6–2, 1–6, 1–6; von Cramm–Henkel d. del Castillo–Zappa 6–1, 6–2, 6–3. **Ireland d. Switzerland 3–2, Dublin:** G. L. Rogers d. B. Maneff 6–2, 6–3, 3–6, 3–6, 6–0 and lost to H. C. Fisher 6–3, 2–6, 3–6, 2–6; T. G. McVeagh d. M. Ellmer 6–3, 4–6, 6–4, 11–9 and lost to Fisher 1–6, 6–3, 8–6, 0–6, 2–6; Rogers–McVeagh d. Fisher–H. Steiner 5–7, 6–4, 6–1, 6–4.

FOURTH ROUND

Yugoslavia d. Austria 4–1, Vienna: F. Puncec d. G. von Metaxa 6–4, 6–3, 6–1; J. Pallada d. A. Bawarowski 3–6, 6–4, 6–3, 3–6, 7–5 and d. von Metaxa 8–6, 6–3, 2–6, 3–6, 6–4; F. Kukuljevic d. Bawarowski 5–7, 6–4, 1–6, 6–2, 6–3; Kukuljevic–D. Mitic lost to Bawarowski–von Metaxa 6–4, 3–6, 4–6, 6–4, 2–6 **Germany d. Ireland 5–0, Berlin:** G. von Cramm d. G. L. Rogers 6–1, 6–2, 6–3 and d. T. G. McVeagh 6–2, 6–3, 6–1; H. Henkel d. McVeagh 6–1, 8–6, 6–2 and d. Rogers 6–2, 6–0, 6–0; von Cramm–Henkel d. Rogers–McVeagh 6–0, 6–1, 6–4.

FINAL ROUND

Germany d. Yugoslavia 3–2, Zagreb: G. von Cramm d. J. Pallada 6–4, 6–2, 6–8, 6–2; H. Henkel d. F. Puncec 6–1, 6–2, 6–4; von Cramm–Henkel d. D. Mitic–F. Kukuljevic 8–6, 4–6, 6–3, 4–6, 6–3; von Cramm lost to Puncec def.; Henkel lost to Pallada def.

North American Zone

FIRST ROUND

USA d. Mexico 5–0, Houston: J. D. Budge d. E. Reyes 6–3, 6–1, 6–1; B. M. Grant d. D. Hernandez 3–6, 6–2, 6–3, 6–3; W. L. Allison–J. van Ryn d. M. A. Mestre–F. Martinez 6–0, 6–1, 6–2; Budge d. Hernandez 6–1, 6–1, 6–3; Grant d. Reyes 6–4, 13–11, 6–2. **Australia d. Cuba def.**

FINAL ROUND

Australia d. USA 3–2, Philadelphia: A. K. Quist d. W. L. Allison 6–3, 5–7, 6–4, 6–1; J. H. Crawford lost to J. D. Budge 2–6, 3–6, 6–4, 6–1, 11–13; Crawford–Quist d. Budge–C. G. Mako 4–6, 2–6, 6–4, 7–5, 6–4; Crawford d. Allison 4–6, 6–3, 4–6, 6–2, 6–2; Quist lost to Budge 2–6, 2–6, 4–6.

INTER-ZONE FINAL

Australia d. Germany 4–1, London: A. K. Quist lost to G. von Cramm 6–4, 4–6, 6–4, 4–6, 9–11; J. H. Crawford d. H. Henkel 6–2, 6–2 def.; Crawford–V. B. McGrath d. von Cramm–Henkel 6–4, 4–6, 6–4, 6–4; McGrath d. Henkel 6–3, 5–7, 6–4, 6–4; Crawford d. H. Denker 6–3, 6–1, 6–4.

CHALLENGE ROUND

Great Britain d. Australia 3–2, London: H. W. Austin d. J. H. Crawford 4–6, 6–3, 6–1, 6–1; F. J. Perry d. A. K. Quist 6–1, 4–6, 7–5, 6–2; G. P. Hughes–C. R. D. Tuckey lost to Crawford–Quist 4–6, 6–2, 5–7, 8–10; Austin lost to Quist 4–6, 6–3, 5–7, 2–6; Perry d. Crawford 6–2, 6–3, 6–3.

1937: USA
European Zone

FIRST ROUND

Belgium d. Hungary 3–2, Budapest: C. Naeyaert d. E. Gabory 7–5, 4–6, 4–6, 6–0, 6–4 and lost to G. Dallos 5–7, 6–4, 2–6, 3–3 def.; A. Lacroix lost to Dallos 6–4, 9–7, 4–6, 3–6, 3–6 and d. Gabory 6–1, 6–2, 6–4; L. de Borman–P. Geelhand d. Gabory–E. Ferenczy 2–6, 1–6, 6–4, 6–3, 6–1. **Switzerland d. Ireland 3–2, Montreux:** M. Ellmer lost to G. L. Rogers 6–8, 6–1, 1–6, 3–6 and d. T. G. McVeagh 5–7, 8–6, 6–4, 6–1; H. C. Fisher d. McVeagh 6–4, 6–2, 6–1 and d. Rogers 6–3, 6–4,

4–6, 2–6, 6–2; B. Maneff–Fisher lost to Rogers–McVeagh 0–6, 1–6, 7–5, 7–5, 4–6. **South Africa d. Holland 5–0, Amsterdam:** V. G. Kirby d. D. Teshmacher 6–2, 7–5, 8–6; N. G. Farquharson d. T. Hughan 6–1, 6–1, 6–1 and d. Teshmacher 9–7, 6–1, 6–3; E. Fannin d. Hughan 6–2, 7–5, 3–6, 6–3; Farquharson–Kirby d. Hughan–A. C. van Swol 6–4, 6–3, 6–2. **New Zealand d. China 3–2, Brighton:** A. C. Stedman d. W. C. Choy 6–4, 6–0, 6–2 and lost to Kho Sin Kie 4–6, 4–6, 6–1, 4–6; C. E. Malfroy d. Choy 6–1, 6–3, 6–1 and lost to Kho Sin Kie 0–6, 3–6, 6–4, 2–6; Stedman–Malfroy d. Kho Sin Kie–Wat Tsui Pui 6–3, 6–8, 6–3, 6–2.

SECOND ROUND

Italy d. Monaco 3–0, Bologna: G. de Stefani d. V. Landau 6–2, 6–0, 6–3; V. Canapele d. G. Medecin 6–0, 6–1, 6–0; V. Taroni–F. Quintavalle d. Landau–Medecin 6–1, 6–3, 6–3. **Germany d. Austria 3–2, Munich:** G. von Cramm d. G. von Metaxa 6–3, 6–4, 6–3 and lost to A. Baworowski 10–8 def.; H. Henkel d. Bawarowski 6–1, 6–4, 6–1; E. Dettmer lost to H. Redl 6–8, 1–6, 6–3, 1–6; von Cramm–Henkel d. Bawarowski–von Metaxa 8–6, 11–9, 7–5. **Sweden d. Greece 3–2, Stockholm:** K. Schroder d. L. Stalios 6–3, 6–3, 6–4 and d. G. Nicholaides 6–2, 6–4, 6–4; S. Karlberg lost to Nicholaides 6–4, 2–6, 2–6, 3–6 and lost to Stalios 2–6, 2–6, 3–6; Schroder–C. Ostberg d. Nicholaides–Stalios 6–2, 6–2, 8–10, 3–6, 8–6. **Belgium d. Switzerland 4–1, Brussels:** A. Lacroix lost to H. C. Fisher 4–6, 2–6, 6–8 and d. M. Ellmer 6–0, 6–4, 6–1; C. Naeyaert d. Ellmer 13–11, 6–3, 6–3 and d. Fisher 4–6, 6–0, 4–6, 6–3, 7–5; Lacroix–L. de Borman d. H. Steiner–B. Maneff 6–2, 6–4, 6–1. **South Africa d. New Zealand 4–1, Brighton:** N. G. Farquharson lost to A. C. Stedman 5–7, 3–6, 6–3, 2–6; V. G. Kirby d. C. E. Malfroy 7–5, 6–2, 6–3 and d. E. D. Andrews 6–2, 6–4, 6–3; E. E. Fannin d. D. C. Coombe 6–4, 6–4, 6–3; Farquharson–Kirby d. Andrews–Malfroy 7–5, 6–2, 6–2. **Yugoslavia d. Rumania 5–0, Belgrade:** J. Pallada d. T. Caralulis 6–3, 6–0, 2–6, 6–2 and d. O. Schmidt 6–4, 6–3, 5–7, 6–0; F. Puncec d. Schmidt 6–3, 6–3, 7–5 and d. Caralulis 6–4, 1–6, 6–3, 6–2; F. Kukuljevic–D. Mitic d. Schmidt–Caralulis 7–5, 6–3, 4–6, 6–2. **Czechoslovakia d. Poland 5–0, Warsaw:** R. Menzel d. K. Tarlowski 6–3, 6–4, 2–6, 6–3; and d. J. Hebda 7–5, 6–3, 6–3; L. Hecht d. Hebda 6–2, 6–0, 3–6, 6–1; J. Siba d. Tarlowski 6–3, 6–4, 6–3; J. Caska–Hecht d. Hebda–I. Tloczynski 6–1, 5–7, 6–1, 6–4. **France d. Norway 5–0, Paris:** B. Destremau d. F. Jenssen 6–0, 6–3, 6–3 and d. D. Bjurstedt 7–5, 6–2, 6–1; M. Bernard d. Bjurstedt 2–6, 6–1, 6–0, 6–0; Y. Petra d. Jenssen 6–1, 6–3, 4–6, 7–5; Bernard–Petra d. J. Beer–Jenssen 6–2, 6–2, 6–2.

THIRD ROUND

Germany d. Italy 4–1, Milan: G. von Cramm d. V. Canapele 6–1, 6–4, 1–6, 6–4 and d. G. de Stefani 6–0, 6–1, 6–4; H. Henkel lost to de Stefani 2–6, 3–6, 7–5, 2–6 and d. Canapele 3–6, 6–3, 6–1, 6–4; von Cramm–Henkel d. V. Taroni–F. Quintavalle 6–3, 6–1, 6–1. **Belgium d. Sweden 3–2, Brussels:** A. Lacroix lost to K. Schroder 3–6, 6–3, 0–6, 6–4, 2–6 and d. S. Martensson 6–2, 6–0, 6–3; C. Naeyaert d. Martensson 6–1, 6–2, 6–1 and lost to Schroder 9–7, 2–6, 0–6, 3–6; Lacroix–L. de Borman d. Schroder–C. Ostberg 6–0, 6–4, 6–4. **Yugoslavia d. South Africa 4–1, Zagreb:** F. Puncec d. V. G. Kirby 1–6, 6–0, 6–3, 2–6, 6–4 and d. N. G. Farquharson 6–1, 6–1, 6–1; J. Pallada d. Kirby 6–1, 6–4, 6–2 and d. Farquharson 3–6, 3–6, 6–3, 6–0, 6–3; F. Kukuljevic–D. Mitic lost to Farquharson–Kirby 2–6, 3–6, 2–6. **Czechoslovakia d. France 4–1, Prague:** R. Menzel d. B. Destremau 6–0, 6–3, 6–4 and d. C. Boussus 6–2, 6–3, 6–4; L. Hecht d. Boussus 2–6, 6–1, 7–5, 6–0 and d. Destremau 6–3, 6–3, 6–1; Menzel–Hecht lost to J. Borotra–Y. Petra 3–6, 6–2, 2–6, 3–6.

FOURTH ROUND

Germany d. Belgium 4–1, Berlin: G. von Cramm d. C. Naeyaert 6–3, 6–0, 6–4; E. Dettmer lost to A. Lacroix 4–6, 6–3, 2–6, 6–8; H. Henkel d. Lacroix 6–1, 6–1, 6–1 and d. Naeyaert 6–3, 6–2, 6–2; von Cramm–Henkel d. Lacroix–L. de Borman 6–4, 6–3, 6–4. **Czechoslovakia d. Yugoslavia 3–0, Prague:** R. Menzel d. J. Pallada 6–2, 6–1, 6–0; L. Hecht d. F. Puncec 7–5, 6–2, 6–3; Menzel–Hecht d. Pallada–Puncec 2–6, 6–1, 6–0, 7–9, 6–1.

FINAL ROUND

Germany d. Czechoslovakia 4–1, Berlin: G. von Cramm d. R. Menzel 3–6, 4–6, 6–4, 6–3, 6–2 and d. L. Hecht 6–3, 7–5, 6–2; H. Henkel d. Hecht 6–1, 7–5, 7–5; H. Denker lost to F. Cejnar 6–4, 6–3, 4–6, 4–6, 2–6; von Cramm–Henkel d. Hecht–J. Caska 6–1, 6–2, 10–12, 6–0.

American Zone

FIRST ROUND

USA d. Japan 5–0, San Francisco: J. D. Budge d. F. Nakano 6–1, 6–1, 6–0; F. Parker d. J. Yamagishi 6–3, 2–6, 8–6, 6–1; Budge–C. G. Mako d. Yamagishi–Nakano 6–0, 6–1, 6–4; Parker d. Nakano 6–0, 6–3, 6–2; Budge d. Yamagishi 6–2, 6–2, 6–4. **Australia d. Mexico 5–0, Mexico City:** A. K. Quist d. E. Reyes 6–3, 6–1, 6–3 and d. R. Tapia 6–2, 6–4, 4–6, 6–3; V. B. McGrath d. Tapia 6–2, 6–4, 6–4; J. Bromwich d. Reyes

6–2, 6–2, 7–5; J. H. Crawford–Quist d. A. Unda–D. Hernandez 6–2, 6–3, 6–3.

FINAL ROUND

USA d. Australia 5–0, New York: J. D. Budge d. J. H. Crawford 6–1, 6–3, 6–2; B. M. Grant d. J. Bromwich 6–2, 7–5, 6–1; Budge–C. G. Mako d. Crawford–V. B. McGrath 7–5, 6–1, 8–6; Budge d. Bromwich 6–2, 6–3, 5–7, 6–1; Grant d. Crawford 6–0, 6–2, 7–5.

INTER-ZONE FINAL

USA d. Germany 3–2, London: B. Grant lost to G. von Cramm 3–6, 4–6, 2–6; J. D. Budge d. H. Henkel 6–2, 6–1, 6–3; C. G. Mako–Budge d. von Cramm–Henkel 4–6, 7–5, 8–6, 6–4; Grant lost to Henkel 5–7, 6–2, 3–6, 4–6; Budge d. von Cramm 6–8, 5–7, 6–4, 6–2, 8–6.

CHALLENGE ROUND

USA d. Great Britain 4–1, London: F. A. Parker lost to H. W. Austin 3–6, 2–6, 5–7; J. D. Budge d. C. E. Hare 15–13, 6–1, 6–2; Budge–C. G. Mako d. C. R. D. Tuckey–F. H. D. Wilde 6–3, 7–5, 7–9, 12–10; Parker d. Hare 6–2, 6–4, 6–2; Budge d. Austin 8–6, 3–6, 6–4, 6–3.

1938: USA
European Zone

FIRST ROUND

France d. Holland 3–2, Scheveningen: B. Destremau d. T. Hughan 6–4, 6–2, 6–2 and lost to A. C. van Swol 3–6, 0–6, 6–8; Y. Petra d. Hughan 6–3, 6–2, 6–2 and d. van Swol 6–0, 6–3, 6–2; Petra–H. Bolelli lost to Hughan–van Swol 8–6, 6–1, 1–6, 5–7, 2–6. **Poland d. Denmark 5–0, Warsaw:** J. Hebda d. H. Plougmann 6–2, 6–2, 6–1 and d. F. Bekevold 6–4, 7–5, 6–1; I. Tloczynski d. Plougmann 6–0, 6–2, 6–1 and d. Bekevold 6–2, 6–3, 6–2; Hebda–Tloczynski d. E. Ulrich–N. K. Koerner 6–2, 6–3, 6–8, 6–3. **Italy d. Ireland 4–1, Dublin:** G. de Stefani d. H. J. Ryan 6–2, 6–2, 6–2 and lost to G. L. Rogers 5–7, 6–2, 3–6, 2–6; V. Canapele d. T. G. McVeagh 6–0, 6–2, 6–0 and d. Rogers 5–7, 6–3, 1–6, 6–3, 6–1; V. Taroni–F. Quintavalle d. Rogers–McVeagh 6–3, 4–6, 6–1, 6–2. **Yugoslavia d. Czechoslovakia 3–2, Zagreb:** F. Puncec d. L. Hecht 7–5, 6–3, 6–3; J. Pallada lost to R. Menzel 2–6, 2–6, 1–6; Puncec–D. Mitic lost to Menzel–F. Cejnar 9–11, 6–3, 7–9, 2–6; Puncec d. Menzel 3–6, 6–1, 6–1, 6–2; Mitic d. Cejnar 3–6, 7–5, 4–6, 6–2, 2–1 def. **Great Britain d. Rumania 3–2, Harrogate:** C. M. Jones lost to C. Caralulis 3–6, 6–3, 2–6, 6–8 and lost to O. Schmidt 3–6, 1–6, 6–0, 6–2, 6–8; D. W. Butler–F. H. D. Wilde d. Caralulis–Schmidt 8–6, 7–5, 6–2; R. A. Shayes d. Schmidt 6–3, 6–2, 6–2 and d. Caralulis 6–3, 6–0, 6–3.

SECOND ROUND

Germany d. Norway 5–0, Berlin: H. Henkel d. F. Jenssen 6–0, 6–0, 6–1; G. von Metaxa d. J. Haanes 2–6, 5–7, 6–2, 6–3, 7–5 and d. Jenssen 6–1, 6–0, 6–0; R. Goepfert d. Haanes 6–3, 8–6, 6–2; Henkel–von Metaxa d. Haanes–Jenssen 6–1, 6–2, 6–3.   **France d. Monaco 5–0, Versailles:** B. Destremau d. G. Medecin 6–3, 6–0, 6–1; Y. Petra d. A. Noghes 6–1, 6–1, 6–0; P. Pellizza d. Medecin 6–2, 6–1, 3–6, 6–4; H. Bolelli d. Noghes 6–1, 6–1, 6–2; Bolelli–Pellizza d. Medecin–V. Landau 6–2, 6–1, 6–3.   **Italy d. Poland 3–2, Milan:** G. de Stefani lost to I. Tloczynski 8–6, 6–4, 2–6, 2–6 def.; V. Taroni lost to J. Hebda 3–6, 6–3, 1–6, 4–6; V. Canapele d. Hebda 6–1, 7–9, 6–2, 7–9, 6–2 and d. Tloczynski 6–2, 6–1, 2–6, 6–2; Taroni–F. Quintavalle d. Tloczynski–C. Spychala 11–9, 2–6, 6–4, 3–6, 7–5.   **Sweden d. Switzerland 4–1, Stockholm:** K. Schroder d. H. C. Fisher 8–6, 6–2, 6–0 and d. B. Maneff 3–6, 1–6, 6–2, 6–4, 6–2; N. Rohlsson d. Fisher 3–6, 4–6, 6–4, 6–3, 6–1 and lost to Maneff 1–6, 4–6, 6–2, 1–6; Schroder–Rohlsson d. Fisher–Maneff 6–2, 5–7, 6–4, 7–5.   **Belgium d. Greece 5–0, Athens:** A. Lacroix d. L. Stalios 6–1, 6–2, 6–1; C. Naeyaert d. J. Michailides 6–1, 6–4, 9–7 and d. Stalios 6–4, 6–3, 6–2; P. Geelhand d. Michailides 6–4, 6–3, 6–3; Lacroix–L. de Borman d. Stalios–Michailides 6–2, 6–1, 6–1.   **Yugoslavia d. Great Britain 5–0, Zagreb:** F. Puncec d. R. A. Shayes 6–4, 4–6, 6–2, 6–4 and d. D. W. Butler 6–3, 6–2, 3–6, 6–3; D. Mitic d. Butler 6–3, 6–1, 6–4 and d. Shayes 6–2, 6–3, 11–9; Mitic–Puncec d. Butler–F. H. D. Wilde 7–5, 6–3, 3–6, 5–7, 6–3.   **India d. Austria def.; Hungary d. New Zealand def.**

THIRD ROUND

Germany d. Hungary 3–1, Budapest: H. Henkel d. G. Dallos 6–4, 11–9, 6–0 and v. E. Gabory 6–1, unfin.; G. von Metaxa d. Dallos 6–2, 3–6, 6–3, 6–2 and lost to Gabory 5–7, 4–6, 6–4, 6–2, 5–7; Henkel–von Metaxa d. Dallos–J. Asboth 5–7, 6–1, 8–6, 6–3.   **France d. Italy 4–1, Paris:** Y Petra d. V. Taroni 6–0, 6–2, 6–3; B. Destremau d. V. Canapele 3–6, 6–0, 6–2, 7–5 and lost to Taroni 6–8, 7–5, 4–6, 2–6; P. Pellizza d. L. Bossi 4–6, 6–4, 5–7, 6–3, 7–5; H. Bolelli–Pellizza d. Taroni–F. Quintavalle 9–7, 6–3, 6–4.   **Yugoslavia d. Sweden 4–1, Zagreb:** J. Pallada d. N. Rohlsson 7–5, 7–5, 6–1 and lost to K. Schroder 5–7, 6–1, 2–6, 8–6, 3–6; F. Puncec d. Rohlsson 6–2, 6–3, 6–3 and d. Schroder def.; Puncec–F. Kukuljevic d. Schroder–Rohlsson 6–3, 9–7, 6–3.

Belgium d. India 4–1, Brussels: A. Lacroix d. S. L. R. Sawhney 6–4, 6–3, 4–6, 6–3 and d. Ghaus Mohammed Khan 7–5, 0–6, 2–6, 7–5, 6–3; C. Naeyaert lost to Ghaus Mohammed Khan 7–5, 6–2, 3–6, 1–6, 7–9; P. Geelhand d. Sawhney def.; Lacroix–L. de Borman d. Sawhney–Ghaus Mohammed Khan 4–6, 3–6, 6–3, 7–5, 6–4.

FOURTH ROUND

Germany d. France 3–2, Berlin: H. Henkel d. Y. Petra 4–6, 6–1, 11–9, 6–2; G. von Metaxa d. B. Destremau 6–4, 7–5, 5–7, 5–7, 6–3 and lost to Petra 7–9, 6–8, 4–6; H. Redl lost to Destremau 8–6, 4–6, 4–6, 2–6; Henkel–von Metaxa d. Petra–J. Lesueur 4–6, 6–4, 2–6, 10–8, 6–4.

Yugoslavia d. Belgium 5–0, Brussels: F. Puncec d. J. van den Eynde 2–6, 6–0, 6–1, 6–2 and d. A. Lacroix 6–4, 6–1, 6–2; J. Pallada d. Lacroix 6–4, 6–1, 6–2 and d. van den Eynde 6–3, 6–3, 6–1; F. Kukuljevic–D. Mitic d. L. de Borman–P. Geelhand 6–3, 6–3, 3–6, 10–8.

FINAL ROUND

Germany d. Yugoslavia 3–2, Berlin: H. Henkel d. J. Pallada 6–3, 7–5, 6–1 and lost to F. Puncec 1–6, 5–7, 3–6; G. von Metaxa d. Pallada 1–6, 6–4, 6–1, 3–6, 12–10; H. Redl lost to F. Kukuljevic 4–6, 3–6, 2–6; Henkel–von Metaxa d. Puncec–Kukuljevic 1–6, 7–9, 7–5, 6–4, 6–4.

American Zone

FIRST ROUND

Japan d. Canada 5–0, Montreal: J. Yamagishi d. R. Murray 6–1, 6–3, 6–3 and d. D. Cameron 6–4, 6–1, 6–0; F. Nakano d. R. Wilson 6–2, 6–3, 6–2 and d. Murray 6–4, 6–3, 6–0; Yamagishi–Nakano d. Wilson–M. Laird Watt 6–3, 3–6, 6–3, 7–5. **Australia d. Mexico 5–0, Kansas City:** J. E. Bromwich d. R. Tapia 6–4, 6–4, 6–4; A. K. Quist d. D. Hernandez 6–1, 7–5, 6–4 and d. Tapia 6–1, 6–1, 6–4; L. Schwartz d. Hernandez 6–4, 6–1, 6–2; Bromwich–Quist d. Hernandez–Tapia 6–1, 6–0, 6–3.

FINAL ROUND

Australia d. Japan 3–2, Montreal: J. E. Bromwich lost to J. Yamagishi 0–6, 6–3, 5–7, 4–6 and lost to F. Nakano 1–6, 6–1, 4–6, 6–3, 12–12 def.; A. K. Quist d. Yamagishi 6–4, 6–4, 2–6, 9–7 and d. Nakano 6–3, 4–6, 9–7, 6–1; Bromwich–Quist d. Nakano–Yamagishi 6–2, 6–4, 6–3.

THE STORY OF THE DAVIS CUP

INTER-ZONE FINAL
Australia d. Germany 5–0, Boston: J. E. Bromwich d. H. Henkel 6–2, 6–3, 6–3 and d. G. von Metaxa 6–3, 6–2, 6–1; A. K. Quist d. Henkel 6–1, 6–0, 8–6 and d. von Metaxa 6–3, 6–2, 6–1; Bromwich–Quist d. Henkel–von Metaxa 6–2, 6–1, 6–4.

CHALLENGE ROUND
USA d Australia 3–2, Philadelphia: R. L. Riggs d. A. K. Quist 4–6, 6–0, 8–6, 6–1; J. D. Budge d. J. E. Bromwich 6–2, 6–3, 4–6, 7–5; Budge–C. G. Mako lost to Bromwich–Quist 6–0, 3–6, 4–6, 2–6; Budge d. Quist 8–6, 6–1, 6–2; Riggs lost to Bromwich 4–6, 6–4, 0–6, 2–6.

1939: AUSTRALIA
European Zone

FIRST ROUND
Yugoslavia d. Ireland 5–0, Zagreb: F. Puncec d. R. F. Egan 6–2, 6–0, 6–4 and d. G. L. Rogers 6–4, 6–2, 6–4; D. Mitic d. Egan 7–5, 6–3, 6–2 and d. Rogers 7–5, 6–2, 3–6, 3–6, 6–3; Puncec–Mitic d. Rogers–Egan 6–1, 6–4, 6–2. **Hungary d. Rumania 3–2, Bucharest:** E. Gabory d. O. Schmidt 4–6, 4–6, 6–4, 6–2, 1–0 def. and lost to C. Caralulis 6–3, 2–6, 3–6, 5–7; J. Asboth d. C. Caralulis 1–6, 6–3, 7–9, 10–8, 6–4 and d. Schmidt 1–6, 6–2, 6–3, 6–8, 6–3; G. Dallos–M. Csiko lost to Caralulis–Schmidt 8–6, 6–4, 2–6, 2–6, 4–6. **Poland d. Holland 4–1, Warsaw:** A. Bawarowski d. A. C. van Swol 9–7, 6–3, 6–0 and d. T. Hughan 0–6, 6–3, 6–4, 6–2; I. Tloczynski d. Hughan 6–0, 6–2, 6–1 and d. van Swol 13–11, 4–6, 6–3, 6–2; Tloczynski–J. Hebda lost to van Swol–Hughan 4–6, 4–6, 10–12. **Germany d. Switzerland 5–0, Vienna:** H. Henkel d. H. C. Fisher 6–2, 2–6, 6–1, 6–3; R. Menzel d. B. Maneff 6–8, 6–3, 5–7, 6–2, 6–3 and d. Fisher 8–6, 6–4, 6–2; H. Redl d. Maneff 6–1, 6–2, 6–2; Henkel–G. von Metaxa d. Maneff–Fisher 6–2, 6–2, 6–4.

SECOND ROUND
Belgium d. India 3–2, Brussels: A. Lacroix d. G. Mohammed Khan 6–1, 6–3, 5–7, 6–0 and d. Y. Savoor 6–2, 6–2, 6–4; C. Naeyaert lost to Mohammed Khan 8–10, 2–6, 1–6 and d. Savoor 6–0, 10–8, 1–6, 6–3; P. Geelhand–J. van den Eynde lost to Mohammed Khan–Savoor 4–6, 4–6, 7–5, 4–6. **Italy d. Monaco 3–0, Naples:** G. de Stefani d. G. Medecin 6–1, 6–2, 6–2; V. Canapele d. A. Noghes 6–0, 6–3, 6–1; G. Vido–G. Cucelli d. V. Landau–Noghes 6–3, 6–1, 6–0. **Yugoslavia d. Hungary**

366

4–1, Budapest: F. Puncec lost to J. Asboth 5–7, 6–4, 5–7, 9–11 and d. E. Gabory 6–1, 6–1, 6–4; D. Mitic d. Gabory 6–3, 0–6, 2–6, 6–1, 6–1 and d. Asboth 9–7, 2–6, 10–8, 6–3; Puncec–Mitic d. Asboth–Gabory 6–1, 4–6, 6–2, 7–5. **Germany d. Poland 3–2, Warsaw:** H. Henkel lost to I. Tloczynski 4–6, 8–6, 4–6, 6–3, 3–6 and d. A. Bawarowski 6–4, 6–2, 6–3; R. Menzel d. Bawarowski 7–5, 6–3, 2–6, 2–6, 6–4 and lost to Tloczynski 6–2, 1–6, 7–5, 2–6, 7–9; Henkel–G. von Metaxa d. J. Hebda–Bawarowski 5–7, 6–4, 6–2, 6–2. **Sweden d. Denmark 4–1, Djursholm:** K. Schroder d. N. Holst 6–4, 6–2, 6–3 and d. H. Plougmann 6–1, 6–1, 6–1; M. Hultman lost to Plougmann 1–6, 0–6, 3–6 and d. Holst 6–1, 6–3, 6–1; Schroder–N. Rohlsson d. Plougmann–A. Wium 6–1, 8–6, 6–0. **Great Britain d. New Zealand 3–2, Brighton:** C. E. Hare d. A. D. Brown 6–3, 6–4, 6–3 and d. C. E. Malfroy 7–5, 6–4, 6–4; R. A. Shayes lost to Malfroy 6–4, 2–6, 2–6, 7–5, 3–6 and d. Brown 6–3, 6–4, 7–5; Hare–F. H. D. Wilde lost to Malfroy–D. C. Coombe 3–6, 6–2, 3–6, 2–6. **France d. China 4–1, Paris:** B. Destremau d. Kho Sin Kie 5–7, 6–3, 1–6, 7–5, 6–0; C. Boussus d. W. C. Choy 1–6, 6–4, 6–4, 6–1; Y. Petra lost to Kho Sin Kie 6–2, 7–9, 3–6, 4–6; P. Pelizza d. J. H. Ho 7–5, 4–6, 6–2, 6–4; Petra–Pelizza d. Kho Sin Kie–Choy 6–2, 6–0, 6–3. **Norway d. Czechoslovakia def.**

THIRD ROUND

Belgium d. Norway 3–0, Brussels: A. Lacroix d. J. Haanes 6–1, 6–4, 6–2; C. Naeyaert d. S. Rinde 6–1, 6–0, 6–0; P. Geelhand–L. de Borman d. L. Anderson–Haanes 6–0, 6–1, 5–7, 6–2. **Yugoslavia d. Italy 3–2, Rome:** F. Puncec d. G. de Stefani 6–4, 6–1, 7–5 and d. V. Canapele 13–11, 6–1, 6–8, 6–3; D. Mitic lost to Canapele 3–6, 3–6, 5–7 and lost to de Stefani 1–6, 4–6, 6–4, 3–6; Puncec–Mitic d. V. Taroni–G. Cucelli 6–2, 6–2, 6–0. **Germany d. Sweden 4–1, Berlin:** H. Henkel d. K. Schroder 5–7, 3–6, 6–2, 8–6, 6–3; R. Menzel d. M. Hultman 6–0, 6–2, 6–1 and d. Schroder 2–6, 6–3, 6–3, 6–3; R. Goepfert d. Hultman 6–2, 6–3, 6–3; Henkel–G. von Metaxa lost to Schroder–N. Rohlsson 2–6, 6–1, 3–6, 3–6. **Great Britain d. France 3–2, London:** C. E. Hare d. B. Destremau 6–2, 6–3, 3–6, 14–12; R. A. Shayes lost to C. Boussus 2–6, 4–6, 0–6 and d. B. Destremau 6–3, 4–6, 6–4, 7–5; L. Shaffi lost to Boussus 0–6, 2–6, 5–7; Hare–F. H. D. Wilde d. Y. Petra–P. Pelizza 6–3, 6–3, 3–6, 4–6, 6–3.

FOURTH ROUND

Yugoslavia d. Belgium 3–2, Zagreb: F. Puncec d. A. Lacroix 1–6, 6–3, 6–3, 7–5 and d. P. Geelhand 6–3, 8–6, 6–3; D. Mitic d. Geelhand 6–1, 6–4, 6–1 and lost to Lacroix 3–6, 2–6, 8–6, 2–6; Puncec–Mitic lost to Lacroix–L. de Borman 2–6, 2–6, 3–6. **Germany d. Great Britain 5–0, Berlin:** H. Henkel d. R. A. Shayes 6–2, 6–3, 6–1; R. Menzel d. C. E. Hare 6–0, 6–1 def. and d. Shayes 6–1, 6–1, 6–0; G. von Metaxa d. F. H. D. Wilde 3–6, 6–0, 6–2, 6–3; Henkel–von Metaxa d. Wilde–L. Shaffi 6–4, 6–2, 6–2.

FINAL ROUND

Yugoslavia d. Germany 3–2, Zagreb: F. Puncec d. R. Goepfert 6–3, 6–1, 6–0 and d. H. Henkel 10–8, 6–3, 6–0; D. Mitic lost to Henkel 0–6, 1–6, 6–4, 4–6 and d. Goepfert 6–1, 6–2, 6–3; Puncec–F. Kukuljevic lost to Henkel–R. Menzel 7–9, 6–4, 4–6, 6–3, 1–6.

North American Zone

FIRST ROUND

Australia d. Mexico 5–0, Mexico City: J. E. Bromwich d. D. Hernandez 6–0, 6–0, 6–0 and d. R. Tapia 6–1, 6–3, 6–1; A. K. Quist d. Tapia 6–1, 6–4, 6–2 and d. D. Hernandez 11–9, 6–3, 6–2; Bromwich–Quist d. Hernandez–Tapia 8–6, 6–0, 6–1. **Cuba d. Canada 3–1, Havana:** R. Morales d. B. Hall 6–1, 6–2, 6–2 and d. E. Tarshis 6–2, 6–4, 3–6, 0–6, 6–4; J. Aguero lost to Tarshis 5–7, 7–5, 3–6, 4–6; Morales–L. Nodarse d. W. Pedlar–P. Pearson 9–7, 4–6, 6–4, 4–6, 6–1.

SECOND ROUND

Australia d. Philippines 5–0, Long Beach: A. K. Quist d. A. Sanchez 6–1, 6–2, 6–2 and d. F. Ampon 7–5, 6–4, 6–3; J. E. Bromwich d. Ampon 8–6, 9–7, 6–3 and d. Sanchez 6–1, 6–1, 6–3; Quist–Bromwich d. Ampon–Sanchez 7–5, 6–4, 6–2. **Cuba d. Japan def.**

FINAL

Australia d. Cuba 5–0, Havana: J. E. Bromwich d. J. Aguero 8–6, 6–0, 6–2 and d. R. Morales 8–6, 8–6, 6–1; A. K. Quist d. Morales 6–0, 6–2, 6–2 and d. Aguero 6–1, 6–0, 6–0; Quist–Bromwich d. Morales–L. Nodarse 6–1, 6–0, 6–3.

South American Zone: Brazil withdrew.

INTER–ZONE FINAL

Australia d. Yugoslavia 4–1, New York: J. E. Bromwich lost to F. Puncec 2–6, 6–8, 6–0, 2–6 and d. D. Mitic 6–1, 6–3, 6–2; A. K. Quist d. Mitic 6–0, 6–4, 6–3 and d. F. Kukuljevic 6–2, 6–3, 6–4; Quist–Bromwich d. Puncec–Kukuljevic 6–2, 6–3, 6–3.

CHALLENGE ROUND

Australia d. USA 3–2, Philadelphia: J. E. Bromwich lost to R. L. Riggs 4–6, 0–6, 5–7; A. K. Quist lost to F. Parker 3–6, 6–2, 4–6, 6–1, 5–7; Bromwich–Quist d. J. Kramer–J. Hunt 5–7, 6–2, 7–5, 6–2; Quist d. Riggs 6–1, 6–4, 3–6, 3–6, 6–4; Bromwich d. Parker 6–0, 6–3, 6–1.

1940–45: NO CONTESTS

1946: USA
European Zone

FIRST ROUND

Switzerland d. Spain 3–2, Barcelona: J. Spitzer d. H. Castella 6–0, 6–1, 6–4; lost to L. Carles 9–7, 5–7, 5–7, 6–3, 2–6; H. Huonder d. Castella 3–6, 6–3, 6–1, 4–6, 6–4; lost to Carles 3–6, 4–6, 3–6; R. Buser–Spitzer d. J. Bartroli–Carles 5–7, 8–6, 11–9, 9–7. **France d. Great Britain 5–0, Paris:** Y. Petra d. D. W. Barton 6–4, 6–4, 6–3; d. D. MacPhail 6–0, 6–2, 6–1; P. Pellizza d. MacPhail, 6–1, 6–2, 6–2; d. Barton 6–2, 6–3, 6–1; B. Destremau–M. Bernard d. J. S. Olliff–H. Billington 13–11, 4–6, 7–5, 6–1. **Czechoslovakia d. Turkey def; Yugoslavia d. Egypt 5–0, Zagreb:** F. Puncec d. A. Shafie 6–0, 6–1, 6–3; D. Mitic d. A. Najar 7–5, 6–1, 6–3; d. Shafie 6–0, 6–1, 6–3; J. Pallada d. Najar 6–0, 6–1, 6–2; Mitic–Pallada d. M. Talaat–J. Grandguillot 6–2, 6–4, 3–6, 10–8. **China d. Denmark 4–1, Copenhagen:** Kho Sin Kie d. W. Rasmussen 6–0, 6–1, 6–0; d. J. Ipsen 6–0, 6–1, 6–4; W. C. Choy d. J. Ipsen 6–2, 6–2, 6–3; K. Lo lost to E. Bjerre 6–3, 4–6, 1–6, 3–6; Kho Sin Kie–Choy d. Ipsen–P. Thielsen 5–7, 6–2, 6–4, 7–5. **Belgium d. Monaco 5–0, Brussels:** J. van den Eynde d. R. Gallepe 6–0, 6–0, 6–2; d. V. Landau 6–2, 6–3, 6–1; P. Washer d. Landau 6–1, 6–1, 6–1; d. Gallepe 6–1, 6–0, 6–2; Washer–P. Geelhand d. Gallepe–Landau 6–1, 6–2, 6–1. **Sweden d. Holland 5–0, Stockholm:** L. Bergelin d. I. Rinkel 5–7, 6–0, 6–4, 6–2; d. A. C. van Swol 7–5, 6–3, 6–1; T. Johansson d. van Swol 8–6, 6–4, 7–5; d. Rinkel 9–7, 6–1, 6–1; Bergelin–Johansson d. Rinkel–van Swol 6–4, 5–7, 4–6, 7–5, 6–2.

SECOND ROUND

France d. Switzerland 3–2, Montreux: Y. Petra d. H. Huonder 10–8, 6–0, 6–1; d. J. Spitzer 6–3, 6–3, 6–4; P. Pellizza lost to Spitzer 2–6, 3–6, 2–6; lost to Huonder 5–7, 4–6, 5–7; Petra–M. Bernard d. Spitzer–R. Buser 6–0, 6–1, 6–2. **Yugoslavia d. Czechoslovakia 3–2, Prague:** F.

Puncec d. J. Vodicka 6–3, 7–5, 7–5; lost to J. Drobny 3–6, 2–6, 4–6; D. Mitic d. Drobny 3–6, 6–4, 0–6, 6–1, 6–3; d. Vodicka 6–2, 6–0, 6–0; Mitic–J. Pallada lost to Drobny–J. Caska 8–10, 2–6, 4–6. **Belgium d. China 3–2, Brussels:** J. van den Eynde lost to Kho Sin Kie 3–6, 5–7, 3–6; d. W. C. Choy 4–6, 6–1, 6–3, 6–4; P. Washer d. Choy 7–5, 6–4, 6–2; lost to Kho Sin Kie 6–1, 7–5, 3–6, 4–6, 1–6; Washer–P. Geelhand d. Kho Sin Kie–Choy 5–7, 6–3, 6–0, 3–6, 6–2. **Sweden d. Ireland 5–0, Stockholm:** L. Bergelin d. C. A. Kemp 2–6, 6–2, 6–2, 6–4; d. R. F. Egan 6–4, 6–2, 6–0; T. Johansson d. Egan 6–2, 7–5, 1–6, 3–6, 6–3; d. Kemp 3–6, 6–1, 6–3, 2–6, 6–3; Bergelin–Johansson d. Kemp–Egan 3–6, 6–1, 6–3, 2–6, 6–3.

SEMI-FINAL ROUND

Yugoslavia d. France 3–2, Paris: D. Mitic lost to Y. Petra 6–2, 6–8, 4–6, 6–3, 6–8; d. M. Bernard 6–3, 4–6, 3–6, 6–0, 6–3; F. Puncec lost to Bernard 6–2, 1–6, 6–0, 5–7, 3–6; d. Petra 6–3, 3–6, 6–4, 7–9, 6–0; Mitic–Puncec d. B. Destremau–P. Pellizza 8–10, 8–6, 6–3, 5–7, 10–8. **Sweden d. Belgium 4–1, Stockholm:** L. Bergelin d. J. Peten 3–6, 6–3, 6–1, 6–1; d. P. Washer 7–5, 3–6, 6–3, 9–7; T. Johansson lost to Washer 2–6, 1–6, 4–6; d. Peten 6–3, 6–3, 6–0; Bergelin–Johansson d. Washer–P. Geelhand 4–6, 6–2, 6–4, 6–4.

FINAL ROUND

Sweden d. Yugoslavia 3–2, Varberg: L. Bergelin lost to J. Pallada 2–6, 2–6, 3–6; d. D. Mitic 5–7, 3–6, 6–3, 6–2, 10–8; T. Johansson lost to Mitic, 6–4, 6–1, 1–6, 2–6, 0–6; d. Pallada 6–3, 6–4, 6–4; Bergelin–Johansson d. Pallada–Mitic 6–1, 3–6, 3–6, 8–6, 6–2.

American Zone

SEMI-FINAL ROUND

USA d. Philippines 5–0, St Louis: F. A. Parker d. F. H. Ampon 6–0, 6–0, 6–0; W. F. Talbert d. A. J. Sanchez 6–1, 6–3, 6–0; Parker d. Sanchez 6–1, 6–4, 6–0; F. R. Schroeder d. Ampon 6–2, 6–2, 6–4; Talbert–G. Mulloy d. Ampon–C. L. Carmona 6–1, 6–3, 6–1. **Mexico d. Canada 5–0, Mexico City:** R. Vega d. B. Macken 6–4, 6–2, 7–5; A. Vega d. H. Rochon 7–5, 6–2, 6–4; R. Vega d. Rochon 6–3, 8–6, 6–4; A. Vega d. D. McDiarmid 6–0, 6–0, 6–3; A. and R. Vega d. L. Watt–Macken 6–3, 6–4, 6–3.

FINAL ROUND

USA d. Mexico 5–0, Orange: F. A. Parker d. R. Vega 6–0, 6–0, 6–2; W. F. Talbert d. A. Vega 6–1, 6–2, 6–1; G. Mulloy d. F. Guerrero 6–3, 6–4, 6–4; F. A. Parker d. A. Vega 6–3, 6–3, 6–2; Talbert–Mulloy d. R. and A. Vega 6–0, 9–7, 6–2.

INTER-ZONE FINAL

USA d. Sweden 5–0, New York: J. A. Kramer d. T. Johansson 6–2, 6–2, 6–2; F. A. Parker d. L. Bergelin 6–0, 6–3, 6–1; W. F. Talbert–G. Mulloy d. Bergelin–Johansson 3–6, 9–7, 3–6, 6–0, 8–6; Kramer d. Bergelin 6–2, 6–2, 8–6; Parker d. Johansson 9–7, 6–2, 6–1.

CHALLENGE ROUND

USA d. Australia 5–0, Melbourne: F. R. Schroeder d. J. E. Bromwich 3–6, 6–1, 6–2, 0–6, 6–3; J. A. Kramer d. D. Pails 8–6, 6–2, 9–7; Kramer–Schroeder d. Bromwich–A. K. Quist 6–2, 7–5, 6–4; Kramer d. Bromwich 8–6, 6–4, 6–4; G. Mulloy d. Pails 6–3, 6–3, 6–4.

1947: USA
European Zone

FIRST ROUND

Belgium d. Luxembourg 5–0, Brussels: P. Washer d. G. Wertheim 6–2, 6–2, 6–1; d. G. Wampach 7–5, 1–6, 6–2, 6–2; J. Peten d. Wertheim, 6–2, 6–0, 6–0; d. Wampach 4–6, 6–2, 9–7, 3–6, 6–3; Washer–P. Geelhand d. Wampach–Wertheim 6–4, 6–3, 6–2. **Egypt d. Spain 3–2, Barcelona:** A. Najar d. M. Szavoszt 6–3, 6–3, 7–9, 3–6, 6–3; lost to J. Bartroli 3–6, 1–6, 3–6; A. Shafie d. L. Carles 3–6, 6–3, 6–4, 7–5; lost to Szavoszt 2–6, 6–3, 4–6, 6–3, 4–6; M. Talaat–M. Coen d. Bartroli–Carles 6–4, 3–6, 6–3, 3–6, 6–4. **Czechoslovakia d. Sweden 3–2, Malmo:** V. Cernik lost to T. Johansson 5–7, 4–6, 8–6, 2–6; lost to L. Bergelin 4–6, 8–6, 1–6, 1–6; J. Drobny d. Bergelin 4–6, 6–1, 6–4, 6–4; d. Johansson 6–1, 2–6, 6–3, 4–6, 6–4; Drobny–Cernik d. Bergelin–Johansson 6–1, 7–9, 7–5, 6–2. **Switzerland d. Greece 4–1, Athens:** J. Spitzer d. Manouilidis 6–2, 7–5, 6–1; d. L. Stalios 1–6, 8–6, 6–0, 6–1; H. Huonder lost to Stalios 6–2, 8–10, 3–6, 3–6; d. Manouilidis 6–0, 6–1, 6–1; Spitzer–Huonder d. Stalios–G. Nicholaides 5–7, 6–8, 6–0, 9–7, 6–1.

SECOND ROUND

Great Britain d. Poland 3–2, Warsaw: A. J. Mottram d. J. Hebda 2–6, 6–1, 6–1, 6–3; d. W. Skonecki 6–4, 6–2, 7–5; D. W. Barton lost to

Skonecki 3–6, 5–7, 11–13; lost to Hebda 6–2, 3–6, 4–6, 6–4, 4–6; G. L. Paish–D. W. Butler d. Hebda–Skonecki 6–2, 6–4, 6–3. **South Africa d. Holland 4–1, Amsterdam:** E. W. Sturgess d. H. Wilton 4–6, 6–1, 6–3, 6–2; d. A. C. van Swol 6–2, 7–5, 2–6, 6–3; E. Fannin d. van Swol 3–6, 6–3, 7–5, 6–2; d. Wilton 7–9, 6–3, 6–1, 6–3; Sturgess–Fannin lost to van Swol–I. Rinkel 3–6, 1–6, 0–6. **Yugoslavia d. Ireland 3–2, Dublin:** D. Mitic d. C. A. Kemp 8–10, 7–9, 6–3, 6–4, 6–1; J. Pallada d. J. R. McHale 6–3, 6–3, 6–3; lost to Kemp 6–4, 1–6, 0–6, 3–6; J. Solc lost to McHale 7–9, 1–6, 5–7; Mitic–Pallada d. Kemp–R. F. Egan 6–2, 6–4, 6–2. **Belgium d. Egypt 4–1, Brussels:** P. Washer d. A. Shafie 6–2, 2–6, 6–0, 8–6; d. A. Najar 6–2, 6–4, 6–2; P. Geelhand d. Najar 4–6, 6–3, 0–6, 6–3, 6–2; lost to Shafie 4–6, 4–6, 5–7; A. Lacroix–Washer d. M. Talaat–M. Coen 6–4, 6–1, 6–3. **Czechoslovakia d. Switzerland 4–1, Prague:** J. Drobny d. H. Huonder 6–1, 6–1, 6–1; d. J. Spitzer 6–2, 6–1, 6–2; V. Cernik lost to Spitzer 2–6, 6–4, 6–0, 5–7, 1–6; d. Huonder 6–3, 6–3, 6–4; Drobny–Cernik d. Spitzer–H. Pfaff, 6–1, 6–2, 6–3. **New Zealand d. Norway 3–2, Oslo:** R. S. McKenzie lost to J. Staubo 2–6, 3–6, 6–3, 2–6; d. J. Haanes 6–4, 0–6, 6–3, 9–7; J. A. Barry lost to Haanes 0–6, 5–7, 4–6; d. Staubo 4–6, 7–5, 3–6, 7–5, 6–2; McKenzie–J. E. Robson d. Haanes–D. Brem 4–6, 6–4, 6–4, 6–2. **France d. India 5–0, Paris:** B. Destremau d. S. C. Misra 6–0, 6–3, 6–3; d. D. K. Bose 6–0, 6–1, 6–2; M. Bernard d. Ghaus Mohammed Khan 6–3, 6–2, 6–0; d. Misra 6–4, 6–3, 6–1; Bernard–P. Pellizza d. Misra–J. M. Mehta 6–3, 6–2, 6–3. **Monaco d. Denmark def.**

THIRD ROUND
South Africa d. Great Britain 4–1, Scarborough: E. W. Sturgess d. A. J. Mottram 5–7, 6–2, 6–1, 6–3; d. D. W. Butler 6–1, 6–1, 6–0; E. Fannin d. Butler 6–4, 4–6, 9–7, 3–3 def; lost to Mottram 4–6, 7–5, 2–6, 5–7; Sturgess–Fannin d. Mottram–G. L. Paish 6–1, 4–6, 2–6, 6–3, 6–4. **Yugoslavia d. Belgium 4–1, Brussels:** D. Mitic lost to P. Washer 4–6, 3–6, 6–1, 3–6; d. P. Geelhand 6–0, 6–3, 6–4. J. Pallada d. Washer 6–3, 6–2, 6–0; d. Geelhand 6–1, 4–6, 6–3, 6–3; Mitic–Pallada d. Washer–A. Lacroix 2–6, 1–6, 6–2, 6–1, 6–2. **Czechoslovakia d. New Zealand 5–0, Prague:** J. Drobny d. J. E. Robson 6–2, 6–2, 8–6; V. Cernik d. R. S. McKenzie 6–3, 6–4, 7–5; d. Robson 5–3, 6–0, 6–0; F. Vrba d. J. A. Barry 6–4, 6–2, 6–2; Drobny–Cernik d. McKenzie–Robson 6–2, 4–6, 9–7, 3–6, 10–8. **France d. Monaco 5–0, Paris:** M. Bernard d. A. Noghes 6–1, 6–2, 6–0; B. Destremau d. V. Landau 6–3, 6–2, 6–1; d. Noghes 7–5, 6–2, 6–1; R. Abdesselam d. Landau 6–2, 6–1, 6–0; P. Pellizza–Abdesselam d. Landau–G. Medecin 6–2, 6–1, 6–0.

Yugoslavia d. South Africa 3–2, Zagreb: D. Mitic d. E. W. Sturgess 3–6, 7–5, 6–2, 3–6, 6–3; d. E. Fannin 6–2, 6–3, 6–4; J. Pallada d. Fannin 6–1, 6–4, 7–5; lost to Sturgess 6–3, 3–6, 0–6, 7–5, 3–6; Mitic–Pallada lost to Sturgess–Fannin 3–6, 5–7, 5–7.   **Czechoslovakia d. France 4–1, Prague:** J. Drobny d. B. Destremau 6–2, 6–0, 6–1; d. M. Bernard 6–3, 2–6, 6–4, 4–6, 6–4. V. Cernik d. Bernard 2–6, 9–7, 6–4, 4–6, 6–4; Cernik lost to Destremau def.; Drobny–Cernik d. J. Borotra–Y. Petra 10–8, 14–12, 6–3.

FINAL ROUND
Czechoslovakia d. Yugoslavia 4–0, Zagreb: J. Drobny d. J. Pallada 6–3, 8–6, 2–6, 6–3; V. Cernik d. D. Mitic 3–6, 6–0, 2–6, 6–1, 6–2; Drobny d. Mitic 1–6, 6–3, 6–4, 4–6, 6–1; Drobny–Cernik d. Mitic–Pallada 6–3, 6–1, 6–3.

American Zone

FINAL ROUND
Australia d. Canada 5–0, Montreal: D. Pails d. H. Rochon 6–1, 6–4, 6–2; d. B. Macken 6–4, 6–2, 6–2; G. E. Brown d. Macken 6–4, 6–4, 6–1; d. Rochon 6–3, 9–7, 6–2; J. E. Bromwich–C. Long d. G. McNiel–E. Lanthier 6–2, 6–1, 6–0.

INTER-ZONE FINAL
Australia d. Czechoslovakia 4–1, Montreal: J. E. Bromwich d. J. Drobny 6–2, 7–5, 6–4; d. V. Cernik 6–1, 6–1, 6–1; D. Pails lost to Drobny 3–6, 4–6, 6–4, 4–6; d. Cernik 6–3, 4–6, 3–6, 6–2, 6–3; Bromwich–C. Long d. Drobny–Cernik 6–2, 6–2, 6–2;

CHALLENGE ROUND
USA d. Australia 4–1, New York: J. A. Kramer d. D. Pails 6–2, 6–1, 6–2; F. R. Schroeder d. J. E. Bromwich 6–4, 5–7, 6–3, 6–4; Kramer–Schroeder lost to Bromwich–C. Long 4–6, 6–2, 2–6, 4–6; Schroeder d. Pails 6–3, 8–6, 4–6, 9–11, 10–8; Kramer d. Bromwich 6–3, 6–2, 6–2.

1948: USA
European Zone

FIRST ROUND

Great Britain d. India 3–2, Harrogate: A. J. Mottram d. S. C. Misra 6–0, 6–3, 7–9, 7–5; d. D. K. Bose 6–3, 6–4, 6–4; H. F. Walton lost to Bose 3–6, 3–6, 2–6; lost to Misra 6–2, 6–8, 7–9, 2–6; A. J. Mottram–G. L. Paish d. Misra–S. L. R. Sawhny 6–3, 7–5, 6–2. **France d. Rumania 3–2, Bucharest:** M. Bernard lost to C. Caralulis 6–3, 4–6, 3–6, 2–6; d. G. Viziru 6–2, 6–1, 6–4; B. Destremau lost to Viziru 3–6, 2–6, 5–7; d. Caralulis 6–2, 6–4, 7–5; M. Bernard–H. Bolelli d. Caralulis–Viziru 6–3, 8–6, 8–6. **Hungary d. Austria 5–0, Budapest:** J. Asboth d. A. Specht 6–2, 6–2, 6–0; d. H. Redl 6–4, 6–2, 6–2; A. A. Stolpa d. Specht 4–6, 6–0, 6–1, 4–6, 6–3; d. Redl 6–3, 4–6, 6–4, 4–6, 6–3; Asboth–K. Feher d. Redl–Specht 6–2, 6–3, 8–6. **Sweden d. Spain 5–0, Barcelona:** L. Bergelin d. M. Szavoszt 6–4, 6–2, 4–6, 6–3; and d. P. Castella def.; T. Johansson d. Castella 6–3, 6–2, 6–1; d. M. Szavoszt 6–3, 11–9, 6–3; Bergelin–Johansson d. J. Bartroli–Szavoszt 7–5, 6–4, 6–4. **Switzerland d. Pakistan 3–2, Montreux:** Huonder lost to I. Ahmed 2–6, 4–6, 3–6; d. M. Alam 6–1, 6–1, 6–2; M. Albrecht d. Alam 6–1, 6–1, 6–2; lost to Ahmed 1–6, 5–7, 6–1, 6–4, 4–6; Albrecht–Huonder d. Ahmed–Alam 7–5, 6–4, 6–4. **Italy d. Poland def.; Yugoslavia d. Turkey 5–0, Zagreb:** D. Mitic d. Gurel 6–1, 6–1, 6–0; J. Pallada d. F. Kizil 6–1, 1–6, 8–6, 6–3; Mitic–Pallada d. Kizil–Cihat 6–2, 6–3, 6–3; Pallada d. Gorel 6–4, 6–2; S. Laszlo d. B. Belig 6–2, 6–4. **Ireland d. Luxembourg 5–0, Dublin:** C. A. Kemp d. G. Wampach 7–5, 6–3, 6–8, 6–4; d. G. Wertheim 6–0, 6–2, 6–4; G. P. Jackson d. Wertheim 7–5, 6–1, 6–1; d. Wampach 7–5, 6–4, 6–2, 6–0; Kemp–T. G. McVeagh d. Wertheim–Wampach 10–8, 6–4, 6–3. **Denmark d. Egypt 3–2, Copenhagen:** T. Ulrich d. A. Shafie 6–1, 7–5, 5–7, 5–7, 8–6; lost to M. Coen 6–2, 1–6, 10–8, 10–12, 0–6; K. Nielsen d. Shafie 6–3, 6–1, 8–6; d. A. Najar 3–6, 6–2, 6–2, 6–3; Nielsen–Ulrich lost to Shafie–Coen 5–7, 8–6, 8–6, 4–6, 3–6.

SECOND ROUND

Holland d. Portugal 5–0, Scheveningen: A. C. van Swol d. J. Roquette 6–0, 6–3, 6–2; d. E. Ricciardi 6–4, 6–2, 6–4; A. L. van Meegeren d. Ricciardi 6–2, 6–1, 6–1; d. Roquette 6–1, 6–1, 6–3; van Swol–I. Rinkel d. Ricciardi–J. da Sylva 6–1, 6–0, 6–3. **Great Britain d. Norway 4–1, Oslo:** A. J. Mottram d. J. Staubo 6–2, 6–1, 6–1; d. J. Haanes 6–1, 6–0, 5–7, 6–1; G. L. Paish lost to Haanes 2–6, 6–4, 3–6, 2–6; d. Staubo 4–6, 6–4, 6–1, 6–2; Mottram–H. Billington d.

Haanes–Staubo 6–1, 7–5, 6–3. **Hungary d. France 4–1, Paris:** J. Asboth lost to M. Bernard 1–6, 4–6, 6–4, 2–6; d. R. Abdesselam 7–5, 6–1, 6–2; A. A. Stolpa d. Abdesselam 2–6, 6–4, 6–3, 8–6; d. Bernard 1–6, 3–6, 6–0, 6–3, 6–4; Stolpa–Asboth d. Bernard–B. Destremau 6–3, 6–3, 6–8, 2–6, 6–2. **Sweden d. Switzerland 5–0, Stockholm:** L. Bergelin d. M. Albrecht 7–5, 6–3, 6–3; d. H. Huonder 6–2, 6–4, 6–1; T. Johansson d. Huonder, 6–2, 6–4, 6–3; d. Albrecht 11–9, 0–6, 6–2, 6–4; Bergelin–Johansson d. Albrecht–Huonder 6–1, 6–1, 6–3. **Italy d. Yugoslavia 3–2, Zagreb:** G. Cucelli lost to D. Mitic 7–5, 6–8, 1–6, 2–6; lost to J. Pallada 7–5, 4–6, 1–6, 4–6; M. del Bello d. Pallada 6–2, 6–3, 6–8, 9–7; d. Mitic 7–5, 6–4, 8–6; Cucelli–del Bello d. Mitic–Pallada 6–0, 6–3, 1–6, 7–5. **Denmark d. Ireland 3–2, Dublin:** T. Ulrich d. C. A. Kemp 8–6, 6–3, 6–4; lost to G. P. Jackson 4–6, 8–6, 6–2, 2–6, 3–6; K. Nielsen d. Jackson 6–4, 2–6, 6–4, 5–7, 6–4; d. Kemp 6–4, 8–6, 6–3; Nielsen–Ulrich lost to Kemp–Jackson 0–6, 3–6, 8–6, 6–3, 2–6. **Czechoslovakia d. Brazil 4–1, Prague:** J. Drobny d. E. Petersen 6–2, 6–2, 6–2; d. M. Fernandez 6–0, 4–1 def.; F. Vrba lost to Fernandez 2–6, 4–6, 3–6; d. Petersen 7–9, 6–3, 6–4, 6–3; Drobny–V. Zabrodsky d. Petersen–Fernandez 6–3, 6–4, 6–0. **Belgium d. Argentina 3–2, Brussels:** J. Peten d. H. Weiss 6–1, 1–6, 6–2, 6–3; lost to E. Morea 6–1, 6–3, 6–8, 4–6, 8–10; P. Washer d. Morea 6–1, 7–5, 6–2; d. Weiss 8–6, 4–6, 6–4, 6–4; Peten–Washer lost to Morea–A. D. Russell 10–8, 3–6, 2–6, 6–8.

THIRD ROUND

Great Britain d. Holland 4–1, Edgbaston: A. J. Mottram d. A. C. van Swol 6–3, 6–4, 9–11, 6–3; d. A. L. van Meegeren 6–3, 6–4, 6–3; G. L. Paish d van Meegeren 6–3, 6–2, 3–6, 7–9, 6–1; d. van Swol 6–1, 2–6, 7–5, 1–6, 6–4; Mottram–Paish lost to van Swol–I. Rinkel 3–6, 7–5, 2–6, 6–1, 4–6. **Sweden d. Hungary 3–2, Budapest:** I. Bergelin d. A. A. Stolpa 5–7, 6–4, 6–2, 6–1; lost to J. Asboth 4–6, 3–6, 4–6; T. Johansson lost to Asboth 6–3, 7–9, 4–6, 0–6; d. Stolpa 7–5, 6–1, 6–4; Bergelin–Johansson d. Asboth–Stolpa 5–7, 6–3, 7–5, 7–5. **Italy d. Denmark 5–0, Turin:** G. Cucelli d. K. Nielsen 6–4, 4–6, 6–1, 6–1; d. T. Ulrich 6–3, 6–3, 6–1; M. del Bello d. Ulrich 6–3, 6–3, 6–3; d. Nielsen 6–2, 7–5, 6–3; Cucelli–del Bello d. Nielsen–Ulrich 6–2, 6–3, 8–6. **Czechoslovakia d. Belgium 3–2, Prague:** J. Drobny d. P. Washer 6–2, 6–4, 6–2; d. J. Peten 6–4, 6–3, 6–1; V. Cernik lost to Peten 4–6, 6–2, 1–6, 4–6; lost to Washer 4–6, 6–2, 4–6, 3–6; Drobny–Cernik d. Washer–P. Geelhand 7–5, 4–6, 6–1, 6–3.

Sweden d. Great Britain 4–1, Stockholm: L. Bergelin d. A. J.
Mottram 6–3, 6–2, 6–3; d. G. L. Paish 4–6, 6–4, 6–1, 6–2; T. Johansson
d. Paish 6–2, 2–6, 8–6, 6–1; lost to Mottram 3–6, 6–2, 2–6, 2–6;
Bergelin–Johansson d. Mottram–Paish 2–6, 7–5, 6–4, 6–3.
Czechoslovakia d. Italy 3–2, Milan: J. Drobny d. G. Cucelli 6–3, 3–6,
6–2, 6–3; d. M. del Bello 11–9, 6–3, 6–2; V. Cernik d. del Bello 6–2,
6–4, 7–9, 6–3; lost to Cucelli 2–6, 6–2, 3–6, 3–6; Drobny–Cernik lost to
Cucelli–del Bello 1–6, 6–8, 2–6.

FINAL ROUND
Czechoslovakia d. Sweden 4–1, Prague: J. Drobny d. L. Bergelin 6–0,
6–3, 7–5; V. Cernik d. T. Johansson 6–4, 4–6, 6–3, 6–3; Drobny–Cernik
d. Bergelin–Johansson 6–2, 6–1, 6–2; V. Zabrodsky lost to Johansson
3–6, 6–3, 2–6, 3–6; F. Vrba d. B. Fornstedt 6–3, 6–1, 6–3.

American Zone

FIRST ROUND
Mexico d. Canada 4–1, Montreal: A. Vega d. B. Macken 6–4, 6–1,
6–3; d. H. Rochon 6–2, 6–1, 6–3; F. Guerrero d. W. Stohlberg 12–10,
6–1, 6–2; lost to Rochon 2–6, 5–7, 4–6; Vega–G. Palafox d. B.–J. Macken
6–2, 6–3, 6–4.   **Australia d. Cuba 3–0, Havana:** A. K. Quist d. J.
Etcheverry 6–1, 6–0, 6–0; O. W. Sidwell d. J. Aguero 6–3, 6–1, 6–4;
Sidwell–C. Long d. Aguero–R. Morales 7–5, 6–2, 6–3.

FINAL ROUND
Australia d. Mexico 4–1, Mexico City: A. K. Quist d. G. Palafox 6–4,
6–1, 6–4; lost to A. Vega 7–9, 4–6, 2–6; O. W. Sidwell d. Vega 2–6,
8–6, 3–6, 6–4, 7–5; d. F. Guerrero 6–1, 6–4, 6–2; C. Long–G. E. Brown
d. Vega–Palafox 6–0, 6–2, 6–2.

INTER-ZONE FINAL
Australia d. Czechoslovakia 3–2, Boston: A. K. Quist d. V. Cernik
6–2, 13–11, 6–0; lost to J. Drobny 8–6, 6–3, 16–18, 3–6, 5–7; O. W.
Sidwell d. Drobny 6–3, 6–2, 9–11, 14–12; d. Cernik 7–5, 6–4, 6–2; C.
Long–G. E. Brown lost to Drobny–Cernik 8–10, 6–4, 3–6, 4–6.

CHALLENGE ROUND
USA d. Australia 5–0, New York: F. A. Parker d. O. W. Sidwell 6–4,
6–4, 6–4; F. R. Schroeder d. A. K. Quist 6–3, 4–6, 6–0, 6–0; W. F.

Talbert–G. Mulloy d. Sidwell–C. Long 8–6, 9–7, 2–6, 7–5; Parker d. Quist 6–2, 6–2, 6–3; Schroeder d. Sidwell 6–2, 6–1, 6–1.

1949: USA
European Zone

FIRST ROUND

France d. Luxembourg 5–0, Mondorf–les–Bains: P. Remy d. G. Wertheim 6–0, 6–1, 6–1; d. G. Wampach 6–1, 6–3, 5–7, 6–3; R. Abdesselam d. Wampach 6–1, 6–2, 7–5; H. Bolelli d. Wertheim 6–0, 6–2, 6–1; Bolelli–Remy d. Wampach–Wertheim 6–2, 6–1, 6–1. **Denmark d. Israel 5–0, Copenhagen:** K. Neilsen d. A. Weiss 6–1, 6–2, 6–1; d. Y. Finkelkraut 6–1, 6–3, 6–1; T. Ulrich d. Finkelkraut 6–0, 6–1, 6–2; d. Weiss 6–4, 3–6, 1–6, 6–0, 6–3; Nielsen–Ulrich d. R. Gornitsky–Finkelkraut 6–2, 6–3, 6–0. **Czechoslovakia d. Monaco 5–0, Prague:** J. Drobny d. G. Pasquier 6–0, 6–1, 6–0; d. A. Noghes 6–2, 6–2, 6–1; V. Cernik d. Noghes 6–3, 6–2, 6–2; d. Pasquier 6–1, 6–0, 6–4; Drobny–Cernik d. Pasquier–Noghes 6–1, 6–2, 6–0. **Great Britain d. Portugal 5–0, Lisbon:** A. J. Mottram d. J. Roquette 8–6, 6–3, 7–5; d. J. da Silva 7–5, 3–6, 7–5, 6–0; G. L. Paish d. da Silva 6–4, 6–1, 6–3; N. R. Lewis d. Roquette 6–2, 1–6, 6–1, 7–5; Mottram–Paish d. Roquette–da Silva 6–0, 6–2, 6–1. **Egypt d. Argentine def.; Chile d. Ireland 3–2, Dublin:** R. Balbiers d. G. P. Jackson 6–2, 4–6, 6–3, 6–0; d. C. A. Kemp 10–8, 10–8, 6–4; M. Taverne lost to Kemp 3–6, 6–4, 4–6, 3–6; lost to Jackson 1–6, 3–6, 2–6; Balbiers–Taverne d. Kemp Jackson 6–2, 6–3, 6–4. **Italy d. Turkey def.; South Africa d. Holland 5–0, Scheveningen:** E. W. Sturgess d. A. C. von Swol 6–4, 6–3, 6–2; d. A. L. van Meegeren 6–2, 6–3, 6–1; E. E. Fannin d. van Meegeren 6–3, 6–2, 6–4; S. Levy d. J. P. A. Linck 6–4, 6–3, 6–4; Sturgess–Fannin d. van Swol–I. Rinkel 7–5, 6–3, 6–4.

SECOND ROUND

Hungary d. Belgium 4–1, Budapest: J. Asboth d. P. Washer 6–2, 6–1, 6–3; d. J. Peten 6–3, 6–1, 6–3; A. A. Stolpa d. Peten 6–0, 8–6, 3–6, 6–1; Z. Katona lost to J. Brichant 4–6, 4–6, 6–0, 4–6; Asboth–Stolpa d. Washer–Brichant 6–1, 3–6, 7–5, 6–4. **Switzerland d. Greece def.; France d. Denmark 4–1, Paris:** M. Bernard d. K. Nielsen 3–6, 11–9, 6–3, 6–3; R. Abdesselam d. T. Ulrich 6–0, 6–3, 6–0; lost to Nielsen 4–6, 6–3, 5–7, 4–6; J. Thomas d. E. Bjerre 3–6, 6–4, 6–0, 6–0; Bernard–H. Bolelli d. Nielsen–Bjerre 6–3, 6–4, 6–4. **Czechoslovakia d. Great Britain 4–1, Wimbledon:** J. Drobny d. A. J. Mottram 6–4, 6–3, 8–6;

d. G. L. Paish 6–3, 6–0, 6–3; V. Cernik lost to Mottram 2–6, 4–6, 4–6; d. Paish 6–3, 2–6, 6–4, 6–4; Drobny–Cernik d. Mottram–Paish 6–3, 6–3, 6–1. **Chile d. Egypt 3–2, Edgbaston:** R. Balbiers d. Shafie 6–0, 6–2, 6–2; d. M. Coen 2–6, 6–4, 8–6, 6–1; M. Taverne lost to Coen 3–6, 4–6, 2–6; lost to Shafie 3–6, 9–11, 9–11; Balbiers–Taverne d. Coen–M. Talaat 6–4, 6–2, 6–4. **Italy d. South Africa 4–1, Milan:** G. Cucelli d. E. Fannin 7–5, 7–5, 6–3; d. E. W. Sturgess 6–1, 2–6, 6–0, 6–4; V. Canepele lost to Sturgess 3–6, 1–6, 4–6; d. Fannin 6–4, 7–5, 6–4; Cucelli–M. del Bello d. Sturgess–Fannin 6–3, 7–9, 10–8, 2–6, 8–6. **Yugoslavia d. Austria 4–1, Vienna:** D. Mitic d. L. Czajkovsky 6–2, 6–2, 6–2; d. H. Redl 11–9, 5–7, 6–2, 5–7, 8–6; M. Branovic lost to Redl 3–6, 4–6, 6–1, 6–4, 4–6; d. Czajkovsky 6–4, 6–3, 6–4; Mitic–J. Pallada d. Redl–Hardwich 6–1, 6–1, 6–4. **Sweden d. Norway 5–0, Stockholm:** L. Bergelin d. H. Hessen 6–4, 6–1, 6–3; d. J. Staubo 6–1, 4–6, 6–4, 6–4; T. Johansson d. Staubo 6–0, 6–3, 6–3; d. Hessen 6–1, 6–2, 6–3; Bergelin–Johansson d. Hessen–Staubo 6–4, 6–4, 6–4.

THIRD ROUND

Hungary d. Switzerland 5–0, Budapest: A. A. Stolpa d. H. Huonder 6–1, 0–6, 6–4, 7–5; d. M. Albrecht 6–1, 6–2, 7–5; J. Asboth d. Albrecht 6–3, 6–3, 5–7, 6–0; d. Huonder 6–1, 6–2, 6–1; Asboth–Stolpa d. Huonder–R. Buser 3–6, 6–3, 6–4, 7–5. **France d. Czechoslovakia 3–2, Paris:** R. Abdesselam d. V. Cernik 6–4, 6–3, 2–6, 6–1; lost to J. Drobny 4–6, 1–6, 3–6; M. Bernard d. Drobny 3–6, 6–3, 9–7, 7–5; d. Cernik 6–4, 6–2, 6–1; Bernard–H. Bolelli lost to Drobny–Cernik 6–4, 6–4, 3–6, 4–6, 4–6. **Italy d. Chile 4–1, Turin:** G. Cucelli d. M. Taverne 6–1, 6–0, 6–4; d. R. Balbiers 6–4, 8–6, 7–5; M. del Bello lost to Balbiers 3–6, 4–6, 6–4, 3–6; d. Taverne 8–10, 6–0, 6–1 def; Cucelli–del Bello d. Balbiers–Taverne 6–3, 6–3, 4–6, 6–4. **Yugoslavia d. Sweden 3–2, Zagreb:** J. Pallada d. L. Bergelin 5–7, 6–3, 6–2, 6–3; lost to T. Johansson 6–4, 4–6, 2–6, 6–4, 3–6; D. Mitic lost to Johansson 4–6, 6–0, 7–5, 3–6, 4–6; d. Bergelin 6–3, 10–8, 6–4; Pallada–Mitic d. Bergelin–Johansson 6–2, 7–5, 6–4.

SEMI-FINAL ROUND

France d. Hungary 3–2, Budapest: M. Bernard lost to J. Asboth 6–3, 0–6, 0–6, 3–6; d. A. A. Stolpa 6–2, 6–4, 6–1; R. Abdesselam d. Stolpa 6–1, 6–3, 6–8, 6–8, 8–6; lost to Asboth 2–6, 5–7, 7–9; Bernard–H. Bolelli d. Asboth–K. Feher 6–1, 6–2, 6–3. **Italy d. Yugoslavia 4–1, Rome:** G. Cucelli d. D. Mitic 5–7, 6–2, 6–1, 7–5; V. Canepele d. J. Pallada 6–4, 6–4, 6–1; lost to Mitic 1–6, 4–6, 3–6; M. del Bello d. Pallada 6–3, 6–1, 7–5; Cucelli–del Bello d. Mitic–Pallada 6–4, 6–0, 7–5.

FINAL ROUND
Italy d. France 3–2, Paris: G. Cucelli d. R. Abdesselam 1–6, 6–8, 10–8, 6–4, 6–2; d. M. Bernard 8–6, 3–6, 4–6, 6–0, 6–1; M. del Bello lost to Bernard 4–6, 3–6, 6–4, 6–2, 8–10; lost to Abdesselam 3–6, 4–6, 2–6; Cucelli–del Bello d. Bernard–H. Bolelli 3–6, 6–1, 4–6, 6–0, 6–2.

American Zone

FIRST ROUND
Australia d. Canada 4–1, Montreal: F. A. Sedgman d. H. Rochon 6–4, 6–2, 6–2; d. B. Macken 6–2, 6–2, 6–0; O. W. Sidwell lost to Macken 6–3, 5–7, 3–6, 7–5, 6–8; d. L. Main 8–6, 4–6, 6–4, 6–1; J. E. Bromwich–Sedgman d. Macken–W. Stohlberg 6–3, 6–2, 6–2. **Mexico d. Cuba 4–1, Havana:** A. Vega d. J. Aguero 7–5, 1–6, 6–1, 6–2; R. Vega d. J. Weiss 6–4, 0–6, 6–0, 10–8; M. Varela d. J. Pardo 6–3, 6–0, 6–2; L. Refkohl lost to Aguero, 4–6, 2–6, 4–6; A. and R. Vega d. Aguero–Weiss 6–3, 6–3, 5–7, 6–4.

FINAL
Australia d. Mexico 5–0, Wilmington: F. A. Sedgman d. A. Vega 12–10, 4–6, 6–4, 1–6, 6–3; J. E. Bromwich d. R. Vega 6–0, 6–2, 6–1; d. A. Vega 6–0, 6–1, 6–4; O. W. Sidwell d. M. Varela 6–2, 6–2, 6–1; Bromwich–Sedgman d. A. and R. Vega 6–0, 6–4, 6–2.

INTER-ZONE FINAL
Australia d. Italy 5–0, New York: O. W. Sidwell d. G. Cucelli 6–2, 6–4, 2–6, 6–2; d. M. del Bello 6–1, 6–1, 6–0; F. A. Sedgman d. del Bello 6–0, 6–4, 6–4; d. Cucelli 1–6, 6–1, 6–2, 6–2; J. E. Bromwich–Sedgman d. Cucelli–del Bello 2–6, 6–2, 6–2, 6–1.

CHALLENGE ROUND
USA d. Australia 4–1, New York: F. R. Schroeder d. O. W. Sidwell 6–1, 5–7, 4–6, 6–2, 6–3; R. Gonzales d. F. A. Sedgman 8–6, 6–4, 9–7; W. F. Talbert–G. Mulloy lost to Sidwell–J. E. Bromwich 6–3, 6–4, 8–10, 7–9, 7–9; Schroeder d. Sedgman 6–4, 6–3, 6–3; Gonzalez d. Sidwell 6–1, 6–3, 6–3.

1950: AUSTRALIA
European Zone

FIRST ROUND

Philippines d. Pakistan 5–0, Manila: R. Deyro d. I. Ahmed 6–2, 6–0, 6–3; d. M. Alam 6–0, 6–2, 6–0; F. H. Ampon d. Alam 6–0, 6–1, 6–0; d. Ahmed 6–0, 6–4, 6–0; Ampon–C. Carmona d. Ahmed–Alam 6–3, 6–1, 6–1. **Sweden d. Holland 4–1, Scheveningen:** L. Bergelin d. A. L. van Meegeren 6–1, 6–2, 6–2; d. J. P. A. Linck 6–3, 6–2, 6–1; T. Johansson d. Linck 6–2, 6–2, 6–4; d. van Meegeren 6–1, 6–2, 6–4; Bergelin–Johansson lost to A. C. van Swol–I. Rinkel 3–6, 7–5, 6–2, 6–8, 1–6. **Norway d. Hungary def; Yugoslavia d. Austria 5–0, Zagreb:** J. Pallada d. H. Redl 6–3, 6–2, 6–2; d. A. Huber 7–5, 6–4, 6–4; M. Branovic d. Huber 6–2, 6–1, 6–4; d. Redl 8–6, 6–1, 6–2; J. Pallada–P. Milojkovic d. Huber–Redl 7–5, 6–1, 7–5. **Belgium d. Finland 4–1, Brussels:** P. Washer d. P. Forsman 6–2, 6–0, 6–2; J. Brichant d. S. Salo 6–4, 8–6, 6–4; d. Forsman 8–6, 6–2, 7–5; J. Peten lost to Salo 1–6, 1–6, 6–4, 6–2, 3–6; Brichant–Washer d. Salo–Forsman 6–4, 6–2, 6–3. **Italy d. Great Britain 3–2, Eastbourne:** G. Cucelli d. A. J. Mottram 5–7, 6–3, 7–5, 6–4; d. G. L. Paish 1–6, 6–2, 4–6, 6–4, 8–6; del Bello lost to Mottram 3–6, 3–6, 6–8; lost to Paish 4–6, 6–4, 3–6, 6–4, 3–6; Cucelli–M. del Bello d. Mottram–Paish 9–7, 6–2, 6–4.

SECOND ROUND

Poland d. Israel 5–0, Warsaw: W. Skonecki d. F. Weiss 6–3, 6–2, 6–4; d. J. Buntmann 6–2, 6–0, 6–2; S. Piatek d. Buntmann 4–6, 6–0, 8–6, 6–1; d. Weiss 6–1, 6–0, 4–6, 4–6, 6–2; Skonecki–Piatek d. Weiss–Y. Finkelkraut 7–5, 6–3, 6–4. **Ireland d. Monaco 5–0, Dublin:** C. A. Kemp d. V. G. Pasquier 6–3, 6–2, 6–2; M. Murphy d. A. Noghes 6–3, 2–6, 6–3, 6–2; d. Pasquier 6–0, 7–5, 4–6, 6–1; J. D. Hackett d. Noghes 8–6, 11–9, 6–3; M. Murphy–Hackett d. Noghes–Pasquier 6–3, 7–5, 7–5. **Philippines d. Peru def.; Sweden d. Norway 5–0, Oslo:** L. Bergelin d. J. Haanes 6–1, 6–2, 6–3; T. Johansson d. Hessen 7–5, 6–2, 3–6, 8–6; d. Haanes 6–2, 6–3, 8–6; S. Davidson d. Hessen 6–3, 6–3, 6–4; Bergelin–Davidson d. Hessen–Haanes 6–1, 6–1, 6–2. **Belgium d. Yugoslavia 3–2, Zagreb:** P. Washer d. M. Branovic 6–4, 6–1, 6–1; lost to D. Mitic 3–6, 4–6, 6–4, 3–6; J. Brichant d. Branovic 6–4, 6–2, 6–4; lost to Mitic 5–7, 1–6, 3–6; Washer–Brichant d. Mitic–J. Pallada 6–4, 6–4, 5–7, 3–6, 6–4. **Italy d. Luxembourg 5–0, Luxembourg:** R. del Bello d. G. Wertheim 6–1, 6–2, 6–2; d. G. Wampach 6–1, 7–5, 6–4; G. Cucelli d. Wampach 6–2, 6–2, 6–1; M. del Bello d. Wertheim 6–3, 6–0, 6–2; Cucelli–M. del Bello d. Wertheim–Wampach 6–0, 6–2, 6–1.

Denmark d. Egypt 3–0, Copenhagen: K. Nielsen d. A. Shafie 6–4, 3–6, 8–6, 6–1; T. Ulrich d. M. Coen 6–1, 6–0, 6–0; Nielsen–Ulrich d. Coen–Shafie 2–6, 9–7, 6–4, 6–3. **France d. Switzerland 4–0, Paris:** B. Destremau d. M. Albrecht 6–1, 6–2, 6–1; d. G. Grange 6–2, 6–3, 8–6; J. Thomas d. Grange 6–0, 6–1, 7–5; v. Albrecht 7–5, 6–4, 1–6, 0–1 unfin.; Abdesselam–P. Remy d. J. P. Blondel–R. Buser 6–3, 6–4, 8–6.

THIRD ROUND

Poland d. Ireland 3–2, Warsaw: W. Skonecki d. M. Murphy 9–7, 6–3, 6–2; d. C. A. Kemp 6–3, 6–2, 6–0; S. Piatek d. Kemp 6–1, 6–1, 9–7; lost to Murphy 6–0, 2–6, 3–6, 2–6; Skonecki–J. Chytrowski lost to J. D. Hackett–Murphy 8–10, 10–8, 14–12, 5–7, 1–6. **Sweden d. Philippines 5–0, Stockholm:** L. Bergelin d. F. H. Ampon 6–4, 4–6, 6–1, 6–2; T. Johansson d. R. Deyro 6–2, 3–6, 6–2, 6–3; d. Ampon 6–8, 8–10, 6–4, 6–1, 6–1; S. Davidson d. Deyro 6–1, 6–0, 6–1; Bergelin–Davidson d. Ampon–C. Carmona 6–2, 6–3, 6–3. **Italy d. Belgium 3–2, Brussels:** G. Cucelli d. J. Brichant 6–2, 5–7, 6–4, 6–2; lost to P. Washer 2–6, 9–11, 4–6; R. del Bello d. Brichant 6–4, 6–1, 6–3; lost to Washer 4–6, 1–6, 1–6; Cucelli–del Bello d. Washer–Brichant 4–6, 6–2, 6–2, 8–6. **Denmark d. France 3–2, Copenhagen:** K. Nielsen d. M. Bernard 6–3, 4–6, 6–1, 6–2; d. B. Destremau 6–2, 3–6, 6–4, 6–3; T. Ulrich lost to Destremau 9–7, 4–6, 0–6, 4–6; lost to Bernard 3–6, 4–6, 0–6; Nielsen–Ulrich d. P. Remy–J. Thomas 7–5, 6–4, 12–10.

SEMI-FINAL ROUND

Denmark d. Italy 4–1, Copenhagen: K. Nielsen d. G. Cucelli 6–3, 7–5, 0–6, 0–6, 6–4; d. R. del Bello 6–3, 7–5, 6–4; T. Ulrich d. R. del Bello 6–0, 6–2, 6–2; d. Cucelli 3–6, 6–2, 6–2, 6–3; Nielsen–Ulrich lost to Cucelli–M. del Bello 2–6, 4–6, 2–6. **Sweden d. Poland 5–0, Båstad:** T. Johansson d. S. Piatek 6–1, 6–1, 6–3; d. W. Skonecki 6–3, 6–3, 6–3; L. Bergelin d. Skonecki, 6–2, 6–2, 1–6, 6–1; S. Davidson d. Piatek 6–0, 6–2, 6–2; Johansson–Davidson d. Skonecki–Piatek 6–4, 6–0, 7–5.

FINAL ROUND

Sweden d. Denmark 4–0, Båstad: T. Johansson d. T. Ulrich 6–1, 4–6, 6–3, 6–1; d. K. Nielson 3–6, 7–5, 6–0, 4–6, 6–2; S. Davidson d. Nielsen 7–5, 3–6, 6–2, 6–4; L. Bergelin–Davidson d. Nielsen–Ulrich 6–2, 6–2, 6–2.

American Zone

FIRST ROUND
Australia d. Canada 5–0, Montreal: F. A. Sedgman d. B. Macken 7–5,
6–2, 6–1; d. L. Main 6–1, 6–2, 6–3; K. McGregor d. Main 6–1, 6–2,
7–5; d. Macken 6–4, 6–4, 6–4; J. E. Bromwich–Sedgman d. H.
Rochon–G. Robinson 6–2, 6–4, 6–4. **Mexico d. Cuba 5–0, Havana:**
A. Puente d. J. Weiss 5–7, 7–5, 1–6, 6–1, 7–5; G. Palafox d. J. Aguero
1–6, 6–2, 6–1, 6–3; R. Ortega d. J. Etcheverry 7–5, 6–2, 2–6, 6–4; A.
Millet d. O. Garrido 6–1, 6–2, 6–3; Palafox–Millet d. Weiss–Aguero 6–1,
6–4, 9–7.

FINAL ROUND
Australia d. Mexico 4–1, Mexico City: F. A. Sedgman d. G. Palafox
6–4, 6–4, 6–2; d. A. Vega 2–6, 6–4, 6–2, 4–6, 6–2; J. E. Bromwich d.
A. Vega 3–6, 6–0, 6–2, 6–2; K. McGregor lost to Palafox 4–6, 4–6, 8–6,
6–3, 3–6; Sedgman–Bromwich d. Palafox–Vega 6–4, 7–5, 6–2.

INTER-ZONE FINAL
Australia d. Sweden 3–2, Rye: F. A. Sedgman lost to L. Bergelin 6–2,
2–6, 5–7, 6–1, 3–6; d. T. Johansson 6–4, 7–5, 6–3; J. E. Bromwich d.
Johansson 6–2, 6–3, 6–0; lost to Bergelin 3–6, 2–6, 6–1, 9–7, 3–6;
Bromwich–Sedgman d. Bergelin–S. Davidson 6–1, 7–5, 7–5.

CHALLENGE ROUND
Australia d. USA 4–1, New York: F. A. Sedgman d. T. P. Brown
6–0, 8–6, 9–7; K. McGregor d. F. R. Schroeder 13–11, 6–3, 6–4;
Sedgman–J. E. Bromwich d. Schroeder–G. Mulloy 4–6, 6–4, 6–2, 4–6,
6–4; Sedgman d. Schroeder 6–2, 6–2, 6–2; McGregor lost to Brown
11–9, 10–8, 9–11, 1–6, 4–6.

1951: AUSTRALIA
European Zone

FIRST ROUND
Switzerland d. Luxembourg 5–0, Lucerne: J. Spitzer d. G. Wertheim
6–0, 6–4, 6–2; d. G. Wampach 6–1, 12–10, 6–2; M. Albrecht d.
Wampach 6–3, 6–8, 6–1, 6–0; d. Wertheim 6–1, 6–2, 6–1; P. Blondel–R.
Buser d. Wampach–Wertheim 3–6, 7–9, 6–3, 6–2, 6–2. **Germany d.
Yugoslavia 3–2, Zagreb:** E. Buchholz lost to M. Branovic 6–4, 7–5,
2–6, 2–6, 4–6; lost to D. Mitic 3–6, 10–12, 4–6; G. von Cramm d. Mitic

6–0, 6–2, 8–6; d. Branovic 6–1, 5–7, 9–7, 6–4; von Cramm–R. Goepfert d. Mitic–J. Pallada 6–2, 7–9, 6–4, 6–4. **Egypt d. Norway 3–2, Oslo:** M. Coen lost to J. Haanes 2–6, 2–6, 3–6; lost to J. Staubo 6–4, 3–6, 3–6, 3–6; A. Shafie d. Staubo 6–8, 6–3, 7–5, 6–2; d. Haanes 6–1, 6–4, 6–3; Shafie–Coen d. Haanes–S. Lie 11–9, 6–4, 6–3. **Brazil d. Finland 4–1, Helsinki:** A. Procopio d. P. Forsman 6–4, 6–4, 4–6, 2–6, 6–1; A. Vieira d. S. Salo 6–1, 6–1, 6–4; d. Forsman 2–6, 6–4, 7–5, 0–6, 6–2; R. Cardozo lost to Salo 3–6, 4–6, 4–6; Vieira–Procopio d. Salo–Forsman 6–4, 6–4, 6–1. **Holland d. Monaco 4–1, The Hague:** J. P. A. Linck d. G. Pasquier 3–6, 6–2, 6–4, 9–7; lost to A. Noghes 6–3, 8–10, 6–3, 5–7, 2–6; A. C. van Swol d. Noghes 2–6, 6–4, 6–2, 6–0; d. Pasquier 6–1, 6–1, 6–2; Rinkel–van Swol d. Noghes–Pasquier 6–1, 6–2, 6–2.

SECOND ROUND

Italy d. South Africa 3–2, Milan: G. Cucelli d. S. Levy 9–11, 6–0, 6–4, 7–5; lost to E. W. Sturgess 3–6, 2–6, 6–4, 7–9; R. del Bello lost to Sturgess 3–6, 1–6, 5–7; d. Levy 6–4, 6–3, 6–2; Cucelli–M. del Bello d. Sturgess–Norgarb 13–11, 6–4, 6–4. **Poland d. Switzerland 4–1, Zurich:** S. Piatek d. M. Albrecht 5–7, 4–6, 7–5, 6–0, 6–1; d. J. Spitzer 8–6, 6–4, 6–4; W. Skonecki d. Spitzer 4–6, 6–2, 6–2, 7–5; d. Albrecht 3–6, 1–6, 7–5, 6–3, 6–3; Skonecki–Piatek lost to Spitzer–R. Buser 6–3, 5–7, 1–6, 6–3, 4–6. **Germany d. Denmark 4–1, Berlin:** G. von Cramm d. K. Nielsen 6–2, 6–4, 6–0; d. T. Ulrich 6–4, 6–2, 6–4; E. Buchholz lost to Ulrich 6–2, 3–6, 4–6, 4–6; d. Nielsen 2–6, 3–6, 6–3, 6–3, 6–4; von Cramm–R. Goepfert d. Nielsen–Ulrich 6–4, 6–4, 6–2. **Belgium d. Egypt 4–1, Brussels:** J. Brichant d. M. Coen 6–1, 6–1, 6–0; d. A. Shafie 6–3, 6–1, 6–4; P. Washer d. Shafie 4–6, 6–2, 7–5, 6–4; J. Peten lost to Coen 4–6, 6–1, 5–7, 4–6; Washer–Brichant d. Shafie–Coen 6–2, 7–5, 2–6, 6–2. **Philippines d. Brazil 4–1, Paris:** R. Deyro lost to A. Vieira 3–6, 2–6, 7–9; d. R. Cardozo 6–3, 7–5, 6–3; F. H. Ampon d. A. Procopio 6–1, 6–0, 6–1; d. Vieira 8–6, 3–6, 6–0, 6–0; Ampon–C. Carmona d. Vieira–Procopio 3–6, 6–2, 6–1, 7–5. **Holland d. Ireland 3–2, The Hague:** L. Krijt d. J. D. Hackett 6–3, 4–6, 6–4, 6–2; lost to G. P. Jackson 2–6, 3–6, 9–7, 5–7; A. C. van Swol lost to Jackson 7–5, 6–4, 4–6, 3–6, 4–6; d. Hackett 6–2, 6–4, 6–1; van Swol–I. Rinkel d. Hackett–C. A. Kemp 6–3, 6–1, 6–2. **Great Britain d. France 3–2, London:** G. L. Paish lost to P. Remy 3–6, 2–6, 3–6; A. J. Mottram d. B. Destremau 6–3, 1–6, 6–8, 6–2, 6–3; d. Remy 6–2, 6–4, 6–4; A. G. Roberts lost to Destremau 5–7, 2–6, 8–6, 6–3, 3–6; Mottram–Paish d. Remy–R. Abdesselam 7–5, 6–3, 6–8, 6–4. **Sweden d. Austria 5–0, Vienna:** S. Davidson d. G. Specht 6–1, 8–6, 6–0; d. H. Redl 6–4, 1–6, 6–4, 6–1;

383

T. Johansson d. Specht 6–1, 7–5, 5–7, 6–4; L. Bergelin d. Redl 7–9, 6–2, 6–1, 6–1; Bergelin–Davidson d. Redl–A. Huber 6–3, 7–5, 6–2.

THIRD ROUND

Italy d. Poland 5–0, Milan: G. Cucelli d. S. Piatek 8–6, 6–0, 6–2; R. del Bello d. J. Radzyo 7–9, 6–3, 7–5, 6–1; d. Piatek 6–4, 6–0, 1–6, 6–2; G. Merlo d. Radzyo 6–1, 6–1, 6–3; Cucelli–M. del Bello d. Piatek–J. Chitrowski 6–2, 6–3, 6–2. **Germany d. Belgium 3–2, Cologne:** G. von Cramm d. P. Washer 5–7, 6–3, 6–4, 6–4; d. J. Brichant 6–0, 6–2, 3–6, 6–3; E. Buchholz lost to Brichant 1–6, 3–6, 2–6; lost to Washer 6–3, 3–6, 6–8, 3–6; von Cramm–R. Goepfert d. Washer–Brichant 8–6, 3–6, 6–2, 6–3. **Philippines d. Holland 4–1, Noordwijk:** F. H. Ampon d. J. P. A. Linck 6–1, 6–3, 5–7, 6–1; R. Deyro d. L. Krijt 6–4, 6–0, 6–1; d. Linck 6–1, 6–4, 4–6, 6–2; C. Carmona d. Krijt 6–3, 6–3, 6–1; Ampon–Carmona lost to A. C. van Swol–I. Rinkel 7–5, 3–6, 5–7, 4–6. **Sweden d. Great Britain 5–0, Scarborough:** L. Bergelin d. G. L. Paish 9–7, 6–1, 6–3; d. A. J. Mottram 3–6, 5–7, 6–3, 6–4, 6–2; S. Davidson d. Mottram 4–6, 7–5, 6–2, 8–6; d. Paish 2–6, 7–5, 6–1, 6–4; Bergelin–Davidson d. Mottram–Paish 2–6, 6–3, 9–7, 10–8.

SEMI-FINAL ROUND

Germany d. Italy 3–2, Munich: G. von Cramm d. G. Cucelli 6–2, 4–6, 8–6, 7–5; d. R. del Bello 7–5, 6–4, 4–6, 6–4; E. Buchholz lost to R. del Bello 2–6, 6–1, 8–6, 1–6, 4–6; lost to Cucelli 2–6, 3–6, 4–6; von Cramm–R. Goepfert d. Cucelli–M. del Bello 6–4, 6–2, 4–6, 9–7. **Sweden d. Philippines 5–0, Båstad:** L. Bergelin d. R. Deyro 6–1, 6–3, 6–2; d. F. H. Ampon 6–3, 6–1, 0–6, 1–6, 6–2; S. Davidson d. Ampon 6–1, 6–4, 4–6, 0–6, 6–3; d. Deyro 6–4, 4–6, 3–6, 8–6, 7–5; Bergelin–Davidson d. Ampon–C. Carmona 6–3, 8–6, 6–4.

FINAL ROUND

Sweden d. Germany 5–0, Båstad: L. Bergelin d. G. von Cramm 6–4, 6–1, 6–4; d. E. Buchholz 6–1, 5–7, 6–4, 6–3; S. Davidson d. Buchholz 6–2, 6–1, 6–4; d. H. Gulz 6–0, 6–2, 6–1; Bergelin–Davidson d. von Cramm–R. Goepfert 9–7, 9–7, 8–10, 6–2.

American Zone

FIRST ROUND

USA d. Japan 5–0, Louisville: R. Savitt d. F. Nakano 7–5, 6–3, 6–2; H. Flam d. J. Kumamaru 7–5, 6–0, 7–5; W. F. Talbert–T. Trabert d.

Nakano–G. Fujikura 6–0, 6–2, 10–8; Savitt d. Kumamaru 6–4, 6–2, 3–6, 6–1; Trabert d. Nakano 6–4, 7–5, 6–0.

SECOND ROUND
USA d. Mexico 5–0, New York: A. Larsen d. A. Vega 7–5, 6–3, 4–6, 7–5; H. Flam d. M. Llamas 6–1, 6–2, 6–4; V. Seixas–Flam d. A. and R. Vega 6–4, 6–2, 6–0; Flam d. R. Vega 6–3, 6–3, 6–3; Seixas d. Llamas 6–3, 8–6, 6–1. **Canada d. Cuba 5–0, Montreal:** L. Main d. J. Aguero 6–4, 6–0, 7–5; H. Rochon d. O. Garrido 6–1, 6–3, 6–2; B. Macken d. J. Weiss 3–6, 6–4, 6–1, 6–4; d. R. Garrido 6–2, 6–4, 6–2; Main–Rochon d. Weiss–I. Inepeaguero 6–4, 6–0, 6–4.

FINAL ROUND
USA d. Canada 5–0, Montreal: T. Trabert d. L. Main 6–1, 6–2, 6–3; R. Savitt d. B. Macken 6–3, 6–1, 6–3; B. Patty–Trabert d. H. Rochon–Macken 6–4, 6–3, 6–2; A. Larsen d. Rochon 6–2, 6–1, 6–3; Patty d. Main 6–3, 6–3, 6–2.

INTER-ZONE FINAL
USA d. Sweden 5–0, Melbourne: F. R. Schroeder d. L. Bergelin 6–2, 6–2, 6–4; T. Trabert d. S. Davidson 6–3, 6–4, 9–7; Schroeder–Trabert d. Bergelin–Davidson 10–12, 6–0, 6–3, 6–2; Schroeder d. Davidson 6–2, 6–2, 6–1; Trabert d. Bergelin 6–1, 10–8, 6–4.

CHALLENGE ROUND
Australia d. USA 3–2, Sydney: M. G. Rose lost to V. Seixas 3–6, 4–6, 7–9; F. A. Sedgman d. F. R. Schroeder 6–4, 6–3, 4–6, 6–4; Sedgman–K. McGregor d. Schroeder–T. Trabert 6–2, 9–7, 6–3; Rose lost to Schroeder 4–6, 11–13, 5–7; Sedgman d. Seixas 6–4, 6–2, 6–2.

1952: AUSTRALIA
European Zone

FIRST ROUND
Switzerland d. Turkey 4–1, Istanbul: J. Spitzer d. N. Bari 6–2, 6–0, 8–6; E. Balestra d. F. Kizil 4–6, 6–4, 6–2, 4–6, 6–4; lost to Bari 2–6, 6–3, 3–6, 5–7; P. Blondel d. B. Cevansir 6–3, 6–2, 6–3; J. P. and P. Blondel d. Cevansir–Bari 6–4, 6–2, 5–7, 6–2. **France d. Norway 5–0, Oslo:** P. Remy d. S. Lie 6–4, 6–3, 6–3; B. Destremau beat N. E. Hessen 6–1, 6–4, 6–3; d. Lie 6–4, 8–6, 6–0; R. Haillet d. Hessen 6–1, 6–3, 6–3; R. Abdesselam–Remy d. Lie–Hessen 6–1, 6–3, 6–2. **Chile d. Austria**

4–1, Vienna: R. Balbiers d. G. Specht 6–0, 6–2, 6–3; d. H. Redl 6–4, 3–6, 6–3, 1–6, 6–1; L. Ayala d. A. Huber 7–5, 12–10, 7–5; d. Specht 6–1, 6–2, 6–1; Ayala–C. Sanhueza lost to Huber–Redl 2–6, 7–5, 2–6, 4–6. **Egypt d. Luxembourg 5–0, Mondorf–les–Bains:** A. Ismail d. P. Decker 6–1, 6–1, 6–0; A. Shafie d. G. Wertheim 6–1, 6–3, 6–2; d. Decker 6–0, 6–0, 6–1; M. Coen d. Wertheim 6–2, 0–6, 6–2, 6–2; Shafie–Coen d. Wertheim–Klees 6–2, 6–2, 6–2. **Yugoslavia d. Finland 4–1, Helsinki:** V. Petrovic d. P. Forsman 2–6, 6–4, 8–6, 6–3; lost to S. Salo 8–6, 6–1, 5–7, 4–6, 5–7; J. Pallada d. Forsman 6–2, 6–1, 6–0; d. Salo def.; Petrovic–Pallada d. Salo–Forsman 5–7, 6–3, 6–2, 6–3. **Monaco d. Ireland 4–1, Monaco:** G. Pasquier lost to C. A. Kemp 5–7, 4–6, 6–8; d. J. D. Hackett 4–6, 6–2, 6–4, 4–6, 6–3; A. Noghes d. Hackett 9–11, 8–10, 6–3, 6–4, 8–6; d. Kemp 6–4, 6–4, 6–4; Noghes–Pasquier d. Hackett–Kemp 6–1, 6–2, 2–6, 6–2.

SECOND ROUND

Argentina d. Switzerland 5–0, Lausanne: E. Morea d. J. Spitzer 6–2, 6–2, 6–3; A. D. Russell d. M. Albrecht 6–2, 2–6, 6–1, 6–2; d. Spitzer 6–2, 6–3, 6–8, 6–1; S. Soriano d. P. Blondel 6–2, 6–2, 6–2; Morea–Russell d. J. P. and P. Blondel 6–3, 6–2, 6–4. **France d. Holland 4–1, Paris:** B. Destremau lost to H. Wilton 3–6, 6–8, 6–1, 2–6; d. A. C. van Swol 5–7, 7–5, 6–1, 7–5; P. Remy d. van Swol 6–1, 6–2, 1–6, 6–3; R. Haillet d. Wilton 6–2, 3–6, 6–2, 6–3; Remy–R. Abdesselam d. van Swol–I. Rinkel 6–1, 6–4, 6–3. **Sweden d. Chile 5–0, Stockholm:** S. Davidson d. L. Ayala 4–6, 3–6, 7–5, 8–6, 6–1; T. Johansson d. R. Balbiers 6–4, 7–5, 6–4; d. Ayala 3–6, 6–2, 6–4, 6–2; A. Eliaeson d. Balbiers 6–2, 3–6, 6–3, 3–6, 6–4; Johansson–N. Rohlsson d. Ayala–Balbiers 6–3, 2–6, 6–3, 4–6, 6–4. **Belgium d. Hungary 4–1, Brussels:** P. Washer d. Asboth 6–2, 6–0, 6–4; d. A. A. Stolpa 6–4, 6–2, 6–0; J. Brichant d. Asboth 3–6, 7–5, 6–4, 6–0; lost to Stolpa 3–6, 5–7, 8–6, 6–2, 5–7; Washer–Brichant d. Asboth–Stolpa 6–3, 6–4, 6–4. **Italy d. Egypt 5–0, Rome:** F. Gardini d. A. Shafie 6–0, 6–3, 6–3; d. M. Coen 6–0, 6–1, 6–1; R. del Bello d. Coen 6–1, 7–5, 6–1; d. Shafie 7–5, 7–5, 2–6, 7–5; G. Cucelli–M. del Bello d. Shafie–Coen 6–2, 6–3, 6–2. **Great Britain d. Yugoslavia 3–2, Belgrade:** A. J. Mottram d. V. Petrovic 8–6, 6–1, 6–2; d. J. Pallada 6–3, 7–5, 6–2; G. L. Paish lost to Pallada 7–9, 8–6, 3–6, 5–7; R. Becker lost to Petrovic 1–6, 6–2, 6–4, 2–6, 1–6; J. C. Gregory–Mottram d. Pallada–S. Laszlo 6–4, 1–6, 9–11, 6–2, 6–2. **Denmark d. Monaco 5–0, Monaco:** K. Nielsen d. G. Pasquier 6–0, 6–2, 6–3; d. A. Noghes 6–2, 6–3, 6–4; T. Ulrich d. Noghes 6–2, 6–2, 6–4; d. Pasquier 0–6, 6–2, 6–1, 3–6, 6–0; Nielsen–Ulrich d. Noghes–Pasquier 3–6, 6–3, 1–6, 6–2, 6–1. **Germany d. Brazil 3–2, Dusseldorf:** G. von Cramm lost to A. Vieira 8–10, 2–6,

8–6, 6–3, 1–6; d. E. Saller 6–2, 6–2, 6–4; E. Buchholz d. Saller 4–6, 6–3, 6–3, 6–4; lost to Vieira 8–10, 7–5, 3–6, 4–6; von Cramm–R. Goepfert d. Vieira–Saller 6–3, 7–5, 6–3.

THIRD ROUND

France d. Argentina 3–2, Paris: B. Destremau d. A. D. Russell 5–7, 6–3, 6–3, 6–4; lost to E. Morea 2–6, 2–6, 2–6; P. Remy d. Russell 6–4, 7–5, 6–3; lost to Morea 4–6, 5–7, 3–6; Remy–R. Abdesselam d. Morea–Russell 6–2, 6–4, 6–4. **Belgium d. Sweden 3–2, Brussels:** P. Washer d. T. Johansson 1–6, 6–3, 7–5, 6–4; lost to S. Davidson 6–1, 7–5, 5–7, def; J. Brichant d. Davidson 6–4, 8–6, 7–5; lost to Johansson 1–6, 3–6, 2–6; Washer–Brichant d. Johansson–N. Rohlsson 3–6, 6–2, 6–1, 7–5. **Italy d. Great Britain 4–1, Bologna:** R. del Bello d. A. J. Mottram 8–6, 6–2, 6–2; d. G. L. Paish 6–3, 6–4, 6–2; F. Gardini d. Mottram 4–6, 4–6, 6–3, 6–1, 6–0; d. Paish 6–2, 6–3, 6–3; G. Cucelli–M. del Bello lost to Mottram–Paish 3–6, 1–6, 8–6, 2–6. **Denmark d. Germany 4–1, Copenhagen:** K. Nielsen d. E. Buchholz 7–5, 6–2, 6–4; d. H. Hermann 6–3, 6–3, 6–2; T. Ulrich d. Buchholz, 6–3, 6–3, 6–0; lost to Hermann 1–6, 3–6, 2–6; Nielsen–Ulrich d. R. Goefert–Hermann 7–9, 14–16, 8–6, 6–3, 6–3.

SEMI-FINAL ROUND

Belgium d. France 3–2, Paris: P. Washer d. R. Abdesselam 7–5, 6–1, 6–3; d. P. Remy 6–0, 6–0, 6–3; J. Brichant lost to Remy 6–3, 6–3, 8–10, 4–6, 1–6; d. Abdesselam 8–6, 6–8, 15–13, 6–1; Washer–Brichant lost to Remy–M. Bernard 1–6, 2–6, 6–1, 6–4, 1–6. **Italy d. Denmark 4–1, Milan:** F. Gardini d. K. Nielsen 8–6, 6–4, 6–4; d. T. Ulrich 6–0, 6–4, 7–5; R. del Bello–Ulrich 6–4, 6–4, 6–3; lost to Nielsen 3–6, 1–6, 4–6; G. Cucelli–M. del Bello d. Nielsen–Ulrich 8–6, 6–4, 2–6, 4–6, 6–0.

FINAL ROUND

Italy d. Belgium 3–1, Milan: F. Gardini d. P. Washer 8–6, 6–1, 3–6, 2–6, 6–4; d. J. Brichant 4–6, 6–1, 0–6, 6–2, 6–2; R. del Bello lost to Brichant 7–5, 1–6, 5–7, 6–0, 4–6; G. Cucelli–M. del Bello d. Washer–Brichant 6–3, 6–1, 5–7, 3–6, 6–3.

American Zone

FIRST ROUND

USA d. Japan 5–0, Cincinnati: A. Larsen d. J. Kumamaru 6–2, 3–6, 6–3, 6–2; V. Seixas d. A. Miyagi 6–3, 6–1, 6–0; W. F. Talbert–G.

Mulloy d. F. Nakano–Kumamaru 6–2, 3–6, 6–3, 6–2; Seixas d. Nakano 6–2, 6–1, 6–2; Larsen d. Miyagi 6–1, 3–6, 6–1, 5–7, 6–3.

SEMI-FINAL ROUND
USA d. Cuba 5–0, Havana: H. Stewart d. J. Weiss 7–5, 6–0, 6–4; B. Bartzen d. O. Garrido 6–0, 6–2, 6–1; G. Mulloy–Stewart d. P. Aguero–Weiss 6–0, 6–4, 6–2; Stewart d. O. Garrido 10–8, 6–3, 6–0; Bartzen d. R. Garrido 6–2, 6–1, 6–0. **Canada d. Mexico 5–0, Montreal:** L. Main d. P. Vega 6–2, 6–0, 6–2; d. M. Llamas 6–4, 3–6, 6–8, 6–4, 6–1; B. Macken d. Llamas 3–6, 4–6, 6–1, 6–1, 6–4; d. M. Galeana 6–2, 6–3, 6–4; Main–H. Rochon d. Llamas–Galeana 6–3, 6–2, 6–4.

FINAL ROUND
USA d. Canada 4–1, Montreal: H. Flam d. H. Rochon 6–2, 8–6, 6–2; V. Seixas d. L. Main 6–2, 6–3, 6–4; Seixas–Flam d. B. Macken–Main 6–3, 3–6, 6–3, 6–4; Flam d. Main 6–2, 6–2, 6–3; R. Perry lost to Macken 3–6, 13–11, 4–6, 4–6.

Eastern Zone

FINAL ROUND
Italy d. India 3–2, Brisbane: F. Gardini d. N. Kumar 6–1, 5–7, 7–5, 6–2; d. S. C. Misra 8–6, 8–6, 1–6, 6–4; R. del Bello lost to Misra 5–7, 4–6, 1–6; lost to Kumar 2–6, 6–8, 6–4, 3–6; M. del Bello–G. Cucelli d. Misra–Kumar 1–6, 1–6, 6–2, 6–2, 13–11.

INTER-ZONE FINAL
USA d. Italy 5–0, Sydney: V. Seixas d. F. Gardini 5–7, 3–6, 6–3, 8–6, 6–3; T. Trabert d. G. Cucelli 6–3, 6–1, 6–3; Seixas–Trabert d. M. del Bello–Cucelli 6–4, 6–3, 6–2; H. Richardson d. R. del Bello 7–5, 6–3, 5–7, 6–3; Trabert d. Gardini 6–3, 5–7, 7–5, 6–3.

CHALLENGE ROUND
Australia d. USA 4–1, Adelaide: F. A. Sedgman d. V. Seixas 6–3, 6–4, 6–3; K. McGregor d. T. Trabert 11–9, 6–4, 6–1; Sedgman–McGregor d. Seixas–Trabert 6–3, 6–4, 1–6, 6–3; Sedgman d. Trabert 7–5, 6–4, 10–8; McGregor lost to Seixas 3–6, 6–8, 8–6, 3–6.

1953: AUSTRALIA
European Zone

FIRST ROUND

Finland d. Ireland 4–1, Helsinki: P. Forsman lost to J. D. Hackett 7–5, 6–3, 2–6, 1–6, 1–6; d. G. P. Jackson 6–2, 7–5, 4–6, 3–6, 7–5; S. Salo d. Jackson 6–1, 6–2, 6–3; d. Hackett 6–3, 6–4, 6–0; Forsman–Salo d. Jackson–Hackett 7–5, 6–4, 6–4. **Austria d. Egypt 4–1, Cairo:** A. Huber lost to M. Coen 6–2, 6–1, 2–6, 1–6, 3–6; d. A. Shafie 3–6, 7–5, 6–1, 6–3; H. Redl d. Shafie 6–1, 6–2, 1–6, 2–6, 11–9; d. Coen 2–6, 6–2, 6–4, 3–6, 6–1; Huber–Redl d. Coen–Shafie 3–6, 7–5, 6–1, 6–3. **Yugoslavia d. Switzerland 5–0, Novisad:** J. Pallada d. E. Balestra 6–1, 1–6, 6–2, 6–4; V. Petrovic d. M. Albrecht 1–6, 6–1, 6–4, 6–2; I. Panajotovic d. Balestra 8–10, 6–2, 6–2, 6–4; P. Milojkovic d. J. P. Blondel 1–6, 6–3, 6–4 def.; Pallada–Petrovic d. J. P. and P. Blondel 3–6, 6–4, 7–5, 6–4. **Norway d. Luxembourg 5–0, Oslo:** N. E. Hessen d. G. Wampach 6–2, 4–6, 3–6, 10–8, 6–3; R. Pape d. G. Wertheim 6–3, 6–2, 6–1; d. Wampach 6–3, 6–4, 6–2; F. Sokol d. Wertheim 6–3, 6–4, 6–1; Pape–Hessen d. Wampach–Wertheim 6–1, 15–13, 6–3. **Holland d. Ceylon 5–0, The Hague:** A. C. van Swol d. D. Scharenguivel 6–3, 6–2, 6–2; d. L. P. Ernst 6–4, 6–0, 6–3; H. Wilton d. Ernst 6–2, 6–2, 5–7, 6–3; d. Scharenguivel 3–6, 1–6, 7–5, 6–1, 7–5; van Swol–Wilton d. Scharenguivel–D. L. Fonseka 6–2, 7–5, 6–3. **Spain d. Israel 5–0, Barcelona:** C. Ferrer d. M. Apel 6–1, 6–1, 6–0; d. A. Weiss 6–3, 6–0, 6–3; J. M. Draper d. Weiss 2–6, 5–7, 6–2, 6–2, 6–3; E. Martinez d. Dubitzky 6–4, 6–1, 9–7; Draper–F. Olozaga d. Apel–Weiss 6–1, 6–3, 8–6.

SECOND ROUND

Philippines d. Finland 5–0, Helsinki: F. H. Ampon d. S. Salo 6–0, 6–2, 6–1; d. P. Forsman 6–2, 6–0, 6–0; R. Deyro d. Forsman 6–3, 6–2, 4–6, 6–0; d. Salo 6–3, 6–2, 3–6, 3–6, 8–6; Ampon–Deyro d. Forsman–Salo 6–3, 6–0, 6–2. **Denmark d. Austria 5–0, Vienna:** K. Nielsen d. H. Redl 6–1, 6–1, 6–2; d. A. Huber 7–5, 6–1, 10–8; T. Ulrich d. Huber 3–6, 7–5, 6–3, 6–4; d. Redl 6–4, 6–3, 2–6, 6–4; Nielsen–Ulrich d. Redl–Huber 6–4, 3–6, 4–6, 6–4, 6–1. **Germany d. South Africa 3–2, Berlin:** E. Koch d. I. C. Vermaak 6–8, 6–3, 6–4, 6–2; lost to W. R. Seymour 4–6, 6–4, 4–6, 4–6; G. von Cramm d. Seymour 6–1, 6–2, 7–5; d. Vermaak 6–1, 6–3, 6–1; H. Hermann–R. Goepfert lost to Seymour–B. M. Woodroffe 6–3, 6–3, 2–6, 4–6, 5–7. **France d. Yugoslavia 4–1, Zagreb:** P. Remy d. J. Pallada 6–2, 6–2, 6–8, 6–4; R. Haillet d. V. Petrovic 6–3, 7–9, 6–4, 6–8, 8–6; d. I. Panajotovic 3–6, 6–2, 6–4, 6–1; R. Abdesselam lost to Petrovic 6–8, 2–6, 1–6; M. Bernard–Remy d.

Petrovic–P. Milojkovic 6–2, 6–4, 9–7. **Belgium d. Hungary 5–0,**
Budapest: P. Washer d. A. Jancso 6–2, 3–6, 6–1, 6–1; d. J. Asboth 4–6,
11–9, 6–3 def.; J. Brichant d. Asboth 6–2, 6–3, 4–6, 10–8; d. Jancso 6–4,
6–2, 6–2; Brichant–Washer d. Z. Katona–D. Vad 6–2, 6–2, 6–4. **Great**
Britain d. Norway 5–0, Oslo: G. L. Paish d. R. Pape 4–6, 6–0, 6–3,
6–2; A. J. Mottram d. S. Lie 6–3, 6–2, 6–1; d. Pape 6–2, 6–3, 5–1 def.; G.
D. Oakley d. N. E. Hessen 6–4, 6–2, 6–0; Paish–Mottram d. Pape–Hessen
7–5, 6–0, 6–3. **Italy d. Holland 5–0, Schleveningen:** G. Merlo d. H.
Wilton 6–3, 6–2, 6–1; d. A. C. van Swol 0–6, 2–6, 7–5, 6–4, 7–5; R. del
Bello d. van Swol 6–4, 1–6, 6–3, 3–6, 6–1; d. A. L. van Meegeren 4–6,
6–1, 6–2, 6–3; M. del Bello–O. Sirola d. van Swol–Wilton 6–2, 7–5,
6–1. **Sweden d. Spain 5–0, Barcelona:** L. Bergelin d. J. M. Draper
6–3, 6–1, 6–4;d. C. Ferrer 6–2, 6–1, 4–6, 6–2; S. Davidson d. Ferrer 6–4,
2–6, 3–6, 6–1, 6–1; d. Martinez 6–4, 10–8, 7–5; T. Johansson–Davidson d.
F. Olozaga–Draper 6–2, 6–0, 6–2.

THIRD ROUND
Denmark d. Philippines 4–1, Copenhagen: K. Nielsen d. F. H.
Ampon 8–6, 6–3, 8–6; d. R. Deyro 6–2, 6–3, 6–4; T. Ulrich d. Deyro
6–3, 6–2, 6–4; lost to Ampon 4–6, 2–6, 3–6; Neilsen–Ulrich d.
Ampon–Deyro 6–3, 6–8, 6–3, 8–6. **France d. Germany 4–1, Paris:**
P. Remy lost to G. von Cramm 4–6, 0–6, 4–6; d. E. Koch 6–2, 6–4, 6–2;
R. Haillet d. Koch 6–1, 6–3, 6–1; d. von Cramm 1–6, 2–6, 6–1, 7–5,
6–4; Remy–J. Ducos de la Haille d. von Cramm–R. Goepfert 2–6, 6–4,
3–6, 6–2, 6–4. **Belgium d. Great Britain 4–1, Brussels:** P. Washer
d. A. J. Mottram 7–5, 6–4, 7–5; d. G. L. Paish 6–2, 6–2, 6–2; J. Brichant
d. Paish 6–4, 4–6, 6–2, 6–1; d. Mottram 7–5, 6–4, 6–0; Washer–Brichant
lost to Mottram–Paish 8–6, 1–6, 2–6, 4–6. **Italy d. Sweden 4–1, Turin:**
F. Gardini d. L. Bergelin 7–9, 1–6, 6–2, 7–5, 6–3; G. Merlo d. S.
Davidson 4–6, 6–3, 6–3, 7–5; d. S. Stockenberg 6–4, 6–0, 6–2; O. Sirola
lost to Davidson 3–6, 6–3, 7–5, 3–6, 4–6; G. Cucelli–M. del Bello d.
Bergelin–Davidson 6–2, 1–6, 6–2, 6–3.

SEMI-FINAL ROUND
Denmark d. France 4–1, Paris: K. Nielsen d. R. Haillet 3–6, 6–2, 6–4,
6–2; d. P. Remy 12–10, 1–6, 0–6, 6–0, 6–4; T. Ulrich lost to Remy 6–2,
1–6, 1–6, 2–6; d. Haillet 6–4, 6–2, 5–7, 6–4; Nielsen–Ulrich d. Remy–J.
Ducos de la Haille 0–6, 6–3, 3–6, 6–3, 8–6. **Belgium d. Italy 3–2,**
Brussels: P. Washer d. F. Gardini 6–4, 14–16, 2–6, 6–4, 6–3; d. G. Merlo
6–2, 6–2, 6–4; J. Brichant lost to Merlo 6–4, 1–6, 6–4, 4–6, 8–10; d.
Gardini 6–2, 7–5, 4–6, 9–7; Washer–Brichant lost to G. Cucelli–M. del
Bello 3–6, 6–2, 5–7, 1–6.

FINAL ROUND

Belgium d. Denmark 3–2, Copenhagen: P. Washer d. T. Ulrich 4–6, 6–4, 7–5, 6–1; lost to K. Nielsen 6–8, 8–6, 2–6, 4–6; J. Brichant lost to Nielsen 1–6, 5–7, 6–3, 6–3, 3–6; d. Ulrich 7–5, 5–7, 6–3, 6–3; Washer–Brichant d. Nielsen–Ulrich 4–6, 3–6, 9–7, 6–1, 6–4.

American Zone

FIRST ROUND

Canada d. Mexico 3–2, Montreal: H. Rochon d. M. Llamas 6–2, 6–3, 6–4; lost to F. Contreras 4–6, 4–6, 5–7; L. Main d. Contreras 9–11, 8–6, 6–3, 8–6; d. Llamas 6–2, 6–3, 6–3; Rochon–R. Bedard lost to Llamas–Contreras 2–6, 4–6, 6–2, 2–6. **USA d. Japan 5–0, Vancouver:** T. Trabert d. K. Kamo 4–6, 1–6, 6–1, 6–2, 6–2; H. Richardson d. A. Miyagi 6–0, 6–3, 8–6; T. Brown–Trabert d. Kamo–Miyagi 6–2, 6–2, 3–6, 6–3; Richardson d. Kamo 0–6, 6–2, 6–1, 6–2; Brown d. M. Kimura 6–2, 6–0, 6–1.

SEMI-FINAL ROUND

Canada d. Cuba 3–2, Montreal: H. Rochon d. R. Garrido 6–2, 6–1, 6–4; L. Main d. O. Garrido 6–2, 5–7, 6–3, 6–2; P. Willey lost to R. Garrido 3–6, 4–6, 6–3, 9–11; R. Bedard lost to O. Garrido 7–9, 6–2, 3–6, 2–6; Main–Willey d. R. and O. Garrido 6–3, 6–4, 6–2. **USA d. West Indies 5–0, Kingston:** G. Mulloy d. I. McDonald 6–1, 6–3, 6–0; B. Bartzen d. R. Cooper 6–1, 6–2, 6–2; R. Perry–Mulloy d. E. Arias–McDonald 6–2, 6–3, 6–3; Bartzen d. McDonald 6–3, 6–1, 6–3; Perry d. Cooper 6–2, 6–2, 6–3.

FINAL ROUND

USA d. Canada 5–0, Montreal: T. Trabert d. H. Rochon 6–2, 6–3, 8–6; V. Seixas d. L. Main 6–1, 6–1, 6–4; Seixas–Trabert d. P. Willey–Main 3–6, 6–2, 6–3, 6–2; S. Clark d. Willey 7–5, 6–2, 6–0; B. Bartzen d. R. Bedard 6–4, 7–5, 1–6, 6–0.

INTER-ZONE FINALS

Belgium d. India 5–0, Perth: P. Washer d. S. C. Misra 6–3, 6–4, 6–3; d. R. Krishnan 6–1, 6–1, 6–1; J. Brichant d. R. Krishnan 3–6, 3–6, 6–4, 6–3, 6–0; d. S. C. Misra 6–4, 4–6, 7–5, 6–4; P. Washer–J. Brichant d. S. C. Misra–R. Krishnan 6–8, 6–3, 7–5, 7–5. **USA d. Belgium 4–1, Brisbane:** T. Trabert d. P. Washer 6–4, 6–2, 6–4; V. Seixas lost to J. Brichant 3–6, 9–11, 6–2, 1–6; W. F. Talbert–Trabert d. Brichant–Washer

6–3, 6–2, 4–6, 9–7; Trabert d. Brichant 6–4, 6–3, 6–1; Seixas d. Washer 6–2, 7–5, 8–6.

CHALLENGE ROUND

Australia d. USA 3–2, Melbourne: L. Hoad d. V. Seixas 6–4, 6–2, 6–3; K. Rosewall lost to T. Trabert 3–6, 4–6, 4–6; Hoad–R. Hartwig lost to Seixas–Trabert 2–6, 4–6, 4–6; Hoad d. Trabert 13–11, 6–3, 2–6, 3–6, 7–5; Rosewall d. Seixas 6–2, 2–6, 6–3, 6–4.

1954: USA
European Zone

FIRST ROUND

Brazil d. Switzerland 3–1, Montreux: R. Falkenburg d. E. Balestra 6–2, 7–5, 6–4; A. Vieira d. P. Blondel 6–1, 6–2, 6–3; d. Balestra 6–2, 6–1, 6–3; Falkenburg–Vieira lost to J. P. and P. Blondel 3–6, 6–8, 6–4, 6–3, 2–6. **Yugoslavia d. Monaco 4–1, Monte Carlo:** V. Petrovic d. G. Pasquier 6–1, 7–5, 7–5; J. Pallada d. A. Noghes 6–4, 6–2, 6–1; I. Panajotovic lost to Pasquier 6–1, 6–3, 5–7, 4–6, 4–6; I. Plecevic d. Noghes 6–2, 6–3, 6–2; Pallada–Petrovic d. Noghes–Pasquier 6–2, 6–2, 9–7. **Spain d. Holland 4–1, The Hague:** E. Martinez d. L. Krijt 6–3, 6–0, 6–3; d. A. E. Dehnert 6–3, 6–3, 3–6, 6–8, 6–3; C. Ferrer d. Dehnert 7–5, 6–1, 6–1; J. M. Draper lost to Krijt 4–6, 6–4, 3–6, 4–6; Ferrer–Draper d. Dehnert–A. L. van Meegeren 6–4, 6–3, 6–4. **Egypt d. Turkey 4–1, Cairo:** A. Shafie d. S. Gurel 6–1, 6–0, 6–2; I. Adel d. N. Bari 5–7, 6–3, 6–0, 6–4; A. Ismail d. Bari 5–7, 6–3, 6–0, 6–4; D. Acobas lost to S. Gurel 5–7, 5–7, 7–5, 6–2, 5–7; Adel–Acobas d. Bari–Gurel 6–1, 6–1, 6–3. **Austria d. Ireland 3–2, Vienna:** F. Saiko d. R. V. Gotto 6–2, 6–1, 6–4; d. G. P. Jackson 7–5, 6–4, 6–2; H. Redl lost to Jackson 6–3, 9–7, 4–6, 6–5, retd.; d. Gotto 3–6, 6–4, 6–4, 6–3; Redl–Saiko lost to Jackson–Gotto 3–6, 1–6, 6–3, 3–6. **Norway d. Finland 3–2, Helsinki:** R. Pape lost to S. Salo 5–7, 8–6, 2–6, 4–6; d. L. H. Krause 6–1, 6–3, 6–2; F. Sohol d. Krause 6–2, 6–4, 6–3; lost to Salo 4–6, 2–6, 3–6; Pape–N. E. Hessen d. Salo–C. Lincoln 7–5, 6–4, 4–6, 6–2. **Hungary d. New Zealand 3–2, Budapest:** J. Asboth d. J. E. Robson 6–3, 4–6, 6–2, 6–0; d. J. A. Barry 6–4, 7–5, 6–2; A. Adam d. Barry 6–0, 3–6, 6–3, 8–6; lost to M. A. Otway 3–6, 2–6, 2–6; Adam–A. Jancso lost to Robson–Otway 1–6, 1–6, 6–2, 2–6.

SECOND ROUND

Great Britain d. Brazil 4–1, Eastbourne: A. J. Mottram d. R. Falkenburg 8–6, 6–4, 6–0; d. A. Vieira 6–3, 6–4, 6–3; G. L. Paish lost to

Vieira 6–8, 7–5, 4–6, 2–6; G. D. Oakley d. Falkenburg 6–1, 5–7, 6–2, 4–6, 6–4; Mottram–Paish d. Falkenburg–Vieira 5–7, 6–1, 6–2, 6–1. **Belgium d. Yugoslavia 5–0, Brussels:** P. Washer d. V. Petrovic 6–3, 6–1, 6–3; d. I. Panajotovic 6–0, 6–4, 6–1; J. Brichant d. Panajotovic 6–1, 6–4, 6–4; d. Petrovic 6–0, 7–5, 6–2; Washer–Brichant d. J. Pallada–Petrovic 6–4, 6–2, 6–2. **Italy d. Spain 5–0, Madrid:** O. Sirola d. E. Martinez 6–2, 4–6, 6–4, 6–4; d. C. Ferrer 6–1, 8–6, 7–5; M. del Bello d. Martinez 6–2, 7–5, 6–3; N. Pietrangeli d. Ferrer 6–4, 6–3, 2–6, 6–2; G. Cucelli–M. del Bello d. Ferrer–J. Bartroli 6–3, 6–3, 5–7, 6–4. **Sweden d. Egypt 5–0, Cairo:** S. Davidson d. I. Adel 6–4, 6–4, 6–4; d. A. Shafie 6–0, 6–0, 6–1; L. Bergelin d. Shafie 6–0, 6–2, 6–1; d. Adel 6–1, 6–3, 6–3; Bergelin–Davidson d. Adel–D. Acobas 6–2, 6–3, 3–6, 6–2. **India d. Austria 3–0, Vienna:** N. Kumar d. H. Redl 4–6, 6–3, 6–4, 7–5; R. Krishnan d. F. Saiko 6–0, 6–2, 7–5; Kumar–N. Nath d. Saiko–Redl 6–3, 6–3, 6–4. **France d. Norway 5–0, Oslo:** R. Haillet d. R. Pape 7–5, 6–2, 4–6, 6–4; d. N. E. Hessen 6–4, 6–3, 6–4; J. C. Molinari d. Hessen 6–3, 3–6, 6–3, 6–2; d. Pape 6–3, 6–3, 5–7, 8–6; J. Ducos de la Haille–P. Remy d. Pape–Hessen 6–4, 6–2, 6–4. **Hungary d. Germany 4–1, Budapest:** J. Asboth d. E. Buchholz 6–2, 3–6, 6–3, 10–8; d. H. Hermann 7–5, 6–3, 6–0; A. Jancso d. Buchholz 6–0, 6–1, 6–4; A. Adam d. E. Koch 3–6, 6–4, 6–2, 6–1; Jancso–I. Sikorski lost to Buchholz–Hermann 2–6, 4–6, 5–7. **Denmark d. Luxembourg 5–0, Luxembourg:** T. Ulrich d. G. Wampach 6–4, 6–4, 6–0; d. G. Wertheim 6–0, 6–2, 6–3; K. Nielsen d. Wertheim 6–2, 6–0, 6–0; d. Wampach 6–3, 6–1, 6–2; Nielsen–Ulrich d. Wertheim–Wampach 6–4, 9–7, 6–0.

THIRD ROUND

Belgium d. Great Britain 3–2, Scarborough: J. Brichant d. A. J. Mottram 4–6, 6–3, 5–7, 6–2, 7–5; lost to G. L. Paish 1–6, 5–7, 3–6; P. Washer d. Paish 6–3, 6–0, 6–4; d. Mottram 7–5, 6–4, 6–4; Washer–Brichant lost to Mottram–Paish 1–6, 5–7, 3–6. **Sweden d. Italy 5–0, Stockholm:** S. Davidson d. M. del Bello 6–1, 6–2, 6–2; d. N. Pietrangeli 6–4, 2–6, 6–4, 6–1; L. Bergelin d. Pietrangeli 7–5, 6–1, 3–6, 6–4; d. O. Sirola 6–2, 6–3, 2–6, 6–1; Davidson–Bergelin d. G. Cucelli–M. del Bello 4–6, 7–5, 2–6, 6–4, 6–3. **France d. India 4–1, Paris:** R. Haillet d. R. Krishnan 6–4, 6–4, 8–6; d. N. Kumar 3–6, 9–11, 6–4, 8–6, 6–0; P. Remy d. Kumar 6–3, 6–4, 6–1; J. C. Molinari lost to Krishnan 4–6, 4–6, 2–6; Remy–J. Ducos de la Haille d. Kumar–N. Nath 6–2, 6–2, 3–6, 7–5. **Denmark d. Hungary 4–1, Copenhagen:** K. Nielsen d. J. Asboth 6–0, 6–4, 6–1; d. A. Adam 4–6, 6–2, 6–3, 6–3; T. Ulrich lost to Adam 6–3, 6–3, 4–6, 1–6, 5–7; d. Asboth 0–6, 7–5, 6–3, 6–2; Nielsen–Ulrich d. A. Jancso–I. Sikorski 5–7, 6–2, 6–1, 6–4.

SEMI-FINAL ROUND
Sweden d. Belgium 3–2, Båstad: S. Davidson d. J. Brichant 6–3, 6–3,
4–6, 6–4; d. P. Washer 7–5, 5–7, 8–6, 6–2; L. Bergelin lost to Washer
4–6, 5–7, 4–6; lost to Brichant 7–5, 8–6, 5–7, 2–6, 8–10; Davidson–T.
Johansson d. Washer–Brichant 6–3, 6–8, 3–6, 9–7, 6–3. **France d.
Denmark 4–1, Copenhagen:** P. Remy d. T. Ulrich 5–7, 1–6, 6–3, 10–8,
6–1; d. K. Nielsen 6–3, 9–7, 6–2; R. Haillet lost to Nielsen 6–1, 7–9, 4–6,
5–7; d. Ulrich 6–3, 2–6, 7–5, 6–3; Remy–Haillet d. Nielsen–Ulrich 6–2,
12–10, 6–3.

FINAL ROUND
Sweden d. France 5–0, Paris: S. Davidson d. P. Remy 6–1, 3–6, 6–3,
6–4; d. R. Haillet 6–4, 6–4, 4–6, 6–3; L. Bergelin d. Haillet 4–6, 7–5,
3–6, 6–3, 6–0; d. Remy 6–2, 6–3, 6–8, 6–4; Davidson–T. Johansson d.
Remy–J. Ducos de la Haille 6–3, 6–4, 3–6, 9–7.

American Zone

FIRST ROUND
Mexico d. Japan 3–2, Mexico City: F. Contreras lost to A. Miyagi
5–7, 1–6, 6–3, 3–6; M. Llamas d. K. Kamo 4–6, 7–5, 7–5, 6–1; d. Miyagi
6–3, 6–2, 8–6; R. Ortega lost to Kamo 5–7, 4–6, 7–5, 4–6; G.
Palafox–Contreras d. Kamo–Miyagi 11–9, 4–6, 4–6, 6–2, 6–4. **Canada
d. Chile 3–2, Toronto:** L. Main d. L. Ayala 4–6, 6–3, 4–6, 8–6, 6–3; d.
A. Hammersley 6–4, 11–13, 3–6, 6–4, 6–3; R. Bedard d. R. Balbiers
6–3, 7–5, 7–5; lost to Ayala 1–6, 3–6, 1–6; Main–P. Willey lost to
Ayala–Hammersley 11–13, 3–6, 0–6. **USA d. West Indies 5–0, Port
of Spain:** H. Richardson d. G. Inglefield 6–2, 6–2, 6–0; S. Clark d. R.
Legall 6–2, 6–0, 6–3; H. Burrows–Clark d. J. Northnagel–Legall 6–0,
6–1, 6–3; Richardson d. D. Phang 6–0, 6–0, 6–2; Burrows d. Inglefield
6–0, 6–0, 6–3.

SEMI-FINAL ROUND
Mexico d. Canada 4–1, Mexico City: M. Llamas d. L. Main 6–3, 6–4,
6–3; d. P. Willey 6–1, 6–1, 6–4; G. Palafox d. R. Bedard 8–6, 6–3, 3–6,
6–0; d. Main 8–6, 3–6, 6–3, 1–6, 6–4; F. Guerrero–F. Contreras lost to
Main–B. Macken 5–7, 7–5, 3–6, 2–6. **USA d. Cuba 5–0, St
Petersburg:** S. Clark d. R. Garrido 6–0, 9–7, 7–5; H. Richardson d. O.
Garrido 6–2, 6–3, 6–1; H. Burrows–Clark d. R. and O. Garrido 6–2,
6–4, 6–3; Burrows d. O. Garrido 6–4, 6–4, 6–4; Richardson d. R. Garrido
6–1, 6–2, 6–2.

FINAL ROUND

USA d. Mexico 4–1, Mexico City: V. Seixas lost to G. Palafox 4–6, 4–6, 5–7; T. Trabert d. M. Llamas 6–4, 6–3, 8–6; Seixas–Trabert d. Palafox–Llamas 6–2, 3–6, 6–1, 6–4; Seixas d. Llamas 6–4, 2–6, 6–3, 6–2; Trabert d. Palafox 14–12, 6–1, 6–2.

INTER-ZONE FINAL

USA d. Sweden 5–0, Brisbane: T. Trabert d. S. Davidson 6–4, 6–3, 6–4; V. Seixas d. L. Bergelin 5–7, 6–2, 6–4, 5–7, 6–2; Seixas–Trabert d. Bergelin–Davidson 6–3, 6–4, 6–3; Trabert d. Bergelin 6–2, 6–2, 3–6, 6–2; Richardson d. Davidson 6–0, 6–3, 6–3.

CHALLENGE ROUND

USA d. Australia 3–2, Sydney: T. Trabert d. L. Hoad 6–4, 2–6, 12–10, 6–3; V. Seixas d. K. Rosewall 8–6, 6–8, 6–4, 6–3; Seixas–Trabert d. Hoad–Rosewall 6–2, 4–6, 6–2, 10–8; Trabert lost to Rosewall 7–9, 5–7, 3–6; Seixas lost to R. Hartwig 6–4, 3–6, 2–6, 3–6.

1955: AUSTRALIA
European Zone

FIRST ROUND

Austria d. Finland 5–0, Vienna: A. Huber d. R. Nyyssonen 8–6, 6–0, 6–1; d. S. Salo 6–4, 6–3, 7–5; F. Saiko d. Salo 6–2, 6–2, 6–2; d. Nyyssonen 6–3, 6–3, 6–1; H. Redl–Saiko d. Salo–L. H. Krause 7–5, 6–1, 6–0. **Egypt d. Turkey 4–1, Istanbul:** A. Ismail d. B. Cevansir 2–6, 6–2, 7–5, 7–5; d. N. Bari 6–4, 4–6, 10–8, 6–4; M. Badr El Din d. Bari 6–1, 3–6, 4–6, 7–5, 16–14; d. E. Balas 6–3, 6–0, 6–0; Ismail–D. Acobas lost to Cevansir–Balas 1–6, 4–6, 4–6. **Germany d. Ireland 4–1, Dusseldorf:** E. Buchholz d. G. P. Jackson 7–9, 7–5, 6–2, 6–0; C. Biederlack d. B. A. Haughton 6–0, 6–0, 7–5; lost to Jackson 3–6, 2–6, 2–6; R. Huber d. Haughton 6–1, 6–2, 6–0; Buchholz–H. Hermann d. Jackson–R. V. Gotto 6–1, 6–2, 6–2. **South Africa d. Norway 4–1, Oslo:** I. C. Vermaak d. N. E. Hessen 6–1, 6–1, 6–2; W. R. Seymour d. G. Sjovall 6–3, 6–3, 6–0; lost to F. Sohol 3–6, 4–6, 6–2, 4–6; G. L. Forbes d. F. D. Jagge 6–2, 6–1, 6–2; A. Segal–Vermaak d. Jagge–Sjovall 6–3, 6–4, 6–1. **Argentina d. Monaco 3–2, Monte Carlo:** A. D. Russell d. G. Pasquier 3–6, 6–3, 6–0, 6–0; lost to Y. Medecin def.; E. Morea d. Medecin 6–1, 6–1, 6–0; lost to G. Pasquier def.; Morea–Russell d. Pasquier–Medecin 6–3, 6–1, 6–2. **Switzerland d. Holland 3–2, Basle:** P. Blondel lost to A. E. Dehnert 5–7, 6–2, 4–6, 4–6; d. A. C. van Swol 0–6, 6–2, 9–7, 3–6,

12–10; M. Froesch d. J. van Dalsum 6–0, 6–1, 6–4; d. Dehnert 6–3, 6–3, 6–0; P. Blondel–Froesch lost to Dehnert–van Dalsum 3–6, 6–0, 6–3, 1–6, 2–6. **Chile d. Yugoslavia 5–0, Karlovac:** L. Ayala d. J. Panajotovic 6–3, 6–1, 6–4; d. V. Petrovic 6–0, 6–4, 6–3; A. Hammersley d. Petrovic 6–3, 3–6, 4–6, 7–5, 6–2; d. L. Jagec 6–3, 6–4, 6–2; Ayala–Hammersley d. Petrovic–Jagec 6–4, 6–4, 6–4. **Czechoslovakia d. Portugal 5–0, Lisbon:** V. Zabrodsky d. D. Cohen 6–0, 6–1, 6–2; d. J. da Silva 6–4, 6–2, 6–0; J. Javorsky d. da Silva 6–0, 6–1, 6–3; d. Cohen 6–2, 6–0, 6–1; Zabrodsky–Javorsky d. da Silva–A. A. Gomes 6–1, 6–0, 6–0.

SECOND ROUND

Great Britain d. Austria 4–1, Vienna: R. Becker lost to A. Huber 4–6, 7–9, 6–0, 4–6; d. F. Saiko 6–2, 6–3, 6–2; A. J. Mottram d. Saiko 10–8, 6–2, 6–4; d. Huber 6–3, 5–7, 2–6, 6–4, 6–4; Mottram–G. L. Paish d. Huber–H. Redl 6–2, 6–2, 6–4. **India d. Egypt 5–0, Cairo:** N. Kumar d. A. Ismail 6–0, 6–3, 4–6, 2–6, 6–1; d. M. Badr El Din 6–1, 1–6, 6–4, 5–7, 6–2; R. Krishnan d. Badr El Din 6–0, 6–2, 6–2; d. A. Shafie 6–1, 9–7, 6–3; Kumar–Krishnan d. D. Acobas–Ismail 6–3, 6–3, 6–4. **Italy d. Germany 5–0, Munich:** F. Gardini d. R. Huber 6–0, 6–3, 6–3; d. C. Biedelack 6–2, 6–0, 6–1; G. Merlo d. Huber 6–2, 6–3, 6–3; d. Biederlack 6–1, 8–6, 6–1; O. Sirola–N. Pietrangeli d. E. Buchholz–H. Hermann 6–1, 6–4, 2–6, 8–6. **Denmark d. South Africa 3–2, Copenhagen:** K. Nielsen d. I. C. Vermaak 4–6, 6–1, 6–2, 1–6, 8–6; d. A. Segal 6–2, 6–3, 9–7; J. Ulrich d. Segal 3–6, 6–3, 6–2, 6–4; lost to G. L. Forbes 6–2, 1–6, 9–11, 3–6; Nielsen–S. Hojberg lost to Segal–Vermaak 11–9, 13–15, 1–6, 5–7. **France d. Argentina 3–2, Paris:** P. Remy d. A. D. Russell 6–4, 6–1, 6–4; lost to E. Morea 7–9, 3–6, 4–6; R. Haillet lost to Morea 2–6, 4–6, 6–8; d. Russell 6–4, 2–6, 6–3, 6–2; Remy–M. Bernard d. Morea–Russell 6–4, 6–3, 6–4. **Sweden d. Switzerland 5–0, Montreux:** S. Davidson d. M. Froesch 6–1, 7–5, 6–0; L. Bergelin d. P. Blondel 6–2, 6–1, 0–6, 6–2; d. Froesch 2–6, 6–4, 6–2, 6–0; U. Schmidt d. P. Blondel 6–2, 6–3, 6–4; Davidson–U. Schmidt d. R. Buser–P. Blondel 6–4, 6–2, 6–1. **Chile d. Hungary 3–2, Budapest:** A. Hammersley d. J. Asboth 6–2, 6–3, 4–6, 10–12, 6–4; lost to A. Adam 6–3, 5–7, 7–5, 5–7, 1–6; L. Ayala d. Adam 6–3, 6–3, 6–3; d. Asboth 3–6, 6–3, 5–7, 6–2, 6–0; Ayala–Hammersley lost to Asboth–Adam 5–7, 5–7, 4–6. **Belgium d. Czechoslovakia 5–0, Prague:** P. Washer d. J. Javorsky 6–0, 6–1, 3–6, 6–4; d. V. Zabrodsky 6–2, 6–1, 3–6, 6–4; J. Brichant d. Zabrodsky 8–6, 6–3, 2–6, 6–4; d. Javorsky 6–2, 11–9, 3–6, 10–8; Washer–Brichant d. Javorsky–Zabrodsky 6–1, 3–6, 6–3, 9–7.

THIRD ROUND

Great Britain d. India 3–2, Manchester: R. Becker d. N. Kumar 6–2, 7–9, 6–2, 6–3; d. R. Krishnan 13–11, 6–3, 6–3; A. J. Mottram lost to Krishnan 4–6, 0–6, 2–6; d. Kumar 2–6, 9–7, 4–6, 7–5, 6–3; Mottram–G. L. Paish lost to Kumar–Krishnan 6–2, 6–1, 3–6, 5–7, 4–6. **Italy d. Denmark 5–0, Copenhagen:** F. Gardini d. K. Nielsen 6–2, 6–3, 6–1; G. Merlo d. T. Ulrich 6–3, 6–4, 3–6, 6–0; d. Nielsen 6–0, 4–6, 6–2, 4–6, 7–5; N. Pietrangeli d. J. Ulrich 6–4, 6–2, 6–3; O. Sirola–Pietrangeli d. Nielsen–Ulrich 16–14, 6–3, 6–1. **Sweden d. France 3–2, Stockholm:** S. Davidson lost to P. Remy 3–6, 6–3, 6–2, 2–6, 1–6; d. R. Haillet 11–9, 6–2, 9–7; L. Bergelin d. Haillet 3–6, 6–2, 6–3, 6–3; d. Remy 1–6, 6–1, 6–2, 6–2; Davidson–U. Schmidt lost to Remy–M. Bernard 4–6, 7–5, 4–6, 6–1, 2–6. **Chile d. Belgium 3–2, Brussels:** L. Ayala d. P. Washer 6–1, 8–6, 6–1; d. J. Brichant 1–6, 6–1, 7–9, 6–1, 7–5; A. Hammersley lost to Brichant 7–5, 4–6, 6–8, 6–8; d. Washer 6–2, 4–6, 6–4, 0–6, 6–4; Ayala–Hammersley lost to Brichant–Washer 4–6, 6–0, 4–6, 6–4, 4–6.

SEMI-FINAL ROUND

Italy d. Great Britain 5–0, Edgbaston: F. Gardini d. W. A. Knight 7–9, 6–2, 6–4, 6–1; N. Pietrangeli d. R. Becker 6–3, 7–9, 6–4, 8–6; d. Knight 3–6, 4–6, 6–4, 6–3, 6–4; O. Sirola d. Becker 10–8, 6–2, 7–5; Sirola–Pietrangeli d. M. G. Davies–R. K. Wilson 4–6, 11–9, 8–6, 6–3. **Sweden d. Chile 3–2, Båstad:** S. Davidson lost to L. Ayala 6–1, 5–7, 5–7, 3–6; d. A. Hammersley 6–1, 6–1, 6–3; L. Bergelin d. Hammersley 5–7, 7–5, 6–2, 6–3; lost to Ayala 4–6, 6–4, 2–6, 1–6; Davidson–T. Johansson d. Ayala–Hammersley 6–0, 6–1, 6–4.

FINAL ROUND

Italy d. Sweden 4–1, Milan: F. Gardini d. S. Davidson 6–4, 0–6, 3–6, 6–1, 6–3; d. S. Stockenberg 6–4, 6–1, 6–4; G. Merlo d. L. Bergelin 6–1, 6–8, 6–8, 8–6, 6–1; O. Sirola lost to Davidson 2–6, 6–8, 4–6; Sirola–N. Pietrangeli d. Davidson–T. Johansson 6–3, 6–4, 2–6, 2–6, 6–1.

Eastern Zone

FIRST ROUND

Philippines d. Burma 5–0, Rangoon: F. H. Ampon d. Ko Ko 6–1, 6–1, 6–0; R. Deyro d. Maung 6–0, 6–0, 6–2; d. Thaung 6–1, 6–2, 6–2; J. M. Jose d. Maung 6–3, 6–4, 6–2; Ampon–Deyro d. Maung–Thaung 6–0, 6–0, 6–0.

FINAL ROUND

Japan d. Philippines 3–2, Tokyo: K. Kamo d. R. Deyro 6–4, 6–8, 6–1, 2–6, 7–5; d. F. H. Ampon 1–6, 6–4, 6–2, 6–0; A. Miyagi d. Ampon 3–6, 6–4, 1–6, 6–0, 6–3; lost to Deyro 2–6, 3–6, 4–6; Kamo–Miyagi lost to Ampon–Deyro 3–6, 3–6, 2–6.

American Zone

FIRST ROUND

Australia d. Mexico 5–0, Chicago: K. R. Rosewall d. G. Palafox 6–3, 7–5, 6–2; d. E. Reyes 6–2, 6–4, 6–3; R. N. Hartwig d. Reyes 6–0, 3–6, 6–3, 6–1; d. Palafox 6–3, 6–3, 6–3; L. A. Hoad–Hartwig d. Palafox–F. Guerrero 6–1, 6–2, 6–4. **Brazil d. Cuba 4–1, Havana:** R. Falkenburg d. R. Garrido 6–2, 6–3, 6–1; R. Moreira d. O. Garrido 6–1, 6–4, 5–7, 8–6; lost to R. Garrido 6–2, 4–6, 3–6, 2–6; J. Aguero d. O. Garrido 3–6, 7–5, 6–4, 6–4; Falkenburg–Moreira d. J. Weiss–O. Garrido 7–9, 6–4, 6–3, 6–1. **West Indies d. Pakistan def.**

SEMI-FINAL ROUND

Australia d. Brazil 4–1, Louisville: K. R. Rosewall d. J. Aguero 7–5, 6–0, 4–6, 6–3; d. R. Falkenburg 6–2, 6–2, 6–3; L. A. Hoad d. Falkenburg 3–6, 8–6, 7–5, 6–1; lost to R. Moreira 4–6, 4–6, 4–6; Hoad–R. N. Hartwig d. Falkenburg–Moreira 6–2, 6–4, 6–1. **Canada d. West Indies 5–0, Montreal:** R. Bedard d. I. A. McDonald 6–2, 3–6, 6–4, 6–2; L. Main d. F. R. Mott–Trille 12–10, 6–3, 2–6, 6–4; d. McDonald 6–2, 4–6, 7–5, 2–6, 6–4; D.Fontana d. P. Philips 6–0, 6–3, 6–3; Bedard–Fontana d. McDonald–Mott–Trille 12–10, 6–3, 2–6, 6–4.

FINAL ROUND

Australia d. Canada 5–0, Montreal: K. R. Rosewall d. R. Bedard 6–0, 6–1, 4–6, 6–2; d. H. Rochon 6–1, 6–2, 6–1; L. A. Hoad d. D. Fontana 9–7, 7–5, 6–1; R. N. Hartwig d. L. Main 6–3, 6–3, 6–3; Hoad–Hartwig d. Bedard–Fontana 6–3, 3–6, 6–3, 6–4;

INTER-ZONE FINALS

Australia d. Japan 4–0, New York: K. Rosewall d. A. Miyagi 6–4, 6–4, 6–1; R. N. Hartwig d. Miyagi 3–6, 6–0, 6–3, 9–7; d. K. Kamo 8–6, 6–8, 6–3, 5–7, 6–3; L. A. Hoad–Hartwig d. Kamo–Miyagi 6–3, 6–3, 6–4. **Australia d. Italy 5–0, Philadelphia:** L. A. Hoad d. F. Gardini 6–3, 6–2, 6–0; d. N. Pietrangeli 9–7, 6–2, 6–3; K. R. Rosewall d. Pietrangeli 8–6, 3–6, 6–1, 6–4; d. O. Sirola 6–4, 4–6, 6–1, 6–4; Hoad–R. N. Hartwig d. Sirola–Pietrangeli 7–5, 13–11, 7–5.

CHALLENGE ROUND

Australia d. USA 5–0, New York: K. Rosewall d. V. Seixas 6–3, 10–8, 4–6, 6–2; L. Hoad d. T. Trabert 4–6, 6–3, 6–3, 8–6; Hoad–R. N. Hartwig d. Seixas–Trabert 12–14, 6–4, 6–3, 3–6, 7–5; Hoad d. Seixas 7–9, 6–1, 6–4, 6–4; Rosewall d. H. Richardson 6–4, 3–6, 6–1, 6–4.

1956: AUSTRALIA
European Zone

FIRST ROUND

Czechoslovakia d. Pakistan 5–0, Prague: J. Javorsky d. K. Saeed 6–1, 6–2, 6–3; d. I. Ahmed 6–3, 4–6, 6–3, 6–2; J. Parma d. Ahmed 4–6, 11–9, 6–3, 2–6, 6–4; d. Saeed 6–2, 6–2, 8–6; Javorsky–V. Zabrodsky d. Ahmed–Saeed 6–3, 10–8, 5–7, 6–2. **Poland d. Austria 3–2, Vienna:** W. Skonecki d. A. Huber 6–2, 6–3, 6–4; d. F. Saiko 6–3, 5–7, 6–2, 6–3; A. Licis lost to Saiko 6–2, 4–6, 4–6, 4–6; d. Huber 2–6, 6–0, 6–4, 6–3; Skonecki–J. Piatek lost to Huber–Saiko 3–6, 3–6, 1–6. **Ireland d. Finland 4–1, Dublin:** J. D. Hackett d. R. Nyyssonen 6–3, 6–3, 6–1; d. S. Salo 6–2, 6–3, 6–1; G. P. Jackson lost to Salo 3–6, 6–3, 6–2, 2–6, 3–6; d. Nyyssonen 6–2, 6–3, 6–3; Hackett–Jackson d. Salo–Nyyssonen 6–3, 12–10, 3–6, 6–3. **Switzerland d. Luxembourg 3–2, Esch-Sur-Alzette:** P. Blondel d. G. Wertheim 6–4, 6–3, 6–4; B. Dupont lost to G. Wampach 4–6, 4–6, 7–5, 6–1, 0–6; d. Wertheim 6–1, 6–1, 6–1; E. Balestra lost to Wampach 4–6, 1–6, 6–4, 2–6; R. Buser–P. Blondel d. Wampach–Wertheim 6–2, 6–1, 6–1. **Spain d. Monaco 3–2, Monte Carlo:** E. Martinez d. R. Borghini 6–4, 7–5, 5–7, 7–5; lost to G. Pasquier 3–6, 8–10, 6–0, 1–6; J. M. Draper d. Borghini 5–7, 6–3, 7–5, 6–1; lost to Pasquier 6–3, 4–6, 6–1, 2–6, 4–6; Martinez–F. Olozaga d. Borghini–Pasquier 8–6, 6–3, 6–0. **Norway d. Israel 4–1, Oslo:** F. Soehol d. A. Avidan 6–1, 6–3, 6–3; d. E. Davidman 7–5, 6–8, 2–6, 6–3, 6–4; G. Sjowall d. Davidman 6–1, 6–2, 6–3; d. Avidan 6–2, 6–0, 6–1; Sjowall–Soehol lost to Avidan–Davidman 4–6, 6–2, 3–6, 6–8. **Yugoslavia d. Egypt 4–1, Belgrade:** I. Plecevic d. M. Badr El Din 2–6, 6–1, 6–1, 2–6, 6–3; lost to A. Ismail 6–1, 6–1, 4–6, 6–8, 2–6; J. Pallada d. Ismail 6–2, 6–4, 6–4; I. Panajotovic d. Badr El Din 6–2, 6–1, 6–2; Panajotovic–Plecevic d. Ismail–D. Acobas 6–2, 6–3, 4–6, 6–3. **Holland d. Turkey 5–0, Ankara:** A. E. Dehnert d. N. Bari 11–9, 2–6, 7–5, 6–4; d. S. Fenmen 9–7, 6–1, 8–6; J. van Dalsum d. Fenmen 6–3, 6–2, 6–3; d. Bari 0–6, 6–3, 6–4, 8–6; Dehnert–van Dalsum d. Bari–Fenmen 7–5, 6–2, 6–3.

SECOND ROUND

Denmark d. Czechoslovakia 4–1, Prague: K. Nielsen d. J. Parma 8–6, 6–2, 8–6; lost to J. Javorsky 5–7, 6–2, 7–5, 4–6, 5–7; T. Ulrich d. Javorsky 6–4, 6–3, 7–5; d. Parma 3–6, 6–3, 8–6, 6–4; Nielsen–Ulrich d. Javorsky–V. Zabrodsky 8–6, 6–4, 5–7, 7–5.   **Italy d. Poland 5–0, Warsaw:** G. Merlo d. W. Skonecki 6–0, 6–2, 6–3; d. A. Licis 6–3, 6–3, 7–5; N. Pietrangeli d. Licis 6–4, 6–4, 7–5; d. Skonecki 6–2, 6–2, 6–1; Pietrangeli–O. Sirola d. J. Piatek–J. Radzio 6–0, 6–2, 6–3.   **Germany d. Ireland 4–1, Dublin:** R. Huber d. G. P. Jackson 8–6, 6–4, 9–7; d. J. D. Hackett 6–4, 3–6, 6–3, 6–4; F. Feldbausch d. Hackett 6–0, 5–7, 6–3, 3–6, 6–1; d. Jackson 6–0, 6–4, 3–6, 4–6, 6–1; Feldbausch–P. Scholl lost to Jackson–Hackett 2–6, 4–6, 4–6.   **France d. Switzerland 5–0, Lausanne:** R. Haillet d. P. Blondel 6–2, 6–4, 6–1; d. M. Froesch 8–6, 6–3, 6–4; P. Darmon d. Froesch 11–9, 1–6, 6–2, 6–8, 6–2; d. P. Blondel 6–1, 6–1, 6–2; P. Remy–M. Bernard d. P. Blondel–R. Buser 6–1, 6–3, 6–3. **Belgium d. Spain 4–1, Barcelona:** J. Brichant d. J. M. Couder 6–3, 7–5, 6–1; d. E. Martinez 6–2, 6–2, 8–6; G. Mezzi d. Martinez 6–4, 6–2, 6–4; lost to Couder 6–8, 6–2, 3–6, 4–6; Brichant–Mezzi d. Couder–F. Olozaga 6–2, 6–1, 6–4.   **Sweden d. Norway 5–0, Oslo:** S. Davidson d. G. Sjowall 9–7, 4–6, 6–2, 6–3; U. Schmidt d. N. E. Hessen 6–1, 6–1, 6–3; d. Sjowall 2–6, 6–3, 6–0, 6–2; B. Axelsson d. Hessen 6–3, 6–3, 6–2; Davidson–T. Johansson d. Sjowall–Hessen 6–2, 6–3, 7–5.   **Great Britain d. Yugoslavia 5–0, Belgrade:** R. Becker d. J. Pallada 6–4, 6–0, 6–2; d. I. Panajotovic 6–1, 6–3, 6–0; W. A. Knight d. Panajotovic 6–4, 6–4, 6–2; M. G. Davies d. Plecevic 6–1, 6–3, 6–1; Knight–Davies d. Panajotovic–Plecevic 6–2, 8–6, 6–2.   **Chile d. Holland 5–0, The Hague:** L. Ayala d. A. E. Dehnert 6–3, 6–1, 6–0; d. J. van Dalsum 7–5, 6–4, 6–4; A. Hammersley d. van Dalsum 8–6, 6–4, 6–2; d. Dehnert 6–1, 6–2, 6–2; Ayala–Hammersley d. Dehnert–van Dalsum 6–1, 6–8, 6–3, 6–2.

THIRD ROUND

Italy d. Denmark 4–1, Bologna: G. Merlo d. T. Ulrich 6–0, 6–4, 6–2; lost to K. Nielsen 7–9, 6–1, 3–6, 4–6; N. Pietrangeli d. Nielsen 8–6, 6–4, 4–6, 2–6, 6–4; d. Ulrich 4–6, 6–2, 6–1, 6–0; Pietrangeli–O. Sirola d. Nielsen–T. Ulrich 6–4, 6–2, 3–6, 6–3.   **France d. Germany 4–1, Duisburg:** P. Remy d. R. Huber 6–4, 6–2, 3–6, 6–3; R. Haillet d. P. Scholl 8–6, 6–1, 7–5; d. F. Feldbausch 6–2, 6–3, 6–2; P. Darmon lost to Scholl 2–6, 0–6, 4–6; M. Bernard–Remy d. Feldbausch–Scholl 6–3, 6–2, 6–2.   **Sweden d. Belgium 4–1, Brussels:** S. Davidson d. J. Brichant 6–3, 2–6, 7–9, 6–1, 6–3; d. G. Mezzi 6–3, 6–1, 6–1; T. Johansson d. Mezzi 2–6, 6–4, 6–0, 6–4; U. Schmidt lost to Brichant 0–6, 2–6, 3–6;

Davidson–Johansson d. Brichant–Mezzi 6–3, 5–7, 6–4, 2–6, 6–4. **Great Britain d. Chile 3–2, Bristol:** R. Becker lost to L. Ayala 6–3, 4–6, 3–6, 6–3, 3–6; d. A. Hammersley 6–4, 6–1, 6–1; W. A. Knight d. Hammersley 6–3, 6–3, 6–4; lost to Ayala 6–1, 3–6, 3–6, 0–6; Becker–J. E. Barrett d. Ayala–Hammersley 6–1, 6–4, 9–7.

SEMI-FINAL ROUND

Italy d. France 3–2, Paris: G. Merlo lost to P. Remy 5–7, 8–6, 2–6, 2–6; d. P. Darmon 6–3, 4–6, 9–7, 6–4; N. Pietrangeli lost to Darmon 6–3, 3–6, 3–6, 6–2, 3–6; d. Remy 6–3, 8–6, 6–2; Pietrangeli–O. Sirola d. Remy–M. Bernard 6–2, 6–2, 2–6, 6–1. **Sweden d. Great Britain 4–1, Stockholm:** S. Davidson d. W. A. Knight 6–1, 6–3, 10–8; lost to M. G. Davies 4–6, 1–6, 1–6; U. Schmidt d. R. Becker 3–6, 1–6, 6–2, 6–1, 6–2; d. Knight 6–0, 6–8, 4–6, 6–3, 6–4; Davidson–T. Johansson d. Becker–Davies 6–3, 8–6, 7–5.

FINAL ROUND

Italy d. Sweden 5–0, Båstad: N. Pietrangeli d. S. Davidson 6–4, 3–6, 6–1, 6–4; d. U. Schmidt 7–5, 6–3, 1–6, 6–3; G. Merlo d. Schmidt 5–7, 6–2, 7–5, 6–1; O. Sirola d. T. Johansson 6–4, 1–6, 6–2, 6–1; Pietrangeli–Sirola d. Davidson–Johansson 6–4, 5–7, 6–2, 6–3.

Eastern Zone

FIRST ROUND

India d. Ceylon 5–0, Colombo: N. Kumar d. R. Ferdinands 6–2, 6–4, 6–2; d. B. L. Pinto 6–4, 7–9, 6–1, 6–0; R. Krishnan d. P. Ernst 6–0, 6–1, 6–2; d. F. J. de Saram 6–1, 6–1, 6–2; Kumar–Krishnan d. Ferdinands–Pinto 7–5, 6–2, 6–2.

FINAL ROUND

India d. Japan 3–2, Tokyo: R. Krishnan d. A. Miyagi 6–3, 6–0, 6–3; d. K. Kamo 6–8, 6–3, 6–4, 7–5; N. Kumar lost to Kamo 2–6, 6–4, 6–2, 4–6, 0–6; lost to Miyagi 4–6, 1–6, 1–6; Kumar–Krishnan d. Miyagi–Kamo 6–4, 6–3, 6–1.

American Zone

FIRST ROUND

Canada d. West Indies 5–0, Port of Spain: R. Bedard d. P. Phillips 6–1, 6–1, 6–4; d. I. A. McDonald 6–0, 6–1, 6–0; D. Fontana d. McDonald 7–5, 6–1, 4–6, 6–3; H. Rochon d. Phillips 6–3, 6–2, 6–4; Bedard–Fontana d. Legall–Waddell 6–0, 6–1, 6–4.

SECOND ROUND

USA d. Canada 4–1, Victoria: H. Richardson d. D. Fontana 6–1, 6–2, 6–2; H. Flam d. R. Bedard 2–6, 6–2, 6–1, 11–9; B. MacKay–R. Holmberg d. Bedard–Fontana 6–3, 3–6, 10–12, 6–4, 6–3; Richardson d. Bedard 6–4, 6–4, 13–11; MacKay lost to P. Willey 16–14, 4–6, 3–6, 6–8. **Mexico d. Brazil 4–1, Mexico City:** M. Llamas d. Aguero 3–6, 6–2, 6–1, 6–1; G. Palafox d. A. Vieira 3–6, 1–6, 7–5, 6–1, 6–4; lost to Aguero 6–4, 5–7, 4–6, 3–6; A. Palafox d. P. Bueno 6–3, 9–7, 6–1; Llamas–G. Palafox d. Vieira–E. Saller 6–3, 6–3, 9–7.

FINAL ROUND

USA d. Mexico 4–1, New York: V. Seixas d. M. Llamas 6–4, 6–2, 6–4; H. Richardson d. P. Contreras 6–3, 6–4, 6–4; B. MacKay–S. Giammalva lost to Llamas–Contreras 13–11, 4–6, 6–1, 6–8, 3–6; Richardson d. Llamas 6–3, 6–3, 6–1; Giammalva d. E. Reyes 6–4, 6–1, 6–3.

INTER-ZONE FINALS

USA d. Italy 4–1, New York: H. Richardson d. N. Pietrangeli 6–3, 6–2, 6–3; V. Seixas d. O. Sirola 6–3, 11–9, 6–4; Richardson–Seixas d. Pietrangeli–Sirola 1–6, 6–3, 6–4, 6–2; M. Green lost to Pietrangeli 6–3, 4–6, 3–6, 4–6; S. Giammalva d. Sirola 12–10, 6–3, 6–2. **USA d. India 4–1, Perth:** H. Flam d. R. Krishnan 7–5, 4–6, 10–8, 2–6, 6–4; V. Seixas d. N. Kumar 6–4, 6–1, 6–2; S. Giammalva–Seixas d. Kumar–Krishnan 6–2, 3–6, 6–4, 6–4; M. Green lost to Krishnan 5–7, 4–6, 4–6; Giammalva d. Kumar 6–3, 6–4, 6–2.

CHALLENGE ROUND

Australia d. USA 5–0, Adelaide: L. Hoad d. H. Flam 6–2, 6–3, 6–3; K. Rosewall d. V. Seixas 6–1, 6–4, 4–6, 6–1; Hoad–Rosewall d. S. Giammalva–Seixas 1–6, 6–1, 7–5, 6–4; Rosewall d. Giammalva 4–6, 6–1, 8–6, 7–5; Hoad d. Seixas 6–2, 7–5, 6–3.

1957: AUSTRALIA
European Zone

FIRST ROUND

Mexico d. Yugoslavia 5–0, Belgrade: M. Llamas d. I. Panajotovic 6–2, 6–4, 6–4; d. I. Plecevic 6–3, 6–4, 6–3; F. Contreras d. Plecevic 7–5, 6–2, 6–2; G. Palafox d. Panajotovic 6–1, 6–4, 7–5; Llamas–Contreras d. S. Nikolia–A. Popovic 6–0, 6–3, 6–3. **Hungary d. Ireland def.; New Zealand d. Lebanon 5–0, Beirut:** J. E. Robson d. N. Hajjar 6–0, 6–0, 6–1; d. S. Khoury 6–3, 6–2, 6–2; C. T. Parker d. Khoury 4–6, 12–10, 6–1, 6–2; L. Gerrard d. R. Karaoglan 6–1, 6–0, 6–2; Robson–Parker d. E. Attieh–Khoury 4–6, 11–9, 6–3, 6–3. **Czechoslovakia d. Switzerland 4–1, Lugano:** J. Javorsky d. P. Blondel 6–0, 6–4, 6–4; d. M. Froesch 6–1, 6–4, 6–1; J. Parma lost to Froesch 2–6, 4–6, 8–6, 6–4, 1–6; d. P. Blondel 6–2, 4–6, 6–0, 6–4; Javorsky–J. Krajcik d. R. Buser–P. Blondel 6–4, 6–2, 6–3. **South Africa d. Spain 4–0, Barcelona:** G. L. Forbes d. J. M. Couder 7–5, 4–6, 7–5, 4–6, 6–3; T. T. Fancutt d. E. Martinez 6–3, 3–6, 6–2, 11–9; d. J. M. Couder 6–2, 10–12, 0–6, 6–4, 6–3; Forbes–A. Segal d. Couder–F. Olozaga 6–4, 4–6, 6–3, 1–6, 6–3. **Austria d. Rumania 5–0, Bucharest:** F. Saiko d. C. Zacopceanu 6–1, 6–3, 6–1; d. G. Viziru 5–7, 2–6, 8–6, 6–2, 6–3; A. Huber d. Viziru, 6–1, 6–4, 12–10. **Poland d. Luxembourg 5–0, Mondorf–les–Bains:** W. Skonecki d. L. Wagner 6–2, 6–1, 6–1; d. G. Wertheim 6–0, 6–4, 6–3; A. Licis d. Wertheim 6–0, 6–0, 6–0; d. Wagner 3–6, 6–1, 6–1, 8–6; Skonecki–J. Piatek d. G. Wampach–Wertheim 6–2, 6–4, 6–4. **Holland d. Norway 4–1, The Hague:** J. van Dalsum d. F. Sjowall 6–2, 4–6, 6–2, 4–6, 6–3; A. E. Dehnert d. F. Sohol 1–6, 6–2, 3–6, 7–5, 6–1; d. F. D. Jagge 6–3, 6–2, 6–0; J. H. Goris lost to Jagge 3–6, 4–6, 4–6; Dehnert–van Dalsum d. Sjowall–Jagge 10–8, 6–2, 7–5.

SECOND ROUND

Mexico d. Germany 3–1, Cologne: M. Llamas d. R. Huber 6–3, 7–5, 4–6, 6–4; F. Contreras d. P. Scholl 6–4, 6–1, 6–2; A. Palafox lost to R. Huber 2–6, 8–10, 1–6; Llamas–Contreras d. E. Buchholz–H. Hermann 8–6, 6–3, 4–6, 6–4. **Belgium d. Hungary 4–1, Brussels:** J. Brichant d. A. Stolpa 6–3, 6–2, 6–2; d. J. Asboth 4–6, 6–2, 6–1, 6–2; P. Washer d. Asboth 8–6, 6–1, 6–4; d. Stolpa 6–1, 4–6, 7–5, 2–6, 6–2; Brichant–G. Mezzi lost to Asboth–Stolpa 6–0, 6–3, 4–6, 4–6, 3–6. **Great Britain d. New Zealand 5–0, Eastbourne:** M. G. Davies d. J. E. Robson 6–8, 6–3, 6–2, 6–4; d. C. T. Parker 6–1, 6–2, 6–4; R. K. Wilson d. L. A. Gerrard 6–2, 11–9, 6–2; d. Robson 4–6, 8–6, 6–1, 6–2; Davies–Wilson d. Robson–Gerrard 6–3, 9–7, 6–2. **France d. Czechoslovakia 4–0,**

Lyons: P. Darmon d. K. Krajcik 6–0, 6–1, 6–2; v. J. Javorsky, unfin.; R. Haillet d. Javorsky 6–8, 7–5, 8–6, 6–4; d. Krajcik 6–4, 6–2, 4–3, def.; P. Remy–J. C. Molinari d. Javorsky–Krajcik 9–7, 6–3, 6–3. **Denmark d. South Africa 4–1, Copenhagen:** K. Nielsen d. T. T. Fancutt 2–6, 6–8, 6–4, 7–5, 6–4; d. G. L. Forbes 6–4, 6–2, 1–6, 6–4; T. Ulrich d. Forbes 3–6, 6–3, 6–4, 6–2; d. Fancutt 2–6, 5–7, 6–4, 6–3, 6–3; Nielsen–Ulrich lost to Forbes–A. Segal 11–9, 1–6, 6–3, 6–8, 1–6. **Sweden d. Austria 4–1, Vienna:** S. Davidson d. A. Huber 6–2, 6–0, 6–2; U. Schmidt d. F. Saiko 3–6, 3–6, 6–2, 6–1, 6–2; lost to Huber 7–5, 6–4, 2–6, 2–6, 2–6; J. Lundquist d. F. Hainka 6–2, 6–4, 9–7; Davidson–Schmidt d. Huber–Saiko 6–3, 6–2, 3–6, 6–3. **Poland d. Chile 3–2, Warsaw:** A. Licis d. A. Hammersley 4–6, 6–3, 6–2, 6–4; lost to L. Ayala 2–6, 2–6, 0–6; W. Skonecki d. Ayala 3–6, 9–7, 6–4, 8–6; d. Hammersley 3–6, 7–5, 6–1, 6–3; J. Piatek–J. Radzio lost to Ayala–Hammersley 2–6, 4–6, 3–6. **Italy d. Holland 5–0, The Hague:** G. Merlo d. A. E. Dehnert 6–2, 6–1, 6–1; d. J. van Dalsum 6–8, 6–2, 10–8, 6–3; N. Pietrangeli d. van Dalsum 6–1, 6–1, 6–1; O. Sirola d. Dehnert 6–4, 6–4, 9–7; Sirola–Pietrangeli d. Dehnert–van Dalsum 6–8, 6–2, 10–8, 6–3.

THIRD ROUND

Belgium d. Mexico 3–2, Brussels: J. Brichant d. M. Llamas 1–6, 6–4, 4–6, 6–4, 6–1; d. F. Contreras 8–6, 6–1, 6–3; P. Washer lost to Contreras 7–5, 3–6, 6–4, 4–6, 3–6; d. Llamas 6–4, 6–1, 6–3; Brichant–Washer lost to Llamas–Contreras 4–6, 4–6, 1–6. **Great Britain d. France 3–2, Paris:** M. G. Davies d. P. Darmon 9–7, 6–2, 5–7, 6–4; d. R. Haillet 6–8, 5–7, 6–4, 6–1, 6–4; R. K. Wilson d. Haillet 6–4, 6–3, 6–2; lost to Darmon 6–1, 4–6, 1–6, 6–3, 5–7; Davies–Wilson lost to P. Remy–J. C. Molinari 6–3, 3–6, 1–6, 3–6. **Sweden d. Denmark 4–1, Stockholm:** S. Davidson d. T. Ulrich 6–2, 6–2, 6–2; lost to K. Nielsen 6–3, 4–6, 6–4, 3–6, 0–6; U. Schmidt d. Nielsen 4–6, 8–6, 1–6, 8–6, 9–7; J. Lundquist d. Ulrich 7–5, 6–1, 4–6, 6–4; Davidson–Schmidt d. Nielsen–Ulrich 6–4, 6–3, 6–4. **Italy d. Poland 4–1, Palermo:** G. Merlo d. A. Licis 6–1, 6–4, 6–0; N. Pietrangeli d. W. Skonecki 7–5, 4–6, 7–5, 6–1; A. Maggi d. Skonecki 6–4, 6–0, 6–4; O. Sirola lost to Licis 4–6, 7–9, 0–6; Pietrangeli–Sirola d. Skonecki–J. Piatek 6–2, 9–7, 6–2.

SEMI-FINAL ROUND

Belgium d. Great Britain 3–2, Brussels: P. Washer lost to M. G. Davies 7–5, 3–6, 6–8, 4–6; d. R. K. Wilson 3–6, 6–4, 6–4, 6–0; J. Brichant d. Wilson 6–0, 7–5, 6–4; d. Davies 1–6, 4–6, 6–3, 6–4, 6–2; Brichant–Washer lost to Davies–Wilson 3–6, 4–6, 6–3, 3–6. **Italy d.**

Sweden 4–1, Milan: G. Merlo d. U. Schmidt 6–0, 6–0, 6–3; d. S. Davidson def.; N. Pietrangeli lost to Davidson 6–4, 0–6, 1–6, 1–6; d. Schmidt 7–9, 8–6, 6–2, 6–2; Pietrangeli–O. Sirola d. Davidson–Schmidt 6–4, 6–4, 6–4.

FINAL ROUND

Belgium d. Italy 3–2, Brussels: J. Brichant lost to N. Pietrangeli 4–6, 4–6, 3–6; d. G. Merlo 6–8, 7–5, 6–8, 7–5, 6–1; P. Washer d. Merlo 6–2, 8–6, 6–2; d. Pietrangeli 6–4, 3–6, 6–8, 7–5, 6–2; Brichant–Washer lost to Pietrangeli–O. Sirola 3–6, 2–6, 5–7.

Eastern Zone

FIRST ROUND

India d. Malaya 5–0, Madras: N. Kumar d. Moss 6–4, 7–5, 7–5; d. O. C. Bee 6–1, 7–5, 6–2; R. Krishnan d. Bee 6–2, 6–4, 6–1; d. Moss 6–2, 6–2, 6–4; Krishnan–Kumar d. Bee–K. K. Soon 6–4, 6–3, 6–1.

SEMI-FINAL ROUND

Philippines d. India 3–2, Manila: F. Ampon d. N. Kumar 6–2, 6–1, 6–4; R. Deyro d. R. Krishnan 4–6, 6–2, 2–6, 6–4, 6–3; d. Kumar 6–3, 6–2, 2–6, 6–4; J. Jose lost to Krishnan 2–6, 4–6, 2–6; Ampon–Deyro lost to Krishnan–Kumar 5–7, 1–6, 6–2, 4–6. **Japan d. Ceylon 5–0, Tokyo:** K. Kamo d. R. Ferdinands 6–2, 6–3, 6–2; d. B. Pinto 6–4, 6–1, 6–2; A. Miyagi d. Pinto 6–1, 6–0, 6–2; Okadome d. Ferdinands 6–3, 5–7, 4–6, 6–3, 6–3; Kamo–Miyagi d. Ferdinands–Pinto 6–0, 6–2, 7–5.

FINAL ROUND

Philippines d. Japan 3–2, Manila: F. Ampon d. A. Miyagi 3–6, 6–4, 6–1, 6–4; d. K. Kamo 6–1, 4–6, 5–7, 6–3, 6–1; R. Deyro d. Kamo 6–2, 4–6, 6–1, 2–6, 6–3; E. Dungo lost to Miyagi 6–4, 1–6, 1–6, 4–6; Ampon–Deyro lost to Kamo–Miyagi 4–6, 6–4, 5–7, 2–6.

American Zone

FIRST ROUND

USA d. West Indies 5–0, Port of Spain: V. Seixas d. P. Phillips 6–0, 6–2, 6–0; B. Bartzen d. I. A. McDonald 6–1, 6–0, 6–1; G. Golden–Seixas d. Phillips–McDonald 6–4, 6–0, 6–0; Bartzen d. P. Valdez 6–1, 6–1, 6–1; Golden d. McDonald 8–6, 6–4, 4–6, 6–2. **Venezuela d. Cuba 3–2,**

Caracas: R. Lopez lost to R. Garrido 5–7, 6–8, 4–6; I. Pimentel d. O. Garrido 4–6, 6–2, 6–4, 6–1; d. R. Garrido 6–0, 6–3, 6–2; W. Ploch lost to O. Garrido 2–6, 2–6, 3–6; R. Lopez–I. Pimentel d. R. Karman–R. Garrido 7–5, 9–7, 6–2. **Brazil d. Canada 3–2, Montreal:** C. Fernandes d. R. Bedard 9–7, 6–8, 6–3, 3–6, 7–5; d. D. A. Fontana 6–2, 6–3, 10–8; A. Vieira lost to Fontana 6–4, 2–6, 3–6, 6–3, 3–6; A. Aguero lost to P. Willey 3–6, 3–6, 6–4, 3–6; Fernandes–Vieira d. Fontana–Willey 8–6, 6–2, 7–9, 6–4.

SECOND ROUND

USA d. Venezuela 4–1, Caracas: G. Golden lost to I. Pimentel 8–6, 4–6, 3–6, 3–6; V. Seixas d. R. Lopez 6–1, 6–0, 6–4; B. Bartzen–Seixas d. Lopez–Pimentel 6–4, 6–3, 6–3; Seixas d. Pimentel 6–4, 6–4, 6–2; Bartzen d. Lopez 6–3, 6–3, 6–2. **Brazil d. Israel 5–0, Montreal:** A. Vieira d. A. Avidan 6–1, 6–3, 12–10; d. E. Davidman 4–6, 6–4, 6–3, 6–2; C. Fernandes d. Davidman 6–4, 6–4, 6–2; d. Avidan 7–5, 6–3, 9–7; Vieira–Fernandes d. Avidan–Davidman 1–6, 4–6, 6–4, 6–2, 23–21.

FINAL ROUND

USA d. Brazil 5–0, Boston: S. Giammalva d. A. Vieira 4–6, 7–5, 6–4, 4–6, 6–4; V. Seixas d. C. Fernandes 6–3, 6–3, 6–2; B. MacKay–Seixas d. Vieira–Fernandes 7–5, 9–7, 11–13, 7–5; M. Green d. J. Aguero 8–6, 5–7, 6–3, 4–6, 6–3; MacKay d. Fernandes 7–5, 6–3, 6–0.

INTER-ZONE FINALS

USA d. Philippines 5–0, Adelaide: V. Seixas d. F. Ampon 6–1, 6–1, 6–2; H. Flam d. R. Deyro 6–3, 6–2, 6–2; G. Mulloy–Seixas d. Ampon–Deyro 6–1, 6–3, 6–2; Flam d. Ampon 6–3, 6–2, 6–4; Seixas d. Deyro 6–2, 6–4, 6–3. **USA d. Belgium 3–2, Brisbane:** H. Flam d. J. Brichant 6–3, 4–6, 1–6, 6–3, 6–3; V. Seixas d. P. Washer 6–0, 6–3, 6–4; G. Mulloy–Seixas lost to Brichant–Washer 5–7, 3–6, 6–4, 3–6; Flam lost to Washer 2–6, 3–6, 6–0, 3–6; Seixas d. Brichant 10–8, 6–0, 6–1.

CHALLENGE ROUND

Australia d. USA 3–2, Melbourne: M. J. Anderson d. B. MacKay 6–3, 7–5, 3–6, 7–9, 6–3; A. J. Cooper d. V. Seixas 3–6, 7–5, 6–1, 1–6, 6–3; Anderson–M. G. Rose d. MacKay–Seixas 6–4, 6–4, 8–6; Anderson lost to Seixas 3–6, 6–4, 3–6, 6–0, 11–13; Cooper lost to MacKay 4–6, 6–1, 6–4, 4–6, 3–6.

1958: USA
European Zone

FIRST ROUND

Finland d. Luxembourg 5–0, Mondorf-les-Bains: R. Nyyssonen d.
Baden 6–3, 5–7, 6–2, 3–6, 7–5; S. Salo d. G. Wampach 6–2, 6–2, 8–6;
Salo d. Baden 6–2, 6–2, 2–6, 6–2; Nyyssonen d. Wampach 4–6, 6–1, 6–3,
6–2; Salo–Nyyssonen d. Baden–Wampach 6–1, 5–7, 4–6, 6–4, 6–4.
Switzerland d. Austria 3–2, Berne: E. Balestra d. F. Hainka 6–4, 6–1,
7–5; lost to F. Saiko 7–5, 5–7, 1–6, 0–6; M. Froesch lost to Saiko 3–6,
6–4, 5–7, 4–6; d. Hainka 6–0, 6–4, 6–1; Froesch–P. Blondel d. Hainka–P.
Broeck 6–3, 4–6, 6–4, 10–8. **India d. Monaco 5–0, Monte Carlo:** R.
Krishnan d. G. Pasquier 6–0, 6–1, 6–0; d. R. Borghini 5–7, 6–3, 6–2,
6–0; N. Kumar d. Borghini 6–8, 6–2, 6–3, 6–4; Ali Akta d. Pasquier
6–3, 6–3, 6–4; Krishnan–Kumar d. Borghini–Pasquier 6–0, 6–1, 6–3.
Czechoslovakia d. Yugoslavia 5–0, Zagreb: J. Javorsky d. I. Plecevic
6–4, 6–4, 6–4; d. K. Keretic 6–2, 8–6, 1–6, 6–2; P. Benda d. Keretic
6–3, 4–6, 1–6, 6–3, 6–4; d. Plecevic 3–6, 5–7, 6–1, 6–1, 7–5; Javorsky–M.
Necas d. Plecevic–I. Panajotovic 4–6, 6–4, 6–3, 6–1. **Brazil d. Hungary
3–2, Budapest:** C. Fernandez d. A. Adam 6–2, 7–5, 6–4; d. I. Gulyas
6–2, 6–3, 6–2; I. Ribeiro lost to Gulyas 3–6, 3–6, 7–5, 5–7; lost to Adam
7–5, 8–6, 4–6, 4–6, 4–6; Fernandez–R. Barnes d. Gulyas–Adam 6–4, 2–6,
3–6, 6–2, 6–4. **Germany d. Holland 4–0, Munich:** W. Bungert d. H.
van Dalsum 7–5, 6–4, 6–2; d. P. van Eysden 6–3, 9–7, 6–8, 6–8, 7–5; R.
Huber d. van Eysden 6–1, 7–5, 6–1; Bungert–Huber d. H. van de
Weg–W. Maris 6–2, 6–4, 6–4. **Chile d. Turkey 4–1, Istanbul:** L. Ayala
d. S. Gurel 6–1, 6–1, 6–2; P. Rodriguez d. N. Bari 6–2, 10–8, 6–1; d.
Gurel 6–2, 6–1, 6–2; A. Chondo lost to Bari 6–3, 6–3, 3–6, 0–6;
Ayala–Rodriguez d. Bari–E. Balash 6–2, 6–3, 6–0. **Spain d. Egypt
4–1, Cairo:** A. Gimeno d. Badr El Din 6–4, 6–3, 6–3; d. N. Hassan 3–6,
6–1, 6–0, 6–1; M. Santana lost to El Din 1–6, 6–2, 6–2, 6–8, 4–6; d. A.
Ismali 7–5, 6–1, 1–6, 6–4; Gimeno–J. M. Couder d. El Din–Ismali 6–3,
6–3, 6–1.

SECOND ROUND

Mexico d. Finland 5–0, Helsinki: M. Llamas d. S. Salo 6–3, 4–6, 6–3,
9–7; F. Contreras d. H. Hedman 6–3, 6–0, 6–2; R. Osuna d. Salo 9–11,
10–12, 10–8, 6–3, 6–4; A. Palafox d. Hedman 7–5, 6–3, 7–5;
Palafox–Osuna d. Salo–M. Kinnunen 6–2, 6–1, 6–2. **Poland d.
Switzerland 4–1, Lausanne:** W. Skonecki d. M. Froesch 6–4, 7–5, 6–4;
d. E. Balestra 5–7, 3–6, 6–4, 6–3, 6–2; A. Licis d. Balestra 6–2, 6–1,
6–0; d. Froesch 6–3, 6–1, 6–4; J. Piatek–J. Radzio lost to P.

Blondel–Froesch 2–6, 4–6, 5–7. **Italy d. India 3–2, Florence:** N. Pietrangeli d. N. Kumar 8–6, 8–6, 10–8; O. Sirola d. R. Krishnan 2–6, 7–5, 6–3, 6–3; lost to Kumar 7–5, 5–7, 6–3, 4–6, 4–6; A. Maggi lost to Krishnan 0–6, 6–2, 4–6, 2–6; Pietrangeli–Sirola d. Krishnan–Kumar 1–6, 9–7, 4–6, 6–2, 6–3. **Denmark d. Czechoslovakia 3–2, Copenhagen:** T. Ulrich d. P. Benda 6–1, 6–4, 6–0; K. Nielsen d. J. Javorski 6–2, 8–10, 7–9, 12–10, 6–1; Nielsen d. Benda 5–7, 6–4, 6–4, 6–2; J. Ulrich lost to Javorski 10–8, 3–6, 1–6, 6–4, 5–7; Nielsen–T. Ulrich lost to Javorski–M. Necas 4–6, 3–6, 4–6. **Great Britain d. Brazil 5–0, Eastbourne:** W. A. Knight d. R. Barnes 6–0, 6–2, 6–0; M. G. Davies d. C. Fernandez 6–4, 6–2, 6–3; d. I. Ribeiro 6–2, 6–1, 6–3; R. Becker d. Fernandez 6–3, 6–1, 6–1; Davies–R. K. Wilson d. Fernandez–Barnes 6–2, 6–4, 6–4. **Germany d. Belgium 3–2, Cologne:** R. Huber d. A. Jamar 6–4, 6–2, 6–1; lost to J. Brichant 8–10, 2–6, 6–2, 2–6; W. Bungert lost to Brichant 4–6, 2–6, 8–6, 6–8; d. Jamar 6–2, 6–3, 6–1; Huber–P. Scholl d. Brichant–J. P. Froment 6–2, 6–1, 6–0. **France d. Chile 4–1, Paris:** P. Darmon lost to L. Ayala 7–9, 4–6, 7–5, 1–6; d. P. Rodriguez 6–2, 6–3, 6–2; R. Haillet d. Rodriguez 6–2, 6–4, 6–3; d. Ayala 6–0, 6–4, 6–4; Darmon–P. Remy d. Ayala–Rodriguez 6–2, 6–4, 6–4. **Sweden d. Spain 3–2, Barcelona:** S. Davidson d. A. Gimeno 3–6, 6–2, 6–3, 3–6, 6–3; U. Schmidt d. M. Santana 6–2, 6–3, 7–5; d. Gimeno 6–4, 3–6, 7–5, 6–4; J. Lundquist lost to Santana 6–1, 4–6, 0–6, 4–6; Schmidt–Lundquist lost to Gimeno–A. Arilla 7–9, 6–8, 7–9.

THIRD ROUND

Poland d. Mexico 3–2, Warsaw: W. Skonecki d. M. Llamas 7–5, 6–8, 6–3, 7–5; d. F. Contreras 6–8, 6–2, 8–6, 6–4; A. Licis lost to Llamas 3–6, 5–7, 3–6; d. Contreras 6–2, 6–2, 8–6; J. Radzio–P. Piatek lost to A. Palafox–R. Osuna 3–6, 5–7, 4–6. **Italy d. Denmark 5–0, Copenhagen:** N. Pietrangeli d. T. Ulrich 6–2, 6–3, 6–1; d. K. Nielsen 6–1, 3–6, 6–4, 6–4; O. Sirola d. Nielsen 6–2, 4–6, 7–5, 12–14, 7–5; d. Ulrich 6–8, 6–3, 6–4, 3–6, 6–3; Pietrangeli–Sirola d. Nielsen–Ulrich 6–2, 2–6, 6–3, 6–2. **Great Britain d. Germany 5–0, Scarborough:** R. Becker d. R. Huber 6–1, 8–6, 6–3; d. W. Bungert 6–2, 4–6, 7–5, 6–2; M. G. Davies d. Bungert 6–2, 6–2, 6–3; W. A. Knight d. Huber 6–2, 6–0, 6–4; Davies–R. K. Wilson d. Huber–P. Scholl 6–2, 6–4, 6–3. **France d. Sweden 3–2, Paris:** P. Darmon d. S. Davidson 3–6, 6–3, 6–0, 6–0; d. U. Schmidt 6–3, 6–2, 6–4; R. Haillet d. Schmidt, 6–3, 6–3, 6–4; lost to Davidson 4–6, 4–6, 4–6; Darmon–P. Remy lost to Davidson–Schmidt 3–6, 3–6, 6–2, 4–6.

SEMI–FINAL ROUND

Italy d. Poland 4–1, Warsaw: N. Pietrangeli d. W. Skonecki 6–3, 6–2, 4–6, 6–4; lost to A. Licis 4–6, 2–6, 1–6; O. Sirola d. Licis 6–4, 3–6, 6–4, 6–3; d. Skonecki 1–6, 3–6, 6–0, 6–2, 6–2; Pietrangeli–Sirola d. J. Radzio–P. Piatek 6–3, 6–1, 6–1.   **Great Britain d. France 5–0, Manchester:** M. G. Davies d. P. Remy 4–6, 4–6, 6–3, 6–4, 6–1; R. K. Wilson d. P. Darmon 6–1 9–7, 6–3; d. Remy 6–3, 8–6, 6–4; W. A. Knight d. Darmon 6–2, 4–6, 6–3, 9–7; Davies–Wilson d. Darmon–J. C. Molinari 4–6, 6–3, 6–4, 6–1.

FINAL ROUND

Italy d. Great Britain 4–1, Milan: N. Pietrangeli lost to M. G. Davies 4–6, 3–6, 1–6; d. W. A. Knight 4–6, 6–3, 6–4, 6–1; O. Sirola d. Knight 6–3, 7–5, 6–3; d. Davies 6–3, 6–2, 6–2; Pietangeli–Sirola d. Davies–Knight 6–3, 5–7, 6–4, 4–6, 9–7.

Eastern Zone

FIRST ROUND

Japan d. Thailand 5–0, Tokyo: O. Ishiguro d. Duangdom 6–1, 6–0, 6–3; Kamo d. Karalak 6–4, 6–1, 6–0; Shibata d. Duangdom 6–3, 6–2, 6–4; Ishiguro d. Karalak 6–3, 6–2, 6–3; Kamo–Shibata d. Karalak–Sudasna 4–6, 6–1, 6–4, 9–7.

SECOND ROUND

Philippines d. Japan 3–2, Tokyo: R. Deyro d. K. Kamo 6–2, 6–3, 6–3; F. Ampon d. Ishiguro 6–4, 6–3, 10–8; J. Jose lost to Kamo 3–6, 0–6, 2–6; M. Dungo lost to Ishiguro 2–6, 6–1, 4–6, 1–6; Deyro–Ampon d. Kamo–Shibata 6–4, 6–3, 3–6, 8–6.   **Ceylon d. Malaya 3–1, Kuala Lumpur:** R. W. Ferdinands d. Lim Hee Chin 9–7, 6–0, 6–1; d. Ong Chew Bee 6–4, 6–3, 10–8; B. Pinto lost to Ong Chew Bee 7–9, 3–6, 4–6; R. Praesody v. Lim Hee Chin 4–6, 4–6, 7–5 unfin.; Ferdinands–Pinto d. M. Tay–Khoong Kit Soon 6–2, 6–4, 6–1.

FINAL ROUND

Philippines d. Ceylon 5–0, Manila: F. Ampon d. B. Pinto 6–1, 6–0, 6–1; R. Deyro d. R. W. Ferdinands 6–2, 6–2, 6–1; M. Dungo d. R. Praesody 6–2, 6–3, 7–5; J. Jose d. Ferdinands 6–1, 6–4, 6–3; Jose–Dungo d. Pinto–Ferdinands 6–1, 6–0, 6–4.

American Zone

FIRST ROUND

USA d. Venezuela 5–0, Caracas: B. MacKay d. M. Gambus 6–4, 6–1, 6–2; H. Richardson d. I. Pimentel 6–2, 6–1, 6–3; W. Quillian–MacKay d. Pimentel–Gambus 6–1, 6–4, 7–5; Quillian d. M. Suarez 6–0, 6–0, 6–1 MacKay d. Pimentel 6–3, 6–4, 5–7, 1–6, 6–1. **Canada d. Cuba 5–0, Toronto:** D. A. Fontana d. R. Karman 6–2, 6–2, 6–3; R. Bedard d. Minoso 6–1, 6–0, 6–0; d. Karman 6–2, 6–1, 6–3; P. Willey d. Minoso 6–2, 6–1, 6–3; Fontana–Bedard d. Karman–Minoso 6–2, 6–2, 6–4. **Argentina d. West Indies 5–0, Buenos Aires:** E. Soriano d. P. Valdez 6–2, 7–5, 6–1; E. Morea d. P. Phillips 6–2, 6–2, 6–2; d. Valdez 10–8, 6–3, 6–3; E. Rios d. Phillips 6–3, 6–4, 6–3; A. Russell–Soriano d. F. Valdez–Phillips 6–1, 6–3, 6–4.

SECOND ROUND

USA d. Canada 5–0, Toronto: B. MacKay d. D. Fontana 6–1, 6–2, 7–5; W. Reed d. R. Bedard 9–7, 6–2, 6–4; S. Giammalva–MacKay d. Bedard–Fontana 6–1, 13–11, 6–4; MacKay d. P. Willey 6–8, 6–2, 12–10, 7–5; J. Douglas d. Fontana 4–6, 6–3, 6–3, 6–1. **Argentina d. Israel 5–0, Buenos Aires:** E. Soriano d. E. Davidman 6–3, 2–6, 6–1, 6–0; d. A. Avidan 6–1, 6–3, 6–1; E. Morea d. Avidan 6–3, 6–2, 6–2; d. Davidman 7–5, 3–6, 6–4, 7–5; Morea–Soriano d. Davidman–Avidan 6–3, 6–3, 6–2.

FINAL ROUND

USA d. Argentina 5–0, Rye: B. MacKay d. E. Soriano 6–2, 6–2, 3–6, 6–3; H. Richardson d. E. Morea 6–1, 6–2, 7–9, 6–2; S. Giammalva–MacKay d. Morea–Soriano 6–3, 6–2, 6–2; Richardson d. Soriano 6–4, 6–2, 7–5; MacKay d. Morea 6–2, 6–2, 6–2.

INTER-ZONE FINALS

Italy d. Philippines 5–0, Sydney: O. Sirola d. R. Deyro 8–6, 6–3, 6–4; N. Pietrangeli d. F. Ampon 6–2, 6–2, 7–5; d. M. Dungo 6–2, 6–2, 6–2; G. Merlo d. J. Jose 6–2, 7–5, 6–1; Pietrangeli–Sirola d. Dungo–Jose 6–3, 6–3, 7–5. **USA d. Italy 5–0, Perth:** A. Olmedo d. N. Pietrangeli 5–7, 10–8, 6–0, 6–1; H. Richardson d. O. Sirola 6–4, 6–2, 7–5; Olmedo–Richardson d. Pietrangeli–Sirola 7–9, 6–4, 13–11, 7–5; B. MacKay d. Pietrangeli 6–4, 3–6, 5–7, 8–6, 8–6; Olmedo d. Sirola 20–18, 6–1, 6–4.

CHALLENGE ROUND

USA d. Australia 3–2, Brisbane: A. Olmedo d. M. J. Anderson 8–6, 2–6, 9–7, 8–6; B. MacKay lost to A. J. Cooper 6–4, 3–6, 2–6, 4–6; Olmedo–H. Richardson d. Anderson–N. Fraser 10–12, 3–6, 16–14, 6–3, 7–5; Olmedo d. Cooper 6–3, 4–6, 6–4, 8–6; MacKay lost to Anderson 5–7, 11–13, 9–11.

1959: AUSTRALIA
European Zone

FIRST ROUND

Denmark d. Yugoslavia 4–1, Zagreb: K. Nielsen d. K. Keretic 6–0, 6–3, 6–2; T. Ulrich d. I. Panajotovic 6–2, 6–4, 9–7; Nielsen–Ulrich lost to Panajotovic–B. Jovanovic 6–8, 4–6, 6–4, 6–4, 13–15; Nielsen d. Panajotovic 6–4, 6–4, 6–2; Ulrich d. Jovanovic 4–6, 8–6, 6–3, 6–1. **New Zealand d. Ireland 5–0, Dublin:** L. Gerrard d. G. P. Jackson 6–1, 8–6, 6–4; M. Otway d. J. D. Hackett 6–3, 6–3, 6–1; Gerrard–Otway d. Jackson–Hackett 6–2, 1–6, 6–4, 7–5; Otway d. Jackson 6–2, 6–3, 6–2; Woolf d. J. Buckley 6–4, 6–3, 6–2. **Rumania d. United Arab Republic 3–2, Cairo:** G. Viziru d. Badr el Din 6–1, 6–3, 6–2; I. Nastase lost to K. Moubarek 1–6, 4–6, 6–2, 2–6; G. and M. Viziru d. Nabil Hassan–Fathi Mohamed Aly 6–3, 6–4, 6–3; Nastase lost to Badr el Din 10–8, 0–6, 6–3, 5–7, 1–6; G. Viziru d. Moubarek 6–4, 3–6, 0–6, 8–6, 6–4. **Belgium d. Holland 4–1, Brussels:** J. Brichant d. P. van Eysden 6–1, 6–2, 6–3; J. P. Froment lost to W. Maris 4–6, 4–6, 5–7; Brichant–P. Washer d. Maris–H. van der Weg 6–4, 6–4, 6–0; Froment d. van Eysden 6–3, 6–3, 11–9; Brichant d. Maris 6–2, 6–0, 6–1. **South Africa d. Norway 5–0, Oslo:** G. Forbes d. F. D. Jagge 6–1, 6–1, 6–0; A. Segal d. G. Sjowall 6–2, 6–1, 6–3; Segal–Forbes d. Sjowall–Jagge 6–3, 6–2, 6–3; Segal d. Pape 6–4, 6–0, 7–5; R. Weedon d. Sjowall 7–5, 4–6, 6–1, 6–8, 7–5. **Colombia d. Lebanon 4–1, Beirut:** Alvares d. K. Fawaz 6–0, 6–2, 6–3; Salas lost to S. Khoury 2–6, 6–4, 4–6, 2–6; Alvarez–Salas d. Attieh–Hajar 7–5, 6–3, 4–6, 6–3; Salas d. Fawaz 8–6, 6–1, 6–4; Alvarez d. Khoury 6–0, 9–7, 6–1. **Spain d. Finland 4–0, Helsinki:** A. Gimeno d. S. Salo 6–2, 6–1, 6–2; J. Couder d. R. Nyyssonen 6–2, 6–4, 8–6; Gimeno–J. L. Arilla d. Salo–Nyyssonen 6–4, 6–3, 6–2; M. Santana d. Salo 6–3, 6–1, 6–1. **Switzerland d. Israel 3–2, Tel Aviv:** M. Froesch d. E. Davidman 6–2, 6–4, 9–7; P. Blondel d. A. Avidan 6–2, 6–4, 6–3; Froesch–Blondel lost to Davidman–Avidan 6–4, 4–6, 3–6, 1–6; Froesch d. Avidan 6–4, 6–4, 6–2; Blondel lost to Davidman 3–6, 1–6, 2–6. **Brazil d. West Germany 4–0, Berlin:** C. Fernandes d. W. Bungert

6–2, 6–4, 6–4; R. Barnes d. D. Ecklebe 6–8, 6–3, 6–3, 6–2;
Fernandes–Barnes d. Bungert–Ecklebe 1–6, 10–8, 6–2, 6–2; Fernandes d.
Ecklebe 6–1, 8–6, 6–3; Barnes v. Bungert 10–8, 3–4 unfin. **Sweden d.
Hungary 5–0, Stockholm:** J. E. Lundquist d. A. Adam 6–4, 6–4, 6–3;
U. Schmidt d. I. Gulyas 7–5, 6–4, 6–1; S. Davidson–Schmidt d.
Gulyas–Adam 6–4, 6–1, 9–7; Schmidt d. Adam 2–6, 6–3, 6–4, 7–5;
Lundquist d. Gulyas 6–3, 7–5, 6–1. **Chile d. Austria 3–2, Vienna:**
P. Rodriguez lost to F. Saiko 1–6, 4–6, 5–7; L. Ayala d. F. Hainka 6–4,
6–4, 6–2; Ayala–E. Aguirre d. Saiko–Boeck 8–6, 6–4, 2–6, 6–0;
Rodriguez d. Hainka 1–6, 6–0, 3–6, 6–4, 6–3; Ayala lost to Saiko def.

SECOND ROUND

France d. Denmark 5–0, Copenhagen: P. Darmon d. K. Nielsen 6–2,
7–5, 6–4; R. Haillet d. T. Ulrich 6–4, 8–6, 4–6, 5–1 def.; J. N. Grinda–J.
C. Molinari d. Nielsen–Ulrich 9–7, 6–4, 6–2; Grinda d. Nielsen 9–7, 8–6,
6–0; Molinari d. Hojberg 6–4, 6–2, 6–4. **Rumania d. New Zealand
3–2, Bucharest:** G. Viziru d. M. Otway 3–6, 7–5, 6–0, 6–1; I. Tiriac lost
to L. Gerrard 4–6, 13–15, 6–8; G. and M. Viziru lost to Gerrard–Otway
6–8, 3–6, 2–6; G. Viziru d. Gerrard 6–0, 6–4, 8–6; Tiriac d. Otway 6–3,
2–6, 6–4, 6–4. **Italy d. Belgium 4–1, Brussels:** N. Pietrangeli d. J.
Brichant 6–4, 6–8, 1–6, 6–1, 6–2; O. Sirola d. J. P. Froment 6–2, 6–2,
6–3; Pietrangeli–Sirola d. Brichant–P. Washer 6–2, 6–3, 6–4; S. Tacchini
d. Froment 6–3, 0–6, 6–4, 8–6; Sirola lost to Brichant 7–5, 3–6, 5–7,
12–10, 5–7. **South Africa d. Colombia 5–0, Bournemouth:** I.
Vermaak d. Salas 6–1, 6–1, 6–2; G. Forbes d. Alvarez 6–4, 6–1, 6–3;
Forbes–A. Segal d. Alvarez–Salas 6–4, 6–1, 6–1; R. Weedon d. Salas
6–3, 6–3, 3–6, 6–2; Vermaak d. Alvarez 6–8, 6–2, 8–6, 6–2. **Spain d.
Switzerland 5–0, Madrid:** J. Couder d. M. Froesch 6–2, 6–2, 6–2; A.
Gimeno d. P. Blondel 6–1, 6–0, 6–2; Gimeno–J. L. Arilla d.
Froesch–Blondel 6–2, 6–3, 6–0; Gimeno d. Schorsi 6–4, 6–3, 6–1;
Couder d. Blondel 6–0, 6–2, 6–3. **Brazil d. Poland 3–2, Warsaw:** R.
Barnes lost to W. Skonecki 1–6, 6–4, 7–5, 1–6, 1–6; C. Fernandes d. A.
Licis 7–5, 4–6, 6–4, 6–1; Fernandes–Barnes d. J. Piatek–W. Gasiorek 6–1,
6–1, 8–6; Fernandes lost to Skonecki 6–8, 4–6, 10–8, 1–6; Barnes d.
Licis 6–1, 6–1, 6–2. **Chile d. Sweden 3–2, Stockholm:** P. Rodriguez
lost to J. E. Lundquist 2–6, 4–6, 1–6; L. Ayala d. U. Schmidt 6–4, 6–4,
6–1; Ayala–E. Aguirra d. S. Davidson–Schmidt 2–6, 7–5, 6–3, 7–5; Ayala
d. Lundquist 3–6, 10–8, 6–1, 6–3; Rodriguez lost to Schmidt 1–6, 2–6,
3–6. **Great Britain d. Luxembourg 5–0, Mondorf–les–Bains:** A.
Mills d. J. Offenheim 6–0, 6–0, 6–0; W. Knight d. F. Baden 6–1, 6–2,
2–6, 6–3; Knight–R. Wilson d. Baden–G. Wampach 6–1, 6–1, 6–2; Knight
d. Offenheim 6–0, 6–1, 6–1; Mills d. Baden 6–1, 5–7, 8–10, 6–2, 6–2.

THIRD ROUND

France d. Rumania 5–0, Paris: R. Haillet d. G. Viziru 6–4, 6–2, 6–0;
P. Darmon d. I. Tiriac 6–0, 6–0, 8–6; J. N. Grinda–J. C. Molinari d.
G. and M. Viziru 6–1, 6–1, 6–4; Darmon d. G. Viziru 6–3, 7–5 6–2;
Haillet d. Tiriac 6–3, 6–3, 6–0. **Italy d. South Africa 4–1, Florence**:
O. Sirola d. I. Vermaak 6–4, 6–3, 6–4; N. Pietrangeli d. G. Forbes 7–5,
6–2, 6–4; Pietrangeli–Sirola d. Forbes–A. Segal 6–4, 6–3, 14–12; Sirola
lost to Segal 3–6, 8–10, 6–4, 4–6; G. Merlo d. Vermaak 6–4, 6–2, 6–4.
Spain d. Brazil 3–2, Barcelona: M. Santana d. C. Fernandes 8–10, 6–4,
6–0, 5–7, 6–3; J. Couder d. R. Barnes 6–2, 6–2, 6–8, 9–7; A. Gimeno–
J. L. Arilla lost to Fernandes–Barnes 3–6, 2–6, 11–9, 3–6; Santana d.
Barnes 6–1, 6–1, 6–4; Gimeno lost to Fernandes 1–6, 5–7, 2–6. **Great
Britain d. Chile 3–2, Eastbourne:** R. Wilson d. L. Ayala 6–1, 6–3, 5–7,
6–2; M. G. Davies d. P. Rodriguez 6–3, 6–4, 6–2; Wilson–Davies lost
to Ayala–E. Aguirre 6–8, 6–3, 4–6, 12–10, 3–6; Wilson d. Rodriguez 8–6,
6–3, 6–3; Davies lost to Ayala 7–9, 0–6, 2–6.

SEMI-FINAL ROUND

Italy d. France 4–1, San Remo: O. Sirola d. P. Darmon 6–1, 6–1, 3–6,
8–6; N. Pietrangeli d. R. Haillet 6–4, 6–2, 6–1; Pietrangeli–Sirola d. J.
N. Grinda–Darmon 6–3, 6–2, 7–5; G. Merlo lost to G. Pilet 1–6, 6–4,
3–6, 4–6; Pietrangeli d. Darmon 3–6, 6–4, 9–7, 6–1. **Spain d. Great
Britain 3–2, Barcelona:** A. Gimeno d. M. G. Davies 9–7, 6–3, 2–6, 6–2;
M. Santana lost to W. Knight 7–9, 1–6, 3–6; Gimeno–J. Couder lost to
Davies–R. K. Wilson 1–6, 6–1, 15–13, 4–6, 1–6; Gimeno d. Knight 7–5,
3–6, 6–3, 7–5; Santana d. Davies 6–2, 3–6, 4–6, 6–0, 6–1.

FINAL ROUND

Italy d. Spain 4–1, Milan: O. Sirola d. J. Couder 2–6, 8–6, 7–5, 2–6,
6–4; N. Pietrangeli d. A. Gimeno 8–6, 6–3, 6–3; Pietrangeli–Sirola d.
Gimeno–Couder 6–4, 8–6, 6–4; S. Tacchini lost to Gimeno 4–6, 1–6, 1–6;
Pietrangeli d. Couder 6–8, 4–6, 6–2, 6–0, 6–4.

Eastern Zone

FIRST ROUND

Japan d. Ceylon 5–0, Tokyo: A. Miyagi d. B. Pinto 6–0, 6–1, 6–0; K.
Kamo d. R. Ferdinands 6–2, 6–0, 6–4; Miyagi–Shibata d. Ferdinands–
Pinto 12–10, 6–3, 6–2; Kamo d. Pinto 6–2, 6–1, 6–2; Matsura d.
Ferdinands 6–4, 7–5, 6–0. **Philippines d. Malaya 5–0, Manila**: F.
Ampon d. Tay 6–1, 6–1, 6–1; R. Deyro d. Chew Bee 6–4, 6–1, 6–2; J.

Jose–E. Dungo d. Tay–Chew Bee 6–3, 6–3, 6–3; Dungo d. Tay 6–2, 6–3, 6–1; Jose d. Chew Bee 6–1, 6–2, 6–3. **India d. Korea def.; Thailand d. Iran def.**

SEMI-FINAL ROUND

India d. Japan 3–2, Tokyo: N. Kumar lost to K. Kamo 3–6, 6–1, 0–6, 6–8; R. Krishnan d. Matsura 6–2, 6–4, 6–4; Krishnan–Kumar d. Shibata–Miyagi 6–3, 6–4, 6–4; Krishnan d. Kamo 3–6, 6–2, 6–0, 7–5; Kumar lost to Matsura 6–3, 3–6, 3–6, 6–4, 3–6. **Philippines d. Thailand 5–0, Bangkok:** R. Deyro d. S. Karalak 6–1, 6–2, 5–7, 6–1; F. Ampon d. Bulkul 6–0, 6–0, 6–3; Deyro–J. Jose d. Karalak–Suthas 6–4, 6–2, 7–5; Ampon d. Karalak 6–0, 4–6, 6–2, 6–1; Deyro d. Bulkul 6–0, 6–0, 6–3.

FINAL ROUND

India d. Philippines 4–1, Calcutta: N. Kumar d. R. Deyro 6–2, 6–2, 6–3; R. Krishnan d. F. Ampon 6–2, 6–2, 6–3; Krishnan–Kumar d. Deyro–J. Jose 6–3, 8–6, 6–2; Krishnan d. Jose 6–1, 6–4, 6–1; P. Lall lost to Ampon 6–8, 1–6, 6–4, 6–2, 1–6.

American Zone

FIRST ROUND

Australia d. Mexico 4–1, Mexico City: N. Fraser d. A. Palafox 8–6, 6–0, 2–6, 4–6, 6–3; R. Laver lost to M. Llamas 4–6, 4–6, 3–6; Fraser–R. Emerson d. Llamas–Palafox 6–3, 6–2, 7–5; Laver d. Palafox 6–3, 6–8, 4–6, 7–5, 6–3; Emerson d. Llamas 6–4, 6–2, 4–6, 4–6, 6–0. **Cuba d. West Indies 4–0, Barbados:** R. Garrido d. I. MacDonald 6–4, 7–5, 3–6, 6–3; O. Garrido d. P. Phillips 6–1, 6–2, 9–7; R. and O. Garrido d. P. Valdez–A. Price 6–2, 6–2, 2–6, 6–2; O. Garrido d. MacDonald 0–6, 4–6, 6–3, 6–3, 6–2; R. Garrido v. Phillips 4–6, 6–4, 5–7, 3–1 unfin. **Argentina d. Venezuela def.**

SEMI-FINAL ROUND

Australia d. Canada 5–0, Montreal: R. Emerson d. D. Fontana 6–2, 6–2, 6–4; R. Laver d. R. Bedard 8–6, 6–3, 6–4; N. Fraser–Emerson d. Fontana–Bedard 6–3, 6–3, 6–1; Emerson d. Bedard 4–6, 6–4, 7–5, 6–4; Laver d. Godbout 7–9, 6–4, 6–2, 6–1. **Cuba d. Argentina def.**

FINAL ROUND

Australia d. Cuba 5–0, Montreal: R. Emerson d. R. Garrido 6–0, 6–4, 6–4; N. Fraser d. O. Garrido 6–1, 7–5, 6–3; R. Laver–Emerson d. R.

and O. Garrido 6–4, 6–4, 6–4; R. Mark d. O. Garrido 6–4, 6–4, 6–2; Fraser d. R. Garrido 6–1, 6–2, 6–4.

INTER-ZONE FINALS

Australia d. Italy 4–1, Philadelphia: R. Laver d. N. Pietrangeli 6–4, 2–6, 6–3, 6–3; N. Fraser d. O. Sirola 19–17, 1–6, 6–3, 6–4; Fraser–R. Emerson d. Pietrangeli–Sirola 3–6, 11–9, 6–3, 9–7; Laver d. Sirola 4–6, 6–4, 6–0, 6–3; Emerson lost to Pietrangeli 4–6, 0–6, 4–6. **Australia d. India 4–1, Brookline:** R. Laver lost to R. Krishnan 1–6, 4–6, 10–8, 4–6; N. Fraser d. P. Lall 10–8, 6–4, 6–1; Fraser–Emerson d. Krishnan–Lall 6–3, 7–5, 6–2; Fraser d. Krishnan 6–2, 6–3, 6–4; Laver d. Lall 6–2, 10–8, 6–4.

CHALLENGE ROUND

Australia d. USA 3–2, New York: N. Fraser d. A. Olmedo 8–6, 6–8, 6–4, 8–6; R. Laver lost to B. MacKay 5–7, 4–6, 1–6; Fraser–R. Emerson d. Olmedo–E. Buchholz 7–5, 7–5, 6–4; Laver lost to Olmedo 7–9, 6–4, 8–10, 10–12; Fraser d. MacKay 8–6, 3–6, 6–2, 6–4.

1960: AUSTRALIA
European Zone

FIRST ROUND

Sweden d. South Africa 5–0, Stockholm: U. Schmidt d. I. Vermaak 6–0, 6–8, 6–4, 8–6; J. E. Lundquist d. G. Koenig 6–2, 6–2, 6–4; Schmidt–Lundquist d. Vermaak–A. Gaertner 6–4, 6–2, 6–3; Lundquist d. Gaertner 6–2, 6–8, 3–6, 6–4, 6–1; Schmidt d. Koenig 6–2, 2–6, 6–3, 6–2. **Poland d. Rumania 3–2, Bucharest:** W. Skonecki d. I. Tiriac 7–5, 6–4, 5–7, 7–5; W. Gasiorek lost to G. Viziru 3–6, 6–3, 4–6, 6–2, 3–6; Gasiorek–J. Piatek d. Tiriac–W. Georgescu 5–7, 6–2, 6–4, 6–3; Skonecki lost to Viziru 1–6, 2–6, 4–6; Gasoriek d. Tiriac 4–6, 6–4, 8–6, 6–3. **Germany d. Czechoslovakia 3–2, Hanover:** W. Stuck lost to J. Javorsky 5–7, 6–8, 1–6; C. Kuhnke lost to P. Korda 6–4, 5–7, 6–4, 1–6, 2–6; Kuhnke–Stuck d. Korda–Javorsky 6–4, 3–6, 6–2, 6–2; Stuck d. Korda 6–4, 6–0, 6–1; Kuhnke d. Javorsky 6–3, 6–2, 6–4. **Argentina d. Finland 5–0, Helsinki:** E. Soriano d. R. Nyyssonen 6–4, 7–5, 6–4; R. Aubone d. S. Salo 9–7, 7–5, 4–6, 6–3; Soriano–Aubone d. Salo–M. Kinnunen 6–2, 6–4, 6–3; Soriano d. Salo 7–5, 6–8, 8–6, 6–4; Aubone d. T. Jokinen 6–3, 6–4, 6–3. **Denmark d. Yugoslavia 3–2, Copenhagen:** K. Nielsen lost to B. Jovanovic 6–1, 1–6, 1–6, 4–6; J. Ulrich d. I. Panajotovic 7–5, 5–7, 6–1, 6–1; J. and T. Ulrich d. Jovanovic–

Panajotovic 6–4, 4–6, 6–1, 5–7, 7–5; J. Ulrich d. Jovanovic 5–7, 6–3, 4–6, 6–0, 9–7; Nielsen lost to Panajotovic 4–6, 2–6, 6–3, 6–2, 4–6. **Austria d. Egypt 3–1, Cairo:** F. Saiko d. Fathi Mohamed Aly 6–2, 6–1, 3–6, 6–3; L. Legenstein d. Badr el Din 8–6, 6–3, 5–7, 7–5; F. Hainka–Legenstein d. Aly–Nabil Hassan 6–1, 7–5, 6–3; Legenstein d. Aly 8–10, 6–3, 6–1, 5–4 retd.; Hainka lost to Badr el Din 3–6, 6–2, 1–6, 7–5, retd. **Belgium d. Switzerland 3–2, Geneva:** J. Brichant d. P. Blondel 6–2, 6–2, 6–1; J. P. Froment lost to H. Grimm 6–3, 2–6, 4–6, 2–6; Brichant–P. Washer d. Grimm–E. Schori 6–2, 6–0, 6–2; Froment lost to Blondel 6–3, 2–6, 4–6, 6–1, 5–7; Brichant d. Grimm 6–1, 6–3, 6–0. **Holland d. Norway 3–2, Oslo:** W. Maris d. G. Sjowall 6–3, 6–2, 6–4; P. van Eysden d. T. Moe 4–6, 6–1, 6–4, 6–4; Maris–J. van Dalsum lost to F. D. Jagge–Moe 1–6, 4–6, 6–8; Maris lost to Moe 4–6, 6–8; van Eysden d. Sjowall 6–2, 4–6, 3–6, 6–3, 6–3. **Chile d. Israel 4–1, Tel Aviv:** L. Ayala d. A. Avidan 6–1, 6–1, 6–2; P. Rodriguez lost to E. Davidman 7–9, 6–4, 4–6, 2–6; Ayala–E. Aguirre d. Avidan–Davidman 6–2, 6–1, 6–0; Rodriguez d. Avidan 2–6, 7–5, 6–0, 7–5; Ayala d. Davidman 6–2, 6–1, 6–1. **Monaco d. Luxembourg 3–2, Mondorf–les–Bains:** R. Borghini d. J. Offenheim 2–6, 6–1, 6–4, 6–3; F. Baden d. G. Pasquier 6–4, 6–1, 7–5; Baden–G. Wampach d. Borghini–Pasquier 6–2, 3–6, 4–6, 7–5, 6–2; Pasquier d. Offenheim 6–1, 6–1, 6–1; Borghini d. Baden 6–2, 6–2, 6–3. **Hungary d. Ireland 5–0, Budapest:** A. Adam d. G. P. Jackson 6–3, 6–0, 6–3; I. Gulyas d. J. D. Hackett 6–2, 6–2, 6–1; Gulyas–A. Szikszai d. Hackett–Jackson 7–5, 6–2, 6–2; Gulyas d. Jackson 6–2, 6–3, 2–6, 6–3; F. Komaromi d. Hackett 6–1, 6–2, 7–5.

SECOND ROUND

Sweden d. Spain 3–2, Stockholm: J. E. Lundquist lost to A. Gimeno 6–2, 6–4, 3–6, 2–6; U. Schmidt d. M. Santana 6–2, 6–4, 4–6, 3–6, 6–2; Schmidt–Lundquist d. Gimeno–J. L. Arilla 6–4, 7–5, 6–4; Lundquist d. Santana 9–7, 6–4, 6–3; Schmidt lost to Gimeno 5–7, 3–6, 2–6.
Germany d. Poland 4–1, Warsaw: W. Stuck d. W. Skonecki 8–6, 6–1, 6–1; C. Kuhnke d. W. Gasiorek 7–5, 6–1, 5–7, 6–3; Stuck–Kuhnke d. Gasiorek–J. Piatek 6–1, 7–5, 6–4; Stuck d. Gasiorek 6–3, 7–5, 6–3; W. Bungert d. A. Licis 6–2, 4–6, 6–3, 6–4. **France d. Argentina 5–0, Paris:** R. Haillet d. E. Soriano 6–3, 6–1, 5–7, 6–2; G. Pilet d. R. Aubone 6–0, 6–2, 6–3; J. N. Grinda–J. C. Molinari d. Soriano–Aubone 6–2, 9–11, 15–13, 6–1; Haillet d. Aubone 6–2, 6–1, 6–1; Pilet d. Soriano 6–4, 6–2, 6–2. **Denmark d. Austria 3–2, Vienna:** K. Nielsen d. F. Saiko 1–6, 6–1, 6–4, 6–4; J. Ulrich d. L. Legenstein 4–6, 6–4, 6–3, 1–6, 6–3; Ulrich d. Saiko 6–3, 6–0, 6–2; Nielsen lost to Legenstein 4–6, 4–6, 3–6; J. and T. Ulrich lost to Legenstein–F. Hainka 6–1, 6–3, 0–6, 1–6, 5–7. **Belgium**

d. Brazil 3–2, Brussels: C. de Gronckel lost to C. Fernandes 3–6, 0–6, 6–8; J. Brichant d. R. W. Barnes 6–2, 6–3, 5–7, 6–1; Brichant–P. Washer d. Fernandes–Barnes 6–3, 6–2, 4–6, 9–7; Brichant d. Fernandes 6–1, 6–4, 6–3; de Gronckel lost to Barnes 5–7, 0–6, 8–10. **Great Britain d. Holland 5–0, Scheveningen:** W. A. Knight d. W. Maris 6–0, 6–4, 6–3; M. G. Davies d. P. van Eysden 9–7, 6–4, 6–2; Knight–Davies d. Maris–van Eysden 6–2, 6–2, 6–2; R. Becker d. van Eysden 6–1, 6–0, 6–3; M. J. Sangster d. Maris 6–2, 6–3, 6–3. **Chile d. Monaco 3–2, Monte Carlo:** L. Ayala d. R. Borghini 6–0, 6–2, 6–1; P. Rodriguez d. G. Pasquier 6–1, 6–1, 3–6, 6–4; Ayala–E. Aguirre d. Borghini–A. Viviani 6–3, 6–2, 6–3; Rodriguez lost to Borghini 2–6, 2–6, 1–6; Aguirre lost to Viviani 1–6, 0–6 def. **Italy d. Hungary 3–2, Budapest:** O. Sirola lost to A. Adam 2–6, 6–2, 8–6, 2–6, 1–6; N. Pietrangeli d. I. Gulyas 1–6, 6–2, 6–4, 6–4; Pietrangeli–Sirola d. Gulyas–A. Szikszai 1–6, 6–3, 6–3, 6–3; Pietrangeli d. Adam 6–2, 3–6, 6–2, 6–4; S. Tacchini lost to Gulyas 3–6, 2–6, 6–4, 7–5, 3–6.

THIRD ROUND
Sweden d. Germany 4–1, Dusseldorf: U. Schmidt lost to I. C. Kuhnke 3–6, 4–6, 4–6; J. E. Lundquist d. W. Stuck 8–6, 6–1, 6–2; Schmidt–Lundquist d. Kuhnke–Stuck 6–3, 6–3, 5–7, 9–7; Lundquist d. Kuhnke 6–3, 8–6, 6–4; Schmidt d. Stuck 7–5, 6–2, 6–0. **France d. Denmark 5–0, Paris:** P. Darmon d. K. Nielsen 6–1, 6–2, 6–3; R. Haillet d. J. Ulrich 10–8, 6–2, 2–6, 6–3; J. N. Grinda–J. C. Molinari d. Nielsen–Ulrich 6–3, 9–7, 7–5; Grinda d. J. Leschly 6–2, 6–3, 0–6, 6–3; Haillet d. Nielsen 6–1, 10–8, 6–8, 6–1. **Great Britain d. Belgium 5–0, Scarborough:** W. Knight d. E. Drossart 6–0, 6–2, 6–1 and d. J. Brichant 6–4, 6–2, 6–2; M. G. Davies d. Brichant 3–6, 9–7, 6–1, 8–6; R. Wilson d. Drossart 6–2, 6–1, 6–2; Davies–Wilson d. Brichant–Drossart 6–1, 6–3, 6–4. **Italy d. Chile 3–2, Turin:** O. Sirola lost to L. Ayala 4–6, 6–3, 3–6, 2–6; N. Pietrangeli d. P. Rodriguez 6–1, 6–4, 6–1; Pietrangeli–Sirola d. Ayala–E. Aguirre 6–1, 6–3, 8–6; Pietrangeli lost to Ayala 4–6, 1–6, 1–6; Sirola d. Rodriguez 6–0, 7–5, 6–3.

SEMI-FINAL ROUND
Sweden d. France 3–2, Båstad: J. E. Lundquist d. P. Darmon 6–0, 6–3, 6–1; S. Davidson d. R. Haillet 4–6, 3–6, 6–2, 6–2, 6–3; Lundquist–U. Schmidt d. J. N. Grinda–J. C. Molinari 2–6, 6–4, 6–4, 6–2; Davidson lost to Darmon 2–6, 8–6, 7–9, 4–6; T. Johansson lost to Haillet 7–9, 3–6, 1–6. **Italy d. Great Britain 4–1, London:** N. Pietrangeli d. R. K. Wilson 6–4, 6–3, 4–6, 7–5; O. Sirola d. M. G. Davies 9–7, 7–5, 1–6, 2–6, 6–4; Pietrangeli–Sirola d. Davies–Wilson 6–4, 3–6, 8–6, 6–3; S.

Tacchini lost to Wilson 6–3, 3–6, 6–8, 2–6; Pietrangeli d. Davies 6–4, 6–3, 6–4.

FINAL ROUND
Italy d. Sweden 3–2, Båstad: O. Sirola lost to J. E. Lundquist 4–6, 6–4, 3–6, 3–6; N. Pietrangeli d. U. Schmidt 6–1, 6–4, 4–6, 6–4; Pietrangeli–Sirola d. Schmidt–Lundquist 14–16, 5–7, 6–2, 6–3, 6–2; Sirola d. Schmidt 6–4, 6–2, 6–1; S. Tacchini lost to Lundquist 2–6, 1–6, 1–6.

Eastern Zone

FIRST ROUND
Japan d. Korea 5–0, Tokyo: O. Ishiguro d. Lee Sang Yun 6–1, 6–2, 6–4; J. Furuta d. Am Wha Yung 6–2, 6–2, 6–3; M. Nagasaki–A. Ichiyama d. Lee Sang Yun–Kin Ke Hwan 3–6, 6–4, 6–1, 6–3; Furuta d. Lee Sang Yun 6–2, 7–5, 6–4; Ishiguro d. Am Wha Yung 6–2, 6–2, 6–4.
India d. Ceylon 5–0, Colombo: R. Krishnan d. D. D. N. Selvadurai 6–0, 6–0, 6–1; N. Kumar d. B. Pinto 6–2, 6–3, 6–3; Krishnan–Kumar d. Pinto–R. Ferdinands 6–3, 6–4, 6–1; Krishnan d. Pinto 6–3, 6–2, 6–2; Kumar d. Selvadurai 6–1, 6–2, 6–0.

SEMI-FINAL ROUND
Philippines d. Japan 3–2, Manila: R. Deyro d. M. Nagasaki 6–1, 6–1, 6–4; J. Jose lost to O. Ishiguro 6–4, 3–6, 4–6, 6–0, 3–6; Deyro–Jose d. Ishiguro–Nagasaki 6–2, 7–5, 6–1; Jose d. Nagasaki 0–6, 1–6, 9–7, 6–4, 6–0; E. Dungo lost to Ishiguro 1–6, 4–6, 4–6. **India d. Thailand 5–0, Bangkok:** J. Mukerjee d. Sutiraphan 11–9, 0–6, 6–2, 3–6, 6–3; N. Kumar d. Seri 6–3, 6–2, 6–4; Kumar–Mukerjee d. Sutiraphan–Kravee Sudasna 6–4, 6–2, 3–6, 6–3; Kumar d. Sutiraphan 8–10, 6–3, 6–0, 4–6, 6–2.

FINAL ROUND
Philippines d. India 5–0, Manila: R. Deyro d. N. Kumar 6–0, 6–1, 6–1; F. Ampon d. R. Krishan 6–3, 8–6, 6–1; J. Jose–E. Dungo d. R. Krishnan–Kumar 6–2, 6–2, 6–2. (India def. last two singles.)

American Zone

FIRST ROUND
USA d. Canada 5–0, Quebec: B. Bartzen d. R. Bedard 5–7, 4–6, 6–0, 6–2, 6–2; B. MacKay d. D. Fontana 6–1, 6–3, 6–2; E. Buchholz–C.

McKinley d. Bedard–Fontana 14–12, 6–3, 6–2; MacKay d. Bedard 6–3, 6–3, 3–6, 6–3; Bartzen d. F. Godbout 6–1, 6–1, 6–3. **New Zealand d. West Indies 5–0, Port of Spain:** M. Otway d. P. Valdez 6–0, 6–0, 6–0; L. Gerrard d. A. Price 8–6, 6–2, 6–3; Otway–Gerrard d. Price–Valdez 6–4, 6–2, 6–2; Gerrard d. Valdez 6–1, 6–1, 6–2; Otway d. Price 8–6, 5–7, 0–6, 6–3, 6–2.

SEMI-FINAL ROUND

USA d. Mexico 3–2, Mexico City: B. MacKay lost to R. Osuna 6–3, 6–8, 4–6, 4–6; E. Buchholz d. M. Llamas 4–6, 7–5, 8–6, 7–5; Buchholz–C. McKinley d. Osuna–A. Palafox 2–6, 6–4, 7–9, 6–4, 7–5; MacKay d. Llamas 6–2, 6–4, 1–6, 12–10; C. McKinley lost to E. Reyes 1–2 def. **Venezuela d. New Zealand 3–2, Caracas:** M. Gambus lost to L. Gerrard 6–4, 6–1, 0–6, 1–6, 0–6; I. Pimental d. M. Otway 6–4, 6–8, 6–1, 7–5; Pimental–Gambus d. Gerrard–Otway 6–4, 6–3, 3–6, 8–6; Pimental d. Gerrard 6–3, 6–4, 6–2; S. Corboda lost to Otway 2–6, 0–6, 1–6.

FINAL ROUND

USA d. Venezuela 5–0, Cleveland: B. Bartzen d. I. Pimental 6–0, 6–1, 6–1; B. MacKay d. M. Gambus 6–1, 6–1, 6–0; E. Buchholz–C. McKinley d. Pimental–Gambus 6–4, 6–1, 7–5; MacKay d. Pimental 6–3, 6–3, 6–3; Bartzen d. Gambus 6–1, 6–0, 6–0.

INTER-ZONE FINALS

USA d. Philippines 5–0, Brisbane: B. MacKay d. E. Dungo 6–1, 6–2, 6–0; E. Buchholz d. J. Jose 5–7, 6–1, 6–0, 6–2; D. Ralston–C. McKinley d. Jose–Dungo 6–3, 6–3, 6–3; McKinley d. F. Ampon 6–3, 6–4, 6–2; Ralston d. R. Deyro 6–2, 6–0, 7–5. **Italy d. USA 3–2, Perth:** O. Sirola lost to E. Buchholz 8–6, 5–7, 9–11, 2–6; N. Pietrangeli lost to B. MacKay 6–8, 6–3, 10–8, 6–8, 11–13; Pietrangeli–Sirola d. C. McKinley–Buchholz 3–6, 10–8, 6–4, 13–11; Pietrangeli d. Buchholz 6–1, 6–2, 6–8, 3–6, 6–4; Sirola d. MacKay 9–7, 6–3, 8–6.

CHALLENGE ROUND

Australia d. Italy 4–1, Sydney: N. Fraser d. O. Sirola 4–6, 6–3, 6–3, 6–3; R. G. Laver d. N. Pietrangeli 8–6, 6–4, 6–3; Fraser–R. Emerson d. Pietrangeli–Sirola 10–8, 5–7, 6–2, 6–4; Laver d. Sirola 9–7, 6–2, 6–3; Fraser lost to Pietrangeli 9–11, 3–6, 6–1, 2–6.

1961: AUSTRALIA
European Zone

FIRST ROUND

Belgium d. Chile 3–2, Brussels: J. Brichant d. P. Apey 6–4, 6–1, 6–1; J. Vanderborght lost to P. Rodriguez 2–6, 3–6, 3–6; Brichant–P. Washer d. Rodriguez–E. Aguirre 7–5, 7–5, 4–6, 6–4; Vanderborght lost to Apey 4–6, 6–8, 2–6; Brichant d. Rodriguez 6–1, 7–9, 8–6, 6–1. **Holland d. Switzerland 3–2, Lucerne:** W. Maris d. H. Grimm 6–3, 6–1, 6–2; P. van Eysden lost to M. Froesch 5–7, 2–6, 4–6; Maris–van Eysden d. Grimm–E. Schori 11–9, 6–3, 9–7; Maris lost to Froesch 3–6, 1–6, 3–6; van Eysden d. Grimm 5–7, 6–4, 6–3, 6–2. **West Germany d. Czechoslovakia 3–2, Prague:** W. Bungert d. P. Korda 6–3, 10–8, 2–6, 3–6, 7–5; C. Kuhnke d. J. Javorsky 3–6, 5–7, 7–5, 6–2, 6–3; Bungert–Kuhnke d. Javorsky–J. Parma 8–6, 3–6, 1–6, 6–3, 6–4; Kuhnke lost to Korda 2–6, 2–6, 1–6; D. Ecklebe lost to Javorsky 4–6, 6–2, 6–2, 4–6, 3–6. **Brazil d. United Arab Republic 5–0, Cairo:** C. Fernandes d. Badr el Din 6–1, 3–6, 6–4, 6–3; E. Mandarino d. Fathi Mohamed Aly 6–2, 6–1, 6–3; Fernandes–Mandarino d. Fathi Moh. Aly–Badr el Din 6–3, 6–3, 6–3; Fernandes d. Fathi Moh. Aly 6–8, 6–1, 6–0, 6–1; Mandarino d. Badr el Din 6–2, 6–2, 6–2. **Poland d. Ireland 5–0, Dublin:** W. Skonecki d. J. Buckley 6–4, 4–6, 6–4, 6–4; W. Gasiorek d. G. P. Jackson 6–3, 5–7, 3–6, 8–6, 6–4; Skonecki–Gasiorek d. J. D. Hackett–V. Gotto 6–3, 3–6, 6–3, 4–6, 6–3; Gasiorek d. Buckley 6–4, 6–4, 6–3; J. Orlikowski d. Jackson 6–4, 6–3, 8–6. **Monaco d. Luxembourg 3–2, Monte Carlo:** R. Borghini d. J. Offenheim 6–4, 6–0, 6–2; G. Pasquier lost to F. Baden 5–7, 2–6, 3–6; Borghini–Pasquier d. Offenheim–G. Wampach 6–4, 6–8, 3–6, 6–3, 6–2; Borghini lost to Baden 7–9, 6–1, 6–3, 6–2; Pasquier d. Offenheim 6–2, 6–1, 6–2. **South Africa d. Rumania 5–0, Bucharest:** J. Mayers d. I. Tiriac 6–0, 3–6, 6–2, 12–14, 6–0; A. Segal d. G. Viziru 6–1, 7–5, 6–4; Segal–A. Gaertner d. Viziru–Tiriac 6–2, 6–2, 6–2; Mayers d. Viziru 8–10, 7–5, 3–6, 7–5, 6–0; Gaertner d. Tiriac 6–1, 2–6, 1–6, 6–3, 7–5. **Finland d. Turkey 4–1, Istanbul:** S. Salo d. N. Bari 3–6, 6–3, 6–4, 6–4; R. Nyyssonen d. E. Balas 6–2, 6–1, 6–0; Salo–Nyyssonen d. Bari–Balas 6–1, 12–10, 6–1; M. Kinnunen lost to Balas 3–6, 3–6, 2–6; Nyyssonen d. Z Kipkizil 4–6, 6–3, 6–0, 6–1. **Austria d. Norway 5–0, Vienna:** F. Saiko d. F. D. Jagge 6–4, 6–1, 6–1; L. Legenstein d. T. Moe 4–6, 6–3, 6–2; Saiko–Legenstein d. Jagge–Moe 6–3, 6–1, 6–1; Saiko d. Moe 6–4, 6–1, 6–3; F. Hainka d. Jagge 6–4, 6–1, 6–2. **New Zealand d. Israel 5–0, Tel Aviv:** M. Otway d. G. Dubitzki 6–2, 8–6, 6–0; L. Gerrard d. E. Davidman 6–1, 6–1, 3–6, 6–4; Otway–Gerrard of Dubitzki–Davidman

6–3, 6–2, 6–3; Otway d. Davidman 6–4, 6–2, 8–6; Gerrard d. Dubitzki 6–2, 4–6, 6–0, 6–1. **Spain d. Yugoslavia 3–2, Belgrade:** A. Martinez lost to V. Presecki 6–8, 6–3, 7–9, 0–6; M. Santana d. B. Jovanovic 6–3, 8–6, 6–1; Santana–J. L. Arilla d. Jovanovic–N. Pilic 6–3, 7–5, 7–5; Santana d. Presecki 6–3, 6–2, 6–1; Martinez lost to Jovanovic def. **Hungary d. Denmark 3–2, Aarhus:** J. Katona d. J. Leschley 4–6, 7–5, 7–5, 6–4; I. Gulyas lost to J. Ulrich 7–5, 6–2, 3–6, 2–6, 4–6; Gulyas–V. Szikszai d. J. and T. Ulrich 6–2, 6–2, 4–6, 9–9 def.; I. Katona lost to J. Ulrich 3–6, 0–6, 1–6; Gulyas d. Leschley 7–5, 4–6, 6–4, 6–4.

SECOND ROUND

Italy d. Belgium 3–2, Brussels: N. Pietrangeli lost to J. Brichant 6–2, 6–2, 0–6, 1–6, 1–6; O. Sirola d. E. Drossart 2–6, 6–4, 7–5, 6–2; Sirola–Pietrangeli d. Brichant–J. Vanderborght 7–5, 6–4, 6–3; Pietrangeli d. Drossart 6–3, 6–2, 7–5; Sirola lost to Brichant 1–6, 5–7, 0–6. **West Germany d. Holland 5–0, Scheveningen:** C. Kuhnke d. W. Maris 6–3, 6–1, 7–5; W. Bungert d. P. van Eysden 6–2, 6–4, 6–4; Bungert–Kuhnke d. Maris–van Eysden 7–5, 6–2, 3–6, 8–6; D. Ecklebe d. van Eysden 6–2, 6–3, 6–1; I. Buding d. Maris 6–3, 4–6, 6–0, 3–6, 6–3. **France d. Brazil 4–1, Paris:** P. Darmon d. R. Barnes 1–6, 6–0, 6–4, 6–1; G. Pilet d. C. Fernandes 6–4, 6–1, 6–1; D. Contet–J. Renavand lost to Barnes–Fernandes 4–6, 3–6, 6–4, 9–7, 3–6; Pilet d. Barnes 6–1, 6–4, 4–6, 2–6, 6–4; Darmon d. E. Mandarino 5–7, 6–1, 9–7, 3–3 def. **Poland d. Monaco 4–1, Warsaw:** W. Skonecki d. R. Borghini 6–8, 6–3, 6–4, 6–2; W. Gasiorek d. A. Viviani 6–4, 6–1, 6–2; J. Orlikowski–W. Nowicki d. Borghini–Viviani 6–2, 6–1, 1–6, 3–6, 6–1; Orlikowski lost to Borghini 8–10, 6–3, 6–2, 6–8, 4–6; Nowicki d. Viviani 6–4, 6–4, 6–1. **South Africa d. Finland 4–1, Helsinki:** J. Mayers lost to R. Nyyssonen 6–1, 5–7, 1–6, 0–6; A. Segal d. S. Salo 6–1, 6–2, 6–3; Segal–A. Gaertner d. Nyyssonen–Salo 6–2, 6–0, 6–1; Mayers d. Salo 6–1, 6–2, 6–3; Segal d. Nyyssonen 6–2, 6–3, 6–4. **Great Britain d. Austria 3–2, Vienna:** M. Sangster d. L. Legenstein 7–5, 6–3, 6–3; R. Wilson lost to F. Saiko 2–6, 7–9, 6–4, 2–6; Wilson–Sangster d. Legenstein–F. Hainka 4–6, 12–10, 6–3, 7–5; Wilson d. Legenstein 6–4, 6–4, 6–4; A. Mills lost to Saiko 0–6, 0–6, 3–6. **Spain d. New Zealand 3–2, Madrid:** E. Martinez lost to L. Gerrard 3–6, 4–6, 2–6; M. Santana d. M. Otway 6–3, 6–1, 6–3; A. Arilla–Santana d. Otway–Gerrard 9–7, 6–4, 6–3; Martinez lost to Otway 4–6, 3–6, 6–8; Santana d. Gerrard 6–1, 6–4, 6–2. **Sweden d. Hungary 3–2, Budapest:** U. Schmidt d. Z. Katona 6–3, 6–3, 6–2; J. E. Lundquist d. I. Gulyas 0–6, 7–5, 4–6, 6–4, 6–4; Lundquist–Schmidt lost to Gulyas–A. Szikszai 4–6, 5–7, 3–6; Schmidt d. Gulyas 6–2, 6–3, 6–3; Lundquist lost to Katona 6–8, 6–2, 4–6. def.

THIRD ROUND

Italy d. West Germany 3–2, Munich: N. Pietrangeli d. C. Kuhnke
6–1, 3–6, 6–4, 2–6, 6–1; O. Sirola lost to W. Bungert 4–6, 3–6, 5–7;
Pietrangeli–Sirola d. Bungert–Kuhnke 2–6, 7–5, 3–6, 6–2, 6–1; Sirola lost
to Kuhnke 7–9, 3–6, 6–3, 9–11; Pietrangeli d. Bungert 7–5, 9–11, 6–0, 3–6,
6–4. **France d. Poland 5–0, Warsaw:** P. Darmon d. W. Gasiorek 6–4,
9–7, 6–0; G. Pilet d. W. Skonecki 6–1, 6–4, 3–6, 6–4; Darmon–J.
Renavand d. Skonecki–J. Orlikowski 6–3, 6–4, 6–3; Renavand d. Gasiorek
6–4, 6–2, 1–6, 6–1; D. Contet d. Orlikowski 3–6, 7–5, 4–6, 8–6, 6–3.
Great Britain d. South Africa 4–1, Birmingham: M. Sangster d. J.
Mayers 6–3, 6–2, 6–4; R. K. Wilson, d. A. Segal 6–4, 6–4, 6–4;
Sangster–Wilson lost to Segal–A. Gaertner 9–11, 4–6, 5–7; Wilson d.
Mayers 6–3, 6–3, 6–2; Sangster d. Segal 6–1, 13–15, 6–2, 10–8.
Sweden d. Spain 4–1, Madrid: U. Schmidt d. A. Arilla 6–0, 6–2, 6–2;
J. E. Lundquist lost to M. Santana 6–3, 6–4, 2–6, 2–6, 2–6; S.
Davidson–Schmidt d. Santana–Arilla 6–2, 6–3, 6–2; Lundquist d. Arilla
9–7, 6–4, 6–4; Schmidt d. E. Martinez 6–2, 4–6, 7–5, 6–2.

SEMI-FINAL ROUND

Italy d. France 4–1, Paris: N. Pietrangeli d. P. Darmon 5–7, 6–0, 6–4,
3–6, 6–2; F. Gardini d. G. Pilet 2–6, 6–3, 6–2, 6–3; Pietrangeli–O. Sirola
d. J. N. Grinda–Darmon 4–6, 6–3, 6–4, 7–5; G. Merlo lost to J. Renavand
3–6, 6–0, 6–4, 5–7, 3–6; Gardini d. Grinda 10–8, 6–2, 7–5. **Sweden d.
Great Britain 4–1, Båstad:** J. E. Lundquist d. R. K. Wilson 6–4, 6–3,
5–7, 6–4; U. Schmidt d. M. Sangster 6–2, 6–4, 8–6; Lundquist–Schmidt
lost to Wilson–J. A. Pickard 3–6, 6–3, 1–6, 6–8; Schmidt d. Wilson 9–7,
6–0, 6–4; Lundquist d. Sangster 6–4, 6–4, 6–2.

FINAL ROUND

Italy d. Sweden 4–1, Milan: F. Gardini d. U. Schmidt 6–4, 4–6, 1–6,
6–3, 6–1; N. Pietrangeli lost to J. E. Lundquist 2–6, 5–7, 6–1, 4–6;
Pietrangeli–O. Sirola d. Lundquist–T. Hallberg 6–3, 3–6, 6–3, 6–1;
Pietrangeli d. Schmidt 6–3, 6–2, 3–6, 6–3; Gardini d. Hallberg 6–2, 6–1,
6–0.

Eastern Zone

FIRST ROUND

India d. Indonesia 4–1, Bandung: J. Mukerjea lost to Tan Liep Tijauw
2–6, 1–6, 6–2, 4–6; R. Krishnan d. I. Sumarna 6–2, 6–1, 6–1;
Krishnan–P. Lall d. Sugiarto–Sie Kong Loen 6–2, 6–4, 6–0; Mukerjea d.

Sumarna 6–2, 6–1, 6–1; Lall d. Sugiarto 6–2, 6–1, 8–6. **Thailand d. Ceylon 3–2, Colombo:** S. Karalak d. G. Perera 6–2, 6–2, 6–4; S. Charuchinda lost to B. Pinto 0–6, 3–6, 0–6; Karalak–Charuchinda lost to Pinto–R. Ferdinands 2–6, 2–6, 6–2, 6–8; Karalak d. Pinto 6–4, 1–6, 6–3, 6–1; Charuchinda d. Perera 4–6, 6–4, 8–6, 9–7. **Japan d. Korea def.**

SEMI-FINAL ROUND
India d. Thailand 5–0, Lucknow: J. Mukerjea d. S. Karalak 6–4, 6–3, 6–4; R. Krishnan d. S. Charuchinda 6–0, 6–3, 6–1; Krishnan–P. Lall d. Karalak–Charuchinda 6–0, 6–2, 6–1; Mukerjea d. Charuchinda 6–1, 3–6, 6–1, 7–5; Lall d. Karalak 6–1, 7–5, 6–2. **Japan d. Philippines 3–2, Tokyo:** A. Miyagi lost to R. Deyro 4–6, 5–7, 5–7; O. Ishiguro lost to J. Jose 3–6, 2–6, 3–6; M. Nagasaki–Miyagi d. Jose–E. Dungo 8–6, 6–3, 6–1; Miyagi d. Jose 6–2, 1–6, 6–1, 3–6, 6–4; Ishiguro d. Deyro 6–4, 6–2, 6–4.

FINAL ROUND
India d. Japan 4–1, New Delhi: J. Mukerjea lost to A. Miyagi 2–6, 7–9, 6–2, 2–6; R. Krishnan d. O. Ishiguro 4–6, 6–3, 6–3, 6–3; Krishnan–P. Lall d. Miyagi–M. Nagasaki 6–4, 6–3, 6–4; Krishnan d. Miyagi 6–4, 6–1, 6–4; A. Ali d. Ishiguro 4–6, 6–4, 6–0, 2–6, 6–4.

American Zone

FIRST ROUND
USA d. West Indies 5–0, Bridgetown: C. Crawford d. I. McDonald 6–1, 6–3, 6–2; J. Douglas d. P. Valdez 6–2, 6–1, 6–2; H. Stewart–Douglas d. P. Phillips–McDonald 6–3, 6–3, 5–7, 6–3; Crawford d. Phillips 6–0, 6–0, 6–2; Douglas d. Valdez 6–2, 6–0, 6–1. **Ecuador d. Colombia 5–0, Quayaquil; Mexico d. Canada 3–2, Quebec:** M. Llamas lost to R. Bedard 6–8, 4–6, 0–6; A. Palafox d. F. Godbout 6–4, 2–6, 6–1, 6–1; R. Osuna–Palafox d. Bedard–Godbout 10–12, 9–7, 8–6, 6–4. Llamas d. Godbout 6–0, 6–3, 6–1; Bedard d. Osuna 5–7, 6–3, 6–1, 6–2.

SEMI-FINAL ROUND
USA d. Ecuador 5–0, St Louis: C. McKinley d. M. Olvera 6–4, 1–6, 6–4, 6–2; B. Bartzen d. E. Zuleta 6–0, 6–1, 6–1; D. Ralston–McKinley d. Olvera–Zuleta 6–1, 6–2, 7–5; McKinley d. Zuleta 6–4, 6–4, 1–6, 7–5; Ralston d. Olvera 6–2, 6–4, 6–2. **Mexico d. Morocco 5–0, Casablanca:** A. Palafox d. A. Douglas 6–0, 6–2, 6–1; P. Contreras d. A.

Lahcen 6–3, 6–4, 6–3; R. Osuna–Palafox d. L. Chadli–M. Cohen 6–2, 6–2, 6–1; M. Llamas d. Douglas 6–1, 6–0, 6–0; Osuna d. Chadli 6–1, 7–5, 7–5.

FINAL ROUND
USA d. Mexico 3–2, Cleveland: C. McKinley lost to R. Osuna 3–6, 3–6, 3–6; B. Bartzen d. M. Llamas 4–6, 6–4, 6–4, 6–4; D. Ralston–McKinley lost to A. Palafox–Osuna 4–6, 6–2, 4–6, 3–6; McKinley d. Llamas 6–4, 7–5, 10–8; Bartzen d. Osuna 6–3, 6–3, 7–5.

INTER-ZONE FINALS
USA d. India 3–2, New Delhi: C. McKinley d. J. Mukerjea 6–4, 6–4, 9–7; W. Reed lost to R. Krishnan 4–6, 1–6, 5–7; D. Dell–McKinley d. P. Lall–Krishnan 5–7, 6–0, 6–3, 6–2; Reed d. Mukerjea 6–2, 6–3, 6–3; McKinley lost to Krishnan 3–6, 6–4, 6–1, 3–6, 4–6. **Italy d. USA 4–1, Rome:** F. Gardini lost to J. Douglas 6–4, 6–4, 5–7, 8–10, 0–6; N. Pietrangeli d. W. Reed 2–6, 6–8, 6–4, 6–4, 6–4; Pietrangeli–O. Sirola d. D. Dell–Reed 6–4, 3–6, 6–3, 6–2; Pietrangeli d. Douglas 9–7, 6–3, 6–2; Gardini d. Reed 3–6, 7–5, 3–6, 8–6, 6–4.

CHALLENGE ROUND
Australia d. Italy 5–0, Melbourne: R. Emerson d. N. Pietrangeli 8–6, 6–4, 6–3; R. Laver d. O. Sirola 6–1, 6–4, 6–3; N. Fraser–Emerson d. Pietrangeli–Sirola 6–2, 6–3, 6–4; Laver d. Pietrangeli 6–3, 3–6, 4–6, 6–3, 8–6; Emerson d. Sirola 6–3, 6–3, 4–6, 6–2.

1962: AUSTRALIA
European Zone

FIRST ROUND
Belgium d. Chile 4–1, Brussels: E. Drossart d. P. Apey 7–5, 6–2, 6–2; J. Brichant d. P. Rodriguez 6–0, 7–5, 6–4; Drossart–Brichant d. Rodriguez–E. Aguirre 4–6, 3–6, 6–3, 6–0, 6–2; C. de Gronckel lost to Apey 3–6, 5–7, 6–4, 7–9; Drossart d. Rodriguez 6–4, 4–6, 7–5, 2–6, 6–2. **Finland d. Lebanon 4–1, Beirut:** R. Nyyssonen d. L. Samuel 6–1, 6–0, 6–2; S. Salo lost to K. Fawaz 4–6, 3–6, 5–7; Nyyssonen–Salo d. Fawaz–Samuel 6–2, 5–7, 8–6, 9–7; Salo d. Samuel 6–8, 6–2, 6–2, 6–1; Nyyssonen d. Fawaz 3–6, 6–4, 6–1, 6–0. **Czechoslovakia d. United Arab Republic 3–2, Prague:** P. Strobl d. K. Moubarek 6–1, 6–4, 4–6, 3–6, 6–4; J. Javorsky d. Fathi Mohamed Ali 6–3, 6–2, 6–4; Javorsky–Strobl d. Ali–Badr el Din 6–2, 3–6, 6–0, 6–3; Strobl lost to Mohamed Ali 4–6,

4–6, 2–6. **South Africa d. Switzerland 4–0, Lausanne:** A. Segal d. M. Froesch 6–2, 6–1, 6–3; G. Forbes d. J. Lemann 6–3, 5–7, 3–6, 7–5, 6–1; Forbes–Segal d. P. Blondel–B. Spielmann 6–3, 6–1, 6–2; C. Drysdale d. Lemann 11–9, 6–2, 6–4. **Rumania d. Israel 4–1, Bucharest:** I. Tiriac d. E. Davidman 6–0, 6–3, 6–3; C. Nastase d. G. Dubitzki 6–0, 6–1, 6–1; Tiriac–C. Marmureanu d. Davidman–Dubitzki 6–4, 6–1, 6–4; Nastase lost to Davidman 6–4, 6–1, 1–6, 3–6, 4–6; Tiriac d. Dubitzki 6–3, 6–1, 6–1. **West Germany d. Spain 3–2, Madrid:** I. Buding d. M. Santana 6–3, 1–6, 6–2, 7–5; W. Bungert lost to J. Couder 6–1, 4–6, 2–6, 6–4, 5–7; Bungert–C. Kuhnke d. Santana–J. L. Arilla 9–7, 6–4, 3–6, 11–9; Bungert d. Santana 6–2, 7–5, 6–3; Buding lost to Couder 4–6, 3–6, 2–6. **Brazil d. Monaco 5–0, Monte Carlo:** E. Mandarino d. A. Viviani 6–0, 6–1, 6–0; C. Fernandes d. R. Borghini 6–4, 6–2, 6–2; Mandarino–T. Koch d. Borghini–R. Ruzic 6–0, 6–2, 6–3; Fernandes d. Viviani 6–1, 6–2, 6–3; Koch d. Borghini 7–5, 6–3, 6–1. **Poland d. Norway 5–0, Oslo:** W. Skonecki d. P. Hegna 6–3, 6–1, 6–0; W. Gasiorek d. F. Soehol 6–2, 3–6, 6–2, 6–2; Gasiorek–J. Orlikowski d. A. L. Hansen–Soehol 6–4, 6–4, 6–1; Gasiorek d. Hegna 6–2, 4–6, 6–1, 6–4; Orlikowski d. Soehol 1–6, 2–6, 6–3, 6–3, 6–4. **Austria d. Ireland 4–1, Dublin:** F. Saiko d. G. P. Jackson 7–5, 6–2, 6–1; L. Legenstein d. R. Condy 6–0, 6–2, 6–2; Legenstein–D. Herdy d. D. Arthurs–M. Hickey 6–3, 6–3, 9–7; Saiko d. Arthurs 6–1, 6–2; Jackson d. Hardy 6–4, 1–6, 6–4. **Denmark d. New Zealand 4–1, Copenhagen:** J. Leschley d. J. Souter 6–2, 7–5, 6–4; J. Ulrich d. I. Crookenden 6–2, 1–6, 10–8, 2–6, 10–8; Ulrich–Leschley d. Crookenden–Souter 8–6, 6–3, 6–4; Leschley d. Crookenden 6–2, 3–6, 8–6, 6–0; A. C. Hegelund lost to Souter 3–6, 2–6, 6–4, 0–6. **Hungary d. Luxembourg 5–0:** Z. Katona d. G. Neumann 6–0, 6–2, 6–3; I. Gulyas d. J. Offenheim 6–3, 6–1, 6–1; Gulyas–A. Szikszai d. Offenheim–G. Wampach 6–1, 6–1, 6–3; Gulyas d. Neumann 6–1, 6–2, 6–3; Katona d. Offenheim 6–1, 6–2, 6–2. **USSR d. Holland 5–0, Scheveningen:** T. Lejus d. W. Maris 6–1, 6–1, 6–2; S. Likhachev d. E. Schneider 6–3, 6–1, 4–6, 6–4; Lejus–Likhachev d. Maris–Schneider 6–1, 7–5, 6–2; Likhachev d. P. van Eysden 6–1, 6–1, 6–1; R. Sivoken d. Schneider 7–5, 7–5, 6–2.

SECOND ROUND

Sweden d. Belgium 5–0, Brussels: J. E. Lundquist d. J. Brichant 2–6, 6–3, 6–4, 6–3; U. Schmidt d. E. Drossart 6–2, 6–4, 6–1; Lundquist–Schmidt d. Brichant–Drossart 6–0, 6–3, 6–1; Schmidt d. Brichant 6–2, 4–6, 6–4, 6–2; Lundquist d. Drossart 6–1, 6–2, 6–2. **Czechoslovakia d. Finland 5–0, Helsinki:** J. Javorski d. R. Nyyssonen 8–6, 6–2, 6–4; P. Korda d. P. Sailae 6–0, 9–7, 6–4; Javorski–P. Strobl d. Nyyssonen–S.

Salo 6–0, 3–6, 8–6, 6–4; Strobl d. Sailae 6–2, 6–3, 6–3; Korda d.
Nyyssonen 4–6, 4–6, 6–4, 6–1, 6–3.   **South Africa d. France 3–2,**
Paris: C. Drysdale d. G. Pilet 7–5, 2–6, 6–3, 12–10; G. Forbes lost to G.
Pilet 3–6, 1–6, 2–6; Forbes–A. Segal d. J. C. Barclay–J. Renavand 6–4,
6–1, 6–3; Drysdale lost to Darmon 4–6, 5–7, 2–6; Forbes d. Pilet 6–1,
6–1, 9–7.   **West Germany d. Rumania 5–0, Hanover:** W. Bungert d.
C. Nastase 6–1, 8–6, 6–2; I. Buding d. I. Tiriac 6–4, 6–0, 6–3; Bungert–C.
Kuhnke d. Nastase–Tiriac 6–0, 6–3, 6–4; Bungert d. Tiriac 6–1, 6–2,
6–2; Buding d. Nastase 6–2, 6–2, 6–1.   **Brazil d. Poland 3–0, Warsaw:**
C. Fernandes d. W. Skonecki 6–4, 2–6, 8–6, 6–4; E. Mandarino d. W.
Gasiorek 5–7, 6–2, 6–4, 9–7; R. Barnes–Fernandes d. W. Nowicki–W.
Bierlanowicz 6–3, 6–2, 6–3.   **Great Britain d. Austria 4–1, Vienna:**
W. Knight d. L. Legenstein 6–0, 3–6, 6–2, 6–3; M. Sangster lost to F.
Saiko 3–6, 6–3, 6–2, 4–6, 3–6; Knight–J. A. Pickard d. Saiko–Legenstein
6–0, 6–2, 3–6, 4–6, 6–0; Knight d. Saiko 6–2, 6–4, 9–7; Sangster d. D.
Herdy 10–8, 6–4, 3–6, 7–5.   **Hungary d. Denmark 5–0, Budapest:**
A. Szikszai d. A. C. Hegelund 6–2, 7–5, 6–4; I. Gulyas d. T. Larsen 6–3,
6–0, 6–2; Szikszai–Gulyas d. Hegelund–Larsen 6–3, 6–2, 6–2; Szikszai
d. Larsen 6–2, 6–4, 6–4; Gulyas d. Hegelund 6–0, 6–3, 6–4.   **Italy d.**
USSR 5–0, Rome: N. Pietrangeli d. T. Lejus 6–4, 1–6, 6–3, 6–1; F.
Gardini d. S. Likhachev 6–0, 6–2, 6–3; Pietrangeli–O. Sirola d.
Lejus–Likhachev 7–5, 6–2, 6–3; Pietrangeli d. Likhachev 0–6, 8–6, 8–6,
6–1; Gardini d. Lejus 6–4, 2–6, 6–3, 6–3.

THIRD ROUND

Sweden d. Czechoslovakia 5–0, Stockholm: U. Schmidt d. P. Korda
6–2, 6–4, 6–2; J. E. Lundquist d. J. Javorski 6–0, 10–8, 6–2;
Lundquist–Schmidt d. Javorski–P. Strobl 8–6, 6–3, 6–0; Schmidt d. Korda
6–2, 6–0, 6–4; Schmidt d. Javorski 6–4, 3–6, 6–3, 6–2.   **South Africa d.**
West Germany 3–2, Berlin: C. Drysdale lost to I. Buding 6–4, 5–7,
4–6, 11–9, 3–6; G. Forbes lost to W. Bungert 3–6, 8–6, 6–4, 3–6, 4–6;
Forbes–A. Segal d. Bungert–C. Kuhnke 4–6, 6–4, 6–2, 3–6, 6–3; Forbes
d. Buding 6–3, 6–2, 5–7, 6–4; Drysdale d. Bungert 6–2, 0–6, 8–6, 6–2.
Great Britain d. Brazil 4–1, Eastbourne: M. Sangster d. C. Fernandes
6–4, 6–4, 6–4; W. Knight d. T. Koch 6–3, 6–3, 6–1; Knight–J. A.
Pickard lost to E. Mandarino–R. Barnes 17–19, 6–1, 4–6, 7–9; Knight d.
Fernandes 10–8, 6–3, 3–6, 7–5; Sangster d. Mandarino 4–6, 6–3, 6–3,
2–6, 7–5.   **Italy d. Hungary 4–1, Brescia:** F. Gardini d. Z. Katona 6–1,
6–3, 6–1; N. Pietrangeli lost to I. Gulyas 6–1, 4–6, 3–6, 2–6;
Pietrangeli–O. Sirola d. Gulyas–A. Szikszai 1–6, 6–2, 6–1, 4–6, 6–3;
Pietrangeli d. Katona 6–0, 6–2, 6–3; Gardini d. Gulyas 6–1, 2–6, 6–3,
6–2.

SEMI-FINAL ROUND

Sweden d. South Africa 4–1, Båstad: U. Schmidt lost to C. Drysdale 3–6, 2–6, 6–3, 3–6; J. E. Lundquist d. G. Forbes 6–2, 6–4, 6–1; Schmidt–Lundquist d. Drysdale–A. Segal 6–4, 6–2, 9–7; Lundquist d. Drysdale 6–4, 6–4, 6–2; Schmidt d. Segal 11–9, 6–4, 6–1. **Italy d. Great Britain 5–0, Milan:** N. Pietrangeli d. M. Sangster 6–3, 4–6, 7–5, 8–6; F. Gardini d. W. A. Knight 6–1, 6–8, 6–3, 6–1; Pietrangeli–O. Sirola d. Knight–J. A. Pickard 6–3, 6–4, 6–8, 6–3; Pietrangeli d. Pickard 8–6, 6–0, 6–1; Gardini d. Sangster 6–1, 6–3, 6–0.

FINAL ROUND

Sweden d. Italy 4–1, Båstad: U. Schmidt lost to F. Gardini 3–6, 6–3, 5–7, 3–6; J. E. Lundquist d. N. Pietrangeli 6–2, 6–4, 6–1; Lundquist–Schmidt d. Pietrangeli–O. Sirola 6–1, 3–6, 6–8, 6–4, 9–7; Lundquist d. Gardini 6–0, 6–2, 6–1; Schmidt d. Pietrangeli 6–1, 8–6, 6–3.

Eastern Zone

FIRST ROUND

Iran d. Malaya 3–2, Tehran: R. Akbari lost to Azeman 3–6, 1–6; T. Akbari d. Billiap 6–0, 6–2, 6–1; T. Akbari–A. Yessai d. Azeman–Billiap 6–0, 10–8, 3–6, 6–3; R. Akbari lost to Billiap 4–6, 6–3, 5–7, 4–6; T. Akbari d. Azeman 10–8, 6–3, 5–7, 6–0. **India d. Pakistan 5–0, Lahore:** P. Lall d. M. Pirzada 6–3, 6–1, 6–2; R. Krishnan d Saeed Hai 6–4, 6–2, 6–2; Lall–Akhtar Ali d. I. Ahmed–Naaem 9–7, 6–2, 7–5; Lall d. Saeed Hai 8–6, 6–1, 6–3; Ali d. Pirzada 6–2, 7–5, 4–6, 6–4. **Japan d. Korea 5–0, Seoul:** O. Ishiguro d. Sang Yun Lee 6–3, 6–1, 4–6, 6–2; N. Fujii d. Yong Ho Chung 6–3, 6–0, 6–0; Ishiguro–Fujii d. Sang Yun Lee–Yong Ho Chung 6–0, 6–2, 6–3; Fujii d. Doo Hwan Kim 6–0, 6–3, 6–3; S. Suga d. Tong Won Lee 6–4, 6–2, 6–1. **Philippines d. Ceylon 4–0, Colombo:** J. Jose d. B. Pinto 6–2, 6–1, 6–4; R. Deyro d. R. Praesody 6–4, 6–4, 6–2; Jose–Deyro d. Pinto–Praesody 6–2, 6–1, 6–2; E. Dungo d. P. Kumar 6–2, 5–7, 6–3, 6–0; Jose v. Praesody 5–0 unfin.

SEMI-FINAL ROUND

India d. Iran 4–0, Jaipur: P. Lall d. R. Akbari 6–1, 6–2, 6–0; J. Mukerjea d. T. Akbari 6–0, 6–2, 6–4; Lall–Mukerjea d. A. Yassai–T. Akbari 6–3, 6–2, 6–2; Akhtar Ali d. R. Akbari 6–0, 6–2, 6–2; Lall v.T. Akbari 6–4 unfin. **Philippines d. Japan 3–2, Manila:** R. Deyro lost to A. Miyagi 1–6, 6–1, 4–6, 2–6; J. Jose d. O. Ishiguro 7–5, 6–2, 6–3; Jose–Deyro d. Miyagi–M. Fujii 6–3, 6–3, 6–4; Deyro d. Ishiguro 6–1, 6–2, 7–5; E. Dungo lost to Fujii 2–6, 0–6, 1–6.

427

FINAL ROUND
India d. Philippines 5–0, New Delhi: J. Mukerjea d. J. Jose 9–11, 7–5,
6–0, 6–4; R. Krishnan d. F. Ampon 6–1, 8–6, 6–1; P. Lall–Mukerjea d.
R. Deyro–Jose 6–3, 3–6, 9–7, 6–1; Lall d. Jose 6–3, 6–1, 6–0; Mukerjea
d. Ampon 6–1, 6–3, 3–6, 6–1.

American Zone

FIRST ROUND
USA d. Canada 5–0, Cleveland: C. McKinley d. F. Godbout 6–4, 3–6,
6–3, 6–4; J. Douglas d. D. Fontana 6–4, 6–2, 5–7, 6–4; D. Ralston–
McKinley d. Godbout–Fontana 11–9, 7–5, 6–1; McKinley d. H. Fauquier
6–3, 6–0, 6–2; Ralston d. Godbout 6–2, 9–7, 6–4.

SEMI-FINAL ROUND
Yugoslavia d. British Caribbean 4–1, Trinidad: B. Jovanovic d. I.
McDonald 6–1, 6–1, 6–1; N. Pilic d. P. Valde 6–2, 6–1, 6–0; Jovanovic–
Pilic d. Valde–A. Price 6–2, 6–0, 6–1; Pilic d. Price 6–0, 6–2, 6–3;
Jovanovic lost to Valde 6–2, 4–6, 1–4 def. **Mexico d. USA 3–2,**
Mexico City: R. Osuna lost to C. McKinley 2–6, 5–7, 3–6; A. Palafox
d. J. Douglas 6–3, 6–1, 3–6, 7–5; Osuna–Palafox d. D. Ralston–
McKinley 8–6, 10–12, 3–6, 6–3, 6–2; Osuna d. Douglas 9–7, 6–3, 6–8,
3–6, 6–1; M. Llamas lost to McKinley 6–2, 6–4, 5–7, 3–6, 3–6.

FINAL ROUND
Mexico d. Yugoslavia 4–1, Mexico City: A. Palafox d. B. Jovanovic
6–4, 1–6, 6–3, 6–3; R. Osuna d. N. Pilic 6–4, 6–4, 6–2; Osuna–Palafox
d. Jovanovic–Pilic 6–4, 2–6, 6–3, 7–5; P. Contreras lost to Pilic 2–6, 2–6,
7–9; M. Llamas d. V. Presechi 6–0, 6–1, 6–1.

INTER-ZONE FINALS
Mexico d. Sweden 3–2, Mexico City: A. Palafox lost to J. E. Lundquist
6–8, 6–1, 6–8, 4–6; R. Osuna d. U. Schmidt 6–3, 16–14, 1–6, 6–2;
Palafox–Osuna d. Lundquist–Schmidt; Palafox lost to Schmidt 9–11, 6–3,
3–6, 6–1, 1–6; Osuna d. Lundquist 3–6, 6–4, 6–3, 1–6, 6–3. **Mexico**
d. India 5–0, Madras: A. Palafox d. J. Mukerjea 9–7, 6–2, 6–2; R. Osuna
d. R. Krishnan 8–6, 2–6, 7–5, 6–8, 6–4; Osuna–Palafox d. Mukerjea–P.
Lall 10–8, 12–10, 6–4; M. Llamas d. Lall 6–2, 6–2, 6–3; F. Contreras d.
A. Ali 6–4, 2–6, 5–7, 6–4, 6–3.

CHALLENGE ROUND

Australia d. Mexico 5–0, Brisbane: R. G. Laver d. R. Osuna 6–2, 6–1, 7–5; N. A. Fraser d. A. Palafox 7–9, 6–3, 6–4, 11–9; R. Emerson–Laver d. Osuna–Palafox 7–5, 6–2, 6–4; Fraser d. Osuna 3–6, 11–9, 6–1, 3–6, 6–4; Laver d. Palafox 6–1, 4–6, 6–4, 8–6.

1963: USA
European Zone

PRELIMINARY ROUND

Israel d. Turkey 4–1, İstanbul: E. Davidman d. Z. Kipkizil 6–2, 6–1, 6–1; G. Dubitsky lost to N. Bari 6–3, 2–6, 1–6, 1–6; Davidman–Dubitsky d. Bari–E. Bales 6–2, 6–3, 6–3; Dubitsky d. Kipkizil 7–5, 8–6, 8–6; Davidman d. Bari 6–3, 1–6, 6–4, 3–6, 6–3. **United Arab Republic d. Lebanon 5–0, Beirut:** B. S. Ibrahim d. E. Samuel 6–1, 6–2, 6–4; F. M. Aly d. K. Fawaz 1–6, 6–1, 6–2, 6–2; Ibrahim–Aly d. Fawaz–E. Attieh 6–1, 6–2, 6–0. **Portugal d. Luxembourg 3–2, Estoril:** D. Cohen d. J. Offenheim 6–0, 6–4, 4–6, 6–3; V. Pinto d. F. Baden 6–4, 2–6, 7–5, 7–5; A. Gomes–M. Diniz lost to Baden–G. Wampach 5–7, 5–7, 5–7; Cohen lost to Baden 4–6, 4–6, 3–6; Pinto d. Offenheim 6–2, 6–0, 6–1. **Greece d. Ireland 3–2, Dublin:** N. Kalogeropoulos d. D. Arthurs 1–6, 7–5, 6–4, 4–6, 6–4; N. Kalyvas d. P. Jackson 6–2, 7–5, 4–6, 6–1; Kalogeropoulos–D. Kanellopoulos lost to Arthurs–M. Hickey 6–3, 2–6, 3–6, 6–3, 1–6; Kalyvas lost to Arthurs 4–6, 6–3, 6–1, 2–6, 3–6; Kalogeropoulos d. Hickey 6–0, 6–3, 6–2.

FIRST ROUND

Rhodesia & Nyasaland d. Holland 4–1, Scheveningen: A. Bey lost to P. van Eysden 6–3, 7–9, 3–6, 3–6; F. Saloman d. W. Maris 6–3, 6–1, 6–3; Bey–Saloman d. Maris–van Eysden 6–3, 6–3, 6–3; Bey d. Maris 3–6, 3–6, 8–6, 6–4, 6–4; Saloman d. van Eysden 3–6, 6–3, 1–6, 6–3, 6–3. **Yugoslavia d. Monaco 5–0, Split:** N. Pilic d. R. Borghini 6–2, 6–2, 7–5; B. Jovanovic d. A. Viviani 6–1, 6–1, 6–1; Pilic–Jovanovic d. Borghini–Viviani 6–2, 6–4, 6–2; S. Jelic d. Borghini 6–2, 5–7, 6–2, 6–3; V. Presecki d. Viviani 6–3, 6–3, 6–3. **Austria d. Israel 5–0, Vienna:** F. Hainka d. G. Dubitsky 6–2, 6–0, 6–0; D. Herdy d. E. Davidman 6–1, 3–6, 6–2, 4–6, 6–2; Herdy–P. Pokorny d. Davidman–Dubitsky 0–6, 6–3, 10–8, 6–1; Pokorny d. Dubitsky 6–4, 6–1, 6–2; Hainka d. Davidman 6–4, 6–1, 6–3. **Rumania d. Switzerland 5–0, Bucharest:** I. Tiriac d. P. Blondel 6–1, 6–1, 6–1; A. Bardan d. B. Schweitzer 3–6, 4–6, 6–3, 6–3, 6–0; Tiriac–P. Marmureanu d. Blondel–J. Auberson 6–2, 7–5, 6–3; Tiriac

d. Schweitzer 6–3, 6–4, 6–1; Bardan d. Blondel 6–2, 6–2, 6–2. **Denmark d. Czechoslovakia 4–1, Copenhagen:** J. Ulrich d. J. Javorsky 6–4, 6–1, 8–6; J. Leschley d. P. Strobl 6–2, 6–4, 6–1; Ulrich–Leschley lost to Javorsky–Strobl 4–6, 4–6, 4–6; Ulrich d. Strobl 6–1, 6–3, 6–3; Leschley d. S. Koudelta 9–7, 6–1, 6–2. **Norway d. Portugal 5–0, Estoril:** G. Sjowall d. A. Gomes 6–3, 6–4, 6–4; Simsoel d. V. Pinto 6–3, 2–6, 6–4, 6–4; J. Bibow–P. Soehol d. M. Diniz–J. Roquete 7–9, 12–10, 6–2, 6–2; Soehol d. Gomes 6–3, 8–6, 6–2; P. Hegna d. Pinto 6–4, 6–4, 6–4. **Chile d. United Arab Republic 5–0, Cairo:** E. Aguirre d. I. Shafei 6–1, 6–4, 2–6, 3–6, 8–6; P. Rodriguez d. Fathi Mahomed Aly 6–3, 6–4, 6–4; Aguirre–J. Pinto d. F. M. Aly–Shafei 6–4, 6–2, 6–1; Rodriguez d. Shafei 6–0, 6–2, 6–2; Aguirre d. F. M. Aly 6–2, 6–2 def. **USSR d. Finland 5–0, Helsinki:** M. Mozer d. P. Petersen–Dyggve 6–3, 6–1, 6–4; T. Lejus d. T. Jokinen 6–0, 6–3, 6–2; Lejus–S. Lichatchev d. S. Salo–M. Kinnunen 6–1, 6–4, 6–0; Lejus d. Petersen–Dyggve 7–5, 6–0, 6–2; Mozer d. Jokinen 6–4, 6–4, 6–2. **Belgium d. Hungary 3–2, Budapest:** J. Brichant lost to I. Gulyas 2–6, 1–6, 2–6; E. Drossart d. F. Komaromi 8–6, 9–7, 6–4; Brichant–Drossart d. Gulyas–A. Szikszai 6–1, 6–3, 1–6, 6–3; Brichant d. Komaromi 6–3, 8–6, 6–2. **Brazil d. Greece 3–2, Athens:** E. Mandarino d. N. Kalyvas 6–1, 9–7, 6–1; R. Barnes d. N. Kalogeropoulos 4–6, 6–0, 7–5, 6–2; Barnes lost to Kalyvas 6–4, 1–6, 3–6, 6–1, 4–6; Mandarino d. Kalogeropoulos 6–1, 6–1, 6–3; Brazil def. doubles. **France d. Poland 5–0, Paris:** J. Barclay d. W. Bielanowcz 6–1, 6–0, 6–2; P. Darmon d. S. Szczukiewiecz 6–0, 6–1, 6–1; P. Buest–D. Contet d. Bielanowicz–Szczukiewiecz 6–2, 6–3, 6–2; Barclay d. Szczukiewicz 6–4, 6–2, 6–3; Darmon d. Bielanowicz 6–0, 6–3, 6–1. **Spain d. West Germany 3–2, Cologne:** M. Santana d. W. Bungert 9–7, 8–6, 6–3; J. Couder lost to C. Kuhnke 4–6, 4–6, 6–8; J. and A. Arilla lost to Bungert–Kuhnke 0–6, 4–6, 6–3, 3–6; Santana d. Kuhnke 6–2, 6–4, 6–0; Couder d. Bungert 3–6, 4–6, 6–3, 7–5, 6–3.

SECOND ROUND

Sweden d. Rhodesia & Nyasaland 3–2, Stockholm: J. E. Lundquist lost to A. Bey 6–3, 5–7, 6–0, 5–7, 5–7; U. Schmidt d. F. Saloman 6–3, 6–1, 6–2; Lundquist–Schmidt d. Bey–Saloman 6–3, 9–7, 6–1; Schmidt d. Bey 6–4, 6–0, 6–4; Lundquist lost to Saloman 6–1, 1–6, 2–6, 2–6.
Yugoslavia d. Austria 5–0, Zagreb: N. Pilic d. D. Herdy 6–3, 6–3, 6–2; B. Jovanovic d. F. Hainka 6–3, 6–3, 6–2; Jovanovic–Pilic d. Herdy–P. Pokorny 6–2, 7–5, 6–4; V. Presecki d. Herdy 6–2, 2–6, 4–6, 6–3, 7–5; S. Jelic d. D. Schultheiss 6–4, 7–5, 6–4. **South Africa d. Rumania 3–2, Bucharest:** A. Segal d. A. Bardan 6–4, 6–3, 6–4; G. Forbes lost to I. Tiriac 4–6, 7–5, 5–7, 4–6; Forbes–Segal d. Tiriac–Bardan

6–2, 7–9, 6–2, 6–2; Forbes d. Bardan 6–2, 6–4, 6–0; Segal lost to Tiriac 1–6, 11–13, 3–6. **Denmark d. Norway 4–1, Copenhagen:** J. Ulrich d. P. Hegna 7–5, 2–6, 6–2, 6–3; J. Leschley d. G. Sjowall 6–3, 6–2, 6–3; Ulrich–Leschley d. Sjowall–Hegna 11–9, 6–2, 6–4; Ulrich lost to Sjowall 2–6, 2–6, 4–6; C. Hedelund d. Hegna 6–1, 3–6, 6–4. **USSR d. Chile 4–1, Moscow:** T. Lejus lost to P. Rodriguez 7–9, 0–6, 7–9; M. Mozer d. E. Aguirre 7–9, 3–6, 6–2, 6–4, 6–4; Lejus–S. Lichachev d. Aguirre– Rodriguez 4–6, 6–0, 1–6, 7–5, 6–2; Lejus d. Aguirre 6–3, 6–3, 6–4; Mozer d. Pinto 3–6, 6–1, 7–5, 6–4. **Great Britain d. Belgium 5–0, Brussels:** W. Knight d. J. Brichant 6–3, 6–2, 6–8, 6–2; M. Sangster d. E. Drossart 8–6, 7–5, 6–4; R. Wilson–J. A. Pickard d. Brichant–Drossart 6–8, 2–6, 6–3, 7–5, 11–9; Knight d. Drossart 6–0, 6–3, 3–6, 6–4; Sangster d. Brichant 4–6, 6–4, 6–1, 6–2. **France d. Brazil 4–1, Paris:** P. Darmon d. E. Mandarino 6–4, 6–2, 6–4; J. Barclay lost to R. Barnes 3–6, 6–8, 2–6; P. Buest–D. Contet d. Barnes–C. Fernandes 2–6, 12–10, 6–2, 6–2; Barclay d. Mandarino 3–6, 6–2, 6–0, 6–4; Darmon d. Barnes 6–3, 6–4, 6–1. **Spain d. Italy 4–1, Barcelona:** M. Santana lost to N. Pietrangeli 4–6, 4–6, 6–3, 6–8; J. Couder d. F. Gardini 9–7, 7–5, 6–1; Santana–J. Arilla d. Pietrangeli–O. Sirola 7–5, 6–4, 6–1; Santana d. Gardini 6–1, 6–1, 10–8; Couder d. Pietrangeli 3–6, 6–3, 6–3, 6–3.

THIRD ROUND

Sweden d. Yugoslavia 4–1, Stockholm: U. Schmidt d. N. Pilic 3–6, 6–1, 6–2, 6–1; J. E. Lundquist d. B. Jovanovic 6–0, 5–7, 6–2, 6–4; Lundquist–Schmidt d. Jovanovic–Pilic 6–2, 3–6, 6–4, 6–1; Lundquist d. Pilic 6–3, 4–6, 13–11, 6–3; Schmidt lost to Jovanovic 6–2, 4–6, 5–7, 5–7. **South Africa d. Denmark 4–1, Copenhagen:** C. Drysdale d. C. Hedelund 6–1, 6–2, 6–0; G. Forbes d. J. Ulrich 6–2, 6–2, 6–4; Forbes–A. Segal d. Hedelund–Ulrich 10–8, 6–2, 6–4; Segal lost to Ulrich 3–6, 7–9, 6–3, 3–6; Forbes d. Hedelund 6–2, 6–4, 7–5. **Great Britain d. USSR 4–1, Eastbourne:** M. Sangster d. A. Metreveli 6–4, 6–3, 6–3; R. K. Wilson lost to T. Lejus 7–5, 4–6, 8–10, 4–6; Sangster–W. Knight d. Lejus–S. Likhachev 6–2, 6–3, 4–6, 15–13; Wilson d. Metreveli 7–5, 8–6, 6–2; Sangster d. Lejus 6–4, 6–4, 6–3. **Spain d. France 4–1, Barcelona:** M. Santana d. J. Barclay 6–1, 6–2, 6–2; J. Couder lost to P. Darmon 4–6, 2–6, 0–6; Santana–J. Arilla d. P. Buest–D. Contet 7–5, 6–2, 6–2; Santana d. Darmon 6–3, 6–4, 10–8; Couder d. Barclay 6–2, 6–1, 6–1.

SEMI–FINAL ROUND

Sweden d. South Africa 5–0, Båstad: J. E. Lundquist d. C. Drysdale 3–6, 3–6, 6–0, 6–3, 6–0; U. Schmidt d. G. Forbes 6–4, 6–4, 3–6, 6–4; Lundquist–Schmidt d. Forbes–A. Segal 8–6, 5–7, 7–5, 6–3; Lundquist d.

Forbes 6–2, 6–3, 6–2; Schmidt d. Drysdale 6–2, 3–6, 7–5, 6–0.   **Great Britain d. Spain 4–1, Bristol:** M. Sangster d. J. L. Arilla 6–2, 6–4, 6–4; R. K. Wilson lost to M. Santana 4–6, 4–6, 8–6, 6–2, 5–7; Sangster–Wilson d. Santana–Arilla 8–10, 7–5, 9–7, 4–6, 6–1; Wilson d. Arilla 6–4, 7–5, 6–3; Sangster d. Santana 6–4, 7–5, 3–6, 4–6, 7–5.

FINAL ROUND
Great Britain d. Sweden 3–2, London: M. Sangster d. J. E. Lundquist 3–6, 6–2, 4–6, 12–10, 9–7; R. K. Wilson lost to U. Schmidt 4–6, 6–4, 4–6, 6–4, 4–6; Sangster–Wilson d. Lundquist–Schmidt 22–20, 6–4, 6–3; Wilson lost to Lundquist 6–3, 6–2, 2–6, 2–6, 1–6; Sangster d. Schmidt 7–5, 6–2, 9–11, 3–6, 6–3.

Eastern Zone

FIRST ROUND
Pakistan d. Ceylon 4–0, Colombo: M. Pirzada d. R. Praesody 6–1, 6–3, 6–4; S. Qutubuddin d. G. N. Perera 6–4, 6–4, 6–1; I. Ahmed–Pirzada d. B. Pinto–P. S. Kumara 9–7, 5–7, 9–7, 6–4; Z. Rahim d. Praesody 6–1, 3–6, 6–1, 2–6, 6–4; Pirzada v. Perera 6–1, 6–3 unfin.

SECOND ROUND
Malaya d. Burma 3–2, Kuala Lumpur: S. A. Azman d. J. Ba Maung 4–6, 6–1, 6–3, 6–1; Kwok Yoke Yen lost to Than Lwin 4–6, 2–6, 2–6; Azman–Yen d. Maung–Lwin 16–14, 6–0, 3–6, 1–6, 6–4; Azman d. Lwin 6–0, 6–2, 6–2; Yen lost to Maung 4–6, 5–7, 2–6.   **India d. Pakistan 4–1, Poona:** R. Krishnan d. S. Qutubuddin 6–0, 6–3, 6–0; J. Mukerjea d. M. Pirzada 6–3, 6–4, 6–2; Mukerjea–A. Ali d. I. Ahmad–Pirzada 3–6, 5–7, 6–3, 6–4, 6–2; Mukerjea d. Qutubuddin 6–2, 6–3, 6–4; Ali lost to Z. Rahim 8–6, 2–6, 6–1, 5–7, 3–6.   **Philippines d. New Zealand 3–1, Manila:** J. Jose d. L. A. Gerrard 2–6, 6–3, 6–3, 9–7; F. Ampon d. I. S. Crookenden 4–6, 6–4, 1–6, 6–4, 6–1; Jose–R. Deyro lost to Gerrard–J. Robson 4–6, 3–6, 6–3, 3–6; Ampon d. Gerrard 6–1, 4–6, 6–3, 6–4.   **Japan d. Korea 5–0, Fukuoka:** O. Ishiguro d. S. Yun Lee 6–2, 1–6, 6–3, 6–2; K. Watanabe d. H. Kim 6–3, 6–2, 7–5; A. Miyagi–M. Fujii d. Doo Shung Pack–S. Y. Lee 3–6, 6–0, 6–2, 6–1; Ishiguro d. Too Hwan 6–2, 6–2, 6–0; Wantanabe d. S. Y. Lee 6–4, 2–6, 6–3, 6–2.

SEMI–FINAL ROUND
India d. Malaya 4–0, Kuala Lumpur: R. Krishnan d. S. A. Azman 6–1, 6–1, 6–0; J. Mukerjea d. B. Yap 6–1, 6–0, 6–2; Mukerjea–A. Ali

d. Azman–K. Yoke 6–4, 6–2, 6–4; Mukerjea d. Azman 6–2, 6–2, 6–3; Ali
v. Yap 6–3, 6–2 unfin. **Japan d. Philippines 4–1, Tokyo:** A. Miyagi
d. J. Jose 3–6, 6–1, 6–2, 7–5; O. Ishiguro d. F. Ampon 6–3, 6–0, 3–6,
6–3; Miyagi–M. Fujii d. Jose–E. Dungo 6–4, 3–6, 7–5, 8–6; Ishiguro lost
to Jose 6–0, 2–6, 1–6, 8–10; Miyagi d. Ampon 2–6, 6–3, 6–4, 8–6.

FINAL ROUND
India d. Japan 3–2, Tokyo: R. Krishnan d. A. Miyagi 7–5, 4–6, 6–0,
6–0; J. Mukerjea lost to O. Ishiguro 2–6, 3–6, 2–6; Mukerjea–P. Lall d.
Miyagi–M. Fujii 6–4, 3–6, 2–6, 5–7; Krishnan d. Ishiguro 6–2, 7–5;
Mukerjea lost to Miyagi 3–6, 2–6, 6–3, 5–7.

American Zone

FIRST ROUND
USA d. Iran 5–0, Teheran: E. Scott d. R. Akbari 6–4, 6–1, 6–0; A. Fox
d. T. Akbari 6–2, 6–2, 6–2; D. Dell–Scott d. R. and T. Akbari 6–0, 6–1,
6–4; Fox d. R. Akbari 6–1, 6–0, 6–1; Dell d. T. Akbari 6–3, 6–4, 6–4.
Mexico d. Canada 4–1, Vancouver: R. Osuna d. F. Godbout 6–3, 6–1,
6–2; A. Palafox d. H. Fauquier 9–7, 6–4, 6–1; Osuna–Palafox d.
Fauquier–K. Carpenter 6–3, 7–5, 6–4; Palafox d. Godbout 6–3, 6–3, 6–1;
J. Arradando lost to Carpenter 2–6, 3–6, 6–3, 6–1, 3–6. **Ecuador d.
British Caribbean 3–2, Guayaquil:** F. Guzman d. L. Lumsden 6–1,
6–3, 6–3; E. Zuleta d. P. Valdez 6–4, 6–3, 6–1; Guzman–Zuleta lost to
Lumsden–Valdez 4–6, 6–3, 4–6, 5–7; Zuleta d. Lumsden 6–1, 6–4, 6–1;
Guzman lost to Valdez 4–6, 5–7, 7–9.

SEMI-FINAL ROUND
USA d. Mexico 4–1, Los Angeles: C. McKinley lost to R. Osuna 2–6,
6–3, 2–6, 6–2, 3–6; D. Ralston d. A. Palafox 6–1, 6–4, 3–6, 6–3;
McKinley–Ralston d. Osuna–Palafox 6–1, 6–3, 8–6; Ralston d. Osuna
6–1, 6–3, 7–5; McKinley d. Palafox 6–4, 6–4, 4–6, 6–3. **Venezuela d.
Ecuador 3–1, Caracas:** J. Notz lost to E. Zuleta 3–6, 3–6, 4–6; I. Pimental
d. F. Guzman 6–2, 6–1, 6–0; Pimental–Notz d. Guzman–Zuleta 6–3,
6–4, 6–2; Pimental d. Zuleta 6–3, 6–2, 6–1; Notz v. Guzman 6–0, 3–6,
3–6, 7–5 unfin.

FINAL ROUND
USA d. Venezuela 5–0, Denver: D. Ralston d. O. Bracamonte 6–2,
6–1, 6–2; M. Riessen d. I. Pimental 8–6, 6–4, 6–4; Ralston–Riessen d.
Pimental–Bracamonte 7–5, 8–6, 6–3; A. Ashe d. Bracamonte 6–1, 6–1,
6–0; Ralston d. Pimental 18–16, 9–7, 6–4.

INTER-ZONE FINALS

USA d. Great Britain 5–0, Bournemouth: C. McKinley d. M. Sangster 7–5, 6–2, 7–5; M. Froehling d. W. Knight 4–6, 8–6, 6–4, 6–4; D. Ralston–McKinley d. R. Wilson–Sangster 6–4, 6–8, 9–7, 6–2; McKinley d. Knight 8–6, 6–2, 6–3; Froehling d. Sangster 6–1, 4–6, 6–0, 6–4. **USA d. India 5–0, Bombay:** C. McKinley d. P. Lall 6–4, 6–3, 6–0; D. Ralston d. R. Krishnan 6–4, 6–1, 13–11; McKinley–Ralston d. J. Mukerjea–Lall 6–8, 6–3, 12–10, 6–4; M. Riessen d. Lall 6–3, 2–6, 6–0, 6–1; McKinley d. Krishnan 10–8, 6–8, 6–2, 2–6, 6–0.

CHALLENGE ROUND

USA d. Australia 3–2, Adelaide: D. Ralston d. J. Newcombe 6–4, 6–1, 3–6, 4–6, 7–5; C. McKinley lost to R. Emerson 3–6, 6–3, 5–7, 5–7; McKinley–Ralston d. Emerson–N. Fraser 6–3, 4–6, 11–9, 11–9; Ralston lost to Emerson 2–6, 3–6, 6–3, 2–6; McKinley d. Newcombe 10–12, 6–2, 9–7, 6–2.

1964: USA

European Zone

FIRST ROUND

Great Britain d. Austria 5–0, Birmingham: W. Knight d. D. Herdy 6–0, 6–4, 6–1; R. Taylor d. E. Blanke 6–2, 6–2, 6–4; M. Sangster–A. Mills d. Herdy–P. Pokorny 6–2, 6–3, 3–6, 3–6, 7–5; Taylor d. Pokorny 5–7, 7–5, 6–3, 6–2; Knight d. Blanke 6–0, 6–0, 6–2. **Ireland d. Switzerland 3–2, Dublin:** P. Jackson lost to D. Sturdza 15–17, 6–4, 3–6, 6–4, 2–6; D. Arthurs d. J. Siegrist 7–5, 6–4, 7–5; Arthurs–Jackson lost to Sturdza–M. Werren 3–6, 5–7, 5–7; Jackson d. Siegrist 6–3, 6–4, 6–4; Arthurs d. Sturdza 3–6, 6–4, 4–6, 7–5, 6–3. **Yugoslavia d. Luxembourg 3–0, Belgrade:** B. Jovanovic d. F. Baden 6–2, 6–0, 6–4; N. Pilic d. J. Offenheim 6–1, 6–0, 6–1; Jovanovic–Pilic d. Baden–Offenheim 6–1, 6–0, 6–4. **Argentina d. Turkey 5–0, Istanbul:** E. Soriano d. N. Bari 6–4, 6–1, 6–3; R. Aubone d. Z. Kipkzil 6–0, 6–1, 6–2; Soriano–Aubone d. Bari–E. Balash 6–0, 6–2, 6–2; Soriano d. Kipkzil 6–1, 6–0, 6–0; Aubone d. Bari 6–2, 6–4. **South Africa d. Poland def.; Norway d. Portugal 4–1, Oslo:** G. Sjowall d. D. Cohen 6–2, 6–2, 6–1; F. Soehol lost to A. V. Pinto 2–6, 3–6, 2–6; F. D. Jagge–J. Bibow d. Pinto–J. Roquette 6–0, 6–3, 6–3; Sjowall d. Pinto 9–11, 8–6, 7–5, 7–5; Soehol d. Cohen 3–6, 6–2, 6–3, 6–3. **France d. Bulgaria 5–0, Dijon:** P. Darmon d. N. Tchouparov 6–0, 6–1, 6–0; P. Barthes d. R. Rangelov 6–0, 6–2, 6–0; P. Beust–D. Contet d. Rangelov–Tchouparov 6–3, 6–4,

434

6–4; Darmon d. Rangelov 6–4, 6–3, 6–3; Barthes d. Tchouparov 6–1, 6–1, 6–3. **Holland d. Hungary 3–2, The Hague:** T. Okker lost to I. Gulyas 3–6, 1–6, 3–6; J. Hajer d. A. Szikszai 2–6, 4–6, 9–7, 8–6, 6–2; Hajer–Okker d. Gulyas–Szikszai 6–3, 1–6, 2–6, 9–7, 6–1; Okker d. Szikszai 6–4, 3–6, 6–3, 6–3; Hajer lost to Gulyas 2–6, 2–6, 1–6. **USSR d. Morocco 4–1, Casablanca:** T. Lejus d. L. Chadli 6–2, 8–6, 6–4; A. Metreveli lost to H. Bouchaib 5–7, 6–2, 6–8, 1–6; Lejus–S. Likhachev d. Chadli–Bouchaib 6–3, 6–3, 6–1; Metrevli d. Chadli 8–6, 6–1, 4–6, 6–4; Lejus d. Bouchaib 6–0, 2–6, 6–2, 6–4. **West Germany d. Belgium 5–0, Brussels:** I. Buding d. C. de Gronckel 4–6, 3–6, 6–4, 6–4, 6–1; C. Kuhnke d. E. Drossart 6–4, 6–4, 1–6, 6–3; W. Bungert–G. Stuck d. Drossart–J. Brichant 6–4, 6–4, 6–2; Bungert d. de Gronckel 2–6, 6–4, 7–5, 6–4; Buding d. Drossart 8–10, 6–3, 11–9, 6–2. **Denmark d. Finland 5–0, Copenhagen:** J. Ulrich d. H. Hedman 5–7, 6–4, 6–4, 7–5; T. Ulrich d. R. Nyyssonen 6–1, 4–6, 3–6, 8–6, 6–4; J. Ulrich–J. Leschly d. Nyyssonen–P. Saela 6–0, 6–2, 2–6, 6–1; J. Ulrich d. Nyyssonen 7–5, 6–4, 6–3; T. Ulrich d. Hedman 6–1, 6–3, 6–2. **Spain d. Brazil 4–1, Barcelona:** J. Couder lost to T. Koch 4–6, 6–8, 2–6; M. Santana d. R. Barnes 6–1, 6–0, 7–5; Santana–L. Arilla d. Koch–Barnes 6–4, 7–5, 4–6, 7–5; Santana d. Koch 6–4, 6–3, 6–1; Couder d. Barnes 6–1, 9–7, 7–5. **Rhodesia and Nyasaland d. Israel 4–1, Tel Aviv:** F. Salomon d. G. Dubitzky 6–3, 6–1, 6–0; A. Bey d. E. Davidman 2–6, 6–3, 6–0, 6–3; Salomon–Bey d. Davidman–Dubitzky 6–4, 10–8, 7–5; Salomon lost to Davidman 1–6, 7–5, 4–6, 6–1, 3–6; Bey d. D. Asz 6–2, 6–1, 6–1. **Italy d. United Arab Republic 4–1. Czechoslovakia d. Rumania def.; Sweden d. Greece 4–1, Athens:** U. Schmidt d. N. Kalogeropoulos 8–6, 6–2, 6–3; J. E. Lundquist d. N. Kalyvas 6–2, 7–5, 6–0; Lundquist–Schmidt d. Kalogeropoulos–Kalyvas 6–3, 6–3, 6–3; B. Homstrom lost to Kalogeropoulos 2–6, 4–6, 2–6; Schmidt d. Kalyvas 6–4, 1–6, 3–6, 6–3, 6–0.

SECOND ROUND

Great Britain d. Ireland 5–0, Eastbourne: M. J. Sangster d. D. Arthurs 6–2, 6–2, 6–2; W. A. Knight d. P. H. Jackson 6–0, 6–0, 6–1; Knight–Sangster d. Arthurs–M. Hickey 6–3, 6–4; 6–2; Knight d. Arthurs 6–1, 6–2, 3–6, 6–1; Sangster d. Jackson 6–2, 6–4, 6–2. **Yugoslavia d. Argentina 5–0, Belgrade:** B. Jovanovic d. E. Soriano 3–6, 6–4, 6–1, 6–3; N. Pilic d. R. Aubone 6–3, 6–1, 6–2; Jovanovic–Pilic d. Soriano–Aubone 7–5, 4–6, 5–7, 6–3, 7–5; Jovanovic d. Aubone 6–1, 6–1, 6–3; Pilic d. Soriano 6–4, 6–4, 7–5. **South Africa d. Norway 5–0, Oslo:** K. Diepraam d. G. D. Jagge 6–1, 6–2, 6–3; C. Drysdale d. S. Hansen 6–3, 6–0, 6–2; Drysdale–Diepraam d. Hansen–Jagge 6–1, 6–4, 10–8; Drysdale

d. Jagge 6–3, 6–2, 6–2; Diepraam d. Hansen 6–2, 6–4, 6–2.   **France d. Holland 5–0, Paris:** P. Darmon d. J. Hayer 7–5, 6–0, 6–2; P. Barthes d. T. Okker 6–1, 6–4, 7–5; Darmon–D. Contet d. Hayer–Okker 6–3, 13–11, 3–6, 6–3; Darmon d. Okker 6–3, 4–6, 6–1, 6–1; Barthes d. Hayer 6–3, 6–1, 6–1.   **West Germany d. Russia 4–1, Dusseldorf:** I. Buding d. T. Lejus 6–2, 6–3, 2–6, 6–4; C. Kuhnke d. A. Metreveli 6–3, 6–4, 6–2; Bungert–Kuhnke lost to Lejus–S. Likachev 6–4, 3–6, 3–6, 3–6; Kuhnke d. Lejus 9–7, 6–4, 6–3; Buding d. A. Metreveli 9–7, 11–9, 6–0.   **Denmark d. Spain 3–2, Copenhagen:** J. Ulrich lost to M. Santana 0–6, 1–6, 2–6; J. Leschly d. J. Couder 1–6, 6–8, 6–3, 6–2, 6–4; Ulrich–Leschly d. Santana–L. Arilla 6–3, 4–6, 6–4, 6–4; Ulrich d. Couder 6–4, 5–7, 6–4, 6–2; Leschly lost to Santana 2–6, 1–6, 2–6.   **Italy d. Rhodesia and Nyasaland 5–0, Genoa:** G. Merlo d. F Saloman 6–2, 0–6, 7–5, 4–6, 7–5; N. Pietrangeli d. A. Bey 6–2, 6–2, 6–1; Pietrangeli–G. Maioli d. Saloman–Bey 4–6, 9–7, 6–2, 3–6, 7–5; Pietrangeli d. Saloman 6–2, 6–1, 6–3; Merlo d. Bey 6–2, 6–3, 6–2.   **Sweden d. Czechoslovakia 5–0, Prague:** J. Lundquist d. S. Koudelka 7–5, 6–4, 6–0; U. Schmidt d. Holececk 6–2, 6–4, 6–4; Lundquist–Schmidt d. Koudelka–Holececk 6–3, 13–11, 6–3; Lundquist d. Holececk 6–3, 6–3, 6–4; Schmidt d. Koudelka 3–6, 6–3, 6–2, 6–4.

THIRD ROUND

Great Britain d. Yugoslavia 3–2, Manchester: M. Sangster d. B. Jovanovic 6–2, 6–4, 6–3; R. Wilson lost to N. Pilic 6–8, 8–6, 3–6, 3–6; Sangster–Wilson d. Jovanovic–Pilic 6–2, 4–6, 6–3, 6–2; Sangster lost to Pilic 14–16, 11–9, 3–6, 4–6; Wilson d. Jovanovic 6–4, 7–5, 0–6, 3–6, 6–2. **France d. South Africa 3–2, Paris:** P. Darmon lost to K. Diepraam 2–6, 10–8, 6–3, 7–9, 1–6; P. Barthes lost to A. Segal 6–3, 8–6, 6–8, 4–6, 4–6; J. N. Grinda–F. Jauffret d. Diepraam–Segal 9–7, 6–4, 6–2; Barthes d. Diepraam 6–2, 0–6, 6–2, 3–6, 6–2; Darmon d. Segal 6–2, 6–1, 6–2. **West Germany d. Denmark 4–1, Munich:** W. Bungert d. J. Leschly 6–1, 3–6, 11–9, 6–2; C. Kuhnke d. J. Ulrich 6–2, 6–4, 3–6, 6–2; Leschly–Ulrich d. W. Stuck–Kuhnke 6–3, 6–3, 1–6, 6–3; Bungert d. Ulrich 6–4, 3–6, 6–4, 6–3; Kuhnke d. Leschly 7–5, 4–6, 6–3, 6–4. **Sweden d. Italy 3–1, Turin:** J. E. Lundquist d. S. Tacchini 6–3, 6–1, 6–3; U. Schmidt lost to N. Pietrangeli 3–6, 4–6, 1–6; Lundquist–Schmidt d. Pietrangeli–G. Maioli 6–4, 7–5, 10–8; Schmidt d. Tacchini 6–2, 6–2, 3–6, 6–3.

SEMI–FINAL ROUND

France d. Great Britain 3–2, Bristol: P. Barthes lost to M. Sangster 3–6, 8–10, 11–13; P. Darmon d. W. Knight 0–6, 7–5, 6–2, 6–8, 7–5;

Sangster–R. Wilson d. J. N. Grinda–F. Jauffret 6–4, 6–8, 10–8, 6–4;
Darmon d. Sangster 8–10, 3–6, 6–4, 8–6, 6–2; Barthes d. Knight 6–4,
6–4, 6–1. **Sweden d. West Germany 3–2, Båstad:** U. Schmidt lost to
W. Bungert 4–6, 1–6, 1–6; J. E. Lundquist d. C. Kuhnke 6–4, 6–4, 6–3;
Lundquist–Schmidt lost to Bungert–Kuhnke 6–2, 3–6, 1–6, 6–2, 2–6;
Schmidt d. Kuhnke 3–6, 6–4, 6–1, 6–4; Lundquist d. Bungert 3–6, 6–3,
8–6, 7–5.

FINAL ROUND
Sweden d. France 4–1, Båstad: U. Schmidt lost to P. Darmon 9–7,
8–6, 4–6, 4–6, 1–6; J. E. Lundquist d. P. Barthes 6–8, 6–1, 6–3, 7–5;
Lundquist–Schmidt d. J. N. Grinda–F. Jauffret 6–4, 9–7, 8–6; Lundquist
d. Darmon 3–6, 7–5, 6–4, 6–1; Schmidt d. Barthes 6–2, 6–4, 6–8, 6–2.

Eastern Zone A

FIRST ROUND
Philippines d. Korea 4–1, Manila: F. Ampon d. Choong Yang Im 6–1,
6–2, 6–0; J. Jose d. Doo Whan Kim 6–0, 6–4, 6–3; S. Ang–D. Jose d.
Choong Yang Im–Doo Whan Kim 6–4, 6–1, 7–5; Ang d. Doo Whan
Kim 6–4, 6–1, 6–4; D. Jose lost to Choong Yang Im 6–2, 4–6, 3–6, 6–2,
3–6.

SEMI-FINAL ROUND
Philippines d. Japan 5–0, Manila: F. Ampon d. O. Ishiguro 2–6, 6–0,
6–2, 6–4; J. Jose d. K. Watanabe 6–3, 5–7, 6–3, 6–3; Jose–R. Deyro d.
Ishiguro–Watanabe 7–5, 6–2, 6–3; Ampon d. Watanabe 6–2, 6–4, 3–6,
4–6, 6–0; Deyro d. Ishiguro 6–1, 6–1, 6–4.

Eastern Zone B

FIRST ROUND
Vietnam d. Malaysia 5–0, Kuala Lumpur: Luu Hoang Duc d. S. A.
Azman 6–2, 7–5, 4–6, 3–6, 6–4; Vo Van Bay d. Tan Song Kean 6–4,
6–1, 3–6, 6–3; Bay–Duc d. Azman–S. Osman 9–7, 8–6, 7–5; Duc d. Kean
6–2, 6–1, 8–6; Bay d. Azman 6–2, 6–3, 6–2. **India d. Ceylon 5–0,
Hyderabad:** J. Mukerjea d. L. Fernando 6–2, 6–2, 6–2; P. Lall d. B.
Pinto 6–1, 6–3, 6–3; Lall–S. P. Misra d. Pinto–Fernando 6–4, 3–6, 6–4,
6–3; Lall d. Fernando 6–1, 6–4, 6–3; Misra d. Pinto 6–4, 6–2, 6–4. **Iran
d. Burma def.**

SECOND ROUND

Vietnam d. Iran 3–2, Teheran: Vo Van Bay lost to T. Akbari 2–6, 1–6, 6–4, 3–6; Luu Hoang Duc d. R. Akbari 12–10, 6–4, 6–0; Vo Van Bay–Luu Hoang Duc d. T. and R. Akbari 2–6, 6–4, 6–2, 7–5; Vo Van Bay d. R. Akbari 6–3, 6–2, 6–1; Luu Hoang Duc lost to T. Akbari 3–6, 5–7, 1–6. **India d. Pakistan 4–0, Lahore:** A. Ali d. Z. Rahim 6–3, 6–4, 6–4; P. Lall d. M. Pirzada 6–0, 6–2, 7–5; Ali–Lall d. Pirzada–A. Inayat 6–4, 6–2, 6–4; S. P. Misra d. Rahim 6–4, 3–6, 9–7, 13–11; Ali v. M. Iqbal 6–3, 7–5, 3–3 unfin.

SEMI-FINAL ROUND

India d. Vietnam 5–0, Saigon: P. Lall d. Luu Hoang Duc 7–5, 6–4, 6–3; J. Mukerjea d. Vo Van Bay 7–5, 6–4, 4–6, 4–6, 6–3; Lall–Mukerjea d. Luu Hoang Duc–Vo Van Bay 4–6, 6–4, 6–3, 6–4; Mukerjea d. Luu Hoang Duc 6–3, 6–1, 6–4; Lall d. Vo Van Bay 6–4, 6–4, 6–3.

EASTERN ZONE FINAL

Philippines d. India 3–2: J. Jose lost to J. Mukerjea 5–7, 6–3, 3–6, 2–6; F. Ampon d. P. Lall 6–0, 6–3, 7–5; Jose–R. Deyro lost to Mukerjea–Lall 3–6, 6–1, 6–3, 2–6, 7–9; Ampon d. Mukerjea 6–4, 6–1, 6–1; Jose d. Lall 6–4, 8–6, 3–6, 6–4.

American Zone

FIRST ROUND

Australia d. Canada 5–0, Montreal: R. Emerson d. K. Carpenter 6–2, 6–1, 6–2; J. Newcombe d. F. Godbout 6–3, 6–3, 4–6, 7–5; Emerson–A. Roche d. Godbout–Carpenter 6–2, 6–2, 6–2; Roche d. Godbout 6–2, 6–1, 6–1; Newcombe d. R. Getz 6–3, 6–0, 6–4. **Mexico d. New Zealand 3–1, Mexico City:** A. Palafox d. L. Gerrard 6–2, 8–6, 6–4; R. Osuna d. I. Crookenden 6–2, 10–8, 5–7, 6–4; Osuna–Palafox d. Gerrard–Crookenden 7–5, 7–5, 4–6, 6–4; V. Zarazua lost to Crookenden 4–6, 4–6, 6–3, 6–8; J. Loyo-Mayo v. Gerrard 6–4, 6–4, 4–6, 3–6 unfin. **British Caribbean d. Venezuela def.**

SEMI-FINAL ROUND

Australia d. Mexico 4–1, Mexico City: F. Stolle lost to R. Osuna 2–6, 5–7, 4–6; R. Emerson d. A. Palafox 8–6, 6–3, 6–3; Emerson–Stolle d. Osuna–Palafox 18–16, 7–9, 7–9, 6–4, 10–8; Stolle d. Palafox 6–3, 6–2, 6–4; Emerson d. Osuna 6–3, 6–4, 11–9. **Chile d. British Caribbean 3–2, Bridgetown:** P. Rodriguez d. D. Tate 6–4, 6–2, 7–5; E. Aguirre lost to R. Russell 5–7, 4–6, 6–3, 7–9; Rodriguez–Aguirre lost to Russell–A. Price 6–2, 4–6, 5–7, 4–6; Rodriguez d. Russell 6–2, 1–6, 7–5, 6–1; Aguirre d. Tate 6–3, 9–11, 1–6, 6–2, 6–4.

FINAL ROUND

Australia d. Chile 5–0: F. Stolle d. P. Cornejo 6–1, 6–0, 6–0; R. Emerson d. P. Rodriguez 6–3, 6–2, 8–6; Emerson–Stolle d. Rodriguez– E. Aguirre 6–4, 6–4, 6–4; J. Newcombe d. Aguirre 6–2, 6–2, 6–4; Stolle d. Rodriguez 6–0, 6–4, 6–4.

INTER-ZONE FINALS

Sweden d. Philippines 5–0: U. Schmidt d. F. Ampon 6–0, 6–1, 6–2; J. E. Lundquist d. J. Jose 6–1, 3–6, 6–1, 6–0; Schmidt–Lundquist d. R. Deyro–Jose 6–3, 5–7, 6–3, 6–3; Lundquist d. Ampon 6–1, 6–1, 6–4; Schmidt d. Jose 6–2, 6–1, 6–2. **Australia d. Sweden 5–0, Bastad:** R. Emerson d. J. E. Lundquist 2–6, 4–6, 6–3, 6–2, 7–5; F. Stolle d. U. Schmidt 6–4, 6–3, 10–8; Emerson–Stolle d. Lundquist–Schmidt 6–2, 6–1, 6–0; Emerson d. Schmidt 3–6, 6–4, 6–3, 6–2; Stolle d. Lundquist 5–7, 6–4, 6–0, 6–3.

CHALLENGE ROUND

Australia d. USA 3–2, Cleveland: F. Stolle lost to C. McKinley 1–6, 7–9, 6–4, 2–6; R. Emerson d. D. Ralston 6–3, 6–4, 6–2; Emerson–Stolle lost to McKinley–Ralston 4–6, 6–4, 6–4, 3–6, 4–6; Stolle d. Ralston 7–5, 6–3, 3–6, 9–11, 6–4; Emerson d. McKinley 3–6, 6–2, 6–4, 6–4.

1965: AUSTRALIA
European Zone

FIRST ROUND

Sweden d. Poland 4–1, Stockholm: J. E. Lundquist d. T. Nowicki 6–1, 6–1, 6–0; L. Olander lost to W. Gasiorek 3–6, 7–9, 3–6; Lundquist–L. Bergelin d. M. Rybarczyk–Nowicki 7–5, 4–6, 2–6, 6–1, 6–3; Olander d. Nowicki 6–4, 0–6, 6–2, 9–7; Lundquist d. Gasiorek 6–3, 6–1, 3–6, 8–6. **Czechoslovakia d. Monaco def.; Italy d. Portugal 5–0, Pescara:** G. Maioli d. J. Roquette 6–0, 6–3, 6–0; N. Pietrangeli d. A. V. Pinto 6–3, 6–2, 6–1; Pietrangeli–Maioli d. Pinto–J. Lagos 6–2, 6–3, 6–2; Pietrangeli d. Roquette 6–1, 6–0, 6–0; Maioli d. Pinto 6–2, 6–3, 6–2. **Brazil d. Hungary 3–2, Budapest:** R. Barnes lost to I. Gulyas 3–6, 0–6, 2–6; T. Koch d. A. Korpas 6–3, 6–2, 8–6; Barnes d. Gulyas–A. Szikszai 7–5, 6–8, 6–1, 6–2; Barnes d. Korpas 8–6,

8–6, 7–5; Koch lost to Gulyas 6–3, 7–5, 4–6, 4–6, 1–6. **West Germany d. Switzerland 5–0, Essen:** I. Buding d. T. Stalder 6–1, 6–0, 6–3; W. Bungert d. D. Sturdza 6–3, 4–6, 7–9, 7–5, 7–5; C. Kuhnke–H. Elschenbroich d. Sturdza–M. Werren 10–8, 6–2, 6–4; Bungert d. Stalder 6–2, 2–6, 7–5, 3–6, 6–2; Buding d. Sturdza 6–4, 6–4, 3–6, 6–1. **Luxembourg d. Turkey 3–2, Mondorf–les–Bains:** F. Baden d. Z. Kipkzil 7–5, 6–1, 6–4. T. Brasseur lost to N. Bari 3–6, 0–6, 5–7; Baden–Neumann lost to Bari–E. Balas 2–6, 6–4, 7–9, 6–4, 2–6; Baden d. Bari 6–4, 7–5, 6–2; Brasseur d. Kipkzil 3–6, 6–2, 4–6, 8–6, 6–2. **Spain d. Greece 5–0, Barcelona:** J. L. Arilla d. N. Kalyvas 6–2, 6–1, 6–1; M. Santana d. N. Kalogeropoulos 6–2, 6–0, 6–4; Arilla–Santana d. Kalogeropoulos–P. Gavrilidis 6–1, 6–2, 6–2; J. M. Couder d. Kalyvas 6–1, 6–1, 6–4; Arilla d. Kalogeropoulos 6–3, 6–2, 6–2. **Chile d. Belgium 3–1, Brussels:** J. P. Bravo d. E. Drossart 6–3, 6–4, 3–6, 6–1; E. Aguirre d. J. Brichant 6–4, 3–6, 6–3, 6–1; Aguirra–P. Pabst d. Drossart–C. de Gronkel 2–6, 6–4, 11–9, 7–5; Aguirre lost to Drossart 2–6, 4–6, 2–6; Brichant v. Bravo 8–6, 8–6, 3–5 unfin. **Norway d. United Arab Republic def.; South Africa d. Holland 4–0, The Hague:** C Drysdale d. J. Hajer 6–0, 6–2, 6–1; K. Diepraam d. T. Okker 7–5, 6–4, 6–3; Drysdale–Diepraam d. Okker–P. van Eysden 6–2, 6–2, 6–2; Drysdale d. Okker 6–2, 6–1, 6–2; Diepraam v. Hajer 1–6, 6–4, 4–6, 9–7, 3–3 unfin. **Denmark d. Ireland 3–0, Dublin:** T. Ulrich d. P. H. Jackson 6–1, 6–1, 6–1; J. Ulrich d. D. Arthurs 6–3, 6–1, 6–1; Ulrich–Ulrich d. Arthurs–M. P. Hickey 6–3, 6–1, 6–4. **Great Britain d. Israel 4–1,:** R. Taylor d. O. Shay 6–1, 6–0, 6–1; M. Sangster lost to E. Davidman 6–3, 6–2, 5–7, 5–7, 4–6; Sangster–R. K. Wilson d. Davidman–D. Asz 6–1, 6–1, 6–3; Sangster d. Shay 6–1, 6–1, 6–0; Taylor d. Davidman 6–1, 8–6, 7–5. **Rhodesia d. USSR def.; Yugoslavia d. Morocco 5–0, Zagreb:** N. Pilic d. L. Chaldi 6–1, 6–3, 4–6, 6–4; B. Jovanovic d. M. Bouchaib 6–2, 6–1, 6–0; Jovanovic–Pilic d. Laroussi–Bouchaib 6–2, 6–4, 6–1; Pilic d. Bouchaib 6–2, 6–4, 6–1; Jovanovic d. Chaldi 6–1, 6–4. def. **Austria d. Finland 4–1, Helsinki:** G. Pazderka lost to P. Saila 4–6, 6–3, 6–2, 6–3, 4–6; N. Klatil d. S. Stahle 6–1, 6–4, 2–6, 6–0; Pazderka–Klatil d. Saila–R. Suominen 6–0, 6–1, 9–7; Pazderka d. Stahle 6–2, 4–6, 6–2, 6–1; Klatil d. Saila 6–0, 6–4, 6–3.

SECOND ROUND

Czechoslovakia d. Sweden 3–2, Stockholm: M. Holecek lost to J. E. Lundquist 4–6, 8–10, 2–6; J. Javorsky d. L. Olander 6–4, 6–4, 6–3; Javorsky–S. Kudelka d. Lundquist–Olander 4–6, 6–3, 6–4, 7–5; Javorsky lost to Lundquist 4–6, 2–6, 3–6; Holecek d. Olander 6–0, 6–1, 6–4. **Italy d. Brazil 3–2, Milan:** N. Pietrangeli d. R. Barnes 6–4, 9–7, 6–3; G.

Merlo d. T. Koch 6–4, 6–2, 6–4; Pietrangeli–G. Maioli lost to Barnes–J. E. Mandarino 2–6, 4–6, 5–7; Pietrangeli d. Koch 7–5, 6–3, 6–2; Merlo lost to Barnes 4–6, 7–9, 6–2, 3–6. **West Germany d. Luxembourg 5–0, Wiesbaden:** W. Bungert d. T. Brasseur 6–0, 6–4, 6–1; C. Kuhnke d. F. Baden 6–3, 6–0, 6–0; I. Buding–H. Elschenbroich d. Baden–Brasseur 6–3, 6–2, 6–2; Kuhnke d. Brasseur 6–1, 6–1, 6–0; Bungert d. Baden 7–5, 6–4, 4–6, 6–3. **Spain d. Chile 5–0, Barcelona:** J. M. Couder d. J. Pinto 6–2, 6–3, 6–3; J. L. Arilla d. O. Pabst 6–3, 6–1, 6–3; Couder–Arilla d. E. Aguirre–Pinto 6–3, 6–4, 6–1; Couder d. P. Cornejo 6–4, 6–3, 9–7; J. Gisbert d. Aguirre 6–3, 6–2, 6–1. **South Africa d. Norway 5–0, Oslo:** K. E. Diepraam d. G. Sjowall 6–4, 6–1, 6–4; C. Drysdale d. F. D. Jagge 6–1, 6–0, 6–1; Diepraam–Drysdale d. Jagge–J. Bibow 6–1, 3–6, 6–1, 6–3; R. Maud d. N. M. Elvig 6–1, 6–0, 6–1; Diepraam d. Jagge 6–2, 6–2, 6–0. **Great Britain d. Denmark 3–1, Copenhagen:** R. Taylor lost to T. Ulrich 4–6, 3–6, 3–6; M. Sangster d. J. Ulrich 5–7, 8–6, 6–0, 4–6, 7–5; Sangster–R. Wilson d. J. and T. Ulrich 10–8, 6–0, 6–3; Sangster d. T. Ulrich 9–11, 6–4, 6–4, 6–4; R. Taylor v. J. Ulrich 6–8, 5–6 unfin. **Yugoslavia d. Rhodesia 5–0, Zagreb:** N. Pilic d. R. Stilwell 6–0, 3–6, 6–4, 6–1; B. Jovanovic d. R. Dowdeswell 6–0, 6–1, 7–5; Pilic–Jovanovic d. Stilwell–Dowdeswell 3–6, 7–5, 7–5, 6–1; Jovanovic d. Stilwell 8–6, 6–1, 6–1; Pilic d. Dowdeswell 7–5, 10–8, 6–0. **France d. Austria 5–0, Vienna:** P. Darmon d. N. Klatil 4–6, 6–1, 6–1, 7–5; P. Barthes d. G. Pazderka 6–1, 6–0, 6–1; Barthes– F. Jauffret d. Pazderka–P. Pokorny 4–6, 6–3, 3–6, 6–2, 6–2; Barthes d. Klatil 6–4, 6–2, 9–7; Darmon d. Pazderka 6–1, 6–0, 6–0.

THIRD ROUND

Czechoslovakia d. Italy 3–2, Prague: M. Holecek d. G. Merlo 6–4, 5–7, 8–6, 6–1; J. Javorsky lost to N. Pietrangeli 3–6, 4–6, 6–2, 4–6; Javorsky–Holecek d. Pietrangeli–S. Tacchini 2–6, 6–4, 7–5, 6–4; Javorsky d. Merlo 1–6, 6–4, 8–6, 6–3; Holecek lost to Pietrangeli 2–6, 2–6, 2–6. **Spain d. West Germany 4–1, Barcelona:** J. Gisbert lost to I. Buding 3–6, 5–7, 6–1, 4–6; M. Santana d. W. Bungert 6–2, 6–3, 6–3; Santana– J. L. Arilla d. Bungert–C. Kuhnke 6–2, 2–6, 6–3, 6–1; Santana d. Buding 6–2, 6–4, 6–3; Gisbert d. Bungert 2–6, 2–6, 6–0, 7–5, 6–1. **South Africa d. Great Britain 3–2, Eastbourne:** K. Diepraam d. M. Sangster 4–6, 7–5, 6–3, 2–6, 9–7; C. Drysdale d. R. Taylor 6–1, 6–2, 7–5; Diepraam–A. Segal lost to Sangster–R. Wilson 6–8, 3–6, 6–3, 6–4, 3–6; Drysdale d. Sangster 6–4, 4–6, 6–0, 6–3; Diepraam lost to Taylor 5–7, 6–3, 4–6, 2–6. **France d. Yugoslavia 5–0, Paris:** P. Barthes d. B. Jovanovic 6–3, 7–9, 7–5, 6–1; P. Darmon d. N. Pilic 6–4, 6–4, 4–6, 3–6,

441

7–5; Barthes–F. Jauffret d. Jovanovic–Pilic 6–3, 6–2, 6–4; Darmon d.
Jovanovic 6–4, 6–2, 2–6, 6–2; Barthes d. Pilic 9–7, 2–6, 6–3, 7–5.

SEMI-FINAL ROUND
Spain d. Czechoslovakia 4–1, Prague: J. Gisbert d. M. Holecek 6–3,
6–1, 6–4; M. Santana d. J. Javorsky 6–3, 6–4, 6–4; Santana–J. L. Arilla
d. Javorsky–Holecek 6–2, 6–2, 6–3; Gisbert lost to Javorsky 6–4, 2–6,
6–4, 2–6, 5–7; Santana d. Holecek 6–1, 6–4, 6–4.   **South Africa d. France
4–1, Paris:** C. Drysdale d. P. Barthes 6–4, 6–2, 6–2; K. Diepraam lost
to P. Darmon 9–7, 2–6, 4–6, 6–4, 4–6; F. McMillan–Diepraam d.
Barthes–F. Jauffret 6–0, 2–6, 6–1, 7–5; Diepraam d. Barthes 6–2, 6–3,
2–6, 4–6, 8–6; Drysdale d. Darmon 0–6, 6–3, 6–1, 6–2.

FINAL ROUND
Spain d. South Africa 4–1, Barcelona: M. Santana d. C. Drysdale 6–3,
6–3, 6–2; J. Gisbert d. K. Diepraam 6–2, 6–1, 3–6, 3–6, 6–2; Santana–J.
L. Arilla d. Diepraam–F. McMillan 9–7, 4–6, 6–3, 6–2; Gisbert lost to
Drysdale 2–6, 6–4, 3–6, 2–6; Santana d. Diepraam 6–1, 6–3, 6–3.

Eastern Zone B

FIRST ROUND
South Vietnam d. Pakistan 4–1, Kuala Lumpur: Vo Van Bay lost to
H. Rahim 6–3, 6–3, 5–7, 5–7, 1–6; Luu Hoang Duc d. M. Iqbal 7–5,
6–1, 6–4; Vo Van Bay–Luu Hoang Duc d. Rahim and A. Inayat 7–5,
7–5, 6–1; Vo Van Bay d. Iqbal 6–3, 6–1, 6–3; Luu Hoang Duc d. Rahim
6–2, 6–4, 6–2.   **India d. Iran 5–0, Teheran:** J. Mukerjea d. T. Akbari
2–6, 6–3, 6–3, 6–3; P. Lall d. N. Nemati 6–2, 6–2, 6–2; Lall–Mukerjea
d. Akbari–Nemati 6–4, 6–1, 6–2; S. P. Misra d. I. Koodah 6–0, 6–0, 6–2;
Lall d. Akbari 6–3, 6–0, 6–4.

SECOND ROUND
South Vietnam d. Malaysia 5–0, Saigon: Luu Hoang Duc d. A. S.
Azman 6–1, 7–5, 6–2; Vo Van Bay d. Sharin Osman 6–2, 6–3, 6–3; Vo
Van Thanh d. A. S. Azman 6–0, 6–1, 6–0; Luu Hoang Duc d. S. Osman
6–2, 6–2, 6–1; Vo Van Bay–Vo Van Thanh d. Asman–K. Yoke 6–3,
6–2, 6–1.   **India d. Ceylon 5–0, Colombo:** J. Mukerjea d. G. N. Perera
6–3, 6–3, 6–3; P. Lall d. B. Pinto 6–2, 6–2, 6–1; Lall–Mukerjea d.
Pinto–Perera 6–4, 6–2, 6–2; R. Yenkatesan d. Pinto 6–0, 2–6, 6–0, 6–1;
S. P. Misra d. Perera 6–1, 6–3, 6–4.

FINAL ROUND
India d. South Vietnam 4–0, Vijayawada: P. Lall d. Vo Van Thanh
6–3, 6–3, 6–1; J. Mukerjea d. Luu Hoang Duc 6–1, 6–2, 6–0;
Lall–Mukerjea d. Luu Hoang Duc–Vo Van Thanh 6–1, 6–4, 3–6, 8–6; R.
Venkatesan d. Luu Hoang Duc 6–2, 6–3, 6–8, 6–3; S. P. Misra v. Vo
Van Thanh 6–2, 6–4, 0–1 unfin.

Eastern Zone A

FIRST ROUND
Japan d. Philippines 5–0, Tokyo: I. Konishi d. A. Villanueva 9–7, 6–2,
6–0; O. Ishiguro d. S. Ang 10–8, 6–2, 6–4; Ishiguro–K. Watanabe d.
Ang–A. Cruz 2–6, 6–3, 3–6, 7–5, 6–0; Konishi d. D. Contreras 6–0, 6–1,
6–2; Watanabe d. Villanueva 8–6, 6–1, 6–2.

SECOND ROUND
Japan d. Korea 5–0, Seoul: O. Ishiguro d. Choong Yang Im 6–1, 7–5,
6–3; K. Watanabe d. Yung Ho Chung 6–0, 6–0, 6–4; M. Motoi–I.
Watanabe d. Choong Yang Im–Yung Ho Chung 6–2, 6–3, 6–4; Motoi
d. Too Hwan Kim 5–7, 6–3, 6–3, 6–3; K. Watanabe d. Se Hyun Paik
6–0, 6–0, 6–2.

ZONE FINAL ROUND
India d. Japan 4–1, Tokyo: J. Mukerjea d. K. Watanabe 6–0, 6–4, 7–5;
R. Krishnan d. O. Ishiguro 6–4, 6–2, 6–2; Krishnan–Mukerjea lost to
Ishiguro–Watanabe 3–6, 4–6, 6–2, 4–6; Krishnan d. Watanabe 8–6, 6–2,
9–7; Mukerjea d. Ishiguro 5–7, 5–7, 6–2, 8–6, 6–4.

American Zone

FIRST ROUND
New Zealand d. British Caribbean 4–1, Nassau: I. Crookenden d. P.
Valdez 6–2, 6–3, 6–2; L. Gerrard d. R. Russell 6–2, 6–3, 6–1;
Crookenden–Gerrard d. Russell–A. Price 6–3, 6–4, 3–6, 6–1; Crookenden
d. Russell 3–6, 8–6, 6–2, 3–6, 6–2; Gerrard lost to Valdez def.

SEMI-FINAL ROUND
Mexico d. New Zealand 5–0, Mexico City: R. Osuna d. L. Gerrard
6–2, 6–3, 6–3; A. Palafox d. I. Crookenden 3–6, 6–2, 6–1, 6–1;
Osuna–Palafox d. Gerrard–Crookenden 6–4, 6–4, 6–2; Osuna d.

Crookenden 1–6, 6–2, 7–9, 6–4, 6–2; Palafox d. Gerrard 6–2, 3–6, 8–6, 6–3. **USA d. Canada 5–0, Bakersfield:** E. Scott d. H. Fauquier 6–3, 6–2, 4–6, 6–4; A. Ashe d. K. Carpenter 6–3, 6–3, 6–1; C. McKinley–M. Riessen d. Fauquier–Carpenter 9–7, 6–2, 6–3; Scott d. Carpenter 6–3, 7–5, 7–5; Ashe d. Fauquier 6–4, 6–0, 6–4.

FINAL ROUND
USA d. Mexico 4–1, Dallas: A. Ashe d. R. Osuna 6–2, 6–3, 9–7; D. Ralston d. A. Palafox 6–2, 6–3, 6–2; H. Richardson–Ralston lost to Osuna–Palafox 6–8, 4–6, 5–7; Ashe d. Palafox 6–1, 6–4, 6–4; Ralston d. Osuna 6–0, 6–2, 6–4.

INTER-ZONE FINALS
Spain d. USA 4–1, Barcelona: J. Gisbert d. D. Ralston 3–6, 8–6, 6–1, 6–3; M. Santana d. F. Froehling 6–1, 6–4, 6–4; J. L. Arilla–Santana d. C. Graebner–Ralston 4–6, 3–6, 6–3, 6–4, 11–9; Gisbert d. Froehling 6–3, 3–6, 6–4, 2–6, 6–3; J. Couder lost to Ralston 6–4, 4–6, 3–6, 3–6. **Spain d. India 3–2:** J. Gisbert lost to R. Krishnan 2–6, 0–6, 1–6; M. Santana d. J. Mukerjea 6–0, 6–4, 6–4; Santana–J. Arilla d. Mukerjea–P. Lall 8–6, 6–2, 10–8; Santana d. Krishnan 6–3, 6–3, 6–3; Gisbert lost to Mukerjea 6–4, 5–7, 2–6, 6–3, 4–6.

CHALLENGE ROUND
Australia d. Spain 4–1, Sydney: F. Stolle d. M. Santana 10–12, 3–6, 6–1, 6–4, 7–5; R. Emerson d. J. Gisbert 6–3, 6–2, 6–2; J. Newcombe–A. Roche d. J. L. Arilla–Santana 6–3, 4–6, 7–5, 6–2; Emerson lost to Santana 6–2, 3–6, 4–6, 13–15; F. Stolle d. Gisbert 6–2, 6–4, 8–6.

1966: AUSTRALIA
European Zone A

FIRST ROUND
Spain d. Yugoslavia 4–1, Barcelona: J. Gisbert lost to N. Pilic 4–6, 3–6, 6–1, 5–7; M. Santana d. B. Jovanovic 6–3, 6–3, 6–3; J. L. Arilla–Santana d. Jovanovic–Pilic 4–6, 6–2, 7–5, 6–4; Gisbert d. Jovanovic 6–0, 6–4, 6–3; Santana d. Pilic 6–1, 6–3, 1–6, 6–2. **Brazil d. Denmark 5–0, Copenhagen:** E. Mandarino d. T. Ulrich 6–4, 6–1, 6–1; T. Koch d. J. Leschly 8–6, 6–3, 6–0; Mandarino–Koch d. Ulrich–Leschly 4–6, 6–1, 6–3, 6–3; Mandarino d. Leschly 6–2, 6–4, 8–6; P. Tavares d. C. E. Hedelund 8–6, 6–2, 6–4. **Poland d. Sweden 3–2, Stettin:** P. Jamroz d. C. Holm 12–10, 6–4, 6–4; W. Gasiorek d. B. Holmstrom 10–8, 6–3,

6–0; Gasiorek–W. Nowicki d. Holmstrom–L. Olander 7–9, 6–4, 6–2,
9–7; Jamroz lost to Holmstrom 1–6, 0–6, 1–6; Gasiorek lost to Holm 3–6,
3–6, 0–6. **United Arab Republic d. Turkey 5–0, Instanbul:** M.
Sombol d. S. Gurel 3–6, 6–1, 6–1, 7–5; F. M. Ali d. T. Gursoy 6–1, 6–2,
6–1; Ali–S. Moubarek d. D. Atas–Gursoy 6–1, 6–2, 6–3. Sombol d. Atas
6–1, 6–1, 6–2; Ali d. E. Berki 6–1, 6–2, 6–0. **France d. Rumania 4–1,
Paris:** F. Jauffret d. I. Tiriac 6–4, 6–4, 6–1; P. Darmon d. I. Nastase
6–1, 6–2, 6–2; D. Contet–P. Beust d. Nastase–Tiriac 6–4, 2–6, 3–6, 6–0,
6–2; Darmon lost to Tiriac 6–3, 0–6, 3–6, 3–6; Jauffret d. Nastaste 6–1,
6–3, 8–6. **Canada d. Finland 4–1, Helsinki:** H. Fauquier d. P. Saila
3–6, 8–6, 6–3, 6–0; M. Belkin d. R. Suominen 6–1, 6–3, 1–6, 6–3;
Fauquier–K. Carpenter d. Suominen–Saila 9–7, 6–8, 6–0, 6–4; R.
Puddicombe lost to Suominen 6–3, 3–6, 6–8, 1–6; Belkin d. Saila 6–3,
6–0, 6–4. **Czechoslovakia d. Austria 5–0, Bratislava:** J. Kodes d. E.
Blanke 4–6, 3–6, 6–4, 6–4, 6–2; J. Javorsky d. P. Pokorny 6–3, 3–6,
6–4, 6–4; Javorsky–Kodes d. Blanke–Pokorny 1–6, 6–1, 4–6, 6–2, 6–4;
Kodes d. Pokorny 2–6, 6–4, 8–6, 6–3; Javorsky d. Blanke 6–1, 6–0, 6–3.
Israel d. Portugal 3–2, Lisbon: E. Davidman d. A. V. Pinto 6–1, 5–7,
2–6, 6–0, 6–4; J. Schalen lost to J. Lagos 4–6, 2–6, 1–6; Davidman–J.
Stabholz d. Lagos–M. Roquette 6–3, 3–6, 2–6, 6–3, 7–5; Schalen lost to
Pinto 0–6, 1–6, 4–6; Davidman d. Lagos 7–5, 6–4, 6–3.

SECOND ROUND

Brazil d. Spain 3–2, Barcelona: T. Koch lost to J. Gisbert 6–3, 4–6,
1–6, 4–6; E. Mandarino lost to M. Santana 5–7, 5–7, 4–6;
Koch–Mandarino d. J. L. Arilla–Gisbert 3–6, 6–2, 7–5, 5–7, 6–4; Koch
d. Santana 7–5, 6–2, 6–1; Mandarino d. Gisbert 7–5, 3–6, 9–11, 8–6,
8–6. **Poland d. United Arab Republic 4–1, Warsaw:** W. Gasiorek d.
E. M. Sombol 8–6, 7–5, 6–0; P. Jamroz lost to F. Mohamed Ali 6–4,
3–6, 0–6, 3–6; Gasiorek–T. Nowicki d. Ali–Sombol 6–3, 6–2, 8–6; Jamroz
d. Sombol 6–4, 6–4, 6–8, 6–3; Gasiorek d. Ali 6–4, 6–1, 6–2. **France
d. Canada 5–0, Paris:** F. Jauffret d. M. Belkin 6–1, 4–6, 6–3, 6–4; P.
Darmon d. H. Fauquier 6–4, 6–2, 6–3; D. Contet–P. Beust d. Fauquier–
K. Carpenter 6–4, 9–7, 6–3; Jauffret d. Fauquier 6–2, 6–2, 1–6, 0–6, 6–0;
Darmon d. Belkin 6–8, 1–6, 7–5, 6–0, 6–1. **Czechoslovakia d. Israel
5–0, Prague:** J. Kodes d. J. Stabholz 6–1, 6–1, 6–3; J. Javorski d. J.
Shalem 6–0, 6–0, 6–0; Javorski–Kodes d. Stabholz–Shalem 6–1, 6–1,
6–2; Pala d. Stabholz 6–2, 6–0, 6–2; Kodes d. Shalem 6–3, 7–5, 6–0.

SEMI-FINAL ROUND

Brazil d. Poland 4–1, Warsaw: E. Mandarino d. T. Nowicki 6–2, 6–2,
6–3; T. Koch lost to W. Gasiorek 7–9, 1–6, 5–7; Koch–Mandarino d.

Gasiorek–Nowicki 6–1, 10–8, 7–5; Koch d. Nowicki 6–3, 6–4, 6–1; Mandarino d. Gasiorek 6–2, 6–1, 6–2. **France d. Czechoslovakia 4–1, Paris:** F. Jauffret d. J. Javorsky 14–12, 1–6, 6–2, 6–1; P. Darmon d. J. Kodes 4–6, 6–4, 6–0, 10–8; D. Contet–P. Buest lost to Javorsky–Kodes 10–8, 7–5, 3–6, 4–6, 2–6; Jauffret d. Kodes 3–6, 1–6, 6–3, 6–4, 6–4; Darmon d. Javorsky 6–2, 6–4, 6–0.

FINAL ROUND
Brazil d. France 4–1, Paris: E. Mandarino d. P. Darmon 3–6, 6–3, 6–2, 6–1; T. Koch d. F. Jauffret 2–6, 6–1, 6–3, 6–2; Koch–Mandarino d. D. Contet–P. Buest 3–6, 6–4, 5–7, 6–3, 6–4; Mandarino d. Jauffret 6–4, 6–1, 5–7, 6–2; Koch lost to Darmon 4–6, 7–9, 2–6.

European Zone B

FIRST ROUND
Switzerland d. Luxembourg 5–0, Mondorf–les–Bains: D. Sturdza d. T. Brasseur 6–0, 6–1, 6–3; T. Stalder d. J. Neumann 7–5, 0–6, 6–4, 6–1; Sturdza–M. Werren d. F. Baden–Brasseur 6–3, 6–3, 6–3; Stalder d. Brasseur 6–1, 6–3, 6–2; Sturdza d. Neumann 6–1, 6–4, 6–4. **West Germany d. Norway 5–0, Freiburg:** W. Bungert d. G. Sjowall 4–6, 6–0, 6–3, 4–6, 6–2; I. Buding d. M. Elvik 6–1, 6–1, 6–0; Buding–H. Elschenbroich d. F. D. Jagge–Elvik 6–2, 7–5, 6–0; Bungert d. Elvik 6–2, 6–1, 6–1; Buding d. Sjowall 6–0, 6–3, 6–0. **Hungary d. Greece 4–1, Budapest:** A. Szikszai lost to N. Kalogeropoulos 6–2, 1–6, 6–3, 2–6, 2–6; I. Gulyas d. N. Kalyvas 6–1, 6–2, 6–0; Gulyas–Szikszai d. Kalogeropoulos–N. Gavrilidis 6–4, 5–7, 6–4, 6–4; Gulyas d. Kalogeropoulos 3–6, 9–7, 6–3, 9–7; Szikszai d. Kalyvas 6–1, 6–0, 6–2. **Great Britain d. New Zealand 4–1, London:** R. Taylor d. B. Fairlie 7–5, 8–6, 6–2; M. Sangster d. L. Gerrard 6–4, 6–2, 6–2; Sangster–R. K. Wilson d. Gerrard–Fairlie 6–1, 6–0, 6–4; Sangster lost to Fairlie 3–6, 7–5, 2–6, def.; Taylor d. Gerrard 6–2, 6–3, 2–6, 6–1. **Morocco d. Monaco 4–1, Monte Carlo:** H. Bouchaib d. P. Landau 6–2, 6–3, 6–3. C. Lachen d. A. Viviani 6–2, 6–0, 6–2; Ben Ali–A. Laroussi lost to Landau–Truchi 2–6, 3–6, 4–6; Lachen d. Landau 6–4, 8–6, 6–1; Bouchaib d. Viviani 7–5, 6–2, 6–2. **Italy d. USSR 4–1, Bologna:** N. Pietrangeli d. T. Lejus 6–1, 6–3, 6–1; S. Tacchini d. A. Ivanov 5–7, 6–4, 6–4, 6–2; G. Maioli–G. di Maso lost to Lejus–S. Likhachev 5–7, 0–6, 3–6; Tacchini d. Lejus 6–1, 6–3, 6–2; Pietrangeli d. Ivanov 6–3, 6–1, 6–4. **Holland d. Ireland 5–0, Scheveningen:** T. Okker d. P. Jackson 6–0, 6–4, 6–1; J. Hajer d. M. Hickey 6–2, 6–1, 6–1; Okker–P. van Eysden d. Jackson–D. Arthurs 6–3,

6–2, 6–3; Okker d. Hickey 6–3, 6–4, 6–2; Hajer d. Jackson 6–0, 6–1, 6–0. **South Africa d. Belgium 5–0, Brussels:** C. Drysdale d. P. Hombergen 6–4, 6–1, 6–4; K. Diepraam d. E. Drossart 2–6, 6–2, 2–6, 8–6, 6–3; Diepraam–F. D. McMillan d. C. de Gronkel–Hombergen 6–1, 8–6, 7–5; Diepraam d. Hombergen 10–12, 6–4, 4–6, 6–1, 6–3; Drysdale d. de Gronkel 6–0, 6–2, 6–3.

SECOND ROUND

West Germany d. Switzerland 4–1, Lugano: I. Buding d. T. Sturdza 6–2, 6–3, 6–1; W. Bungert d. T. Stalder 6–2, 6–2, 6–1; Buding–H. Elschenbroich d. Sturdza–M. Werren 6–2, 3–6, 6–3, 10–8; Bungert lost to Sturdza 6–4, 3–6, 6–2, 5–7, 4–6; Buding d. Stalder 6–2, 6–2, 6–2.
Great Britain d. Hungary 3–2, Budapest: M. Sangster lost to I. Gulyas 6–4, 3–6, 4–6, 6–2, 5–7; R. Taylor d. A. Szikszai 6–4, 6–2, 2–6, 6–2; Sangster–R. K. Wilson d. Gulyas–Szikszai 6–2, 6–4, 11–13, 6–4; Sangster lost to Szikszai 1–6, 2–6, 6–3, 3–6; Taylor d. Gulyas 16–18, 6–3, 6–1, 6–4.
Italy d. Morocco, def.; South Africa d. Holland 4–1, Scheveningen: K. Diepraam d. J. Hajer 4–6, 6–2, 6–0, 6–4; C. Drysdale d. T. Okker 6–3, 6–4, 4–6, 6–2; Diepraam–F. McMillan d. Okker–Hajer 7–5, 8–6, 6–1; Diepraam lost to Okker 3–6, 2–6, 6–8; Drysdale d. Hajer 6–2, 6–1, 6–0.

SEMI-FINAL ROUND

West Germany d. Great Britain 3–2, Hanover: I. Buding d. M. Sangster 6–1, 6–4, 3–6, 6–3; W. Bungert d. R. Taylor 6–1, 2–6, 13–11, 6–4; Bungert–Buding lost to R. Wilson–Sangster 6–0, 8–10, 1–6, 5–7; Bungert d. Sangster 6–3, 6–3, 12–10; Buding lost to Taylor 2–6, 6–3, 2–6, 1–1 def. **South Africa d. Italy 3–2, Rome:** C. Drysdale lost to S. Tacchini 6–1, 1–6, 4–6, 4–6; K. Diepraam lost to N. Pietrangeli 2–6, 3–6, 6–1, 3–6; F. McMillan–Diepraam d. G. di Maso–G. Maioli 3–6, 9–11, 6–3, 6–4, 6–4; Drysdale d. Pietrangeli 6–3, 6–3, 4–6, 2–6, 6–2; Diepraam d. Tacchini 6–4, 7–5, 6–3.

FINAL ROUND

West Germany d. South Africa 3–2, Munich: W. Bungert d. C. Drysdale 6–3, 0–6, 8–6, 6–4; I. Buding d. K. Diepraam 6–2, 6–1, 1–6, 6–4; Buding–H. Elschenbroich lost to Diepraam–F. McMillan 1–6, 7–5, 6–1, 5–7, 5–7; Bungert d. Diepraam 12–10, 6–2, 6–3; Buding lost to Drysdale 4–6, 9–7, 5–7, 0–6.

Eastern Zone A

FIRST ROUND

Philippines d. Korea 3–2, Seoul: F. Ampon d. Doo Hwan Kim 3–6, 6–4, 6–3, 6–1; R. Deyro lost to Chong Yang Im 2–6, 4–6, 5–7; A. Villanueva–S. Ang d. Chong Yang Im–Doo Hwan Kim 6–3, 5–7, 6–2, 4–6, 6–1; Ampon d. Chong Yang Im 6–2, 6–2, 6–3; Deyro lost to Doo Hwan Kim 9–7, 4–6, 3–6, 6–3, 4–6.

SECOND ROUND

Japan d. Philippines 3–2, Manila: K. Watanabe d. F. Ampon 7–5, 6–4, 6–3; O. Ishiguro lost to R. Deyro 4–6, 6–1, 6–2, 1–6, 1–6; Ishiguro–Watanabe d. S. Ang–E. Cruz 6–1, 6–2, 7–5; Watanabe d. Deyro 6–2, 6–4, 6–2; Ishiguro lost to Ampon 4–6, 3–6, 1–6.

Eastern Zone B

FIRST ROUND

Ceylon d. Vietnam def.

SECOND ROUND

Ceylon d. Malaysia 4–1, Kuala Lumpur: P. S. Kumara d. S. A. Azman 6–2, 6–2, 6–2; B. Pinto d. B. Yap 6–3, 6–3, 6–4; Pinto–Kumara d. Azman–M. Tay 2–6, 12–10, 6–3, 4–6, 9–7; Kumara d. Yap 6–4, 2–6, 6–1, 6–3; G. N. Perera lost to Azman 1–6, 6–2, 6–1, 4–6, 1–6. **India d. Iran 5–0, Ahmedabad:** S. P. Misra d. T. Akbari 6–2, 3–6, 6–3, 6–4; P. Lall d. N. Nemati 6–2, 6–3, 6–1. Lall–Misra d. Akbari–Nemati 6–2, 6–4, 6–4; Misra d. Nemati 7–5, 6–0, 6–0; R. Venkatesan d. E. Nemati 6–1, 6–1, 6–0.

THIRD ROUND

India d. Ceylon 5–0, Madras: P. Lall d. P. S. Kumara 6–2, 6–4, 6–4; S. P. Misra d. B. Pinto 9–7, 6–2, 6–2; Lall–Misra d. Pinto–Kumara 6–3, 6–2, 6–2; R. Venkatesan d. G. N. Perera 6–1, 4–6, 6–1, 6–3; Misra d. Kumara 6–4, 6–3, 6–3.

ZONE FINAL ROUND

India d. Japan 4–1: R. Krishnan d. O. Ishiguro 6–3, 2–6, 6–2, 10–8; P. Lall lost to K. Watanabe 3–6, 6–4, 3–6, 6–3, 7–9; Krishnan–Lall d. Ishiguro–Watanabe 6–2, 6–3, 6–3; Lall d. Ishiguro 2–6, 8–6, 7–5, 10–8; Krishnan d. Watanabe 6–2, 7–5, 6–0.

American Zone

FIRST ROUND

British Caribbean d. Venezuela 3–2, Caracas: R. Russell d. H. Hose 4–6, 6–3, 5–7, 8–6, 6–0; L. Lumsden lost to I. Pimentel 5–7, 0–6, 2–6; Russell–Lumsden lost to Pimentel–E. Alvarez 7–5, 2–6, 7–5, 4–6, 3–6; Lumsden d. Hose 6–4, 9–7, 1–6, 6–0; Russell d. Pimentel 6–4, 9–7, 1–6, 2–6, 8–6. **Argentina d. Chile 3–2, Buenos Aires:** E. Soriano lost to P. Rodriguez 6–1, 5–7, 4–6, 3–6; R. Aubone d. P. Cornejo 8–6, 6–1, 3–6, 5–7, 6–2; Aubone–Soriano d. Rodriguez–O. Pabst 3–6, 5–7, 6–2, 7–5, 6–2; Soriano d. Cornejo 6–2, 9–7, 6–2; Aubone lost to Rodriguez 1–6, 1–6, 0–6.

SEMI-FINAL ROUND

USA d. British Caribbean 4–1, Kingston: A. Ashe d. L. Lumsden 6–0, 6–1, 6–2; C. Richey d. R. Russell 6–2, 6–4, 6–0; Ashe–C. Pasarell lost to Russell–Lumsden 4–6, 9–7, 12–14, 6–4, 4–6; Richey d. Lumsden 6–3, 6–3, 6–2; Ashe d. Russell 8–6, 6–4, 8–6. **Mexico d. Argentina 4–1, Mexico City:** R. Osuna d. R. Aubone 6–2, 6–2, 7–5; I. Garcia d. E. Soriano 6–2, 6–3, 6–1; Osuna–M. Lara lost to Aubone–Soriano 5–7, 6–3, 10–12, 8–6, 12–14; Garcia d. Aubone 6–2, 6–4, 6–3; Osuna d. Soriano 9–7, 4–6, 14–12, 4–6, 7–5.

FINAL ROUND

USA d. Mexico City 5–0, Cleveland: C. Graebner d. J. Loyo-Mayo 6–0, 4–6, 6–1, 3–6, 6–3; D. Ralston d. R. Osuna 6–4, 2–6, 7–5, 6–1; Ralston–Graebner d. Osuna–Loyo-Mayo 6–1, 6–4, 6–0; C. Richey d. M. Lara 11–13, 6–0, 12–10, 6–4; Graebner d. Osuna 6–3, 6–4, 6–4.

INTER-ZONE FINALS

Brazil d. USA 3–2, Porto Alegre: T. Koch lost to D. Ralston 4–6, 4–6, 0–6; E. Mandarino d. C. Richey 5–7, 6–3, 7–5, 6–3; Koch–Mandarino lost to A. Ashe–Ralston 5–7, 4–6, 6–4, 2–6; Koch d. Richey 6–1, 7–5, 6–1; Mandarino d. Ralston 4–6, 6–4, 4–6, 6–4, 6–1. **India d. West Germany 3–2, Calcutta:** R. Krishnan d. W. Bungert 7–5, 7–5, 6–4; J. Mukerjea d. I. Buding 2–6, 7–5, 6–3, 6–4; Mukerjea–P. Lall lost to Bungert–Buding 1–6, 8–10, 4–6; Mukerjea d. Bungert 4–6, 8–6, 8–6, 6–3; Lall lost to Buding 6–4, 3–6, 6–3, 1–6, 4–6. **India d. Brazil 3–2, Calcutta:** J. Mukerjea lost to T. Koch 2–6, 2–6, 3–6; R. Krishnan d. E. Mandarino 5–7, 6–2, 6–2, 6–3; Krishnan–Mukerjea d. Koch–Mandarino 7–5, 3–6, 6–3, 3–6, 6–3; Mukerjea lost to Mandarino 7–9, 6–3, 4–6, 6–3, 5–7; Krishnan d. Koch 3–6, 6–4, 10–12, 7–5, 6–2.

CHALLENGE ROUND
Australia d. India 4–1, Melbourne: F. Stolle d. R. Krishnan 6–3, 6–2,
6–4; R. Emerson d. J. Mukerjea 7–5, 6–4, 6–2; J. Newcombe–A. Roche
lost to Krishnan–Mukerjea 6–4, 5–7, 4–6, 4–6; Emerson d. Krishnan 6–0,
6–2, 10–8; Stolle d. Mukerjea 7–5, 6–8, 6–3, 5–7, 6–3.

1967: AUSTRALIA
European Zone A

FIRST ROUND
Bulgaria d. Portugal 5–0: K. Yashmakov d. A. V. Pinto 6–4, 5–7, 6–2,
6–4; R. Rangelov d. J. Lagos 6–1, 6–2, 6–4; Rangelov d. Pinto 6–1, 6–1,
6–2; Yashmakov d. Lagos 6–1, 6–2, 5–7, 6–1.   **Great Britain d. Canada
4–1, London:** M. Sangster lost to M. Belkin 2–6, 3–6, 6–3, 1–6; R.
Taylor d. R. Bedard 6–4, 3–6, 6–3, 1–6, 7–5; R. Wilson–Taylor d. K.
Carpenter–Belkin 3–6, 4–6, 8–6, 7–5, 12–10; Taylor d. Belkin 2–6, 2–6,
6–4, 7–5, 6–3; Sangster d. Bedard 6–4, 6–4, 6–1.   **Rumania d. Belgium
4–1, Bucharest:** I. Tiriac lost to E. Drossart 4–6, 2–6, 7–9; I. Nastase
d. P. Hombergen 6–3, 5–7, 6–1, 6–0; Tiriac–Nastase d. Drossart–C. de
Gronckel 6–4, 6–0, 6–4; Nastase d. Drossart 6–2, 5–7, 10–8, 6–2; Tiriac
d. Hombergen 8–6, 7–5, 6–8, 3–1. def.   **Spain d. United Arab
Republic 5–0, San Sebastian:** L. Arilla d. S. Mourad 7–5, 6–4, 6–3; M.
Santana d. El Moataz Sonbol 6–0, 7–5, 6–4; Santana–Arilla d. Fathy
Mohammed Aly–Mourad 6–1, 6–2, 6–3; Santana d. Mourad 7–5, 6–2,
6–3; M. Orantes d. Sonbol 6–1, 6–2, 6–2.   **Greece d. Switzerland 3–2,
Geneva:** P. Gavrilidis lost to M. Werren 5–7, 2–6, 3–6; N. Kalo d. D.
Sturdza 3–6, 6–3, 7–9, 6–2, 6–3; Gavrilidis–Kalo d. Sturdza–E. Schori
3–6, 9–7, 6–2, 7–5; Kalo d. Werren 6–2, 6–3, 6–3; Gavrilidis lost to Sturdza
2–6, 2–6, 2–6.   **Chile d. Czechoslovakia 3–2, Prague:** J. Pinto Bravo
d. M. Holecek 6–3, 6–2, 6–1; P. Rodriguez d. J. Kodes 3–6, 6–1, 6–3,
4–6, 6–0; P. Cornejo–Pinto Bravo lost to Kodes–Holecek 1–6, 4–6, 3–6;
Pinto Bravo lost to Kodes 2–6, 3–6, 3–6; Rodriguez d. Holecek 3–6, 6–3,
1–6, 6–3, 7–5.   **Denmark d. Finland 4–1, Helsinki:** T. Ulrich d. P.
Saila 6–2, 6–3, 6–3; J. Ulrich d. R. Suominen 1–6, 6–1, 5–7, 6–1, 7–5;
T. and J. Ulrich d. Suominen–Saila 2–6, 6–3, 6–1, 6–4; J. Ulrich lost to
Saila 6–2, 4–6, 4–6, 6–4, 4–6; T. Ulrich d. Suominen 6–1, 6–4, 4–6,
6–1.   **USSR d. West Germany 3–2, Dusseldorf:** A. Metreveli d. I.
Buding 7–5, 6–3, 1–6, 9–7; T. Lejus lost to W. Bungert 3–6, 2–6, 5–7;
S. Likhachev–Metreveli d. Bungert–Buding 6–3, 6–4, 9–11, 9–7; Lejus
lost to Buding 4–6, 6–4, 6–8, 2–6; Metreveli d. Bungert 6–2, 4–6, 4–6,
6–2, 7–5.

SECOND ROUND

Great Britain d. Bulgaria 5–0, Sofia: R. Taylor d. K. Yashmakov 6–4, 6–2, 6–0; M. Sangster d. R. Rangelov 6–4, 6–2, 6–2; R. Wilson–M. Cox d. B. Pampoulov–S. Velov 6–0, 6–0, 6–0; Sangster d. Yashmakov 6–4, 6–2, 6–3; Taylor d. Rangelov 6–2, 6–1, 6–0. **Spain d. Rumania 3–2, Bucharest:** J. Gisbert lost to I. Tiriac 1–6, 2–6, 7–5, 6–0, 2–6; M. Santana d. I. Nastase 0–6, 6–3, 6–3, 6–3; Santana–Gisbert lost to Nastase–Tiriac 5–7, 5–7, 4–6; Gisbert d. Nastase 6–3, 4–6, 9–7, 6–4; Santana d. Tiriac 6–2, 8–6, 7–5. **Chile d. Greece 3–2, Athens:** P. Rodriguez d. N. Kalo 6–4, 6–1, 6–1; J. Pinto Bravo d. P. Gavrilidis 6–1, 8–6, 6–3; Pinto Bravo–E. Aguirre lost to Kalo–Gavrilidis 9–7, 6–3, 4–6, 2–6, 6–8; Pinto Bravo lost to Kalo 5–7, 6–8, 6–2, 6–2, 2–6; Rodriguez d. Gavrilidis 3–6, 2–6, 6–1, 6–1, 6–1. **USSR d. Denmark 3–2, Copenhagen:** T. Lejus d. T. Ulrich 6–2, 6–1, 3–6, 6–3; A. Metreveli lost to J. Leschly 5–7, 8–6, 2–6, 10–8, 3–6; Metreveli–S. Lichachev d. Leschly–J. Ulrich 4–6, 6–3, 6–3, 6–1; Lejus lost to Leschly 3–6, 5–7, 3–6; Metreveli d. T. Ulrich 6–3, 6–1, 6–2.

SEMI-FINAL ROUND

Spain d. Great Britain 3–2, Eastbourne: L. Arilla lost to R. Taylor 6–3, 3–6, 4–6, 2–6; M. Santana d. M. Sangster 8–10, 6–3, 5–7, 9–7, 6–0; Santana–Arilla d. R. Wilson–Sangster 7–5, 12–10, 6–4; Santana d. Taylor 6–4, 6–3, 7–5; Arilla lost to Sangster 4–6, 11–9, 4–6, 3–6. **USSR d. Chile 3–0, Moscow:** A. Metreveli d. J. Pinto Bravo 6–3, 6–2, 5–7, 6–1; T. Lejus d. P. Rodriguez 6–4, 6–1, 6–8, 6–0; Metreveli–S. Likhachev d. Pinto Bravo–P. Cornejo 7–5, 6–1, 6–2.

FINAL ROUND

Spain d. USSR 4–1, Barcelona: M. Santana d. T. Lejus 6–3, 6–4, 6–1; J. Gisbert d. A. Metreveli 3–6, 2–6, 6–3, 7–5, 6–2; Santana–L. Arilla lost to Metreveli–S. Likhachev 3–6, 6–3, 4–6, 4–6; Santana d. Metreveli 6–0, 6–3, 6–3; Gisbert d. Lejus 2–6, 6–4, 6–3, 6–0.

European Zone B

FIRST ROUND

Brazil d. Yugoslavia 3–2, Zabreb: E. Mandarino d. Z. Franulovic 6–3, 6–2, 6–4; T. Koch lost to N. Pilic 2–6, 4–6, 6–3, 1–6; Mandarino–Koch d. B. Jovanovic–Pilic 5–7, 6–3, 9–7, 7–5; Mandarino d. Pilic 2–6, 7–5, 6–4, 6–4; Koch lost to Franulovic 2–6, 10–8, 2–6, 4–6. **Poland d. Israel 5–0, Warsaw:** M. Rybarczyk d. J. Stabholz 6–1, 6–3, 6–2; W.

Gasiorek d. E. Davidman 6–3, 6–2, 6–4; T. Nowicki–B. Lewandowski d. Davidman–Stabholz 6–1, 6–1, 6–4; Lewandowski d. Stabholz 6–3, 6–4, 6–3; Rybarczyk d. Davidman 6–4, 6–3, 6–1. **Italy d. Austria 5–0, Verona:** N. Pietrangeli d. P. Pokorny 6–0, 6–3, 6–1; G. Maioli d. D. Schultheiss 6–0, 6–1, 6–2; Maioli–V. Crotta d. Pokorny–H. Holzer 7–5, 7–5, 7–5; Maioli d. Pokorny 6–3, 6–0, 6–1; Pietrangeli d. Schultheiss 8–6, 4–6, 6–1, 7–5. **Luxembourg d. Ireland 3–2, Mondorf:** F. Baden d. P. Jackson 6–3, 7–5, 6–4; T. Brasseur lost to M. Hickey 6–8, 1–6, 7–5, 2–6; Baden–Brasseur lost to Jackson–Hickey 6–3, 1–6, 1–6, 2–6; Baden d. Hickey 10–8, 6–2, 6–1; Brasseur d. Jackson 6–3, 11–9, 5–7, 7–5. **France d. Norway 5–0, Paris:** G. Goven d. E. Raastad 6–0, 6–2, 6–1; F. Jauffret d. N. Martin 6–3, 6–4, 6–2; P. Beust–D. Contet d. Martin–A. Melander 6–2, 6–4, 6–2; Jauffret d. Raastad 6–0, 6–4, 6–0; Goven d. Martin 6–0, 6–3, 6–0. **Hungary d. Sweden 4–1, Budapest:** I. Gulyas d. O. Bengtson 6–2, 3–6, 7–5, 6–1; A. Szikszai lost to J. E. Lundquist 4–6, 2–6, 6–4, 2–6; Gulyas–Szikszai d. Lundquist–Bengtson 6–3, 4–6, 6–3, 6–3; Gulyas d. Lundquist 8–6, 7–5, 6–1; Szikszai d. Bengtson 6–2, 6–4, 6–1. **South Africa d. Holland 3–2, The Hague:** R. Hewitt d. T. Okker 4–6, 6–1, 6–0, 2–6, 6–2; C. Drysdale lost to J. Hajer 5–7, 8–10, 3–6; Hewitt–F. McMillan d. Okker–Hajer 6–3, 6–4, 6–1; Hewitt d. Hajer 6–1, 4–6, 8–6, 6–1; Drysdale lost to Okker 2–6, 2–6, 6–0, 5–7. **Monaco d. Turkey 5–0, Monte Carlo:** P. Landau d. T. Gursoy 6–0, 6–1, 7–5; A. Viviani d. Z. Grenli 6–1, def.; Landau–F. Truchi d. Gursoy–B. Ambar 6–4, 6–4, 6–0; A. Vatrican d. Ambar 7–5, 6–4, 7–5; Viviani d. Gursoy 6–4, 1–6, 3–6, 6–4, 6–4.

SECOND ROUND

Brazil d. Poland 5–0, Warsaw: E. Mandarino d. T. Nowicki 6–1, 6–0, 6–4; T. Koch d. W. Gasiorek 6–2, 6–2, 6–1; Mandarino–Koch d. Nowicki–Gasiorek 8–6, 6–2, 6–4; Koch d. Nowicki 7–5, 6–2, 6–4; Mandarino d. Gasiorek 6–4, 6–2, 6–4. **Italy d. Luxembourg 5–0, Piacenza:** N. Pietrangeli d. F. Baden 6–1, 6–3, 6–3; G. Maioli d. T. Brasseur 6–1, 6–0, 6–2; Maioli–V. Crotta d. Baden–Brasseur 6–2, 6–3, 6–3; Pietrangeli d. Brasseur 6–2, 6–2, 6–0; Maioli d. Baden 6–2, 6–1, 6–4. **France d. Hungary 5–0, Paris:** G. Goven d. E. Raastad 6–0, 6–2, 6–1; F. Jauffret d. N. Martin 6–3, 6–4, 6–2; P. Beust–D. Contet d. Martin–A. Melander 6–2, 6–4, 6–2; Jauffret d. Raastad 6–0, 6–4, 6–0; Goven d. Martin 6–0, 6–3, 6–0. **South Africa d. Monaco 5–0, Monte Carlo:** C. Drysdale d. P. Landau 6–1, 6–4, 7–5; R. Hewitt d. A. Viviani 6–0, 6–0, 6–0; Hewitt–F. McMillan d. Landau–F. Truchi 6–1, 6–1, 6–2; R. Maud d. Viviani 6–1, 6–2, 6–4; R. Moore d. Landau 3–6, 6–2, 6–3, 6–4.

SEMI-FINAL ROUND

Brazil d. Italy 3–1, Naples: E. Mandarino d. N. Pietrangeli 2–6, 9–7, 6–4, 6–3; T. Koch d. G. Maioli 6–0, 6–3, 7–5; Mandarino–Koch d. Maioli–V. Crotta 6–3, 6–4, 6–2; Koch lost to Pietrangeli 7–5, 6–2, 4–6, 0–6, 0–6; Mandarino v. Maioli 6–1, 6–1, 4–6, 4–6, 5–5 unfin. **South Africa d. France 5–0, Paris:** R. Hewitt d. F. Jauffret 6–1, 6–1, 4–6, 9–7; C. Drysdale d. P. Darmon 6–1, 6–2, 6–1; Hewitt–F. McMillan d. P. Beust–D. Contet 9–11, 6–1, 6–3, 6–1; Drysdale d. Jauffret 6–1, 6–2, 7–5; R. Maud d. Contet 9–7, 6–2, 6–3.

FINAL ROUND

South Africa d. Brazil 5–0, Durban: R. Hewitt d. T. Koch 6–4, 9–11, 11–9, 6–2; C. Drysdale d. E. Mandarino 6–2, 8–6, 6–2; Hewitt–F. McMillan d. Koch–Mandarino 1–6, 4–6, 6–3, 6–4, 6–3; Hewitt d. Mandarino 1–6, 3–6, 6–4, 6–2, 6–0; Drysdale d. Koch 6–3, 8–6, 6–4.

Eastern Zone A

FIRST ROUND

Philippines d. South Korea 5–0, Manila: R. Deyro d. Kim Doo Hwan 6–2, 6–2, 6–0; F. Ampon d. Chung Yang Im 7–5, 6–1, 6–2; S. Ang–E. Cruz d. Im–Hwan 2–6, 6–2, 6–3, 6–2; Ang d. Hwan 6–4, 6–0, 6–1; Cruz d. Im 6–4, 6–4, 6–0.

SECOND ROUND

Philippines d. Vietnam 5–0, Manila: E. Cruz d. Vo Van Bay 6–2, 6–3, 6–2; F. Ampon d. Vo Van Thanh 6–4, 6–1, 6–1; Cruz–S. Ang d. Vo Van Bay–Luu Hoang Duc 4–6, 19–17, 6–2, 6–3; Ang d. Luu Hoang Duc 6–3, 6–4, 6–1; Cruz d. Thanh 12–10, 9–7, 6–1. **Japan d. Indonesia 5–0, Jakarta:** K. Yanagi d. G. Widjaja 6–2, 6–4, 7–5; I. Konishi d. S. Soetarjo 6–1, 6–2; I. Watanabe–I. Kabeyashi d. Soetarjo–Widjaja 6–8, 6–3, 6–3, 8–10, 6–3; Konishi d. Widjaja 6–1, 6–3, 6–2; Yanagi d. Soetarjo 1–6, 6–2, 6–4, 4–6, 6–1.

SEMI-FINAL ROUND

Japan d. Philippines 5–0, Tokyo: K. Watanabe d. S. Ang 6–2, 6–0, 6–2; I. Konishi d. F. Ampon 6–1, 6–0, 6–4; I and K. Watanabe d. R. Deyro–Ang 6–2, 6–2, 6–4; Konishi d. Ang 6–4, 6–3, 6–2; K. Watanabe d. Ampon 6–0, 6–1, 6–1.

Eastern Zone B

FIRST ROUND

India d. Ceylon 5–0, Colombo: J. Mukerjea d. L. Fernando 6–3, 6–4, 6–3; S. P. Misra d. P. S. Kumara 6–0, 6–2, 6–4; Mukerjea–Misra d. B. Pinto–Kumara 6–4, 11–9, 6–3; R. Venkethasan d. Fernando 6–2, 6–0, 6–0; Mukerjea d. Arichandran 6–0, 6–1, 6–1. **Iran d. Malaysia def.**

SEMI-FINAL ROUND

India d. Iran 4–1, Teheran: S. P. Misra d. E. Nemati 6–4, 6–1, 6–0; J. Mukerjea d. T. Akbari 7–5, 6–4, 5–7, 6–3; Mukerjea–Misra d. H. and T. Akbari 6–4, 6–3, 6–3; Mukerjea d. I. Khodai 6–4, 7–5, 6–4; Misra lost to T. Akbari 2–6, 0–3 def.

FINAL ROUND

India d. Japan 4–1, New Delhi: P. Lall d. K. Watanabe 6–2, 6–4, 6–2; J. Mukerjea d. I. Konishi 3–6, 6–3, 5–7, 9–7, 6–3; Lall–R. Krishnan d. K. and I. Watanabe 6–2, 6–4, 4–6, 6–0; Mukerjea lost to K. Watanabe 8–6, 2–6, 2–6, 1–6; Lall d. Konishi 6–2, 9–7, 6–3.

American Zone North

FIRST ROUND

USA d. British Caribbean 5–0, Port of Spain: C. Pasarell d. L. Lumsden 6–2, 6–2, 6–1; C. Richey d. R. Russell 6–2, 1–6, 7–5, 6–4; M. Riessen–C. Graebner d. Russell–Lumsden 6–4, 6–2, 6–2; Pasarell d. Russell 6–2, 6–2, 6–2; Richey d. Lumsden 6–2, 6–4, 4–6, 6–2. **Mexico d. New Zealand 4–1, Mexico City:** R. Osuna lost to B. Fairlie 4–6, 6–2, 3–6, 6–4, 3–6; M. Lara d. O. Parun 6–1, 6–1, 6–1; Osuna–L. Garcia d. Fairlie–K. Woolcott 11–9, 4–6, 6–4, 6–4; Lara d. Fairlie 6–2, 6–1, 10–8; Osuna d. Parun 6–4, 6–1, 6–2.

SEMI-FINAL ROUND

USA d. Mexico 4–1, Mexico City: C. Richey lost to R. Osuna 3–6, 6–4, 6–1, 3–6, 1–6; A. Ashe d. M. Lara 7–5, 6–2, 7–5; C. Graebner–M. Riessen d. Osuna–J. Loyo Mayo 6–4, 6–3, 7–5; Ashe d. Osuna 8–6, 6–3, 6–2; Richey d. Lara 8–6, 3–6, 6–3, 2–6, 6–4.

American Zone South

FIRST ROUND

Argentina d. Venezuela 5–0, Buenos Aires: J. Ganzabal d. H. Hose
6–1, 6–2, 6–2; R. Aubone d. J. Moros 5–7, 6–3, 6–3, 6–0; Aubone–E.
Soriano d. Moros–Hose 6–1, 8–6, 7–5; Ganzabal d. J. Andrew 6–1, 6–4,
6–0; Soriano d. Hose 6–0, 8–6, 6–1.

SEMI-FINAL ROUND

Ecuador d. Argentina 4–1, Buenos Aires: F. Guzman lost to J.
Ganzabal 6–2, 4–6, 2–6, 1–6; M. Olvera d. R. Aubone 6–4, 6–1, 5–7, 6–0;
Olvera–Guzman d. Aubone–E. Soriano 6–3, 4–6, 6–4, 3–6, 6–4; Guzman
d. Aubone 6–3, 6–3, 6–1; Olvera d. Ganzabal 6–2, 6–2, 8–6.

FINAL ROUND

Ecuador d. USA 3–2, Guayaquil: F. Guzman lost to C. Richey 2–6,
6–2, 6–8, 4–6; M. Olvera d. A. Ashe 4–6, 6–4, 6–4, 6–2; Olvera–Guzman
d. C. Graebner–M. Riessen 0–6, 9–7, 6–3, 4–6, 8–6; Guzman d. Ashe
0–6, 6–4, 6–2, 0–6, 6–3; Olvera lost to Richey 7–5, 4–6, 5–7, 6–4, 0–6.

INTER-ZONE FINALS

Spain d. Ecuador 5–0, Barcelona: M. Santana d. F. Guzman 6–2, 6–1,
6–1; J. Gisbert d. M. Olvera 6–3, 6–3, 6–2; Santana–L. Arilla d.
Guzman–Olvera 7–5, 6–8, 3–6, 9–7, 6–1; Santana d. Olvera 6–3, 6–4,
6–1; Gisbert d. Guzman 6–3, 2–6, 0–6, 6–2, 6–1.   **South Africa d.
India 5–0, Barcelona:** R. Hewitt d. R. Krishnan 3–6, 6–3, 6–2, 2–6, 8–6;
C. Drysdale d. J. Mukerjea 6–1, 6–0, 6–0; Hewitt–P. McMillan d.
Mukerjea–Krishnan 6–2, 7–5, 6–2; Drysdale d. Krishnan 7–5, 6–4, 3–6,
6–3; R. Maud d. Mukerjea 6–1, 6–2, 6–3.   **Spain d. South Africa 3–2,
Johannesburg:** M. Santana d. R. Moore 6–3, 6–2, 6–4; M. Orantes lost
to C. Drysdale 4–6, 2–6, 4–6; Santana–L. Arilla d. F. McMillan–
Drysdale 6–4, 6–3, 13–11; Orantes lost to Moore 4–6, 6–0, 4–6, 6–2, 4–6;
Santana d. Drysdale 6–3, 6–3, 3–6, 6–2.

CHALLENGE ROUND

Australia d. Spain 4–1, Brisbane: R. Emerson d. M. Santana 6–4, 6–1,
6–1; J. Newcombe d. M. Orantes 6–3, 6–3, 6–2; Newcombe–A. Roche
d. Santana–Orantes 6–4, 6–4, 6–4; Newcombe lost to Santana 5–7, 4–6,
2–6; Emerson d. Orantes 6–1, 6–1, 2–6, 6–4.

1968: USA
European Zone A

FIRST ROUND

Spain d. Holland 3–2, Valencia: M. Santana d. J. Hajer 6–4, 9–7, 6–3; J. M. Gisbert lost to T. S. Okker 5–7, 3–6, 5–7; Santana–J. L. Arilla d. Okker–Hajer 1–6, 4–6, 6–3, 6–4, 6–3; Santana lost to Okker 4–6, 6–3, 3–6, 7–5, 4–6; Gisbert d. Hajer 7–5, 6–1, 6–0.   **Sweden d. Rhodesia 4–1, Bandol, France:** O. Bengtson d. A. Bey 6–3, 6–2, 6–4; H. Nerell lost to F. Salomon 6–2, 4–6, 5–7, 6–1, 5–7; Bengston–Nerell d. Bey–Salomon 6–2, 6–3, 6–0; Bengston d. Salomon 6–1, 6–3, 6–4; Nerell d. D. Irvine 2–6, 5–7, 6–3, 6–3, 6–3.   **Finland d. Portugal 4–1, Helsinki:** P. Petersen–Dyggve d. A. V. Pinto 3–6, 6–2, 7–5, 3–6, 6–4; T. Jokinen d. J. Lagos 5–7, 7–5, 4–6, 7–5, 6–3; H. Hedman–Petersen–Dyggve d. Pinto–Roquete 6–3, 6–3, 6–3; Jokinen lost to Pinto 4–6, 4–6, 2–6; Petersen–Dyggve d. Lagos 6–4, 6–4, 6–4.   **Great Britain d. France 3–0, Bournemouth:** R. K. Wilson d. F. Jauffret 6–3, 3–6, 1–6, 6–4, 6–1; M. Cox d. G. Goven 3–6, 4–6, 6–1, 7–5, 7–5; Cox–Wilson d. P. Beust–D. Contet 1–6, 6–2, 3–6, 6–4, 7–5.   **USSR d. Greece 4–1, Tbilisi:** T. Lejus lost to N. Kalogeropoulos 10–8, 4–6, 4–6, 1–6; A. Metreveli d. P. Gavrilides 6–2, 6–4; 6–3; Metreveli–S. Likhachev d. Gavrilides–Kalogeropoulos 6–4, 4–6, 6–3, 7–5; Lejus d. Gavrilides 6–2, 6–1, 6–0; Metreveli d. Kalogeropoulos 3–6, 6–2, 1–6, 8–6, 6–2. **Yugoslavia d. New Zealand 4–0, Zagreb:** Z. Franulovic d. O. Parun 5–7, 7–5, 6–1, 6–3; B. Jovanovic d. B. Fairlie 2–6, 7–5, 7–5, 6–4; Jovanovic–Franulovic d. Fairlie–R. N. Hawkes 6–1, 6–4, 6–4; Jovanovic d. Parun 6–0, 6–1, 6–2; Franulovic v. Fairlie 6–2, 7–5, 3–6, 1–6, 1–2 unfin.   **Italy d. Hungary 5–0, Cagliari, Sardinia:** M. F. Mulligan d. I. Gulyas 6–4, 3–6, 6–3, 2–6, 7–5; N. Pietrangeli d. P. Szoke 6–3, 6–2, 6–1; Mulligan–Pietrangeli d. Gulyas–A. Szikszai 7–5, 9–7, 2–6, 11–9; Pietrangeli d. Gulyas 6–4, 6–2, 2–6, 1–6, 7–5; Mulligan d. Szoke 4–6, 7–5, 6–4, 6–1.   **Monaco d. Ireland 3–1, Monte Carlo:** P. Landau d. P. Mockler 6–2, 6–3, 5–7, 6–2; A. Viviani lost to M. P. Hickey 4–6, 4–6, 2–6; Landau–F. Trucchi d. Hickey–P. Jackson 5–7, 6–4, 6–4, 4–6, 6–2; Landau d. Hickey 4–6, 6–4, 8–6, 6–4.

QUARTER-FINAL ROUND

Spain d. Sweden 3–1, Barcelona: J. M. Gisbert d. O. Bengtson 6–2, 6–2, 6–3; M. Santana d. H. Nerell 6–1, 6–4, 6–2; Santana–J. L. Arilla lost to Bengtson–Nerell 4–6, 5–7, 6–4, 5–7; Gisbert d. Nerell 10–8, 6–0, 7–9, 3–6, 7–5.   **Great Britain d. Finland 5–0, London:** M. Sangster d. P. Saila 6–4, 8–6, 6–4; M. Cox d. P. Petersen–Dyggve 6–2, 6–4, 6–0;

P. R. Hutchins–R. Wilson d. H. Hedman–Saila 6–1, 6–2, 6–1; Sangster d. Petersen–Dyggve 7–5, 6–2, 6–2; Cox d. Saila 6–4, 4–6, 6–1, 6–4. **USSR d. Yugoslavia 5–0, Moscow:** A. Metreveli d. B. Jovanovic 6–3, 6–4, 6–4; T. Lejus d. Z. Franulovic 6–3, 2–6, 8–6, 7–5; S. Likhachev–Metreveli d. Franulovic–Jovanovic 6–2, 11–9, 8–6; Metreveli d. Franulovic 6–3, 6–2, 9–7; Lejus d. Jovanovic 7–5, 4–6, 6–3, 6–2. **Italy d. Monaco 5–0, Beila, Italy:** N. Pietrangeli d. A. Vatrican 6–1, 6–2, 6–1; M. F. Mulligan d. F. Trucchi 6–0, 6–0, 6–1; E. Castigliano–E. di Matteo d. Trucchi–A. Manigley 6–3, 6–1, 6–3; Mulligan d. Manigley 6–0, 6–0, 6–0; Castigliano d. Trucchi 6–2, 6–2, 6–1.

SEMI-FINAL ROUND

Spain d. Great Britain 4–1, Barcelona: M. Santana d. M. Cox 6–1, 6–3, 6–3; J. M. Gisbert d. P. Hutchins 6–1, 6–3, 6–1; Santana–M. Orantes d. Cox–R. Wilson 4–6, 6–3, 6–3, 6–3; Santana d. Hutchins 6–4, 6–3, 6–4; Gisbert lost to Cox 6–4, 3–6, 3–6, 3–6. **Italy d. USSR 3–2, Reggio Emilia:** N. Pietrangeli d. T. Lejus 6–4, 4–6, 6–1, 6–2; M. F. Mulligan lost to A. Metreveli 3–6, 1–6, 3–6; Pietrangeli–Mulligan d. S. Likhachev–Metreveli 6–3, 4–6, 6–2, 6–4; Pietrangeli lost to Metreveli 0–6, 0–6, 1–6; Mulligan d. Lejus 6–2, 6–4, 7–5.

FINAL ROUND

Spain d. Italy 3–2, Barcelona: M. Santana d. N. Pietrangeli 6–3, 3–6, 4–6, 6–4, 6–2; J. M. Gisbert d. M. F. Mulligan 6–4, 2–6, 6–2, 6–4; J. L. Arilla–M. Orantes lost to Mulligan–Pietrangeli 5–7, 2–6, 6–3, 3–6; Gisbert d. Pietrangeli 8–6, 6–4, 6–2; Orantes lost to Mulligan 6–4, 6–4, 5–7, 3–6, 0–4 def.

European Zone B

FIRST ROUND

Bulgaria d. Turkey 5–0, Sofia: K. Yashmakov d. R. Aydin 6–1, 6–2, 6–3; S. Velev d. T. Gursoy 6–0, 6–0, 6–2; Yashmakov–L. Genov d. Aydin–N. Gurak 6–3, 3–6, 9–11, 6–3, 6–4; Genov d. Gursoy 6–1, 6–4, 3–6, 6–4; Velev d. Aydin 6–1, 6–1, 6–0. **West Germany d. Switzerland 4–1, Freiburg:** W. P. Bungert d. T. Stalder 6–4, 6–2, 7–5; I. D. Buding d. D. Sturdza 10–8, 6–1, 6–8, 6–1; K. Meiler–J. Fassbender lost to Sturdza–M. Werren 6–4, 2–6, 6–4, 1–6, 4–6; Buding d. Stalder 6–1, 11–9, 6–1; Bungert d. Sturdza 1–6, 6–2, 2–6, 6–2, 7–5. **Belgium d. Poland 3–2, Brussels:** E. Drossart d. B. L. Lewandowski 6–2, 6–4, 5–7, 2–6, 7–5; P. Hombergen lost to W. Gasiorek 6–4, 1–6, 1–6, 1–6;

Drossart–Hombergen d. Gasiorek–T. Nowicki 6–3, 4–6, 6–4, 6–2; Drossart lost to Gasiorek 1–6, 2–6, 2–6; Holmbergen d. Lewandowski 6–4, 4–6, 6–3, 3–6, 6–2. **Czechoslavia d. Brazil 3–2, Prague:** J. Kodes d. T. Koch 6–2, 6–3, 3–6, 7–5; J. Kukal lost to J. E. Mandarino 3–6, 6–4, 2–6, 1–6; Kodes–M. Holecek d. Koch–Mandarino 6–4, 6–4, 4–6, 7–5; Kukal lost to Koch 4–6, 2–6, 4–6; Kodes d. Mandarino 8–6, 6–4, 8–6. **Norway d. Luxembourg 4–1, Luxembourg:** F. Prydz d. T. Brasseur 6–2, 8–6, 6–4; N. M. Elvik lost to F. Baden 9–7, 6–4, 1–6, 2–6, 6–8; Elvik–E. Melander d. Baden–Brasseur 7–5, 8–6, 7–5; Elvik d. Brasseur 6–3, 6–3, 6–2; Prydz d. Baden 6–3, 6–3, 3–6, 4–6, 6–2. **Rumania d. Denmark 4–1, Bucharest:** I. Nastase d. T. Ulrich 6–4, 6–4, 6–2; I. Tiriac d. J. Ulrich 6–0, 2–6, 6–4, 9–7; Nastase–Tiriac lost to J. Leschly–T. Ulrich 6–3, 7–9, 2–6, 3–6; Tiriac d. T. Ulrich 6–1, 6–3, 6–1; Nastase d. J. Ulrich 6–2, 11–9, 4–6, 4–6, 6–4. **Iran d. Israel 4–1, Teheran:** H. Akbari d. J. Stabholz 6–2, 6–2, 5–7, 6–3; T. Akbari d. E. Davidman 7–5, 6–4, 6–4; E. Nemati–I. Khodai d. Davidman–I. Froman 6–1, 6–4, 6–4; T. Akbari d. Stabholz 6–1, 6–2, 8–6; H. Akbari lost to Davidman 1–6, 2–6, 3–6. **South Africa d. Austria, 5–0, Linz:** R. J. Moore d. D. Herdy 6–1, 6–2, 6–4; R. A. J. Hewitt d. D. Schultheiss 6–1, 6–1, 6–3; Hewitt–F. D. McMillan d. Herdy–F. Kolbinger 6–3, 6–1, 6–2; Moore d. Schultheiss 6–0, 6–2, 6–1; McMillan d. Herdy 6–4, 4–6, 6–4, 6–0.

QUARTER FINAL ROUND

West Germany d. Bulgaria 5–0, Sofia: I. D. Buding d. S. Velev 6–4, 6–1, 6–3; W. P. Bungert d. K. Yashmakov 6–2, 6–0, 7–5; K. Meiler–J. Fassbender d. Velev–Yashmakov 11–9, 6–2, 6–2; Buding d. Yashmakov 6–3, 6–2, 6–2; Bungert d. Velev 3–6, 6–1, 6–1, 6–3. **Czechoslovakia d. Belgium 3–2, Brussels:** J. Kodes d. E. Drossart 4–6, 6–3, 4–6, 6–2, 6–1; M. Holecek lost to P. Hombergen 4–6, 5–7, 6–3, 7–9; Holecek–Kodes d. Drossart–C. de Gronckel 6–3, 6–1, 6–2; Kodes lost to Hombergen 6–3, 6–2, 4–6, 2–6, 4–6; Holecek d. Drossart 6–3, 6–1, 3–6, 5–7, 6–2. **Rumania d. Norway 5–0, Oslo:** I. Nastase d. F. Prydz 4–6, 6–0, 8–6, 6–0; I. Tiriac d. N. Martin 6–2, 6–2, 6–4; Nastase–Tiriac d. J. E. Ross–E. Melander 6–2, 8–6, 6–3; Nastase d. Martin 6–2, 6–3, 6–1; Tiriac d. Prydz 6–1, 6–4, 6–2. **South Africa d. Iran 5–0, Teheran:** R. A. J. Hewitt d. T. Akbari 6–4, 10–8, 6–3; R. R. Maud d. I. Khodai 6–4, 6–3, 6–3; Hewitt–F. D. McMillan d. Khodai–E. Nemati 6–2, 6–2, 6–2; Hewitt d. Khodai 6–4, 6–1, 6–2; Maud d. Akbari 7–5, 6–3, 6–1.

SEMI–FINAL ROUND

West Germany d. Czechoslovakia 4–1: W. P. Bungert d. J. Kodes 6–2, 6–4, 6–0; I. D. Buding lost to M. Holecek 6–1, 3–6, 2–6, 3–6;

Bungert–Buding d. Holecek–Kodes 5–7, 6–1, 7–5, 3–6, 12–10; Buding d. Kodes 8–6, 6–3, 6–3; Bungert d. Holecek 8–6, 6–3, 6–4.   **South Africa d. Rumania def.**

FINAL ROUND

West Germany d. South Africa 3–2, Dusseldorf: W. P. Bungert d. R. A. J. Hewitt 9–7, 7–5, 7–5; I. D. Buding d. R. J. Moore 6–3, 4–6, 10–8, 6–8, 6–4; Buding–J. Fassbender lost to Hewitt–F. D. McMillan 4–6, 2–6, 4–6; Bungert d. Moore 6–1, 6–1, 6–1; Buding lost to Hewitt 5–7, 2–6, 6–2, 3–6.

American Zone South

FIRST ROUND

Venezuela d. Argentina 3–2, Caracas: H. Hose d. M. Vasques 4–6, 6–3, 8–6, 6–1; J. Andrew d. N. Herrero 13–15, 6–4, 7–5, 6–4; Hose–J. Moros lost to Vasquez–R. Aubone 1–6, 4–6, 8–10; Andrew lost to Vasquez 1–6, 4–6, 1–6; Hose d. Herrero 6–2, 6–2, 6–2.

SECOND ROUND

Chile d. Peru 3–0, Lima: J. Pinto Bravo d. T. Gonzales 6–3, 6–1, 6–2; P. Cornejo d. A. Acuna 8–6, 6–3, 6–0; Cornejo–Pinto Bravo d. Acuna–Gonzales 3–6, 6–3, 6–3, 6–3.   **Ecuador d. Venezuela 3–0, Caracas:** M. Olvera d. J. Moros 6–3, 6–3, 6–4; J. Guzman d. J. Andrew 2–6, 6–2, 6–3, 6–2; Guzman–Olvera d. Andrew–Y. Savy 6–2, 6–3, 6–1.

FINAL ROUND

Ecuador d. Chile 4–1, Guayaquil: M. Olvera lost to J. Pinto Bravo 6–3, 9–7, 4–6, 4–6, 1–6; J. Guzman d. P. Cornejo 3–6, 5–7, 8–6, 6–4, 6–3; Olvera–Guzman d. Cornejo–P. Rodriguez 3–6, 7–9, 6–3, 11–9, 6–1; Olvera d. Cornejo 5–7, 5–7, 12–10, 6–2, 7–5; Guzman d. Pinto Bravo def.

American Zone North

SECOND ROUND

USA d. British Caribbean 5–0, Richmond: C. Graebner d. R. Russell 6–1, 7–5, 6–2; A. Ashe d. L. Lumsden 6–1, 6–1, 6–0; S. Smith–R. Lutz d. Russell–Lumsden 6–2, 6–3, 6–3; Ashe d. Russell 6–3, 6–2, 6–4; Lutz d. Lumsden 6–0, 6–2, 6–1.   **Mexico d. Canada 5–0, Mexico City:** R.

459

Osuna d. H. Fauquier 6–3, 6–2, 6–4; J. Loyo-Mayo d. M. Belkin 16–14, 4–6, 6–3, 6–3; Osuna–V. Zarazua d. Belkin–K. Carpenter 6–3, 6–4, 6–3; Loyo-Mayo d. Fauquier 6–3, 1–6, 1–6, 6–0, 6–3; Osuna d. Carpenter 6–2, 6–3, 6–2.

FINAL ROUND
USA d. Mexico 5–0, Berkeley: A. Ashe d. R. Osuna 6–0, 6–3, 6–0; C. Graebner d. J. Loyo-Mayo 6–3, 8–6, 4–6, 6–4; S. Smith–R. Lutz d. Osuna–V. Zarazua 4–6, 6–3, 9–7, 10–8; Graebner d. Osuna 10–8, 6–3, 6–2; Ashe d. Loyo-Mayo 6–4, 8–6, 6–2.

AMERICAN ZONE FINAL
USA d. Ecuador 5–0, Charlotte: A. Ashe d. J. Guzman 6–3, 6–3, 6–2; C. Graebner d. M. Olvera 6–2, 6–1, 6–2; Graebner–R. Lutz d. Guzman–Olvera 6–3, 6–2, 7–5; Graebner d. Guzman 4–6, 6–3, 6–4, 6–4; Ashe d. Olvera 6–1, 6–3, 6–0.

Eastern Zone A

FIRST ROUND
Indonesia d. Vietnam def.

SECOND ROUND
Philippines d. Indonesia 4–1, Manila: E. Cruz d. D. Moerdono 4–6, 6–2, 6–2, 6–3; F. Ampon d. G. Widjojo 6–4, 3–6, 6–3, 3–0 def; M. Dungo–F. Deyro lost to S. Sugiarto–A. Widjojo 2–6, 3–6, 6–4, 3–6; Cruz d. G. Widjojo 6–2, 6–3, 4–6, 6–3; Ampon d. Moerdono 7–5, 4–6, 6–1, 6–1. **Japan d. Korea 5–0, Tokyo:** T. Sakai d. Ek–Son Lee 6–1, 6–2, 6–8, 6–1; K. Watanabe d. Yung–Ho Chung 6–1, 6–1, 6–4; K. and I. Watanabe d. Chung–Moon II Kim 6–4, 6–4, 6–2; J. Kamiwazumi d. Kim 8–6, 8–6, 6–1; Sakai d. Chung 6–1, 6–1, 6–1.

THIRD ROUND
Japan d. Philippines 4–1, Tokyo: I. Konishi d. F. Ampon 1–6, 6–1, 8–6, 6–2; K. Watanabe d. E. Cruz 4–6, 6–2, 6–0, 6–2; K. and I. Watanabe d. Cruz–F. Deyro 6–1, 6–2, 6–2; Konishi d. Cruz 6–1, 6–0, 6–4; T. Sakai lost to Ampon 5–7, 6–1, 4–6, 3–6.

Eastern Zone B

SECOND ROUND

Ceylon d. Malaysia 4–1: B. Pinto lost to S. A. Azman 4–6, 4–6, 6–3, 6–3, 4–6; P. S. Kumara d. B. Yap 6–0, 6–2, 6–4; Pinto–F. W. Ferdinands d. Azman–M. Tay 6–8, 6–2, 7–5; Pinto d. Yap 6–3, 6–3, 7–5; Kumara d. Azman 8–6, 6–3, 6–2.

THIRD ROUND

India d. Ceylon 3–2, Guahati: S. Minotra d. R. W. Ferdinands 6–2, 5–7, 6–2, 6–8, 8–6; J. Mukerjea d. P. Kumara 5–7, 6–4, 6–3, 6–2; G. Misra–A. Amritraj d. Kumara–Ferdinands 6–4, 6–4, 6–4; A. Amritraj lost to Ferdinands 5–7, 6–4, 1–6, 7–9; Minotra lost to Kumara 2–6, 1–6, 6–2, 0–6.

EASTERN ZONE FINAL

India d. Japan 4–1, Tokyo: P. Lall d. K. Yanagi 6–2, 6–4, 6–3; R. Krishnan d. K. Watanabe 6–2, 3–6, 6–3, 6–2; Krishnan–J. Mukerjea d. K. and I. Watanabe 6–2, 6–2, 5–7, 1–6, 6–0; Krishnan d. Yanagi 6–4, 6–3, 6–1; Lall lost to K. Watanabe 6–8, 1–6, 2–6.

INTER-ZONE FINALS

USA d. Spain 4–1, Cleveland: C. E. Graebner lost to M. Santana 2–6, 3–6, 3–6; A. Ashe d. J. Gisbert 6–2, 6–4, 6–2; Graebner–C. M. Pasarell d. Gisbert–Santana 11–13, 17–15, 7–5, 6–2; Graebner d. Gisbert 9–7, 6–3, 6–1; Ashe d. Santana 11–13, 7–5, 6–3, 13–15, 6–4. **India d. West Germany 3–2, Munich:** P. Lall d. I. Buding 2–6, 6–2, 6–3, 6–4; R. Krishnan lost to W. Bungert 6–4, 0–6, 6–8, 5–7; Krishan–J. Mukerjea d. Bungert–J. Fassbender 6–2, 6–2, 6–3; Krishnan d. Buding 6–2, 7–5, 6–2; Lall lost to Bungert 1–6, 6–4, 4–6, 3–6. **USA d. India 4–1, Puerto Rico:** A. Ashe d. P. Lall 6–2, 5–7, 6–2, 6–4; C. E. Graebner lost to R. Krishnan 5–7, 6–4, 2–6, 1–6; S. R. Smith–R. C. Lutz d. Krishnan–J. Mukerjea 6–2, 6–3, 6–2; Ashe d. Krishnan 6–1, 6–3, 6–3; Graebner d. Lall 9–11, 9–7, 7–5, 6–4.

CHALLENGE ROUND

USA d. Australia 4–1, Adelaide: C. E. Graebner d. W. Bowrey 8–10, 6–4, 8–6, 3–6, 6–1; A. Ashe d. R. Ruffels 6–8, 7–5, 6–3, 6–3; S. R. Smith–R. C. Lutz d. Ruffels–J. Alexander 6–4, 6–4, 6–2; Graebner d. Ruffels 3–6, 8–6, 2–6, 6–3, 6–1; Ashe lost to Bowrey 6–2, 3–6, 9–11, 6–8.

1969: USA
European Zone A

FIRST ROUND

Monaco d. Bulgaria 3–2, Monte Carlo: P. Landau d. L. Genov 7–5,
10–12, 6–2, 4–6, 6–4; A. Viviani lost to K. Yashmankov 3–6, 6–3, 6–2,
2–6, 1–6; Landau–F. Truchi d. M. Pampulov–B. Pampulov 6–3, 3–6,
2–6, 7–5, 6–2; Landau d. Yashmankov 7–5, 6–2, 3–6, 7–5; Viviani lost
to Genov 6–8, 8–6, 6–8, 5–7. **Czechoslovakia d. Denmark 3–2,
Copenhagen:** J. Kodes d. J. Leschly 6–2, 6–2, 6–3; M. Holecek lost to
J. Ulrich 6–0, 4–6, 4–6, 6–3, 5–7; Kodes–J. Kukal d. Leschly–J. Ulrich
8–6, 9–11, 6–2, 6–4; Kodes d. J. Ulrich 6–2, 6–2, 6–4; Holecek lost to
Leschly 0–6, 6–3, 5–7, 2–6. **Poland d. Hungary 3–2, Warsaw:** W.
Gasiorek d. P. Szoke 7–9, 6–4, 7–9, 6–0, 6–2; M. Rybarczyk d. I. Gulyas
6–4, 6–4, 7–5; T. Nowicki–Rybarczyk lost to S. Baranyi–R. Machan 3–6,
4–6, 4–6; Rybarczyk d. Szoke 11–9, 6–4, 3–6, 6–4; Gasiorek lost to Gulyas
6–8, 4–6, 6–1, 6–3, 3–6. **South Africa d. Iran 5–0, Cape Town:** R.
Maud d. T. Akbari 6–4, 6–3, 8–6; R. A. J. Hewitt d. T. Khodai 6–3,
6–1, 6–1; Hewitt–F. D. McMillan d. Khodai–E. Nemati 6–2, 6–0, 6–1;
Maud d. Khodai 6–1, 6–0, 6–1; Hewitt d. Akbari 6–4, 6–3, 6–3.
Ireland d. Luxembourg 5–0, Cork: M. Hickey d. T. Brasseur 5–7,
6–3, 6–4, 6–4; P. Jackson d. J. Neumann 8–6, 7–5, 6–2; Hickey–Jackson
d F. Baden–Brasseur 6–2, 18–16, 8–6; Jackson d. Brasseur 6–4, 6–1, 6–3;
Hickey d. Neumann 6–2, 7–5, 6–2. **Great Britain d. Switzerland 5–0,
Zurich:** M. Cox d. T. Stalder 6–4, 8–6, 6–2; G. R. Stilwell d. D. Sturdza
8–6, 6–4, 6–1; Cox–P. W. Curtis d. Sturdza–M. Werren 6–1, 6–3, 6–3;
Cox d. Sturdza 6–3, 6–0, 4–6, 6–2; Stilwell d. Stalder 6–2, 6–0, 6–2.
Sweden d. Finland 4–1, Helsinki: O. Bengtson d. G. Berner 5–7, 6–2,
6–3, 6–4; H. Nerell d. H. Hedman 6–2, 6–0, 6–4; Bengtson–M. Carlstein
d. Hedman–Berner 6–0, 6–2, 6–3; Nerell lost to Berner 6–3, 4–6, 1–6,
3–6; Bengtson d. Hedman 6–4, 6–0, 6–3. **West Germany d. New
Zealand 4–1, Cologne:** W. Bungert d. O. Parun 6–4, 9–7, 6–0; C.
Kuhnke d. B. Fairlie 6–3, 6–1, 6–4; I. Buding–Kuhnke d. Fairlie–Parun
6–2, 6–3, 6–4; Bungert lost to Fairlie 0–6, 5–7, 0–6; Kuhnke d. Parun
7–5, 6–4, 3–6, 6–4.

SECOND ROUND

Czechoslovakia d. Monaco 5–0, Monte Carlo: J. Kukal d. R. Ruzic
6–1, 6–2, 6–1; V. Zednik d. F. Truchi 6–1, 6–1, 6–1; J. Kodes–Kukal
d. Truchi–A. Vatrican 6–0, 6–1, 6–2; Zednik d. A. Viviani 6–0, 7–5, 6–3;
Kukal d. Vatrican 6–1, 6–1, 6–0. **South Africa d. Poland def.; Great
Britain d. Ireland 5–0, Eastbourne:** G. R. Stilwell d. P. Jackson 6–2,

6–2, 6–1; M. Cox d. M. Hickey 6–2, 6–2, 6–3; Cox–P. W. Curtis d. Jackson–Hickey 6–2, 6–3, 6–2; Cox d. Jackson 6–3, 6–2, 6–1; Stilwell d. Hickey 8–6, 6–4, 6–1. **West Germany d. Sweden 4–1, Båstad:** C. Kuhnke d. O. Bengtson 6–3, 7–5, 6–3; W. Bungert d. J. E. Lundquist 6–3, 6–4, 6–4; I. Buding–Kuhnke lost to Bengtson–H. Nerell 3–6, 3–6, 3–6; Bungert d. Bengtson 9–11, 6–3, 6–4, 6–1; Kuhnke d. Lundquist 3–6, 3–6, 6–4, 9–7, 6–3.

SEMI-FINAL ROUND
South Africa d. Czechoslovakia def.; Great Britain d. West Germany 3–2, Edgbaston: M. Cox d. C. Kuhnke 4–6, 6–3, 6–4, 6–2; G. R. Stilwell d. W. Bungert 9–7, 6–3, 7–5; Cox–P. W. Curtis lost to Bungert–Kuhnke 8–10, 19–17, 11–13, 6–3, 2–6; Stilwell lost to Kuhnke 4–6, 12–14, 5–7; Cox d. Bungert 6–3, 2–6, 8–10, 7–5, 6–2.

FINAL ROUND
Great Britain d. South Africa 3–2, Bristol: M. Cox d. R. Maud 3–6, 6–3, 6–4, 3–6, 6–4; G. R. Stilwell lost to R. A. J. Hewitt 9–7, 3–6, 6–3, 2–6, 3–6; Cox–P. W. Curtis d. Hewitt–F. D. McMillan 6–4, 3–6, 4–6, 6–4, 9–7; Stilwell d. Maud 8–6, 11–9, 6–3; Cox lost to Hewitt 6–3, 0–6, 6–4, 3–6, 7–9.

European Zone B

PRELIMINARY ROUND
United Arab Republic d. Lebanon 5–0, Cairo: I. El Shafei d. M. Khoder 6–0, 6–1, 6–2; A. El Daoudi d. A. Ramadan 6–0, 6–2, 6–1; El Shafei–El Daoudi d. J. Khouayess–T. Kettanen 6–0, 6–2, 6–3; El Daoudi d. Khoder 6–3, 6–3, 6–1; M. Sombol d. Khouayess 6–1, 6–1, 6–4. **Israel d. Turkey def.**

FIRST ROUND
Spain d. Rhodesia 5–0, Lisbon: M. Orantes d. F. Saloman 6–2, 7–5, 8–6; M. Santana d. H. Irvine 6–2, 6–1, 6–3; Orantes–Santana d. F. Saloman–A. Saloman 6–3, 6–3, 6–4; J. Gisbert d. Irvine 6–3, 6–4, 7–5; Santana d. F. Saloman 6–0, 6–2, 6–2. **Yugoslavia d. France 3–2, Maribor:** N. Spear lost to F. Jauffret 3–6, 2–6, 1–6; Z. Franulovic d. G. Goven 6–3, 6–3, 7–5; Franulovic–Spear d. P. Beust–D. Contet 6–2, 6–2, 6–4; Spear lost to Goven 3–6, 2–6, 1–6; Franulovic d. Jauffret 6–3, 6–3, 6–3. **Rumania d. United Arab Republic 3–2, Bucharest:** I. Tiriac lost to I. El Shafei 3–6, 3–6, 3–6; I. Nastase d. M. Sonbol 6–4, 6–0, 6–4;

Nastase–Tiriac d. El Shafei–Sonbol 6–3, 6–4, 6–0; Tiriac d. Sonbol 6–4, 3–6, 6–4, 6–3; Nastase lost to El Shafei 2–6, 6–1, 3–6, 1–6. **Israel d. Portugal 4–1, Lisbon:** J. Stabholz d. J. Lagos 6–2, 6–3, 6–0; E. Davidman d. V. Pinto 6–2, 4–6, 3–6, 7–5, 6–3; Davidman–I. Froman d. Pinto–J. Roquette 6–3, 6–0, 6–1; Stabholz lost to Pinto 1–6, 4–6, 4–6; Davidman d. O. Silva 6–3, 6–2, 6–2. **USSR d. Greece 4–1, Athens:** A. Metreveli d. P. Gavrilides 6–0, 6–1, 6–1; T. Lejus d. N. Kalogeropoulos 5–7, 3–6, 6–4, 6–2, 4–0 def.; Metreveli–S. Likhachev d. Kalogeropoulos–E. Argyriou 6–2, 6–2, 3–6, 6–2; Lejus d. Gavrilides 6–1, 1–6, 6–4, 6–4; V. Korotkov d. Argyriou 6–2, 6–3. **Canada d. Holland 3–2, Scheveningen:** F. Godbout lost to J. Hordijk 1–6, 2–6, 1–6; M. Belkin d. M. Fleury 6–4, 6–4, 6–0; Belkin–H. Fauquier d. Fleury–Hordijk 6–4, 6–4, 5–7, 6–2; Godbout lost to Fleury 5–7, 2–6, 8–6, 3–6; Belkin d. Hordijk 6–1, 6–1, 6–2. **Italy d. Belgium 4–1, Genoa:** N. Pietrangeli d. P. Hombergen 6–3, 6–2, 6–3; E. Castigliano d. E. Drossart 6–4, 4–6, 6–4, 5–7, 6–1; V. Crotta–P. Marzano lost to Drossart–Hombergen 2–6, 3–6, 5–7; Pietrangeli d. Drossart 7–5, 6–4, 7–9, 6–4; Castigliano d. Hombergen 3–6, 6–3, 6–4, 6–4. **Austria d. Norway 5–0, Oslo:** E. Blanke d. J. E. Ross 6–2, 6–4, 6–4; D. Herdy d. D. Jagge 6–1, 6–4, 6–1; Blanke–Herdy d. S. L. Gaitung–Ross 6–2, 7–5, 6–1; Blanke d. Jagge 6–2, 6–2, 4–6, 6–3; Herdy d. Ross 6–2, 6–4, 6–0.

SECOND ROUND

Spain d. Yugoslavia 5–0, Zagreb: M. Orantes d. Z. Franulovic 7–5, 6–4, 8–6; M. Santana d. B. Jovanovic 6–1, 6–1, 6–3; Orantes–Santana d. Franulovic–Jovanovic 8–6, 6–1, 7–5; Santana d. Franulovic 6–4, 3–6, 9–7, 6–2; Orantes d. Jovanovic 6–2, 6–4, 6–4. **Rumania d. Israel 5–0, Bucharest:** I. Nastase d. J. Stabholz 6–2, 6–2, 6–0; I. Tiriac d. E. Davidman 6–2, 7–5, 6–2; Nastase–Tiriac d. Davidman–I. Froman 6–2, 6–0, 6–4; Tiriac d. Stabholz 6–2, 6–2, 6–0; Nastase d. Davidman 6–0, 6–2, 6–4. **USSR d. Canada 4–1, Moscow:** A. Metreveli d. J. Sharpe 6–0, 6–0, 6–4; T. Lejus lost to M. Belkin 9–7, 3–6, 6–4, 2–6, 7–9; Metreveli–S. Likhachev d. H. Fauquier–Sharpe 6–2, 6–3, 6–2; Lejus d. Sharpe 6–4, 6–4, 6–4; Metreveli d. Belkin 2–6, 8–9 def. **Italy d. Austria 5–0, Bari:** N. Pietrangeli d. D. Herdy 6–1, 8–6, 6–3; E. Castigliano d. E. Blanke 1–6, 6–3, 3–6, 4–4 def.; V. Crotta–P. Marzano d. Herdy–H. Kary 6–2, 6–2, 6–4; Pietrangeli d. Blanke 3–6, 7–5, 6–2, 1–6, 8–6; Castiglia no d. P. Schulteiss 3–6, 6–1, 6–2, 6–1.

SEMI-FINAL ROUND

Rumania d. Spain 4–1, Valencia: I. Nastase d. J. L. Arilla 6–4, 8–6,
6–2; I. Tiriac d. M. Orantes 6–4, 6–3, 4–6, 1–6, 6–3; Nastase–Tiriac d.
Arilla–Orantes 6–4, 6–8, 9–7, 7–9, 8–6; Tiriac d. Arilla 6–2, 3–6, 6–2,
6–4; P. Marmureanu lost to Orantes 1–6, 1–6, 1–6.   **USSR d. Italy 5–0,
Moscow:** T. Lejus d. N. Pietrangeli 6–4, 6–4, 6–8, 6–3; A. Metreveli d.
E. Castigliano 6–1, 6–2, 6–3; Metreveli–S. Likhachev d. V. Crotta–P.
Marzano 7–5, 6–4, 8–6; Metreveli d. Pietrangeli 6–2, 6–2, 6–2; Lejus d.
Castigliano 4–6, 3–6, 6–4, 7–5, 6–2.

FINAL ROUND

Rumania d. USSR 4–1, Bucharest: I. Tiriac d. T. Lejus 6–3, 6–3, 8–6;
I. Nastase d. A. Metreveli 6–4, 6–2, 7–5; Nastase–Tiriac d. Metreveli–S.
Likhachev 6–8, 6–1, 6–8, 6–4, 8–6; Nastase d. Lejus 4–6, 6–3, 6–2, 6–2;
S. Dron lost to V. Korotkov 1–6, 4–6, 4–6.

Eastern Zone

FIRST ROUND

Philippines d. Indonesia 3–0, Djakarta: E. Cruz d. A. Wijono 6–2,
5–7, 4–6, 6–2, 6–2; R. Deyro d. S. Soertarjo 6–3, 8–6, 6–2; Cruz–A.
Marcial d. G. Widjojo–Soetarjo 6–3, 6–4, 4–6, 9–7.

SECOND ROUND

Japan d. Philippines 5–0, Tokyo: K. Watanabe d. R. Deyro 6–2, 6–1,
6–2; K. Yanagi d. E. Cruz 6–1, 6–3, 6–2; Watanabe–J. Kawamori d.
Cruz–A. Marcial 6–4, 6–4, 6–3; Yanagi d. Deyro 6–1, 6–1, 6–2; Watanabe
d. Cruz 6–3, 6–4, 6–4.   **South Vietnam d. South Korea 3–2, Seoul:**
L. H. Duc d. Y. H. Chung 4–6, 6–0, 7–5, 9–7; V. V. Thanh d. K. T.
H. Kim 6–4, 6–3, 3–6, 4–6, 7–5; Duc–V. V. Bay d. T. K. Kim–Chung
6–0, 6–0, 6–0; Duc lost to K. T. H. Kim 3–6, 6–2, 4–6, 2–6; Thanh lost
to Chung 4–6, 7–5, 6–2, 3–6, 6–8.   **India d. Malaysia 5–0, Kuala
Lumpur:** G. Misra d. S. A. Azman 6–1, 6–1, 6–1; R. Krishnan d. B.
Yap 6–2, 6–3, 6–1; Misra–A. Amritraj d. M. Tay–Yap 6–4, 6–3, 6–4;
Amritraj d. Azman 6–2, 6–2, 6–4; Misra d. R. Bakar 6–2, 6–0, 6–4.

SEMI-FINAL ROUND

Japan d. South Vietnam def.; India d. Ceylon 4–1, Colombo: R.
Krishnan d. P. Kumara 6–0, 6–0, 6–0; S. Misra d. R. Ferdinands 6–3,
6–3, 6–3; A. Amritraj–G. Misra lost to Ferdinands–B. Pinto 6–2, 9–7,
12–14, 5–7, 4–6; S. Misra d. Kumara 6–2, 6–2, 6–2; Amritraj d. S.
Melwani 6–2, 6–2, 6–1.

FINAL ROUND

India d. Japan 5–0, Poona: R. Krishnan d. I. Konishi 6–2, 6–4, 6–4; P. Lall d. K. Watanabe 6–2, 6–3, 6–4; Lall–J. Mukerjea d. K. Watanabe–J. Watanabe 6–3, 13–11, 7–9, 6–4; Lall d. Konishi 6–3, 6–1, 6–1; S. Misra d. K. Watanabe 6–3, 6–3, 5–7, 6–2.

American Zone North

FIRST ROUND

Mexico d. British Caribbean 4–1, Bridgetown, Barbados: R. H. Osuna d. R. Russell 6–1, 6–3, 6–2; V. Zarazua lost to D. Tate 3–6, 7–9, 4–6; Osuna–Zarazua d. Russell–A. Price 6–4, 9–7, 8–6; Osuna d. Tate 6–3, 6–2, 6–1; Zarazua d. Russell 6–4, 3–6, 6–3, 2–6, 6–4.

FINAL ROUND

Mexico d. Australia 3–2, Mexico City: R. H. Osuna d. R. Ruffels 9–7, 3–6, 7–5, 6–3; J. Loyo-Mayo lost to W. W. Bowrey 6–4, 3–6, 2–6, 5–7; Osuna–V. Zarazua d. P. Dent–J. Alexander 18–16, 12–10, 6–4; Loyo-Mayo lost to Ruffels 3–6, 6–4, 4–6, 8–10; Osuna d. Bowrey 6–2, 3–6, 8–6, 6–3.

American Zone South

FIRST ROUND

Colombia d. Venezuela 3–2, Caracas: W. Alvarez lost to J. Andrew 6–2, 4–6, 6–8, 5–7; J. Velasco lost to H. Hose 2–6, 6–8, 6–8; Alvarez–Velasco d. Andrew–Hose 6–1, 4–6, 4–6, 6–3, 6–4; Alvarez d. Hose 0–6, 2–6, 6–2, 6–4, 6–4; Velasco d. Andrew 6–2, 6–3, 6–2. **Chile d. Argentina 3–2, Santiago:** J. Fillol d. E. Soriano 6–2, 6–3, 6–2; P. Cornejo d. J. Ganzabal 5–7, 4–6, 6–1, 6–3, 6–3; Cornejo–Fillol lost to Ganzabal–Soriano 6–4, 4–6, 7–5, 2–6, 7–9; Fillol lost to Ganzabal 3–6, 7–5, 1–6, 1–6; Cornejo d. Soriano 6–1, 6–2, 6–3.

SEMI-FINAL ROUND

Brazil d. Colombia 3–2, Bogota: T. Koch lost to J. Velasco 6–3, 1–6, 4–6, 4–6; J. E. Mandarino d. W. Alvarez 9–7, 6–2, 7–5; Koch–Mandarino d. Alvarez–Velasco 7–5, 6–1, 6–2; Koch d. Alvarez 6–2, 7–5, 6–2; Mandarino lost to Valasco 2–6, 1–6, 3–6. **Chile d. Ecuador 4–1, Santiago:** P. Cornejo d. P. Guzman 6–3, 1–6, 8–6, 6–4; J. Fillol d. M. Olvera 7–5, 6–0, 0–6, 6–2; J. P. Bravo–Cornejo d. Guzman–Olvera

10–8, 6–1, 6–4; Fillol lost to Guzman 6–3, 0–6, 6–4, 3–6, 4–6; Cornejo
d. Olvera 6–3, 6–3, 6–3.

FINAL ROUND
Brazil d. Chile 3–2, Santiago: J. E. Mandarino lost to J. Fillol 6–3,
6–3, 4–6, 6–8, 8–10; T. Koch d. P. Cornejo 7–5, 6–3, 6–4; Koch–
Mandarino d. Cornejo–Fillol 6–2, 6–2, 6–2; Mandarino lost to Cornejo
4–6, 6–3, 6–2, 0–6, 4–6; Koch d. Fillol 6–4, 2–6, 4–6, 6–2, 7–5.

AMERICAN ZONE FINAL
Brazil d. Mexico 4–1, Sao Paolo: J. E. Mandarino d. M. Lara 4–6,
6–2, 6–4, 5–7, 6–3; T. Koch d. J. Loyo-Mayo 7–5, 6–1, 6–3; Koch–
Mandarino d. Loyo-Mayo–L. Garcia 19–17, 6–3, 6–4; Mandarino lost to
Loyo-Mayo 6–2, 7–5, 5–7, 3–6, 5–7; Koch d. Garcia 4–6, 6–1, 6–2, 6–4.

INTER-ZONE FINALS
Great Britain d. Brazil 3–2, Wimbledon: G. R. Stilwell d. J. E.
Mandarino 6–3, 8–6, 8–6; M. Cox lost to T. Koch 6–4, 13–11, 3–6,
6–8, 6–8; Cox–P. W. Curtis lost to Koch–Mandarino 6–4, 4–6, 4–6, 4–6;
Stilwell d. Koch 7–5, 6–4, 6–4; Cox d. Mandarino 6–3, 18–16, 3–6, 6–2.
Rumania d. India 4–0, Bucharest: I. Tiriac d. P. Lall 6–2, 6–3, 6–2; I.
Nastase d. J. Mukerjea 6–2, 6–4, 4–6, 4–6, 6–1; Nastase–Tiriac d. Lall–
Mukerjea 6–2, 6–2, 6–3; P. Marmureanu d. G. Misra 6–2, 6–2, 6–3; S.
Dron v. A. Amritraj 6–3, 6–2, 8–10 unfin. **Rumania d. Great Britain
3–2, Wimbledon:** I. Tiriac d. M. Cox 6–4, 6–4, 6–3; I. Nastase lost to
G. R. Stilwell 4–6, 6–4, 1–6, 2–6; Nastase–Tiriac d. Cox–Stilwell 10–8,
3–6, 6–3, 6–4; Tiriac lost to Stilwell 3–6, 2–6, 2–6; Nastase d. Cox 3–6,
6–1, 6–4, 6–4.

CHALLENGE ROUND
USA d. Rumania 5–0, Cleveland: A. Ashe d. I. Nastase 6–2, 15–13,
7–5; S. Smith d. I. Tiriac 6–8, 6–3, 5–7, 6–4, 6–4; B. Lutz–Smith d.
Nastase–Tiriac 8–6, 6–1, 11–9; Smith d. Nastase 4–6, 4–6, 6–4, 6–1, 11–9;
Ashe d. Tiriac 6–3, 8–6, 3–6, 4–0 def.

1970: USA
European Zone A

FIRST ROUND
Rumania d. Iran 4–1, Teheran: I. Nastase d. T. Akbari 10–8, 6–0, 6–8,
5–7, 6–3; I. Tiriac d. H. Akbari 6–0, 6–1, 6–4; Nastase–Tiriac d. H and T.

Akbari 6–3, 3–6, 6–3, 6–3; Nastase d. H. Akbari 6–2, 4–6, 6–2, 6–3; P. Marmureanu lost to T. Akbari 1–6, 4–6, 3–6. **Greece d. Holland 4–1, Athens:** P. Gavrilides lost to J. Hordijk 4–6, 8–6, 1–6, 1–6; N. Kalogeropoulos d. P. Soeters 7–5, 8–6, 6–2; Gavrilides–Kalogeropoulos d. N. Fleury–Hordijk 4–6, 6–2, 6–2, 6–2; Gavrilides d. Soeters 6–3, 6–4, 6–2; Kalogeropoulos d. Hordijk 6–1, 6–2, 6–4. **Yugoslavia d. Poland 3–2, Maribor:** N. Spear d. M. Rybarczyk 6–0, 3–6, 6–0, 6–2; N. Franulovic d. W. Gasiorek 4–6, 6–2, 2–6, 6–3, 6–2; Franulovic–Spear lost to Rybarczyk–T. Nowicki 4–6, 6–3, 3–6, 6–1, 3–6; Franulovic d. Rybarczyk 6–1, 6–1, 6–2; Spear lost to Gasiorek 6–8, 6–4, 4–6, 6–2, 1–6. **Ireland d. Luxembourg 3–0, Luxembourg:** P. Jackson d. G. Logelin 4–6, 6–8, 7–5, 6–1, 6–2; W. Brown d. T. Brasseur 3–6, 6–4, 6–4, 9–11, 6–4; Brown–J. McGrath d. Brasseur–Logelin 6–1, 6–1, 6–1. **Austria d. Great Britain 3–2, Edinburgh:** P. Pokorny d. J. G. Clifton 6–1, 4–6, 8–6, 6–1; H. Kary d. G. Battrick 7–5, 6–3, 6–1; Pokorny–R. Hoskowitz lost to Battrick–P. W. Curtis 6–2, 6–8, 4–6, 0–6; Pokorny lost to Battrick 4–6, 2–6, 7–9; Kary d. Clifton 6–3, 6–2, 6–4. **France d. Switzerland 4–1, Geneva:** F. Jauffret d. W. Burgener 6–3, 4–6, 6–3, 6–4; G. Goven lost to D. Sturdza 8–10, 5–7, 6–4, 3–6; J. Chanfreau–J. Rouyer d. Sturdza–M. Werren 9–11, 6–2, 6–3, 6–1; Goven d. Burgener 6–1, 5–7, 6–3, 6–4; Jauffret d. Sturdza 6–3, 6–4, 6–3. **Spain d. Sweden 5–0, Stockholm:** M. Orantes d. O. Bengtson 7–5, 6–4, 6–4; M. Santana d. J. E. Lundquist 6–2, 6–4, 4–6, 6–0; Orantes–J. Gisbert d. Bengtson–H. Nerell 10–8, 6–3, 8–6; Santana d. Bengtson 11–9, 4–6, 6–4, 6–2; Gisbert d. Lundquist 4–6, 6–2, 6–0, 6–0. **Bulgaria d. Turkey 5–0, Istanbul:** S. Velev d. T. Gursoy 6–3, 6–2, 4–6, 6–0; K. Yashmakov d. R. Aydin 6–3, 6–0, 6–2; Velev–Yashmakov d. Gursoy–Aydin 6–3, 6–4, 4–6, 6–2; T. Guenov d. Gursoy 6–3, 6–2, 6–1; Velev d. B.Ambar 6–3, 6–1, 6–0.

SECOND ROUND
Rumania d. Greece 5–0, Bucharest: I. Nastase d. N. Kalogeropoulos 6–2, 7–5, 6–4; I. Tiriac d. P. Gavrilides 6–0, 6–1, 6–0; Nastase–Tiriac d. Kalogeropoulos–E. Argyriou 6–4, 6–1, 6–2; V. Marcu d. Argyriou 6–1, 6–3, 6–4; S. Muresan d. Gavrilides 8–6, 3–6, 6–2, 6–3.
Yugoslavia d. Ireland 5–0, Dublin: N. Spear d. W. Brown 6–3, 6–2, 6–4; Z. Franulovic d. P. Jackson 6–2, 6–3, 3–6, 3–6, 6–3; Franulovic–Spear d. Brown–J. McGrath 6–1, 7–5, 6–4; Franulovic d. Brown 6–3, 6–1, 6–3; Spear d. Jackson 7–5, 6–1, 6–1. **France d. Austria 5–0, Paris:** G. Goven d. P. Pokorny 6–4, 6–1, 6–2; F. Jauffret d. H. Kary 12–10, 1–6, 6–3, 6–4; J. Chanfreau–J. P. Rouyer d. Kary–Pokorny 6–2, 6–4, 12–10; Jauffret d. Pokorny 6–3, 6–3, 6–4; Goven d. Kary 6–3, 6–3, 6–1. **Spain d. Bulgaria 5–0, Barcelona:** M. Santana d. K.

Yashmakov 6–1, 6–1, 7–5; J. Gisbert d. L. Guenov 6–2, 6–2, 6–2; M. Orantes–Gisbert d. B. Pampoulov–S. Velev 6–4, 8–6, 6–2; Santana d. Velev 6–0, 6–2, 6–0; Gisbert d. Yashmakov 6–3, 6–2, 6–0.

SEMI-FINAL ROUND

Yugoslavia d. Rumania 3–2, Maribor: N. Spear lost to I. Tiriac 6–1, 4–6, 4–6, 2–6; Z. Franulovic d. I. Nastase 6–3, 3–6, 6–2, 6–1; Franulovic–Spear lost to Nastase–Tiriac 5–7, 8–6, 1–6, 3–6; Spear d. Nastase 7–5, 8–6, 6–2; Franulovic d. Tiriac 1–6, 5–7, 6–4, 6–4, 6–0.
Spain d. France 5–0, Paris: M. Santana d. G. Goven 6–1, 6–8, 6–2, 2–6, 6–3; M. Orantes d. F. Jauffret 3–6, 6–4, 6–1, 6–2; Santana–J. Gisbert d. J. L. Rouyer–J. B. Chanfreau 6–4, 6–4, 8–6; Santana d. Jauffret 7–5, 6–3, 6–2; Orantes d. Goven 6–2, 6–3, 6–2.

FINAL ROUND

Spain d. Yugoslavia 4–1, Barcelona: M. Orantes d. N. Spear 6–4, 6–2, 6–2; M. Santana d. Z. Franulovic 6–4, 6–4, 1–6, 6–4; Santana–J. Gisbert d. Franulovic–Spear 6–4, 6–1, 6–2; Orantes lost to Franulovic 7–5, 6–4, 4–6, 6–8, 2–6; Santana d. Spear 6–2, 6–1, 7–5.

European Zone B

FIRST ROUND

Monaco d. Portugal 4–1, Lisbon: P. Landau d. V. Pinto 6–4, 6–2, 6–3; F. Truchi lost to R. Peralta 2–6, 0–6, 5–7; Landau–Truchi d. Peralta–M. Dinis 3–6, 6–4, 7–5, 6–4; Truchi d. Pinto 3–6, 2–6, 10–8, 6–4, 6–2; Landau d. Peralta 6–3, 6–4, 3–6, 6–2. **USSR d. Hungary 3–2, Budapest:** V. Korotkov lost to S. Baranyi 6–4, 3–6, 6–1, 1–6, 3–6; A. Metreveli d. I. Gulyas 9–7, 6–2, 6–3; Metreveli–S. Likhachev d. Baranyi–B. Machen 6–4, 4–6, 6–3, 8–6; Metreveli d. Baranyi 6–4, 6–1, 6–2; Korotkov lost to Gulyas 3–6, 6–4, 0–6, 4–6. **Rhodesia d. Israel def.; Czechoslovakia d. Italy 3–2, Turin:** J. Kodes d. M. di Domenico 6–3, 1–6, 3–6, 6–4, 6–4; J. Kukal lost to A. Panatta 6–8, 3–6, 3–6; Kodes–Kukal lost to di Domenico–Panatta 4–6, 6–2, 2–6, 6–3, 3–6; Kukal d. di Domenico 7–9, 6–4, 7–5, 9–7; Kodes d. Panatta 6–3, 6–2, 6–2. **United Arab Republic d. Norway 4–1, Cairo:** M. Sonbol d. F. Prydz 6–3, 6–1, 6–4; A. Daoudi d. J. Ross 6–1, 6–2, 6–3; Daoudi–A. Ghani lost to Prydz–Ross 5–7, 6–2, 4–6, 1–6; Daoudi d. Prydz 7–9, 5–7, 6–2, 9–7, 6–4; Sonbol d. Ross def. **West Germany d. Denmark 4–1, Bad Homburg:** C. Kuhnke d. J. Ulrich 6–3, 6–2, 6–3; W. Bungert lost to C. E. Hedelund 2–6, 4–6, 6–3, 5–7; Kuhnke–I. Buding d. Ulrich–Hedelund 6–1, 6–1, 6–4; Kuhnke

d. Hedelund 6–0, 7–5, 6–1; Bungert d. Ulrich 7–5, 6–2, 2–6, 3–6, 6–3.
Belgium d. Finland 4–1, Helsinki: P. Hombergen d. G. Berner 6–4,
6–2, 6–2; E. Drossart lost to P. Saila 7–5, 2–6, 3–6, 4–6; Hombergen–
Drossart d. Berner–Saila 6–0, 4–6, 6–3, 6–0; Drossart d. Berner 2–6, 7–5,
6–3, 8–6; Hombergen d. Saila 6–4, 6–2, 5–7, 3–6, 6–4.

SECOND ROUND
USSR d. Monaco 5–0, Monte Carlo: A. Metreveli d. A. Vatrican 6–0,
6–1, 6–4; V. Korotkov d. F. Truchi 6–2, 6–0, 6–1; Metreveli–S.
Likhachev d. Truchi–Vatrican 6–0, 4–6, 6–3, 6–2; Korotkov d. Vatrican
6–0, 6–0, 6–0; Metreveli d. Truchi 6–2, 6–4, 6–2. **Czechoslovakia d.
Rhodesia def.; West Germany d. United Arab Republic 5–0, West
Berlin:** W. Bungert d. M. A. Ghani 6–2, 6–4, 1–6, 6–2; C. Kuhnke d.
M. Sonbol 6–0, 6–2, 6–2; I. Buding–Kuhnke d. Ghani–Sonbol 6–0, 6–3,
6–0; Bungert d. Sonbol 10–8, 6–2, 6–3; J. Fassbender d. Ghani 6–1, 6–1,
6–3. **Belgium d. South Africa def.**

SEMI-FINAL ROUND
USSR d. Czechoslovakia 3–2, Moscow: T. Lejus lost to J. Kodes 6–2,
3–6, 3–6, 5–7; A. Metreveli d. J. Kukal 6–1, 6–0, 6–2; Metreveli–S.
Likhachev d. Kodes–Kukal 8–6, 1–6, 2–6, 8–6, 6–4; Lejus lost to Kukal
6–3, 4–6, 3–6, 2–6; Metreveli d. Kodes 6–4, 4–6, 6–3, 6–3. **West
Germany d. Belgium 5–0, Nuremburg:** W. Bungert d. P. Hombergen
6–2, 6–1, 3–6, 6–3; C. Kuhnke d. E. Drossart 6–4, 6–2, 6–3; I.
Buding–Kuhnke d. Hombergen–Drossart 4–6, 6–3, 7–5, 4–6, 10–8;
Bungert d. Drossart 2–6, 6–2, 6–0, 6–3; Kunhke d. Hombergen 6–2,
6–2, 6–0.

FINAL ROUND
West Germany d. USSR 3–2, Dusseldorf: W. Bungert d. V. Korotkov
6–4, 7–9, 6–4, 6–3; C. Kuhnke lost to A. Metreveli 1–6, 1–6, 8–10;
Bungert–I. Buding d. Metreveli–S. Lihkachev 5–7, 1–6, 8–6, 6–2, 7–5;
Kuhnke d. Korotkov 6–1, 6–1, 5–7, 6–2; Bungert lost to Metreveli 4–6,
5–5, def.

Eastern Zone A

FIRST ROUND
Japan d. Hong Kong 5–0, Hong Kong: K. Yanagi d. Ling Fong 6–2,
6–2, 6–2; I. Kobayashi d. Kenneth Tsui 6–2, 6–3, 6–3; K. and I.
Watanabe d. Tsui–Winson Wei Chung 6–4, 6–3, 6–1; Kobayashi d. Fong

6–3, 6–2, 6–1; I. Watanabe d. Tsui 6–0, 6–0, 6–2. **Australia d. Korea def.; Vietnam d. Indonesia 3–1.**

SEMI-FINAL ROUND

Japan d. South Vietnam 5–0, Tokyo: K. Watanabe d. Vo Van Thanh 6–3, 6–3, 6–1; I. Kobayashi d. Vo Van Bay 6–4, 6–4, 9–11, 6–2; Y. Tezuka–H. Koromatsu d. Vo Van Thanh–Vo Van Bay 6–1, 8–6, 6–1; Watanabe d. Vo Van Bay 6–2, 6–3, 6–4; Kobayashi d. Vo Van Thanh 6–4, 8–6, 6–3. **Australia d. Philippines 5–0, Manila:** R. O. Ruffels d. E. Cruz 6–4, 6–2, 6–4; R. D. Crealy d. R. Deyro 6–2, 4–6, 6–2, 6–1; Crealy–A. Stone d. Cruz–A. Marcial 6–3, 6–4, 6–4; Ruffels d. Deyro 6–1, 6–0, 6–2; J. Alexander d. Cruz 8–6, 6–3, 6–3.

FINAL ROUND

Australia d. Japan 5–0, Tokyo: A. Stone d. K. Watanabe 8–6, 7–9, 6–4, 6–0; R. D. Crealy d. I. Kobayashi 6–4, 6–2, 2–6, 6–4; R. O. Ruffels–Stone d. J. Kawamori–T. Koura 7–5, 5–7, 6–2, 6–4; Crealy d. Watanabe 9–11, 6–2, 6–1, 3–6, 6–3; Ruffels d. Kobayashi 6–2, 6–2, 6–0.

Eastern Zone B

FIRST ROUND

Ceylon d. Malaysia 3–0, Kuala Lumpur: B. Pinto d. S. A. Azman 6–1, 6–2, 6–1; R. Ferdinands d. Tan Song Kean 7–5, 6–3, 6–1; Pinto–Ferdinands d. Azman–Kean 4–6, 6–3, 3–6, 6–0, 6–0. **India d. Pakistan 3–1, Patna, India:** J. Mukerjea d. H. Rahim 4–6, 5–7, 10–8, 6–2 def.; P. Lall d. M. Iqbal 13–11, 6–4, 6–4; Mukerjea–Lall d. Rahim–Iqbal 6–4, 6–1, 6–4; S. Menon lost to Iqbal 6–8, 1–6, 4–6; V. Amritraj v. A. Elahi 7–5, 7–5, 8–10, 5–5 unfin.

FINAL ROUND

India d. Ceylon 5–0, Bombay: J. Mukerjea d. B. Pinto 6–3, 6–1, 6–4; P. Lall d. P. S. Kumara 6–0, 6–3, 6–2; S. Menon–V. Amritraj d. Pinto–Kumara 6–3, 6–4, 5–7, 6–4; Amritraj d. Kumara 6–1, 6–0, 6–3; Menon d. Pinto 6–3, 6–1, 4–6, 8–6.

ZONE FINAL

India d. Australia 3–1, Bangalore: J. Mukerjea d. R. D. Crealy 3–6, 6–8, 6–4, 6–3, 6–2; P. Lall d. R. O. Ruffels 6–2, 6–8, 6–3, 3–6, 14–12; Lall–Mukerjea lost to A. Stone–J. Alexander 13–15, 4–6, 4–6; Lall d. Crealy 8–6, 6–2, 6–2; Mukerjea v. Ruffels 6–3, 7–5, 4–6, 3–6, 6–6 unfin.

American Zone South

FIRST ROUND

Brazil d. Venezuela 4–1, Caracas: E. Mandarino d. J. Andrew 7–5, 5–7, 6–2, 6–1; T. Koch d. H. Hose 6–2, 6–8, 6–0, 1–6, 8–6; Koch–Mandarino d. Andrew–Hose 6–2, 9–7, 6–2; R. Berner lost to Hose 4–6, 4–6, 3–6; Koch d. Andrew 6–4, 6–2, 6–1. **Chile d. Argentina 3–2, Buenos Aires:** P. Cornejo d. G. Vilas 3–6, 0–6, 6–2, 6–2, 6–2: J. Fillol lost to J. Ganzabal 6–4, 6–1, 4–6, 4–6, 2–6; Cornejo–Fillol d. L. Alvarez–T. Vasquez 6–3, 6–2, 6–1; Fillol lost to Vilas 5–7, 4–6, 6–3, 3–6; Cornejo d. Ganzabal 6–3, 3–6, 6–4, 6–2. **Colombia d. Ecuador 3–2, Bogota:** I. Molina d. P. Guzman 3–6, 7–5, 6–4, 6–1; J. Velasco d. M. Olvera 4–6, 3–6, 6–1, 6–1, 6–1; Molina–Velasco d. Guzman–Olvera 6–2, 7–5, 1–6, 9–7; A. Betancourt lost to Guzman 3–6, 4–6, 3–6; Molina lost to Olvera 4–6, 7–5, 6–8, 4–6.

SEMI-FINAL ROUND

Brazil d. Chile 3–2, Sao Paulo: T. Koch d. P. Cornejo 1–6, 3–6, 6–2, 6–2, 6–1; E. Mandarino lost to J. Fillol 1–6, 6–3, 1–6, 7–5, 7–9; Koch–Mandarino d. Cornejo–Fillol 6–4, 6–4, 10–12, 6–4; Mandarino lost to Cornejo 5–7, 6–4, 6–2, 3–6, 2–6; Koch d. Fillol 6–1, 6–3, 4–6, 4–6, 8–6. **Colombia d. Uruguay 5–0, Bogota:** J. Velasco d. G. Stapff 6–1, 6–0, 6–0; I. Molina d. A. Laborde 6–1, 6–2, 6–0; Molina–Velasco d. Stapff–Laborde 6–2, 6–1, 6–0; Velasco d. Laborde 6–0, 6–3, 6–3; A. Betancourt d. Stapff 6–1, 6–0, 6–0.

FINAL ROUND

Brazil d. Colombia 3–2, Sao Paulo: F. Tavarez lost to J. Velasco 5–7, 1–6, 8–6, 4–6; E. Mandarino d. I. Molina 6–2, 6–2, 6–3; Mandarino–C. Fernandes lost to Velasco–Molina 5–7, 2–6, 6–4, 3–6; Mandarino d. Velasco 4–6, 8–6, 6–3, 6–2; Tavarez d. Molina 4–6, 2–6, 6–3, 9–7, 6–3.

American Zone North

FIRST ROUND

Canada d. British Caribbean 5–0, Winnipeg: J. Sharpe d. R. Russell 6–8, 7–5, 4–6, 6–1, 6–1; M. Belkin d. L. Lumsden 6–2, 4–6, 6–1, 3–6, 6–0; Belkin–Sharpe d. Lumsden–Russell 6–2, 6–2, 6–2; P. Burwash d. L. Rolle 6–1, 6–1, 6–1; Sharpe d. Lumsden 6–4, 6–1, 6–0. **New Zealand d. Mexico 3–2, Mexico City:** B. Fairlie lost to J. Loyo-Mayo 3–6, 6–3, 6–3, 0–6, 2–6; O. Parun d. V. Zarazua 1–6, 6–2, 6–4, 7–5; Fairlie–Parun lost to Loyo–Mayo–Zarazua 9–11, 3–6, 3–6; Parun d. Loyo–Mayo 8–6, 6–4, 6–4; Fairlie d. Zarazua 8–10, 8–6, 6–1, 6–1.

FINAL ROUND

Canada d. New Zealand 3–2, Winnipeg: M. Belkin lost to be B. Fairlie 3–6, 2–6, 4–6; J. Sharpe d. O. Parun 6–2, 2–6, 6–0, 1–6 def.; Belkin–Sharpe d. Fairlie–Parun 6–2, 11–9, 6–3; Sharpe lost to Fairlie 4–6, 2–6, 0–6; Belkin d. Parun 6–2, 3–6, 7–5, 6–3.

AMERICAN ZONE FINAL

Brazil d. Canada 3–2, Sao Paulo: T. Koch d. J. Sharpe 9–7, 7–5, 5–7, 8–6; E. Mandarino lost to M. Belkin 2–6, 4–6, 2–6; Koch–Mandarino d. Belkin–Sharpe 6–3, 3–6, 0–6, 6–4, 6–3; Koch lost to Belkin 8–6, 6–8, 3–6, 4–6; Mandarino d. Sharpe 6–1, 6–0, 6–2.

INTER–ZONE FINALS

West Germany d. India 5–0, Poona: W. Bungert d. J. Mukerjea 6–2, 7–5, 6–3; C. Kuhnke d. P. Lall 6–4, 6–3, 6–3; Bungert–Kuhnke d. Lall–Mukerjea 6–2, 4–6, 13–11, 6–3; Bungert d. Lall 6–4, 6–3, 5–7, 13–11; Kuhnke d. Mukerjea 11–9, 8–6, 6–4. **Spain d. Brazil 4–1, Sao Paulo:** M. Orantes d. T. Koch 6–1, 6–3, 3–6, 6–1; M. Santana d. E. Mandarino 3–6, 6–3, 2–6, 6–0, 6–4; Santana–J. Gisbert d. Koch–Mandarino 6–1, 6–4, 6–4; Orantes d. Mandarino 3–6, 6–1, 6–3, 6–3; Santana lost to Koch 5–7, 8–10, 6–4 def. **West Germany d. Spain 4–1, Dusseldorf:** W. Bungert lost to M. Orantes 4–6, 8–10, 9–11; C. Kuhnke d. M. Santana 6–4, 6–8, 12–10, 6–2; Kuhnke–Bungert d. Santana–J. Gisbert 6–4, 12–10, 6–3; Kuhnke d. Orantes 6–3, 6–3, 7–5; Bungert d. Gisbert 6–4, 6–1, 6–3.

CHALLENGE ROUND

USA d. West Germany 5–0, Cleveland: A. Ashe d. W. Bungert 6–2, 10–8, 6–2; C. Richey d. C. Kuhnke 6–3, 6–4, 6–2; B. Lutz–S. Smith d. Kuhnke–Bungert 6–3, 7–5, 6–4; Richey d. Bungert 6–4, 6–4, 7–5; Ashe d. Kuhnke 6–8, 10–12, 9–7, 13–11, 6–4.

1971: USA
European Zone A

FIRST ROUND

Portugal d. Turkey 4–1, Lisbon: V. Pinto d. R. Aydin 6–4, 6–0, 6–0; R. Peralta d. T. Gursoy 6–3, 6–3, 6–0; Pinto–Peralta d. Aydin–Gursoy 7–5, 6–3, 6–0; J. Silva lost to Aydin 7–5, 6–4, 2–6, 3–6, 2–6; J. Vilela d.

Gursoy 6–0, 6–3, 6–4. **Czechoslovakia d. United Arab Republic 4–1, Cairo:** J. Kodes d. I. Mahmoud 6–2, 6–4, 6–1; F. Pala d. M. Sonbol 6–2, 6–1, 7–5; J. Kuka–V. Zednik d. Mahmoud–A. Daoudi 6–3, 6–4, 6–2; Pala d. Mahmoud 6–4, 6–2, 6–3; Kodes lost to Sonbol 5–7, 3–6, 4–6. **Belgium d. Greece 3–1, Athens:** E. Drossart lost to N. Kalogeropoulos 2–6, 6–2, 4–6, 6–4, 3–6; P. Hombergen d. P. Gavrilidis 6–1, 6–2, 3–6, 6–3; Hombergen–Drossart d. Kalogeropoulos–Gavrilidis 7–5, 6–3, 6–3; Drossart d. Gavrilidis 6–4, 6–4, 6–1; Hombergen v. Kalogeropoulos 3–6, 6–4, 6–2, 3–6, 6–6 unfin. **USSR d. Denmark 5–0, Copenhagen:** V. Korotkov d. J. Ulrich 6–3, 6–2, 6–0; A. Metreveli d. J. Leschly 6–4, 6–3, 6–2; Metreveli–S. Likhachev d. Leschly–Ulrich 6–0, 6–4, 6–4; Metreveli d. Ulrich 6–2, 6–1, 6–2; Korotkov d. Leschly 9–7, 3–6, 6–0, 6–3. **Finland d. Ireland 5–0, Helsinki:** G. Berner d. R. Brown 6–1, 6–4, 6–3: P. Saila d. M. Hickey 6–3, 6–2, 6–8, 6–2; Berner–Saila d. P. Jackson–Hickey 6–4, 4–6, 13–11, 6–0; Berner d. Hickey 6–3, 6–1, 6–2; Saila d. Brown 6–3, 6–1, 6–0. **France d. Sweden 5–0, Båstad:** P. Proisy d. O. Bengtson 6–3, 6–2, 6–3; P. Barthes d. H. Zahr 6–1, 6–4, 6–1; Barthes–F. Jauffret d. Bengston–H. Nerell 6–3, 15–13, 8–6, 7–5; Proisy d. Nerell 6–2, 6–3, 6–1; Barthes d. Bengtson 6–3, 6–3, 4–6, 3–6, 6–3.

SECOND ROUND

Czechoslovakia d. Portugal 5–0, Prague: F. Pala d. V. Pinto 6–1, 6–1, 6–1; J. Kodes d. R. Peralta 8–6, 6–0, 6–2; Kodes–J. Kukal d. Peralta–Pinto 6–0, 6–2, 6–1; Kukal d. Pinto 6–2, 6–0, 6–2; Pala d. Peralta 6–1, 6–2, 6–1. **USSR d. Belgium 4–1, Brussels:** A. Metreveli d. E. Drossart 6–3, 6–2, 6–2; V. Korotkov lost to P. Hombergen 3–6, 3–6, 1–6; Metreveli–S. Likhachev d. Hombergen–Drossart 7–5, 4–6, 13–11, 6–3; Metreveli d. Hombergen 6–0, 6–2, 6–0; Korotkov d. Drossart 3–6, 6–3, 5–7, 9–7, 8–6. **France d. Finland 3–0, Paris:** F. Jauffret d. G. Berner 7–5, 6–2, 6–2; P. Proisy d. P. Saila 6–4, 6–0, 6–2; P. Dominguez–Proisy d. Berner–Saila 6–4, 7–5, 7–5; Proisy v. Berner 6–3, 6–3, 4–6, 3–0 unfin. **Spain d. Switzerland 4–0, Basle:** M. Orantes d. M. Werren 6–1, 6–1, 6–4; J. Gisbert d. T. Sturdza 6–2, 6–4, 6–3; Orantes–Gisbert d. L. Manta–Werren 6–4, 9–7, 6–2; Orantes d. Sturdza 7–5, 9–7, 7–9, 8–6; A. Munoz v. Werren 23–21, 3–1 unfin.

SEMI-FINAL ROUND

Czechoslovakia d. USSR 4–1, Prague: J. Kodes lost to A. Metreveli 5–7, 6–3, 6–4, 5–7, 3–6; F. Pala d. V. Korotkov 6–3, 6–4, 7–5; Kodes–J. Kukal d. Metreveli–S. Likhachev 3–6, 6–4, 2–6, 7–5, 6–3; Kodes d. Korotkov 6–0, 6–3, 7–5; Pala d. Metreveli 6–0, 6–4, 2–0 def. **Spain**

d. France 4–1, Barcelona: J. Gisbert lost to F. Jauffret 2–6, 3–6, 2–6;
M. Orantes d. P. Proisy 6–1, 6–2, 6–3; Gisbert–Orantes d. Jauffret–P.
Barthes 6–3, 4–6, 6–3, 6–2; Orantes d. Jauffret 6–4, 7–9, 6–4, 5–7, 7–5;
Gisbert d. Proisy 6–2, 6–3, 6–4.

FINAL ROUND
Czechoslovakia d. Spain 3–2, Prague: F. Pala lost to M. Orantes 6–2,
4–6, 2–6, 5–7; J. Kodes d. J. Gisbert 6–3, 4–6, 9–7, 7–5; Kodes–J. Kukal
lost to Gisbert–Orantes 4–6, 9–11, 4–6; Pala d. Gisbert 6–0, 6–1, 6–1;
Kodes d. Orantes 7–5, 4–6, 7–5, 6–4.

European Zone B

FIRST ROUND
Hungary d. Poland 5–0, Budapest: I. Gulyas d. T. Nowicki 6–3, 6–3,
2–6, 6–3; S. Baranyi d. W. Gasiorek 1–6, 6–3, 6–1, 6–4; Baranyi–B.
Machan d. Nowicki–J. Niedzwiedzki 6–4, 6–4, 6–2; Baranyi d. Nowicki
6–4, 6–4, 6–0; Gulyas d. Gasiorek 6–4, 9–7, 6–0. **Luxembourg d.
Monaco 5–0, Luxembourg:** F. Baden d. F. Truchi 6–1, 6–4, 7–5; T.
Brasseur d. A. Viviani 6–3, 7–5, 6–4; Baden–Brasseur d. Truchi–Balaret
6–2, 6–3, 7–5; Baden d. Viviani 6–4, 3–6, 9–7, 6–3; Brasseur d. Truchi
6–4, 9–7, 6–2. **Yugoslavia d. Great Britain 3–0, Zagreb:** Z.
Franulovic d. G. Battrick 6–2, 6–2, 6–0; B. Jovanovic d. S. Matthews
6–2, 6–4, 9–11, 2–6, 6–4; Jovanovic–Franulovic d. Battrick–Matthews
7–5, 5–7, 0–6, 7–5, 6–0. **Italy d. Bulgaria 5–0, Perugia:** M. di
Domenico d. B. Pampoulov 3–6, 6–2, 6–1, 6–3; A. Panatta d. L. Guenov
6–1, 6–3, 6–3; di Domenico–Panatta d. M and B. Pampoulov 6–4, 6–4,
6–4; A. Zugarelli d. Guenov 6–4, 6–2, 6–3; E. di Matteo d. Pampoulov
6–3, 6–3, 6–1. **Rumania d. Holland 5–0, Bucharest:** I. Tiriac d. F.
Hemmes 7–5, 6–1, 6–3; I. Nastase d. J. Hordjik 6–2, 6–2, 6–3;
Nastase–Tiriac d. Hemmes–Hordjik 6–2, 6–2, 6–3; Tiriac d. Hordjik 6–1,
6–1, 6–1; Nastase d. Hemmes 6–0, 6–2, 6–4. **Israel d. Norway 4–1,
Tel Aviv:** Y. Stabholz d. E. Melander 3–6, 6–4, 6–4, 6–0; Y. Shalem d.
J. E. Ross 10–12, 6–4, 6–3, 6–0; E. Davidman–I. Froman lost to
Melander–F. Prydz 7–5, 4–6, 3–6, 4–6; Shalem d. Melander 6–1, 5–7,
6–1, def.; Stabholz d. Ross 7–5, 3–6, 6–2, 1–6, 6–1.

SECOND ROUND
West Germany d. Austria 4–1, Augsburg: W. Bungert d. P. Pokorny
5–7, 1–6, 7–5, 8–6, 6–2; C. Kuhnke lost to H. Kary 6–4, 6–2, 0–6, 0–6,
5–7; J. Fassbender–H. J. Pohmann d. R. Hoskowitz–E. Blanke 6–2, 6–4,

6–3; Kuhnke d. Pokorny 6–3, 6–1, 6–4; Bungert d. Kary 6–3, 3–6, 6–3, 2–6, 7–5. **Hungary d. Luxembourg 5–0, Budapest:** S. Baranyi d. G. Logelin 6–2, 6–1, 6–2; I. Gulyas d. J. Hoffenheim 6–3, 6–2, 6–0; Baranyi–R. Machan d. Hoffenheim–Logelin 6–2, 6–2, 6–1; Gulyas d. Logelin 6–2, 6–1, 6–1; Baranyi d. Hoffenheim 6–1, 6–1, 6–1.
Yugoslavia d. Italy 3–2, Zagreb: Z. Franulovic d. N. Pietrangeli 7–5, 8–6, 6–1; B. Jovanovic d. A. Panatta 6–0, 3–6, 4–6, 6–3, 6–2; Franulovic–Jovanovic d. M. di Domenico–Panatta 3–6, 6–0, 4–6, 7–5, 6–3; Jovanovic lost to Pietrangeli 2–6, 2–6, 1–6; Z. Ivancic lost to A. Zugarelli 4–6, 3–6, 2–6. **Rumania d. Israel 5–0, Tel Aviv:** I. Tiriac d. Y. Stabholz 6.0, 6–0, 6–0; I. Nastase d. J. Shalem 6–1, 6–2, 6–3; S. Dron–Tiriac d. I. Froman–Stabholz 6–2, 6–2, 6–3; Tiriac d. Shalem 6–2, 6–0, 6–3; Nastase d. Stabholz 6–0, 6–0, 6–1.

SEMI-FINAL ROUND
West Germany d. Hungary 4–1, Munich: C. Kuhnke d. I. Gulyas 3–6, 6–4, 6–2, 2–6, 6–3; W. Bungert d. S. Baranyi 5–7, 6–3, 6–3, 6–3; J. Fassbender–H. J. Pohmann d. P. Szoke–Baranyi 5–7, 6–3, 6–2, 4–6, 6–4; Bungert d. Gulyas 6–3, 6–4, 7–5; Kuhnke lost to Baranyi 1–6, 8–10, 2–6.
Rumania d. Yugoslavia 4–1, Bucharest: I. Nastase d. Z. Franulovic 7–5, 6–2, 6–3; I. Tiriac d. B. Jovanovic 6–4, 7–5, 2–6, 6–4; Nastase–Tiriac d. Franulovic–Jovanovic 6–0, 6–4, 9–7; Tiriac lost to Franulovic 4–6, 0–6, 6–4, 3–6; Nastase d. Jovanovic 4–6, 6–4 ret.

FINAL ROUND
Rumania d. West Germany 5–0, Bucharest: I. Tiriac d. C. Kuhnke 6–2, 3–6, 6–2, 7–5; I. Nastase d. W. Bungert 6–2, 6–3, 6–2; Nastase–Tiriac d. J. Fassbender–H. J. Pohmann 8–6, 6–4, 6–4; Nastase d. Kuhnke 6–0, 6–4, 6–4; P. Marmureanu d. Bungert 6–1, 7–5, 6–1.

Eastern Zone A

FIRST ROUND
Australia d. Hong Kong 5–0, Hong Kong: C. Dibley d. L. Hsu 6–1, 6–2, 6–2; J. Cooper d. K. Tsui 6–2, 6–4, 6–2; Dibley–R. Giltinan d. Tsui–Ling Fong 6–2, 6–3, 6–4; Cooper d. Hsu 6–3, 6–1, 6–0; Dibley d. C. Chang 6–2, 6–2, 6–1.

SECOND ROUND
Australia d. Indonesia 3–2, Jakarta: R. Case d. A. Wijono 6–2, 2–6, 4–6, 6–3, 6–3; R. Giltinan d. G. Widjojo 8–6, 6–4, 0–6, 6–4; J. Cooper–

C. Dibley d. J. Wulur–B. Aznar 6–2, 6–0, 6–1; Cooper lost to Wijono 4–6, 4–6, 8–10; Dibley lost to Widjojo 1–6, 6–4, 5–7, 1–6. **Japan d. Philippines 4–1, Manila:** J. Kuki d. R. Deyro 6–1, 6–4, 6–2; T. Sakai lost to E. Cruz 5–7, 1–6, 7–5, 6–8; J. Kawamori–T. Koura d. Deyro–Cruz 6–2, 8–6, 3–6, 8–6; Kuki d. Cruz 6–0, 3–6, 6–2, 6–1; Sakai d. Deyro 6–4, 6–2, 6–3.

FINAL ROUND

Japan d. Australia 3–2, Tokyo: K. Yanagi d. J. Cooper 6–3, 6–4, 2–6, 1–6, 6–3; T. Sakai d. C. Dibley 5–7, 8–6, 6–3, 6–2; J. Kawamori–T. Koura lost to Dibley–R. Giltinan 1–6, 6–3, 9–11, 1–6; Yanagi lost to Dibley 3–6, 4–6, 7–5, 6–3, 6–8; Sakai d. Cooper 6–1, 15–13, 8–6.

Eastern Zone B

FIRST ROUND

India d. Ceylon 3–0, Colombo: G. Misra d. P. S. Kumara 6–2, 13–11, 6–2; J. Mukerjea d. B. Pinto 7–5, 8–6, 7–5; Mukerjea–P. Lall d. Pinto–R. Wattegedera 6–2, 6–3, 6–4. **Pakistan d. Malaysia 5–0, Lahore:** H. Rahim d. S. A. Azman 6–2, 6–2, 6–2; M. Iqbal d. T. S. Kean 6–3, 6–3, 6–1; Rahim–Iqbal d. Azman–Kean 6–2, 6–1, 6–3; M. Mohammed d. Kean 7–5, 7–5, 7–5; Iqbal d. Azman 6–1, 6–3, 6–0.

FINAL ROUND

India d. Pakistan def.

ZONE FINAL

India d. Japan 3–2, Tokyo: J. Mukerjea d. T. Sakai 6–0, 6–0, 6–4; P. Lall lost to K. Yanagi 6–3, 3–6, 1–6, 2–6; Mukerjea–Lall d. Sakai–J. Kamiwazumi 7–9, 6–1, 3–6, 6–1, 8–6; Lall d. Sakai 6–2, 6–2, 6–4; Mukerjea lost to Yanagi 4–6, 3–6, 0–6.

American Zone South

FIRST ROUND

Brazil d. Bolivia 5–0, Porto Alegre: J. E. Mandarino d. O. Chiarella 6–1, 6–3, 6–2; T. Koch d. R. Benavides 6–0, 6–1, 6–1; Mandarino–L. Tavares d. Benavides–Chiarella 6–2, 6–2, 6–0; Mandarino d. Benavides 6–0, 6–2, 6–3; Koch d. Chiarella 6–1, 6–0, 6–1. **Ecuador d. Venezuela 4–1, Guayaquil:** M. Olvera d. H. Hose 6–2, 6–4, 6–3; P.

Guzman d. J. Andrew 6–1, 6–3, 6–0; Guzman–Olvera d. Andrew–Hose 6–3, 6–4, 6–1; Guzman lost to Hose 8–6, 4–6, 5–7, 4–6; Olvera d. Andrew 6–2, 6–0, 6–3. **Argentina d. Uruguay 5–0, Montevideo:** J. Ganzabal d. F. Barriola 6–1, 6–2, 6–0; Vilas d. G. Stapff 6–0, 6–4, 6–0; R. Cano–Vilas d. E. P. Alvarez–Barriola 6–2, 6–4, 6–4; J. van Kerckhoven d. M. Laborde 6–1, 6–2, 6–1; Cano d. Stapff 6–0, 6–2, 6–2. **Chile d. Colombia 3–2, Bogota:** J. Fillol d. I. Molina 6–4, 6–3, 5–7, 6–3; P. Cornejo lost to J. Velasco 8–6, 6–1, 4–6, 6–8, 1–6; Cornejo–Fillol d. Molina–Velasco 7–5, 7–5, 4–6, 6–3; Fillol lost to Velasco 6–8, 2–6, 3–6; Cornejo d. Molina 6–3, 6–4, 6–2.

SEMI-FINAL ROUND

Brazil d. Ecuador 4–1, Porto Alegre: T. Koch d. M. Olvera 6–3, 3–6, 6–4, 6–1; J. E. Mandarino d. P. Guzman 6–4, 4–6, 6–3, 6–2; Koch–Mandarino d. Guzman–Olvera 6–4, 6–1, 6–1; Koch d. Guzman 6–4, 6–4, 5–7, 6–2; Mandarino lost to Olvera 1–6, 6–2, 6–3, 3–6, 0–6. **Chile d. Argentina 4–1, Santiago:** J. Fillol d. T. Lynch 6–2, 6–4, 6–2; P. Cornejo d. J. Ganzabal 6–4, 6–4, 6–4; Cornejo–Fillol d. R. Cano–Ganzabal 6–2, 6–3, 6–4; Cornejo d. Lynch 6–3, 6–3, 6–4; Fillol lost to Ganzabal 3–6, 6–2, 6–8, 4–6.

FINAL ROUND

Brazil d. Chile 3–2, Santiago: T. Koch d. P. Cornejo 4–6, 6–2, 5–7, 8–6, 6–2; J. E. Mandarino lost to J. Fillol 1–6, 6–8, 6–4, 8–10; Koch–Mandarino d. Cornejo–Fillol 3–6, 2–6, 6–2, 6–2, 8–6; Koch d. Fillol 6–3, 6–2, 6–2; Mandarino lost to Cornejo 6–4, 6–1, 0–6, 3–6, 4–6.

American Zone North

FIRST ROUND

Mexico d. South Korea 5–0, Mexico City: J. Loyo-Mayo d. K. T. Kwan 6–1, 6–1, 7–5; M. Lara d. C. Y. Ho 6–4, 6–1, 6–1; V. Zarazua–R. Ramirez d. Ho–H. K. Sung 6–2, 4–6, 6–3, 6–1; Loyo-Mayo d. Ho 6–0, 6–2, 6–2; Lara d. K. S. Bae 6–2, 6–2, 6–2.

SECOND ROUND

Mexico d. Canada 3–2, Mexico City: M. Lara d. J. Sharpe 6–3, 6–2, 6–2; J. Loyo-Mayo lost to M. Belkin 6–4, 4–6, 2–6, 4–6; Loyo-Mayo–Lara d. Sharpe–Belkin 7–5, 3–6, 6–1, 6–3; Lara lost to Belkin 6–4, 4–6, 5–7, 2–6; Loyo-Mayo d. Sharpe 4–6, 7–5, 6–1, 6–1. **New Zealand d. Caribbean Commonwealth 4–1, Kingston:** O. Parun d. L. Rolle 6–2,

6–2, 6–0; J. Simpson lost to R. Russell 2–6, 4–6, 6–3, 6–8; Parun–Simpson d. R. and C. Russell 6–1, 6–1, 4–6, 6–4; Simpson d. Rolle 7–5, 6–3, 6–0; Parun d. Russell 7–5, 6–2, 6–2.

FINAL ROUND
Mexico d. New Zealand 3–2, Mexico City: J. Loyo-Mayo lost to O. Parun 9–7, 4–6, 1–6, 5–7; M. Lara d. J. Simpson 6–3, 6–3, 6–1; M. Garcia–Lara d. Parun–Simpson 3–6, 6–2, 12–10, 6–3; Lara lost to Parun 5–7, 3–6, 4–6; Loyo-Mayo d. Simpson 6–3, 6–3, 6–2.

ZONE FINAL
Brazil d. Mexico 3–2, Mexico City: T. Koch d. M. Lara 6–4, 6–2, 6–1; J. E. Mandarino lost to J. Loyo-Mayo 4–6, 6–3, 6–4, 5–7, 1–6; Koch–Mandarino lost to Loyo-Mayo–V. Zarazua 6–8, 5–7, 2–6; Mandarino d. Lara 6–4, 6–3, 9–7; Koch d. Loyo-Mayo 7–5, 4–6, 7–9, 6–4, 9–7.

INTER-ZONE FINALS
Rumania d. India 4–1, New Delhi: I. Nastase d. J. Mukerjea 6–3, 6–3, 6–4; I. Tiriac lost to P. Lall 12–14, 3–6, 7–9; Nastase–Tiriac d. Lall–Mukerjea 6–3, 6–8, 8–6, 6–1; Tiriac d. Mukerjea 3–6, 7–5, 6–3 ret. Nastase d. Lall 6–3, 8–10, 6–1, 6–1. **Brazil d. Czechoslovakia 4–1, Porto Alegre:** J. E. Mandarino d. J. Kodes 8–6, 6–4, 6–4; T. Koch d. F. Pala 6–4, 6–4, 6–2; Koch–Mandarino d. Kodes–J. Kukal 8–6, 6–2, 6–4; C. A. Kirmayr lost to Pala 1–6, 6–2, 6–4, 2–6, 4–6; F. Tavares d. V. Zednik 9–7, 5–7, 4–6, 4–5 def. **Rumania d. Brazil 3–2, Sao Paulo:** I. Nastase d. J. E. Mandarino 6–4, 6–1, 6–1; I. Tiriac lost to T. Koch 6–4, 4–6, 3–6, 7–9; Nastase–Tiriac lost to Koch–Mandarino 6–1, 3–6, 3–6, 6–3, 4–6; Nastase d. Koch 6–4, 6–0, 8–6; Tiriac d. Mandarino 6–0, 6–2, 6–4.

CHALLENGE ROUND
USA d. Rumania 3–2, Charlotte: S. R. Smith d. I. Nastase 7–5, 6–3, 6–1; F. A. Froehling d. I. Tiriac 3–6, 1–6, 6–1, 6–3, 8–6; Smith–E. Van Dillen lost to Nastase–Tiriac 5–7, 4–6, 6–8; Smith d. Tiriac 8–6, 6–3, 6–0; Froehling lost to Nastase 3–6, 1–6, 6–1, 4–6.

1972: USA
European Zone A

PRELIMINARY ROUND

Iran d. Israel 4–1, Tel Aviv: H. Akbari d. J. Stabholz 6–2, 6–4, 9–7;
T. Akbari d. J. Shalem 6–1, 6–1, 6–4; H. Akbari–Memati lost to Stabholz–
Y. Wertheimer 2–6, 3–6, 6–2, 3–6; H. Akbari d. Shalem 7–5, 7–9, 7–5,
2–6, 6–3; Taghi d. Stabholz 6–3, 6–2, 6–0.

FIRST ROUND

Rumania d. Switzerland 5–0, Bucharest: I. Tiriac d. M. Werren 6–1,
6–2, 6–2; I. Nastase d. M. Burgener 6–1, 6–2, 6–2; Nastase–Tiriac d.
Werren–F. Blatter 6–0, 6–4, 4–6, 6–1; P. Marmureanu d. Blatter 6–2,
6–2, 6–1; Tiriac d. Burgener 6–3, 6–2, 2–6, 6–0.   **Iran d. United Arab
Republic 4–1, Teheran:** T. Akbari d. E. Mahmoud 6–1, 6–4, 10–8; H.
Akbari d. E. El Daoudi 6–3, 6–3, 6–4; T; Akbari–I. Khodai d.
Mahmoud–Daoudi 6–4, 6–2, 4–6, 8–6; T. Akbari lost to Daoudi 8–6,
4–6, 6–8, 8–6, 3–6; H. Akbari d. Mahmoud 4–6, 7–5, 6–3, 6–0.   **Italy
d. Austria 5–0, Reggio Calabria:** C. Barazzutti d. E. Blanke 6–2, 0–6,
6–1, 6–3; P. Bertolucci d. H. Kary 6–3, 6–1, 6–3; A. Panatta–N.
Pietrangeli d. Blanke–R. Hoskowetz 6–3, 6–4, 6–4; Barazzutti d. Kary
6–8, 6–4, 4–6, 6–3, 6–4; Bertolucci d. Hoskowetz 6–4, 6–2, 6–3.
Holland d. Norway 5–0, Scheveningen: F. Hemmes d. J. E. Ross 6–1,
10–8, 6–2; J. Hordijk d. F. Prydz 6–0, 6–1, 6–0; Hemmes–Hordijk d.
Ross–F. Jagge 6–1, 6–3, 6–3; Hemmes d. Prydz 6–0, 6–2, 6–4; Hordijk
d. Ross 6–1, 7–5, 6–1.   **Poland d. Yugoslavia 3–1, Warsaw:** T.
Nowicki d. N. Spear 4–6, 6–3, 6–2, 6–2; W. Gasiorek lost to B. Jovanovic
3–6, 4–6, 3–6; Nowicki–Gasiorek d. Jovanovic–Spear 6–4, 7–9, 6–2,
6–3; Gasiorek d. Spear 6–2, 7–5, 5–7, 6–4; Spear v. Jovanovic 3–6, 3–6,
unfin.   **Denmark d. Finland 3–2, Helsinki;** T. Christensen lost to P.
Saila 1–6, 3–6, 4–6; C. E. Hedelund d. M. Timonen 6–1, 6–2, 6–4;
Christensen–K. E. Nielsen d. Saila–Timonen 6–2, 11–13, 6–4, 6–3;
Christensen d. R. Suominen 9–7, 6–1, 6–2; Hedelund lost to Saila 6–8,
0–6, 8–10.   **USSR d. Hungary 3–2, Tbilisi:** V. Korotkov lost to P.
Szoke 6–4, 3–6, 2–6, 1–6; A. Metreveli d. S. Baranyi 6–3, 2–6, 6–4, 6–0;
Metreveli–S. Likhachev d. Baranyi–Szoke 6–3, 6–4, 10–8; Korotkov lost
to Baranyi 2–6, 2–6, 2–6; Metreveli d. Szoke 6–3, 6–3, 6–1.   **Morocco
d. Lebanon 5–0, Beirut:** O. Laimina d. K. Issa 2–6, 3–6, 6–3, 6–4,
11–9; N. O. Ahmed d. S. Khoury 6–3, 6–0, 6–4; Laimina–H. Bouchaib
d. Khoury–N. Abouhassoune 3–6, 10–8, 6–3, 6–2; M. El Achraoui d.
Issa 1–6, 7–5, 6–1, 6–2; Laimina d. Khoury 6–0, 6–3, 6–4.

SECOND ROUND

Rumania d. Iran 5–0, Bucharest: I. Nastase d. T. Akbari 6–1, 6–1, 6–3; I. Tiriac d. H. Akbari 6–2, 6–3, 6–3; Nastase–Tiriac d. S. Akbari–I. Khoda 6–1, 6–4, 7–5; T. Ovici d. H. Akbari 6–3, 6–3, 6–1; Tiriac d. T. Akbari 6–2, 4–6, 5–7, 6–3, 6–1. **Italy d. Holland 4–1, San Benedette:** A. Panatta d. J. Hordijk 10–8, 6–2, 6–3; P. Bertolucci d. F. Hemmes 6–0, 6–4, 2–6, 6–3; Panatta–N. Pietrangeli d. Hemmes–Hordijk 3–6, 6–1, 6–4, 6–2; Bertolucci lost to Hordijk 6–1, 6–8, 6–1, 5–7, 6–8; Panatta d. Hemmes 6–1, 6–1, 6–1. **Poland d. Denmark 5–0, Copenhagen:** W. Gasiorek d. C. E. Hedelund 6–4, 6–4, 6–2; T. Nowicki d. K. E. Nielsen 6–1, 6–3, 6–4; Nowicki–W. Finback d. H. Norkaer–Nielsen 6–2, 7–5, 7–5; Gasiorek d. Nielsen 6–4, 6–1, 6–4; Nowicki d. Hedelund 6–1, 6–1, 6–2. **USSR d. Morocco 5–0, Casablanca:** A. Metreveli d. O. Laimina 6–3, 3–6, 6–0, 6–2; V. Korotkov d. A. Ben Omar 6–0, 6–0, 6–2; Metreveli–S. Likhachev d. H. Bouchaib–Laimina 6–2, 6–2, 7–5; Korotkov d. Laimina 3–6, 6–1, 6–2, 6–4; Metreveli d. Zengaoui 6–4, 7–5, 6–0.

SEMI-FINAL ROUND

Rumania d. Italy 4–1, Bucharest: I. Nastase d. C. Barazzutti 7–5, 6–2, 6–0; I. Tiriac d. A. Panatta 8–6, 7–5, 0–6, 6–3; Nastase–Tiriac d. Panatta–N. Pietrangeli 6–2, 9–7, 6–4; P. Marmureanu lost to Barazzutti 4–6, 5–7, 2–6; Nastase d. Panatta 4–6, 6–0, 6–3, 6–1. **USSR d. Poland 4–1, Warsaw:** A. Metreveli d. T. Nowicki 6–3, 6–3, 6–3; T. Kakulia d. W. Gasiorek 8–6, 5–7, 6–3, 2–6, 6–1; Metreveli–S. Likhachev d. Gasiorek–Nowicki 7–5, 6–4, 4–6, 9–7; Metreveli d. Gasiorek 4–6, 7–5, 7–5, 8–6; Kakulia lost to Nowicki def.

FINAL ROUND

Rumania d. USSR 3–2, Tblisi: I. Nastase d. A. Metreveli 6–4, 6–0, 6–4; I. Tiriac lost to T. Kakulia 4–6, 5–7, 1–6; Nastase–Tiriac d. Metreveli–S. Likhachev 6–2, 6–4, 6–3; Tiriac lost to Metreveli 6–2, 4–6, 6–1, 4–6, 3–6; Nastase d. Kakulia 6–2, 6–2, 6–3.

European Zone B

FIRST ROUND

Monaco d. Luxembourg 3–2, Monte Carlo: V. Landau d. J. Neumann 8–6, 6–2, 6–3; F. Trucchi lost to F. Baden 6–4, 5–7, 3–6, 3–6; Landau–Trucchi d. G. Logelin–Neumann 6–3, 6–2, 4–6, 6–1; Landau lost to Baden 4–6, 1–6, 6–2, 6–4, 4–6; Trucchi d. Neumann 6–1, 6–3, 6–3. **Portugal**

d. South Africa def.; France d. Great Britain 4–1, Paris: P. Proisy
d. D. Lloyd 6–1, 6–3, 6–2; P. Barthes d. J. G. Paish 6–0, 6–1, 6–4;
Barthes–G. Goven lost to Lloyd–Paish 3–6, 6–4, 1–6, 3–6; Barthes d.
Lloyd 6–0, 6–3, 6–1; Proisy d. Paish 6–1, 6–0, 6–4.   **Spain d. Bulgaria
5–0, Sofia:** A. Gimeno d. L. Genov 6–3, 6–2, 6–1; M. Orantes d. B.
Pampoulov 6–4, 6–2, 6–2; Gimeno–J. Gisbert d. M. and B. Pampoulov
6–4, 6–4, 7–5; Gimeno d. B. Pampoulov 6–0, 6–2, 7–5; A. Munoz d.
Genov 6–4, 6–1, 6–3.   **Ireland d. Turkey 5–0, Rushbrooke:** P.
Jackson d. B. Ambar 4–6, 6–2, 6–2, 6–3; M. Hickey d. B. Altinkaya 6–3,
6–3, 11–9; Hickey–W. Brown d. Altinkaya–L. Gursoy 6–2, 6–4, 6–0;
K. Reid d. Ambar 6–4, 9–7, 7–5; Jackson d. Altinkaya 8–6, 8–6, 3–6,
6–0.   **West Germany d. Greece 5–0, Athens:** H. Elschenbroich d.
N. Kalogeropoulos 5–7, 6–4, 6–4, 6–2; C. Kuhnke d. P. Gavrilidis 6–0,
7–5, 6–4; J. Fassbender–H. J. Pohmann d. Kalogeropoulos–Gavrilidis 6–3,
6–2, 6–4; Elschenbroich d. Gavrilidis 6–2, 6–1, 6–0; Kuhnke d.
Kalogeropoulos 3–6, 8–6, 6–1, 6–4.   **Sweden d. New Zealand 4–1,
Båstad:** B. Borg d. O. Parun 4–6, 3–6, 6–3, 6–4, 6–4; O. Bengtson d.
J. Simpson 9–7, 6–1, 3–6, 6–3; Bengtson–Borg lost to Parun–Simpson
6–8, 3–6, 7–9; Bengtson d. Parun 6–4, 16–14, 13–11; Borg d. Simpson
9–7, 6–4, 5–7, 6–1.   **Czechoslovakia d. Belgium 3–2, Brussels:** J.
Kodes d. B. Mignot 6–2, 6–2, 6–4; F. Pala d. P. Hombergen 2–6, 6–3,
3–6, 6–3, 10–8; J. Hrebec–J. Kukal lost to Hombergen–E. Drossart 3–6,
8–10, 4–6; Kodes d. Hombergen 10–8, 6–2, 6–2; Pala lost to Mignot 3–6,
4–6, 5–7.

SECOND ROUND

Monaco d. Portugal 3–2, Monte Carlo: F. Trucchi lost to P. Peralta
6–4, 1–6, 4–6, 4–6; V. Landau d. V. Pinto 6–3, 5–7, 6–1, 5–7, 6–3;
Landau–Trucchi d. Peralta–Villela 6–3, 3–6, 6–3, 3–6, 6–3; Trucchi d.
Pinto 6–1, 6–3, 1–6, 6–4; Balleret lost to Villela 2–6, 6–2, 0–6, 4–6.   **Spain
d. France 3–2, Paris:** A. Gimeno d. P. Barthes 5–7, 6–4, 5–7, 6–3, 6–3;
M. Orantes d. P. Proisy 6–0, 6–3, 6–3; Orantes–J. Gisbert d.
Barthes–Proisy 6–4, 8–6, 6–4; A. Munoz lost to P. Dominguez 2–6, 7–9,
3–6; Gimeno lost to Proisy 2–6, 2–6, 11–9, 3–6.   **West Germany d.
Ireland 5–0, Berlin:** C. Kuhnke d. M. Hickey 6–3, 6–3, 6–0; H.
Elschenbroich d. K. Reid 6–2, 6–0, 6–0; J. Fassbender–H. J. Pohmann
d. W. Brown–Hickey 6–3, 6–3, 6–3; Kuhnke d. P. Jackson 6–2, 6–0, 6–3;
Elschenbroich d. Hickey 6–2, 6–0, 6–2.   **Czechoslovakia d. Sweden
3–1, Prague:** J. Kodes d. B. Borg 6–2, 6–3, 7–5; F. Pala lost to O.
Bengtson 8–6, 2–6, 0–6, 3–6; Kodes–J. Kukal d. Bengtson–Borg 8–6, 6–4,
6–3; Pala d. Borg 6–4, 6–4, 6–4; Kodes v. Bengtson 4–6, 2–1 unfin.

SEMI-FINAL ROUND

Spain d. Monaco 5–0, Ariles: M. Orantes d. F. Truchi 6–0, 6–1, 6–0; A. Gimeno d. V. Landau 6–3, 6–2, 6–2; Orantes–J. Gisbert d. Trucchi–Landau 6–0, 6–2, 6–0; A. Munoz d. Landau 6–1, 7–5, 6–1; Gisbert d. B. Balleret 6–1, 6–2, 6–0. **Czechoslovakia d. West Germany 3–2, Dusseldorf:** F. Pala lost to H. Elschenbroich 3–6, 4–6, 6–4, 4–6; J. Kodes d. J. Fassbender 3–6, 6–3, 6–2, 10–8; Kodes–J. Kukal d. H. J. Pohmann–Fassbender 4–6, 6–3, 3–6, 6–2, 19–17; Kodes d. Elschenbroich 6–4, 4–6, 6–2, 1–6, 8–6; Pala lost to Fassbender 4–6, 4–6, 2–6.

FINAL ROUND

Spain d. Czechoslovakia 3–2, Barcelona: J. Gisbert d. J. Kodes 8–6, 6–4, 5–7, 0–6, 6–4; M. Orantes lost to F. Pala 5–7, 4–6, 6–0, 7–5, 4–6; Orantes–Gisbert d. Kodes–J. Kukal 10–12, 6–2, 7–5, 6–4; Gisbert d. Pala 6–3, 6–3, 4–6, 6–0; A. Munoz lost to J. Hrebec 4–6, 0–6, 3–6.

Eastern Zone A

FIRST ROUND

Japan d. Hong Kong 5–0, Hong Kong: J. Kamiwazumi d. Ling Fong 6–2, 6–4, 6–2; J. Kuki d. C. Chang 6–0, 6–0, 6–3; T. Sakai–Kamiwazumi d. K. Tsui–L. Hau 6–4, 6–4, 6–4; Kuki d. Fong 6–0, 6–1, 6–2; Kamiwazumi d. Chang 6–2, 6–3, 6–0. **Vietnam d. Taiwan 5–0, Saigon:** Vo Van Bay d. Lin Chi Yuan 6–0, 6–0, 6–0; Vo Van Thanh d. Tang Fu Shun 6–3, 6–2, 6–3; Vo Van Bay–Vo Van Thanh d. Tang Fu Shun–Sui Chang Lee 6–2, 6–1, 6–0; Ly Allin d. Lin Chi Yuan 6–3, 6–2, 6–1; Vo Van Bay d. Tang Fu Shun 6–2, 6–0, 6–0. **Korea d. Philippines def.**

SEMI-FINAL ROUND

Japan d. Vietnam 3–2, Saigon: T. Sakai lost to Vo Van Bay 13–11, 4–6, 2–6, 3–6; J. Kamiwazumi d. Vo Van Thanh 8–6, 6–3, 6–1; Kamiwazumi–Sakai d. Vo Van Bay–Vo Van Thanh 4–6, 4–6, 6–3, 12–10, 1–3 ret'd; Sakai d. Duong Van Minh 6–1, 6–0, 6–1; Kamiwazumi lost to Vo Van Bay 3–6, 6–8, 6–3, 4–6. **Australia d. Korea 5–0, Seoul:** C. Dibley d. Kim Sung–Bay 6–1, 4–6, 6–4, 6–3; M. J. Anderson d. Chung Yung Ho 4–6, 6–0, 6–2, 7–5; Anderson–G. Masters d. Chung Yung Ho–Kim Moon 7–5, 6–2, 6–2; Dibley d. Chung Yung Ho 7–5, 10–8, 6–1; Anderson d. Kim Sung Bay 6–2, 6–2, 6–2.

FINAL ROUND
Australia d. Japan 4–1, Tokyo: M. J. Anderson d. T. Sakai 6–3, 6–3,
6–3; C. Dibley d. J. Kuki 6–4, 3–6, 3–6, 6–1, 6–3; Anderson–G. Masters
lost to Sakai–J. Kamiwazumi 3–6, 7–9, 6–1, 3–6; Anderson d. Kuki 6–2,
6–3, 6–2; Dibley d. Sakai 4–6, 6–4, 4–6, 7–5, 6–3.

Eastern Zone B

FIRST ROUND
Malaysia d. Pakistan def.; India d. Ceylon 5–0, Lucknow: J.
Mukerjea d. P. S. Kumara 6–3, 6–4, 6–4; P. Lall d. R. Wettegedera 6–1,
6–1, 6–1; Mukerjea–Lall d. B. Pinto Bravo–Kumara 6–3, 6–2, 6–3;
Mukerjea d. Wettegedera 6–2, 6–1, 6–2; Lall d. Kumara 6–4, 6–2, 6–2.

FINAL ROUND
India d. Malaysia 5–0, Kuala Lumpur: J. Mukerjea d. S. A. Azman
6–2, 6–0, 8–6; P. Lall d. Tan Song Kean 6–1, 6–2, 6–0; Lall–Mukerjea
d. Azman–Tan Song Kean 6–3, 6–4, 6–4; Lall d. Azman 6–0, 6–3, 6–4;
Mukerjea d. Tan Song Kean 6–0, 6–4, 6–0.

ZONE FINAL
Australia d. India 5–0, Bangalore: M. J. Anderson d. V. Amritraj 6–4,
6–4, 6–2; G. Masters d. J. Mukerjea 6–3, 6–3, 3–6, 1–6, 6–3; C.
Dibley–Masters d. Mukerjea–P. Lall 6–2, 6–4, 3–6, 6–3; R. Case d. A.
Amritraj 6–1, 8–6, 7–5; Dibley d. Amritraj 7–5, 4–6, 6–3, 6–2.

American Zone South

FIRST ROUND
Chile d. Peru 4–1, Santiago: J. Pinto Bravo d. M. Maurtua 7–5, 6–1,
7–5; P. Rodriguez d. S. Velasco 6–2, 6–3, 6–1; B. Prajoux–Pinto Bravo
d. J. Olmedo–Maurtua 6–1, 6–2, 6–0; Prajoux d. Maurtua 7–5, 6–4, 6–1;
Masalem lost to Velasco 4–6, 2–6, 6–2, 6–4, 5–7. **Colombia d. Ecuador
4–1, Guayaquil:** J. Velasco lost to M. Olvera 2–6, 6–2, 0–6, 7–5, 2–6; I.
Molina d. F. Guzman 6–3, 3–6, 7–5, 6–0; Velasco–Molina d. Olvera–
Guzman 2–6, 6–3, 6–4, 6–4; Velasco d. Guzman 2–6, 6–3, 6–4, 6–4;
Molina d. Olvera 8–6, 6–2, def. **Brazil d. Venezuela 4–0, Rio de
Janeiro:** T. Koch d. H. Hose 6–3, 6–1, 2–6, 3–6, 6–4; J. E. Mandarino
d. J. Andrew 6–2, 4–0, def.; Koch–Mandarino d. Hose–C. Suero 6–1,

6–3, 6–2; L. Tavares d. Suero 6–1, 6–1, 6–3; C. Kirmayr v. Hose 6–8, 2–0, unfin.

SECOND ROUND

Chile d. Colombia 4–1, Santiago: J. Pinto Bravo d. I. Molina 6–4, 6–3, 6–3; P. Cornejo d. J. Velasco 6–3, 6–4, 9–7; Pinto Bravo–Cornejo lost to Molina–Velasco 6–2, 7–5, 18–20, 5–7, 4–6; Cornejo d. Molina 6–3, 6–4, 1–6, 6–8, 6–4; Pinto Bravo d. Velasco 2–6, 5–7, 9–7 def.
Brazil d. Argentina 3–2, Rio de Janeiro: T. Koch d. G. Vilas 4–6, 6–3, 10–8, 6–3; J. E. Mandarino d. J. Ganzabal 4–6, 6–2, 6–3 unfin.; Koch–Mandarino lost to Vilas–R. Cano 6–2, 3–6, 8–6, 4–6, 4–6; Koch d. H. Roman 4–6, 6–4, 6–3, 1–6, 6–1; L. Tavares lost to Vilas 1–6, 0–6, 3–6.

FINAL ROUND

Chile d. Brazil 3–2, Rio de Janeiro: J. Fillol d. J. E. Mandarino 5–7, 8–6, 7–5, 6–1; J. Pinto Bravo d. T. Koch 7–5, 6–1, 6–0; P. Cornejo–Fillol lost to Koch–Mandarino 4–6, 1–6, 3–6; Pinto Bravo d. Mandarino 6–3, 2–6, 6–2, 6–2; Fillol lost to Koch 1–6, 6–4, 2–6, 3–6.

American Zone North

FIRST ROUND

USA d. Commonwealth Caribbean 4–1, Kingston: E. van Dillen d. L. Lumsden 6–1, 6–4, 6–2; T. Gorman d. R. Russell 6–4, 6–2, 7–5; S. R. Smith–Van Dillen d. Lumsden–Russell 6–4, 6–2, 6–0; Van Dillen lost to Russell 2–6, 5–7, 6–3, 6–3, 3–6; Gorman d. C. Russell 6–1, 6–4, 6–3.
Mexico d. Canada 3–2, Vancouver: J. Loyo-Mayo lost to M. Belkin 2–6, 0–6, 6–3, 8–6, 5–7; R. Ramirez d. A. Bardsley 6–4, 8–6, 6–2; Loyo-Mayo–V. Zarazua d. Belkin–D. Power 6–4, 6–0, 3–6, 6–3; Loyo-Mayo d. Bardsley 8–6, 6–4, 6–4; Ramirez lost to Belkin 5–7, 4–6, 2–6.

FINAL ROUND

USA d. Mexico 5–0, Mexico City: T. Gorman d. J. Loyo-Mayo 8–6, 6–3, 7–5; S. R. Smith d. V. Zarazua 6–2, 6–1, 6–2; Smith–E. van Dillen d. Loyo-Mayo–Zarazua 21–19, 6–3, 6–4; Smith d. Loyo-Mayo 6–0, 6–3, 2–6, 6–4; H. Solomon d. O. Martinez 6–4, 6–1, 6–2.

ZONE FINAL

USA d. Chile 5–0, Santiago: S. R. Smith d. J. Pinto Bravo 6–1, 7–5, 6–2; H. Solomon d. P. Cornejo 9–7, 4–6, 6–1, 3–6, 6–2; Smith–E. van

Dillen d. J. Fillol–Cornejo 6–2, 6–4, 4–6, 3–6, 6–3; Solomon d. Pinto
Bravo 6–1, 6–1, 6–2; Smith d. Cornejo 6–4, 1–6, 9–7, 6–1.

INTER-ZONE FINALS
USA d. Spain 3–2, Barcelona: S. Smith lost to A. Gimeno 8–6, 5–7,
3–6, 4–6; H. Solomon d. J. Gisbert 9–7, 7–5, 0–6, 1–6, 6–4; Smith–E.
van Dillen d. Gisbert–Gimeno 6–3, 0–6, 6–2, 6–3; Smith d. Gisbert 11–9,
10–8, 6–4; Solomon lost to Gimeno 3–6, 1–6, 6–2, 2–6. **Rumania d.
Australia 4–1, Bucharest:** I. Tiriac lost to M. Anderson 6–2, 6–2, 6–8,
4–6, 4–6; I. Nastase d. C. Dibley 6–3, 6–0, 6–2; Nastase–Tiriac d.
Dibley–Anderson 6–2, 6–2, 6–2; Tiriac d. Dibley 6–3, 3–6, 11–13, 6–3,
6–0; Nastase d. Anderson 6–2, 6–2, 4–6, 6–3.

FINAL
USA d. Rumania 3–2, Bucharest: S. Smith d. I. Nastase 11–9, 6–2,
6–3; T. Gorman lost to I. Tiriac 6–4, 6–2, 4–6, 3–6, 2–6; Smith–E. van
Dillen d. Nastase–Tiriac 6–2, 6–0, 6–3; Smith d. Tiriac 4–6, 6–2, 6–4,
2–6, 6–0; Gorman lost to Nastase 1–6, 2–6, 7–5, 8–10.

1973: AUSTRALIA
European Zone A

FIRST ROUND
Austria d. Monaco 5–0, Vienna: P. Pokorny d. L. Borfigá 6–0, 6–3,
5–7, 4–6, 7–5; H. Kary d. E. Vanderpol 6–3, 6–2, 6–4; G. Wimmer–E.
Walter d. Borfiga–P. Balleret 6–4, 4–6, 6–1, 6–2; Pokorny d. Vanderpol
def.; Kary d. Borfiga def. **Greece d. Finland 3–2, Athens:** N.
Kalogeropoulos d. G. Berner 2–6, 8–6, 6–4, 1–6, 6–2; N. Kalaidis lost to
M. Timonen 3–6, 3–6, 5–7; Kalogeropoulos–Kalaidis d. P. Saila–
Timonen 8–6, 2–6, 6–3, 3–6, 9–7; Kalaidis lost to Berner 2–6, 2–6, 3–6;
Kalogeropoulos d. Timonen 7–5, 12–10, 6–2. **Norway d. Ireland 5–0,
Dublin:** E. Melander d. M. P. Hickey 7–5, 6–2, 6–4; P. Hegna d. R.
Brown 7–5, 6–0, 6–0; Melander–T. Moe d. Brown–Hickey 2–6, 6–1,
20–22, 6–4, 6–4; F. D. Jagge d. P. Ledbeter 1–6, 6–3, 6–0, 6–2; Hegna
d. P. Jackson 6–4, 7–5, 6–2.

SECOND ROUND
Holland d. Israel 4–1, Tel Aviv: N. Fleury d. R. Lehrner 6–1, 6–4,
9–7; J. Hordijk d. Y. Shalem 6–1, 6–0, 6–2; Fleury–Hordijk d. Y.
Stabholz–Y. Wertheimer 10–8, 6–4, 6–2; Fleury lost to Shalem 7–5, 5–7,
6–8, 2–6; Hordijk d. Lehrner 6–3, 6–1, 6–4. **New Zealand d. Austria**

3–2, Vienna: O. Parun lost to H. Kary 6–3, 6–2, 3–6, 3–6, 1–6; B. Fairlie
d. P. Pokorny 6–1, 6–3, 3–6, 6–0; Fairlie–Parun d. Kary–Pokorny 6–1,
6–2, 6–4; Parun d. Pokorny 6–4, 6–1, 6–3; Fairlie lost to Kary 4–6, 3–6,
3–6. **Hungary d. Greece 4–1, Athens:** B. Taroczy d. N.
Kalogeropoulos 6–1, 5–7, 8–6, 8–6; S. Baranyi d. N. Kalaidis 6–4, 6–0,
6–1; Taroczy–B. Machan d. Kalogeropoulos–Kalaidis 6–4, 6–1, 9–7;
Baranyi lost to Kalogeropoulos 1–6, 5–7, 4–6; Taroczy d. Kalaidis 6–1,
6–8, 6–2, 6–3. **Norway d. Denmark 3–2, Oslo:** P. Hegna d. L.
Elvstrom 7–5, 6–4, 6–2; E. Melander d. T. Christensen 6–3, 6–4, 9–11,
6–3; J. E. Ross–T. Moe lost to Elvstrom–Christensen 6–8, 5–7, 6–3, 3–6;
Melander lost to Elvstrom 6–2, 6–4, 3–6, 4–6, 2–6; Hegna d. Christensen
5–7, 6–1, 6–3, 6–2.

THIRD ROUND

Rumania d. Holland 3–2, Scheveningen: T. Ovici lost to T. S. Okker
7–5, 2–6, 1–6, 1–6; I. Nastase d. J. Hordijk 6–3, 6–3, 6–2; Nastase–D.
Haradau lost to Okker–Hordijk 6–8, 8–6, 1–6; Ovici d. N. Fleury 6–2,
6–3, 6–4; Nastase d. Okker 6–4, 6–2, 6–4. **New Zealand d. Yugoslavia
3–2, Zagreb:** O. Parun d. B. Jovanovic 1–6, 6–3, 6–2, 6–2; B. Fairlie
lost to Z. Franulovic 2–6, 8–6, 6–2, 2–6, 1–6; Fairlie–Parun d.
Franulovic–Jovanovic 6–0, 6–3, 6–4; Parun d. Franulovic 6–3, 4–6, 6–2,
6–2; Fairlie lost to Jovanovic 3–6, 2–6, 0–6. **USSR d. Hungary 3–2,
Budapest:** T. Kakulia d. B. Taroczy 1–6, 6–0, 6–8, 7–5, 7–5; A. Metreveli
d. S. Baranyi 6–2, 6–2, 6–4; Metreveli–S. Likhachev lost to Taroczy–B.
Machan 8–10, 2–6, 6–2, 0–6; Metreveli d. Taroczy 6–4, 6–4, 6–3; Kakulia
lost to Baranyi 6–4 def. **France d. Norway 5–0, Oslo:** P. Proisy d. P.
Hegna 6–1, 6–1, 6–2; F. Jauffret d. E. Melander 6–0, 6–3, 6–2; J. B.
Chanfreau–W. N'Godrella d. T. Moe–Melander 7–5, 6–3, 7–5; Proisy
d. Melander 6–0, 6–0, 6–3; Jauffret d. Hegna 6–0, 6–3, 6–2.

SEMI-FINAL ROUND

Rumania d. New Zealand 4–1, Bucharest: T. Ovici d. B. Fairlie 6–1,
3–6, 3–6, 6–0, 6–2; I. Nastase d. O. Parun 6–1, 8–6, 6–2; Nastase–I.
Santeiu d. Fairlie–Parun 6–1, 8–6, 6–3; Nastase d. Fairlie 4–6, 6–0, 6–3,
6–0; Ovici lost to Parun 3–6, 5–7, 2–6. **USSR d. France 3–2, Moscow:**
T. Kakulia lost to F. Jauffret 4–6, 4–6, 4–6; A. Metreveli d. P. Proisy
6–3, 6–8, 7–5, 6–2; Metreveli–S. Likhachev lost to Jauffret–P. Barthes
4–6, 5–7, 9–11; Kakulia d. Proisy 6–3, 6–3, 6–4; Metrevli d. Jauffret 6–1,
6–3, 4–6, 4–6, 6–4.

FINAL

Rumania d. USSR 3–2, Bucharest: T. Ovici lost to A. Metreveli 5–7,
5–7, 2–6; I. Nastase d. T. Kakulia 6–0, 6–3, 6–0; Nastase–I. Santeiu lost

to Metreveli–S. Likhachev 0–6, 6–3, 4–6, 7–5, 2–6; Nastase d. Metreveli 6–0, 6–2, 6–4; Ovici d. Kakulia 6–3, 6–3, 6–1.

European Zone B

FIRST ROUND

Switzerland d. Portugal 5–0, Lisbon: P. Kanderal d. V. Pinto 8–6, 6–2, 6–3; D. Sturdza d. P. Peralta 6–3, 6–3, 6–3; Sturdza–M. Werren d. Peralta–Vaz Pinto 6–2, 6–2, 10–8; Kanderal d. Peralta 6–1, 6–0, 6–4; Sturdza d. Pinto 3–6, 6–1, 6–1, 8–6. **Egypt d. Turkey 5–0, Cairo:** A. Daoudi d. A. Kocak 8–6, 6–2, 6–0; I. Mahmoud d. B. Altinkaya 6–3, 6–1, 6–0; Mahmoud–Daoudi d. H. Ozdemir–Altinkaya 6–0, 6–2, 6–3; A. Hassan d. Altinkaya 6–3, 6–3, 6–3; M. Sonbol d. Kocak 6–2, 6–3, 6–1. **Bulgaria d. Iran 5–0, Sofia:** B. Pampoulov d. T. Akbari 6–4, 6–2, 4–6, 8–10, 6–3; L. Guenov d. H. Akbari 6–2, 8–6, 6–2; B. and M. Pampoulov d. H. and T. Akbari 6–2, 6–3, 6–4; B. Pampoulov d. H. Akbari 6–0, 6–3, 11–9; Guenov d. T. Akbari 6–4, 6–4, 6–4. **Morocco d. Luxembourg 5–0, Casablanca:** A. Ben Aamar d. J. Brucher 6–1, 6–0, 6–2; O. Laimina d. J. Neumann 8–6, 6–1, 2–6, 6–4; Laimina–H. Bouchaib d. Brucher–Neumann 6–1, 6–4, 8–6; Bouchaib d. Neumann 6–3, 6–4, 4–6, 6–3; A. Chinois d. Brucher 6–3, 6–2, 2–6, 6–4.

SECOND ROUND

Germany d. Switzerland 3–0, Geneva: J. Fassbender d. D. Sturdza 0–6, 6–3, 6–2, 6–2; H. Elschenbroich d. P. Kanderal 9–7, 6–4, 7–5; Fassbender–H. J. Pohmann d. Sturdza–M. Werren 6–4, 18–16, 6–4. **Egypt d. Poland 4–1, Cairo:** I. Mahmoud d. T. Nowicki 2–6, 7–5, 6–3, 9–7; I. El Shafei d. J. Niedzweiski 6–3, 7–5, 6–1; El Shafei–A. Daoudi d. Nowicki–Niedzweiski 6–1, 7–5, 4–6, 3–6, 6–3; Daoudi lost to W. Fibak 1–6, 5–7, 6–3, 7–5, 1–6; Mahmoud d. Niedzweiski 4–6 def. **Bulgaria d. Belgium 3–2, Sofia:** M. Pampoulov lost to P. Hombergen 5–7, 3–6, 7–9; L. Guenov lost to B. Mignot 6–3, 2–6, 1–6, 2–6; B. and M. Pampoulov d. Hombergen–Mignot 5–7, 6–3, 7–5, 6–4; B. Pampoulov d. Mignot 6–4, 9–7, 6–2; Guenov d. Hombergen 5–7, 6–2, 3–6, 12–10, 6–3. **Sweden d. Morocco 4–1, Rabat:** B. Borg d. O. Laimina 6–3, 6–2, 6–1; T. Johansson d. A. Ben Aamar 6–0, 6–4, 6–4; Borg–O. Bengtson d. Ben Aamar–Kunuba 7–5, 6–2, 6–1; Borg d. Ben Aamar 6–1, 6–0, 6–1; Johansson lost to Laimina 4–6, 0–6, 1–6.

THIRD ROUND

Germany d. Great Britain 4–1, Munich: J. Fassbender d. M. Cox 6–3, 6–4, 1–6, 9–7; K. Meiler d. R. Taylor 6–3, 6–4, 6–4; Fassbender–H. J.

Pohmann d. D. Lloyd–Taylor 7–5, 4–6, 6–3, 6–4; Fassbender d. Taylor 6–4, 8–6, 6–3; Meiler lost to Cox 6–4, 0–6, 4–6, 2–6. **Czechoslovakia d. Egypt 4–1, Cairo:** J. Kodes d. I. Mahmoud 6–4, 6–4, 6–1; J. Hrebec d. I. El Shafei 8–6, 6–4, 3–6, 3–6, 13–11; Kodes–J. Kukal d. El Shafei–A. Daoudi 6–1, 6–4, 6–2; F. Pala d. Daoudi 6–1, 3–6, 6–2, 4–6, 6–4; Hrebec lost to Mahmoud 6–1, 6–8, 2–5 def. **Italy d. Bulgaria 5–0, Reggio Emilia:** P. Bertolucci d. B. Pampoulov 8–6, 6–1, 6–4; A. Panatta d. L. Guenov 6–1, 6–2, 6–3; Bertolucci–Panatta d. B. and M. Pampoulov 6–2, 7–5, 6–4; Bertolucci d. Guenov 6–3, 6–3, 6–3; Panatta d. B. Pampoulov 6–4, 3–6, 6–3, 6–3. **Spain d. Sweden 3–2, Båstad:** M. Orantes d. B. Borg 6–1, 6–2, 6–1; A. Gimeno d. O. Bengtson 6–4, 6–4, 3–6, 6–8, 6–1; A. Munoz–Orantes lost to Bengtson–R. Norbeg 3–6, 3–6, 8–6, 3–6; Orantes d. Bengtson 8–6, 6–4, 6–1; Munoz lost to Borg 7–5, 3–6, 3–6, 6–3, 5–7.

SEMI-FINAL ROUND

Czechoslovakia d. Germany 3–2, Prague: J. Kodes d. K. Meiler 6–3, 6–4, 6–1; J. Hrebec d. J. Fassbender 6–1, 7–9, 6–2, 6–3; Kodes–J. Kukal lost to H. J. Pohmann–Fassbender 2–6, 6–3, 6–8, 7–9; Kodes d. Fassbender 6–2, 6–1, 7–5; Hrebec lost to Fassbender 1–6, 1–6, 5–7. **Italy d. Spain 3–2, Turin:** C. Barazzutti d. M. Santana 7–5, 1–6, 6–4, 6–4; A. Zugarelli d. J. Higueras 7–5, 6–3, 6–2; P. Marzano–G. Maioli lost to J. Gisbert–Higueras 3–6, 1–6, 6–4, 4–6; Barazzutti d. Higueras 6–4, 6–3, 6–1; Zugarelli lost to Santana 6–2, 3–6, 3–6, 2–6.

FINAL

Czechoslovakia d. Italy 4–1, Prague: J. Kodes lost to C. Barazzutti 5–7, 6–3, 4–6, 2–6; J. Hrebec d. A. Zugarelli 12–10, 6–1, 6–1; Kodes–F. Pala d. G. Maioli–P. Marzano 6–2, 8–6, 6–4; Hrebec d. Barazzutti 9–7, 6–1, 6–4; Kodes of Zugarelli 6–1, 6–3, 0–6, 6–2.

Eastern Zone

FIRST ROUND

Indonesia d. Hong Kong 5–0: G. Widjojo d. Tao Po 6–0, 6–0, 6–0; A. Wijono d. K. C. Tsui 6–2, 6–1, 6–2; Widjojo–Wijono d. Tsui–Winston Wei Jr 6–3, 6–3, 6–4; Justedjo Tarik d. Tsui 6–1, 6–2, 6–3; S. Samudra d. Tao Po 7–5; 6–0, 6–2. **Japan d. Korea 4–1, Seoul:** J. Kamiwazumi lost to Kim Sung Dae 6–8, 1–6, 4–6; J. Kuki d. Kim Moon II 6–4, 6–4, 6–2; T. Sakai–Kamiwazumi d. Moon II–Chung Yung Ho 6–2, 6–2, 2–6, 3–6, 6–3; Kamiwazumi d. Moon II 6–2, 1–6, 6–0, 6–0; Kuki d. Sung Dae

7–5, 7–5, 6–0. **Pakistan d. Malaysia 3–0, Kuala Lumpur:** M. Iqbal d. Z. Meah 6–0, 6–4, 6–1; S. Meer d. S. A. Azman 6–0, 6–0, 6–2; Iqbal–Meer d. Chow Weng Wah–Lee Wai Ching 6–2, 6–4, 6–2; Iqbal v. Azman 6–1, 1–4, unfin. **Vietnam d. Ceylon 3–0, Penang:** Vo Van Bay d. P. S. Kumara 6–4, 6–3, 4–6, 6–4; Vo Van Thanh d. B. Pinto 6–4, 6–3, 4–6, 6–4; Vo Van Bay–Ly Alline d. Pinto–Kumara 6–1, 6–2, 12–14, 6–4.

SECOND ROUND
Japan d. Indonesia 3–0, Tokyo: J. Kamiwazumi d. G. Widjojo 6–1, 6–4, 7–5; T. Sakai d. A. Wijono 6–3, 6–4, 6–1; Kamiwazumi–K. Hirai d. Widjojo–Wijono 6–3, 6–2, 7–5. **Pakistan d. Vietnam 4–1, Kuala Lumpur:** S. Meer d. Vo Van Thanh 6–2, 6–4, 5–7, 9–11, 6–2; M. Iqbal d. Vo Van Bay 6–4, 6–4, 8–6; Iqbal–Meer d. Bay–Ly Alline 6–4, 3–6, 4–6, 6–3, 10–8; Iqbal d. Thanh 6–4, 6–3, 6–1; Meer lost to Bay 8–6, 0–6, 3–6, 2–6.

SEMI-FINAL ROUND
Australia d. Japan 4–1, Tokyo: M. J. Anderson d. T. Sakai 6–2, 9–7, 3–6, 6–1; J. D. Newcombe d. J. Kamiwazumi 6–2, 7–5, 6–1; Newcombe–G. Masters d. Kamiwazumi–Sakai 6–4, 7–5, 6–4; Newcombe lost to Sakai 6–8, 4–6, 6–4, 6–0, 3–6; Anderson d. Kamiwazumi 4–6, 4–6, 6–4, 6–4, 8–6. **India d. Pakistan 4–0, Kuala Lumpur:** V. Amritraj d. S. Meer 6–1, 6–4, 6–4, 8–6; A. Amritraj d. M. Iqbal 6–2, 6–2, 6–2; V. and A. Amritraj d. Iqbal–Meer 6–3, 6–4, 6–4; V. Amritraj d. Iqbal 2–6, 6–3, 6–4, 2–3, def.; C. Mukerjea v. Meer 4–6, unfin.

FINAL ROUND
Australia d. India 4–0, Madras: J. D. Newcombe d. A. Amritraj 6–2, 6–1, 6–0; M. J. Anderson d. V. Amritraj 6–1, 6–2, 6–1; Newcombe–G. Masters d. P. Lall–V. Amritraj 4–6, 6–2, 7–5, 6–3; J. Cooper d. Lall 4–6, 6–0, 8–6, 6–1; Newcombe v. V. Amritraj 12–10, 3–6 unfin.

American Zone South

FIRST ROUND
Argentina d. Ecuador 5–0, Buenos Aires: G. Vilas d. R. Ycaza 6–2, 6–3, 6–2; J. Ganzabal d. M. Olvera 6–4, 8–6, 6–2; Vilas–R. Cano d. Olvera–Ycaza 6–4, 6–3, 6–4; H. Romani d. Ycaza 6–1, 6–1, 6–2; Vilas d. Olvera 6–3, 6–2, 6–0.

SECOND ROUND

Argentina d. Brazil 4–1, Buenos Aires: J. Ganzabal lost to J. E. Mandarino 3–6, 8–6, 3–6, 4–6; G. Vilas d. J. Lehmann 6–2, 6–3, 1–6, 6–2; Vilas–R. Cano d. L. Tavarez–C. Kirmayr 4–6, 6–4, 6–2, 6–1; Ganzabal d. Lehmann 10–8, 7–5, 6–4; Vilas d. Kirmayr 4–6, 7–5, 6–0, 6–2.   **South Africa d. Uruguay 5–0, Punta Del Este:** F. D. McMillan d. A. Laborde 6–0, 6–2, 6–1; P. Cramer d. G. Stapff 6–0, 6–1, 4–6, 6–1; McMillan–Cramer d. M. Laborde–L. Damiani 6–3, 6–2, 6–2; Cramer d. Laborde 6–0, 6–1, 6–0; R. J. Moore d. Stapff 10–8, 6–0, 6–3.

SEMI-FINAL ROUND

Argentina d. South Africa 4–1, Montevideo: J. Ganzabal d. P. Cramer 6–2, 6–0, 3–6, 6–0; G. Vilas d. B. Mitton 6–1, 6–3, 6–4; Vilas–R. Cano lost to D. Joubert–Mitton 3–6, 6–2, 6–1, 6–8, 3–6; Vilas d. Joubert 6–2, 6–2, 6–1; Ganzabal d. Mitton def.

FINAL ROUND

Chile d. Argentina 3–2, Buenos Aires: J. Fillol lost to G. Vilas 3–6, 3–6, 0–6; P. Cornejo d. J. Ganzabal 6–4, 6–2, 5–7, 6–4; Fillol–Cornejo lost to Vilas–R. Cano 6–3, 4–6, 6–4, 3–6, 4–6; Cornejo d. Vilas 6–1, 9–7, 2–6, 6–1; Fillol d. Ganzabal 7–5, 9–11, 5–7, 6–2, 6–1.

American Zone North

FIRST ROUND

Colombia d. Canada 4–1, Bogota: I. Molina d. M. Belkin 9–7 def.; J. Velasco d. T. Bardsley 5–7, 6–1, 6–3, 6–1; Molina–Velasco d. Bardsley–D. McCormick 6–3, 6–4, 6–3; J. Restrepo lost to Bardsley 6–8, 5–7, 1–6; Velasco d. McCormick 6–2, 6–3, 7–5.

SECOND ROUND

Colombia d. Commonwealth Caribbean 3–2, Bogota: I. Molina d. R. Russell 6–3, 6–1, 6–4; J. Velasco d. L. Rolle 6–1, 6–2, 6–1; Molina–Velasco lost to M. Valdez–A. Price 3–6, 4–6, 6–1, 6–0, 4–6; Velasco lost to Russell 3–6, 6–3, 6–3, 4–6, 2–6; Molina d. Rolle 6–3, 6–1, 6–0.   **Mexico d. Venezuela 4–1, Mexico City:** R. Ramirez d. J. Andrew 6–2, 6–4, 6–3; V. Zarazua lost to H. Hose 5–7, 3–6, 6–3, 1–6; Zarazua–Ramirez d. Hose–Andrew 6–4, 6–2, 6–2; Ramirez d. Hose 6–2, 6–4, 7–5; Zarazua d. Andrew 6–4, 6–4, 6–3.

SEMI-FINAL ROUND

Mexico d. Colombia 5–0, Mexico City: R. Ramirez d. I. Molina 6–3, 6–8, 6–4, 6–2; J. Loyo-Mayo d. J. Velasco 5–7, 6–2, 5–7, 6–3, 7–5; Ramirez–V. Zarazua d. Molina–Velasco 6–3, 3–6, 8–6, 6–3; Loyo-Mayo d. Molina 2–6, 6–4, 6–1, 6–3; Ramirez d. Velasco 6–1, 6–3, 6–3.

FINAL ROUND

USA d. Mexico 4–1, Mexico City: T. Gorman lost to R. Ramirez 4–6, 2–6, 3–6; H. Solomon d. J. Loyo-Mayo 7–5, 6–4, 7–5; Gorman–E. van Dillen d. Ramirez–V. Zarazua 7–5, 12–14, 6–3, 6–4; Solomon d. Ramirez 8–6, 7–5, 7–5; R. Stockton d. L. Baraldi 2–6, 6–1, 6–3, 8–6.

ZONE FINAL

USA d. Chile 4–1, Little Rock: T. Gorman d. J. Fillol 17–15, 6–4, 4–6, 6–3; S. R. Smith d. P. Cornejo 7–9, 6–2, 8–6, 6–4; Smith E. van Dillen d. Cornejo–Fillol 7–9, 37–39, 8–6, 6–1, 6–3; Gorman d. Cornejo 6–3, 6–1, 6–1; Smith lost to Fillol def.

INTER-ZONE FINALS

USA d. Rumania 4–1, Alamo: M. C. Riessen lost to I. Nastase 2–6, 4–6, 2–6; S. R. Smith d. T. Ovici 7–5, 6–1, 6–3; Smith–E. van Dillen d. Nastase–I. Santeiu 6–2, 7–5, 6–2; Riessen d. Ovici 6–1, 4–6, 6–1, 7–5; Smith d. Nastase 5–7, 6–2, 6–3, 4–6, 6–3. **Australia d. Czechoslovakia 4–1, Melbourne:** R. Laver d. J. Kodes 6–3, 7–5, 7–5; J. D. Newcombe lost to J. Hrebec 4–6, 10–8, 4–6, 5–7; K. R. Rosewall–Laver d. Kodes–V. Zednik 6–4, 14–12, 7–9, 8–6; Laver d. Hrebec 5–7, 6–3, 6–4, 4–6, 6–4; Newcombe d. Kodes 6–2, 6–2, 6–4.

FINAL

Australia d. USA 5–0, Cleveland: J. D. Newcombe d. S. R. Smith 6–1, 3–6, 6–3, 3–6, 6–4; R. Laver d. T. Gorman 8–10, 8–6, 6–8, 6–3, 6–1; Laver–Newcombe d. Smith–E. Van Dillen 6–1, 6–2, 6–4; Newcombe d. Gorman 6–2, 6–1, 6–3; Laver d. Smith 6–3, 6–4, 3–6, 6–2.

1974: SOUTH AFRICA
European Zone A

PRELIMINARY ROUND

Turkey d. Lebanon 3–2, Istanbul: A. Kocak d. K. Miri 6–4, 6–3, 6–0; H. Ozdemir lost to N. Abouhassoun 1–6, 1–6, 5–7; T. Gursoy–Kocak

d. A. Wilkinson–E. Wilkinson 6–2, 6–1, 6–3; Ozdemir lost to Miri 6–4, 8–10, 3–6, 1–6; Kocak d. Abouhassoun 3–6, 6–1, 6–0, 6–4.

FIRST ROUND

Turkey d. Luxembourg 5–0, Istanbul: R. Aydin d. J. Neumann 6–0, 6–4, 6–4; T. Gursoy d. G. Logelin 6–4, 6–3, 7–5; Aydin–Gursoy d. Neumann–Logelin 6–1, 6–4, 7–5; H. Ozdemir d. Logelin 6–3, 8–6, 6–1; A. Kocak d. Neumann 6–0, 6–2, 6–3.

SECOND ROUND

Portugal d. Ireland 4–1, Lisbon: J. Viela d. K. Menton 6–4, 6–3, 4–6, 6–4; R. Peralta d. M. Hickey 7–5, 6–4, 6–8, 6–8, 8–6; Viela–A. V. Pinto lost to Hickey–D. Early 3–6, 6–4, 3–6, 6–2, 5–7; Viela d. Hickey 7–9, 6–3, 6–2, 6–3; Peralta d. P. Ledbetter 6–1, 2–6, 6–2, 6–3. **Austria d. Switzerland 3–2, Zurich:** P. Pokorny lost to P. Kanderal 3–6, 3–6, 9–7, 6–8; H. Kary d. M. Burgener 6–3, 9–7, 6–2; Kary–Pokorny d. Burgener–Kanderal 7–5, 6–4, 6–4; Kary lost to Kanderal 6–8, 5–7, 3–6; Pokorny d. Burgener 6–3, 6–4, 6–0. **Poland d. Hungary 3–2, Warsaw:** J. Niedzwiedzki lost to B. Taroczy 2–6, 6–4, 3–6, 2–6; W. Fibak d. P. Szoke 6–4, 3–6, 6–2, 6–4; Fibak–T. Nowicki d. B. Machan–Taroczy 4–6, 16–14, 6–3, 7–5; Niedzwiedzki lost to Szoke 6–3, 1–6, 3–6, 4–6; Fibak d. Taroczy 4–6, 6–4, 5–7, 7–5, 6–4. **Finland d. Turkey 5–0, Helsinki:** G. Berner d. H. Ozdemir 6–0, 6–1, 6–0; M. Timonen d. R. Aydin 6–1, 6–1, 6–1; J. Narakka–Timonen d. Ozdemir–T. Gursoy 9–7, 6–4, 6–2; Timonen d. Gursoy 6–2, 6–2, 6–0; Berner d. Aydin 6–2, 6–1, 6–1.

THIRD ROUND

France d. Portugal 5–0, Porto: F. Jauffret d. J. Viela 6–0, 6–3, 6–1; G. Goven d. J. Cruz 6–1, 6–1, 6–4; W. N'Godrella–J. F. Caujolle d. Viela–R. Peralta 1–6, 9–7, 6–1, 2–6, 6–2; Jauffret d. Cruz 6–1, 6–0, 6–2; Goven d. Viela 6–2, 6–4, 4–6, 4–6, 6–3. **Austria d. New Zealand 3–1, Vienna:** P. Pokorny lost to O. Parun 4–6, 2–6, 2–6; H. Kary d. J. Simpson 6–4, 6–3, 7–5; Kary–Pokorny d. Parun–Simpson 3–6, 7–6, 3–6, 6–3, 6–2; Pokorny d. Simpson 6–1, 6–2, 9–11, 6–3; Kary v. Parun 6–8, 6–4, 2–6, 7–7 unfin. **Sweden d. Poland 4–1, Båstad:** B. Borg d. T. Nowicki 2–6, 6–2, 0–6, 6–1, 6–1; L. Johansson d. W. Fibak 6–4, 2–6, 6–3, 7–5; Borg–O. Bengston d. Nowicki–Fibak 6–4, 6–8, 6–2, 6–4; Borg d. Fibak 6–0, 6–4, 6–3; Johansson lost to Nowicki 0–6, 3–6, 11–13. **Holland d. Finland 4–1, Scheveningen:** R. Thung d. P. Saila 6–2, 6–4, 6–4; J. Hordijk d. G. Berner 8–6, 6–1, 7–5; Thung–F. Hemmes d.

Saila–J. Narakka 6–3, 6–3, 8–6; Thung lost to Berner 4–6, 6–2, 3–6, 6–8; Hordijk d. Saila 6–0, 6–1, 6–1.

QUARTER-FINAL ROUND

France d. Austria 3–1, Vienna: F. Jauffret lost to H. Kary 5–7, 1–6, 7–9; G. Goven d. P. Pokorny 6–2, 5–2, 6–2; P. Barthes–Jauffret d. Kary–Pokorny 7–5, 6–4, 6–2; Jauffret d. Pokorny 6–4, 6–2, 6–3.
Sweden d. Holland 4–1, Båstad: B. Borg d. R.Thung 4–6, 6–4, 6–1, 6–1; L. Johansson d. J. Hordijk 5–7, 4–6, 6–0, 6–1, 6–2; Borg–O. Bengtson d. Thung–F. Hemmes 6–2, 7–9, 6–1, 6–1; Johansson lost to Thung 6–4, 6–4, 1–6, 3–6, 3–6; Borg d. Hemmes 6–3, 6–3, 6–1.

SEMI-FINAL ROUND

Rumania d. France 3–2, Bucharest: I. Nastase lost to F. Jauffret 6–2, 4–6, 3–6, 2–6; T. Ovici d. P. Barthes 6–1, 10–8, 6–2; Nastase–I. Tiriac d. Barthes–Jauffret 6–2, 6–4, 9–7; Ovici lost to Jauffret 2–6, 4–6, 6–4, 5–7; Nastase d. Barthes 6–2, 6–2, 6–3. **Italy d. Sweden 3–2, Båstad:** P. Bertolucci lost to B. Borg 5–7, 1–6, 0–6; A. Panatta d. L. Johansson 8–6, 6–1, 4–6, 6–1; Panatta–Bertolucci d. Borg–O. Bengtson 6–1, 5–7, 7–5, 6–4; Bertolucci d. Johansson 3–6, 6–3, 5–7, 7–5, 8–6; Panatta lost to Borg 4–6, 6–4, 7–9, 3–6.

FINAL ROUND

Italy d. Rumania 3–2, Mestre: C. Barazzutti lost to I. Nastase 7–9, 0–6, 1–6; A. Panatta d. I. Tiriac 6–1, 6–3, 6–2; P. Bertolucci–Panatta d. Nastase–Tiriac 6–4, 8–6, 6–8, 4–6, 6–2; Barazzutti d. Tiriac 6–3, 6–0, 6–0; Panatta lost to Nastase 0–6, 0–6, 5–7.

European Zone B

PRELIMINARY ROUND

Morocco d. Nigeria 3–2: Nait Omar lost to T. Onibokun 3–6, 6–3, 1–6, 6–1, 6–8; Laimina Omar d. L. Awopegba 7–5, 6–2, 6–2; Nait–Laimina d. Onibokun–Awopegba 7–5, 6–4, 6–4; Nait lost to Awopegba 4–6, 3–6, 1–6; Laimina d. Onibokun 6–1, 6–4, 6–4. **Iran d. Israel 4–1, Teheran:** T. Akbari d. F. Kaplan 6–1, 6–3, 6–3; H. Akbari d. Y. Shalem 6–4, 6–4, 6–4; A. Madani–K. D. Javan d. Y. Wertheimer–R. Porges 6–4, 6–2, 3–6, 6–3; T. Akbari d. Shalem 6–2, 6–2, 4–6, 9–7; H. Akbari lost to Kaplan 6–3, 5–7, 1–6, 8–6, 3–6.

FIRST ROUND
United Arab Republic d. Morocco 3–0, Cairo: A. Daoudi d. A. Ben
Omar 6–2, 6–1, 6–1; I. El Shafei d. Laimina Omar 6–3, 7–5, 6–0;
Daoudi–El Shafei d. A. Ben–Laimina 6–1, 10–8, 6–1.

SECOND ROUND
United Arab Republic d. Bulgaria 3–1, Cairo: A. Daoudi d. B.
Pampulov 6–1, 2–6, 6–2, 6–1; I. Mahmoud lost to L. Genov 3–6, 3–6, 2–6;
Daoudi–Mahmoud d. B. and M. Pampulov 3–6, 6–3, 6–3, 6–8, 6–2;
Daoudi d. Genov 8–6, 7–5, 6–4; Mahmoud v. B. Pampulov 14–12, 6–3,
4–6 unfin. **Belgium d. Greece 5–0, Brussels:** P. Hombergen d. N.
Kelaidis 6–3, 6–4, 6–1; B. Mignot d. N. Kalogeropoulos 6–2, 7–5, 1–6,
6–4; Hombergen–Mignot d. Kelaidis–Kalogeropoulos 6–1, 6–2, 9–7;
Mignot d. Kelaidis 6–3, 6–1, 6–1; Hombergen d. Kalogeropoulos 6–1,
6–4, 6–3. **Denmark d. Monaco 3–2, Monte Carlo:** L. Elvstrom d. L.
Borfiga 6–2, 6–4, 6–4; T. Christensen lost to B. Balleret 2–6, 5–7, 3–6;
Christensen–L. Nielsen d. Balleret–Borfiga 4–6, 6–2, 6–2, 5–7, 8–6;
Christensen lost to Borfiga 1–6, 1–6, 2–6; Elvstrom d. Balleret 6–2, 6–4,
6–2. **Norway d. Iran 4–1, Oslo:** P. Hegna d. H. Akbari 6–1, 7–5, 6–1;
T. Moe lost to T. Akbari 2–6, 6–3, 5–7, 5–7; Hegna–Moe d. A.
Madani–K. D. Javan 6–1, 6–2, 6–2; Hegna d. T. Akbari 6–2, 7–5, 4–6,
6–2; Moe d. H. Akbari 6–4, 6–2, 6–3.

THIRD ROUND
United Arab Republic d. Great Britain 5–0, Cairo: I. El Shafei d. D.
A. Lloyd 6–1, 6–4, 6–3; A. Daoudi d. J. M. Lloyd 7–5, 7–5, 4–6, 4–6,
6–2; El Shafei–Daoudi d. D. A. and J. M. Lloyd 10–8, 6–4, 6–4; Daoudi
d. D. A. Lloyd 8–6, 6–3, 6–4; El Shafei d. J. M. Lloyd 6–1, 8–6, 6–1.
Yugoslavia d. Belgium 3–2, Brussels: Z. Franulovic d. P. Hombergen
3–6, 6–3, 6–2, 3–6, 10–8; N. Pilic d. B. Mignot 8–6, 6–2, 6–2;
Franulovic–Pilic lost to Hombergen–Mignot 8–6, 3–6, 7–9, 5–7;
Franulovic lost to Mignot 4–6, 1–6, 6–1, 3–6; Pilic d. Hombergen 7–5,
8–6, 3–6, 6–2. **West Germany d. Denmark 5–0, Berlin:** H. J.
Pohmann d. K. E. Nielsen 6–0, 6–0, 6–3; K. Meiler d. L. Elvstrom
4–6, 6–0, 6–3, 6–0; Pohmann–J. Fassbender d. Nielsen–Elvstrom 6–2,
6–0, 6–1; Fassbender d. T. Christensen 6–1, 6–0, 6–1; Meiler d. Nielsen
1–6, 7–5, 6–1, 6–1. **Spain d. Norway 5–0, Barcelona:** J. Higueras d.
T. Moe 6–1, 6–2, 6–2; M. Orantes d. P. Hegna 6–0, 6–1, 6–1; Higueras–
Orantes d. Moe–F. Pryndz 6–4, 6–3, 6–0; Orantes d. Moe 6–1, 6–1, 6–1;
Higueras d. Hegna 6–3, 6–3, 6–3.

QUARTER-FINAL ROUND

Yugoslavia d. United Arab Republic 3–2, Cairo: Z. Franulovic lost to I. El Shafei 2–6, 3–6, 2–6; N. Pilic d. A. Daoudi 6–0, 6–4, 6–0; Franulovic–Pilic d. El Shafei–Daoudi 6–3, 6–1, 6–0; Pilic lost to El Shafei 6–2, 7–9, 6–2, 3–6 def.; Franulovic d. Daoudi 6–2, 7–5, 6–3. **West Germany d. Spain 3–2, Dusseldorf:** K. Meiler d. M. Orantes 3–6, 4–6, 6–4, 6–4, 6–3; J. Fassbender lost to J. Higueras 6–8, 3–6, 6–2, 3–6; Fassbender–H. J. Pohmann d. Orantes–A. Munoz 6–3, 6–4, 4–6, 6–4; Meiler d. Higueras 6–3, 6–2, 6–1; Fassbender lost to Orantes 4–6, 2–6, 0–6.

SEMI-FINAL ROUND

USSR d. Yugoslavia 3–1, Donetsk: A. Metreveli d. B. Jovanovic 6–4, 6–1, 6–1; T. Kakulia lost to N. Pilic 7–5, 6–8, 5–7, 1–6; Metreveli–V. Korotkov d. Jovanovic–Pilic 6–1, 6–1, 3–6, 6–3; Kakulia d. Jovanovic 6–2, 6–4, 6–0. **Czechoslovakia d. West Germany 3–2, Munich:** J. Kodes d. H. J. Pohmann 6–4, 6–1, 6–3; J. Hrebec lost to K. Meiler 3–6, 6–1, 6–3, 11–13, 4–6; Kodes–V. Zednik lost to J. Fassbender–Pohmann 4–6, 0–6, 2–6; Kodes d. Meiler 6–1, 7–5, 6–0; Hrebec d. Pohmann 6–4, 6–1, 6–8, 12–10.

FINAL ROUND

USSR d. Czechoslovakia 3–2, Donetsk: A. Metreveli d. F. Pala 6–2, 6–4, 3–6, 6–2; T. Kakulia lost to J. Kodes 4–6, 2–6, 3–6; Metreveli–V. Korotkov lost to Kodes–V. Zednik 4–6, 1–6, 3–6; Metreveli d. Kodes 4–6, 6–3, 4–6, 6–3, 7–5; Kakulia d. Pala 6–3, 4–6, 6–4, 2–6, 6–4.

Eastern Zone

FIRST ROUND

Philippines d. Indonesia 3–1, Manila: E. Cruz d. A. Wijono 6–1, 6–3, 6–2; R. Ranon d. G. Widjojo 2–6, 4–6, 6–3, 6–3, 6–2; Cruz–J. Hernandez d. Widjojo–Wijono 1–6, 6–2, 6–0, 6–2; B. Dimalanta lost to V. Hadiman 11–9, 4–6, 0–6, 3–6. **Japan d. Korea 3–0, Tokyo:** K. Hirai d. K. Bae–Sung 6–4, 6–4, 6–4; T. Sakai d. K. Moon–Il 6–3, 6–0, 6–1; Hirai–K. Tanabe d. Bae–Sung–K. Moon–Il 6–4, 6–1, 6–1.

SECOND ROUND

Pakistan d. Malaysia 4–1, Karachi: S. Meer d. A. Baba 6–3, 6–0, 6–1; M. Iqbal d. L. W. Ching 6–0, 6–4, 3–6, 6–4; Meer–Iqbal d. Ching–C. W. Wah 6–4, 8–6, 6–3; I. Majeed d. Ching 6–3, 6–2, 6–3; F. Mahmood lost to Wah 3–6, 6–2, 4–6, 1–2 def. **Philippines d. Hong Kong 5–0, Manila:** E. Cruz d. C. Chang 6–1, 6–0, 6–2; R. Ranon d. H. Ny 6–2, 6–0, 6–1; J. Hernandez–B. Dimalanta d. Ny–H. Ruslie 6–0, 6–2, 6–1; Dimalanta d. Ruslie 6–4, 6–2, 6–1; Ranon d. M. Y. Lung 6–0, 6–0, 6–4. **Japan d. Vietnam 3–0:** T. Sakai d. Dinh Quoc Tuan 6–0, 6–2, 6–0; K. Hirai d. Vo Van Bay 6–0, 6–3, 6–1; Hirai–Sakai d. Bay–Ly Alline 6–3, 6–1, 6–4. **Taiwan d. Sri Lanka def.**

QUARTER-FINAL ROUND
Pakistan d. Philippines 4–1, Lahore: M. Iqbal lost to E. Cruz 4–6, 6–8, 2–6; S. Meer d. R. Ranon 6–2, 6–2, 6–1; Iqbal–Meer d. Cruz–J. Hernandez 6–8, 6–4, 6–4, 6–2; Meer d. Cruz 10–8, 6–0, 6–1; M. Mohammad d. B. Dimalanta 6–3, 6–4, 6–2. **Japan d. Taiwan 3–0.**

SEMI-FINAL ROUND
Australia d. Pakistan 3–0, Rawalpindi: A. D. Roche d. H. Rahim 5–7, 6–3, 6–1, 6–3; S. Ball d. S. Meer 6–4, 7–5, 16–14; Roche–C. Dibley d. Rahim–Meer 20–18, 6–4, 6–3. **India d. Japan 4–1, Kanpur:** V. Amritraj d. T. Sakai 3–6, 6–0, 3–6, 6–2, 6–2; A. Amritraj d. K. Hirai 6–4, 12–10, 6–3; V. and A. Amritraj d. Hirai–Sakai 6–3, 8–6, 8–6; S. Menon d. K. Tanabe 6–3, 6–2, 6–2; J. Singh lost to Sakai 6–4, 3–6, 2–6, 3–6.

FINAL
India d. Australia 3–2, Calcutta: J. Singh d. R. Giltinan 11–9, 9–11, 12–10, 8–6; V. Amritraj lost to J. Alexander 12–14, 15–17, 8–6, 2–6; V. and A. Amritraj d. Alexander–C. Dibley 17–15, 6–8, 6–3, 16–18, 6–4; Singh lost to Alexander 6–8, 4–6, 3–6; V. Amritraj d. Giltinan 6–1, 5–7, 6–4, 6–4.

American Zone South

FIRST ROUND
Ecuador d. Uruguay 5–0, Guayaquil: R. Ycaza d. G. Stapff 7–9, 11–9, 6–1, 4–6, 7–5; M. Olvera d. J. L. Damiani 6–2, 6–3, 6–0; Olvera–Ycaza d. Stapff–Damiani 6–4, 6–4, 6–1; Olvera d. Stapff 6–0, 6–1, 6–1; Ycaza d. Damiani 10–8, 6–3, 7–5. **South Africa d. Brazil 5–0, Montevideo:** E. C. Drysdale d. J. E. Mandarino 6–3, 6–0, 6–0; R. A. J. Hewitt d. T. Koch 6–2, 6–1, 3–6, 6–3; F. D. McMillan–Hewitt d. Koch–Mandarino 6–0, 6–0, 6–1; Drysdale d. C. Kirmayr 2–6, 6–4, 2–6, 6–4, 6–3; Hewitt d. R. Carvalhaes 6–0, 6–3, 6–3.

SECOND ROUND
South Africa d. Ecuador 5–0, Guayaquil: R. A. J. Hewitt d. M.
Olvera 6–4, 6–2, 6–4; R. J. Moore d. E. Andrade 6–2, 6–2, 6–1; Hewitt–
F. D. McMillan d. Olvera–F. Guzman 6–3, 6–3, 6–2; Moore d. Olvera
6–3, 6–2, 6–3; Hewitt d. Andrade 6–0, 6–0, 6–0.

THIRD ROUND
South Africa d. Argentina def.

FINAL ROUND
South Africa d. Chile 3–2, Bogota: C. Drysdale d. P. Cornejo 1–6,
6–2, 6–2, 6–3; R. A. J. Hewitt d. J. Fillol 6–2, 6–4, 6–4; Hewitt–F. D.
McMillan d. Cornejo–Fillol 7–9, 4–6, 6–2, 6–4, 6–4; Hewitt lost to
Cornejo 2–6, 3–6, 6–3, 3–6; Drysdale lost to Fillol 6–4, 4–6, 5–7, 0–6.

American Zone North

FIRST ROUND
Canada d. Commonwealth Caribbean 3–2, Jamaica: A. Bardsley d.
L. Rolle 6–1, 6–4, 7–5; D. McCormick lost to R. Russell 6–8, 9–11,
6–4, 0–6; Bardsley–McCormick d. D. Pratt–Russell 6–4, 6–2, 7–5;
McCormick d. Rolle 6–3, 6–3, 6–4; Bardsley lost to Russell 1–6, 4–6,
4–6.

SECOND ROUND
Colombia d. Venezuela 3–2, Bogota: J. Velasco d. H. Hose 9–7, 7–5,
7–5; J. Acudelo d. J. Andrew 6–4, 6–2, 4–6, 8–6; J. Velasco–N. Velasco
lost to Andrew–Hose 7–5, 6–4, 2–6, 4–6, 5–7; Acudelo lost to Hose 1–6,
5–7, 2–6; J. Velasco d. Andrew 6–3, 6–1, 6–2. **Mexico d. Canada
4–1, Mexico City:** J. Loyo-Mayo d. R. Genois 6–4, 10–8, 3–6, 6–2; R.
Ramirez d. A. Bardsley 6–1, 6–3, 6–2; Ramirez–L. Baraldi d. Bardsley–
D. McCormick 6–1, 6–3, 4–6, 5–7, 7–5; Loyo-Mayo d. McCormick 6–1,
6–2, 6–1; Baraldi lost to Genois 7–9, 4–6, 4–6.

THIRD ROUND
Colombia d. Mexico 3–1, Cali, Colombia: J. Velasco d. J. Loyo-Mayo
6–3, 6–4, 6–3; I. Molina d. R. Ramirez 6–1, 6–1, 7–5; Molina–Velasco
lost to V. Zarázua–Ramirez 6–2, 8–10, 3–6, 4–6; Molina d. Loyo-Mayo
7–5, 1–6, 6–3, 6–3.

FINAL ROUND

Colombia d. USA 4–1, Bogota: J. Velasco d. H. Solomon 6–1, 3–6, 4–6, 6–3, 7–5; I. Molina d. E. Van Dillen 6–4, 7–5, 6–2; Molina–Velasco lost to C. Pasarell–Van Dillen 4–6, 11–13, 4–6; Velasco d. Van Dillen 6–0, 6–4, 5–7, 6–3; Molina d. Solomon 6–2, 6–1, 6–0.

ZONE FINAL

South Africa d. Colombia 3–2, Bogota: R. Moore d. I. Molina 6–8, 6–3, 7–5, 6–4; R. A. J. Hewitt d. J. Velasco 6–1, 6–3, 6–2; F. D. McMillan–Hewitt d. Molina–Velasco 6–3, 6–0, 6–3; Moore lost to Velasco 2–6, 6–4, 3–6, 9–7, 2–6; B. Bertram lost to A. Betancour 2–6, 6–4, 6–8, 6–8.

INTER–ZONE FINALS

India d. USSR 3–1, Poona: V. Amritraj d. T. Kakulia 6–4, 11–9, 6–3; A. Amritraj lost to A. Metreveli 4–6, 7–9, 3–6; A. and V. Amritraj d. V. Korotkov–Metreveli 13–15, 7–5, 19–17, 6–3; A. Amritraj d. Kakulia 6–2, 8–10, 4–6, 6–3, 6–3. **South Africa d. Italy 4–1, Johannesburg:** R. A. J. Hewitt d. A. Zugarelli 4–6, 6–0, 9–7, 4–6, 6–1; R. Moore d. A. Panatta 4–6, 6–4, 6–3, 6–4; Hewitt–F. D. McMillan d. Panatta–P. Bertolucci 7–5, 6–4, 10–8; Hewitt lost to Panatta 3–6, 6–8, 2–6; Moore d. Zugarelli 6–3, 7–5, 6–3.

FINAL

South Africa d. India def.

1975: SWEDEN
European Zone A

FIRST ROUND

Israel d. Luxembourg 5–0, Tel Aviv: Y. Shalem d. Storck 6–0, 6–1, 6–1; Y. Wertheimer d. Claude 6–2, 6–2, 6–2; R. Porges–Y. Stabholz d. J. Offenheim–Claude 6–1, 6–1, 10–8; Shalem d. Claude 6–3, 6–1, 6–3; Wertheimer d. Storck 6–1, 6–3, 6–1. **Iran d. Lebanon 5–0, Teheran:** T. Akbari d. K. Miri 6–1, 6–2, 6–1; A. Madani d. A. Ramadan 6–2, 6–3, 6–2; Madani–Akbari d. Miri–Ramadan 10–8, 6–1, 6–2; Seleh d. Ramadan 7–5, 11–9, 6–4; K. D. Javan d. Miri 8–6, 6–3, 6–2.

SECOND ROUND

Switzerland d. Israel 5–0, Tel Aviv: D. Sturdza d. Y. Shalem 6–2, 6–3, 6–3; P. Kanderal d. Y. Stabholz 6–2, 6–1, 6–0; M. Werren–Sturdza

d. Stabholz–Y. Wertheimer 9–7, 6–3, 7–5; Kanderal d. Shalem 6–2, 6–1, 4–6, 6–1; Sturdza d. Stabholz 6–4, 6–3, 5–7, 8–6.   **Poland d. Portugal 5–0, Warsaw:** J. Niedzwiedzki d. J. Vilela 6–2, 6–4, 6–0; H. Drzymalsky d. D. Cruz 6–2, 6–1, 6–4; W. Fibak–Niedzwiedzki d. Vilela–Cruz 6–1, 6–0, 6–2; Drzymalsky d. Vilela 7–5, 6–4, 7–5; Niedzwiedzki d. Cruz 6–1, 6, 6–2.   **Denmark d. Greece 4–1, Copenhagen:** L. Elvstrom d. N. Kelaidis 6–3, 4–6, 4–6, 7–5, 6–4; T. Christensen d. N. Kalogeropoulos 6–3, 3–6, 12–10, 4–6, 6–3; Christensen–Elvstrom d. Kalogeropoulos–Kelaidis 10–12, 2–6, 6–1, 9–7, 8–6; Elvstrom lost to Kalogeropoulos 5–7, 5–7, 6–2, 7–9; Christensen d. Kelaidis 4–6, 6–2, 6–3, 4–6, 6–5 def.
Great Britain d. Iran 5–0, London: R. Taylor d. M. Bahrami 6–0, 6–0, 6–2; J. M. Lloyd d. A. Madani 6–1, 7–5, 6–2; M. Farrell–Lloyd d. Madani–K. D. Javan 6–1, 6–1, 6–1; Lloyd d. Bahrami 7–5, 7–5, 6–4; Taylor d. Madani 6–1, 6–3, 6–1.

THIRD ROUND

Germany d. Switzerland 5–0, Freiburg: H. J. Pohmann d. D. Sturdza 4–6, 6–4, 6–2, 6–0; K. Meiler d. P. Kanderal 6–2, 6–2, 6–4; J. Fassbender–Pohmann d. Sturdza–M. Werren 6–4, 6–2, 6–4; Meiler d. M. Hurlimann 6–0, 6–2, 8–6; H. Elschenbroich d. Kanderal 6–4, 6–0, 6–2.
Sweden d. Poland 4–1, Warsaw: B. Andersson lost to W. Fibak 1–6, 6–8, 6–2; B. Borg d. H. Drzymalski 6–0, 6–0, 6–2; Borg–O. Bengtson d. Fibak–I. Niedzwiedzki 6–4, 6–2, 6–4; Borg d. Fibak 6–4, 6–1, 8–6; Andersson d. Drzymwalski 6–3, 6–0, 6–2.   **Spain d. Denmark 5–0, Murcia:** J. Higueras d. T. Christensen 6–3, 6–4, 6–1; M. Orantes d. L. Elvstrom 6–3, 6–3, 6–0; Orantes–J. Gisbert d. Christensen–Elvstrom 6–1, 6–4, 6–1; A. Munoz d. Christensen 6–0, 6–3, 6–0; Higueras d. Elvstrom 6–3, 6–0, 6–2.   **Great Britain d. Austria 4–0, Vienna:** R. Taylor d. H. Kary 6–3, 1–6, 8–6, 6–1; C. J. Mottram d. G. Wimmer 6–1, 6–1, 6–0; Mottram–Taylor d. Kary–Wimmer 6–4, 6–3, 6–1; Taylor d. Wimmer 6–2, 6–4, 2–6, 4–6, 6–2; J. M. Lloyd v. Kary 2–6, 6–3, 6–4, 4–5 unfin.

QUARTER-FINAL ROUND

Sweden d. Germany 3–2, Berlin: B. Andersson lost to H. J. Pohmann 6–1, 0–6, 3–6, 0–6; B. Borg d. K. Meiler 6–1, 14–12, 8–6; O. Bengtson–R. Norberg lost to J. Fassbender–Pohmann 2–6, 3–6, 1–6; Borg d. Pohmann 3–6, 6–0, 6–0, 6–3; Andersson d. Meiler 7–5, 6–1, 6–2.   **Spain d. Great Britain 3–2, Barcelona:** M. Orantes d. C. J. Mottram 6–4, 6–1, 6–2; J. Higueras lost to R. Taylor 4–6, 6–1, 3–6, 3–6; Orantes–J. Gisbert d. Mottram–Taylor 6–4, 6–4, 4–6, 6–0; Higueras lost to Mottram 1–6, 0–6, 3–6; Orantes d. Taylor 6–3, 3–6, 7–5, 5–7, 7–5.

SEMI-FINAL ROUND

Sweden d. USSR 3–2, Yurmala, USSR: B. Andersson d. A. Volkov
6–1, 6–4, 6–4; B. Borg d. A. Metreveli 7–5, 6–3, 6–3; Borg–O. Bengtson
lost to T. Kakulia–Metreveli 1–6, 4–6, 6–8; Andersson lost to Metreveli
3–6, 7–5, 2–6, 3–6; Borg d. Volkov 8–6, 6–1, 6–0. **Spain d. Rumania
3–2, Barcelona:** M. Orantes d. T. Ovici 6–2, 6–2, 3–6, 6–2; J. Higueras
lost to I. Nastase 0–6, 6–8, 6–4, 1–6; Orantes–J. M. Gisbert d. Nastase–I.
Tiriac 3–6, 4–6, 6–3, 7–5, 6–2; Orantes lost to Nastase 2–6, 2–6, 4–6;
Higueras d. Ovici 6–2, 2–6, 6–1, 5–7, 6–3.

FINAL ROUND

Sweden d. Spain 3–2, Barcelona: B. Andersson lost to M. Orantes
1–6, 3–6, 4–6; B. Borg d. J. Higueras 6–3, 6–1, 6–1; O. Bengtson–Borg
lost to Orantes–J. M. Gisbert 4–6, 3–6, 1–6; Borg d. Orantes 6–4, 6–2,
6–2; Andersson d. Higueras 3–6, 6–4, 6–3, 6–0.

European Zone B

FIRST ROUND

Nigeria d. Kenya 5–0, Lagos: Awopegba d. Rana 6–3, 6–4, 5–7, 6–3;
Allan d. Shretta 6–4, 3–6, 2–6, 6–2, 6–4; Allan–Awopegba d. Shretta–
Rana 7–9, 6–3, 11–13, 7–5, 10–8; Allan d. Rana 6–2, 7–5, 6–3; Ajay d.
Shretta 6–0, 6–2, 6–1. **Turkey d. Ireland 3–2, Istanbul:** Altinkaya d.
K. Menton 6–1, 6–1, 4–6, 6–2; R. Aydin d. P. Ledbetter 6–3, 6–1, 0–6,
6–2; Altinkaya–Aydin d. M. Hickey–K. Reid 2–6, 6–2, 7–5, 6–4; H. Gerek
lost to Reid 7–5, 3–6, 3–6, 1–6; H. Ozdemir lost to Menton 0–6, 1–6,
1–6.

SECOND ROUND

Monaco d. Nigeria 4–1, Monte Carlo: L. Borfiga d. Allan 6–3, 6–2,
6–1; Vanderpol d. Awopegba 6–3, 6–2, 6–1; B. Balleret–Vanderpol d.
Allan–Awopegba 6–1, 6–2, 3–6, 6–3; Borfiga d. Awopegba 7–5, 6–4, 6–0;
Vanderpol lost to Allan 6–1, 3–6, 3–6, 5–7. **Hungary d. Finland 4–1,
Helsinki:** B. Machan lost to G. Berner 6–1, 7–9, 8–6, 6–8, 1–6; B.
Taroczy d. P. Saila 6–1, 6–3, 6–1; Machan–Taroczy d. M. Timonen–M.
Horsma 8–6, 7–9, 6–2, 6–3; Machan d. Saila 7–5, 6–8, 6–4, 6–4; Taroczy
d. Berner 3–6, 6–3, 6–4, 6–2. **Belgium d. Norway 5–0, Brussels:**
B. Mignot d. F. Ulleberg 6–0, 6–1, 6–4; P. Hombergen d. P. Hegna 6–3,
6–4, 6–2; Hombergen–Mignot d. Hegna–Ulleberg 6–1, 6–4, 6–3;
Mignot d. Hegna 6–2, 6–2, 6–0; Hombergen d. Ulleberg 7–5, 6–3, 6–2.
Bulgaria d. Turkey 5–0, Sofia: L. Genov d. R. Aydin 6–3, 6–0, 6–1;

B. Pampoulov d. H. Ozdemir 6–1, 6–3, 6–1; B. and M. Pampoulov d. Aydin–Ozdemir 6–0, 6–1, 6–3; M. Pampoulov d. Ambar 6–3, 6–0, 6–2; Petrov d. Ozdemir 6–3, 6–2, 7–9, 6–0.

THIRD ROUND

United Arab Republic d. Monaco 3–1, Monte Carlo: A. el Dawoodi d. E. Vanderpol 6–2, 6–2, 7–5; I. el Shafei d. L. Borfiga 6–4, 6–2, 7–5; El Shafei–Dawoodi d. Vanderpol–B. Balleret 6–3, 6–1, 6–4; M. Ghani lost to Balleret 5–7, 7–9, 6–4, 4–6.   **Hungary d. Holland 5–0, Budapest:** B. Taroczy d. R. Thung 7–5, 6–0, 6–1; S. Baranyi d. L. Sanders 6–4, 6–2, 6–4; Taroczy–B. Machan d. Sanders–N. Fleury 6–2, 8–6, 6–1; Taroczy d. Sanders 6–3, 6–4, 6–2; Baranyi d. Thung 6–0, 4–6, 6–0, 6–3. **France d. Belgium 4–1, Paris:** P. Dominguez d. P. Hombergen 6–1, 7–5, 6–1; F. Jauffret d. B. Mignot 8–6, 7–5, 6–1; Dominguez–Jauffret lost to Hombergen–Mignot 1–6, 6–4, 3–6, 14–16; Dominguez d. Mignot 6–2, 7–5, 7–5; Jauffret d. Hombergen 2–6, 6–1, 6–1, 10–8.   **Yugoslavia d. Bulgaria 4–1, Zagreb:** N. Pilic d. L. Genov 6–3, 6–4, 6–1; N. Spear lost to B. Pampoulov 6–0, 6–3, 3–6, 8–10, 2–6; Pilic–Spear d. B. and M. Pampoulov 6–1, 6–3, 7–5; Pilic d. B. Pampoulov 6–0, 6–2, 6–0; Spear d. Genov 6–1, 6–0, 6–1.

QUARTER-FINAL ROUND

Hungary d. United Arab Republic 3–2, Cairo: S. Baranyi lost to I. El Shafei 2–6, 4–6, 6–2, 4–6; B. Taroczy d. A. el Dawoodi 6–2, 6–3, 6–3; Taroczy–B. Machan d. El Shafei–Dawoodi 6–2, 6–4, 6–3; Taroczy lost to El Shafei 7–9, 2–6, 13–15; Baranyi d. el Dawoodi 6–1, 5–7, 6–3, 4–6, 6–2.   **France d. Yugoslavia 3–0, Paris:** P. Dominguez d. Z. Franulovic 12–10, 8–6, 6–2; F. Jauffret d. N. Pilic 6–3, 7–5, 2–6, 6–3; Dominguez–Jauffret d. Franulovic–Pilic 9–7, 3–6, 6–2, 6–3; Dominguez v. Pilic 3–6, 8–6, 3–6 unfin.

SEMI-FINAL ROUND

Czechoslovakia d. Hungary 4–1, Prague: J. Kodes d. B. Taroczy 6–3, 4–6, 6–8, 7–5, 8–6; J. Hrebec d. S. Baranyi 6–2, 3–6, 6–3, 6–3; Hrebec–Kodes d. Taroczy–R. Machan 6–3, 6–3, 6–4; Hrebec lost to Taroczy 4–6, 1–6, 2–6; Kodes d. Baranyi 8–6, 4–6, 3–6, 7–5, 6–4. **France d. Italy 3–2, Paris:** F. Jauffret d. A. Panatta 6–1, 6–4, 8–6; P. Dominguez lost to C. Barazzutti 6–4, 0–6, 1–6, 3–6; Dominguez–Jauffret lost to P. Bertolucci–Panatta 1–6, 4–6, 1–6; Dominguez d. Panatta 6–3, 1–6, 7–5, 6–3; Jauffret d. Barazzutti 6–2, 4–6, 6–3, 3–6, 6–3.

FINAL ROUND

Czechoslovakia d. France 3–2, Prague: J. Kodes d. P. Dominguez
6–1, 6–4, 1–6, 6–0; J. Hrebec d. F. Jauffret 6–4, 4–6, 6–3, 2–6, 6–0;
Kodes–Hrebec lost to Dominguez–P. Proisy 3–6, 6–3, 4–6, 6–1, 3–6;
Hrebec lost to Dominguez 6–4, 3–6, 4–6, 4–6; Kodes d. Jauffret 6–1,
7–5, 6–1.

Eastern Zone

FIRST ROUND

**South Korea d. Taiwan def.; South Vietnam d. Malaysia 5–0, Kuala
Lumpur:** Vo Van Thanh d. Lee Wai Ching 6–4, 6–2, 6–3; Ta Duy Bau
d. Zainudin Meah 5–7, 3–6, 6–4, 7–5, 6–2; Thanh–Ly Alline d. Meah–Ran
Poh Seng 8–6, 6–2, 1–6, 6–3; Thanh d. Meah 6–4, 6–4, 6–1; Bau d. Ching
8–6, 6–2, 6–4. **Sri Lanka d. Hong Kong def.; Philippines d.
Pakistan 3–2, Manila:** E. Cruz d. M. Mohammad 6–3, 6–4, 8–6; R. Rafon
lost to S. Meer 2–6, 3–6, 5–7; Cruz–M. Dominguez d. Mohammad–Meer
6–1, 6–4, 3–6, 6–3; Rafon d. Mohammad 6–4, 11–9, 12–10; Funtera lost
to Meer 1–6, 1–6, 0–6.

SECOND ROUND

**South Vietnam d. South Korea 3–2, Saigon; Philippines d. Sri
Lanka 3–1, Colombo:** A. Marcial d. L. Fernando 6–4, 6–3, 7–9, 4–6,
6–1; R. Rafon d. S. Suresh 6–4, 2–6, 6–1, 7–5; Marcial–M. Dominguez
d. N. and A. Fernando 6–2, 6–2, 6–1; R. Funtera lost to A. Fernando
2–6, 6–4, 1–6, 6–1, 3–6; Dominguez v. Suresh 1–6, 3–6, 3–2 unfin.
Japan d. Indonesia 5–0, Jakarta: J. Kamiwazumi d. G. Wijojo 6–4, 6–3,
6–4; T. Sakai d. A. Wijono 6–4, 6–3, 6–1; K. Hirai–S. Kato d.
Wijojo–Wijono 6–3, 3–6, 6–2, 4–6, 8–6; Hirai d. Hadiman 6–4, 6–4, 7–5;
Kato d. S. Sangitan 6–3, 8–6, 6–3.

THIRD ROUND

New Zealand d. Vietnam 5–0, Auckland: O. Parun d. Vo Van Thanh
6–1, 6–1, 6–1; B. Fairlie d. Banu 6–2, 6–2, 6–2; Fairlie–Parun d. Quoc–Ming
6–4, 6–2, 7–5; R. Simpson d. Van Thanh 6–1, 6–1, 6–2; J. Simpson d.
Banu 6–1, 6–1, 6–2. **Japan d. Philippines 5–0, Tokyo.**

SEMI-FINAL ROUND

New Zealand d. India 3–1, Lucknow: O. Parun d. V. Amritraj 4–6,
6–2, 10–12, 6–3, 6–4; B. Fairlie d. A. Amritraj 3–6, 6–8, 9–7, 6–4, 7–5;
Parun–Fairlie lost to V. and A. Amritraj 11–13, 4–6, 6–4, 4–6; Parun d.

A. Amritraj 5–7, 6–4, 6–3, 6–8, 6–2; Fairlie v. V. Amritraj 3–6, 6–8, 7–5 unfin. **Australia d. Japan 4–1, Adelaide:** J. D. Newcombe d. J. Kuki 6–1, 6–2, 6–3; P. Dent lost to T. Sakai 1–6, 6–4, 6–2, 4–6, 4–6; J. D. Alexander–Newcombe d. K. Hirai–Sakai 6–3, 5–7, 6–1, 3–6, 6–3; Newcombe d. Sakai 6–4, 6–3, 6–3; Dent d. Kuki 8–6, 6–4, 6–3.

FINAL ROUND
Australia d. New Zealand 4–0, Auckland: J. D. Newcombe d. B. Fairlie 7–5, 6–3, 7–5; K. R. Rosewall d. O. Parun 6–2, 6–4, 6–2; G. Masters–Newcombe d. Fairlie–Parun 6–4, 6–4, 7–5; Rosewall d. Fairlie 6–1, 9–11, 7–5, 9–7; Masters v. Parun 3–6, 8–10 unfin.

American Zone

FIRST ROUND
Uruguay d. Ecuador def.; USA d. Commonwealth Caribbean 5–0, Nassau: A. R. Ashe d. R. Russell 6–2, 6–1, 6–1; T. Gorman d. L. Rolle 6–4, 6–2, 6–4; E. Van Dillen–C. Pasarell d. J. Antonas–Rolle 6–2, 6–1, 6–1; Pasarell d. Rolle 1–6, 11–9, 6–1, 4–6, 6–2; Gorman d. Russell 6–2, 3–6, 6–1, 6–3. **Mexico d. Canada 4–1, Quebec:** R. Ramirez d. D. McCormick 6–0, 6–2, 6–4; J. Loyo-Mayo d. A. Bardsley 6–2, 6–2, 6–2; Ramirez–V. Zarazua d. R. Genois–P. Lamarche 6–1, 6–0, 6–2; Loyo-Mayo lost to McCormick 6–4, 4–6, 8–10, 2–6; R. Chavez d. Genois 0–6, 6–4, 6–3, 13–11.

SECOND ROUND
Argentina d. Uruguay 5–0, Montevideo: J. Ganzabal d. G. Stapff 6–4, 6–1, 6–1; R. Cano d. H. Roverano 6–1, 6–1, 6–4; Cano–Ganzabal d. J. L. Damiani–M. Laborde 6–4, 6–2, 6–4; Cano d. Stapff 6–2, 6–0, 6–1; T. Lynch d. Roverano 6–0, 6–1, 6–3. **Brazil d. Bolivia 5–0, Sao Paulo:** T. Koch d. R. Benavides 6–2, 6–2, 6–1; J. E. Mandarino d. E. Gorostiaga 6–0, 6–1, 6–2; Koch–Mandarino d. Benavides–Gorostiaga 6–4, 6–1, 6–2; Mandarino d. Benavides 6–3, 10–8, 6–8, 6–1; Koch d. Gorostiaga def. **Mexico d. USA 3–2, Palm Springs:** R. Ramirez d. S. R. Smith 3–6, 6–4, 6–1, 8–6; R. Chavez lost to R. Tanner 1–6, 3–6, 3–6; Ramirez–V. Zarazua d. R. C. Lutz–D. Stockton 4–6, 6–3, 6–8, 6–4, 6–4; Ramirez d. Tanner 7–5, 7–9, 6–4, 6–2; Chavez lost to Smith 2–6, 7–9, 1–6.

THIRD ROUND
Brazil d. Argentina 3–2, Sao Paulo: T. Koch d. R. Cano 6–3, 7–5, 2–6, 6–1; J. E. Mandarino lost to G. Vilas 6–8, 2–6, 13–11, 4–6;

Koch–Mandarino d. Cano–Vilas 6–1, 6–3, 7–5; Koch lost to Vilas 4–6, 3–6, 1–6; Mandarino d. Cano 2–6, 8–6, 3–6, 6–2, 6–1. **South Africa d. Mexico def.**

SEMI-FINAL ROUND
Chile d. Brazil 4–1, Santiago: J. Fillol d. T. Koch 6–2, 7–5, 8–6; P. Cornejo d. J. E. Mandarino 6–2, 7–5, 6–4; Cornejo–Fillol d. Koch–Mandarino 6–2, 6–2, 6–4; Fillol d. L. F. Tavares 6–3, 6–4, 6–2; J. Pinto Bravo lost to Koch 2–6, 3–6, 3–6. **South Africa d. Colombia def.**

FINAL ROUND
Chile d. South Africa 5–0, Santiago: P. Cornejo d. B. Mitton 4–6, 6–4, 6–2, 7–5; J. Fillol d. R. J. Moore 6–3, 6–3, 0–6, 3–6, 6–3; Cornejo–Fillol d. F. D. McMillan–Moore, 7–5, 6–2, 6–4; Fillol d. Mitton 2–6, 6–2, 3–6, 6–1, 7–5; Cornejo d. Moore 6–3, 6–4, 4–6, 6–3.

INTER-ZONE FINALS
Sweden d. Chile 4–1, Båstad: B. Borg d. P. Cornejo 3–6, 6–4, 7–5, 6–3; B. Andersson lost to J. Fillol 3–6, 2–6, 3–6; Borg–O. Bengtson d. Cornejo–Fillol 7–5, 6–2, 3–6, 6–3; Andersson d. Cornjeo 6–3, 14–12, 6–1; Borg d. Fillol 6–1, 6–2, 6–1. **Czechoslovakia d. Australia 3–1, Prague:** J. Kodes d. J. Alexander 6–4, 2–6, 7–5, 6–4; J. Hrebec d. A. D. Roche 3–6, 4–6, 6–1, 6–3, 6–3; F. Pala–V. Zednik lost to Alexander–P. Dent 3–6, 6–3, 2–6, 3–6; Kodes d. Roche 6–3, 6–1, 6–4; Hrebec v. Alexander 6–8, 3–6, 6–1, 6–6 unfin.

FINAL
Sweden d. Czechoslovakia 3–2, Stockholm: B. Borg d. J. Hrebec 6–1, 6–3, 6–0; O. Bengtson lost to J. Kodes 6–4, 2–6, 5–7, 4–6; Bengtson–Borg d. Kodes–Zednik 6–4, 6–4, 6–4; Borg d. Kodes 6–4, 6–2, 6–2; Bengtson lost to Hrebec 6–2, 3–6, 1–6, 4–6.

1976: ITALY
European Zone A

FIRST ROUND
Israel d. Turkey def.

SECOND ROUND
Ireland d. Rhodesia def.; Belgium d. Holland 4–1, Brussels: P. Hombergen d. L. Sanders 6–4, 3–6, 6–4, 6–4; B. Mignot d. T. S. Okker

505

6–3, 6–3, 12–14, 6–4; Hombergen–Mignot d. N. Fleury–Sanders 6–2, 4–6, 6–4, 6–4; Hombergen d. F. Hemmes 6–4, 8–6, 6–3; Mignot lost to Sanders 3–6, 5–7, 6–3, 3–6. **Denmark d. Finland 4–1, Copenhagen:** T. Christensen d. M. Timonen 6–1, 8–6, 7–5; L. Elvstrom d. G. Berner 6–4, 7–5, 13–11; Christensen–Elvstrom d. M. Horsma–Timonen 2–6, 9–7, 6–2, 6–2; Elvstrom lost to Timonen 1–6, 3–6, 1–6; Christensen d. Berner 6–3, 6–2, 1–6, 3–6, 6–4. **Monaco d. Israel 4–1, Monte Carlo:** B. Balleret d. Y. Shalem 6–0, 6–3, 6–1; L. Borfiga d. J. Wertheimer 6–2, 5–7, 6–3, 6–1; Borfiga–E. Vanderpol lost to J. Stabholz–Wertheimer 3–6, 6–3, 2–6, 4–6; Balleret d. Wertheimer 6–3, 6–4, 6–4; Borfiga d. Shalem 6–2, 6–0, 6–3.

THIRD ROUND

Egypt d. Ireland 4–1, Cairo: A. Ghani Mohamed d. M. P. Hickey 6–2, 6–2, 6–3; A. Gawed Mohamed d. Arden 6–3, 6–2, 6–2; A. Ghani Mohamed–Mubarek d. Hickey–S. J. Sorensen 6–2, 7–5, 6–3; A. Gawed Mohamed lost to Hickey 6–2, 6–4, 4–6, 4–6, 6–8; A. Ghani Mohamed d. Menton 8–6, 6–3, 1–6, 6–0. **Hungary d. Belgium 5–0, Brussels:** B. Taroczy d. P. Hombergen 6–4, 6–1, 6–1; P. Szoke d. B. Mignot 6–1, 8–6, 9–7; Szoke–Taroczy d. Hombergen–Mignot 6–2, 6–8, 6–4, 2–6, 6–3; Taroczy d. Mignot 6–2, 9–7, 4–6, 2–6, 6–3; Szoke d. Hombergen 10–8, 6–2, 6–3. **Germany d. Denmark 5–0, Fribourg:** H. J. Pohmann d. C. E. Hedelund 6–2, 6–2, 6–3; U. Pinner d. J. Rud 6–2, 6–0, 6–1; Pohmann–J. Fassbender d. Hedelund–K. Greger 6–2, 7–5, 6–4; Pohmann d. Rud 6–2, 6–1, 6–2; Pinner d. Hedelund 7–5, 6–0, 6–0. **USSR d. Monaco 5–0, Tblisi:** T. Kakulia d. L. Borfiga 7–5, 6–3, 6–4; V. Borisov d. B. Balleret 7–5, 6–2, 10–8; Kakulia–K. Pugayev d. Borfiga–Balleret 5–7, 6–3, 6–3, 6–3; Pugayev d. E. Vanderpol 6–0, 6–2, 6–2; Borisov d. Borfiga 6–4, 9–7, 7–5.

QUARTER-FINAL ROUND

Hungary d. Egypt 5–0, Budapest: P. Szoke d. A. Ghani Mohamed 6–2, 6–4, 6–0; B. Taroczy d. I. El Shafei 4–6, 6–3, 6–1, 6–1; Szoke–Taroczy d. El Shafei–Mohamed 6–0, 6–1, 6–2; Szoke d. El Shafei 6–1, 6–8, 6–2, 6–4; Taroczy d. Mohamed 6–2, 6–1, 6–4. **USSR d. Germany 4–1, Bad Homburg:** A. Metreveli d. U. Pinner 8–10, 6–3, 6–4, 6–2; T. Kakulia d. K. Meiler 0–6, 2–6, 1–1 def.; Metreveli–Kakulia d. H. J. Pohmann–J. Fassbender 4–6, 6–1, 5–7, 9–7, 6–4; Kakulia lost to Pinner 4–6, 5–7, 5–7; Metreveli d. Fassbender 6–3, 3–6, 6–1, 6–3.

SEMI-FINAL ROUND

Hungary d. Czechoslovakia 3–1, Budapest: B. Taroczy d. J. Kodes 6–3, 6–0, 6–3; P. Szoke lost to J. Hrebec 2–6, 3–6, 3–6; Szoke–Taroczy

d. Hrebec–Kodes 6–3, 6–4, 2–6, 3–6, 6–4; Taroczy d. Hrebec 6–3, 6–3, 6–2; Szoke v. Kodes 6–4, 3–6, 6–3, 3–6 unfin. **USSR d. Spain 4–1, Donetsk:** A. Metreveli d. M. Orantes 6–4, 2–6, 6–4, 6–4; T. Kakulia d. A. Munoz 6–2, 6–1, 6–3; Kakulia–Metreveli lost to Orantes–J. Gisbert 1–6, 6–8, 3–6; Metreveli d. Munoz 6–3, 6–3, 4–6, 6–4; Kakulia d. A. Gimenez 6–2, 6–4.

FINAL ROUND
USSR d. Hungary 4–1, Tblisi: A. Metreveli d. S. Benyik 6–3, 7–5, 6–3; T. Kakulia lost to B. Taroczy 3–6, 3–6, 4–6; Kakulia–Metreveli d. Szoke–Taroczy 12–10, 6–0, 6–4; Metreveli d. Taroczy 7–5, 6–1, 9–7; Kakulia d. Benyik 6–4, 6–8, 3–6, 6–3, 6–1.

European Zone B

PRELIMINARY ROUND
Nigeria d. Algeria def.

FIRST ROUND
Iran d. Nigeria def.; Portugal d. Luxembourg 5–0, Luxembourg: J. Vilela d. A. Neu 6–1, 6–4, 6–1; J. Largos d. T. Stark 6–2, 6–1, 7–5; A. va Pincto–Vilela d. J. Brucher–F. Claude 6–4, 9–7, 6–0; Vilela d. Stark 6–1, 6–2, 6–3; Largos d. Neu 6–0, 6–3, 6–1.

SECOND ROUND
Switzerland d. Iran 3–2, Teheran: P. Kanderal d. T. Akbari 6–2, 6–4, 7–5; H. Gunthardt lost to K. Derafshijavan 4–6, 5–7, 6–3, 8–6, 3–6; Kanderal–M. Werren d. Derafshijavan–A. Madani 6–4, 6–1, 6–4; Kanderal d. Derafshijavan 6–2, 6–2, 6–4; Gunthardt lost to Akbari 1–6, 6–2, 4–6, 3–6. **Austria d. Bulgaria 4–1, Sofia:** P. Feigl d. B. Pampoulov 3–6, 2–6, 6–4, 6–1, 6–2; H. Kary d. L. Genov 3–6, 6–1, 6–1, 6–3; Feigl–Kary d. B. and M. Pampoulov 6–4, 6–4, 8–10, 7–5; Kary d. L. Petrov 6–4, 6–0, 6–0; Feigl lost to Genov 1–6, 8–10, 3–6. **Poland d. Norway 5–0, Warsaw:** W. Fibak d. P. Hegna 2–6, 6–4, 6–0, 6–0; J. Niedzwiedzki d. E. Ulleberg 6–8, 6–3, 7–5, 6–2; Fibak–T. Nowicki d. Hegnal–Ulleberg 6–0, 7–5, 6–0; Fibak d. Ulleberg 6–1, 6–2, 6–0; Niedzwiedzki d. Hegna 6–3, 5–7, 6–4, 6–2. **Greece d. Portugal 4–1, Greece:** N. Kalogeropoulos d. Vilela 6–3, 6–2, 6–2; N. Kelaides d. J. Lagos 6–4, 6–2, 6–1; Kalogeropoulos–Kelaides d. Vilela–Lagos 5–7, 6–3, 6–4, 6–2; Kelaides lost to Vilela 3–6, 6–3, 7–5, 4–6, 3–6; Kalogeropoulos d. Largos 6–1, 6–2, 6–1.

THIRD ROUND

Great Britain d. Switzerland 4–1, Zurich: C. J. Mottram d. D. Sturdza 6–2, 7–5, 6–2; R. Taylor d. P. Kanderal 3–6, 10–12, 6–3, 6–2, 6–2; Mottram–J. M. Lloyd lost to Kanderal–Sturdza 12–10, 3–6, 3–6, 4–6; Taylor d. Sturdza 6–4, 3–6, 6–2, 6–3; Mottram d. Kanderal 6–2, 6–2, 6–3. **Rumania d. Austria 4–1, Vienna:** D. Haradau lost to H. Kary 2–6, 4–6, 1–6; I. Nastase d. P. Feigl 6–1, 6–3, 7–5; Nastase–V. Marcu d. Feigl–Kary 6–4, 8–6, 3–6, 6–3; Nastase d. Kary 6–3, 7–5, 6–1; Haradau d. Feigl 7–5, 4–6, 0–6, 8–6, 7–5. **Italy d. Poland 5–0, Florence:** A. Panatta d. M. Dobrowolski 6–1, 6–0, 6–3; P. Bertolucci d. H. Drymalski 7–9, 6–4, 6–4, 6–2; Panatta–Bertolucci d. Drymalski–J. Jasinski 6–1, 6–4, 8–6; Bertolucci d. Dobrowolski 6–4, 6–4, 6–3; Panatta d. Drymalski 6–1, 6–0, 6–4. **Yugoslavia d. Greece 5–0, Zagreb:** N. Pilic d. N. Kalogeropoulos 6–3, 6–2, 6–2; Z. Franulovic d. N. Kelaidis 6–4, 6–0. 6–2; Franulovic–Pilic d. Kalogeropoulos–Kelaidis 6–3, 6–3, 7–9, 6–2; Pilic d. Kelaidis 6–2, 6–3, 7–5; Franulovic d. Kalogeropoulos 6–4, 6–0, 6–0.

QUARTER-FINAL ROUND

Great Britain d. Rumania 5–0, Eastbourne: R. Taylor d. V. Sotiriu 6–1, 6–1, 6–4; C. J. Mottram d. D. Haradau 6–2, 6–0, 6–2; Mottram–Taylor d. Haradau–V. Marcu 6–2, 6–1, 6–4; Mottram d. Sotiriu 6–2, 6–0, 6–4; Taylor d. Haradau 6–1, 5–7, 6–3, 6–1. **Italy d. Yugoslavia 5–0, Bologna:** C. Barazzutti d. Z. Franulovic 6–1, 7–5, 6–4; A. Panatta d. N. Pilic 6–3, 6–4, 6–3; P. Bertolucci–Panatta d. Franulovic–Pilic 6–2, 9–7, 7–5; Panatta d. Franulovic 6–1, 1–6, 6–3; Barazzutti d. Pilic 0–6, 6–4, 6–4.

SEMI-FINAL ROUND

Great Britain d. France 4–1, Eastbourne: R. Taylor d. P. Proisy 3–6, 6–2, 6–3, 6–2; J. M. Lloyd d. F. Jauffret 4–6, 6–2, 6–4, 4–6, 8–6; D. A. and J. M. Lloyd d. Jauffret–Proisy 6–2, 6–4, 9–11, 6–3; J. M. Lloyd lost to Proisy 1–6, 0–6, 4–6; Taylor d. Jauffret 6–2, 6–3, 6–1. **Italy d. Sweden 4–0, Rome:** A. Panatta d. R. Norberg 6–2, 6–2, 7–5; C. Barazzutti d. K. Johansson 6–2, 6–4, 3–6, 3–6, 6–2; P. Bertolucci–Panatta d. O. Bengtson–Norberg 7–5, 6–2, 7–5; A. Zugarelli d. Johansson 7–5, 5–7, 8–6, 4–6, 8–6; Barazzutti v. Norberg 6–4, 2–6 unfin.

FINAL ROUND

Italy d. Great Britain 4–1, Wimbledon: A. Zugarelli d. R. Taylor 6–1, 7–5, 3–6, 6–1; A. Panatta d. J. M. Lloyd 5–7, 6–3, 6–3, 2–6, 6–4; P. Bertolucci–Panatta lost to J. M and D. A. Lloyd 8–6, 6–3, 3–6, 16–18,

2–6; Panatta d. Taylor 3–6, 6–2, 6–4, 6–4; Zugarelli d. J. M. Lloyd 4–6, 6–8, 6–1, 6–1, 6–1.

American Zone

FIRST ROUND

Canada d. Colombia 5–0, Montreal: A. Bardsley d. O. Agudelo 6–0, 6–3, 6–2; D. Power d. A. Betancour 6–4, 22–24, 2–6, 6–3, 7–5; Bardsley–R. Genois d. Agudelo–Betancour 6–2, 9–7, 6–4; Bardsley d. J. Restrepo 6–2, 6–4, 6–2; Genois d. Agudelo 6–1, 6–4, 7–5. **Mexico d. Commonwealth Caribbean 5–0, Mexico City:** L. Baraldi d. R. Russell 6–2, 6–1, 6–4; M. Lara d. J. Antonas 6–1, 6–3, 6–2; R. Chavez–A. Gonzales d. A. Price–M. Valdes 6–4, 6–4, 6–4; Lara d. Russell 6–0, 6–0, 6–4; Baraldi d. Antonas 6–3, 6–1, 6–1. **Brazil d. Bolivia def.; Peru d. Uruguay 3–2:** E. Maynetto lost to F. Barriola 5–7, 1–6, 4–6; M. Maurtua d. G. Stapff 6–1, 6–0, 6–4; Maurtua–Maynetto d. Barriola–A. Laborde 6–3, 3–6, 6–4, 3–6, 7–5; Maurtua d. Barriola 7–5, 6–1, 6–4; Maynetto lost to Stapff 6–8, 6–2, 5–7, 7–9.

SECOND ROUND

Mexico d. Canada 3–2, Mexico City: J. Loyo-Mayo d. R. Genois 4–6, 6–1, 6–2, 8–6; M. Lara d. D. Power 6–2, 6–1, 6–2; L. Baraldi–R. Chavez lost to A. Bardsley–Genois 6–2, 4–6, 4–6, 8–6, 4–6; Loyo-Mayo lost to Power 6–4, 2–6, 6–1, 1–6, 5–7; Lara d. Genois 4–6, 6–2, 1–6, 6–1, 7–5. **USA d. Venezuela 5–0, Tucson:** J. Connors d. H. Hose 6–4, 6–1, 6–3; R. Tanner d. J. Andrew 6–4, 6–3, 6–2; E. van Dillen–R. Stockton d. Andrew–Hose 6–2, 6–2, 7–5; Connors d. Andrew 6–2, 6–1, 6–2; Tanner d. Hose 3–6, 6–3, 6–2, 6–4. **Brazil d. Peru 5–0, Brasilia:** C. Kirmayr d. Acuna 6–0, 6–0, 6–0; J. E. Mandarino d. M. Maurtua 6–4, 4–6, 6–2, 4–6, 6–3; Kirmayr–F. Gentil d. Maurtua–Carlos 6–2, 6–3, 6–3; Mandarino d. Acuna 6–1, 6–3, 3–6, 7–5; Kirmayr d. Maurtua 6–1, 6–4, 6–1. **Argentina d. Ecuador 5–0, Guayaquil:** J. Ganzabal d. R. Ycaza 8–6, 6–2, 3–6, 11–9; R. Cano d. G. Nunez 3–6, 6–1, 4–6, 6–2, 6–2; L. Alvarez–Cano d. M. Olvera–Ycaza 6–4, 6–3, 11–13, 6–4; Ganzabal d. Nunez 6–1, 6–1, 6–0; Cano d. Ycaza 6–4, 6–4, 7–5.

THIRD ROUND

Mexico d. USA 3–2, Mexico City: M. Lara lost to J. Connors 2–6, 1–6, 6–3, 6–4, 5–7; R. Ramirez d. B. Gottfried 6–1, 6–4, 6–2; Lara–Ramirez d. R. Stockton–R. Tanner 6–4, 8–6, 3–6, 6–3; Lara lost to Gottfried 6–3, 2–6, 6–3, 6–8, 1–6; Ramirez d. Connors 2–6, 6–3, 6–3,

6–4. **Argentina d. Brazil 5–0, Buenos Aires:** R. Cano d. L. F. Tavarez 6–3, 6–4, 7–5; L. Alvarez d. C. Kirmayr 6–4, 6–1, 6–1; Alvarez–Cano d. Kirmayr–Tavarez 3–6, 6–3, 6–4, 6–3; Alvarez d. Tavarez 6–3, 6–3, 10–8; Caviglia d. Enck 6–4, 6–4, 6–4.

SEMI-FINAL ROUND
South Africa d. Mexico def.; Chile d. Argentina 3–2, Santiago: J. Fillol d. R. Cano 6–8, 6–4, 6–1, 6–2; P. Cornejo lost to G. Vilas 2–6, 8–6, 1–6, 6–4, 2–6; Cornejo–Fillol d. Cano–Vilas 4–6, 6–4, 7–5, 6–4; Cornejo d. Cano 3–6, 6–2, 8–6, 7–5; Fillol lost to Vilas 3–6, 1–6, 2–6.

FINAL ROUND
Chile d. South Africa 3–2, Santiago: P. Cornejo lost to B. Mitton 4–6, 6–3, 5–7, 5–7; J. Fillol d. R. J. Moore 7–5, 8–6, 6–3; Cornejo–Fillol lost to B. Bertram–F. D. McMillan 6–3, 10–8, 2–6, 4–6, 3–6; Cornejo d. Moore 5–7, 6–2, 10–8, 7–5; Fillol d. Mitton 7–5, 6–3, 4–6, 6–2.

Eastern Zone

FIRST ROUND
India d. Thailand 5–0, Amritsar; Pakistan d. Malaysia 5–0, Kuala Lumpur: Meer Mohammad Khan d. Tan Poh Seng 6–2, 6–2, 6–2; Saeed Meer d. Mohammad Akbar Baba 6–3, 6–0, 6–3; Meer–Khan d. Zain-ud-Din Meah–Seng 6–2, 6–4, 7–5; Khan d. Meah 7–9, 6–2, 6–0, 6–3; Meer d. Seng 6–4, 6–0, 6–2.

SECOND ROUND
Philippines d. Taiwan 4–0, Taipei: E. Cruz d. Tang Fu Shan 6–4, 6–1, 6–2; M. Dominguez d. Lin Teng Wen 6–1, 6–0, 6–1; Cruz–Dominguez d. Tang Fu Shan–Ling Ten Wen 6–3, 6–1, 6–3; A. Marcial d. Y. Lin 6–0, 6–0, 6–2. **India d. Japan 3–2, Tokyo:** V. Amritraj d. J. Sakai 7–5, 7–5, 0–6, 6–2; A. Amritraj lost to J. Kamiwazumi 5–7, 6–8, 7–9; A. and V. Amritraj d. Sakai–K. Haiai 6–3, 4–6, 2–6, 6–3, 6–4; A. Amritraj d. Sakai 3–6, 6–0, 6–4, 6–3; S. Menon lost to J. Kuki 6–4, 3–6, 1–6, 4–6.
Pakistan d. Sri Lanka 4–0, Colombo: Meer Mohammad Khan d. L. Fernando 6–3, 2–6, 6–1, 6–0; Saeed Meer d. A. Perera 6–4, 6–1, 6–0; Meer–Khan d. Fernando–S. Melvani 6–3, 6–4, 6–3; Meer d. Fernando 6–2, 6–4, 7–5; Tayyab Ifitkhar v. Perera 2–6, 6–4, 3–3 unfin.
Indonesia d. Korea 3–2, Djakarta: A. Wijono lost to Kim Moon III 8–6, 4–6, 9–11, 3–6; G. Widjojo lost to Kim Sung Bai 6–3, 1–6, 7–9, 2–6; Yustdjo Tarik–Hadiman d. Chai Bo Kil–Chun Sang Nam 6–4, 8–6,

6–1; Wijono d. Kim Sung Bai 6–2, 6–4, 9–7; Widjojo d. Kim Moon III 6–2, 6–3, 7–5.

THIRD ROUND

India d. Philippines 4–1, Manila: C. Mukerjea d. E. Cruz 3–6, 6–4, 6–3, 3–6, 6–4; S. Menon d. A. Dominguez 6–2, 6–4, 6–3; Menon–Mukerjea d. Cruz–Dominguez 6–4, 6–2, 4–6, 6–4; Mukerjea d. Dominguez 2–6, 2–6, 6–3, 6–4, 9–7; Menon lost to Cruz def.
Indonesia d. Pakistan 4–1, Karachi: G. Widjojo lost to S. Meer 6–2, 10–12, 7–9, 2–6; A. Wijono d. M. Mohammed 6–1, 6–4, 6–4; Widjojo–Wijono d. Meer–A. Hussain 6–2, 7–5, 11–9; Wijono d. Meer 3–6, 6–2, 6–3, 3–6, 6–4; Widjojo d. Mohammed 9–7, 6–1.

SEMI-FINAL ROUND

New Zealand d. India 3–2, Auckland: B. Fairlie d. A. Amritraj 6–2, 6–4, 7–5; O. Parun lost to V. Amritraj 6–4, 3–6, 6–8, 5–7; Fairlie–Parun d. A. and V. Amritraj 6–1, 6–1, 15–13; Fairlie lost to V. Amritraj 3–6, 8–10, 1–6; Parun d. A. Amritraj 6–2, 9–7, 6–4. **Australia d. Indonesia 5–0, Hobart:** A. D. Roche d. A. Wijono 6–0, 6–0, 6–0; J. D. Newcombe d. G. Widjojo 6–1, 6–2, 7–5; Newcombe–Roche d. Wijono–Widjojo 6–3, 6–2, 6–1; Newcombe d. Wijono 6–2, 6–1, 6–1; Roche d. Paris 6–3, 6–2, 6–2.

FINAL ROUND

Australia d. New Zealand 3–1, Brisbane–Nottingham, England: R. Case lost to B. Fairlie 6–3, 8–10, 1–6, 6–2, 4–6; J. D. Newcombe d. O. Parun 8–6, 6–3, 7–5; Newcombe–A. D. Roche d. Fairlie–Parun 6–1, 3–6, 6–3, 7–5 (played 28, 29 February and 2 March in Brisbane); Newcombe d. Fairlie 8–6, 5–7, 11–9, 6–3 (played 19 June, Nottingham, England).

INTER-ZONE FINALS

Chile d. USSR def.; Italy d. Australia 3–2, Rome: C. Barazzutti d. J. D. Newcombe 7–5, 6–1, 6–4; A. Panatta lost to J. Alexander 5–7, 3–6, 4–6; Panatta–P. Bertolucci d. Newcombe–A. D. Roche 6–3, 6–4, 6–3; Barazzutti lost to Alexander 2–6, 2–6, 7–5, 6–4, 2–6; Panatta d. Newcombe 5–7, 8–6, 6–4, 6–2.

FINAL ROUND

Italy d. Chile 4–1, Santiago: C. Barazzutti d. J. Fillol 7–5, 4–6, 7–5, 6–1; A. Panatta d. P. Cornejo 6–3, 6–1, 6–3; P. Bertolucci–Panatta d. Cornejo–Fillol 3–6, 6–2, 9–7, 6–3; Panatta d. Fillol 8–6, 6–4, 3–6, 10–8; A. Zugarelli lost to B. Prajoux 4–6, 4–6, 2–6.

1977: AUSTRALIA
European Zone A

FIRST PRELIMINARY ROUND
Algeria d. Morocco def.

SECOND PRELIMINARY ROUND
Iran d. Algeria 5–0: T. Akbar d. M. Abdeslam 6–0, 6–4, 6–3; K. D. Javan d. B. Sebti 6–2, 6–2, 7–5; E. Nemati–M. Khodai d. Abdeslam–Sebti 6–2, 6–2, 6–3; Khodai d. S. Moussa 6–0, 6–1, 6–3; Nemati d. Abdeslam 6–1, 6–3, 6–2.

FIRST ROUND
Poland d. Norway 5–0, Posnan: T. Nowicki d. P. Hegna 6–3, 6–3, 6–2; W. Fibak d. O. Foss Abrehamson 6–0, 6–0, 6–0; Fibak–J. Niedzwiedzki d. Hegna–J. Munch–Soegaard 6–0, 8–6, 6–3; Nowicki d. Abrehamson 6–2, 6–2, 6–1; Fibak d. Hegna 6–1, 5–7, 7–5, 6–3.
Switzerland d. Rhodesia 3–2, Scheuren: H. Guenthardt d. R. McKenzie 6–1, 6–2, 6–0; N. Hurlimann lost to C. Dowdeswell 5–7, 5–7, 6–0, 3–6; Guenthardt–P. Kanderal d. Dowdeswell–S. Towers 8–6, 10–8, 6–4; Guenthardt lost to Dowdeswell 6–0, 7–9, 2–6, 3–6; Hurlimann d. McKenzie 6–2, 6–1, 6–0. **Belgium d. Bulgaria 3–2, Brussels:** B. Mignot lost to L. Jenov 6–1, 2–6, 6–3, 1–6, 0–6; P. Hombergen d. B. Pampoulov 8–6, 6–1, 5–7, 4–6, 6–0; Hombergen–Mignot d. B. and M. Pampoulov 6–3, 6–4, 6–2; Mignot d. M. Pampoulov 6–2, 6–4, 6–4; Hombergen lost to Jenov 6–2, 3–6, 6–4, 3–6, 1–6.
Ireland d. Iran 3–2, Dublin: G. Sorensen lost to M. Bahrami 7–5, 9–11, 3–6, 6–2, 2–6; J. McArdle d. K. D. Javan 6–4, 6–2, 4–6, 15–17, 6–3; M. Hickey–Sorensen d. Bahrami–Javan 6–2, 2–6, 6–4, 6–4; Sorensen d. Javan 7–5, 6–3, 6–3; McArdle lost to Bahrami 3–6, 9–11, 2–6.

SECOND ROUND
Poland d. W. Germany 3–1, Warsaw: J. Niedzwiedzki lost to U. Pinner 9–11, 2–6, 1–6; W. Fibak d. K. Meiler 6–0, 6–1, 6–1; Fibak–T. Nowicki d. Meiler–J. Fassbender 4–6, 8–10, 6–3, 6–4, 6–3; Fibak d. Pinner 10–8, 6–3, 6–4. **France d. Switzerland 3–2, Zurich:** P. Dominguez d. P. Kanderal 6–3, 16–14, 6–4; R. L. Haillet d. H. Guenthardt 6–3, 6–3, 6–3; Dominguez–Haillet d. Kanderal–D. Sturdza 4–6, 9–7, 4–6, 6–1, 6–4; Haillet lost to Kanderal 13–15, 5–7, 6–2, 3–6; Dominguez lost to Guenthardt 6–8, 3–6, 8–10. **Rumania d. Belgium 5–0, Bucharest:** I. Nastase d. B. Boileau 6–1, 6–4, 6–1; D. Haradau d. J. P. Richer 6–1, 6–3, 6–3; Nastase–I. Tiriac d. Demuynck–Steveaux 6–2, 6–1, 6–4; Haradau d.

Boileau 6–1, 6–2, 6–3; Nastase d. Richer 6–2, 6–2, 6–2. **Czechoslovakia d. Ireland 5–0, Prague:** T. Smid d. P. Ledbetter 6–0, 6–0, 6–2; J. Hrebec d. J. McArdle 6–0, 6–1, 6–2; Smid–G. Granat d. McArdie–J. O'Brien 6–0, 6–0, 6–2; Hrebec d. Ledbetter 6–0, 6–1, 6–0; F. Pala d. McArdle 6–2, 6–3, 6–0.

QUARTER-FINAL ROUND

France d. Poland 5–0, Warsaw: P. Dominguez d. H. Drzymalski 8–6, 6–2, 6–4; F. Jauffret d. T. Nowicki 6–0, 6–0, 6–2; Dominguez–J. Jauffret d. Nowicki–H. Niedzewski 6–8, 10–8, 1–6, 3–6, 6–2; Dominguez d. Nowicki 3–6, 7–5, 8–6, 9–7; Jauffret d. Drzymalski 6–4, 6–0.
Rumania d. Czechoslovakia 3–1, Bucharest: D. Haradau lost to J. Kodes 6–2, 2–6, 2–6, 3–6; I. Nastase d. J. Hrebec 6–1, 1–0 def.; Nastase–I. Tiriac d. Kodes–Hrebec 6–1, 6–3, 6–3; Nastase d. Kodes 6–2, 6–2, 6–4; Haradau v. Hrebec 1–6, 6–3 unfin.

SEMI-FINAL ROUND

France w.o. USSR disqualified. Rumania d. Great Britain 4–1, Bucharest: I. Nastase d. J. Feaver 6–1, 6–2, 4–6, 6–4; D. Haradau d. J. M. Lloyd 2–6, 7–5, 6–0, 6–1; Nastase–I. Tiriac d. D. A. and J. M. Lloyd 9–7, 2–6, 6–4, 9–7; T. Marcu lost to R. A. Lewis 6–4, 1–6, 1–6, 3–6; Haradau d. Feaver 5–7, 6–3, 4–6, 6–1, 6–3.

FINAL ROUND

France d. Rumania 3–2, Paris: F. Jauffret d. I. Nastase 3–6, 0–6, 6–4, 6–3, 6–1; P. Proisy d. D. Haradau 6–2, 6–4, 8–6; Jauffret–P. Dominguez lost to Nastase–I. Tiriac 3–6, 4–6, 6–3, 5–7; Jauffret d. Haradau 6–1, 6–4, 6–4; Proisy lost to Nastase 4–6, 6–4, 6–8, 1–6.

European Zone B

FIRST PRELIMINARY ROUND
Turkey d. Kenya def.

SECOND PRELIMINARY ROUND
Israel d. Turkey 5–0, Tel Aviv: S. Glickstein d. M. Gurlar 7–5, 6–1, 6–0; Y. Wertheimer d. C. Atas 6–0, 6–0, 6–2; Sher–Wertheimer d. Gurlar–A. Yenilmez 6–1, 6–1, 6–0; Wertheimer d. Gurlar 6–1, 6–3, 6–1; Glickstein d. Yenilmez 6–0, 6–3, 6–0. **Finland d. Luxembourg 5–0, Mondorf–les–Bains:** L. Palin d. F. Claude 6–3, 6–2, 6–2; G. Berner d.

M. Weitzel 6–0, 6–0, 6–1; Berner–P. Saila d. Claude–Weitzel 6–0, 6–3, 6–1; Palin d. Genevo 6–1, 6–2, 6–1; Berner d. Claude 6–2, 6–1, 6–1.

FIRST ROUND

Holland d. Israel 5–0, Holland: L. Sanders d. S. Glickstein 6–2, 6–4, 6–1; F. Hemmes d. Y. Wertheimer 5–7, 8–6, 1–6, 6–4, 6–0; Hemmes–Sanders d. Glickstein–Wertheimer 4–6, 6–2, 6–2, 6–2; Hemmes d. Glickstein 6–4, 6–2, 6–4; Sanders d. Wertheimer 6–3, 6–0, 6–1. **Greece d. Denmark 3–1, Athens:** N. Kelaides d. C. E. Hedelund 6–3, 4–6, 6–8, 6–3, 10–8; N. Kalogeropoulos d. T. Christensen 6–1, 6–3, 6–4; Kalogeropoulos–Kelaides lost to Christensen–Hedelund 2–6, 4–6, 2–6; Kalogeropoulos d. Hedelund 6–2, 6–3, 6–4; Kelaides v. Christensen 4–6, 6–1, 7–5, 7–9 unfin. **Monaco d. Portugal 4–1, Lisbon:** B. Balleret d. J. Vilela 0–6, 6–2, 6–3, 6–3; L. Borfiga d. S. Cruz 6–2, 6–4, 6–3; Balleret–Borfiga d. Vilela–Peralta 6–1, 7–5, 6–2; Balleret d. Cruz 5–7, 7–5, 5–7, 6–3, 6–2; Borfiga lost to Vilela 6–4, 6–2, 4–6, 2–3 def. **Austria d. Finland 5–0, Vienna:** P. Feigl d. P. Saila 6–4, 6–2, 6–3; H. Kary d. M. Timonen 6–4, 6–2, 6–3; Kary–C. Letcher d. G. Berner–Saila 10–8, 6–1, 6–2; Feigl d. Timonen 6–2, 6–4, 6–4; Kary d. Saila 6–1, 6–1, 6–3.

SECOND ROUND

Yugoslavia d. Holland 5–0, Scheveningen: N. Pilic d. F. Hemmes 6–0, 6–3, 6–2; Z. Franulovic d. L. Sanders 3–6, 6–1, 6–4, 5–7, 6–2; Franulovic–Pilic d. Sanders–R. Thung 6–0, 9–7, 3–6, 6–4; Franulovic d. Hemmes 6–4, 6–2, 4–6, 6–1; Pilic d. Sanders 7–5, 6–3, 6–2. **Spain d. Greece 5–0, Athens:** J. Higueras d. N. Kelaidis 6–0, 6–0, 6–1; M. Orantes d. N. Kalogeropoulos 6–1, 6–2, 6–0; A. Munoz–J. Soler d. Kelaidis–Kalogeropoulos 6–3, 3–6, 6–2, 8–6; Higueras d. Kalogeropoulos 6–4, 6–0, 6–2; Orantes d. Kelaidis 6–2, 6–3, 6–2. **Sweden d. Monaco 5–0, Uppsala:** R. Norberg d. B. Balleret 9–7, 3–6, 6–4, 6–3; K. Johansson d. L. Borfiga 6–1, 6–1, 6–1; J. Norback–D. Palm d. Balleret–Borfiga 7–5, 6–2, 6–2; Norberg d. Borfiga 6–3, 6–2, 6–2; Johansson d. Balleret 6–1, 6–1, 6–2. **Austria d. Egypt 5–0, Vienna:** C. Letcher d. A. Ghani 6–0, 6–0, 6–1; H. Kary d. I. El Shafei 6–2, 7–5, 3–6, 6–3; Kary–Letcher d. El Shafei–I. El Sarka 6–2, 6–2, 7–9, 6–2; Kary d. El Sarka 6–2, 6–0, 6–2; Letcher d. El Shafei 6–2, 6–2, 6–0.

QUARTER-FINAL ROUND

Spain d. Yugoslavia 4–1, Belgrade: M. Orantes d. Z. Ilin 6–1, 6–3, 6–2; J. Higueras lost to N. Pilic 3–6, 2–6, 1–6; A. Munoz–Orantes d. Pilic–Ilin 7–5, 3–6, 6–2, 8–6; Higueras d. Ilin 6–3, 6–1, 4–6, 6–2; Orantes d. Pilic 7–5, 6–2, 6–2. **Sweden d. Austria 5–0, Stockholm:** R. Norberg

d. C. Letcher 4–6, 4–6, 6–3, 6–2, 6–2; K. Johansson d. H. Kary 4–6, 7–5, 6–4, 6–3; O. Bengtson–Norberg d. Kary–Letcher 6–4, 6–4, 6–3; Norberg d. P. Feigl 9–7, 6–4, 6–4; Johansson d. Letcher 6–1, 6–3, 6–3.

SEMI-FINAL ROUND

Spain d. Hungary 3–2, Budapest: J. Higueras d. J. Benyik 6–4, 6–1, 6–1; M. Orantes lost to B. Taroczy 5–7, 6–4, 6–1, 1–6, 1–6; Higueras–Orantes lost to P. Szoke–Taroczy 2–6, 3–6, 6–4, 1–6; Orantes d. Benyik 11–9, 6–3, 6–2; Higueras d. Taroczy 0–6, 8–6, 6–4, 6–4. **Italy d. Sweden 4–1, Bastad:** A. Panatta d. B. Andersson 7–5, 6–4, 6–4; C. Barazzutti d. R. Norberg 6–3, 6–1, 6–2; P. Bertolucci–Panatta d. J. Norback–Norberg 6–3, 6–3, 3–6, 6–4; A. Zugarelli lost to Norback 1–6, 6–3, 2–6, 2–6; Barazzutti d. Anderson 4–6, 6–2, 6–1, 6–3.

FINAL ROUND

Italy d. Spain 3–2, Barcelona: C. Barazzutti lost to J. Higueras 4–6, 4–6, 1–6; A. Panatta d. M. Orantes 6–4, 3–6, 6–3, 6–1; Barazzutti–Panatta d. A. Munoz–Higueras 6–4, 7–5, 6–4; Barazzutti d. Orantes 7–5, 7–5, 6–1; Panatta lost to J. Soler 1–6, 0–6.

American Zone

FIRST ROUND

Bolivia d. Peru 4–1, La Paz: J. C. Alvarado lost to F. Maynetto 4–6, 2–6, 2–6; R. Benavides d. L. A. Olmedo 6–0, 6–1, 6–2; Alvarado–Benavides d. Maynetto–Olmedo 6–4, 6–2, 6–2; Benavides d. Maynetto 6–1, 8–6, 6–1; Alvarado d. C. Hohnhold 6–2, 6–0, 6–1. **Ecuador d. Uruguay 3–2, Montevideo:** C. Nunez lost to J. L. Damiani 1–6, 6–3, 2–6, 6–4, 2–6; R. Ycaza d. H. L. Roverano 9–7, 5–7, 9–7, 6–3; Ycaza–Nunez d. Damiani–Roverano 3–6, 8–6, 6–4, 6–4; Ycaza d. Damiani 6–4, 6–2, 6–1; Nunez lost to Roverano 3–6, 6–8, 1–6. **Venezuela d. Colombia 4–0, Caracas:** H. Hose d. J. Restrepo 6–2, 6–4, 6–4; J. Andrew d. O. Agudelo 7–5, 12–10, 6–2; Andrew–Hose d. Agudelo–Restrepo 5–7, 9–7, 6–2, 6–3; F. Winckelmann d. Rodrigo Ramirez 6–3, 6–1, 6–3; Hose v. Agudelo 6–4, 5–7, 6–3, 1–1 unfin. **Canada d. Commonwealth Caribbean 5–0, Ottawa:** J. Boyce d. J. Antonas 6–2, 6–2, 6–4; B. Genois d. L. Rolle 6–3, 6–4, 3–6, 6–1; G. Halder–D. Power d. Antonas–Rolle 4–6, 6–3, 2–6, 7–5, 6–4; Genois d. Antonas 9–7, 6–0, 6–2; Boyce d. Rolle 5–7, 9–7, 6–4, 6–4.

SECOND ROUND

Brazil d. Bolivia 4–1, Sao Paulo: T. Koch d. J. C. Alvarado 6–1, 4–6, 6–1, 6–0; C. Kirmayr d. R. Benavides 6–0, 6–1, 7–5; Kirmayr–Koch d. Alvarado–Benavides 6–1, 6–2, 6–2; Goes d. Chiarella 6–0, 6–0, 6–4; Kirmayr lost to Alvarado def.   **Argentina d. Ecuador 4–1, Buenos Aires:** R. Cano d. R. Ycaza 6–3, 3–6, 6–1, 6–2; F. Fontana d. M. Olvera 5–7, 8–6, 6–1, 6–4; Cano–J. L. Clerc d. Ycaza–L. Nunez 6–3, 3–6, 8–6, 6–2; Clerc d. Nunez 6–3, 6–1, 6–1; Fontana lost to Ycaza 3–6, 10–12, 3–6.   **USA d. Venezuela 4–1, Caracas:** R. Stockton d. J. Andrew 6–2, 6–4, 9–7; V. Gerulaitis d. H. Hose 3–6, 6–4, 6–3, 6–4; F. McNair–S. Stewart d. Hose–Andrew 8–6, 6–3, 6–4; Stockton lost to Hose 4–6, 6–3, 9–11, 7–9; Gerulaitis d. Andrew 6–3, 1–6, 6–3, 7–5.   **Mexico d. Canada 3–2, Ottawa:** J. Loyo-Mayo d. R. Genois 6–3, 9–7, 3–6, 6–4; R. Chavez lost to D. Power 2–6, 6–3, 6–8, 2–6; M. Lara–Loyo-Mayo d. J. Boyce–Genois 3–6, 9–7, 6–3, 6–4; Chavez d. Genois 6–4, 7–5, 2–6, 0–6, 6–1; Loyo-Mayo lost to Power 8–10, 4–6, 10–8, 4–6.

QUARTER-FINAL ROUND

Argentina d. Brazil 3–2, Sao Paulo: R. Cano lost to T. Koch 6–3, 5–7, 4–6, 1–6; G. Vilas d. C. Kirmayr 10–6, 6–1 def.; Vilas–E. Alvarez lost to Koch–Kirmayr 5–7, 4–6, 6–4, 4–6; Vilas d. Koch 4–6, 6–1, 6–2, 6–4; Cano d. Kirmayr 3–6, 6–2, 6–0, 6–0.   **USA d. Mexico 4–1, Tucson:** R. Tanner d. R. Ramirez 7–5, 6–4, 6–4; A. R. Ashe d. R. Chavez 6–4, 6–4, 6–4; R. C. Lutz–S. R. Smith d. E. Montano–Ramirez 6–2, 6–3, 6–4; Tanner d. Chavez 6–1, 6–3, 2–6, 6–3; Ashe lost to Ramirez 3–6, 4–6, 4–6.

SEMI-FINAL ROUND

Argentina d. Chile 4–1, Buenos Aires: R. Cano d. P. Cornejo 8–6, 4–6, 6–2, 6–8, 6–2; G. Vilas d. J. Fillol 8–6, 3–6, 6–2, 6–3; Vilas–E. Alvarez lost to Cornejo–Fillol 3–6, 0–6, 8–10; Cano d. Fillol 6–4, 6–4, 6–4; Vilas d. Cornejo 6–1, 6–1, 6–3.   **USA d. South Africa 4–1, Newport Beach:** R. Tanner d. B. Bertram 6–4, 6–2, 1–6, 6–4; B. Gottfried d. R. J. Moore 6–4, 6–2, 6–3; R. C. Lutz–S. R. Smith d. Bertram–F. D. McMillan 7–5, 6–1, 3–6, 6–3; Tanner lost to Moore 7–9, 4–6, 7–5, 2–6; Gottfried d. Bertram 6–4, 6–3, 6–4.

FINAL ROUND

Argentina d. USA 3–2, Buenos Aires: R. Cano d. R. L. Stockton 3–6, 6–4, 8–6, 6–4; G. Vilas d. B. E. Gottfried 6–4, 6–0, 6–2; Cano–E. Alvarez lost to F. McNair–S. Stewart 3–6, 3–6, 3–6; Vilas d. Stockton 5–7, 6–2, 6–2, 6–2; Cano lost to Gottfried 5–7, 5–7, 0–6.

Eastern Zone

FIRST ROUND

Thailand d. Malaysia 4–1: S. Champisri d. M. Akbar Baba 6–0, 6–2, 6–3; Chana Techasen lost to Eddie Chiew 5–7, 6–4, 3–6, 2–6; Champisri–P. Boratisa d. Akbar Baba–Chiew 6–3, 7–5, 8–6; Champisri d. Chiew 6–4, 8–6, 6–3; P. Kaimarn d. R. Anchant 6–3, 6–3, 6–3. **Philippines d. Sri Lanka 4–0, Manila;** M. Dominguez d. E. de Silva 6–1, 6–1, 6–2; E. Cruz d. A. Fernando 6–1, 6–1, 6–4; Cruz–Dominguez d. de Silva–Fernando 6–2, 6–3, 6–1; A. Marcial d. de Silva 6–0, 6–1, 6–1; R. Rafon v. Fernando 2–1 unfin. **Japan d. Taiwan 5–0, Tokyo:** J. Kamiwazumi d. Fu-shun Taug 6–4, 6–4, 6–2; K. Hirai d. Kuang-yung Hsu 6–3, 6–2, 6–3; Y. Tezuka–S. Nishio d. Taug–Hsu 6–3, 6–4, 6–4; Kamiwazumi d. Chi-yuan Lin 6–1, 6–1, 6–4; Tezuka d. Ten-wen Lin 6–1, 6–1, 6–2. **Korea d. Pakistan def.**

SECOND ROUND

Thailand d. Philippines def.; Japan d. Korea 3–2, Seoul: J. Kamiwazumi d. Choi Boo Kil 6–2, 6–1, 6–2; K. Hirai d. Chang Nam 6–4, 5–7, 6–3, 6–2; Kamiwazumi–Hirai d. Kil–Nam 3–6, 6–3, 6–4, 6–4; S. Tanabe lost to Kil 5–7, 3–6, 6–2, 2–6; S. Kato lost to Nam 3–6, 5–7, 1–6.

QUARTER-FINAL ROUND

Indonesia d. Thailand 5–0, Jakarta: G. Widjojo d. C. Techasen 6–1, 6–3, 6–3; Y. Tarik d. S. Champisri 6–3, 6–4, 3–6, 6–0; Widjojo–Tarik d. Champisri–P. Kaimarn 6–3, 6–1, 10–8; L. Wijono d. Kaimarn 7–5, 3–6, 8–6, 6–1; S. Sangitan d. C. T. Chason 6–2, 6–4, 6–3. **India d. Japan 3–2, New Delhi:** S. Menon lost to J. Kamiwazumi 6–8, 2–6, 6–8; A. Amritraj d. K. Hirai 6–2, 3–6, 6–1, 7–5; A. and V. Amritraj d. Kamiwazumi–Hirai 6–3, 6–3, 6–2; Menon lost to Hirai 7–5, 6–4, 8–10, 5–7, 1–6; A. Amritraj d. Kamiwazumi 8–6, 6–1, 6–4.

SEMI-FINAL ROUND

New Zealand d. Indonesia 5–0, Auckland: O. Parun d. A. Wyono 6–4, 6–0, 6–4; B. Fairlie d. Y. Tarik 3–6, 6–1, 6–2, 2–6, 9–7; Fairlie–Parun d. Wyono–G. Wijojo 7–5, 6–4, 6–2; C. Lewis d. Tarik 6–2, 6–2, 6–0; Fairlie d. Wyono 6–3, 6–2, 8–6. **Australia d. India 5–0, Perth:** M. Edmondson d. V. Amritraj 6–2, 7–5, 2–6, 8–6; J. G. Alexander d. A. Amritraj 6–0, 6–2, 6–1; Alexander–P. Dent d. A and V. Amritraj 6–3, 6–2, 6–3; Edmondson d. A. Amritraj 6–2, 9–7, 10–8; Dent d. S. Menon 9–7, 11–9, 6–4.

FINAL ROUND
Australia d. New Zealand 4–0, Auckland: M. Edmondson d. O. Parun
6–3, 7–5, 5–7, 6–4; J. G. Alexander d. B. Fairlie 6–3, 6–2, 6–3;
Alexander–P. Dent d. Fairlie–Parun 6–1, 3–6, 4–6, 6–1, 6–4; Alexander
d. Parun 9–11, 4–6, 6–4, 6–3, 6–4; Edmondson v. C. J. Lewis 6–4, 4–6,
6–4 unfin.

INTER-ZONE FINALS
Australia d. Argentina 3–2, Buenos Aires: P. Dent lost to G. Vilas
2–6, 6–4, 5–7, 3–6; J. Alexander d. R. Cano 6–4, 6–0, 6–0; Dent–
Alexander d. Cano–Vilas 6–2, 4–6, 9–7, 4–6, 6–2; Dent d. Cano 6–4, 6–4,
6–3; Alexander lost to Vilas 4–6, 5–7, 6–4, 2–6. **Italy d. France 4–1,
Paris:** A. Panatta d. P. Dominguez 6–4, 4–6, 6–4, 3–6, 6–3; C. Barazzutti
d. F. Jauffret 6–4, 2–6, 2–6, 6–2, 6–1; Panatta–P. Bertolucci d.
Dominguez–Jauffret 6–1, 3–6, 9–7, 6–1; Panatta d. Jauffret 6–2, 6–1;
Barazzuti lost to Dominguez 2–6, 6–0, 6–8.

FINAL ROUND
Australia d. Italy 3–1, Sydney: A. D. Roche d. A. Panatta 6–3, 6–4,
6–4; J. G. Alexander d. C. Barazzutti 6–2, 8–6, 4–6, 6–2; Alexander–P.
Dent lost to Panatta–P. Bertolucci 4–6, 4–6, 5–7; Alexander d. Panatta
6–4, 4–6, 2–6, 8–6, 11–9; Roche v. Barazzutti 12–12 unfin.

1978: USA
European Zone A

FIRST ROUND
Israel d. Finland 4–0, Tel Aviv: Y. Wertheimer d. G. Berner 3–6, 6–0,
6–2, 6–4; S. Glickstein d. M. Timonen 2–6, 6–2, 6–3, 6–2;
Wertheimer–Glickstein d. Berner–Timonen 6–2, 6–1, 3–6, 2–6, 6–1;
Wertheimer d. Timonen 6–2, 6–3, 6–3. **Monaco d. Luxembourg
5–0, Monaco:** L. Borfiga d. J. Brucher 6–4, 6–1, 6–2; B. Balleret d. M.
Klensch 6–1, 6–2, 6–1; Balleret–Borfiga d. C. Fernand–T. Storck 6–2,
6–0, 6–3; Balleret d. Brucher 6–0, 6–3, 6–1; Borfiga d. Klensch 6–3, 6–1,
6–4. **Holland d. Greece 4–1, Zeist:** L. Sanders d. N. Kelaidis 7–5, 6–1,
6–2; W. Fok lost to N. Kalogeropoulos 4–6, 6–0, 5–7, 6–3, 3–6;
Sanders–Fok d. Kelaids–Kalogeropoulos 6–1, 6–2, 6–3; Fok d. Kelaidis
6–2, 4–6, 2–6, 6–0, 6–1; Sanders d. Kalogeropoulos 8–6, 6–4, 3–6, 8–6.
Iran d. Algeria 4–1, Algeria: M. Bahrami d. A. Mahmoudi 6–3, 6–4,
6–4; M. Khodaei d. K. Boudjemline 6–2, 6–1, 6–2; Bahrami–K.

Darafshi–Javan d. Mahmoudi–Boudjemline 3–6, 6–4, 6–1, 6–2; Khodaei lost to Mahmoudi 4–6, 4–6, 2–6; Bahrami d. H. Younes 6–3, 6–4, 8–6.

SECOND ROUND
Austria d. Israel 3–2, Tel Aviv: P. Feigl d. S. Glickstein 6–4, 6–3, 1–6, 9–7; H. Kary lost to S. Krulevitz 6–4, 6–4, 4–6, 1–6, 2–6; Feigl–Kary d. Krulevitz–Y. Wertheimer 8–6, 6–4, 7–5; Feigl lost to Krulevitz 4–6, 6–8, 3–6; Kary d. Glickstein 3–6, 7–9, 6–4, 8–6, 6–3. **Great Britain d. Monaco 5–0, Monte Carlo:** J. M. Lloyd d. L. Borfiga 6–2, 6–1, 6–4; R. A. Lewis d. B. Balleret 8–6, 4–6, 10–12, 7–5, 6–1; D. A. and J. M. Lloyd d. L. and M. Borfiga 6–2, 6–1, 6–1; Lewis d. L. Borfiga 2–6, 2–6, 8–6, 6–1, 6–1; J. M. Lloyd d. Balleret 6–1, 6–2. **Czechoslovakia d. Holland 3–1, Prague:** J. Kodes lost to T.S. Okker 6–4, 7–9, 6–0, 3–6, 4–6; J. Hrebec d. L. Sanders 6–2, 7–5, 6–3; Kodes–T. Smid d. Okker–Sanders 9–7, 6–2, 6–2; Hrebec d. Okker 6–3, 2–6, 6–1, 6–4; Smid v. Sanders 4–6, 3–6 unfin. **Poland d. Iran 4–1, Warsaw:** W. Fibak d. M. Khoadai 6–0, 7–5, 6–0; C. Dobrowolski lost to M. Bahrami 6–8, 4–6, 6–4, 6–3, 3–6; Fibak–I. Nowicki d. Bahrami–K. Derafshidjavan 6–1, 6–1, 6–4; Fibak d. Bahrami 6–3, 6–1, 6–2; Dobrowolski d. Khoadai 6–1, 6–0, 6–4.

QUARTER-FINAL ROUND
Great Britain d. Austria 5–0, Bristol: J. M. Lloyd d. P. Feigl 7–5, 6–2, 2–6, 9–7; C. J. Mottram d. H. Kary 6–2, 6–3, 6–1; Mottram–D. A. Lloyd d. Feigl–C. Letcher 4–6, 6–3, 4–6, 6–4, 6–3; R. A. Lewis d. R. Reininger 3–6, 6–4, 8–6, 6–4; Mottram d. Feigl 6–4, 6–3, 6–1.
Czechoslovakia d. Poland 3–2, Prague: J. Kodes d. H. Drzymalski 6–0, 6–3, 7–5; J. Hrebec lost to W. Fibak 5–7, 5–7, 4–6; Kodes–T. Smid d. Fibak–T. Nowicki 8–6, 6–3, 7–5; Kodes lost to Fibak 6–8, 4–6, 2–6; Hrebec d. Dryzmalski 6–1, 6–1, 3–6, 6–4.

SEMI-FINAL ROUND
Great Britain d. France 3–2, Paris: C. J. Mottram d. Y. Noah 3–6, 6–3, 9–7, 6–3; J. M. Lloyd d. E. Deblicker 6–2, 6–2, 4–6, 3–6, 6–3; J. M. and D. A. Lloyd lost to Noah–F. Jauffret 3–6, 1–6, 5–7; Mottram d. Deblicker 7–5, 6–4, 6–1; J. M. Lloyd lost to Noah 3–6, 2–6, 5–7.
Czechoslovakia d. Rumania 5–0, Prague: P. Slozil d. A. Dirzu 6–2, 6–4, 7–5; T. Smid d. D. Haradau 7–5, 6–1, 6–8, 6–1; Slozil–Smid d. Dirzu–F. Segarceanu 6–4, 6–2, 6–4; Slozil d. Segarceanu 6–3, 6–4; Smid d. Dirzu 6–3, 6–2.

FINAL ROUND
Great Britain d. Czechoslovakia 5–0, Eastbourne: J. M. Lloyd d. J.
Hrebec 9–7, 6–3, 4–6, 5–7, 12–10; C. J. Mottram d. I. Lendl 6–4, 7–5,
7–5; D. A. Lloyd–M. Cox d. J. Kodes–T. Smid 6–4, 13–15, 6–4, 2–6,
6–4; Cox d. Lendl 6–2, 6–4, 6–3; Mottram d. Hrebec 5–7, 3–6, 6–3,
6–4, 6–0.

European Zone B

PRELIMINARY ROUND
Morocco d. Turkey 5–0, Casablanca: M. Dislam d. A. Yenilmez 6–3,
6–2, 6–3; O. Laimina d. R. Aydin 6–1, 6–0, 6–1; Laimina–Dislam d.
Aydin–Yenilmez 6–2, 6–0, 6–0; H. Saber d. Yenilmez 6–3, 6–4, 6–2; M.
Dlimi d. C. Cika 6–0, 6–3, 7–5.

FIRST ROUND
Morocco d. Norway 4–1, Casablanca: H. Saber d. F. Prydz 6–2, 6–3,
6–3; O. Laimina d. P. Hegna 7–5, 5–7, 6–1, 3–6, 7–5; M. Dislam–M.
Dlimi d. Prydz–E. Ulleberg 6–3, 6–8, 6–8, 10–8, 7–5; Saber lost to Hegna
3–6, 1–6, 1–6; Laimina d. Prydz 6–2, 6–2, 6–2. **Ireland d. Portugal
4–1, Dublin:** K. Menton d. A. Marta 6–2, 7–5, 4–6, 4–6, 6–3; S. Sorensen
d. S. Cruz 6–2, 6–4, 10–8; M. Hickey–Sorensen d. M. Soares–M. Sousa
6–1, 6–2, 6–2; Sorensen d. Marta 6–0, 6–2, 6–4; Menton lost to Cruz 5–7,
4–6, 4–6. **Belgium d. Denmark 3–2, Brussels:** T. Stevaux lost to
L. Elvstrom 6–3, 6–0, 1–6, 4–6, 6–8; B. Boileau d. T. Ulrich 5–7, 3–6,
6–2, 6–3, 6–4; Boileau–Stevaux lost to Elvstrom–T. Christensen 2–6,
7–5, 3–6, 3–6; Stevaux d. Ulrich 6–3, 6–1, 6–3; Boileau d. Elvstrom 6–2,
6–2, 6–1, **Switzerland d. Egypt 5–0, Lucerne:** M. Hurlimann d. T.
El–Sakka 6–0, 6–1, 6–3; H. Gunthardt d. M. Fattah 6–0, 6–1, 6–2; P.
Kanderal–D. Sturdza d. El–Sakka–Fattah 6–1, 6–1, 6–3; Gunthardt d.
El–Sakka 6–1, 6–0, 6–0; Kanderal d. Fattah 6–0, 4–6, 10–8, 7–5.

SECOND ROUND
Yugoslavia d. Morocco 5–0, Casablanca: D. Savic d. O. Laimina 4–6,
6–2, 6–2, 6–4; Z. Ilin d. M. Dislam 6–0, 6–4, 6–2; Ilin–Savic d.
Dislam–A. Dlimi 7–5, 6–4, 8–6; Savic d. Dislam 6–4, 6–2, 6–2; Ilin d.
Laimina 4–6, 6–3, 6–1, 6–0. **Sweden d. Ireland 5–0, Dublin:** B. Borg
d. M. P. Hickey 6–1, 6–1, 6–0. K. Johansson d. S. Sorensen 3–6, 3–6,
9–7, 6–3, 6–2; O. Bengtson–T. Svensson d. Hickey–Sorensen 4–6, 6–2,
6–4, 6–1; Borg d. Sorensen 6–0, 6–2, 6–0; Johansson d. K. Newton 6–0,
6–0, 6–0. **Hungary d. Belgium 4–1, Pin Pecs, Hungary:** P. Szoke d.

B. Boileau 7–5, 6–4, 6–1; B. Taroczy d. P. Hombergen 12–10, 6–3, 6–3; Taroczy–Szoke d. Boileau–T. Stevaux 6–3, 8–10, 6–2, 6–1; Szoke d. Hombergen 6–3, 6–2, 6–2; J. Benyik lost to Boileau 6–3, 4–6, 1–6, 6–3, 3–6. **West Germany d. Switzerland 5–0, Zurich:** P. Elter d. M. Burgener 6–4, 6–3, 6–2; U. Pinner d. H. Gunthardt 8–10, 4–6, 6–2, 6–4, 8–6; Pinner–R. Probst d. P. Kanderal–D. Sturdza 6–4, 6–2, 6–3; Pinner d. Burgener 2–6, 6–4, 6–4, 6–2; Elter d. Gunthardt 6–3, 9–7, 2–6, 9–7.

QUARTER-FINAL ROUND

Sweden d. Yugoslavia 3–2, Belgrade: K. Johansson lost to Z. Franulovic 6–3, 9–11, 5–7, 5–7; B. Borg d. Z. Ilin 6–0, 6–0, 6–2; O. Bengtson–Borg d. Franulovic–Ilin 4–6, 6–2, 6–0, 6–0; T. Svensson lost to Ilin 6–4, 4–6, 6–3, 0–6, 3–6; Borg d. Franulovic 6–2, 6–2, 9–7. **Hungary d. West Germany 3–2, Budapest:** B. Taroczy d. U. Pinner 6–1, 6–2, 6–1; P. Szoke lost to P. Elter 6–4, 4–6, 2–6, 3–6; Szoke–Taroczy d. Pinner–R. Probst 6–1, 4–6, 7–5, 6–2; Taroczy d. Elter 6–0, 6–1, 6–4; Szoke lost to Pinner 2–6, 2–6, 3–6.

SEMI-FINAL ROUND

Sweden d. Spain 3–2, Båstad: K. Johansson d. J. Higueras 6–2, 6–2, 5–7, 6–2; B. Borg d. M. Orantes 6–2, 5–7, 6–3, 6–3; Borg–O. Bengtson lost to Orantes–Higueras 6–3, 2–6, 2–6, 4–6; Johansson lost to Orantes 4–6, 4–6, 5–7; Borg d. Higueras 6–1, 6–4, 6–2. **Hungary d. Italy 4–1, Budapest:** P. Szoke lost to C. Barazzutti 6–2, 1–6, 5–7, 3–6; B. Taroczy d. A. Panatta 6–4, 6–3, 11–9; Szoke–Taroczy d. P. Bertolucci–Panatta 6–3, 6–2, 6–4; Szoke d. Panatta 6–3, 3–6, 6–0, 8–6; Taroczy d. Barazzutti 6–3, 6–4, 6–4.

FINAL ROUND

Sweden d. Hungary 3–1, Båstad: K. Johansson d. B. Taroczy 7–5, 6–2, 6–4; B. Borg d. P. Szoke 6–2, 6–0, 6–0; O. Bengtson–T. Svensson lost to Tarozcy–Szoke 2–6, 1–6, 10–12; Johansson d. Szoke 3–6, 7–5, 6–1, 3–6, 6–1; Svensson v. Taroczy 2–6, 6–4, 5–5, unfin.

American Zone

FIRST ROUND

Bolivia d. Peru 5–0, Lima: M. Martinez d. F. Maynetto 6–3, 6–3, 4–6, 7–5; R. Benavides d. M. Maurtua 6–2, 6–4, 4–6, 7–5; Benavides–J. C. Alvarado d. Maurtua–Maynetto 3–6, 8–6, 6–2, 5–7, 6–3; Martinez d. Maurtua 6–4, 4–6, 6–4, 10–8; Alvarado d. L. A. Olmedo 6–0, 6–1, 6–3.

Uruguay d. Ecuador 3–2, Montevideo: J. L. Roverano d. R. Pazmino 6–2, 6–2, 6–1; J. L. Damiani lost to R. Ycaza 4–6, 5–7, 1–6; Damiani–Roverano d. M. Olvera–Ycaza 6–3, 6–2, 6–2; Damiani d. Pazmino 6–1, 6–0, 6–2; Roverano lost to Ycaza 5–7, 2–6, 4–6.

SECOND ROUND

Chile d. Bolivia 5–0, Santiago: B. Prajoux d. M. Martinez 6–4, 6–1, 6–3; H. Gildemeister d. R. Benavides 6–2, 6–2, 6–1; J. Fillol–P. Cornejo d. J. C. Alvarado–Benavides 3–6, 6–2, 6–0, 8–6; Gildemeister d. Martinez 6–3, 6–1, 6–3; Prajoux d. Benavides 6–1, 6–1, 6–1. **Uruguay d. Brazil 4–1, Montevideo:** J. L. Damiani d. T. Koch 7–5, 6–4, 6–0; H. L. Roverano d. C. Kirmayr 0–6, 6–2, 6–3, 4–6, 7–5; Damiani–Roverano d. Koch–Kirmayr 9–7, 6–3, 6–2; Damiani d. J. Hocevar 6–3, 6–4, 6–4; Roverano lost to F. Gentil 1–6, 3–6, 7–5, 5–7.

QUARTER-FINAL ROUND

South Africa d. Colombia 4–1, Johannesburg: B. Bertram d. J. Velasco 0–6, 3–6, 6–4, 12–10, 6–1; R. J. Moore lost to I. Molina 5–7, 2–6, 6–4, 2–6; R. A. J. Hewitt–F. D. McMillan d. A. Betancour–Molina 6–0, 8–6, 6–2; Bertram d. Molina 3–6, 6–3, 6–4, 6–4; Moore d. Betancour 6–3, 6–3, 6–2. **Chile d. Uruguay 5–0, Santiago:** J. Fillol d. H. Roverano 9–7, 6–3, 6–0; H. Gildemeister d. J. L. Damiani 6–2, 6–2, 6–2; P. Cornejo–B. Prajoux d. Roverano–Damiani 8–6, 6–0, 6–2; Fillol d. Damiani 8–6, 6–0, 6–2; Gildemeister d. Roverano 6–1, 6–4, 6–2.

SEMI-FINAL ROUND

USA d. South Africa 4–1, Nashville: V. Gerulaitis d. B. Mitton 2–6, 6–2, 6–1, 7–5; H. Solomon d. B. Bertram 4–6, 6–0, 6–3, 6–1; S. Stewart–F. McNair lost to R. A. J. Hewitt–F. D. McMillan 0–6, 3–6, 4–6; Solomon d. Mitton 7–5, 6–4, 6–2; Gerulaitis d. Bertram 6–3, 6–3, 6–0. **Chile d. Argentina 3–2, Santiago:** H. Gildemeister d. G. Vilas 9–7, 6–3, 3–6, 6–4; J. Fillol d. R. Cano 6–2, 6–3, 6–3; Fillol–P. Cornejo lost to Vilas–J. Clerc 4–6, 3–6, 3–6; Gildemeister d. Cano 6–4, 7–5, 6–4; Fillol lost to Vilas 3–6, 4–6, 0–6.

FINAL ROUND

USA d. Chile 3–2, Santiago: B. Gottfried d. J. Fillol 6–4, 7–5, 6–2; H. Solomon d. H. Gildemeister 7–5, 3–6, 6–3, 6–1; Gottfried–J. McEnroe d. Fillol–B. Prajoux 3–6, 6–3, 8–6, 6–3; Solomon lost to Fillol 3–6, 2–6; Gottfried lost to Gildemeister 6–4, 5–7, 10–12.

Eastern Zone

FIRST ROUND

Pakistan d. Malaysia 4–0, Rawalpindi: S. Meer d. Mohd Akbar Baba 6–4, 6–2, 6–1; A. Hussain d. A. Cheah 6–1, 6–0, 6–3; Meer–M. Mohammad d. E. Chien–Baba 6–3, 6–2, 6–2; Mohammad d. Cheah 6–0, 6–0, 6–0; J. Ahmed v. Baba 11–9, 6–2, 6–6 unfin. **Philippines d. Thailand 5–0, Manila:** E. Cruz d. Somparn Champisri 6–2, 6–3, 6–3; R. Rafon d. Pichet Boratisa 6–2, 6–2, 6–4; A. Marshall–R. Gabriel d. Champisri–Boratisa 6–3, 6–2, 6–2; Rafon d. Prasert Kaiman 6–0, 6–1, 6–2; Gabriel d. Chana Techasen 6–3, 6–0, 8–6. **Japan d. Taiwan 5–0, Tokyo:** K. Hirai d. H. Z. Hsu 6–2, 6–0, 6–2; T. Fukui d. C. R. Wu 6–1, 6–3, 6–1; Hirai–S. Nishio d. Hsu–Wu 6–2, 6–3, 6–4; T. Yamamoto d. D. W. Lin 6–2, 12–10, 6–1; Nishio d. D. W. Lin 6–2, 12–10, 6–1.

SECOND ROUND

S. Korea d. Pakistan 3–2, Seoul: M. Kim lost to S. Meer; C Ju d. M. Mohammad 6–2, 6–2, 6–2; Ju–B. Kim d. Meer–M. Iqbal 6–3, 6–4, 4–6, 7–5; M. Kim d. Mohammad 6–2, 6–2, 6–2; Ju lost to Meer 2–6, 2–6, 0–6. **Japan d. Philippines 4–1, Manila:** K. Hirai d. A. Marcial 6–4, 3–6, 6–4, 6–0; T. Fukui lost to R. Rafon 6–3, 6–4, 0–6, 3–6, 2–6; Hirai–S. Nishio d. R. Gabriel–M. Valleramos 5–7, 6–0, 6–2, 6–2; Hirai d. Rafon 6–2, 2–6, 7–5; T. Tamamoto d. Marcial 7–5, 6–4, 6–3.

QUARTER-FINAL ROUND

India d. S. Korea 4–1, Coimbatore, India: S. Menon d. K. Moon 6–4, 8–6, 6–2; A. Amritraj d. J. Chang Nam 6–3, 6–1, 6–2; V. and A. Amritraj d. Nam–K. Bong Suk 6–1, 6–3, 8–6; Menon lost to C. Book II 6–3, 6–2, 1–6 def.; R. Krishnan d. Moon II 6–2, 6–1, 6–2. **Japan d. Indonesia 4–1, Tokyo:** T. Fukui d. A. Wyono 6–0, 6–2, 6–4; K. Hirai d. G. Widjojo 8–6, 6–2, 7–5; Hirai–S. Nishio lost to Widjojo–Wyono 6–2, 1–6, 6–3, 4–6, 2–6; Fukui d. Widjojo 6–4, 6–1, 6–3; T. Yamamoto d. J. Tarik 8–6, 6–3, 7–9, 3–6, 6–3.

SEMI-FINAL ROUND

New Zealand d. India 4–1, New Delhi: C. J. Lewis d. S. Menon 6–4, 6–3, 7–5; O. Parun d. A. Amritraj 6–4, 3–6, 9–7, 6–3; Lewis–B. Fairlie d. A. Amritraj–Menon 2–6, 14–16, 12–10, 6–2, 6–2; Parun lost to Menon 3–6, 4–6, 2–6; R. Simpson d. R. Krishnan 4–6, 6–4, 6–2, 6–4. **Australia d. Japan 5–0, Tokyo:** G. Masters d. J. Kuki 6–1, 6–3, 6–2; P. Dent d. K. Hirai 6–2, 10–8, 6–0; Masters–A. Stone d. H. Kamiwazumi–Hirai

6–4, 6–4, 6–1; K. Warwick d. Kuki 2–6, 5–7, 6–3, 6–3, 6–1; Stone d. T. Fukui 6–3, 7–5, 3–6, 2–6, 6–2.

FINAL ROUND

Australia d. New Zealand 4–0, Adelaide: A. D. Roche d. C. J. Lewis 13–11, 6–3, 6–2; J. G. Alexander d. B. E. Fairlie 6–4, 6–4, 6–4; Alexander–Roche d. Fairlie–Lewis 6–3, 6–4, 12–14, 4–6, 6–1; Alexander d. Lewis 8–10, 16–14, 6–1, 9–7; A Stone v. Fairlie 2–6, 6–1 unfin.

INTER-ZONE FINALS

USA d. Sweden 3–2, Gothenburg: A. R. Ashe lost to B. Borg 4–6, 5–7, 3–6; V. Gerulaitis d. K. Johansson 6–2, 6–1, 6–4; S. R. Smith–R. C. Lutz d. Borg–O. Bengston 2–6, 6–3, 3–6, 7–5, 6–3; Ashe d. Johansson 6–2, 6–0, 7–5; Gerulaitis lost to Borg 3–6, 1–6.   **Great Britain d. Australia 3–2, Crystal Palace, London:** C. J. Mottram d. A. D. Roche 8–6, 3–6, 7–5, 6–4; J. M. Lloyd d. J. G. Alexander 7–5, 6–2, 6–2; D. A. Lloyd–M. Cox d. R. Case–G. Masters 8–6, 3–6, 6–4, 6–3; J. M. Lloyd lost to Roche 3–6, 3–6, 2–6; Mottram lost to Alexander 2–6, 3–6, 2–6.

FINAL ROUND

USA d. Great Britain 4–1, Palm Springs: J. McEnroe d. J. M. Lloyd 6–1, 6–2, 6–2; B. Gottfried lost to C. J. Mottram 6–4, 6–2, 8–10, 4–6, 3–6; S. R. Smith–R. C. Lutz d. M. Cox–D. A. Lloyd 6–2, 6–2, 6–3; McEnroe d. Mottram 6–2, 6–2, 6–1; Gottfried d. J. M. Lloyd 6–1, 6–2, 6–4.

1979: USA
European Zone A

FIRST ROUND

All byes.

SECOND ROUND

Egypt d. Portugal 5–0, Cairo: A. El Gawap d. S. Cruz 3–6, 3–6, 6–1, 6–3, 6–1; I. El Shafei d. J. Vilela 6–4, 6–1, 6–3; El Shafei–T. El Sakka d. Vilela–L. Filipe 8–6, 6–2, 6–2; El Sakka d. Filipe 6–4, 6–2, 6–4; A. El Mehelmy d. M. Sousa 6–4, 3–6, 6–3, 6–0.   **USSR d. Monaco 4–1, Monte Carlo:** T. Kakulia d. L. Borfiga 6–1, 4–6, 6–4, 6–3; A. Metreveli d. B. Balleret 6–3, 3–6, 7–5, 6–2; Metreveli–Kakulia d. Balleret–M. Borfiga 6–1, 7–5, 6–4; Kakulia lost to Balleret 4–6, 6–2, 6–1, 4–6, 3–6; Metreveli d. L. Borfiga 6–2, 6–2.   **Denmark d. Greece 4–1, Athens:**

L. Elvstrom d. N. Kalogeropoulos 6–3, 1–0 def.; F. Christensen d. N. Kelaidis 9–11, 2–6, 6–1, 6–4, 6–2; Elvstrom–Christensen lost to P. Mamasis–G. Kalovelonis 6–4, 9–11, 3–6, 6–3, 5–7; Elvstrom d. Kelaidis 6–0, 6–2, 6–1; Christensen d. Mamasis 7–5, 7–5, 4–6, 8–6. **Finland d. Morocco 5–0, Helsinki:** L. Palin d. M. Dislam 6–4, 6–2, 6–1; M. Timonen d. O. Laimina 6–2, 8–6, 4–6, 6–1; R. Tuomola–Palin d. Laimina–Dislam 6–3, 6–1, 6–1; Palin d. Laimina 6–2, 6–2, 6–4; Timonen d. Dislam 6–1, 6–1, 6–3.

THIRD ROUND

Austria d. Egypt 5–0, Vienna: H. Kary d. I. El Shafei 6–3, 3–6, 6–4, 6–2; P. Feigl d. T. El Sakka 11–9, 6–4, 6–3; Kary–Feigl d. El Sakka–El Shafei 7–5, 6–4, 6–4; Feigl d. El Shafei 11–9, 12–10 def.; Kary d. El Sakka 6–4, 6–4, 6–2. **Spain d. USSR 5–0, Barcelona:** J. Higueras d. A. Metreveli 7–5, 6–2, 6–0; M. Orantes d. V. Borisov 6–3, 6–4, 6–0; Higueras–Orantes d. Metreveli–Borisov 7–5, 6–2, 6–0; A. Munoz d. R. Akhmerov 8–6, 6–2; F. Luna d. Borisov 6–1, 6–4. **Italy d. Denmark 5–0, Palermo:** A. Panatta d. M. Mortensen 6–2, 6–0, 6–2; C. Barazzutti d. C. E. Hedelund 6–1, 6–1, 6–2; Panatta–P. Bertolucci d. Hedelund–Mortensen 6–0, 6–8, 6–2, 6–2; Barazzutti d. Mortensen 6–1, 6–1; Panatta d. Hedelund 6–0, 6–3, 6–1. **Poland d. Finland 4–1, Warsaw:** H. Drzymalski lost to L. Palin 2–6, 2–6, 2–6; W. Fibak d. M. Timonen 6–1, 6–2, 6–3; Fibak–T. Nowicki d. Palin–G. Berner 6–3, 6–3, 6–0; Fibak d. Palin 6–0, 6–3, 6–3; Drzymalski d. Timonen 6–3, 6–4, 7–5.

QUARTER-FINAL ROUND

Italy d. Poland 4–1, Warsaw: A. Panatta lost to W. Fibak 2–6, 0–6, 6–2, 4–6; C. Barazzutti d. H. Drzymalski 6–3, 6–2, 6–1; Panatta–Barazzutti d. Fibak–I. Nowicki 6–1, 4–6, 14–12, 6–2; Barazzutti d. Fibak 7–5, 5–7, 3–6, 6–4, 6–2; Panatta d. Drzymalski 6–2, 6–1. **Spain d. Austria 3–2, Vienna:** J. Higueras lost to P. Feigl 3–6, 6–4, 5–7, 9–11; M. Orantes d. H. Kary 14–16, 10–8, 6–3, 6–4; Higueras–Orantes d. Feigl–Kary 14–12, 8–6, 6–4; Orantes d. Feigl 6–3, 17–15, 6–2; Higueras lost to Kary def.

SEMI-FINAL ROUND

Italy d. Hungary 3–2, Rome: A. Panatta d. P. Szoke 6–2, 6–0, 6–3; C. Barazzutti d. B. Taroczy 9–7, 6–2, 3–6, 7–5; Panatta–P. Bertolucci lost to Szoke–Taroczy 3–6, 6–3, 0–6, 6–8; Barazzutti d. Szoke 6–4, 6–1, 6–1; A. Zugarelli lost to Taroczy 4–6, 3–6. **Great Britain d. Spain 4–1, Eastbourne:** C. J. Mottram d. J. Higueras 6–2, 6–3, 6–0; J. M. Lloyd d.

M. Orantes 7–5, 6–1, 3–6, 6–2; M. Cox–D. A. Lloyd d. Higueras–
Orantes 2–6, 6–2, 6–4, 6–4; J. M. Lloyd lost to Higueras 3–6, 0–6, 4–6;
Cox d. A. Munoz 6–1, 6–3, 6–2.

FINAL ROUND
Italy d. Great Britain 4–1, Rome: A. Panatta lost to C. J. Mottram
0–6, 4–6, 4–6; C. Barazzutti d. J. M. Lloyd 6–1, 6–4, 6–4;
Barazzutti–A.Zugarelli d. M. Cox–D. A. Lloyd 7–5, 10–8, 6–1; Panatta
d. J. M. Lloyd 6–3, 6–2, 6–3; Barazzutti d. Mottram 8–6, 7–5.

European Zone B

FIRST ROUND
Iran d. Turkey 5–0, Ankara: M. Bahrami d. H. Ozgenel 6–0, 6–1, 6–0;
M. Khodai d. K. Anbar 6–1, 6–4, 6–2; Bahrami–K. Derafshidjavan d.
Anbar–M. Gurler 6–4, 6–2, 9–7; Ozgenel d. H. Akbari 4–6, 6–3, 6–3,
6–4; Bahrami d. Anbar 6–0, 4–6, 5–7, 6–2, 6–4.

SECOND ROUND
Switzerland d. Iran 3–2, Geneva: H. Gunthardt d. M. Khodai 6–4,
6–2, 1–6, 6–4; S. Gramegna lost to M. Bahrami 6–4, 6–3, 4–6, 4–6, 2–6;
Gunthardt–Gramegna d. Bahrami–K. Derafshidjavan 6–4, 9–7, 6–0;
Gunthardt d. Bahrami 6–2, 3–6, 6–2, 12–14, 11–9; Gramegna lost to
Khodai 2–6, 1–6, 4–6. **Holland d. Norway 4–1, Amersfoort:** R.
Thung lost to P. Hegna 8–6, 5–7, 2–6, 2–6; L. Sanders d. J. E. Rustad
6–3, 6–1, 6–1; Sanders–W. Fok d. Hegna–F. Prydz 6–2, 6–4, 6–1; Thung
d. Rustad 6–3, 6–3, 6–3; Sanders d. Hegna 3–6, 3–6, 6–2, 6–4, 6–0.
Belgium d. Ireland 5–0, Brussels: B. Boileau d. S. Sorensen 6–1, 8–6,
6–0; T. Stevaux d. K. Menton 6–3, 6–1, 6–4; Boileau–Stevaux d. J.
Biscomb–Sorensen 6–0, 6–2, 6–3; Boileau d. Menton 6–1, 6–1, 6–1;
Stevaux d. Sorensen 3–6, 7–9, 9–7, 6–2, 6–4. **Israel d. Nigeria def.**

THIRD ROUND
Switzerland d. Yugoslavia 4–1, Zurich: R. Stadler d. M. Ostoja 3–6,
6–4, 6–2, 6–4; H. Gunthardt d. Z. Ilin 6–4, 6–0, 6–2; Gunthardt–S.
Gramegna lost to Ostoja–Ilin 10–12, 6–3, 7–5, 3–6, 5–7; Stadler d. Ilin
6–1, 6–2, 6–4; Gunthardt d. Ostoja 6–1, 6–3, 6–4. **France d. Holland
3–2, Amsterdam:** P. Portes lost to T. S. Okker 6–3, 4–6, 3–6, 1–6; Y.
Noah d. L. Sanders 6–2, 6–4, 5–7, 6–3; G. Moretton–P. Dominguez
lost to Okker–R. Thung 7–9, 8–6, 2–6, 1–6; Noah d. Okker 8–10, 6–1,
7–9, 6–3, 6–4; Portes d. Sanders 8–6, 6–4, 6–4. **Rumania d. Belgium**

4–1; Brussels: G. Marc d. T. Stevaux 6–2, 7–5, 6–4; I. Nastase d. B. Boileau 6–3, 6–4, 6–2; Marc–Nastase d. Boileau–P. Hombergen 5–7, 6–2, 6–4, 4–6, 6–2; Nastase d. Stevaux 6–0, 6–4, 6–4; Marc lost to Boileau 6–4, 2–6, 3–6, 1–6. **West Germany d. Israel 3–2, Augsburg:** R. Gehring lost to S. Glickstein 6–4, 2–6, 6–2, 7–9, 2–6; U. Pinner d. S. Krulevitz 6–3, 6–3, 7–5; Pinner–W. Zirngibl d. Y. Wertheimer–Glickstein 3–6, 6–3, 6–4, 6–4; Pinner d. Glickstein 6–2, 6–4, 6–2; Gehring lost to Krulevitz 1–6, 6–4, 3–6, 9–7, 4–6.

QUARTER-FINAL ROUND

Rumania d. West Germany 4–1, Bucharest: D. Haradau lost to M. Wuenschig 6–2, 3–6, 3–6, 4–6; I. Nastase d. P. Elter 6–4, 6–4, 6–2; Nastase–G. Marc d. J. Fassbender–U. Marten 6–2, 7–5, 7–5; Haradau d. Elter 6–3, 6–4, 5–7, 6–1; Nastase d. Wuenschig 6–1, 6–3, 7–5. **France d. Switzerland 5–0, Paris:** Y. Noah d. H. Gunthardt 6–0, 6–3, 6–2; D. Bedel d. R. Stadler 2–6, 6–2, 7–5, 6–4; Noah–G. Moretton d. Gunthardt–S. Gramegna 2–6, 6–2, 7–5, 6–3; Noah d. Stadler 6–4, 6–0, 6–2; Bedel d. Gunthardt 2–6, 6–4, 4–6, 14–12, 7–5.

SEMI-FINAL ROUND

Sweden d. Rumania 3–2, Bucharest: S. Simonsson lost to I. Nastase 9–7, 7–5, 5–7, 3–6, 3–6; B. Borg d. D. Haradau 6–3, 6–0, 6–1; Borg–O. Bengtson d. Nastase–I. Marcu 7–5, 6–4, 6–3; Borg d. Nastase 6–3, 6–0, 6–0; Simonsson lost to Haradau 3–6, 4–6, 3–6. **Czechoslovakia d. France 4–1, Paris:** I. Lendl d. Y. Noah 6–3, 6–3, 3–6, 9–7; T. Smid d. G. Moretton 4–6, 4–6, 6–3, 6–3, 8–6; J. Kodes–Smid d. Noah–Moretton 7–5, 6–4, 5–7, 6–2; Lendl d. Moretton 6–1, 6–2, 6–2; Smid lost to Noah 5–7, 1–6, 2–6.

FINAL ROUND

Czechoslovakia d. Sweden 3–2, Prague: T Smid d. K. Johansson 6–4, 6–3, 6–2; I. Lendl lost to B. Borg 4–6, 5–7, 2–6; Smid–J. Kodes d. Borg–O. Bengtson 2–6, 6–3, 6–4, 6–0; Lendl d. Johansson 8–10, 6–4, 6–4, 4–6, 6–1; Smid lost to P. Hjertquist 3–5 def.

Eastern Zone

FIRST ROUND

Taiwan d. Malaysia def.; Pakistan d. Korea 3–2, Peshawar: Saeed Meer lost to Kim Song Souk 7–5, 9–7, 7–9, 4–6, 2–6; Nadir Ali Khan d. Ju Chang Nam 6–3, 6–8, 10–8, 6–4; Khan–Jameel Ahmed lost to

Souk–Nam 6–1, 6–8, 3–6, 1–6; Meer d. Nam 6–0, 6–1, 6–2; Khan d. Souk 6–3, 6–4, 9–7.

SECOND ROUND

Indonesia d. Taiwan 4–0, Jakarta: Y. Tarik d. Hsu Huang Jung 6–4, 6–2, 6–4; A Wijono d. Wu Chang Rung 6–3, 6–1, 6–1; G. Widjojo–Wijono d. Jung–Rung 6–2, 9–7, 6–1; Tarik d. Rung 6–2, 6–2, 3–6, 6–0; Hadiman v. Jung 4–6, 7–5, 4–6, 5–4 unfin. **Pakistan d. Philippines def.**

QUARTER-FINAL ROUND

India d. Indonesia 4–1: S. Menon d. A. Wijono 7–5, 6–0, 6–4; A. Amritraj d. Y. Tarik 6–4, 6–2, 6–4; Amritraj–Menon d. G. Widjojo–Wijono 6–1, 10–8, 6–2; Amritraj lost to Wijono def.; Menon d. Tarik 7–5, 4–6, 6–2, 6–4. **Japan d. Pakistan 4–1, Kasuga:** J. Kuki d. M. Mohammad 6–2, 6–2, 6–1; J. Kamiwazumi lost to Saeed Meer 4–6, 6–3, 5–7, 7–9; Kamiwazumi–K. Hirai d. Meer–Mohammad 6–0, 6–2, 6–2; Kuki d. Meer 6–2, 6–4, 6–4; Hirai d. Mohammad 6–2, 6–2, 6–4.

SEMI-FINAL ROUND

Australia d. India 3–2, Madras: R. Case d. S. Menon 9–7, 6–1, 6–2; J. Alexander d. V. Amritraj 6–4, 8–6, 1–6, 6–3; Case–G. Masters lost to V. and A. Amritraj 8–6, 4–6, 1–6, 3–6; Case lost to V. Amritraj 5–7, 1–6, 5–7; Alexander d. Menon 6–8, 3–6, 6–3, 6–3, 6–4. **New Zealand d. Japan 3–0, Christchurch:** R. Simpson d. J. Kamiwazumi 6–4, 6–4, 6–4; O. Parun d. K. Hirai 6–3, 12–14, 10–8, 6–3; Simpson–B. Fairlie d. Kamiwazumi–Hirai 6–4, 4–6, 6–4, 6–4.

FINAL ROUND

Australia d. New Zealand 3–2, Christchurch: M. Edmondson lost to O. Parun 6–3, 3–6, 3–6, 2–6; J. G. Alexander d. R. Simpson 6–4, 4–6, 7–5, 6–4; Alexander–P. Dent d. Parun–Simpson 6–4, 9–7, 6–3; Edmondson d. Simpson 6–3, 6–2, 6–4; Alexander lost to Parun 5–7, 3–6, 3–6.

American Zone South

FIRST ROUND

Ecuador d. Peru 4–1, Guayaquil: A. Gomez d. A. Franco 6–2, 6–2, 8–6; R. Ycaza d. F. Mayneto 6–4, 4–6, 0–6, 6–3, 6–4; Gomez–Ycaza d. Franco–Mayneto 6–4, 6–3, 6–1; R. Viver d. Franco 5–7, 6–2, 6–2, 6–2;

Gomez lost to Mayneto 3–6, 4–6, 3–6.   **Brazil d. Bolivia 5–0,**
Bolivia: C. Kirmayr d. J. C. Alvarado 6–2, 6–3, 6–0; C. Motta d. M.
Martinez 6–4, 7–5, 6–3; Kirmayr–Keller d. Alvarado–Martinez 6–3, 6–3,
6–4; Motta d. Alvarado 6–4, 6–3, 6–0; J. Soares d. Martinez 6–3, 6–3,
3–6, 0–6, 6–4.

QUARTER–FINAL ROUND
Argentina d. Ecuador 4–1, Guayaquil: R. Cano d. R. Ycaza 3–6, 9–7,
4–6, 6–4, 7–5; J. L. Clerc d. A. Gomez 6–1, 3–6, 8–6, 6–2; E.
Alvarez–Clerc d. Ycaza–Gomez 7–5, 4–6, 7–5, 6–4; Clerc lost to Ycaza
2–6, 3–6; F. Dalla Fontana d. R. Viver 6–4, 12–10.   **Brazil d. Uruguay**
4–0, Itu: C. Kirmayr d. H. Roverano 6–0, 6–2, 6–3; C. Motta d. J. L.
Damiani 3–6, 6–4, 0–6, 6–3, 6–4; Kirmayr–Keller d. Damiani–Roverano
6–2, 11–9, 6–3; Motta d. A. Laborde 6–2, 7–5, 6–1.

SEMI–FINAL ROUND
Argentina d. Brazil 5–0, Argentina: R. Cano d. C. Kirmayr 3–6, 6–3,
6–2, 6–1; J. L. Clerc d. C. Motta 6–1, 6–0, 6–0; Clerc–E. Alvarez d. N.
Keller–Motta 6–4, 6–1, 6–4; Clerc d. J. Soares 6–4, 6–4, 6–0; Cano d.
Motta 6–4, 6–2, 6–0.

FINAL ROUND
Argentina d. Chile 3–2, Buenos Aires: G. Vilas d. J. Fillol 9–7, 6–2,
6–2; J. L. Clerc lost to H. Gildemeister 1–6, 6–2, 3–6, 5–7; Vilas–Clerc
d. P. Cornejo–B. Prajoux 6–2, 6–2, 8–6; Clerc d. Fillol 6–2, 6–1, 6–1;
Vilas lost to Gildemeister 6–2, 1–6, 6–1, 5–7, 2–1 def.

American Zone North

FIRST ROUND
Venezuela d. Commonwealth Caribbean 3–2, Nassau: H. Hose d.
L. Rolle 6–3, 6–4, 6–0; J. Andrew lost to J. Antonas 3–6, 6–0, 6–4, 0–5
def.; Hose–Andrew d. Antonas–Rolle 6–2, 3–6, 6–2, 6–1; Andrew d.
Rolle 6–1, 6–1, 6–1; A. Sojo lost to Antonas 3–6, 6–3, 1–6, 1–6.

QUARTER–FINAL ROUND
Colombia d. Venezuela 4–1, Bogota: J. Velasco d. H. Hose 6–3, 5–7,
5–7, 6–4, 6–4; I. Molina d. J. Andrew 3–6, 6–3, 6–2, 7–5; Molina–
Velasco d. Andrew–Hose 6–4, 8–6, 6–8, 6–4; A. Betancourt lost to Hose
6–3, 1–6, 5–7; O. Agudelo d. A. Sojo 6–3, 6–3.   **Mexico d. Canada 3–2,**
Mexico City: M. Lara d. R. Genois 7–5, 3–6, 9–11, 6–2, 6–4; E. Montano

d. G. Halder 5–7, 7–5, 6–4, 10–8; Lara–R. Ramirez d. Genois–R. Legendre 6–4, 6–4, 6–4; E. Haro lost to J. Picken 1–6, 4–6, 8–6, 4–6; Montano lost to Genois 6–2, 6–8, 3–6.

SEMI-FINAL ROUND

Colombia d. Mexico 3–2, Mexico City: J. Velasco d. R. Chavez 6–2, 6–2, 3–6, 6–8, 8–6; I. Molina d. R. Ramirez 8–6, 8–6, 5–7, 6–3; Molina–Velasco lost to M. Lara–Ramirez 6–3, 3–6, 3–6, 2–6; Velasco lost to Ramirez 1–6, 5–7, 4–6; Molina d. Chavez 6–2, 6–3, 6–2.

FINAL ROUND

USA d. Colombia 5–0, Cleveland: J. P. McEnroe d. A. Betancourt 6–2, 6–1, 6–1; R. Stockton d. I. Molina 6–2, 6–3, 6–4; McEnroe–P. Fleming d. Molina–O. Agudelo 6–4, 6–0, 6–4; Stockton d. Betancourt 6–1, 6–2, 7–5; McEnroe d. Molina 6–4, 6–3, 6–2.

ZONE FINAL

USA d. Argentina 4–1, Memphis: V. Gerulaitis d. J. L. Clerc 6–1, 7–5, 6–1; J. P. McEnroe d. G. Vilas 6–2, 6–3, 6–2; R. C. Lutz–S. R. Smith d. Vilas–Clerc 2–6, 4–6, 11–9, 6–4, 6–1; McEnroe d. Clerc 6–2, 6–3; Gerulaitis lost to Vilas 7–9, 3–0 def.

INTER-ZONE FINALS

Italy d. Czechoslovakia 4–1, Rome: C. Barazzutti lost to T. Smid 1–6, 6–3, 1–6, 6–3, 5–7; A. Panatta d. I. Lendl 6–4, 1–6, 6–0, 6–0; P. Bertolucci–Panatta d. Smid–J. Kodes 6–8, 6–2, 6–1, 6–2; Barazzutti d. Lendl 4–6, 6–1, 6–2, 3–6, 7–5; Panatta d. Smid 6–3, 6–2. **USA d. Australia 4–1, Sydney:** V. Gerulaitis d. M. Edmondson 6–8, 14–16, 10–8, 6–3, 6–3; J. P. McEnroe d. J. G. Alexander 9–7, 6–2, 9–7; R. C. Lutz–S. R. Smith lost to Alexander–P. Dent 7–9, 4–6, 4–6; Gerulaitis d. Alexander 5–7, 6–4, 8–6, 6–2; McEnroe d. Edmondson 6–3, 6–4.

FINAL ROUND

USA d. Italy 5–0, San Francisco: V. Gerulaitis d. C. Barazzutti 6–2, 3–2 def.; J. McEnroe d. A. Panatta 6–2, 6–3, 6–4; R. C. Lutz–S. R. Smith d. Panatta–P. Bertolucci 6–4, 12–10, 6–2; McEnroe d. A. Zugarelli 6–4, 6–3, 6–1; Gerulaitis d. Panatta 6–1, 6–3, 6–3.

RESULTS YEAR BY YEAR

1980: CZECHOSLOVAKIA
European Zone A

FIRST ROUND

Turkey d. Luxembourg 4–1, Luxembourg: B. Altinkaya d. M.
Klensch 6–1, 6–2, 4–6, 6–2; R. Aydin d. J. Jilemnicky 6–2, 6–2, 6–2; K.
Anbar–Altinkaya d. Klensch–P. Genevo 6–0, 7–5, 6–2; Aydin d. Klensch
6–3, 6–2, 6–2; Altinkaya lost to Jilemnicky 9–11, 4–6, 6–4, 4–6.

SECOND ROUND

Israel d. Monaco 4–1, Ramat–Hasharon: S. Krulevitz d. L. Borfiga
6–2, 6–1, 3–6, 6–2; S. Glickstein d. B. Balleret 6–3, 6–1, 6–4; Glickstein–
Y. Wertheimer d. M. Borfiga–Balleret 6–2, 6–1, 6–0; H. Arlozorov lost
to Balleret 8–6, 4–6, 1–6, 4–6; Glickstein d. L. Borfiga 6–3, 6–1, 6–0.
Bulgaria d. Ireland 3–2, Dublin: L. Genov lost to S. Sorensen 4–6,
6–3, 4–6, 3–6; L. Petrov d. K. Menton 6–2, 6–2, 6–2; B. and M.
Pampulov d. J. McArdle–Sorensen 7–5, 3–6, 6–3, 6–4; Genov d. Menton
6–0, 6–4, 6–0; Petrov lost to Sorensen 4–6, 4–6, 6–4, 1–6.   **Holland d.**
Denmark 3–2, Hilversum: L. Sanders d. M. Mortensen 6–3, 6–3, 6–3;
R. Thung lost to L. Elvstrom 1–6, 4–6, 1–6; P. van Min–T. Gorter lost
to Mortensen–Elvstrom 4–6, 6–2, 4–6, 4–6; Thung d. Mortensen 7–5,
3–6, 7–5, 9–7; Sanders d. Elvstrom 7–5, 6–4, 3–6, 6–0.   **Norway d.**
Turkey 4–1, Oslo: T. Randby lost to R. Aydin 6–4, 0–6, 3–6, 4–6; P.
Hegna d. A. Kocak 6–1, 6–1, 6–0; Hegna–J. Munch–Soegaard d.
Aydin–Kocak 6–4, 6–3, 6–2; Hegna d. Aydin 6–1, 6–3, 6–1; Randby d.
Kocak 6–1, 1–6, 6–1, 6–2.

THIRD ROUND

Switzerland d. Israel 4–1, Winterthur: R. Stadler lost to S. Glickstein
6–2, 6–4, 3–6, 3–6, 0–6; H. Gunthardt d. S. Krulevitz 6–1, 6–3, 3–6,
6–3; H. and M. Gunthardt d. Glickstein–Krulevitz 6–4, 6–3, 7–5; Stadler
d. Krulevitz 5–7, 6–2, 6–2, 8–6; H. Gunthardt d. Glickstein 6–3, 6–3, 6–1.
Hungary d. Bulgaria 3–1: J. Benyik d. I. Stamatov 6–1, 6–1, 7–5; B.
Taroczy d. M. Pampulov 6–1, 6–1, 6–3; Taroczy–P. Szoke d.
Pampulov–L. Petrov 6–3, 6–4, 3–6, 8–6; Benyik lost to Petrov 6–3, 7–5,
3–6, 5–7, 6–3.   **Spain d. Holland 4–1, Seville:** F. Luna d. T. S.
Okker 6–2, 6–2, 6–3. J. Higueras d. L. Sanders 6–2, 6–4, 6–3; M.
Orantes–A. Gimenez lost to Okker–H. van Boeckel 6–8, 6–2, 3–6, 11–9,
6–8; Gimenez d. Okker 6–1, 6–1 def.; Luna d. Sanders 6–4, 6–1, 6–4.
West Germany d. Norway 4–0, Hanover: R. Gehring d. J. Munch–
Soegaard 6–1, 6–1, 6–1; K. Meiler d. P. Hegna 6–1, 6–3, 6–1; Meiler–A.

531

Maurer d. R. Felix–Munch–Soegaard 7–5, 6–2, 6–1; Maurer d. Hegna 6–1, 6–0, 6–1.

QUARTER-FINAL ROUND
Switzerland d. Hungary 3–2, Zurich: H. Gunthardt d. J. Benyik 3–6, 7–5, 6–4, 4–6, 6–1; R. Stadler lost to Z. Kuharszky 3–6, 6–4, 6–3, 6–8, 6–4; Gunthardt–Stadler d. P. Szoke–R. Machan 4–6, 6–3, 8–6, 15–13; Stadler lost to Benyik 5–7, 5–7, 5–7; Gunthardt d. Kuharszky 6–1, 6–2, 6–4. **West Germany d. Spain 3–2, Valencia:** U. Pinner lost to F. Luna 0–6, 4–6, 3–6; R. Gehring d. J. Higueras 3–6, 1–6, 6–1, 6–2, 6–1; K. Meiler–Gehring lost to Higueras–A. Gimenez 5–7, 4–6, 9–11; Pinner d. Higueras 6–4, 6–3, 6–3; Gehring d. Luna 3–6, 6–3, 6–3, 6–3.

SEMI-FINAL ROUND
Italy d. Switzerland 5–0, Turin: C. Barazzutti d. H. Gunthardt 6–4, 6–1, 6–4; A. Panatta d. R. Stadler 6–4, 10–8, 6–1; P. Bertolucci–Panatta d. M. and H. Gunthardt 7–9, 10–8, 1–6, 6–4, 6–2; Barazzutti d. Stadler 6–3, 6–4; G. Ocleppo d. I. du Pasquier 6–0, 6–3. **Sweden d. West Germany 4–1, Båstad:** B. Borg d. R. Gehring 6–1, 6–1, 6–2; K. Johansson d. K. Eberhard 6–4, 0–6, 6–2, 6–3; P. Hjertquist–S. Simonsson lost to Gehring–R. Probst 5–7, 3–6, 2–6; Borg d. Eberhard 6–2, 5–7, 6–0, 6–0; Simonsson d. Gehring 3–6, 6–1, 6–0.

FINAL ROUND
Italy d. Sweden 4–1, Rome: C. Barazzutti d. K. Johansson 6–3, 6–3, 6–2; A. Panatta lost to S. Simonsson 6–8, 6–1, 2–6, 6–4, 4–6; P. Bertolucci–Panatta d. S. and H. Simonsson 6–2, 6–3, 7–5; Panatta d. Johansson 3–6, 6–3, 6–4, 1–6, 6–4; Barazzutti d. S. Simonsson 8–6, 6–1.

European Zone B

FIRST ROUND
Morocco d. Algeria 4–1, Paris: M. Dislam lost to D. Boudjemline 2–6, 7–9, 4–6; O. Laimina d. Y. Amier 6–2, 7–5, 6–1; Laimina–H. Saber d. Amier–Boudjemline 6–2, 6–4, 6–3; Dislam d. Amier 6–4, 7–5, 8–6; Laimina d. Boujemline 6–3, 6–0, 6–1.

SECOND ROUND
Belgium d. Morocco 4–1, Casablanca: B. Boileau d. H. Saber 6–3, 6–1, 6–3; T. Stevaux lost to O. Laimina 9–7, 3–6, 1–6, 6–0, 6–8; Boileau–Stevaux d. Laimina–Saber 6–3, 6–0, 10–8; Stevaux d. Saber 6–3,

6–2, 6–1; Boileau d. Laimina 6–3, 6–2, 6–1. **Yugoslavia d. Portugal 5–0, Belgrade:** Z. Ilin d. J. Vilela 6–2, 6–1, 6–0; Z. Franulovic d. J. Cordeiro 6–1, 6–0, 6–0; Franulovic–M. Ostoja d. J. and P. Cordeiro 6–0, 6–1, 6–2; Ilin d. J. Cordeiro 6–0, 6–1, 6–2; Ostoja d. Vilela 2–6, 7–5, 6–4. **USSR d. Greece 5–0, Athens:** A. Zverev d. N. Kalogeropoulos 6–0, 6–3, 6–3; A. Metreveli d. G. Kalovelonis 6–1, 6–4, 6–4; Metreveli–Zverev d. Kalovelonis–Kalogeropoulos 6–4, 6–2, 6–4; Zverev d. Kalovelonis 6–1, 6–4, 6–4; Metreveli d. Kalogeropoulos 6–3, 5–7, 6–4, 7–5. **Finland d. Egypt 5–0, Helsinki:** M. Timonen d. T. El Sakka 6–1, 6–3, 6–3; L. Palin d. A. El Meheilmy 6–0, 6–2, 6–3; Palin–Timonen d. El Sakka–El Meheilmy 6–0, 6–2, 6–1; Timonen d. El Meheilmy 6–2, 6–1, 6–0; Palin d. El Sakka 6–4, 6–1, 6–0.

THIRD ROUND
Austria d. Belgium 3–2, Brussels: H. Kary d. P. Hombergen 4–6, 8–6, 6–2, 6–4; P. Feigl lost to B. Boileau 4–6, 6–3, 5–7, 3–6; Kary–Feigl d. Boileau–Hombergen 6–3, 3–6, 15–13, 15–13; Kary lost to Boileau 6–2, 6–4, 3–6, 5–7, 2–6; Feigl d. Hombergen 7–5, 6–3, 6–4. **Rumania d. Yugoslavia 5–0, Zagreb:** I. Nastase d. Z. Ilin 12–10, 6–3, 4–6, 6–3; F. Segarceanu d. Z. Franulovic 6–4, 7–5, 7–5; Nastase–Sergarceanu d. Franulovic–Ilin 6–4, 12–10, 3–6, 7–5; Segarceanu d. Ilin 2–6, 6–4, 6–3, 6–2; Nastase d. Z. Petkovic 6–2, 6–1, 6–2. **France d. USSR 3–2, Montpelier:** Y. Noah lost to V. Borisov 6–3, 15–13, 4–6, 3–2, 2–6; P. Portes d. S. Leonjuk 6–3, 6–4, 6–3; Noah–Portes d. Borisov–Kakulia 6–4, 6–4, 6–4; Noah d. Leonjuk 6–1, 6–0, 6–2; Portes lost to Borisov 7–5, 2–6, 2–6, 3–6. **Finland d. Poland 5–0, Helsinki:** L. Palin d. T. Nowicki 6–3, 6–3, 7–5; M. Timonen d. H. Drzymalski 6–3, 6–1, 6–1; Palin–Timonen d. Nowick–Drzymalski 7–5, 8–10, 3–6, 6–4, 6–4; Timonen d. Nowicki 6–3, 6–3, 3–6, 6–3; B. Berner d. A. Wisnieski 6–1, 6–1 def.

QUARTER-FINAL ROUND
Rumania d. Austria 3–2, Bucharest: I. Nastase d. H. Kary 6–1, 7–5, 6–4; F. Segarceanu lost to R. Reininger 4–6, 7–5, 5–7, 1–6; Nastase–Segarceanu d. Kary–Reininger 8–6, 6–4, 6–3; Segarceanu lost to Kary 1–6, 6–3, 6–2, 13–15, 5–7; Nastase d. Reininger 6–3, 6–3, 6–3. **France d. Finland 3–2, Toulouse:** P. Portes d. L. Palin 6–2, 1–6, 6–2, 6–0; J. L. Haillet d. M. Timonen 6–1, 6–1, 6–4; Haillet–G. Moretton d. Palin–G. Berner 0–6, 6–1, 6–4, 6–4; Haillet lost to Palin 5–7, 2–6, 8–6, 6–3, 7–9; Portes lost to Timonen 5–7, 6–3, 3–6.

Rumania d. Great Britain 3–2, Bristol: A. Dirzu d. J. Feaver 1–6, 4–6, 6–3, 8–6, 6–4; I. Nastase d. C. J. Mottram 6–3, 6–2, 6–4; Dirzu–Nastase lost to D. A. and J. M. Lloyd 6–4, 5–7, 4–6, 2–6; Dirzu lost to Mottram 5–7, 2–6, 2–6; Nastase d. Feaver 7–5, 8–6, 2–6, 2–6, 6–4. **Czechoslovakia d. France 5–0, Prague:** T. Smid d. C. Roger–Vasselin 6–2, 6–3, 3–6, 6–1; I. Lendl d. P. Portes 6–4, 8–6, 6–4; Smid–P. Slozil d. D. Bedel–Portes 6–3, 7–5, 6–3; Lendl d. Roger–Vasselin 4–6, 7–5, 6–4; Smid d. Portes 6–4, 3–6, 6–2.

FINAL ROUND
Czechoslovakia d. Rumania 4–1, Bucharest: I. Lendl d. D. Haradu 6–4, 6–1, 6–3; P. Slozil d. F. Segarceanu 6–3, 6–3, 6–1; J. Kodes–Lendl d. Haradu–Segarceanu 6–3, 6–2, 6–4; Slozil d. E. Pana 7–5, 6–0; S. Birner lost to Segarceanu 6–2, 2–6, 6–8.

American Zone North

FIRST ROUND
Canada d. Commonwealth Caribbean 5–0, Kingston: J. Brabenec d. J. Antonas 18–20, 8–6, 6–3, 6–4; D. Power d. G. Maharaj 6–2, 6–2, 6–4; Power–R. Bettauer d. Antonas–L. Rolle 7–5, 6–2, 4–6, 7–5; Brabenec d. S. Sarnia 7–5, 6–3, 6–1; Bettauer d. Rolle 6–1, 6–3, 4–6, 6–3.

SECOND ROUND
Mexico d. Canada 4–1, Brantford, Ontario: E. Montano lost to D. Power 2–6, 6–3, 1–6, 7–5, 4–6; M. Lara d. Bettauer 6–2, 6–4, 6–4; Lara–Montano d. J. Brabenec–Power 7–5, 6–4, 10–8; Montano d. Bettauer 7–5, 3–6, 6–3, 2–6, 8–6; Lara d. Power 6–2, 6–2. **Venezuela d. Colombia 4–1, Caracas:** J. Andrew d. A. Cortez 6–2, 6–3, 9–7; H. Hose d. I. Molina 7–5, 8–6, 5–7, 6–2; Andrew–Hose d. Molina–M. Posso 6–3, 6–4, 6–4; F. M. Bet d. Cortez 6–2, 7–5; C. Claverie lost to Posso 3–6, 6–3, 1–6.

SEMI–FINAL ROUND
Mexico d. Venezuela 4–1, Mexico City: M. Lara d. H. Hose 6–3, 3–6, 6–3, 8–6; R. Ramirez d. J. Andrew 6–2, 8–6, 6–2; Lara–Ramirez d. Andrew–Hose 6–3, 6–3, 6–4; Lara d. Andrew 6–4, 3–6, 6–2; J. Rodaz lost to Hose 3–6, 2–6.

FINAL ROUND

USA d. Mexico 3–2, Mexico City: J. P. McEnroe d. R. Ramirez 6–4, 6–4, 6–2; V. Gerulaitis d. M. Lara 6–1, 6–2, 5–7, 6–2; P. Fleming– McEnroe d. Lara–Ramirez 6–3, 6–3, 10–12, 4–6, 6–2; Gerulaitis lost to Ramirez 6–8, 4–6; S. Davis lost to J. Ordez 8–6, 4–6, 4–6.

American Zone South

FIRST ROUND

Uruguay d. Peru 4–1, Lima: D. Perez d. P. Arraya 7–5, 6–4, 9–7; J. Damiani d. F. Maynetto 6–4, 9–7, 6–0; Damiani–H. Roverano d. Maynetto–J. Salked 6–3, 7–5, 3–6, 5–7, 7–5; Damiani d. Arraya 3–6, 6–3, 8–6; Perez lost to Maynetto def.

SECOND ROUND

Chile d. Uruguay 4–1, Montevideo: B. Prajoux d. D. Perez 4–6, 6–2, 6–4, 6–4; H. Gildemeister d. J. Damiani 6–2, 6–3, 6–3; Prajoux– Gildemeister d. Perez–Damiani 6–3, 3–6, 5–7, 8–6, 6–1; Gildemeister d. Perez 6–1, 6–1; Prajoux lost to Damiani 0–6, 4–6. **Brazil d. Ecuador 3–2, Guayaquil:** C. A. Kirmayr d. R. Ycaza 6–1, 6–3, 6–1; C. Motta lost to A. Gomez 9–11, 6–2, 4–6, 6–3, 3–6; Kirmayr–Motta d. Gomez–R. Viver 4–6, 7–5, 9–11, 6–4, 6–4; Motta lost to Viver 4–6, 6–4, 4–6, 4–6; Kirmayr d. Gomez 1–6, 10–8, 9–7, 6–4.

SEMI-FINAL ROUND

Brazil d. Chile 3–1, Sao Paulo: T. Koch d. J. Fillol 7–5, 6–3, 1–6, 6–3; C. Kirmayr lost to H. Gildemeister 4–6, 2–6, 6–2, 1–6; Koch–Kirmayr d. Gildemeister–A. Fillol 3–6, 6–3, 7–5, 6–0; Kimayr d. R. Acuna 6–3, 6–1, 5–7, 7–5.

FINAL ROUND

Argentina d. Brazil 4–1, Sao Paulo: G. Vilas d. T. Koch 6–3, 4–6, 4–6, 6–2, 6–1; J. L. Clerc d. C. Kirmayr 4–6, 2–6, 8–6, 6–3, 7–5; Clerc–Vilas lost to Kirmayr–Koch 2–6, 9–7, 10–12, 3–6; Vilas d. Kirmayr 2–6, 6–3, 6–8, 6–3, 6–3; Clerc d. Koch 6–2, 6–0.

ZONE FINAL

Argentina d. USA 4–1, Buenos Aires: J. L. Clerc d. J. P. McEnroe 6–3, 6–2, 4–6, 14–12; G. Vilas d. B. Gottfried 7–5, 6–4, 6–3; R. Cano–C. Gattiker lost to P. Fleming–McEnroe 0–6, 1–6, 4–6; Vilas d. McEnroe 6–2, 4–6, 6–3, 2–6, 6–4; Clerc d. Gottfried 7–5, 6–4.

Eastern Zone

FIRST ROUND

Thailand d. Philippines def.; Korea d. Pakistan 3–2, Seoul: Bong
Suk Kim lost to Saeed Meer 0–6, 4–6, 2–6; Chang Dae–Jeon d. Ali
Khan 6–0, 6–2, 6–3; Chang Dae-Jeon–Yeong Dae-Jeon lost to Saeed
Meer–Ali Khan 6–2, 4–6, 6–2, 3–6, 2–6; Yeong Dae-Jeon d. Ali Khan
6–3, 6–1, 6–3; Chang Dae-Jeon d. Saeed Meer 6–1, 6–3, 6–2.

SECOND ROUND

Taiwan d. Thailand 3–2, Guam: Wu Chang–Rung d. Supoj Meesawas
2–6, 6–3, 4–6, 6–2, 7–5; Hsu Huang-Jung d. Pranomkorn Pladchurnil
6–3, 1–6, 7–5, 6–4; Hsu Huang-Jung–Wu Chang-Rung lost to Supoj
Meesawas–Pranomkorn Pladchurnil 8–6, 11–9, 3–6, 3–6, 6–8; Wu
Chang-Rung lost to Pranomkorn Pladchurnil 6–2, 5–7, 12–10, 4–6; Hsu
Huang-Jung d. Supoj Meesawas 6–1, 2–6, 6–3, 6–3. **Korea d.
Indonesia 5–0, Seoul:** Chang Dae-Jeon d. Yustedjo Tarik 6–3, 6–0, 6–3;
Choon Ho Kim d. Atet Wijono 6–4, 6–3, 6–2; Choon Ho Kim–Yeong
Dee-Jeon d. Atet Wijono–Gondo Widjojo 6–4, 4–6, 8–6, 3–6, 6–4; Choon
Ho Kim d. Yustedjo Tarik 6–4, 6–4, 6–0; Choon Ho Kim d. Hodimon
6–1, 6–1, 7–5.

THIRD ROUND

Japan d. Taiwan 5–0, Taipei: S. Nishio d. Wu Chang-Rung 5–7, 6–0,
6–3, 6–3; T. Fukui d. Hsu Huang-Jung 6–4, 6–2, 6–1; J. Kamiwazumi–S.
Sakamoto d. Wu Chang-Rung–Hsu Huang-Jung 6–2, 6–2, 6–4; Nishio
d. Hsu Huang-Jung 6–2, 6–4, 10–8; Fukui d. Wu Chang-Rung 6–2,
6–3, 6–4. **Korea d. India 3–2, Seoul:** Chang Ho Kim d. S. Krishnan
6–4, 6–3, 6–2; Choon Ho Kim d. N. Bal 5–7, 6–3, 6–2, 6–1; Choon
Ho Kim–Yeong Dae-Jeon lost to S. Menon–Bal 2–6, 6–8, 4–6; Choon
Ho Kim d. Krishnan 6–4, 8–6, 6–1; Yeong Dae-Jeon lost to Bal 2–6,
6–3, 4–6, 3–6.

SEMI–FINAL ROUND

Australia d. Japan 5–0, Hobart: M. Edmondson d. T. Fukui 6–2, 6–3,
4–6, 6–3; P. McNamara d. S. Nishio 6–4, 6–3, 6–0; B. Drewett–
Edmondson d. J. Kamiwazumi–S. Sakamoto 8–6, 6–1, 6–2; McNamara
d. Fukui 7–5, 6–0, 6–3; Edmondson d. Nishio 2–6, 6–0, 6–2, 6–1. **New
Zealand d. Korea 5–0, Christchurch:** O. Parun d. Choon Ho Kim
7–5, 3–6, 6–2, 10–8; C. Lewis d. Yeong Dae-Jeon 6–2, 6–4, 6–0; Lewis–R.
Simpson d. Choon Ho Kim–Bong Suk Kim 6–1, 6–0, 7–5; Lewis d.
Chang Dae-Jeon 6–3, 6–2, 6–0; Parun d. Bong Suk Kim 6–4, 6–3, 6–1.

FINAL ROUND
Australia d. New Zealand 3–1, Brisbane: J. G. Alexander lost to C. Lewis 7–5, 7–9, 10–8, 4–6, 5–7; P. Dent d. O. Parun 6–2, 5–7, 6–3, 3–6, 6–2; Dent–Alexander d. Lewis–R. Simpson 6–2, 8–6, 9–7; Dent d. Lewis 6–4, 6–3, 6–2.

INTER-ZONE FINAL
Czechoslovakia d. Argentina 3–2, Buenos Aires: P. Slozil lost to J. L. Clerc 3–6, 6–3, 6–4, 2–6, 1–6; I. Lendl d. G. Vilas 7–5, 8–6, 9–7; Lendl–T. Smid d. Clerc–Vilas 6–2, 6–4, 6–3; Lendl d. Clerc 6–1, 7–5, 6–8, 6–2; Slozil lost to Vilas 2–6, 2–6. **Italy d. Australia 3–2, Rome:** A. Panatta d. P. McNamee 5–7, 6–4, 6–0, 6–4; C. Barazzutti lost to P. McNamara 8–10, 6–1, 4–6, 2–6; P. Bertolucci–Panatta d. McNamara–McNamee 2–6, 9–7, 9–7, 2–6, 6–4; Panatta d. McNamara 6–1, 7–5, 6–4; Barazzutti lost to R. Frawley 6–2, 4–6, 6–8.

FINAL ROUND
Czechoslovakia d. Italy 4–1, Prague: T. Smid d. A. Panatta 3–6, 3–6, 6–3, 6–4, 6–4; I. Lendl d. C. Barazzutti 4–6, 6–1, 6–1, 6–2; Lendl–Smid d. P. Bertolucci–Panatta 3–6, 6–3, 3–6, 6–3, 6–4; Smid lost to Barazzutti 6–3, 3–6, 2–6; Lendl d. G. Ocleppo 6–3, 6–3.

1981: USA
Non–Zonal Competition

FIRST ROUND
Argentina d. West Germany 3–2, Munich: G. Vilas d. R. Gehring 6–2, 6–3, 8–6; J. L. Clerc lost to U. Pinner 6–3, 3–6, 4–6, 3–6; Clerc–Vilas d. Gehring–C. Zipf 6–3, 4–6, 6–4, 6–3; Clerc lost to Gehring 1–6, 6–4, 3–6, 1–6; Vilas d. Pinner 6–3, 6–2, 3–6, 6–1. **Rumania d. Brazil 3–2, Timisoara:** F. Segarceanu d. C. Kirmayr 4–6, 7–5, 6–2, 6–2; A. Dirzu lost to T. Koch 2–6, 4–6, 1–6; Dirzu–Segarceanu d. Koch–Kirmayr 0–6, 6–8, 6–4, 7–5; Segarceanu d. Koch 4–6, 6–3, 7–5, 4–6, 6–0; Dirzu lost to Kirmayr 2–6, 0–6. **Great Britain d. Italy 3–2, Brighton:** C. J. Mottram d. A. Panatta 9–7, 3–6, 6–3, 6–4; R. A. Lewis lost to C. Barazzutti 4–6, 6–1, 8–6, 7–9, 4–6; A. M. Jarrett–J. R. Smith d. P. Bertolucci–Panatta 6–1, 3–6, 6–3, 3–6, 7–5; Lewis lost to Panatta 4–6, 2–6, 4–6; Mottram d. Barazzutti 6–3, 6–2, 6–2. **New Zealand d. South Korea 5–0, Seoul:** R. Simpson d. Chang Dal Jeon 6–3, 2–6, 6–1; C. J. Lewis d. Young Dal Jeon 6–1, 6–2, 6–2; Lewis–Simpson d. Bong Soo Kim–Young Dal Jeon 6–3, 6–2, 6–4; Lewis d. Chang Dal Jeon 6–1,

6–4, 7–5; Simpson d. Young Dal Jeon 6–2, 8–6, 6–0. **Sweden d. Japan 5–0, Yokohama:** K. Johansson d. T. Fukui 7–5, 6–2, 6–4; P. Hjertquist d. J. Kamiwazumi 6–3, 7–5, 8–6; A. Jarryd–H. Simonsson d. Kamiwazumi–K. Hirai 6–0, 8–6, 6–2; Hjertquist d. Fukui 6–4, 6–2, 6–0; Johansson d. S. Nishio 6–3, 3–6, 6–2, 6–1. **Australia d. France 3–2, Lyons:** P. McNamara d. Y. Noah 4–6, 8–6, 6–3, 3–6, 6–3; K. Warwick lost to P. Portes 6–4, 2–6, 7–9, 4–6; M. Edmondson–Warwick d. Noah–Portes 6–3, 6–2, 5–7, 6–4; McNamara d. Portes 6–3, 6–0, 6–2; Warwick lost to Noah 2–6, 5–7, 8–10. **Czechoslovakia d. Switzerland 3–2, Zurich:** I. Lendl d. H. Gunthardt 6–3, 7–5, 6–0; T. Smid d. R. Stadler 6–2, 6–1, 6–3; Lendl–Smid lost to H. and M. Gunthardt 3–6, 6–3, 6–2, 3–6, 4–6; Smid d. H. Gunthardt 7–5, 6–2, 8–6; Lendl lost to Stadler 6–6 def. **USA d. Mexico 3–2, Carlsbad:** J. P. McEnroe d. J. Lozano 6–3, 6–1, 6–3; R. Tanner lost to R. Ramirez 6–3, 6–8, 3–6, 10–8, 3–6; M. C. Riessen–S. Stewart lost to Lozano–Ramirez 4–6, 6–3, 7–9, 6–0, 3–6; Tanner d. Lozano 6–2, 6–2, 6–3; McEnroe d. Ramirez 6–4, 6–3, 6–0.

QUARTER-FINAL ROUND

Argentina d. Rumania 3–2, Timisoara: G. Vilas d. A. Dirzu 6–4, 6–4, 6–3; J. L. Clerc d. F. Segarceanu 6–4, 6–2, 6–0; Clerc–Vilas lost to Dirzu–Segarceanu 6–4, 8–10, 3–6, 5–7; Vilas d. Segarceanu 6–4, 6–4, 3–6, 6–1; R. Cano lost to Dirzu 6–4, 2–6 def. **Great Britain d. New Zealand 4–1, Christchurch:** R. A. Lewis d. R. Simpson 4–6, 4–6, 6–4, 6–4, 8–6; C. J. Mottram d. C. J. Lewis 4–6, 6–4, 4–6, 9–7, 6–3; A. M. Jarrett–J. R. Smith d. C. J. Lewis–Simpson 6–3, 6–4, 6–4; R. A. Lewis d. C. J. Lewis 6–2, 6–2; Smith lost to Simpson 6–4, 9–11, 2–6. **Australia d. Sweden 3–1, Båstad:** P. McNamee d. P. Hjertquist 6–3, 8–6, 6–1; P. McNamara d. M. Wilander 6–4, 6–2, 6–1; McNamara–McNamee lost to A. Jarryd–H. Simonsson 9–7, 6–3, 6–8, 2–6, 2–6; McNamee d. Wilander 2–6, 6–4, 6–0, 6–4; McNamara v. Hjertquist 6–6 unfin. **USA d. Czechoslovakia 4–1, New York:** J. P. McEnroe lost to I. Lendl 4–6, 12–14, 5–7; J. S. Connors d. T. Smid 6–3, 6–1, 6–2; R. C. Lutz–S. R. Smith d. Lendl–Smid 9–7, 6–3, 6–2; McEnroe d. Smid 6–3, 6–1, 6–4; Connors d. Lendl 7–5, 6–4.

SEMI-FINAL ROUND

Argentina d. Great Britain 5–0, Buenos Aires: J. L. Clerc d. R. A. Lewis 6–4, 6–4, 6–0; G. Vilas d. C. J. Mottram 6–3, 6–1, 6–1; Clerc–Vilas d. A. M. Jarrett–J. R. Smith 8–6, 8–6, 6–2; Clerc d. Mottram 7–5, 6–4; Vilas d. Lewis 6–0, 6–3. **USA d. Australia 5–0, Portland, Oregon:** J. P. McEnroe d. M. Edmondson 6–3, 6–4, 6–2; R. Tanner d. P.

McNamara 6–4, 6–4, 4–6, 3–6, 6–3; P. Fleming–McEnroe d. P. Dent–
McNamara 8–6, 6–4, 8–6; McEnroe d. McNamara 9–7, 6–0; Tanner d.
Edmondson 4–6, 6–2, 6–3.

FINAL ROUND
USA d. Argentina 3–1, Cincinnati: J. P. McEnroe d. G. Vilas 6–3,
6–2, 6–2; R. Tanner lost to J. L. Clerc 5–7, 3–6, 6–8; P. Fleming–
McEnroe d. Clerc–Vilas 6–3, 4–6, 6–4, 4–6, 11–9; McEnroe d. Clerc 7–5,
5–7, 6–3, 3–6, 6–3; Tanner v. Vilas 11–10 unfin.

RELEGATION ROUND
Germany d. Brazil 3–2, Sao Paulo: U. Pinner d. T. Koch 6–3, 6–3,
6–2; P. Elter lost to C. Kirmayr 5–7, 2–6, 6–3, 2–6; C. Zipf–D. Beutel
d. Kirmayr–M. Hocevar 6–8, 6–4, 6–3, 13–11; Pinner lost to Kirmayr
2–6, 13–11, 19–21, 3–6; Elter d. Koch 7–5, 7–5, 6–3. **Italy d. South
Korea 4–1, San Remo:** C. Barazzutti d. Woo Ryong Lee 6–0, 6–2, 6–3;
A. Panatta d. Choon Ho Kim 6–4, 6–4, 7–5; P. Bertolucci–Panatta d.
Kim–Dong Wook Song 6–2, 7–5, 6–4; Barazzutti lost to Kim 6–2, 6–8,
2–6, 6–2, 1–6; G. Ocleppo d. Chang Dal Jeon 6–3, 8–10, 6–3, 6–4.
France d. Japan 4–1, Paris: G. Moretton lost to T. Fukui 6–1, 6–4 def.;
T. Tulasne d. S. Sakamoto 6–0, 6–0, 6–0; Y. Noah–C. Roger–Vasselin
d. Fukui–T. Yonezawa 8–6, 6–2, 6–4; Roger–Vasselin d. Sakamoto 6–0,
6–4, 6–1; Tulasne d. Fukui 6–1, 8–6, 6–3. **Mexico d. Switzerland
3–2, Tijuana:** R. Ramirez d. H. Gunthardt 6–4, 6–2, 6–1; J. Lozano lost
to R. Stadler 4–6, 6–4, 4–6, 5–7; Ramirez–Lozano d. H. and M.
Gunthardt 3–6, 6–2, 6–0, 6–1; Ramirez d. Stadler 6–1, 6–2, 6–3; J.
Hernandez lost to I. Du Pasquier 4–6, 4–6.

Zonal Competition

American Zone

FIRST ROUND
Venezuela d. Commonwealth Caribbean 4–1, Caracas: C. Claverie
d. J. Anthonas 8–10, 6–3, 3–6, 7–5, 6–1; J. Andrew d. J. Russell 6–4,
6–2, 6–3; Andrew–I. Sauce d. Anthonas–Russell 6–4, 6–4, 6–4; R. Scheller
lost to Anthonas 1–6, 3–6; Claverie d. Russell 6–2, 7–5. **Colombia d.
Canada 3–2, Bogota:** C. Gomez lost to R. Genois 4–6, 2–6, 6–4, 2–6;
A. Cortes d. M. Wostenholme 6–2, 6–2, 6–4. Cortes–C. Behar d.
Genois–S. Bonneau 6–2, 6–3, 10–8; Cortes d. Bonneau 6–4, 2–6, 6–4,
6–3; G. Monroy lost to Wostenholme 4–6, 4–6. **Chile d. Peru 4–1,**

Lima: H. Gildemeister d. F. Maynetto 6–2, 6–3, 6–4; P. Rebolledo d. P. Arraya 4–6, 6–2, 7–5, 6–1; R. Acuna–B. Prajoux d. Maynetto–Arraya 6–4, 6–2, 5–7, 6–2; Rebolledo d. C. Di Laura 7–5, 6–3; Acuna lost to Arraya 7–5, 2–6, 3–6. **Uruguay d. Ecuador 3–2, Guayaquil:** J. L. Damiani d. R. Ycaza 6–4, 4–4 def.; D. Perez lost to A. Gomez 4–6, 3–6, 5–7; Damiani–Perez lost to Gomez–R. Viver 6–3, 7–9, 6–4, 6–8, 3–6; Damiani d. Gomez 4–6, 4–6, 6–2, 6–3, 7–5; Perez d. Viver 6–2, 4–6, 11–9, 6–2.

SEMI-FINAL ROUND
Colombia d. Venezuela 5–0, Bogota: C. Behar d. R. Scheller 2–6, 6–3, 6–2, 6–1; A. Cortes d. J. Andrew 7–5, 3–6, 9–7, 3–2 def.; Behar–C. Gomez d. I. Sauce–A. Sojo 6–4, 6–3, 6–4; Gomez d. Scheller 14–12, 6–2; G. Monroy d. Sauce 3–6, 6–2, 9–7. **Chile d. Uruguay 5–0, Santiago:** P. Rebolledo d. A. Laborde 6–1, 6–1, 6–1; B. Prajoux d. D. Perez 6–4, 7–5, 6–2; H. Gildemeister–Prajoux d. Perez–Laborde 6–1, 6–4, 6–2; R. Acuna d. Perez 6–3, 6–2; Prajoux d. Laborde 6–3, 6–2.

FINAL ROUND
Chile d. Colombia 3–2, Bogota: R. Acuna lost to J. Velasco 6–4, 6–3, 13–15, 4–6, 1–6; H. Gildemeister d. A. Cortes 6–4, 6–2, 6–2; Gildemeister–B. Prajoux d. Velasco–Cortes 6–4, 6–3, 3–6, 6–2; Acuna d. Cortes 8–6, 6–4, 6–3; Prajoux lost to A. Jimenez 1–2 def.

Eastern Zone

FIRST ROUND
Thailand d. Malaysia 5–0, Bangkok: Pichet Boratisa d. Suresh Menon 6–3, 6–0, 4–6, 6–0; Sombat Eaumongkol d. Rudy Foo 6–3, 7–5, 6–4; Boratisa–Eaumongkol d. Menon–Foo 6–2, 6–2, 6–1; Eaumongkol d. Menon 6–1, 6–3, 6–3; Pongkapan Pisaisamonket d. Foo 6–4, 6–1, 3–6, 6–1. **Indonesia d. Taiwan 4–1, Taipei:** S. Tintus d. Wu Chang-Rung 11–9, 6–3, 8–6; Justedjo Tarik d. Hsu Huang-Rung 6–2, 6–2, 6–4; Atet Wyono–Gondo Widjojo lost to Wu Chang-Rung–Hsu Huang-Rung 4–6, 6–3, 3–6, 6–8; Justedjo Tarik d. Wu Chang-Rung 6–3, 4–6, 6–2, 6–2; Tintus d. Hsu Huang-Rung 6–3, 4–6, 7–5, 3–6, 6–3.

SEMI-FINAL ROUND
India d. Thailand 5–0, Bangkok: R. Krishnan d. S. Eaumongkol 6–3, 6–2, 6–2; V. Amritraj d. P. Boratisa 6–2, 6–1, 6–2; V. and A. Amritraj d. Eaumongkol–Boratisa 6–2, 6–4, 6–1; Krishnan d. Boratisa 6–3, 6–2,

6–1; V. Amritraj d. Eaumongkol 6–0, 6–2, 9–7. **Indonesia d.
Pakistan 3–0, Jakarta:** A. Wyono d. Inan Ul Haq 6–1, 6–2, 6–0; J. Tarik
d. Saeed Meer 6–2, 6–1, 8–10, 15–13; G. Widjojo–Wyono d. Nadir Ali
Khan–Altaf Husain 4–6, 6–2, 6–4, 6–1.

FINAL ROUND

India d. Indonesia 3–2, Jakarta: S. Menon d. A. Wyono 6–3, 8–10,
6–2, 6–3; A. Amritraj lost to J. Tarik 9–11, 4–6, 7–5, 9–7, 4–6; A.
Amritraj–Menon d. T. Wigowa–Tarik 3–6, 7–5, 11–9, 6–4; Menon d.
Tarik 6–3, 6–4, 6–2; A. Amitraj d. Wyono 5–6 def.

European Zone A

FIRST ROUND

Algeria d. Zimbabwe def.; Monaco d. Morocco 3–1, Monte Carlo:
B. Balleret d. M. Dislam 6–4, 1–6, 6–4, 6–1; L. Borfiga lost to M.
Dlimi 6–8, 6–2, 6–8, 5–7; Balleret–M. Borfiga d. Dlimi–H. Saber 13–11,
8–6, 6–4; L. Borfiga d. Dislam 2–6, 6–4, 1–6, 7–5, 6–1; Balleret v. Dlimi
3–6, 5–2 unfin. **Egypt d. Greece 5–0, Cairo.** T. El Sakka d. N.
Kalogeropoulos 6–4, 6–3, 6–8, 6–2; I. El Shafei d. G. Kalovelonis 6–4,
6–4, 6–4; El Shafei–El Sakka d. Kalogeropoulos–Kalovelonis 6–3, 6–4,
3–6, 6–3; El Sakka d. Kalovelonis 11–9, 7–5; El Shafei d. Kalogeropoulos
6–1, 6–3.

QUARTER-FINAL ROUND

Spain d. Algeria 5–0, Algiers: J. G. Reuena d. Y. Amier 6–1, 6–2, 6–0;
J. Lopez-Maeso d. D. Boudjemline 8–6, 6–1, 6–1; M. Mir–Lopez-Maeso
d. Amier–Boudjemline 6–4, 6–1, 8–6; Reuena d. Boudjemline 6–3, 6–2,
8–6; S. C. Martinez d. Amier 6–0, 6–4, 6–0. **Monaco d. Poland 3–2,
Monte Carlo:** B. Balleret d. T. Nowicki 2–6, 6–3, 7–5, 3–6, 6–4; L.
Borfiga d. C. Dobrowolski 5–7, 6–1, 2–6, 6–1, 6–0; Balleret–Borfiga lost
to H. Dryzmalski–Nowicki 2–6, 5–7, 1–6; Borfiga lost to Nowicki 8–6,
2–6, 0–6, 4–6; Balleret d. Dobrowolski 2–6, 9–7, 6–3, 6–1. **Hungary
d. Egypt 4–1, Cairo:** R. Machan d. T. El Sakka 6–3, 6–1, 7–5; B.
Taroczy d. l. El Shafei 9–7, 6–4, 6–4; Taroczy–P. Szoke d. El Shafei–El
Sakka 6–4, 8–6, 6–4. Machan d. K. Baligh 6–1, 6–1; J. Benyik lost to El
Sakka 6–3, 1–6, 3–6. **Israel d. Yugoslavia 4–1, Skopje:** S. Glickstein d.
Z. Ilin 6–1, 6–4, 6–4; D. Schneider d. S. Zivojinovic 6–4, 6–4, 10–8;
Glickstein–Schneider d. D. Savic–Zivojinovic 6–3, 6–4, 7–5; S. Perkiss lost
to Ilin 3–6, 2–6, 6–3, 6–3, 0–6; Glickstein d. B. Horvat 3–6, 6–2, 6–1,
6–2.

SEMI-FINAL ROUND
Spain d. Monaco 5–0, Lerida: A. Gimenez d. B. Balleret 6–3, 6–4, 6–1; F. Luna d. L. Borfiga 6–0, 6–1, 6–2; S. Casal–J. Lopez-Maeso d. Balleret–M. Borfiga 7–5, 6–1, 6–1; Lopez-Maeso d. L. Borfiga 6–2, 6–4, 6–0; Luna d. J. Vinceleoni 6–1, 6–4. **Hungary d. Israel 3–2, Tel Aviv:** R. Machan d. D. Schneider 3–6, 6–2, 6–2, 6–8, 7–5; Taroczy lost to S. Glickstein 9–7, 1–6, 3–6, 1–6; P. Szoke–Taroczy d. Schneider–Glickstein 3–6, 9–7, 3–6, 6–4, 6–4; Taroczy d. Schneider 6–3, 6–3, 6–2; Machan lost to Glickstein 0–6, 4–6.

FINAL ROUND
Spain d. Hungary 3–2, Aviles: F. Luna lost to B. Taroczy 4–6, 3–6, 3–6; J. Lopez-Maeso d. R. Machan 6–1, 4–6, 6–1, 9–7; A. Gimenez–S. Casal d. Taroczy–P. Szoke 4–6, 8–6, 10–8, 6–3; Lopez-Maeso lost to Taroczy 6–3, 1–6, 5–7, 3–6; Luna d. Machan 3–6, 10–8, 6–0, 6–2.

European Zone B

FIRST ROUND
Ireland d. Norway 3–2, Oslo: P. Hannon lost to P. Hegna 3–6, 1–6, 4–6; M. Doyle d. T. Randby 6–2, 6–3, 6–0; Doyle–S. Sorensen d. Hegna–B. Naume 6–1, 6–0, 6–2; Doyle d. Hegna 6–2, 6–2, 6–4; Hannon lost to Randby 6–3, 3–6, 6–2, 5–7, 2–6. **Bulgaria d. Luxembourg 5–0, Mondorf-les-Bains:** Y. Stamatov d. A. Navrotchi 6–1, 6–1, 6–3; B. Pampoulov d. J. Goudenbourg 8–6, 6–2, 6–2; M. and B. Pampoulov d. Navrotchi–Goudenbourg 6–2, 6–3, 11–9; Stamatov d. Goudenbourg 8–6, 7–5, 6–3; M. Pampoulov d. F. Claude 7–5, 6–0, 6–1. **Belgium d. Turkey def.; Denmark d. Portugal 5–0, Aarhus:** P. Bastiansen d. M. Soares 6–2, 6–0, 6–2; M. Mortensen d. J. Cordeiro 4–6, 6–4, 6–0, 4–6, 10–8; Bastiansen–Mortensen d. J. and P. Cordeiro 6–1, 11–9, 6–4; Bastiansen d. J. Cordeiro 6–0, 6–1, 6–0; Mortensen d. Soares 6–3, 6–1, 6–0.

QUARTER-FINAL ROUND
Holland d. Ireland 4–1, Eindhoven: L. Sanders d. M. Doyle 8–6, 2–6, 2–6, 6–2, 6–2; E. Wilborts d. S. Sorensen 4–6, 7–5, 6–4, 6–1; M. Albert–H. van Boeckel lost to Doyle–Sorensen 3–6, 6–4, 1–6, 2–6; Wilborts d. Doyle 6–4, 6–8, 12–10, 6–4; Sanders d. Sorensen 6–3, 6–2. **Finland d. Bulgaria 3–2, Helsinki:** L. Palin d. L. Petrov 6–1, 6–2, 6–0; M. Timonen lost to Y. Stamatov 8–10, 6–1, 6–2, 5–7, 0–6; Palin–J. Berner lost to Petrov–Stamatov 7–5, 6–1, 3–6, 5–7, 0–6; Palin d. Stamatov 9–11, 6–2,

6–1, 6–0; Timonen d. Petrov 6–3, 6–2, 4–6, 3–6, 6–0. **USSR d. Belgium 4–1, Yurmala:** K. Pugaev d. B. Boileau 4–6, 6–4, 6–4, 6–1; V. Borisov d. T. Stevaux 2–6, 6–4, 6–2, 4–6, 6–3; Borisov–Pugaev lost to Boileau–A. Brichant 6–4, 7–9, 1–6, 4–6; Pugaev d. Stevaux 5–7, 3–6, 6–4, 6–0, 6–4; A. Zverev d. Brichant 6–1, 2–6, 6–4. **Austria d. Denmark 3–2, Salzburg:** P. Feigl d. M. Mortensen 6–3, 10–8, 6–3; H. Kary d. P. Bastiansen 4–6, 6–3, 6–2, 6–1; Feigl–Kary d. Bastiansen–Mortensen 6–3, 6–4, 1–6, 6–1; R. Reininger lost to Mortensen 3–6, 4–6, 3–6; Feigl lost to Bastiansen 4–6, 6–2, 4–6, 5–7.

SEMI-FINAL ROUND
Holland d. Finland 5–0, Helsinki: L. Sanders d. K. Alkio 6–3, 6–1, 6–1; E. Wilborts d. M. Timonen 6–2, 6–2, 9–7; M. Albert–H. van Boeckel d. L. Palin–G. Berner 7–5, 7–5, 6–2; Sanders d. Timonen 4–6, 6–3, 7–5, 6–4; Wilborts d. Alkio 3–6, 2–6, 6–0, 6–2, 6–4. **USSR d. Austria 4–0, Portschach:** K. Pugaev d. H. Kary 6–4, 6–3, 6–1; V. Borisov d. I. Wimmer 8–6, 6–4, 6–4; Borisov–S. Leonjuk d. Kary–B. Pils 6–4, 6–2, 6–2; Pugaev d. Wimmer 6–4, 6–2, 3–6, 6–3.

FINAL ROUND
USSR d. Holland 5–0, Yurmala: V. Borisov d. E. Wilborts 7–5, 4–6, 6–1, 6–3; A. Zverev d. L. Sanders 6–4, 7–9, 1–6, 9–7, 6–3; Borisov–K. Pugaev d. T. S. Okker–M. Albert 6–4, 6–4, 6–2; S. Leonjuk d. Albert 4–6, 9–7, 6–4, 4–6, 6–4; Zverev d. Wilborts 6–1, 6–3.

1982: USA
Non-Zonal Competition

FIRST ROUND
USA d. India 4–1, Carlsbad: J. P. McEnroe d. V. Amritraj 6–4, 9–7, 7–5; E. Teltscher d. R. Krishnan 6–3, 6–3, 6–4; P. Fleming–McEnroe d. A. and V. Amritraj 6–3, 6–1, 7–5; Teltscher lost to V. Amritraj 3–6, 5–7; McEnroe d. Krishnan 6–1, 5–7, 6–4. **Sweden d. USSR 4–1, Stockholm:** M. Wilander d. V. Borisov 9–7, 6–1, 6–4; A. Jarryd d. A. Zverev 6–1, 3–6, 0–6, 6–3, 6–2; Jarryd–H. Simonsson d. Borisov–K. Pugaev 8–10, 3–6, 6–2, 8–6, 6–0; J. Nystrom lost to Pugaev 4–6, 6–3, 4–6; Wilander d. Zverev 4–6, 10–8, 6–2. **Australia d. Mexico 3–2, Mexico City:** M. Edmondson d. F. Maciel 6–3, 6–4, 6–1; P. McNamara lost to R. Ramirez 2–6, 3–6, 4–6; P. Dent–J. Alexander lost to J. Lozano–Ramirez 6–3, 5–7, 5–7, 7–9; McNamara d. Maciel 6–3, 6–3, 6–0; Edmondson d. Ramirez 6–1, 6–4, 6–2. **Chile d. Rumania 3–2,**

543

Santiago: B. Prajoux lost to I. Nastase 6–1, 7–9, 4–6, 8–6, 2–6; P. Rebolledo d. F. Segarceanu 6–4, 6–2, 6–0; J. Fillol–Prajoux d. A. Dirzu–Segarceanu 8–6, 6–1, 2–6, 6–1; Rebolledo d. Nastase 5–7, 6–4, 6–1, 6–3; Prajoux lost to Segarceanu def. **New Zealand d. Spain 3–2, Christchurch:** R. Simpson d. J. Lopez-Maeso 14–12, 6–3, 7–9, 12–10; O. Parun d. A. Gimenez 6–3, 6–3, 6–2; Parun–Simpson lost to Gimenez–S. Casal 3–6, 6–3, 6–4, 3–6, 4–6; Parun lost to Lopez-Maeso 8–10, 3–6, 7–9; Simpson d. Gimenez 2–6, 5–7, 6–1, 6–3, 6–1. **Italy d. Great Britain 3–2, Rome:** A. Panatta lost to C. J. Mottram 7–5, 5–7, 3–6, 4–6; C. Barazzutti d. R. A. Lewis 11–9, 6–1, 6–1; P. Bertolucci–Panatta d. A. M. Jarrett–J. R. Smith 6–4, 6–3, 6–3; Barazzutti lost to Mottram 4–6, 3–6, 5–7; Panatta d. Lewis 8–6, 6–4, 6–2. **Czechoslovakia d. West Germany 5–0, Prague:** T. Smid d. U. Pinner 9–7, 6–4, 6–1; I Lendl d. R. Gehring 6–1, 6–2, 6–2; P. Slozil–Smid d. C. Zipf–H. Beutel 6–3, 6–3, 6–4; Smid d. Gehring 6–3, 2–6, 6–3; Lendl d. Pinner 6–1, 6–3. **France d. Argentina 3–2, Buenos Aires:** Y. Noah lost to G. Vilas 1–6, 6–4, 5–7, 6–3, 5–7; T. Tulasne d. R. Cano 6–1, 6–3, 6–2; Noah–G. Moretton d. J. Ganzabal–Vilas 6–8, 6–3, 6–2, 6–4; Tulasne lost to Vilas 1–6, 0–6, 1–6; Noah d. Cano 8–6, 6–1, 8–6.

QUARTER-FINAL ROUND

USA d. Sweden 3–2, St Louis: J. P. McEnroe d. A. Jarryd 10–8, 6–3, 6–3; E. Teltscher lost to M. Wilander 4–6, 5–7, 6–3, 6–3, 0–6; P. Fleming–McEnroe d. Jarryd–H. Simonsson 6–4, 6–3, 6–0; B. E. Gottfried lost to Jarryd 2–6, 2–6, 4–6; McEnroe d. Wilander 9–7, 6–2, 15–17, 3–6, 8–6. **Australia d. Chile 4–1, Brisbane:** J. Fitzgerald d. R. Acuna 8–6, 7–5, 6–1; M. R. Edmondson d. P. Rebolledo 6–1, 6–2, 6–3; P. McNamara–P. McNamee d. H. Gildemeister–B. Prajoux 8–6, 2–6, 8–6, 6–2; Edmondson lost to Acuna 4–6, 6–2, 4–6, 4–6; Fitzgerald d. Rebolledo 8–6, 3–6, 4–6, 6–4, 6–2. **New Zealand d. Italy 3–2, Cervia:** C. J. Lewis d. C. Barazzutti 3–6, 6–1, 6–4, 6–3; R. Simpson d. A. Panatta 4–6, 6–3, 5–7, 6–4, 6–2; Lewis–Simpson lost to P. Bertolucci–Panatta 4–6, 4–6, 6–3, 11–13; Lewis d. Panatta 6–4, 6–3, 6–2; B. Derlin lost to Barazzutti 2–6, 3–6. **France d. Czechoslovakia 3–2, Paris:** Y. Noah d. T. Smid 6–3, 5–7, 6–3, 4–6, 6–3; T. Tulasne lost to I. Lendl 3–6, 6–4, 3–6, 11–9, 4–6; H. Leconte–Noah d. Smid–P. Slozil 2–6, 6–3, 6–3, 6–4; Noah d. Lendl 6–2, 3–6, 7–9, 6–3, 6–4.

SEMI-FINAL ROUND

USA d. Australia 5–0, Perth: J. P. McEnroe d. P. McNamara 6–4, 4–6, 6–2, 6–4; G. Mayer d. J. G. Alexander 6–4, 3–6, 6–1, 6–2; P. Fleming–McEnroe d. McNamara–P. McNamee 6–2, 6–2, 3–6, 8–6;

Mayer d. M. R. Edmondson 6–3, 6–3; McEnroe d. Alexander 6–4, 6–3.
France d. New Zealand 3–2, Aix–en–Provence: T. Tulasne d. R.
Simpson 6–3, 4–6, 7–5, 6–2; Y. Noah d. C. J. Lewis 6–3, 6–1, 7–5;
Noah–H. Leconte lost to Lewis–Simpson 3–6, 7–9, 4–6; Tulasne lost to
Lewis 4–6, 2–6, 4–6; Noah d. Simpson 6–2, 6–2, 6–2.

FINAL ROUND
USA d. France 4–1, Grenoble: J. P. McEnroe d. Y. Noah 12–10, 1–6,
3–6, 6–2, 6–3; G. Mayer d. H. Leconte 6–2, 6–2, 7–9, 6–4; P.
Fleming–McEnroe d. Leconte–Noah 6–3, 6–4, 9–7; Mayer lost to Noah
1–6, 0–6; McEnroe d. Leconte 6–2, 6–3.

RELEGATION ROUND
USSR d. India 4–1, Donetsk: F. Pugaev d. S. Menon 2–6, 6–3, 6–4,
6–0; A. Zverev d. V. Amritraj 8–6, 6–1, 6–0; V. Borisov–R. Ashmerov
lost to A. and V. Amritraj 5–7, 5–7, 9–7, 4–6; Zverev d. Menon 6–0,
6–3, 3–6, 6–1; Pugaev d. V. Amritraj 6–3, 6–4. **Rumania d. Mexico
3–2, Mexico City:** I. Nastase d. F. Maciel 6–4, 2–6, 6–4, 10–8; F.
Segarceanu lost to R. Ramirez 5–7, 6–8, 9–7, 2–6; Nastase–Segarceanu
d. Ramirez–J. Lozano 6–3, 6–4, 11–9; Nastase lost to Ramirez 2–6, 1–6,
3–6; Segarceanu d. Maciel 6–1, 6–3, 9–7. **Great Britain d. Spain 3–2,
Barcelona:** A. M. Jarrett d. F. Luna 5–7, 2–6, 7–5, 6–0, 6–3; C. J.
Mottram d. J. Lopez-Maeso 6–2, 6–0, 6–2; Jarrett–J. R. Smith lost to S.
Casal–A. Gimenez 6–4, 2–6, 2–6, 4–6; Jarrett lost to Lopez-Maeso 5–7,
3–6, 6–2, 5–7; Mottram d. Luna 8–6, 8–6, 6–2. **Argentina d. West
Germany 3–2, Buenos Aires:** G. Vilas d. H. Beutel 6–4, 6–1, 7–5; J.
L. Clerc d. A. Maurer 6–4, 4–6, 3–6, 6–3, 6–2; Clerc–Vilas d. Maurer–W.
Popp 6–4, 6–2, 6–4; C. Castellan lost to Beutel 3–6, 0–6; A. Ganzabal
lost to M. Westphal 7–9, 4–6.

Zonal Competition

American Zone

FIRST ROUND
Ecuador d. Bolivia 5–0, La Paz: R. Ycaza d. J. C. Alvarado 6–2, 6–1,
3–6, 6–4; A. Gomez d. R. Benavides 8–10, 6–3, 6–4, 3–6, 6–1;
Gomez–Ycaza d. Alvarado–Benavides 4–6, 6–4, 6–2, 6–1; Gomez d. A.
Zalesky 6–1, 6–3; R. Viver d. Benavides 6–3, 6–2. **Paraguay d. Peru
3–2, Asuncion:** F. Gonzalez d. B. Arraya 6–2, 8–6, 6–4; V. Pecci d. F.
Maynetto 6–4, 7–5, 6–2; Gonzalez–Pecci d. Arraya–Maynetto 4–6, 7–5,

6–4, 6–3; O. E. Napout lost to C. Di Laura 2–6, 2–6; F. Arrellago lost to L. Cuneo 6–4, 4–6, 0–6.

Ecuador d. Brazil 5–0, Fortaleza: R. Ycaza d. D. Oliveira 6–1, 6–1, 6–2; A. Gomez d. M. Braga 6–2, 4–6, 6–3, 6–4; Gomez–Ycaza d. E. Oncins–F. Roese 6–4, 6–4, 6–4; R. Viver d. Roese 6–7, 6–2, 6–2; Ycaza d. Oncins 7–5, 6–3. **Paraguay d. Uruguay 3–2, Montevideo:** F. Gonzalez lost to D. Perez 6–1, 4–6, 6–1, 6–8, 3–6; V. Pecci lost to J. L. Damiani 6–8, 3–6, 6–8; Gonzalez–Pecci d. Damiani–Perez 6–3, 3–6, 9–7, 7–9, 8–6; Gonzalez d. Damiani 6–4, 6–4, 6–3; Pecci d. Perez 6–1, 5–7, 8–6, 6–4. **Colombia d. Commonwealth Caribbean 5–0, Bogota:** A. Cortes d. L. Rolle 6–4, 6–4, 6–3; J. Velasco d. J. Anthonas 9–7, 6–0, 6–4; Cortes–Velasco d. Rolle–Anthonas 6–3, 6–1, 3–6, 6–4; Cortes d. A. Clarke 6–1, 6–4; L. Gonzalez d. Rolle 7–5, 4–6, 6–2, 6–4. **Canada d. Venezuela 4–1, Caracas:** H. Fritz d. J. Andrew 16–14, 11–9, 9–11, 4–6, 11–9; R. Genois d. R. Scheller 6–2, 6–1, 6–3; J. Picken–B. Cowan lost to Andrew–E. Calvo 6–4, 6–4, 5–7, 4–6, 5–7; Picken d. Scheller 6–3, 6–3, 6–4; Cowan d. A. Sojo 7–5, 6–2.

Paraguay d. Ecuador 3–2, Asuncion: V. Pecci d. R. Ycaza 6–1, 10–8, 6–1; F. Gonzalez d. A. Gomez 6–3, 14–12, 6–3; Gonzalez–Pecci lost to Gomez–Ycaza 8–6, 3–6, 2–6, 4–6; Pecci d. Gomez 7–5, 5–7, 6–2, 6–4; Gonzalez lost to Ycaza 6–1, 5–7, 3–6. **Canada d. Colombia 3–2, Montreal:** R. Genois d. J. Velasco 6–2, 8–6, 6–3; G. Michibata lost to A. Cortes 3–6, 4–6, 9–11; H. Fritz–J. Brabenec Jr d. Velasco–Cortes 6–3, 6–3, 6–3; Genois d. Cortes 9–7, 4–6, 3–6, 6–3, 6–3; Michibata lost to Velasco def.

Paraguay d. Canada 4–1, Laval: F. Gonzalez d. G. Michibata 6–3, 3–6, 6–4, 4–6, 6–3; V. Pecci d. R. Genois 6–2, 8–6, 6–3; Gonzalez–Pecci d. B. Cowan–H. Fritz 6–4, 6–4, 6–0; Gonzalez d. Genois 6–3, 7–6; F. Arrellaga lost to Michibata 1–6, 0–6.

Eastern Zone

FIRST ROUND

Philippines d. Hong Kong 3–2, Hong Kong: R. Gabriel d. P. Chi
Yuen 6–2, 2–6, 3–6, 6–1, 6–2; M. Valleramos lost to K. Ng 1–6, 5–7,
3–6; Gabriel–A. Marcial d. M. Bailey–Ng 8–6, 6–2, 6–4; Gabriel lost to
Ng 4–6, 3–6, 4–6; Valleramos d. Yuen 6–1, 6–0, 6–0.   **Taiwan d.
Pakistan def.**

QUARTER-FINAL ROUND

South Korea d. Philippines 4–1, Manila: J. Y. Dae d. M. Valleramos
6–3, 2–6, 6–3, 6–3; K. C. Ho d. R. Z. Meda 12–10, 4–6, 6–3, 6–1;
Dae–S. D. Wook lost to R. Gabriel–A. Marcial 6–3, 4–6, 4–6, 2–6; Dae
d. Marcial 8–6, 6–2, 6–3; Ho d. Valleramos 6–4, 7–5.   **Indonesia d.
Malaysia 4–1, Kuala Lumpur:** A. W. Tintus d. Selvarajoo 6–8, 8–6,
6–2, 6–2; J. Tarik lost to Rudy Foo 6–4, 5–7, 5–7, 6–4, 0–6; Tintus–Tarik
d. Rudy Foo–Adam Malik 6–2, 6–3, 6–2; Tarik d. Selvarajoo 6–2, 6–2,
6–3; Tintus d. Rudy Foo 3–6, 8–6, 6–1, 6–3.   **Thailand d. Sri Lanka
3–1, Colombo:** P. Pladchurnil d. A. Perera 6–2, 6–1, 6–2; S. Eaumongkol
lost to A. Fernando 4–6, 7–5, 4–6, 6–3, 1–6; Pladchurnil–Eaumongkol
d. Evo–Fernando 6–4, 4–6, 6–3, 6–3; Pladchurnil d. Fernando 6–1, 5–7,
4–6, 6–4, 6–2.   **Japan d. Taiwan 4–1, Taipei:** S. Sakamoto d. Wu Chang-
Rung 6–4, 6–3, 5–7, 7–5; S. Nishio d. Hsu Hsuang–Jung 4–6, 3–6, 6–1,
6–2, 6–1; H. Shirato–T. Yonezawa d. Huang–Jung–Chang-Rung 6–2,
6–2, 14–12; Sakamoto d. Huang–Jung 4–6, 6–2, 7–5; Nishio lost to
Chang-Rung 2–6, 2–6.

SEMI-FINAL ROUND

Indonesia d. South Korea 3–2, Jakarta: T. Arianto lost to J. Y. Dae
4–6, 2–6, 2–6; J. Tarik d. K. C. Ho 4–6, 2–6, 6–4, 6–1, 6–2; A.
Wijono–Arianto lost to Dae–S. D. Wook 3–6, 3–6, 2–6; Tarik d. Dae
9–7, 6–0, 9–7; Arianto d. Ho 6–3, 3–6, 6–4, 6–1.   **Japan d. Thailand
3–0, Tokyo:** T. Fukui d. S. Eaumongkol 6–0, 6–3, 5–7, 6–0; S. Nishio
d. P. Pladchurnil 6–2, 6–8, 6–0, 7–5; Fukui–T. Yonezawa d.
Pladchurnil–Eaumongkol 6–1, 6–2, 6–3.

FINAL ROUND

Indonesia d. Japan 4–1, Jakarta: J. Tarik d. T. Fukui 6–4, 9–7, 1–6,
7–5; T. A. Wibowo d. S. Nishio 6–3, 6–3, 9–7; Tarik–I. Hadiman d.
T. Yonezawa–Fukui 6–2, 6–3, 6–3; Wibowo d. E. Takeuchi 6–4, 3–6,
6–4; Hadiman lost to Yonezawa 3–6, 5–7.

European Zone A

FIRST ROUND
Morocco d. Poland 3–2, Casablanca: O. Laimina d. H. Drzymalski
6–4, 6–2, 6–4; M. Dlimi lost to W. Meres 4–6, 6–4, 4–6, 6–3, 3–6;
Laimina–H. Saber d. Drzymalski–Meres 9–7, 6–2, 5–7, 6–3; Saber lost to
Drzymalski 3–6, 6–1, 5–7, 4–6; Laimina d. Meres 6–8, 6–3, 8–6, 6–2.
Ireland d. Luxembourg 5–0, Dublin: S. Sorensen d. J. Goudenbourg
6–1, 6–1, 6–2; M. Doyle d. P. Hoffman 6–0, 6–1, 6–0; T. Burke–P.
Hannon d. Goudenbourg–S. Kinsch 6–2, 6–3, 6–4; Sorensen d. Hoffman
6–2, 6–2, 6–1; Doyle d. Goudenbourg 7–5, 6–4, 6–4. **Greece d.
Turkey 5–0, Ankara:** A. Anastopoulos d. N. Demir 3–6, 6–4, 6–0, 1–6,
6–4; G. Kalovelonis d. Altinkaya 6–3, 6–3, 6–3; Kalovelonis–
Anastopoulos d. Demir–Altinkaya 6–4, 8–10, 3–6, 7–5, 6–0; Anastopoulos
d. Altinkaya 6–4, 6–4, 6–4; Kalovelonis d. Demir 6–2, 7–5, 9–7.

QUARTER-FINAL ROUND
Switzerland d. Morocco 5–0, Casablanca: Y. DuPasquier d. M. Dlimi
6–2, 10–8, 4–6, 6–3; H. Gunthardt d. O. Laimina 2–6, 2–6, 6–1, 6–3,
6–0; H. and P. Gunthardt d. Laimina–Dlimi 8–6, 7–5, 6–2; R. Stadler d.
Laimina 6–4, 6–1, 7–5; H. Gunthardt d. Dlimi 6–3, 6–0, 6–2. **Austria
d. Algeria 5–0, Vienna:** R. Reininger d. D. Boudjemline 6–3, 6–1, 6–4;
H. P. Kandler d. Y. Amier 6–1, 6–0, 6–3; I. Wimmer–G. Mild d.
Boudjemline–Amier 6–3, 6–0, 6–3; Reininger d. Amier 6–1, 6–0, 6–3;
Kandler d. Boudjemline 6–1, 6–3, 9–7. **Ireland d. Monaco 4–1,
Dublin:** S. Sorensen d. B. Balleret 6–3, 6–3, 6–1; M. Doyle d. I. Borfiga
6–1, 6–3, 6–3; T. Burke–Sorensen d. Balleret–Borfiga 5–7, 7–9, 10–8,
6–3, 8–6; Sorensen d. Borfiga 6–1, 6–1, 6–2; P. Hannon lost to C. Carlier
4–6, 1–6, 3–6. **Finland d. Greece 3–2, Athens:** K. Alkio lost to G.
Kalovelonis 1–6, 4–6, 3–6; L. Palin d. T. Anastopoulos 6–2, 6–1, 2–6,
6–1; Palin–Alkio d. Kalovelonis–Anastopoulos 18–16, 6–4, 6–4; Palin d. G.
Kalovelonis 1–6, 6–2, 6–1, 6–3; O. Rahnasto lost to F. Vazoes 7–9, 5–7.

SEMI-FINAL ROUND
Switzerland d. Austria 4–0, Poertschach: H. Gunthardt d. R.
Reininger 6–4, 6–4, 6–1; R. Stadler d. H. P. Kandler 6–1, 6–3, 6–1; H.
and M. Gunthardt d. I. Wimmer–G. Mild 6–2, 6–2, 6–4; H. Gunthardt
d. Kandler 6–3, 7–5, 4–6, 6–4; Stadler v. Reininger 6–8, 6–8, 1–1 unfin.
Ireland d. Finland 4–1, Dublin: M. Doyle d. L. Palin 6–2, 6–1, 6–0;
S. Sorensen d. M. Timonen 6–2, 7–5, 6–3; Doyle–Sorensen d. Palin–K.
Alkio 6–3, 6–4, 6–4; Doyle d. Timonen 6–2, 6–2; R. Dolan lost to Alkio
2–6, 3–6.

FINAL ROUND
Ireland d. Switzerland 4–1, Dublin: M. Doyle d. H. Gunthardt 6–0, 6–4, 6–0; S. Sorensen d. R. Stadler 6–3, 3–6, 8–6, 9–7; Doyle–Sorensen lost to H. and M. Gunthardt 6–8, 2–6, 5–7; Doyle d. Stadler 6–4, 6–2, 6–4; Sorensen d. J. Hlasek 7–5, 7–5.

European Zone B

FIRST ROUND
Yugoslavia d. Norway 5–0, Varazdin: M. Ostoja d. J. Svensen 6–3, 6–1, 6–2; S. Zivojinovic d. M. Ronneberg 6–1, 6–2, 4–6, 7–9, 6–0; Ostoja–Zivojinovic d. G. Pedersen–Svensen 6–2, 6–1, 6–1; Z. Petkovic d. Svensen 9–7, 6–1, 6–1; B. Horvat d. Pedersen 6–3, 6–3, 6–4.
Portugal d. Tunisia 5–0, Oporto: P. Cordeiro d. B. Farhat 6–1, 6–1, 6–3; M. Soares d. A. Zouhir 6–0, 6–2, 6–3; Soares–Cordeiro d. Zouhir–Farhat 6–0, 6–4, 6–3; J. Gueddes d. Hanashi 6–3, 6–2; M. de Sousa d. Zouhir 6–3, 6–1. **Denmark d. Bulgaria 4–1, Sofia:** P. Bastiansen lost to B. Pampoulov 6–8, 6–3, 2–6 def.; M. Mortensen d. Y. Stamatov 6–2, 7–9, 6–3, 5–7, 7–5; Mortensen–Bastiansen d. B. and M. Pampoulov 6–4, 6–4, 6–2; Bastiansen d. Stamatov 6–0, 6–1, 6–0; Mortensen d. B. Pampoulov 6–2, 6–2.

QUARTER-FINAL ROUND
Hungary d. Yugoslavia 3–2, Budapest: B. Taroczy d. S. Zivojinovic 6–2, 6–2, 6–0; J. Benyik lost to M. Ostoja 7–5, 3–6, 1–6, 4–6; Taroczy–P. Szoke d. Zivojinovic–Ostoja 6–2, 7–5, 8–6; Benyik lost to Zivojinovic 8–6, 6–4, 2–6, 3–6, 2–6; Taroczy d. Ostoja 6–3, 6–2, 9–7. **Israel d. Belgium 3–0, Eupen:** S. Perkis d. J. Grandjean 6–3, 3–6, 6–8, 6–0, 7–5; S. Glickstein d. B. Boileau 3–6, 8–6, 6–3, 4–6, 6–4; Glickstein–D. Schneider d. Boileau–T. Stevaux 6–1, 10–12, 7–9, 6–4, 6–2. **Egypt d. Portugal 5–0, Lisbon:** T. El Sakka d. M. Soares 4–6, 6–3, 6–4, 6–4; A. El Mehelmy d. P. Cordeiro 6–4, 6–3, 2–6, 1–6, 8–6; I. El Shafei–El Mehelmy d. Soares–Cordeiro 6–4, 6–2, 6–4; Mehelmy d. Soares 7–5, 6–3; El Sakka d. Cordeiro 9–7, 6–2. **Denmark d. Holland 3–0, Hoersholm:** M. Mortensen d. L. Sanders 6–8, 4–6, 8–6, 6–2, 6–2; P. Bastiansen d. M. Schapers 6–4, 6–3, 6–2; Mortensen–Bastiansen d. Schapers–H. van Boeckel 8–10, 6–4, 6–4, 5–7, 9–7.

SEMI-FINAL ROUND
Hungary d. Israel 4–1, Budapest: B. Taroczy d. S. Perkiss 7–5, 6–4, 6–2; J. Benyik lost to S. Glickstein 1–6, 0–6, 2–6; Taroczy–P. Szoke d.

Glickstein–D. Schneider 3–6, 6–3, 2–6, 7–5, 8–6; Benyik d. Perkiss 5–7, 8–6, 6–2, 9–7; Taroczy d. Glickstein 7–5, 6–2. **Denmark d. Egypt 4–1, Aarhus:** M. Mortensen d. A. El Mehelmy 6–4, 4–6, 6–3, 6–4; P. Bastiansen d. T. El Sakka 6–1, 6–0, 5–7, 6–4; Mortensen–Bastiansen d. El Mehelmy–El Sakka 5–7, 6–1, 6–3, 6–1; Bastiansen d. El Mehelmy 6–3, 6–0; Mortensen lost to El Sakka 1–6, 6–4, 3–6.

FINAL ROUND
Denmark d. Hungary 3–2, Budapest: P. Bastiansen d. R. Machan 4–6, 6–2, 2–6, 6–4, 6–2; M. Mortensen lost to B. Taroczy 1–6, 3–6, 3–6; Bastiansen–Mortensen lost to P. Szoke–Taroczy 2–6, 5–7, 0–6; Bastiansen d. Taroczy 6–4, 6–4, 2–6, 8–6; Mortensen d. Machan 6–2, 3–6, 9–7, 11–9.

1983: AUSTRALIA
Non-Zonal Competition

FIRST ROUND
France d. USSR 4–1, Moscow: Y. Noah d. K. Pugaev 6–4, 6–4, 6–4; H. Leconte d. V. Borisov 13–11, 6–2, 6–2; Leconte–Noah d. Pugaev–S. Leonyuk 6–3, 7–5, 4–6, 4–6, 6–3; Noah d. Borisov 6–2, 6–2; Leconte lost to Pugaev 8–10, 6–4. **Paraguay d. Czechoslovakia 3–2, Asuncion:** F. Gonzalez lost to I. Lendl 3–6, 4–6, 8–10; V. Pecci d. T. Smid 6–3, 3–6, 6–4, 5–7, 6–1; Gonzalez–Pecci d. Lendl–P. Slozil 6–4, 6–4, 6–4; Gonzalez d. Smid 6–3, 12–10, 3–6, 6–3; V. Cabellero lost to J. Navratil 2–6, 0–6. **Australia d. Great Britain 4–1, Adelaide:** P. Cash d. J. M. Lloyd 5–7, 7–5, 6–3, 1–6, 7–5; P. McNamee d. C. J. Mottram 6–3, 6–2, 6–2; M. Edmondson–McNamee d. A. M. Jarrett–Lloyd 6–2, 9–11, 6–3, 6–2; Cash lost to Mottram 6–1, 5–7, 3–6; McNamee d. Lloyd 6–1, 6–2. **Rumania d. Chile 5–0, Timisoara:** F. Segarceanu d. H. Gildemeister 6–3, 3–6, 0–6, 6–3, 9–7; I. Nastase d. R. Acuna 2–6, 6–3, 6–2, 6–4; Nastase–Segarceanu d. Gildemeister–B. Prajoux 6–3, 8–6, 6–4; Segarceanu d. Acuna 6–1, 7–5; Nastase d. Gildemeister 2–6, 6–4, 6–2. **Sweden d. Indonesia 5–0, Bjaerred:** A. Jarryd d. T. Wibowo 6–4, 6–2, 7–5; M. Wilander d. J. Tarik 6–2, 6–2, 6–1; Jarryd–H. Simonsson d. Tarik–I. Hadiman 6–2, 6–3, 6–3; Wilander d. Wibowo 6–3, 6–3; Jarryd d. Tarik 6–3, 6–1. **New Zealand d. Denmark 5–0, Christchurch:** R. Simpson d. M. Mortensen 8–6, 9–11, 6–4, 6–2; C. J. Lewis d. P. Bastiansen 10–8, 6–3, 7–5; Lewis–Simpson d. Bastiansen–Mortensen 8–6, 6–3, 6–4; Simpson d. Bastiansen 6–1, 6–2; Lewis d. Mortensen 11–9, 6–3. **Italy d. Ireland 3–2, Reggio Calabria:** C. Panatta lost to S. Sorensen 6–1, 4–6, 4–6, 1–6; C. Barazzutti d. M. Doyle 6–4, 6–3, 6–1;

P. Bertolucci–A. Panatta d. Doyle–Sorensen 3–6, 6–2, 6–2, 6–4; C. Panatta lost to Doyle 6–1, 3–6, 4–6, 4–6; Barazzutti d. Sorensen 6–0, 6–3, 6–3. **Argentina d. USA 3–2, Buenos Aires:** J. L. Clerc d. J. P. McEnroe 7–4, 6–0, 3–6, 4–6, 7–5; G. Vilas d. G. Mayer 6–3, 6–3, 6–4; Clerc–Vilas lost to P. Fleming–McEnroe 6–2, 8–10, 1–6, 6–3, 1–6; Vilas d. McEnroe 6–4, 6–0, 6–1; R. Ganzabal lost to Mayer 4–6, 6–3, 8–10.

QUARTER-FINAL ROUND

France d. Paraguay 3–2, Marseille: T. Tulasne d. F. Gonzalez 6–3, 8–6, 6–2; H. Leconte d. V. Pecci 6–3, 1–6, 6–2, 6–3; Leconte–G. Moretton lost to Gonzalez–Pecci 4–6, 4–6, 7–9; Tulasne lost to Pecci 1–6, 5–7, 6–4, 2–6; Leconte d. Gonzalez 6–4, 6–4, 7–5.   **Australia d. Rumania 5–0, Brisbane:** P. Cash d. F. Segarceanu 6–2, 6–1, 6–1; M. R. Edmondson d. I. Nastase 4–6, 6–3, 14–12, 6–2; Edmondson–P. McNamee d. Nastase–Segarceanu 8–6, 7–5, 6–0; Cash d. Nastase 6–3, 6–3; Edmondson d. Segarceanu 6–4, 6–3.   **Sweden d. New Zealand 3–2, Eastbourne:** H. Sundstrom lost to R. Simpson 7–9, 8–10, 4–6; M. Wilander d. C. J. Lewis 6–4, 7–5, 6–8, 10–8; A. Jarryd–H. Simonsson d. Lewis–Simpson 6–2, 6–4, 4–6, 6–4; Sundstrom lost to Lewis 9–7, 4–6, 6–4, 3–6, 3–6; Wilander d. Simpson 6–3, 6–3, 6–2.   **Argentina d. Italy 5–0, Rome:** G. Vilas d. A. Panatta 6–2, 6–2, 6–1; J. L. Clerc d. C. Barazzutti 12–10, 6–2, 7–9, 3–6, 6–4; Clerc–Vilas d. Panatta–P. Bertolucci 7–5, 6–3, 6–4; Vilas d. Barazzutti 6–3, 6–1; R. Arguello d. F. Cancellotti 7–5, 6–4.

SEMI-FINAL ROUND

Australia d. France 4–1, Sydney: P. Cash lost to Y. Noah 4–6, 8–10, 3–6; J. Fitzgerald d. H. Leconte 4–6, 10–8, 9–7, 6–2; M. R. Edmondson–P. McNamee d. Leconte–Noah 11–9, 6–4, 6–3; Fitzgerald d. Noah 13–11, 4–6, 6–4, 6–3. Cash d. Leconte 3–6, 9–7, 8–6.   **Sweden d. Argentina 4–1, Stockholm:** M. Wilander d. G. Vilas 6–4, 6–3, 6–4; A. Jarryd d. J. L. Clerc 7–5, 6–2, 6–2; Jarryd–H. Simonsson d. Clerc–Vilas 6–3, 6–3, 6–4; Jarryd lost to Vilas 4–6, 0–6; Wilander d. Clerc 6–1, 6–2.

FINAL ROUND

Australia d. Sweden 3–2, Melbourne: P. Cash lost to M. Wilander 3–6, 6–4, 7–9, 3–6; J. Fitzgerald d. J. Nystrom 6–4, 6–2, 4–6, 6–4; M. R. Edmondson–P. McNamee d. A. Jarryd–H. Simonsson 6–4, 6–4, 6–2; Cash d. Nystrom 6–4, 6–1, 6–1; Fitzgerald lost to Wilander 8–6, 1–6, 0–6.

RELEGATION ROUND

Czechoslovakia d. USSR 4–1, Hrabec Kralova: T. Smid d. A. Zverev 4–6, 8–6, 4–6, 6–4, 6–4; M. Mecir d. A. Chesnokov 8–10, 1–6, 6–3, 6–4, 6–2; L. Pimek–P. Slozil d. Zverev–A. Olkouky 6–0, 6–4, 6–2; Smid d. Chesnokov 6–2, 7–5; Mecir lost to Zverev 3–6, 6–7. **Great Britain d. Chile 4–1, Eastbourne:** J. M. Lloyd d. J. Fillol 6–1, 7–5, 6–8, 6–4; C. J. Mottram d. R. Acuna 6–4, 6–3, 6–3; Lloyd–Mottram d. Fillol–B. Prajoux 6–4, 6–2, 6–1; A. M. Jarrett lost to Acuna 14–12, 7–9, 0–6; Mottram d. Fillol 6–4, 6–2. **Denmark d. Indonesia 4–1, Copenhagen:** M. Mortensen d. J. Tarik 11–9, 6–3, 6–4; P. Bastiansen d. T. Wibowo 13–11, 4–6, 6–1, 6–4; Bastiansen–Mortensen d. Tarik–Wibowo 7–5, 6–2, 6–3; Bastiansen d. Tarik 6–4, 7–5; Mortensen lost to Wibowo 4–6, 4–6. **USA d. Ireland 4–1, Dublin:** J. P. McEnroe d. S. Sorensen 6–3, 6–2, 6–2; E. Teltscher lost to M. Doyle 3–6, 4–6, 4–6; P. Fleming–McEnroe d. Doyle–Sorensen 6–2, 6–3, 6–4; McEnroe d. Doyle 9–7, 6–3, 6–3; Teltscher d. Sorensen 14–16, 10–8, 8–6.

Zonal Competition

American Zone

FIRST ROUND

Brazil d. Peru 4–1, Lima: C. Kirmayr d. C. Di Laura 6–1, 6–4, 6–4; M. Hocevar lost to P. Arraya 3–6, 6–2, 1–6, 3–6; Kirmayr–C. Motta d. Arraya–F. Maynetto 6–4, 6–3, 6–4; Kirmayr d. Arraya 8–6, 7–5, 6–4; Hocevar d. Di Laura 8–6, 6–2.

QUARTER-FINAL ROUND

Uruguay d. Mexico 4–1, Montevideo: J. L. Damiani d. J. Lozana 6–1, 6–2, 6–3; D. Perez d. F. P. Pascal 6–4, 6–2, 6–1; Damiani–Perez lost to Lozano–Pascal 3–6, 2–6, 2–6; Damiani d. Pascal 6–4, 10–8, 6–2; Perez d. F. Maciel 7–5, 0–6, 7–5. **Brazil d. Colombia 5–0, Bogota:** C. Motta d. J. Restrepo 6–1, 6–2, 6–2; C. Kirmayr d. R. Gomez 6–2, 3–6, 6–1, 6–4; Kirmayr–Motta d. Gomez–Restrepo 6–1, 7–9, 7–5, 6–2; Kirmayr d. L. A. Gonzalez 7–5, 0–6, 6–3; Motta d. Gomez 6–2, 7–5. **Ecuador d. Commonwealth Caribbean 5–0, Guayaquil:** A. Gomez d. A. Clarke 6–1, 6–4, 6–3; R. Viver d. S. Sarnia 6–0, 6–1, 6–2; Gomez–R. Ycaza d. L. Rolle–Sarnia 6–1, 6–0, 6–2; Ycaza d. Sarnia 3–2 def.; Viver d. Clarke 6–0, 6–0. **Canada d. Venezuela 3–2, Laval, Quebec:** M. Wostenholme d. J. Andrew 6–2, 2–6, 6–2, 6–4; R. Genois d. C. Claverie 6–4, 6–1, 2–6, 6–3; B. Cowan–J. Brabenec Jr lost to Andrew–I. Calvo

3–6, 6–3, 6–4, 4–6, 4–6; Wostenholme lost to Claverie 6–8, 4–6, 6–2, 3–6; Genois d. Andrew 6–4, 6–3, 6–1.

SEMI-FINAL ROUND

Brazil d. Uruguay 3–2, Montevideo: M. Hocevar d. J. L. Damiani 8–6, 4–6, 4–6, 6–3, 15–13; C. Kirmayr lost to D. Perez 3–6, 6–8, 7–5, 4–6; Kirmayr–C. Motta d. Damiani–Perez 1–6, 4–6, 8–6, 6–2, 6–4; Hocevar lost to Perez 6–8, 5–7, 3–6; Kirmayr d. Damiani 3–6, 7–5, 6–2, 5–7, 6–1. **Ecuador d. Canada 4–1, Guayaquil:** A. Gomez d. G. Michibata 6–2, 6–4, 3–6, 6–2; R. Ycaza d. J. Picken 6–4, 2–6, 6–0, 6–4; Gomez–Ycaza d. J. Brabenec Jr–R. Genois 6–1, 6–1, 6–2; M. Aguirre Jr lost to Picken 1–6, 0–6, R. Viver d. Michibata 6–4, 6–4.

FINAL ROUND

Ecuador d. Brazil 5–0, Guayaquil: A. Gomez d. C. Kirmayr 6–3, 6–2, 6–0; R. Ycaza d. M. Hocevar 7–5, 1–6, 6–2, 6–2; Gomez–Ycaza d. Kirmayr–C. Motta 6–3, 11–9, 3–6, 4–6, 6–1; Ycaza d. Kirmayr 8–6, 6–2; R. Viver d. Hocevar 6–3, 6–4.

Eastern Zone

FIRST ROUND

Sri Lanka d. Hong Kong 3–2, Colombo: A. Fernando lost to M. Bailey 5–7, 3–6, 5–7; F. Sabaratnam d. Kelvin Ng 2–6, 6–2, 6–1, def.; Fernando–Sabaratnam d. Bailey–Pang Chi Yuen 6–4, 3–6, 4–6, 6–4, 6–1; Sabaratnam d. Bailey 7–5, 3–6, 2–6, 6–4, 6–4; A. Perera lost to P. Bailey 2–6, 4–6, 2–6. **Philippines d. Malaysia 5–0, Manila:** R. Gabriel d. A. Malik 6–4, 6–0, 6–2; R. Rafon d. R. Anchant 6–0, 6–0, 6–0; E. Capulong–R. Suarez d. Malik–R. Ramial 6–3, 7–9, 6–2, 7–5; Gabriel d. Ramial 6–2, 6–1; Rafon d. Malik 6–0, 6–0.

QUARTER-FINAL ROUND

India d. Sri Lanka 4–1, Colombo: S. Menon d. F. Sabaratnam 6–0, 6–1, 6–3; V. Amritraj d. A. Fernando 6–3, 6–1, 6–4; A. and V. Amritraj d. Fernando–Sabaratnam 6–2, 6–4, 6–1; S. Vasudevan d. Sabaratnam 6–1, 6–2, 6–0; Menon lost to Fernando 6–4, 1–2, def. **Thailand d. Taiwan 3–2, Tapei:** Pnamkorn Pladchurnil lost to Wu Chang Rung 2–6, 10–8, 4–6, 6–4, 4–6; Sombat Eaumongkol d. Hsu Huang Jung 4–6, 6–4, 6–2, 7–5; Pladchurnil–Eaumongkol d. Rung–Jung 6–3, 6–2, 6–4; Eaumongkol lost to Rung 6–4, 4–6, 2–6, 6–4, 2–6; Pladchurnil d. Jung 4–6, 6–4, 2–6, 6–1, 6–1. **South Korea d. Philippines 4–1, Seoul:** J. Yeong–Dae d.

V. Sison 6–1, 6–4, 8–6; K. Choon–Ho d. R. Rafon 8–6, 6–3, 6–0; L. Woo-Ryong–S. Dong-Wook d. R. Gabriel–Sison 11–9, 6–3, 9–7; Dong-Wook d. M. Valleramos 6–2, 6–2; Choon–Ho lost to Sison 8–10, 3–6. **Japan d. China 3–2, Osaka City:** T. Fukui d. Li Shiquin 6–0, 6–0, 6–1; H. Shirato lost to Liu Shuhua 6–8, 3–6, 6–3, 6–4, 4–6; T. Yonezawa–Shirato lost to Shuhua–Ma Keqin 4–6, 3–6, 6–1, 6–4, 5–7; Fukui d. Shuhua 6–2, 6–2, 6–2; Shirato d. Shiquin 6–2, 7–5, 6–4.

SEMI-FINAL ROUND

India d. Thailand 5–0, New Delhi: V. Amritraj d. Eaumongkol 6–4, 6–0, 6–3; S. Menon d. S. Meesawad 7–5, 6–2, 6–0; A. and V. Amritraj d. Eaumongkol–Meesawad 6–1, 6–2, 6–0; Menon d. Eaumongkol 7–5, 6–3; N. Bal d. Meesawad 6–4, 9–7. **Japan d. Korea 4–1, Nagoya:** T. Fukui d. S. Dong-Wook 2–6, 6–2, 6–1, 7–5; H. Shirato d. L. Woo-Ryong 4–6, 6–1, 6–4, 6–3; S. Nishio–T. Yonezawa d. J. Yeong-Dae–Dong-Wook 7–5, 5–7, 6–3, 3–6, 7–5; Fukui d. Woo-Ryong 6–1, 6–1; Shirato lost to Dong-Wook 5–7, 5–7.

FINAL ROUND

India d. Japan 3–2, Tokyo: R. Krishnan d. T. Fukui 6–4, 6–1, 3–6, 4–6, 6–0; V. Amritraj d. H. Shirato 6–2, 8–6, 6–3; A. and V. Amritraj d. J. Kamiwazumi–T. Yonezawa 6–1, 6–8, 6–4, 6–2; Krishnan lost to Shirato 6–2, 4–6, 5–7; V. Amritraj lost to Fukui 5–7, 3–6.

European Zone A

FIRST ROUND

Belgium d. Poland 5–0, Warsaw: J. Van Langendonck d. W. Rogowski 8–6, 6–8, 6–1, 6–4; B. Boileau d. L. Bienkowski 6–0, 6–2, 6–2; Boileau–J. Grandjean d. H. Dryzmalski–Blenkowski 6–2, 7–5, 6–4; Boileau d. Rogowski 6–3, 6–2; Van Langendonck d. Bienkowski 5–7, 8–6, 6–2. **Monaco d. Luxembourg 4–1, Monte Carlo:** B. Balleret d. M. Klensch 6–0, 6–3, 6–2; M. Borfiga d. J. Goudenbourg 6–3, 10–8, 6–1; Balleret–J. Vincileoni d. Klensch–Goudenbourg 6–1, 6–4, 6–2; Borfiga d. Klensch 6–2, 6–3; A. Viviani lost to Goudenbourg 8–6, 4–6, 5–7. **Holland d. Portugal 4–1, Estoril:** M. Schapers d. P. Cordeiro 6–2, 6–4, 6–4; E. Wilborts d. M. Sousa 6–2, 6–3, 7–5; Schapers–T. Sie d. J and P. Cordeiro 8–6, 6–4, 6–4; Schapers d. Sousa 6–2, 6–2; Wilborts lost to P. Cordeiro 7–5, 1–6, 1–6. **Greece d. Iraq def.**

QUARTER-FINAL ROUND

West Germany d. Belgium 5–0, Eupen: M. Westphal d. J. Van Langendonck 6–3, 6–4, 4–6, 6–1; D. Keretic d. J. Grandjean 4–6, 6–1, 6–3, 6–1; A. Maurer–W. Popp d. Grandjean–Van Langendonck 6–4, 6–4, 6–1; Keretic d. Van Langendonck 6–4, 3–6, 8–6, 6–1; Westphal d. Grandjean 7–5, 6–2.   **Israel d. Monaco 4–1, Monte Carlo:** S. Glickstein d. B. Balleret 7–5, 6–2, 6–2; S. Perkiss d. E. Carlier 6–3, 6–3, 6–1; Glickstein–D. Schneider d. Balleret–A. Vincileoni 1–6, 6–4, 6–2, 13–11; Perkiss lost to Balleret 3–6, 2–6, 4–6; Glickstein d. Carlier 6–2, 6–4, 6–4. **Holland d. Egypt 4–1, Cairo:** H. Van Boeckel d. A. El Mehelmi 6–4, 6–3, 4–6, 6–3; M. Schapers d. K. Baligh 6–2, 6–4, 6–3; Schapers–Van Boeckel d. Baligh–El Mehelmi 6–2, 6–4, 6–2; Van Boeckel d. Baligh 2–6, 6–4, 6–2; Schapers lost to El Mehelmi 4–6, 1–6.   **Switzerland d. Greece 5–0, Ostermundigen:** R. Stadler d. F. Vazeos 6–2, 6–4, 6–1; H. Gunthardt d. G. Kalovelonis 6–1, 6–3, 6–0; M. and H. Gunthardt d. Kalovelonis–Vazeos 6–2, 6–4, 6–1; H. Gunthardt d. Vazeos 6–1, 6–2; Stadler d. Kalovelonis 6–1, 2–6, 6–4.

SEMI-FINAL ROUND

West Germany d. Israel 3–2, Tel Aviv: D. Keretic d. D. Schneider 1–6, 6–4, 6–2, 6–2; M. Westphal d. S. Glickstein 9–7, 1–6, 4–6, 6–4, 6–3; A. Maurer–W. Popp lost to Glickstein–S. Perkis 4–6, 10–8, 5–7, 5–7; Westphal d. Perkiss 2–6, 6–0, 7–5, 11–9; Keretic lost to Glickstein 4–6, 4–6.   **Switzerland d. Holland 3–2, Lugano:** H. Gunthardt d. H. Van Boeckel 5–7, 6–1, 8–6, 6–0; R. Stadler d. M. Schapers 6–1, 6–2, 6–1; H. and M. Gunthardt lost to Schapers–Van Boeckel 6–4, 6–3, 6–8, 5–7, 7–9; Stadler d. Van Boeckel 6–4, 6–4, 6–8, 6–4; H. Gunthardt lost to Schapers def.

FINAL ROUND

West Germany d. Switzerland 3–2, Freiburg: M. Westphal lost to H. Gunthardt 2–6, 2–6, 8–6, 6–2, 2–6; D. Keretic d. R. Stadler 6–0, 6–3, 5–7, 1–6, 6–2; A. Maurer–W. Popp d. H. and M. Gunthardt 6–2, 2–6, 6–1, 6–2; Westphal d. Stadler 7–5, 6–2, 8–10, 6–2; Keretic lost to H. Gunthardt 3–6, 5–7.

European Zone B

FIRST ROUND

Zimbabwe d. Turkey 5–0, Istanbul: O. Lourenco d. N. Demir 6–1, 6–3, 6–1; P. Tuckniss d. M. Guler 6–2, 6–1, 6–2; H. Ismail–Tuckniss

d. Y. Er Kangil–M. Arpacioglou 6–3, 6–4, 6–4; Tuckniss d. Demir 6–4, 2–6, 6–0; Lourenco d. Guler 6–0, 6–2. **Austria d. Morocco 5–0, Ternitz, Austria:** G. Mild d. H. Saber 6–1, 3–6, 6–4, 6–1; R. Reininger d. O. Laimina 6–2, 7–5, 6–4; Mild–H. Kary d. Laimina–M. Dlimi 6–2, 4–6, 6–4, 6–3; Mild d. Laimina 3–6, 6–3, 6–1; Reininger d. Saber 6–1, 7–5. **Norway d. Libya def.; Bulgaria d. Algeria 4–1, Algiers:** Y. Stamatov d. D. Boudjemline 6–4, 6–1, 6–1; K. Lazarov d. K. Harad 6–3, 6–0, 6–1; Stamatov–M. Lazarov d. M. Bouabdullah–N. Abbes 6–2, 7–5, 6–3; Stamatov d. Harad 6–1, 6–4, 6–2; K. Lazarov lost to Boudjemline 8–10, 8–10, 4–6. **Yugoslavia d. Tunisia 3–0, Zagreb:** S. Zivojinovic d. R. Hichen 6–2, 6–2, 6–2; M. Ostoja d. A. Dsoudani 6–0, 6–2, 5–2, def.; Ostoja–Zivojinovic d. Hichen–M. Ben Aziza 6–2, 6–2, 6–3.

QUARTER-FINAL ROUND

Hungary d. Zimbabwe 4–1, Budapest: R. Machan lost to H. Ismail 6–1, 6–2, 6–8, 4–6, 0–6; B. Taroczy d. P. Tuckniss 6–4, 6–2, 6–0; P. Szoke–Taroczy d. Ismail–Tuckniss 6–2, 6–1, 7–5; Machan d. Tuckniss 6–4, 6–0, 7–5; Taroczy d. Ismail 6–2, 7–5. **Austria d. Norway 4–1, Oslo:** R. Reininger d. T. Joensson 6–2, 8–6, 4–6, 6–1; K. Oberparleiter d. M. Roenneberg 7–5, 8–6, 7–5; H. Kary–Reininger d. T. Persson–Roenneberg 6–1, 3–6, 5–7, 6–4, 6–2; Reininger lost to P. Hegna 4–6, 3–6; G. Mild d. Joensson 6–2, 6–4. **Bulgaria d. Finland 3–2, Sofia:** L. Petrov lost to L. Palin 4–6, 2–6, 6–4, 4–6; K. Lazarov d. O. Rahnasto 6–4, 4–6, 6–4, 3–6, 6–3; K. and M. Lazarov d. K. Alki–Palin 4–6, 6–4, 6–3, 6–4; Petrov lost to Rahnasto 6–4, 1–6, 3–6, 6–2, 3–6; K. Lazarov d. Palin 6–1, 6–2, 6–8, 4–6, 6–0. **Yugoslavia d. Spain 3–2, Madrid:** M. Ostoja d. S. Casal 1–6, 4–6, 6–3, 6–1, 6–3; S. Zivojinovic lost to J. Avendano 1–6, 6–4, 6–4, 3–6, 1–6; Ostoja–Zivojinovic d. J. Aguillera–Casal 2–6, 6–1, 6–4, 1–6, 8–6; Zivojinovic d. Casal 5–7, 3–6, 6–4, 6–3, 6–4; G. Prpic lost to A. Tous 6–3, 3–6, 3–6.

SEMI-FINAL ROUND

Hungary d. Austria 3–2, Poertschach: R. Machan lost to B. Pils 6–4, 2–6, 1–6, 10–8, 4–6; B. Taroczy d. P. Feigl 6–1, 6–4, 3–6, 6–4; P. Szoke–Taroczy d. Feigl–G. Mild 6–4, 6–2, 4–6, 6–4; Taroczy d. Feigl 6–1, 6–4, 3–6, 6–4; Machan lost to Pils 8–6, 6–2, 5–7, 1–6, 2–6. **Yugoslavia d. Bulgaria 5–0, Sofia:** M. Ostoja d. K. Lazarov 1–6, 6–3, 4–6, 6–4, 6–3; S. Zivojinovic d. Y. Stamatov 6–3, 6–4, 6–2; Ostoja–Zivojinovic d. K. and M. Lazarov 6–4, 3–6, 6–1, 2–6, 6–4; G. Prpic d. M. Lazarov 6–2, 6–4; Ostoja d. Stamatov 7–5, 6–3.

FINAL ROUND

Yugoslavia d. Hungary 5–0, Zagreb: M. Ostoja d. R. Machan 6–0,
3–6, 6–2, 6–2; S. Zivojinovic d. J. Benyik 6–3, 2–6, 6–2, 7–5;
Ostoja–Zivojinovic d. Machan–P. Szoke 6–4, 6–3, 10–12, 6–3; Ostoja d.
Benyik 7–5, 6–2; Zivojinovic d. Machan def.

1984: SWEDEN
Non-Zonal Competition

FIRST ROUND

Australia d. Yugoslavia 5–0, Perth: P. McNamee d. S. Zivojinovic
9–7, 4–6, 9–7, 10–8; J. Fitzgerald d. M. Ostoja 2–6, 7–5, 6–1, 6–2;
McNamee–M. Edmondson d. Zivojinovic–Ostoja 6–4, 6–1, 6–4;
Fitzgerald d. B. Oresar 6–3, 6–4; McNamee d. B. Horvat 6–4, 10–8.
Italy d. Great Britain 3–2, Telford: G. Ocleppo d. C. Dowdeswell
1–6, 6–2, 9–7, 6–2; C. Barazzutti lost to J. Lloyd 4–6, 6–3, 2–6, 3–6;
Ocleppo–C. Panatta lost to Lloyd–Dowdeswell 9–11, 4–6, 6–3, 6–3, 3–6;
Ocleppo d. Lloyd 2–6, 6–2, 6–3, 6–3; Barazzutti d. Dowdeswell 6–1, 0–6,
6–3, 7–5. **Argentina d. West Germany 4–1, Stuttgart:** G. Vilas d.
H. Beutel 8–6, 8–6, 7–5; J. L. Clerc d. M. Westphal 6–3, 3–6, 6–3, 1–6,
8–6; Vilas–Clerc d. Beutel–A. Maurer 13–11, 6–4, 6–3; Clerc d. Beutel
7–5, 7–5; Vilas lost to Westphal 3–6, 4–6. **USA d. Rumania 5–0,
Bucharest:** J. Connors d. F. Segarceanu 6–2, 6–3, 6–4; J. McEnroe d. I.
Nastase 6–2, 6–4, 6–2; McEnroe–P. Fleming d. Segarceanu–Nastase 6–3,
6–4, 6–4; Connors d. Nastase 6–4, 6–4; McEnroe d. Segarceanu 2–6, 6–2,
6–2. **Czechoslovakia d. Denmark 5–0, Hradec Kralove:** L. Pimek
d. M. Mortensen 10–8, 6–2, 6–4; T. Smid d. P. Bastiansen 6–2, 6–1, 6–2;
Smid–P. Slozil d. Bastiansen–Mortensen 6–4, 6–3, 12–10; Pimek d.
Bastiansen 6–4, 4–6, 6–4; Smid d. Mortensen 8–6, 6–3. **France d. India
4–1, New Delhi:** Y. Noah d. R. Krishnan 6–2, 7–5, 6–2; H. Leconte
d. A. Amritraj 2–6, 6–2, 6–3, 8–6; Noah–Leconte d. Amritraj–S. Menon
7–5, 6–4, 6–4; Leconte lost to Menon 2–6, 7–5, 8–10; Noah d. Amritraj
6–4, 6–4. **Paraguay d. New Zealand 3–2, Christchurch:** F. Gonzalez
d. R. Simpson 6–1, 6–3, 6–8, 2–6, 6–4; V. Pecci d. C. Lewis 4–6, 8–6,
6–4, 2–6, 6–4; Pecci–Gonzalez d. Lewis–Simpson 6–3, 8–10, 6–2, 6–4;
Gonzalez lost to Lewis 3–6, 4–6; Pecci lost to Simpson 3–6, 3–6.
Sweden d. Ecuador 4–1, Norrkoping: A. Jarryd lost to A. Gomez
1–6, 6–2, 6–8, 6–3, 3–6; M. Wilander d. R. Ycaza 6–3, 6–2, 6–1;
Wilander–Jarryd d. Gomez–Ycaza 3–6, 6–3, 6–4, 6–4; J. Nystrom d.
Ycaza 6–2, 6–0, 6–3; Wilander d. Gomez 7–5, 6–4.

QUARTER-FINAL ROUND

Australia d. Italy 5–0, Brisbane J. Fitzgerald d. G. Ocleppo 6–3, 6–1, 4–6, 6–1; P. Cash d. C. Panatta 6–3, 3–6, 6–3, 6–4; M. Edmondson–P. McNamee d. Ocleppo–Panatta 3–6, 7–5, 6–4, 6–3; Fitzgerald d. Panatta 6–4, 8–10, 6–2; Cash d. Ocleppo 9–7, 6–4. **USA d. Argentina 5–0, Atlanta:** J. McEnroe d. J. L. Clerc 6–4, 6–0, 6–2; J. Connors d. M. Jaite 6–3, 6–4, 10–8; McEnroe–P. Fleming d. Clerc–Jaite 7–5, 4–6, 6–3, 6–1; Connors d. Clerc 8–6, 6–2; McEnroe d. Jaite 6–3, 6–4. **Czechoslovakia d. France 3–2, Hradec Kralove:** I. Lendl lost to H. Leconte 3–6, 6–8, 4–6; T. Smid d. G. Forget 6–4, 2–6, 3–6, 6–1, 6–4; Smid–P. Slozil d. Leconte–P. Portes 6–2, 5–7, 7–5, 4–6, 6–2; Lendl d. Forget 11–9, 6–4, 6–2; Smid lost to Leconte 3–6, 3–6. **Sweden d. Paraguay 4–1, Båstad:** H. Sundstrom d. V. Pecci 6–3, 6–4, 2–6, 6–4; A. Jarryd d. F. Gonzalez 6–3, 6–2, 6–4; Jarryd–S. Edberg lost to Pecci–Gonzalez 2–6, 6–8, 6–4, 1–6; Sundstrom d. Gonzalez 6–3, 6–1, 6–2; Jarryd d. O. Napout 6–3, 6–0.

SEMI-FINAL ROUND

USA d. Australia 4–1, Portland: J. McEnroe d. P. Cash 6–3, 6–4, 6–1; J. Connors d. J. Fitzgerald 6–3, 6–3, 6–2; McEnroe–P. Fleming d. M. Edmondson–P. McNamee 6–4, 6–2, 6–3; McEnroe d. Fitzgerald 4–6, 6–2, 6–1; Connors lost to Cash 4–6, 2–6. **Sweden d. Czechoslovakia 5–0, Båstad:** M. Wilander d. T. Smid 7–5, 7–5, 6–2; H. Sundstrom d. I. Lendl 4–6, 3–6, 6–3, 6–1, 6–1; S. Edberg–A. Jarryd d. P. Slozil–Smid 2–6, 5–7, 6–1, 10–8, 6–2; Wilander d. Lendl 6–3, 4–6, 6–2; Sundstrom d. Smid 6–4, 6–4.

FINAL ROUND

Sweden d. USA 4–1, Gothenburg: M. Wilander d. J. Connors 6–1, 6–3, 6–3; H. Sundstrom d. J. McEnroe 13–11, 6–4, 6–3; A. Jarryd–S. Edberg d. McEnroe–P. Fleming 7–5, 5–7, 6–2, 7–5; Wilander lost to McEnroe 3–6, 7–5, 3–6; Sundstrom d. J. Arias 3–6, 8–6, 6–3.

RELEGATION ROUND

Yugoslavia d. Great Britain 4–1, Eastbourne: M. Ostoja d. S. Shaw 5–7, 6–4, 6–2; S. Zivojinovic d. J. Lloyd 4–6, 7–5, 5–7, 6–3, 10–8; Ostoja–Zivojinovic lost to Lloyd–C. Dowdeswell 3–6, 7–9, 1–6; Zivojinovic d. Shaw 8–6, 8–6, 6–3; Ostoja d. Lloyd 6–4, 1–6, 6–2. **West Germany d. Rumania 5–0, Berlin:** H. Schwaier d. A. Marcu 6–2, 6–0, 6–1; M. Westphal d. A. Dirzu 6–2, 7–5, 7–5; H. Beutel–W. Popp d. Dirzu–M. Nastase 6–3, 6–1, 6–4; Westphal d. Marcu 6–0, 8–6; Schwaier d. Dirzu 9–7, 7–5. **India d. Denmark 3–2, Aarhus:** V. Amritraj d. M. Mortensen 6–0, 6–1, 6–2; R. Krishnan d. P. Bastiansen

6–0, 6–1, 6–4; V. and A. Amritraj lost to Bastiansen–Mortensen 4–6, 5–7, 4–6; Krishnan d. Mortensen 6–2, 6–3, 10–8; S. Menon lost to Bastiansen 0–6, 6–4, 1–6. **Ecuador d. New Zealand 4–1, Guayaquil:** A. Gomez d. R. Simpson 6–1, 11–9, 6–0; R. Viver lost to C. Lewis 3–6, 4–6, 3–6; Gomez–R. Ycaza d. Lewis–Simpson 6–3, 6–2, 6–3; Viver d. Simpson 6–4, 3–6, 6–2, 6–4; Gomez d. Lewis 6–2, 6–2.

American Zone

FIRST ROUND

Mexico d. Venezuela 5–0, Caracas: F. Maciel d. F. M. Bet 8–6, 6–3, 6–1; F. P. Pascall d. I. Calvo 9–7, 4–6, 5–7, 6–4, 6–2; Pascall–A. Gonzalez d. Calvo–J. Andrew 6–4, 6–4, 6–4; Pascall d. Bet 5–7, 6–4, 6–4; Gonzalez d. Calvo 6–2, 6–2.

QUARTER-FINAL ROUND

Chile d. Colombia 5–0, Santiago: H. Gildemeister d. A. Jordan 6–2, 4–6, 4–6, 6–0, 6–4; R. Acuna d. R. Gomez 6–2, 6–2, 6–3; B. Prajoux–A. Fillol d. Jordan–R. Perczek 6–3, 6–3, 6–2; Acuna d. Jordan 6–3, 5–7, 6–1; Fillol d. Perczek 7–5, 7–5. **Mexico d. Canada 5–0, Mexico City:** J. Lozano d. G. Michibata 5–7, 6–8, 6–3, 6–3, 6–4; F. Maciel d. D. Segal 6–4, 6–3, 9–11, 6–3; Lozano–F. P. Pascall d. Michibata–B. Cowan 9–7, 6–2, 6–4; Lozano d. Segal 6–3, 6–0; Maciel d. Michibata 5–7, 6–2, 6–3. **Uruguay d. Commonwealth Caribbean 4–1, Barbados:** H. Roverano d. A. Clarke 6–4, 6–2, 6–1; D. Perez d. S. Sarnia 7–5, 6–1, 6–1; Perez–V. Caldarelli d. Sarnia–R. Hale 6–2, 1–6, 6–1, 10–8; Caldaralli lost to J. Tasker 8–10, 5–7; Roverano d. Sarnia 7–5, 6–4. **Brazil d. Peru 5–0, Rio de Janeiro:** M. Hocevar d. C. Di Laura 3–6, 8–6, 6–1, 6–4; C. Motta d. P. Arraya 6–3, 6–2, 6–4; Motta–C. Kirmayr d. Arraya–F. Maynetto 7–9, 6–4, 7–5, 12–10; N. Aertiz d. Di Laura 6–4, 6–2; Hocevar d. J. Izaza 6–4, 3–2, ret.

SEMI-FINAL ROUND

Chile d. Mexico 5–0, Santiago: P. Rebolledo d. F. Perez 6–1, 6–4, 6–8, 3–6, 7–5; H. Gildemeister d. F. Maciel 6–2, 6–2, 6–3; R. Acuna–A. Fillol d. J. Lozano–Perez 6–1, 6–4, 2–6, 6–4; Gildemeister d. Perez 6–1, 2–6, 6–3; Rebolledo d. J. Contreras 6–1, 6–2. **Brazil d. Uruguay 3–2, Rio de Janeiro:** M. Hocevar lost to D. Perez 5–7, 2–6, 0–6; C. Motta d. V. Caldarelli 6–3, 6–1, 6–3; C. Kirmayr–Motta d. P. Pinet–Perez 6–2, 6–3, 6–3; Motta lost to Perez 5–7, 6–3, 2–6, def.; Hocevar d. Caldarelli 8–6, 6–3, 8–6.

FINAL ROUND

Chile d. Brazil 4–1, Santiago: H. Gildemeister d. C. Motta 6–3, 6–4, 6–2; P. Rebolledo d. M. Hocevar 7–5, 7–5, 6–2; A. Fillol–C. Kirmayr lost to R. Acuna–Motta 1–6, 7–9, 2–6; Gildemeister d. Hocevar 6–4, 6–1, 6–4; Rebolledo d. Motta 6–0, 6–3.

Eastern Zone

FIRST ROUND

Pakistan d. Malaysia 4–1, Rawalpindi: I. Haq d. Selvarajoo 6–3, 6–3, 6–3; A. Haq d. A. Malik 6–1, 6–4, 6–2; I. Haq–N. Munir lost to Malik–D. Murali 7–5, 6–2, 7–9, 5–7, 4–6; A. Haq d. Selvarajoo 6–1, 6–1, 6–3; R. Malik d. A. Malik 4–6, 6–4, 6–0. **Hong Kong d. Chinese Taipei 3–2, Taipei:** K. Ng lost to W. Chang-Rung 2–6, 3–6, 7–5, 3–6; M. Bailey d. L. Chung-Hsing 3–6, 6–3, 3–6, 6–1, 6–4; Ng–R. King d. Chang-Rung-Chung-Hsing 6–1, 4–6, 6–4, 8–6; Bailey lost to Chang-Rung 4–6, 7–5, 2–6, 2–6; Ng d. Chung-Hsing 6–3, 7–5, 6–2. **China d. Sri Lanka 4–1, Guangzhou:** L. Shuhua d. A. Fernando 4–6, 6–2, 8–6, 6–3; Y. Wei d. F. Sebaratnam 6–3, 6–1, 6–4; Shuhua–M. Keqin d. Sebaratnam–Fernando 6–4, 6–4, 6–1; L. Shuchen lost to Fernando 3–6, 3–6; Keqin d. A. Perera 6–0, 6–1. **Philippines d. Singapore 5–0, Singapore:** R. Gabriel d. A. Teo 6–3, 6–3, 6–3; F. Barrientos d. M. Hassan 8–6, 6–1, 6–3; Barrientos–A. del Rosario d. Teo–V. Pereira 6–3, 6–4, 6–8, 3–6, 6–1; Barrientos d. Teo 6–2, 6–4, 6–3; Del Rosario d. Hassan 7–5, 6–0, 6–2.

QUARTER-FINAL ROUND

Pakistan d. Indonesia 4–1, Rawalpindi: A. Haq d. Suharyadi 3–6, 7–9, 6–4, 6–1, 7–5; I. Haq d. T. A. Wibowo 6–3, 8–6, 6–1; I. Haq–N. Munir lost to D. Wailan–L. Wijono 6–3, 4–6, 3–6, 2–6; I. Haq d. Suharyadi 3–6, 8–6, 7–5, 8–6; R. Malik d. Wijono 6–2, 6–2. **Thailand d. Hong Kong 5–0, Hong Kong:** S. Eaumongkol d. R. King 4–6, 8–6, 8–6, 1–6, 6–4; P. Pladchurnil d. K. Ng 6–8, 6–3, 6–4, 6–4; Eaumongkol–Pladchurnil d. Ng–King 6–3, 3–6, 9–11, 6–3, 6–2; Pladchurnil d. King 8–6, 6–8, 6–1; Eaumongkol d. Ng 6–3, 1–6, 6–1. **China d. Korea 3–1, Kunming City:** Y. Wei d. S. Dong-Wook 7–5, 6–1, 4–6, 3–6, 6–3; L. Shuhua d. K. Choon-Ho 6–1, 6–2, 6–4; Shuhua–M. Keqin lost to K. Bong-Soo–Y. Jin-Sun 6–1, 6–8, 3–6, 2–6; Wei d. Choon-Ho 6–4, 1–6, 0–6, 6–4, 6–0. **Japan d. Philippines 5–0, Fukuoka:** S. Shiraishi d. M. Tolentino 6–1, 6–1, 6–1; T. Fukui d. V. Sison 6–0, 4–6, 6–3, 7–5; H. Shirato–T.

Yonezawa d. Sison–R. Gabriel 8–6, 7–5, 6–4; Fukui d. F. Barrientos 6–2, 6–1; Shiraishi d. Sison 6–4, 7–5.

SEMI-FINAL ROUND

Pakistan d. Thailand 4–1, Rawalpindi: I. Haq d. P. Pladchurnil 4–6, 1–6, 6–3, 6–1, 6–2; H. Haq d. S. Eaumongkol 4–6, 8–6, 4–6, 6–1, 6–1; I. Haq–R. Malik lost to Pladchurnil–Eaumongkol 3–6, 4–6, 4–6; H. Haq d. Pladchurnil 6–2, 6–4, 6–4; I. Haq d. Eaumongkol 12–10, 6–2, 6–1.

Japan d. China 3–2, Kunming City: T. Fukui d. L. Shuhua 4–6, 4–6, 6–2, 12–10, 7–5; S. Shiraishi d. Y. Wei 6–4, 2–6, 6–1, 6–4; H. Shirato–T. Tsuji lost to Shuhua–M. Keqin 6–0, 6–2, 2–6, 4–6, 0–6; Fukui d. Wei 7–5, 10–8, 6–2; Shiraishi lost to Shuhua 1–6, 2–6.

FINAL ROUND

Japan d. Pakistan 4–1, Rawalpindi: S. Shiraishi d. I. Haq 7–5, 6–1, 6–2; T. Fukui d. H. Haq 6–0, 6–2, 6–1; S. Sakamoto–S. Nishio d. M. Zia–H. Aslam 2–6, 6–3, 6–4, 6–4; Fukui d. I. Haq 6–0, 6–2; Shiraishi lost to H. Haq 6–4, 5–7, 5–7.

European Zone A

FIRST ROUND

Monaco d. Zimbabwe 4–1, Monte Carlo: A. Viviani d. H. Ismail 7–5, 6–2, 6–4; B. Balleret d. O. Lourenco 6–1, 6–2, 3–6, 6–1; Balleret–J. Vincileoni d. Ismail–P. Tuckniss 2–6, 6–4, 2–6, 6–3, 7–5; Viviani lost to Lourenco 0–6, 4–6; Balleret d. Ismail 6–2, 6–4. **Austria d. Lebanon def.; Norway d. Portugal 4–1, Oslo:** M. Roenneberg d. J. Silva 6–2, 6–3, 2–6, 6–0; T. Joensson d. J. Maio 6–3, 6–2, 6–1; Roenneberg–T. Persson d. Maio–Silva 8–6, 6–8, 6–3, 6–4; Roenneberg d. Maio 6–2, 6–3; Joensson lost to Silva 8–6, 0–6, 6–4, 4–6, 3–6. **Poland d. Greece 4–1, Warsaw:** W. Fibak d. T. Bavelas 6–1, 6–3, 6–4; W. Rogowski lost to G. Kalovelonis 2–6, 3–6, 4–6; Fibak–W. Kowalski d. Kalovelonis–C. Efremeglou 9–7, 6–1, 6–2; Fibak d. Kalovelonis 6–2, 6–2, 4–6, 3–6, 6–2; Rogowski d. Bavelas 6–2, 6–4. **Senegal d. Tunisia 3–2, Dakar:** T. Ly lost to A. Soudani 5–7, 6–8, 3–6; N. Kabaz d. A. Zouhir 6–8, 6–4, 4–6, 6–2, 6–4; Kabaz–M. Doumbia d. H. and A. Soudani 3–6, 4–6, 6–4, 6–3, 6–4; Ly d. Zouhir 6–4, 6–2, 6–4; Kabaz lost to A. Soudani 6–4, 5–7, 1–6.

QUARTER-FINAL ROUND

USSR d. Monaco 5–0, Yurmala: A. Zverev d. G. Ganancia 7–5, 6–4, 6–2; A. Chesnokov d. B. Balleret 6–1, 8–6, 6–0; Zverev–S. Leoniuk d.

Balleret–J. Vincileoni 8–6, 5–7, 6–4, 6–0; Zverev d. Balleret 6–2, 8–6; Chesnokov d. Ganancia 6–2, 6–4. **Austria d. Norway 5–0, Vienna:** P. Feigl d. M. Roenneberg 6–2, 6–3, 6–3; B. Pils d. T. Joensson 6–3, 6–0, 6–2; Feigl–A. Antonitsch d. Roenneberg–T. Persson 6–3, 6–2, 6–1; Pils d. Persson 6–1, 6–4; T. Muster d. Joensson 6–0, 6–3. **Israel d. Poland 5–0, Jerusalem:** S. Glickstein d. W. Fibak 6–4, 6–2, 6–2; S. Perkiss d. W. Rogowski 6–1, 6–2, 6–2; Glickstein–Perkiss d. Fibak–W. Kowalski 6–3, 6–2, 9–7; A. Mansdorf d. Rogowski 7–5, 6–2; Perkiss d. Kowalski 6–2, 6–1. **Switzerland d. Senegal 5–0, Disentis:** R. Stadler d. T. Ly 6–1, 6–3, 6–1; J. Hlasek d. Y. Doumbia 6–2, 6–1, 4–6, 6–2; H. and M. Gunthardt d. Doumbia–Ly 6–4, 6–1, 6–3; Hlasek d. Ly 6–4, 6–1, 6–1; Stadler d. Doumbia 6–2, 6–2, 8–6.

USSR d. Austria 3–2, Yurmala: V. Borisov lost to P. Feigl 6–0, 7–9, 6–1, 1–6, 6–8; A. Zverev lost to B. Pils 6–1, 6–3, 6–8, 6–8, 3–6; Borisov–S. Leonuik d. Feigl–A. Antonitsch 6–4, 6–3, 5–7, 6–2; Zverev d. Feigl 4–6, 6–3, 3–6, 8–6, 6–3; Borisov d. Pils 6–4, 6–2, 2–6, 6–2. **Israel d. Switzerland 4–1, Ramat Hasharon:** S. Glickstein d. H. Gunthardt 6–3, 7–5, 6–3; S. Perkiss lost to J. Hlasek 4–6, 2–6, 6–3, 6–4, 3–6; Glickstein–Perkiss d. H. and M. Gunthardt 11–9, 6–3, 3–6, 6–3; Glickstein d. Hlasek 8–6, 14–12, 6–2; Perkiss d. H. Gunthardt 6–4, 6–0.

USSR d. Israel 3–2, Donetsk: A. Chesnokov d. S. Perkiss 7–5, 6–3, 7–5; A. Zverev lost to S. Glickstein 3–6, 6–1, 3–6, 7–5, 6–8; V. Borisov–S. Leoniuk lost to Glickstein–Perkiss 6–2, 11–9, 4–6, 4–6, 3–6; Chesnokov d. Glickstein 6–0, 7–9, 1–6, 6–2, 6–1; Zverev d. Perkiss 2–6, 7–5, 10–8, 6–4.

European Zone B

Egypt d. Luxembourg 5–0, Cairo: T. El Sakka d. J. Goudenbourg 6–3, 6–4, 3–6, 7–5; A. El Mehelmy d. S. Kinsch 6–2, 6–1, 6–3; El Mehelmy–El Sakka d. Goudenbourg–M. Klensch 6–1, 6–1, 6–4; El Sakka d. Kinsch 6–1, 6–3; El Mehelmy d. Goudenbourg 7–9, 7–5, 11–9. **Belgium d. Turkey 5–0, Istanbul:** J. Van Langendonck d. A. Karagoz 6–1, 6–3, 6–3; B. Boileau d. Y. Erkangil 6–4, 6–2, 6–2; Boileau–A. Brichant d. Erkangil–O. Azkara 6–2, 6–0, 6–0; Van Langendonck d. Erkangil 6–3, 6–1; Boileau d. Y. Esin 6–3, 6–1. **Spain d. Algeria 5–0,**

Pamplona: E. Sanchez d. K. Harrad 6–0, 6–0, 6–0; J. Aguilera d. Y. Amier 6–2, 6–1, 6–0; Aguilera–S. Casal d. R. Bouchabou–D. Ghouli 6–2, 6–1, 6–0; Sanchez d. Amier 6–1, 6–1; Aguilera d. Harrad 6–0, 6–2.

Finland d. Morocco 5–0, Casablanca: O. Rahnasto d. S. Houcine 7–5, 6–1, 7–5; L. Palin d. C. Arafa 3–6, 6–3, 3–6, 1–0, ret.; Palin–Rahnasto d. Houcine–D. Mohamed 6–4, 6–4, 9–7; Rahnasto d. Mohamed 6–0, 7–5; K. Alkio d. N. Abdehak 6–0, 6–1.

QUARTER-FINAL ROUND

Hungary d. Egypt 4–1, Budapest: S. Kiss lost to T. Shawki 2–6, 4–6, 5–7; B. Taroczy d. A. El Mehelmy 6–3, 6–2, 6–0; Kiss–Taroczy d. Shawki–El Mehelmy 7–5, 6–1, 6–3; Taroczy d. Shawki 6–0, 6–1, 6–2; Kiss d. El Mehelmy 7–5, 7–5.　**Belgium d. Bulgaria 3–2, Plovdiv:** J. Van Langendonck lost to Y. Stamatov 6–8, 2–6, 5–7; B. Boileau d. L. Petrov 6–2, 6–4, 6–2; Boileau–A. Brichant d. T. Bachev–M. Lazarov 6–4, 6–4, 6–4; Van Langendonck d. Petrov 3–6, 4–6, 6–4, 6–1, 6–3; Boileau lost to Stamatov 0–6, 0–6, 0–6.　**Spain d. Holland 3–2, Amsterdam:** J. Aguilera lost to M. Schapers 6–8, 6–8, 6–2, 6–2, 3–6; Casal d. H. van Boeckel 6–2, 6–2, 6–4; Aguilera–Casal lost to Schapers–van Boeckel 2–6, 1–6, 6–1, 6–4, 3–6; Casal d. Schapers 6–4, 6–3, 6–0; Aguilera d. van Boeckel 7–5, 6–4, 6–4.　**Ireland d. Finland 3–2, Helsinki:** S. Sorensen lost to O. Rahnasto 3–6, 4–6, 4–6; M. Doyle d. L. Palin 6–2, 7–5, 7–5; Doyle–Sorensen d. Palin–Rahnasto 6–4, 6–2, 6–1; Sorensen d. Palin 8–10, 9–7, 6–2, 6–4; Doyle lost to Rahnasto 1–6, 1–6.

SEMI-FINAL ROUND

Hungary d. Belgium 3–2, Brussels: B. Taroczy d. J. Van Langendonck 9–7, 6–0, 6–4; S. Kiss lost to B. Boileau 1–6, 2–6, 5–7; Kiss–Taroczy d. Boileau–A. Brichant 6–8, 6–2, 8–10, 11–9, 6–1; Taroczy d. Boileau 6–2, 6–4, 6–2; Kiss lost to Van Langendonck 3–6, 6–3, 5–7.　**Spain d. Ireland 4–1, Vigo:** J. Aguilera d. M. Doyle 6–3, 6–4, 6–3; E. Sanchez d. S. Sorensen 6–3, 6–0, 6–4; Sanchez–S. Casal d. Doyle–Sorensen 6–4, 6–0, 6–4; Aguilera lost to Sorensen 3–6, 1–6; Sanchez d. M. Nugent 6–0, 6–1.

FINAL ROUND

Spain d. Hungary 4–1, Budapest: J. Aguilera lost to B. Taroczy 2–6, 6–3, 3–6, 8–10; S. Casal d. S. Kiss 6–3, 6–4, 6–2; Casal–E. Sanchez d. Taroczy–Kiss 11–9, 6–3, 6–4; Casal d. Taroczy 6–3, 9–7, 6–4; Aguilera d. Kiss 10–8, 6–4.

SUMMARY

Year	Champion Nation	Runner-up	Venue	Number of competing nations
1900	USA	Great Britain	Boston	2
1901	no competition			
1902	USA	Great Britain	New York	2
1903	Great Britain	USA	Boston	2
1904	Great Britain	USA	London	3
1905	Great Britain	USA	London	5
1906	Great Britain	USA	London	3
1907	Australasia	Great Britain	London	3
1908	Australasia	USA	Melbourne	3
1909	Australasia	USA	Sydney	3
1910	no competition			
1911	Australasia	USA	Christchurch	3
1912	Great Britain	Australasia	Melbourne	3
1913	USA	Great Britain	London	8
1914	Australasia	USA	New York	7
1915–18	no competition			
1919	Australasia	Great Britain	Sydney	5
1920	USA	Australasia	Auckland	6
1921	USA	Japan	New York	12
1922	USA	Australasia	New York	11
1923	USA	Australasia	New York	17
1924	USA	Australasia	Philadelphia	23
1925	USA	France	Philadelphia	23
1926	USA	France	Philadelphia	24
1927	France	USA	Philadelphia	24
1928	France	USA	Paris	24
1929	France	USA	Paris	29
1930	France	USA	Paris	28
1931	France	Great Britain	Paris	30

Year	Champion Nation	Runner-up	Venue	Number of competing nations
1932	France	USA	Paris	29
1933	Great Britain	France	Paris	30
1934	Great Britain	USA	London	27
1935	Great Britain	USA	London	28
1936	Great Britain	Australia	London	24
1937	USA	Great Britain	London	25
1938	USA	Australia	Philadelphia	24
1939	Australia	USA	Haverford	26
1940–45	no competition			
1946	USA	Australia	Melbourne	19
1947	USA	Australia	New York	22
1948	USA	Australia	New York	29
1949	USA	Australia	New York	27
1950	Australia	USA	New York	26
1951	Australia	USA	Sydney	27
1952	Australia	USA	Adelaide	28
1953	Australia	USA	Melbourne	29
1954	USA	Australia	Sydney	31
1955	Australia	USA	New York	35
1956	Australia	USA	Adelaide	33
1957	Australia	USA	Melbourne	36
1958	USA	Australia	Brisbane	37
1959	Australia	USA	New York	40
1960	Australia	Italy	Sydney	41
1961	Australia	Italy	Melbourne	43
1962	Australia	Mexico	Brisbane	42
1963	USA	Australia	Adelaide	49
1964	Australia	USA	Cleveland	49
1965	Australia	Spain	Sydney	44
1966	Australia	India	Melbourne	46
1967	Australia	Spain	Brisbane	48
1968	USA	Australia	Adelaide	50
1969	USA	Rumania	Cleveland	51
1970	USA	West Germany	Cleveland	51
1971	USA	Rumania	Charlotte	47
1972	USA	Rumania	Bucharest	54
1973	Australia	USA	Cleveland	53
1974	South Africa	India (def.)	—	56
1975	Sweden	Czechoslovakia	Stockholm	56
1976	Italy	Chile	Santiago	58
1977	Australia	Italy	Sydney	59
1978	USA	Great Britain	Rancho Mirage	59
1979	USA	Italy	San Francisco	52

Year	Champion Nation	Runner-up	Venue	Number of competing nations
1980	Czechoslovakia	Italy	Prague	54
1981	USA	Argentina	Cincinnati	53
1982	USA	France	Grenoble	58
1983	Australia	Sweden	Melbourne	58
1984	Sweden	USA	Gothenburg	62

INDEX